Mobilizing in Our Own Name

An Anthology by Clarence Thomas

DeClare Publishing

Mobilizing in Our Own Name
MILLION WORKER MARCH

Workers and activists document struggles as they happen in news articles, interviews, letters, posters, photos, speeches, and video transcripts.

An Anthology by Clarence Thomas

MWM logo designed by Leo Robinson

ISBN 978-1-7370819-0-6

Published by the DeClare Publishing

Published May 2021

MillionWorkerMarch.com

Website design by Mildred Center at iyobu-creative.com

Graphic book design by Lallan Schoenstein

Fonts: Encode Sans and Times New Roman

This book is dedicated to the memory of my father, Clarence C. Thomas Sr.

Although he never sought elective office, he was a strong rank-and-file member of ILWU Local 10 who loved the union.

He was a man of courage and conviction who spoke truth to power and fought against discrimination.

CONTENTS

CHAPTER 1   ORGANIZING THE MILLION WORKER MARCH
                LABOR MUST SPEAK IN ITS OWN VOICE

CHAPTER 5

MAY DAY
INTERNATIONAL WORKERS' DAY

CHAPTER 6   THE FIGHT AGAINST WHITE SUPREMACY

CHAPTER 7   INTERNATIONAL SOLIDARITY
2003 – 2017

CHAPTER 8 CONFERENCE ON SOCIALISM
NEW YORK CITY • MAY 2006

CHAPTER 11   OCCUPY OAKLAND
'SHUT IT DOWN'

CHAPTER 12   THE STRUGGLE CONTINUES!

Million Worker March
A 21st Century Initiative

Workers from all over the country and from around the world, waged and unwaged, converged on Washington, D.C., on October 17, 2004, just before the U.S. presidential election. The Million Worker March Movement put forward an independent workers agenda: health care and education; the right to a living wage for all; an end to the war in Iraq and on workers at home; repeal of the Patriot Act and all repressive legislation; amnesty for undocumented workers; and more.

Despite tremendous opposition from the Democratic Party and AFL-CIO, the Million Worker March became a reality led by African American trade union members.

Commentary

I was inspired and compelled to do an anthology on the Million Worker March (MWM), which convened, on the steps of the Lincoln Memorial in Washington D.C., Oct. 17, 2004, for the purpose of documenting this important struggle so that others may learn from it as a tool for future independent worker struggles. Writing or editing a book is a major challenge especially for an activist engaged in as many struggles as I've been engaged in.

Yes, I did say I was compelled to make this book a reality. Completing this project keeps a promise to my elders that it would be done while they are still with us. My mom Charlene Thomas, who turned 92 in October 2020, and her life-long friend Barbara Phillips, have been patiently awaiting the completion of this book. I kid my mother about her having been on the employer's payroll since 1944. She is the daughter, spouse, niece, and mother of longshore workers.

I am retired from the waterfront, but not the struggle, as I'm sure many of you are that will hopefully read this book.

MWM is born

Today, Trent Willis is president of ILWU Local 10. Trent is also a third-generation longshore worker, whose father known as 'Buster' came on the waterfront in 1963, the same year as Leo Robinson and my dad, Clarence Thomas Sr. But on January 15, 2004, when he called me, brother Trent was a young, emerging, rank-and-file leader and business agent for the local.

He wanted my opinion on an idea: What did I think of organizing a Million Worker March in Washington, D.C.? When I asked what motivated the idea for the MWM, he explained that as a young trade unionist his generation had not been a part of militant working class mobilization of the past. "Business unionism," operating unions as "top down hierarchies," where workers and bosses have common interests, was and continues to be a dominant trend in the labor movement. When I asked him when he thought we should do it, he said, "In 2004, before the election." The hour was late and I had a 3 a.m. start for my next job. I couldn't help but reflect on the massive turn out, grandeur, and organizing that went into the Million Man March (1995). Together with many members of the local, including Brother Leo Robinson, I experienced it. A million worker march?

The last thing I wanted to do was to be dismissive of this young member. He already had certainly earned the respect of many of us veterans of the local. Trent represented Local 10 at the 2003 U.S. Labor Against the War (USLAW) founding conference in Chicago. With all of this in mind, I told him I would talk to Brother Leo Robinson to get his thoughts on the idea.

Brother Leo was always open for late night calls especially on union meeting nights Although then a pensioner but still a strategist, Leo wanted the 411 from the union meetings. When he heard Trent's proposal, the first thing Leo asked was, "What did you say?" I answered, "I told Trent that I would call you." At Leo's suggestion, we met three days later at my house – Leo, Trent and then President of Local 10 Henry 'Hammering Hank' Graham.

Shaping the MWM Details of the meeting – two points

Two things stand out in my mind about that initial meeting: the first thing I recall was that I had a copy of President Franklin D. Roosevelt's *Second Bill of Rights* on my dining room table; and the second was Leo's concern that the MWM resolution would not be "blind-sided" or "red-baited" before it got off the ground.

This approach reflected Leo's experience in building movements, and his understanding of how conservative business union advocates viewed the history and reputation of Local 10 in the labor movement.

We agreed that the language had to be embraced by a broad cross-section of the labor movement. We found a key in Pres. Roosevelt's Jan. 11, 1944, State of the Union Address: "*the second bill of rights.*" Roosevelt contended that "Political Rights" protected by the U.S. Bill of Rights had proven inadequate to ensure U.S. citizens' equality in the pursuit of happiness. It is for that reason, that the third Whereas, in the Resolution, proposing a Million Worker March reads as follows:

> "Whereas, Franklin D. Roosevelt in his State of the Union address acknowledged rights saying "We have come to the realization of the fact that true individual freedom cannot exist without economic security and independence. Necessitous men are not free men."

It was the consensus of the framers of the MWM resolution, that references to Roosevelt and the 'economic bill of rights' were a strategic decision to enhance support for the MWM resolution. Although that strategy initially proved effective, we eventually faced the opposition of the Democratic Party and AFL-CIO, two of the most powerful forces with influence over organized labor.

The Resolution proposing a Million Worker March was adopted at the Local 10 membership meeting in February 2004. On May 22, 2004, the ILWU Longshore Caucus, representing dock workers at all 29 ports on the West Coast, unanimously adopted the call for the Million Worker March. The MWM Kick-Off Rally was held at the ILWU Local 10 William "Bill" Chester hiring hall, attended by around 250 people including ILWU rank-and-filers, other labor activists, and featured labor officials.

The gathering set out to build committees in cities across the country reaching out to local unions, community organizations, and student groups. During the Rally, the pending endorsement of the MWM by the Coalition of Black Trade Unionists (CBTU), endorsement of New York City American Federation of State, County and Municipal Employees (AFCSME), District Council 1707, and other major unions was announced demonstrating enthusiasm for the project.

Local 10 President Henry Graham opened the Rally, saying, "I am proud to welcome you to our longshore hiring hall, not only because of our history of struggle for the rights of working people, but because we are about to embark upon a great mobilization that recalls to us our finest moments. We defended the rights of South African workers. We fought to defend working people in El Salvador and in Nicaragua. We stood by our fellow dock workers in Liverpool. And in each instance, we shut the port down in solidarity!

"We are gathered here tonight saying enough is enough! We have issued a call to our brothers and sisters across this country. … A call to mobilize against the constant attacks on labor. … We are about to embark on a great mobilization which calls for absolute solidarity!"

Trent Willis and I co-chaired the Kick-Off Rally. The speakers were: Maria Guillen, vice president SEIU Local 790; Danny Glover, actor and activist; Walter Johnson, secretary-treasurer San Francisco Labor Council; Frank Martin Del Campo, president San Francisco Labor Chapter for Latin American Advancement; Ralph Schoenman, co-producer of Pacifica's Taking Aim/Guns and Butter; Chris Silvera, secretary-treasurer Teamsters Local 808 New York and Teamsters National Black Caucus; and

Brenda Stokely, president AFSCME District Council 1707 and Local 215 N.Y. Written greetings were received and read from Donna Dewitt, president South Carolina State AFL-CIO and Saladin Muhammad, national chairperson of Black Workers for Justice.

The following quotes from the Kick-Off Rally published in the May/June 2004 issue of *The Organizer*, showed the unmet demands to which the MWM gave a voice.

Donna Dewitt: Pres. S.C. AFL-CIO, "...Congratulations to ILWU Local 10 for their tireless efforts toward the achievement of justice and equality! They have recognized the struggles of America's working people and extended a call to unite and mobilize our organizations and communities to demand an end to the assault on the working class of America. ILWU was in South Carolina to stand side-by-side with International Longshoremen Association (ILA) Local 1422 President Ken Riley and the Charleston 5. Although I can not be with you today, I send you this message in spirit with urgency."

Saladin Muhammad: "...We send greetings from Black Workers for Justice and from workers in the U.S. South to the important May 22, Kick-Off Rally for the Million Worker March. It will be workers' organized power that will defeat the oppressive policies, direction and rule of corporate greed. The Bush-lead U.S. government in both parties must be challenged and defeated by workers power."

Walter Johnson: "It is appropriate that the seed for the Million Worker March be planted here in San Francisco. Tonight, here in this room is the beginning, but let us keep in mind we can only be successful if we act together. Only this way will the seed spread across America."

Ralph Schoenman: "The time has come to build a genuinely independent Million Worker March in Washington, D.C., in October 2004. The MWM organizers will have to guard against every attempt to take the MWM into safe channels for the corporations and politicians in their service. The organizers, for example, will have to keep their pledge that no Democratic Party politician will be allowed to speak from the podium. This is the only way to keep true to the independent working-class mandate of the Million Worker March."

Chris Silvera: "I am here today to tell you the truth, fighting trade unionism lives on in the longshore union, in ILWU Local 10. When they signed NAFTA, let us not forget it was a democratic president, Bill Clinton, who signed this bill on behalf of corporate America. A number of years ago, I approached AFL-CIO President John Sweeney and told him, 'Hell, if Farrakhan could put a million people in the streets, why can't we in the labor movement do the same?' I never got a response. Well, now it is the time for the Million Worker March. People might tell us along the way that this March will distract from this or that. I say no it won't. We've got to shake these folks in the labor movement and move them out into the streets. We are the working people of this country!"

Brenda Stokely: "I am proud to announce that AFSCME District Council 1707, representing 23,000 members voted unanimously to endorse the Million Worker March. Now we have to get to work, organizing from the ground up, rock by rock, by workplace, union by union. It is about building the strength to make sure we control the government. We've had enough of seeing labor beg on its knees. We should be mad as hell. Our sisters and brothers are dying in Iraq and we are taking it on the chin here at home. We've gotten to this point because we failed to organize and mobilize."

Previous calls for Marches in Washington made by Black workers

In analyzing the Million Worker March and putting it into its historical context you have to first look at the 1940s.

On Jan. 25, 1941, A. Philip Randolph, president of the Brotherhood of Sleeping Car Porters (BSCP), proposed the idea of a national mobilization of 10,000 African Americans for a March on Washington Movement (MOWM). The purpose was to pressure President Franklin D. Roosevelt to end discrimination in the government, the armed forces and to gain jobs in the defense industries, by demonstrating mass Black working class power.

There were many similarities between the MOWM (1941) and MWM (2004). The Marches were intended to be independent, militant, political mass movements led by African American trade unionists organized independently of the Democratic Party and the officialdom of labor, with chapters organized across the country. In 1941, Pres. Roosevelt opposed the MOWM having a march and rally at the U.S. Capitol. In 2004, the Democratic Party did not want the MWM to have a march and rally at the Lincoln Memorial. Both Marches appealed to the 'waged and unwaged' workers and not elected officials.

There were two prominent differences between MOWM and the MWM:

1. The MOWM **canceled its mobilization** because a deal was reached between Randolph and Roosevelt. Pres.

Roosevelt issued Executive Order 8802, which prohibited discrimination in federal vocational and training programs, established the first Fair Employment Practices Committee, and ended discrimination in hiring in defense industries contracting with the government; and

2. Randolph wanted to minimize the participation of whites. He is quoted as saying, "There are some things Negroes must do alone." See tinyurl.com/53vx8c75

In contrast:

1. The MWM happened and 10,000 people **attended** the march and rally at the Lincoln Memorial on Oct. 17, 2004; and

2. MWM reached out to the entire multi-national working class.

The Democratic Party and the officialdom of labor wanted the MWM called off. They offered no concessions, and we were not considering any. They used the excuse that it was the "wrong time," suggesting it should be organized the next year after the presidential election. We continued organizing in our own name.

MWM a tendency in the labor movement

The MWM represented a tendency within the trade union movement that has manifested itself for several decades. That tendency is a Black rank-and-file militancy that is unafraid to express an independent movement that is willing to challenge the more passive traditions of the officialdom of labor and its master, the Democratic Party. An example of this is the League of Revolutionary Black Workers (LRBW) formed in Detroit, Michigan in 1969. The LRBW brought together various revolutionary union movements that were forming inside of the auto industry and other industrial sectors. It was developed during a period of "increasing militancy and revolutionary consciousness" in the Black working class movement.

The MWM was initiated by African American longshore workers of Local 10 of the International Longshore and Warehouse Union (ILWU) in San Francisco. It's the only predominantly African American Local in the entire West Coast Longshore Division, with a long and glorious radical history that is well documented. It is in the vanguard in the fight for economic and social justice in the labor movement. In 1934, Black workers played a key role in the victory of the West Coast Waterfront Strike in San Francisco. The militancy, unity, and power of that victory still reverberates up and down the West Coast today.

ILWU 1934 built in struggle vs white supremacy

In 1934, during the great "West Coast Waterfront Strike," Harry Bridges, Henry Schmidt, and other rank-and-file strike leaders struck a mighty blow against white supremacy as it related to the employers' use of Black workers crossing the picket line during the Strike, as well as challenging discrimination within the labor movement.

They appealed directly to the Black community in the Bay Area through the Black churches to support the Strike and not cross the picket line. The union made a commitment to bring African Americans on the waterfront and to be a part of the union. In so doing, they demonstrated that **Black Lives Matter!** in 1934. And that strategy was the key to winning on the waterfront and successfully organizing the ILWU.

Bruce Nelson, in his book, "Divided We Stand: American Workers and the Struggle for Black Equality," acknowledges 'left wing' militants for challenging "Jim Crow" in the dock workers union on the West Coast. Bridges, Schmidt, and others understood how discrimination was a tool of the bosses in their ending the "shape up" (the discriminatory dispatch system) and undermining the employers' ability to exploit Blacks in scabbing on striking dock workers. Nelson quotes Bridges, "I went directly to them. I said: 'Our union means a new deal for Negroes'. Stick with us and we'll stand for your inclusion in the industry.'" And, he declared, "almost without exception, they stuck with us. They helped us. The employers were frustrated in their attempt to use them for scabs."

Peter Cole, in his book "Dockworker Power: Race and Activism in Durban and the San Francisco Bay Area," explains how these white radical dock workers who understood the intersectionality of race and class stepped forward with the support of C.L. Dellums, Oakland's "most prominent Black labor leader" and uncle to former congressman and mayor of Oakland, Ronald V. Dellums. Dellums said, "… I was interested in breaking up the segregation on the waterfront and breaking up the shape-up system and providing for Negroes to be allowed to work there, because they were human beings and had a right to work – and should work without discrimination."

Men like Dellums, Bridges, and Schmidt knew that all workers needed to be in the union, and that the interests of white and Black workers are inextricably linked. This was a pivotal moment of the 1934 Strike, but an even more significant moment in the history of the struggle of the working class.

Dick Meister in, "Labor – And A Whole Lot More: A Porter Who Dared Protest," describes Dellums thinking upon arriving in Oakland from his native Corsicana, Texas in 1925 in hopes of finding better opportunities. Dellums said, "There were only three ways an African American could make a living in Oakland – on the trains, on ships, and by doing something illegal." C.L. Dellums chose trains and his brother Verney chose ships.

'Fight or be slaves!', were the words of Dellums when the Brotherhood of Sleeping Car Porters (BSCP) was founded in 1925 and remained his credo for the rest of his life. BSCP aimed to improve the working conditions and treatment of African American railroad porters and maids employed by the Pullman Company. The BSCP was the first African American union to be recognized by the American Federation of Labor. Dellums was fired as a Pullman car porter for organizing. In 1968, he succeeded A. Philip Randolph and became the president of the union.

Local 10 was ideologically committed to building Black and white working class consciousness and solidarity. This provided the space and opportunity for Blacks in Local 10 to fully participate and to assert their influence and leadership in the local. It is important to provide some historical context as to how the origins of rank-and-file social conscious, anti-racist, trade unionism came about. It is because of that history Local 10 could make the call for the Million Worker March.

The Rev. Dr. Martin Luther King Jr.

On Sept, 21, 1967, six and one-half months before his assassination, Dr. King spoke at the ILWU Local 10 membership meeting. He was given an honorary lifetime membership in the union. William 'Bill' Chester, introduced Dr. King at that historic union meeting. King said, "I don't feel like a stranger in the midst of the ILWU. We have been strengthened and energized by the support you have given to our struggles. …What we need is a radical distribution of political and economic power so that in a nation almost sick with wealth there will not be so much poverty." He said, "If the nation cannot provide full employment, then it must grant minimum guaranteed annual incomes. We are going to organize the unorganized. Poverty, after all, is not only among the unemployed. Most of the poverty stricken are people who are working every day. We will organize to make clear that everyone

in this country has a right to a living income." See ILWU *The Dispatcher*, Vol 25 No. 20 Sept. 29, 1967. There is an iconic photograph in Local 10's hiring hall that features Dr. King, Thomas L. Berkley, publisher and Chairman of the Oakland Port Board of Commissioners, and Williams 'Bill' Chester. A framed copy of this photo was presented to Martin Luther King III at the MWM event. See page 25.

The MWM Mission Statement reflected Dr. King's statement at Local 10 and the 1968 "Poor People's March on Washington," that he initiated with the Southern Christian Leadership Conference (SCLC) and was carried forward by Ralph Abernathy in the wake of Dr. King's assassination.

The MWM mobilization was not to be denied due to the national election, lack of resources, the undeniable opposition of the AFL-CIO or the Democratic Party. The Million Worker March was born out of the Iraq and Afghanistan war; a workers movement to put peoples' needs above the bipartisan support for the military budget and war machine.

The MWM was held 41 years later at the Lincoln Memorial, where Dr. King gave his "I Had a Dream Speech," and where his son, Martin Luther King III spoke at the MWM in 2004.

Saladin Muhammad wrote in an email to me on Feb. 3, 2005: "Like the March on Washington in the 1940s, the MWM has the potential to set into motion a more politically defined working class based social justice movement similar to the Civil Rights Movement of the 1950s, but with a sharper anti-imperialist working class program reflecting the demands of African Americans, the oppressed, women, workers and the international community for this period. The MWM could help create the basis for the merging of the anti-war movement with the workers and oppressed people's movement to further radicalize both movements as was done with the anti-Vietnam War Movement and the African American Liberation Movement of the 1960s. The MWM in addition to promoting its independent political character must also promote new tactics that help to define its program as one of struggling for power for workers and oppressed peoples."

The working class cannot depend on presidents; we cannot depend on elections and voting to solve our problems. We the people, can solve our problems by organizing and mobilizing, in our own name, as we did with the MWM and breaking from the two parties of the bosses. We need a party that represents the working class and the oppressed.

Local 10, has been referred to disparagingly by some of the conservative members of the Longshore Division, as the 'Black power and commie Local': because the local is predominately Black with a history of militancy and commie because of our rank-and-file radical class conscious trade union activism. After all, Local 10 is the local of the legendary Harry Bridges and Henry Schmidt, two radical rank-and-file strike leaders and co-founders of the ILWU.

The roadblocks begin – Bill Fletcher

Immediately after Local 10 issued the call for the MWM to mobilize at the Lincoln Memorial, many in the labor union thought this was pure 'folly.' Alan Benjamin, who attended the Kickoff Rally, wrote in *The Organizer*, May/June 2004 issue, those in the labor movement who were raising objections to the March said, "This is an election year, and all the resources of labor and community organizations will be devoted to 'Dumping Bush.' No one will get behind the call for the MWM call," some said. There were other concerns and issues that were raised from serious labor activists nationwide. "Local 10 should have built a coalition of unionists and community groups first, before issuing this Call," they said.

William 'Bill' Fletcher, assistant to AFL-CIO president John Sweeney, vice president George Meany Center for Labor Studies, and president & CEO of TransAfrica Forum, was among those that did not endorse the MWM. Fletcher was one of the first persons outside of the initiators of the MWM, to see the resolution before it was even submitted to Local 10's executive board. The occasion was the Northern California Chapter CBTU, Annual Salute to Black Labor Dinner, where he was keynote speaker in February 2004. Brother Leo Robinson and I congratulated him on his speech where he called for Black workers to play a vanguard role in leading a fight back movement and an agenda for working people in the trade union movement; which was exactly what the MWM represented.

When we shared the MWM resolution with Fletcher his response was very positive. We agreed to have follow up discussions and we did.

Bill Fletcher was no stranger to the ILWU. He had an opportunity to interview the legendary Harry Bridges. He spoke of this in his Sept. 12, 2003 speech at the Labor Notes Conference. In 2004, he introduced me in New York City at a SEIU sponsored gathering, where I reported, along with David Bacon, on our visit with Iraqi workers, October 2003.

Fletcher was invited to the May 22 Kick-Off Rally at Local 10. He expressed a willingness to attend if his schedule permitted. However, he raised some specific pre-conditions and concerns before he could endorse the MWM. In an email dated April 29, 2004, he wrote,

> "Thanks, but let me clarify. I have some misgivings about the call for a million worker march. We should discuss this. I believe that a worker mobilization is important. At the same time, I do not believe that a call from a Local union will make it. To move this, and I think back on the Solidarity Day March in 1981, there needs to be significant resources put into it by either the AFL-CIO or at least one or two national unions. Second, I think that the demands need to be very clear and sharp. In other words, there must be a clear focus. Third, there must be broad outreach that really hits at the issue of economic justice. That would mean identifying – prior to a call for such a march – key mass organizations that are focused on working people but may not themselves be unions. So, on the one hand, I am open to speaking about the conditions facing workers. At the same time, I am not prepared to endorse a call for such a march unless I have a MUCH clearer sense as to who has been spoken to; what their responses have been; have national unions been approached; etc. I hope you understand. I cannot speak on behalf of Danny Glover but my guess is that he would share many of these same concerns.
> In unity, Bill Fletcher, Jr."

Brother Fletcher did not attend the Kick-Off Rally.

Notwithstanding the concerns and objections raised by Fletcher and others in and outside the labor movement, including the leadership of the ILWU, the incontrovertible fact was this: the Million Worker March was already a reality. Significant unions, community organizations, renowned figures in entertainment, and academia had already endorsed the MWM.

The MWM's Mission Statement reflected the goal of reaching out to workers organized and unorganized. Most workers are not members of unions. We wanted to reach the broad multi-national working class.

ILWU's opposition

The leadership of the ILWU deliberately acted to undermine the MWM soon after it was adopted at the Longshore Caucus. *The Dispatcher*, the official newspaper of the ILWU did not mention the MWM resolution or its Kick-Off Rally at Local 10 on May 22. It was not until we raised criticism with the International leadership informing them that their actions were tantamount to censoring the MWM mobilization before they acquiesced and printed the story about the Kick-off Rally in the June/July issue of *The Dispatcher.* These attempts to sabotage the mobilization had a chilling effect on our ability to raise funds, both within and outside the ILWU.

We met with Brother James Spinosa, ILWU International President upon his return from the 2004 Democratic National Convention (DNC) in Boston. Brother Spinosa was very forthcoming in describing a meeting with a number of presidents of international labor unions at the home of Sen. Edward Kennedy (D-Mass.), prior to the start of the DNC. Leaders included James P. Hoffa Jr., General President of International Brotherhood of Teamsters (IBT); Andy Stern, President Service Employees International Union (SEIU); and John Sweeney, President AFL-CIO. They discussed how the MWM was a great idea but it was the wrong time. (This was verified in the Sept. 12, 2004 issue of *The Dispatcher.* John Showalter wrote:

> "On the Friday prior to the Convention's start, Spinosa was also invited to Senator Edward Kennedy's (D-MA) home in Hyannis Port, MA, where he rubbed elbows with other national labor leaders.")

Spinosa was justifying not supporting the MWM mobilization because labor officials and democrats believed that it would be a distraction for providing the necessary labor support for John Kerry. His rationale was in direct violation of the ILWU's TEN GUIDING PRINCIPLES upon which our union is based. The first Guiding Principle reads in part as follows:

> "A union is built on its members. The strength, understanding and unity of the membership can determine the union's course and its advancements. The members who work, who make up the union and pay it dues can best determine their own destiny. … In brief, it is the membership of the union which is the best judge of its own welfare; not the officers, not the employers, not the politicians and the fair weather friends of labor." …

Saladin Muhammad wrote under the heading Breaking with Business Unionism, "AFL-CIO, sends a wrong message about the role and power of labor, when it publicly opposes the call for the Million Worker March. The fear by the national trade union bureaucracy of waging a strong and united challenge against the forces and policies of capital has led many trade unions to enter into compromises that are eroding some of the hard fought gains won by their members over the years. This only makes the corporations more arrogant and aggressive in their attacks of unions and the broader working class."

It was no surprise that when we presented a proposal for funding MWM mobilization to the ILWU International al Executive Board (IEB), the proposal was flatly rejected. They refused to provide any type of financial or material support. The IEB as well as the AFL-CIO, were sending a very strong message to the rank-and-file. Obviously, that did not stop the will of the rank-and-file from organizing and mobilizing in our own name at the Lincoln Memorial on October 17.

The rank-and-file overcame and Leo Robinson

Brother Gabriel Prawl, executive board member of ILWU Local 19 in Seattle and the MWM coordinator of the Pacific Northwest, introduced a motion to allow Brother Leo Robinson to address the membership. Prawl was motivated to do this because he was disappointed at the meager $500 donation the local was contributing to the MWM. Robinson had a reputation in the Longshore Division. Members never doubted his commitment to the ILWU and its rank-and-file.

During Robinson's remarks to the Local 19 membership he asserted, "I couldn't stop the MWM even if I wanted to." He made such a compelling case for supporting the MWM, that a white member of the Local stood and made a motion that the Local make a $5,000 contribution to the MWM. The motion passed unanimously!

Peter Cole in his piece, "Leo Robinson: ILWU Activist Led Anti-Apartheid Struggle," wrote, "Robinson was outspoken and not afraid of controversy. He frequently challenged officials and union policies, using his passion and public speaking skills to command respect from his audience."

The MWM could not have happened without the leadership, dedication and sacrifice of Local 10 and Local 34 members and pensioners. For example, pensioner Leo Robinson contributed $50,000 and pensioner Addison "Jr" Hicks was also a large contributor. I lost two qualifying years of retirement benefits due to my organizing for the Million Worker March in 2004 and the subsequent Million Worker March Movement in 2005.

We all understood that solidarity is not an empty slogan. Leo's contribution was truly revolutionary, he placed his money and actions where his beliefs were as he had on other occasions. He demonstrated that indeed the power of the rank-and-file resides in their hip pocket as Harry Bridges had pointed out many times. The MWM was a rank-and-file movement in the truest sense of the word.

The contributions of Danny Glover can not be overstated. Danny was a San Francisco College (SFSC) classmate of mine where we were arrested as student activists. We served on the Black Student Union Central Committee together during the 1968 SFSC student strike.

In Kitty Kelly Epstein and Bernard Stringer's book, "Changing Academia Forever – Black Student Leaders Analyze the movement they led," Danny states, "One of the things that I think is important to observe about the strike is the coalition building. …The coalition politics with progressive white students, Latino students, Asian American students, and First Nation students were key in making the strike successful."

Danny contributed unselfishly his time and money to the building of the MWM. He has been a part of many historical actions initiated by the organizers of the MWM over the last 16 years, as this anthology will attest.

Teamsters National Black Caucus (TNBC)

Brother Chris Silvera, a Jamaican born radical trade unionist, is the longest serving elected principal officer in the Teamsters.

During his leadership, at the 29th Annual Educational Conference of the TNBC in Orlando a motion was made to contribute $10,000 to the MWM, it passed unanimously. C. Thomas Keegel, General Secretary-Treasurer of the International Brotherhood of Teamsters (IBT), who was present, assured the membership that this would get done.

As TNBC Chair, Silvera's bold and courageous leadership motivated the contribution in defiance of the AFL-CIO directive to not devote any resources toward its mobilization.

On Sept. 20, 2004, Mike Mathis, Director of Government Affairs of the Teamsters, sent a memo to local unions and joint council principal officers reading in part:

> "We agree as does the AFL-CIO in principal with the idea of the Million Worker March. However, we also believe that the timing of the March will divert valuable time and resources away from our efforts in the Battle Ground States."

It is clear the memo was intended to stop any further motions on the part of Teamsters to provide any material support to the MWM.

The Teamsters did keep their commitment to donate $10,000 to MWM. The check was sent soon after the successful march. In 2005, IBT contributed another $10,000 to the Million Worker March Movement's, commemoration of the Million More Movement in Washington D.C. See page 71. We welcome their 2004 and 2005 generous contributions which added up to $20,000.

Sister Brenda Stokely was president of AFSCME DC 1707 and Local 215 in New York City. She is a leading radical African American labor activist; a dynamic voice in the anti-war movement for labor; and co-convener of the New York City Labor Against the War (NYCLAW). Stokely's strong and unwavering leadership was critical in the building of MWM on the East Coast. Stokely was retaliated against for her support of the MWM. After the March, she was illegally removed from office and was reinstated by the courts.

Stokely and Silvera were responsible for generating large delegations of union workers to the march from their respective unions. Teamsters and AFSCME members from across the country attended the MWM.

The March

On October 17, 2004, thousands of organized and unorganized workers, immigrant rights groups, anti-war and social justice activists, interfaith and community organizations and international trade unionists from around the world, answered the call from the organizers of the Million Worker March to rally at the Lincoln Memorial, 'mobilizing in our own name.' They were present answering the call with their identifiable banners, posters, tee shirts and jackets, MWM's navy blue and heather gray MWM tee shirts, and buttons, all expressing their agreement with the:

MILLION WORKER MARCH LIST OF DEMANDS:

- Universal Health Care
- Stop Dismantling Public Education
- Enforce All Civil Rights
- Bring the Troops Home Now
- Hands Off Social Security
- Workers Right to Organize
- Tax Relief for the Working Class
- Preserve and Restore Environment
- Truth in Media

- Stop Off-Shoring American Jobs
- Stop Corporate Greed
- Repeal Taft Hartley
- Slash the Military Budget
- National Living Wage
- Repeal Corporate Free Trade Agreements
- Amnesty for All Undocumented Workers

The call of the MWM had come from one of the most well-known labor organizations in the country and the world, famous for its long history of militancy, boldness, and courage in defense of the working class, African Americans and the oppressed. Local 10 initiated the call and the working class at home and abroad answered the call despite threats, intimidation, and the lack of financial support from the top leadership of the Democratic Party and AFL-CIO, including the leadership of the International Longshore and Warehouse Union.

But they still could not oppose its aims and issues. Supporters across the country immediately understood the relevancy and the urgent need to go to Washington and speak in our own name. The Million Worker March was intended to become a movement and not an organization.

The MWM represented a workers fight back movement with a workers agenda, against two political parties acting as one. Those parties try to confine the working class to a corporate agenda of permanent war internationally, and economic insecurity for the working class at home. That is why thousands and thousands of workers organized and unorganized assembled on the Lincoln Memorial that day so that their independent voices were heard. No democrat or republican politicians were allowed to the podium.

The March launched a movement that emerged as a defining struggle of the 21st century for the working class. It had a mission statement, demands and principles. The speakers at the Lincoln Memorial spoke for the vast majority of the people of the U.S. from: New York; Philadel-phia; Baltimore; Washington, D.C.; Charleston; Columbia; Atlanta; Cleveland; Chicago; Decatur; Minneapolis; St. Paul; Houston; Los Angeles; Oakland; San Francisco; Portland; and Seattle.

And the appeal of the MWM was global. The movement we launched was international in scope because we all face the same privatization and austerity. Platform speakers included representatives from: Haiti, Japan and South Africa, just to name a few. Voices and faces both on the stage and in the crowd, was a harbinger of struggles to come. Leaders of major trade union federations and worker organizations from Bangladesh, Brazil, Britain, Canada, India, Hong Kong, Japan, Pakistan, Philippines, Russia, South Korea, and Venezuela sent statements of support and plans for ongoing coordinated struggles. These messages were sent on behalf of 47 million organized workers across the globe.

Simultaneous mobilizations in support of the Million Worker March were held in Seoul, Korea; Madrid, Spain; Paris, France; and Sao Paulo, Brazil, among other cities. There were ten such actions in Japan, spearheaded by Doro Chiba, the Japanese Railway Workers Union that has led the fight against privatization.

Now more than ever workers around the world must act in unity in our own interests. Workers must build an international rank-and-file fight-back movement to defend the rights of workers internationally to achieve economic security and a peaceful world.

Conclusion

The anthology includes: abridged articles, reports from conferences and meetings, endorsers, and interviews from *The ILWU Dispatcher, The Organizer,* and *Workers World* newspapers along with other periodicals. There are also selections from the *Peoples Video Network, Labor Video Project*, from individuals' writings and books on labor, as well as leaflets, photos, posters, speeches and other video transcripts.

Through these documents, the story is told of the Million Worker March and Movement, its roots, and the branches that have grown from it, **mobilizing in our own name.**

Interviewing Delores Lemon-Thomas

Les Blough Editor, Axis of Logic

At the Million Worker March in front of the Lincoln Memorial in Washington D.C., I had the pleasure of interviewing Delores Lemon-Thomas, spouse of Clarence Thomas, one of the chief organizers and a co-founder of the MWM. It was in their dining room in the Bay Area of Northern California that it all began.

Les Blough: I know you've been very busy today, so I want to thank you for giving us this interview.

You have been involved in planning and organizing the MWM from the beginning and that you have sacrificed along with others to bring it to Washington today. Can you tell our readers how the MWM began?

Delores Lemon-Thomas: It all began in our dining room in a discussion with Leo Robinson, a Local 10 retiree, Trent Willis, Business Agent and Henry Graham, Local 10 President. Clarence is rank-and-file but also on the Executive Board of Local 10.

It was Trent's idea. We were all fighting to let the worker's voices be heard, but nobody was listening. So, Trent called

Clarence and said, "Clarence, I think we ought to do a Million Workers March on Washington."

Clarence said, "Let's do it." So he came over with the others to discuss it. By listening to the demands of the workers, they made resolutions and took it back to the membership who passed the resolution. But the International refused to endorse it

LES: Why do you think the big union federations didn't endorse the MWM. Why aren't the top leaders here today?

DLT: Because the leadership of the large unions are following the voices of the politicians, not the workers who elected them. It doesn't matter what Bush or Kerry say. It's about what the workers want. These union leaders are "Anybody But Bush." But, when you look at John Kerry, he would ignore the workers too, he'd just ignore them better! Who's going to speak for health care for workers? Who's going to speak out against outsourcing? For a sustainable wage and the education of our children? The workers have to speak out because the politicians and the union leaders aren't doing it for them. We're listening to their program. But are they listening to our program?

The leadership of the big labor coalitions say, "We don't have the funds." The reason they don't have funds is that the money is all going to the politicians. The AFL-CIO has donated millions to the politicians, but nothing for the workers. All the money for this wonderful event came directly from the workers themselves.

LES: We heard about Mr. Robinson's generous contribution of $50,000 out of his own pocket for the MWM. But I know that you must have sacrificed to make the MWM happen today. Can you tell us about what this has meant to you and your family?

Leo Robinson speaking on the steps of the Lincoln memorial, Oct. 17 2004.

Photo: Don Williams

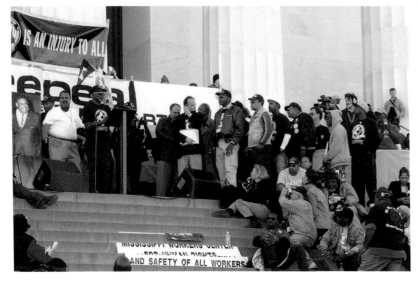

DLT: Actually, Leo Robinson has contributed more than $60,000. Well, Clarence gave up a year of seniority on his job for the MWM. That meant losing a year of health care coverage and not enough income to contribute to his retirement fund. So it cost us in terms of our annual income and it will affect his retirement.

But this is bigger than an annual check and our health care coverage. This is about speaking in our own name and letting people around the country know that we as workers have power.

LES: Can you tell us about your family?

DLT: We have two grown children and two grandchildren. Our families are here today from California. Clarence's mother and father have been activists all their lives. His grandfather, father and great uncle were all longshoremen. His mother has always been an activist too, as a block parent, member of the PTA and other things. She's a very strong woman.

LES: What do you think of the MWM so far today?

DLT: The number of people has exceeded all my expectations. All that networking and sacrifice that has led up to this and all these people are so inspiring!

LES: And how has this year of work and sacrifice affected your marriage and relationship with Clarence?

DLT: Oh, you know I could help Clarence slow down and help him think things through. Sometimes when things became difficult, I took him out to a restaurant, just to get out of the middle of things, to help him calm down. We did that quite a few times. He didn't know anything about the computer. I taught him how to use e-mail and download files and all of that. He would always thank me.

LES: Thank you for taking the time out of your busy schedule to share your thoughts on the MWM and giving us insight into what it takes from all members of a family to build this successful campaign on behalf of working women and men. Thank you for all your sacrifice and hard work to make all of this possible.

DLT: Today is only the beginning!

Les Blough, Editor, *Axis of Logic*
Boston, MA

Delores Lemon-Thomas inspecting the damage to the Lower Ninth Ward home of her uncle, Shep Davis, after Hurricane Katrina in 2005.

Davis was a longshore worker in New Orleans. Chapter 4 is about the consequences of Hurricane Katrina.

Photo: Clarence Thomas

Acknowledgments

My deep appreciation to the membership of the International Longshore and Warehouse Union (ILWU) Local 10 and other locals of the Longshore Division, for the rank-and-file unity that they have demonstrated and displayed in the many struggles that we have chronicled in this anthology.

A special thanks to all my peers because without their experiences, support, and encouragement this book would not have been finished.

I would like to thank the many unions, organizations, movements, and individuals who made the Million Worker March and Movement a reality. Your articles, endorsements, leaflets, labor, photos, speeches, and video transcripts along with your attendance and activism continue to build a fight-back movement to defend the rights of workers everywhere.

I want to express my sincere appreciation to political prisoner Mumia Abu-Jamal, who was on death row at that time, for his resolute support of the Million Worker March and the many struggles that followed, always fighting for the release of all political prisoners.

Finally, I would like to personally acknowledge those who were directly involved in completing this anthology: David Bacon, Mildred Center, Kelly Kane, Cheryl LaBash, Phil Meyer, John Parulis, Bryan G. Pfeifer, Gloria Verdieu, Lallan Schoenstein, Denise Lemon-Price, Bill Hackwell, Gary Wilson, and Michael Letwin.

I am indebted to my wife Delores Lemon-Thomas for her unwavering commitment to do what was called for in completing this book.

THE STRUGGLE CONTINUES

A message from the editor

Early in 2019, Clarence Thomas, an African American labor activist, longshore leader, and an organizer of the 2004 Million Worker March (MWM) said he was working on a book; an Anthology of the Million Worker March Movement.

The Million Worker March and rally was held on October 17, 2004, on the steps of the Lincoln Memorial. It was attended by thousands of workers organized and unorganized representing unions, communities, and grassroots organizations from around the world. Organizers estimate that the March and Rally represented 3.5 million workers. Martin Luther King Jr. III, standing where his father Dr. Martin Luther King Jr., Rep. John Lewis, and A. Philip Randolph spoke at the 1963 March on Washington for Jobs and Freedom, told the crowd that civil rights, workers, and anti-war activists must come together in common cause.

Thomas spoke of the history of the International Longshore and Warehouse Union (ILWU) and the General Strike of 1934 led by Harry Bridges, a native of Australia. The great ILWU emerged out of that strike under the leadership of Bridges. Written into the ILWU contracts which covered all workers are these words, "There will be no discrimination by the employers or by anyone employed by the employers against any worker or any member of the union because of members activities, race, creed, color, national origin, religious, or political beliefs."

– "American Minorities and the Case of Harry Bridges"

W.E.B. Du Bois said, "Harry Bridges' place in history must never be forgotten. His Union today is one of the most extraordinary creations of current democracy… and for the first time in their history colored workers are received into equal membership, with no discrimination…"

The role of ILWU and the MWMM is important and it clearly needs to be documented and recorded. Having recently completed editing, compiling, and publishing the Book, "Black August 1619-2019" with Lallan Schoenstein, we offered to help Clarence finish his book. We were both excited about this publishing project, and the opportunity to work with Clarence, a 30-year veteran of ILWU Local 10.

This book documents the Million Worker March Movement, drawing on articles from the mainstream media, transcribed audio presentations and interviews, as well as media from the union movement, community news, and political organizations. The source and dates of the

Gloria Verdieu, Delores Lemon-Thomas and Clarence Thomas at the U.S./Cuba Labor Exchange Conference in Tijuana 2008.

publications can be found at the end of the article in italic wherever possible.

Many reprints and excerpts are taken from the excellent articles in Workers World newspaper because of the consistent and supportive coverage over the years written by those who were themselves engaged in building the MWM. The articles document the profound significance of Black labor organizing in its own name and its role in leading a struggle to empower and unite the working class.

Another source for the book was the pamphlet "*United! ILWU ranks and 'Occupy' fight 'Wall Street on the Waterfront,'* articles from the pages of WW, compiled by Cheryl LaBash. The 54-page booklet contains reports from September 2011 to February 2012.

I asked Thomas, "Why Million Worker March was chosen as the name?" His response was, "It is not the name that brought people to D.C. it was the demands; **THE ILWU TEN GUIDING PRINCIPLES** are the 'Guiding Principles to Building International Solidarity."

From the Commentary to the index this book should be included as required reading in all Ethnic Studies Curriculum, from kindergarten to high school, trade schools and for those who question the power of workers united. This Anthology defines the true meaning of ILWU's slogan 'An Injury to One is an Injury to All.'

Gloria Verdieu

This book is a compilation of material selected by Clarence Thomas, edited by Delores Lemon-Thomas, Cheryl LaBash, Lallan Schoenstein and Gloria Verdieu.

CHAPTER 1

LABOR MUST SPEAK IN ITS OWN VOICE
Organizing the Million Worker March

Join Us in a Historic Kick-Off Rally of the
MILLION WORKER MARCH
ON WASHINGTON, D.C. – OCTOBER 17

Come Learn About It:

Saturday, May 22 at 8 p.m.
ILWU Local 10 Hiring Hall

400 North Point (@ Mason)
San Francisco

Welcoming Remarks:
Henry Graham, President, ILWU Local 10
Featured Speakers Include:
Danny Glover, Renowned Actor & Activist
Chris Silvera, Secretary-Treasurer, Teamsters Local 808 (N.Y.) and Chair, Teamsters National Black Caucus;
Walter Johnson, Secretary-Treasurer, San Francisco Labor Council
María Guillen, Vice President, SEIU Local 790
Dennis Orton, Black Workers For Justice (BWFJ)
Ralph Schoenman, Co-Producer, Pacifica's Taking Aim/Guns and Butter
Alexander Cockburn, Counterpunch
Frank Martin Del Campo, President, S.F. LCLAA

(For more information contact 510-815-1309 or 707-552-9992)

Partial List of Endorsers of the Million Worker March:

ILWU Local 10; Teamsters Local 808 (Long Island City, N.Y.); Northern California Teamsters Black Caucus; Northern California Chapter, Coalition of Black Trade Unionists; San Francisco Labor Council; Donna Dewitt, President, South Carolina AFL-CIO; Letter Carriers, Local 214; GCIU Local 4-N; San Francisco Chapter, Labor Council for Latin American Advancement (LCLAA); UAW 1981 Chapter 3; AFSCME Local 1072; Charleston, South Carolina Labor Council; Troy (New York) Labor Council; Albany (New York) Labor Council; Jim Houghton, Director, Harlem Fight Back; Dick Gregory; Father Lawrence Lucas, Our Lady of Lourdes, Roman Catholic Church, Harlem; Al Avants, Secretary-Treasurer, UFCW Local 373R; Michael Lewis, IBEW Local 617 (San Mateo); Solano County Peace and Justice Coalition; I.W.W.   (list in formation)

Jobs, health-care and a living wage for all
Workers want to bring the troops home now

LABOR ANTI-WAR CONTINGENT

AN INJURY TO ONE IS AN INJURY TO

MILLION WORKER
Volunteers & funds need!
MARCH
The bosses are attacking us everyday
WE WILL FIGHT BACK
OCTOBER 17, 2004
LINCOLN MEMORIAL · WASHINGTON, D.C.

NATIONAL SAN FRANCISCO ILWU Local 10	BOSTON c/o USWA Local 8751	LONG ISLAND CITY, N.Y. Teamsters	NEW YORK c/o AFSCME District Council 1707	BALTIMORE MILLION WORKER MARCH
415.771.2028	617.524.3507	718.389.1900 x21	212.219.0022 x 5185	410.235.7040
WASHINGTON D.C. Million Worker March	MIDWEST REGION Chicago,IL Local 3506/AFSCME	SOUTHWEST REGION	NORTH CAROLINA Black Workers for Justice	SOUTH CAROLINA AFL-CIO
202.355.8666		713-928-3738	252-977-1419	803-798-8300

MillionWorkerMarch.org

Labor rally kicks off organizing
Million Worker March set for October

Ralph Schoenman

Can labor organize an independent mass mobilization to address the broad range of problems facing the multinational working class here? Though many hurdles need to be overcome, the answer being given is a resounding "Yes!"

On February 26, Local 10 of the International Longshore and Warehouse Union (ILWU) in San Francisco proposed a bold initiative: a Million Worker March on Washington. This plucky union is well known nationally for its leading role in class warfare and in struggles against U.S. imperialist wars. The leaders have educated, organized, and defended their rank-and-file in a period of unprecedented hostility from Washington and Wall Street.

The local union passed a resolution that the call be forwarded to "unions, labor councils and labor organizations, as well as other organizations to which workers belong whether organized or not, so they can take similar action to organize this march as soon as possible." At a kickoff rally here on May 22, they set the date for the march: October 17, 2004.

The May 22 rally sent a strong message that it was time to take the road of independent class struggle and break labor's traditional ties to the Democratic Party. Clarence Thomas, an executive board member of ILWU, Local 10 and a nationally known African-American trade union leader, issued an appeal to support the Million Worker March (MWM):

"This is a Call to working people to unite and mobilize around our own agenda. For the past decade we have been subject to an unrestrained corporate assault. This is the moment; this is the time for us to

Chris Silvera

Larry Holmes

Ralph Schoenman

Sharon Black

Brenda Stokely with other speakers on Sept. 16, 2004 at the National Press Club.
Image captured from a video by Raza Namdar.

Clarence Thomas

Trent Willis speaking at the Juneteenth Rally in 2020

Photo: Amir Aziz

advance our own demands, our own needs and to proclaim a political agenda in our own vital interests." Thomas and Trent Willis, another member of ILWU, Local 10, chaired the rally.

The rally of around 250 participants represented a diverse group of primarily trade union leaders from many parts of the country.

Individual endorsers included community organizers, anti-war representatives and fighters for civil rights like Dick Gregory, Danny Glover and Casey Kasem. The undocumented were represented by the San Francisco Day Laborers Program. Within a short time, the entire ILWU Longshore Division endorsed MWM, in spite of the ILWU International executive board endorsement of John Kerry.

Brenda Stokely gave a passionate appeal to build MWM. She is president of District Council 1707 of the American Federation of State, County, Municipal Employees, AFL-CIO in New York, and a nationally known African American woman who is a labor leader and a strong opponent of the Iraq war.

Chris Silvera, secretary treasurer of Teamsters Local 808 in Long Island City, N.Y., and chairperson of the Teamsters National Black Caucus, reflected on the sentiment of the rally: "Now you can sit around and wait for Kerry to do something. But we are going to Washington to shake the house. We need to take back our country, take back our rights and rip up the Patriot Act."

Among the many speakers was Walter Johnson, secretary treasurer of the San Francisco Central Labor Council. The base of support for the mobilization so far is the West Coast labor movement.

Organizers from Baltimore, St. Louis, Los Angeles, New York, Charleston, S.C., Cleveland and seven other cities agreed to set up centers to build the march.

The labor councils of Charleston, S.C., and five other cities around the country endorsed the proposal.

A call to the rank-and-file

This call comes at a most opportune time. It is an appeal to the rank-and-file, to the disfranchised, the oppressed who labor in the fields, the factories, the mines and the offices. It is a reminder that they have a collective power, a power in numbers that can resist the relentless assault on their living conditions.

It is a call to action against the banks and bosses, led by President George W. Bush, who has written off the workers, organized and unorganized.

The *Wall Street Journal* had gloated on Jan. 23 that "Membership has been in decline since the Reagan years, but the latest report shows a more dramatic fall than usual. Unions don't seem to have the allure that they once did, especially for younger workers. All of which must depress John Sweeney who took over the AFL-CIO some years ago promising organizing. ... The shrinking labor movement has lost clout in the real economy."

The gloating is generated by the overall growth of profits resulting from layoffs, downsizing of wages and benefits, privatizing and outsourcing, which continue unabated without significant resistance. For 1,488 companies tracked by Dow Jones & Co., net income in the first quarter was $159.2 billion, up 23 percent from the first quarter of 2003. (WSJ, May 28, 2004)

These corporate profits are achieved on the backs of the workers, especially through increased productivity, two-tier concessionary contracts and reduced wages and benefits. In the race to the bottom that generates these huge profits, the top leaders of the official labor movement have so far shown neither an independent policy nor a strategy of action to rescue the besieged sisters and brothers.

Million Worker March shows labor on the move

Milt Neidenberg

Timing is often critical when taking on a struggle to advance the cause of the workers and oppressed. A political program is primary for prosecuting the class struggle. On both counts, the proposal for an October 17 Million Worker March (MWM) on Washington gets high marks. Although time is short and resources are slim, fulfillment of this splendid objective will lay the basis for building an independent, class-wide movement.

On Feb. 26, as the election-year rhetoric of the capitalist parties began to heat up, Local 10 of the International Longshore and Warehouse Union (ILWU) in San Francisco proposed this bold initiative. They passed a resolution that a call be sent out to "unions, labor councils and labor organizations, as well as other organizations to which workers belong, whether organized or not, so they can take similar actions to organize this march as soon as possible."

The Million Worker March was born. This militant union is nationally known for its leading role in the struggle against the Iraq war and the anti-labor offensive at home. On April 7, 2003, ILWU Local 10 was involved in a demonstration against the Iraq war. They honored a picket line outside the Oakland terminals of the Stevedoring Services of America (SSA), a major contractor chosen by the Defense Department to rebuild the largest seaport in Iraq. The protest shut SSA down.

The action led to a brutal attack by the Oakland police. The April *ILWU Dispatcher* vividly describes the event: "They unleashed waves of terror with barrages of lethal rubber bullets, concussion grenades and bean bags filled with metal shot and wooden pellets, to break up the picket line. Scores were injured, many sent to the hospital with severe wounds. Twenty-four protesters and an ILWU business agent were arrested."

Marking the one-year anniversary on April 7, 2004, hundreds of protesters held a rally at the Alameda County court house, marched to a SSA terminal and shut down the entire second shift. Two weeks later the Alameda district attorney dropped all charges against the protesters.

Time for independent struggle

Following the victory, on May 22, a MWM kickoff rally was held. It sent a strong message that it is time to take the road of independent class struggle and break labor's traditional ties to the "lesser of two evils," the Democratic Party.

Over 250 participated in the rally, representing labor unionists, community activists and anti-war protesters from around the country.

At the recent American Federation of State, County and Municipal Employees (AFSCME) convention of more than 3,000 delegates held in Anaheim, Ca., Brenda Stokely was among a number of progressive and anti-war delegates who presented a resolution to end the occupation and bring the troops home. It passed overwhelmingly in spite of an effort by International President Gerald McEntee to water it down.

Under Stokely's leadership, District Council 1707 proposed a resolution to support the MWM. The resolution was tabled, but the AFSCME constitution provides avenues for the fight to continue. The Coalition of Black Trade Unionists, the South Carolina State AFL-CIO and numerous other locals and councils have joined the initiative.

The National Education Association (NEA), with 2.7 million members, announced it is backing the MWM. The NEA has affiliates in every state who work in education — from pre-school to university graduate programs. Its affiliates are in more than 13,000 communities across the U.S.

Break with big-business parties

Fearful that this development will undermine the "anybody but Bush" campaign, the American Federation of Labor and Congress of Industrial Organizations (AFL-CIO) leadership opened up an attack on the MWM.

On June 23, AFL-CIO President John Sweeney, through the director of the Field Mobilization Department, sent a memorandum to all State Federations and Central Labor Councils of the AFL-CIO. It read in part, "The AFL-CIO is not a co-sponsor of this effort and we will not be devoting resources or energies toward mobilizing demonstrations this fall. ... We think it is absolutely crucial that we commit the efforts of our labor movement to removing George W. Bush from office."

In a column entitled "Reclaim America," Sweeney praises Kerry's record on behalf of labor. "President Bush's failed policies and Senator John Kerry's (Democrat Mass) plans to create good jobs," Sweeney wrote, "ensure health coverage and restore pride and momentum to a nation tarnished by the Bush administration's domestic heartlessness and international incompetence." (*America at Work*, June/July 2004) By "international incompetence," Sweeney is referring to the U.S. quagmire in Iraq.

The Democrats and Kerry are for internationalizing the conflict and putting more troops and resources into the occupation that has already led to mounting casualties and the diversion of huge amounts of money from social services to the Pentagon. It will only prolong death and destruction for the Iraqi people as well. Kerry voted for the Iraq War and recently the Senate voted 98-0 to expand the Pentagon budget to more than $400 billion.

It would be wise for the AFL-CIO to distance itself from the Democrats' position on the war and to demand: end the occupation and bring the troops home now. The Service Employees International Union, (SEIU) the largest AFL-CIO affiliate, overwhelmingly passed this anti-war resolution at its June convention.

To build an independent, class-wide movement, it is indispensable to break with the two capitalist parties. The AFL-CIO must break the chains binding it to Kerry and the Democratic Party.

Kerry's labor record has to be exposed, not covered up. It has been 10 years since the North American Free Trade Agreement (NAFTA) passed with his blessing, and to this day he is a supporter of NAFTA as an exemplary model for all U.S. imperialist trade agreements. NAFTA has been a horrendous disaster for the workers, oppressed and impoverished. In the U.S., factories have been shut down, thousands of jobs lost, outsourced to low-paid nonunion labor in countries like Mexico, leaving ghost towns in many states.

The Mexican government estimates that between 800,000 and 2.5 million children work instead of attending school. Serious health and safety violations are common in the workplace and sinister environmental dangers pervade the communities surrounding the factories. U.S. corporations collude with local managers. Wall Street bankers and corporate bosses accumulate huge profits as they privatize large swaths of valuable property in underdeveloped countries.

Kerry's cabal

Kerry has surrounded himself with a cabal of these bankers and big-business advisors. He has selected as his running mate Sen. John Edwards from North Carolina, where workers, particularly in the textile industries, have suffered under NAFTA. North Carolina is a "right to work" state, that is, a scab state. Laws that exist there and in 20 other states have decimated every gain made by labor, including the right to organize unions.

The Kerry/Edwards slate is an insult to the 13 million organized workers, as well as millions more who yearn to be in unions.

Kerry supports a miserly raise in the minimum wage from $5.15 to $7 over two years that will keep most low-paid workers and their families in poverty. He was responsible for the defeat of an extension of unemployment insurance, which lost by one vote, by not showing up. Kerry supports the Clinton workfare program, which has created an underclass of workers and eliminated good-paying union jobs, depriving oppressed workers, including many women of color and single mothers, of daycare, decent housing and educational opportunities.

Kerry has no plans for a massive jobs creation program to alleviate the conditions of millions of unemployed workers. He has supported the massive raids by the Immigration and Naturalization Service, now part of the so-called Department of Homeland Security, on the undocumented. And he has not spoken out against the repressive Patriot Act nor supported same-sex marriage.

How can AFL-CIO President John Sweeney, with his line of "anybody but Bush," ignore all this?

The AFL-CIO is racked with problems and internal tensions. Its leadership needs to support, not attack, an independent class-struggle movement that along with the oppressed nationalities will forge the unity that is so necessary and timely. It is a dangerous oversight for the AFL-CIO to key up the rank-and-file and their local unions that their saviors are the Kerry/Edwards ticket.

MWM leaders have eloquently responded to Sweeney's opposition to building an independent class-wide movement. This movement will not go away, regardless of the difficulties and obstacles placed in its way. The labor movement and its allies have an alternative to voting for the capitalist "lesser of two evils," a no-win strategy for the workers and the oppressed nationalities. That alternative is: Build the Oct. 17 Million Worker March on Washington.

Abridged from WW, July 22, 2004.

East Coast rallies kick off organizing

Pam Parker and Steven Ceci

A laid-off federal worker jumped to his feet: "I'm with the Million Worker March. I am now unemployed as a result of privatization. We need this fight."

"I was laid off, too, from my city job," added Denise Lowery, an activist from the African American community. "Neither Bush or Kerry care about us. I have a 15-year-old son and the big question for me is stopping the war. It's people like me who are doing the dying."

This spirit of protest and struggle rang out at a kickoff rally for the MWM held in Washington, D.C. on July 14, 2004 and at another the following day in New York.

The rallies showed that the planned October march, conceived by ILWU, Local 10 in San Francisco as an event where labor could stand up and speak in its own voice, has now taken on a national presence. Leaders of Local 10 were at both rallies.

Many labor and community activists attended the one here, the largest group coming from the American Federation of Teachers (AFT), which was holding its national convention in Washington, D.C.

Unionists from the Service Employees attended, as well as Teamsters, United Food and Commercial Workers, the Newspaper Guild of the Communications Workers, and AFSCME. There was Jobs with Justice, the All People's Congress and the International Action Center (IAC). From the anti-war movement came Act Now to Stop War and End Racism, U.S. Labor Against the War, D.C. United for Peace and Justice, and Women's Global Strike for Peace.

A recurrent theme was to urge labor participation in the protests at both the Democratic and Republican national conventions as part of the buildup to the October 17, MWM. The national leadership of the AFL-CIO has put out a letter

disassociating itself from the MWM, saying labor's resources are needed to defeat Bush in the election. Nevertheless, serious discussions are going on in the labor movement calling into question labor's attachment to the Democratic Party.

'Labor needs an independent voice'

Clarence Thomas, ILWU, Local 10, and Brenda Stokely, president of AFSCME, DC 1707 in New York, were key speakers at the Washington rally. Both will be featured at the July 25 Boston rally protesting the Democratic National Convention.

Thomas explained why labor needs an independent voice. His local has helped formulate a mission statement, resolution and demands that speak to the major needs and rights of workers, from universal health care and funding for education to slashing the military budget.

Local 10 has a distinguished history of international solidarity. It organized actions at West Coast ports for South African workers and shut down the ports around the issue of apartheid. More recently, Thomas' local honored a picket line outside the Oakland terminals of the Stevedoring Services of America, a major contractor chosen by the Defense Department to rebuild the largest seaport in Iraq. The protest shut SSA down.

Thomas was part of a delegation to Iraq with U.S. Labor Against the War. He has since spoken at numerous events calling for the U.S. to bring the troops home now.

Local 10 has secured the support of all the ILWU West Coast locals for the MWM, and has been gathering endorsers from labor conventions and community meetings across the country. The South Carolina International Longshoreman's Association Local 1422, known for its defense of the Charleston Five, has also joined the cause of the march.

'I was laid off, too, from my city job. I have a 15-year-old son and the big question for me is stopping the war. It's people like me who are doing the dying.'
– Denise Lowery

Clipping from the NY Times August 30, 2004

New York co-convener of the MWM, Brenda Stokely, speaks at an Aug. 27, 2004 press conference in front of NYC Hall, above. The press conference was called to denounce police repression and denial of permits for rallies against the Republican National Convention.

Larry Holmes, of the International Action Center (IAC), on the right, commended the MWM organizers and explained why a fight to break the labor movement away from the Democratic Party was needed and long overdue. "Your impact can be seen from the recent letter issued by the AFL-CIO field office. There is a major contradiction between Kerry's program and the desire by union members to bring the troops home now." Holmes pledged to bring anti-war movement support to the march.

Over 50 activists attended the press conference, called on a day's notice. Many held signs condemning police repression during the RNC especially targeting young people.

WW photos: Deirdre Griswold

Brenda Stokely emphasized that the march has to be built from the ground up. She pointed out that the majority of workers are not unionized and need to be mobilized. Stokely helped to organize a three-day strike of thousands of NYC day care workers who are without a contract. Stokely, who recently returned from a trip to Venezuela, proposed that the MWM invite international delegates. This was echoed by a delegate from the AFT.

Stokely is co-convener of the MWM in New York City, along with Chris Silvera, secretary-treasurer of Teamsters Local 808 and president of the Teamsters National Black Caucus (TNBC). Silvera spoke in D.C. on the issue of homeland security and attacks on workers' civil rights.

Larry Holmes, national co-coordinator of the IAC and a member of ANSWER, brought the audience to its feet when he commended the MWM organizers and explained why a fight to break the labor movement away from the Democratic Party was needed and long overdue. "Your impact can be seen from the letter issued by the AFL-CIO field office. There is a major contradiction between Kerry's program and the desire by the membership of the unions, who want and need to bring the troops home now." Holmes mentioned resolutions against the war passed at the Service Employees and AFSCME conventions, and pledged to bring support from the anti-war movement to the march.

Ralph Schoenman, co-producer of

the Pacifica Radio program "Taking Aim," drew applause as he described the hypocrisy at the top level.

Andy Griggs is a soft-spoken and modest organizer who helped win the endorsement for the MWM by the National Education Association, the largest independent union with a membership of 2.7 million teachers and school support personnel. "When I taught in Watts I had to buy supplies for my students out of my pocket," Griggs said. Other teachers in the audience nodded. "We need to stop the war and fund education."

Teamsters Local 639 President Thomas Ratliff hosted the rally, held at his union's hall. Sharon Black, a regional coordinator for the Million Worker March, chaired the panel. Black concluded, "Why should workers' dues go to a politician like Kerry who has refused to promote a real program for workers? What about addressing the issues of the unorganized, unemployed and immigrant workers? Why has the AFL-CIO funneled money to what has amounted to CIA efforts in countries like Venezuela?

"These debates are beginning to breathe fresh air into the union movement. In every way possible, progressive trade unionists, community organizers and anti-war activists should help to ensure the Million Worker March's success. The struggle to wrestle the people's movement away from the capitalist parties has begun."

Abridged from WW, July 22, 2004.

ILWU leader builds support for Million Worker March

John Parker

On Aug. 13, 2004 the International Action Center held a Los Angeles forum on the Million Worker March. The gathering featured honored guest Clarence Thomas, ILWU, Local 10 executive board member and former secretary-treasurer, and Alameda County Central Labor Council member.

Members of several unions, including the United Teachers of Los Angeles, Communication Workers and Service Employees, attended the meeting. Representatives also came from community organizations including Korean Immigrant Workers Advocates, Minjok/Tongshin (news resource and activist organization of the Korean community), Global Women's Strike and Veterans for Peace.

Magda Madrigal of the IAC, who chaired the meeting, is playing a leading role in organizing for Oct. 15 immigrant-rights marches in Los Angeles. She explained the Million Worker March's importance for the progressive movement. And she congratulated Thomas for leading the effort.

Thomas framed the MWM's intentions within the historic tradition of Harry Bridges, founder of the ILWU. It was Bridges who said in the 1930s, during the tumultuous struggles for basic union rights, that "the main issue is the right of labor to organize."

Thomas is leading a battle for the right of labor to organize politically and independent of the two ruling-class parties. The MWM exposes that there is indeed a ruling-class war against workers.

Thomas is bringing these class antagonisms to light by pushing demands that

the candidates of the two parties of capital – John Kerry and George W. Bush – refuse to address.

Thomas spoke of his recent trip to Iraq. He witnessed the devastation to civilians, hospitals and the labor movement there. Saying the war in Iraq must be opposed, he said, "Iraqi Unions have a long history full of drama, sacrifice and bloody confrontation. The movement was once the model of the entire Arab world." He said workers and progressives here must stand in solidarity with workers everywhere.

Johnnie Stevens, from the International Action Center national office in New York and People's Video Network, spoke about the connections between the MWM and the struggle against U.S. terror and occupation in Haiti.

Juan Jose Gutierrez of Latino Movement USA addressed the most recent attacks on immigrant workers and how the MWM's demands coincide with the struggle of the undocumented. He is one of those building for the Oct. 15 demonstrations, calling for justice for immigrants and an end to terrorist Immigration and Naturalization Service raids.

After he spoke, many in the audience enthusiastically suggested ways to build for the Oct. 15 events simultaneously, to increase participation in both demonstrations and strengthen solidarity in Los Angeles.

Million Worker March and Haiti

The MWM demands that Clarence Thomas referred to are resonating loudly amongst workers and community activists alike. He attended an August 14

John Parker helped to organize the August 13 and August 15, 2004 meetings on the MWM and on Haiti. Parker is building support for the MWM in Los Angeles.

Photo: Pat Chin

Juan Jose Gutierrez, national coordinator of Latino Movement USA, announces the "The Great American Boycott 2006," to be held on May 1, 2006, a nationwide day without an immigrant when immigrants and their supporters stay home from work and school and businesses are closed.

Magda Madrigal after becoming a lawyer for immigrant rights in 2010.

Photo: Annelle

Johnnie Stevens
Member, The International Action Center

Johnnie Stevens speaking on the Gil Noble Show, "Like It Is," about the coup that took place in Haiti on Feb. 29, 2004. Haitian President Jean-Bertrand Aristide had been kidnapped and taken by U.S. forces to Bangui, Central African Republic.

Stevens traveled to Africa to meet with Aristide in a delegation of supporters.

PVN photo

Subhi Al-Mashadani, general secretary of the Workers Democratic Trade Union Federation greets Clarence Thomas in Iraq in October 2003.

At the IAC forum in Los Angeles, Thomas spoke of his recent trip to Iraq where he witnessed the devastation to civilians, hospitals and the labor movement. He said, "The war in Iraq must be opposed. Workers and progressives here must stand in solidarity with workers everywhere."

Photo: David Bacon

afternoon planning session at the IAC office, along with representatives of the Peace and Freedom Party in Southern California, United Teachers of Los Angeles, Communication Workers, National Lawyers Guild, Latino Movement USA, Veterans for Peace and ANSWER Los Angeles.

That evening, the theme of solidarity for the MWM extended to a forum on Haiti in South Central Los Angeles. This forum was hosted by Black organizations including the Haiti Solidarity Coalition.

Johnnie Stevens spoke about the parallels between U.S. imperialism's attack on Africa and Central and Latin America, and their connections to the Haitian people's struggle for self-determination. He said that all these developments affect working and poor people here, and helped motivate people to answer the call for a Million Worker March.

Clarence Thomas commented on the need for people to become organizers and participants in the MWM to help build awareness and fight back on issues like U.S. crimes against Haiti.

On August 15, Thomas held meetings with South Central church leaders including the Rev. Andrew Gaither of Faith United Methodist Church and the Rev. Richard Byrd of KRST Unity Center for African Spirituality. At KRST Unity, Thomas addressed the packed church from the pulpit about the MWM. Church members enthusiastically endorsed his effort with applause and Byrd incorporated Thomas' message into his sermon. About one-third of those present signed up to become MWM organizers.

Thus, like Harry Bridges, Clarence Thomas is building the type of unity and leadership in the labor movement that will be a precursor to historic revolutionary change in this country and around the world.

Abridged from WW, Aug. 26, 2004.

There was a large, militant contingent of Haitian workers at the Million Worker March in Washington, D.C.

WW photo: G. Dunkel

Statement of Anti-War 4 Million Worker March
'Chance to unite anti-war and workers' movements'

Appeal sent out via email by the newly formed group, Anti-War 4 the Million Worker March

Dear Activists and Organizers,

This fall in Washington, D.C., you will have a timely and historic opportunity to unite the anti-war movement with an unprecedented and vitally necessary mass march of working people speaking for themselves. This is a rare opportunity that serious anti-war activists can't afford to pass up.

Some of the strongest voices and most active groups in the labor movement, together with the active support and participation of organizations representing every progressive movement and cause, will be "getting on the bus" to D.C. on Oct. 17, for the **Million Worker March**. A sea of workers from every industry, from every union and every place where workers want a union, from every part of the country, will be streaming into the capital to demand things like jobs, a living wage and workers' rights.

They will also express their anger over the senseless dying that is going on every day in Iraq and elsewhere, and their desire that it end now. Why? Because it is working families who bear the burden, it is their loved ones who are sent off to fight and die — and it is their, our, the workers' money that is stolen to pay for war and occupation.

What makes the Million Worker March unique is that the event's principal organizers want to make the anti-war movement's demand to **'End the Occupation of Iraq and Bring the Troops Home Now'** central to the March's message and the goals.

We are asking anti-war activists to set up local "Anti-War 4 the Million Worker March" committees. Start meeting, planning and reserving buses to go to Washington on Oct. 17. Anti-war coalitions and groups need to let us know ASAP if their group can be listed as an "Anti-War 4 the Million Worker March" committee in their locality or region.

We encourage activists to form committees in their unions, schools, work places, churches and communities. It is our hope that "Anti-War 4 MWM" committees will complement the labor union and community-based organizing that is going on across the country for Oct. 17.

YOU CAN HELP

- **Add your name and endorsement to this urgent call.**
- **Set up an Anti-War 4 the MWM committee.**
- **Sending a bus from your city.**

The call for a Million Worker March came from one of the most well-known labor organizations in the country, famous for its long history of militancy, boldness and courage in defense of working people: Local 10 of the International Longshore Workers Union in San Francisco. Over the past few months this call has rolled across the country, picking up the support of scores of labor unions, labor activists and leaders including:

Working people are coming to Washington, D.C., on October 17 because whether their concern is about jobs, or

The call for a **MWM** came from one of the most well-known labor unions in the country, famous for its long history of militancy and courage in defense of working people: **ILWU Local 10 in San Francisco.**

Over the past few months this call has rolled across the country, picking up the support of scores of labor unions and labor activists:

The Coalition Of Black Trade Unionists; Bill Lucy, Secretary-Treasurer, AFSCME; the National Education Association; Transportation Workers Union Local 100 (NY); AFSCME District Council 1707 (NY); S.C. AFL-CIO; Farm Labor Organizing Committee; AFSCME District Council 92 (MD); D.C. Labor Against the War; Int'l ANSWER; Danny Glover; American Indian Movement; ILWU Local 34; Troy & Albany Labor Council (NY); Nat'l Immigration Solidarity Network; NYC Labor Against the War; Global Women's Strike; Teamsters National Black Caucus; Dick Gregory; Mya Shone and Ralph Schoenman, Taking Aim, Pacifica; Nat'l Association of Letter Carriers, Branch 3825; Howard Wallace, co-founder, Pride at Work; Jim Haughton, Director, Harlem Fightback; Justice 4 Homeless, SF; United Steel Workers Local 8751; Int'l Action Center; Ramsey Clark; Nellie Bailey, Harlem Tenants Council; Howard Zinn; Noam Chomsky; AFSCME Local 95, Local 205, Local 215, Local 389, Local 167, Local 1881, Local 1930; ILWU West Coast Longshore Division; CUE Local 3; and many more. For a more extensive list go to page 31.

decent wages, or layoffs, or union busting, or the battle to protect our pensions and Social Security and to make health care a universal right instead of a privilege for the wealthy, with all we face, we had better raise our own voices and act in our own interests instead of relying on the next president, whoever that will be.

And most important, the time for us to speak in our own voice is not after people vote in November, but before. The Million Worker March is about the people telling the president, the candidates, the politicians and the corporate elite who are the real power behind the election campaigns and the politicians to "Shut up!" and listen to us for a change.

Let's make sure that the march in New York against the Republican convention in November isn't the only important date this fall.

We urge all of you to work to make the October 17 Million Worker March in Washington, D.C. the next major event for the entire anti-war movement. If we rise to this challenge, we will put the next president and Congress on notice that we will accept no excuses for prolonging the occupation of Iraq and wasting lives and precious resources that should go toward satisfying people's needs like housing and schools. Moreover, we will have helped to forge a critical alliance between the grass roots of the labor movement and the anti-war movement that would represent a whole new level of unity, potential and power.

Does this sound like something worth working for? Does this sound like something you've been waiting for? You can help make it happen.

In solidarity,

Clarence Thomas,
Co-Chair, Million Worker March Organizing Committee, ILWU Local 10

Brenda Stokely,
President, DC 1707, AFSCME, Co-chair, New York City Labor Against the War

Chris Silvera,
Secretary-Treasurer, Local 808 IBT, President, Teamsters National Black Caucus

Ralph Schoenman,
Communications Coordinator, Million Worker March

Larry Holmes,
International Action Center Steering Committee, ANSWER

Sharon Black,
Washington/Baltimore Coordinator, Million Worker March

Ramsey Clark,
Former U.S. Attorney General

AFSCME Council 92 of the Greater Baltimore & Metropolitan D.C. Area endorses the MWM

AFSCME Council 92 represents 30,000 state workers in Maryland and is the largest of the only two AFSCME Councils.

Andre Powell reported to the Baltimore-D.C. Regional MWM Committee that the vote by AFSCME Council 92 to endorse the March passed overwhelmingly. Although some opposition was expected, none was seen. In fact, long-time members raised their hands to say, "we have to make sure that we have buses from the Council on the 17th ...

Council 92 is an affiliation of multiple AFSCME union locals. This bodies endorsement represents the surging support for the independent mobilization of working people. From Texas to Baltimore to New York, workers are organizing to demand healthcare, housing and education.

Long Island City Union Organizes for MWM

"The point of the march is to change the agenda of our country," said Chris Silvera, secretary treasurer for Teamsters Local 808, which represents building maintenance and Metro North Railroad workers, among others.

Organizers for the MWM, say that "decent paying jobs are disappearing through outsourcing and privatization whose purpose is to break unions and roll back the gains of 100 years of struggle."

Silvera sees an erosion of worker's rights. He blames President Clinton's passage of NAFTA as being a jolt to workers. He notes the march is not against one political party. "The rich has two parties," Silvera said. "They own the Republican Party and they own the Democratic Party. We see it as being the working class against the ruling class."

*– **Queens Chronicle**, New York, Oct. 7, 2004.*

Build the Million Worker March!
A groundswell of union support

Sako Sefiani

On August 27, 2004, the Postal Workers Union, APWU, formally joined the growing list of unions along with other organizations across the country that have endorsed the Million Worker March set for October 17, in Washington, D.C., at the Lincoln Memorial.

The Postal Workers convention took place in the Los Angeles Convention Center Aug. 20-28. With 330,000 members, it is the biggest postal workers' union in the world.

The Postal Workers resolution states:

"Whereas, the majority of Americans are continuing to experience a decline in health care, good wages, job and pension security, education, environmental protection, the protection of unions and are suffering the consequences of a war initiated under false pretenses prior to the United Nation's completing its investigation, and

"Whereas there has been a monopolization of the media and union busting of media workers which has made it difficult for labor's voice to be heard,

"Therefore, be it resolved that APWU endorse the Oct. 17, 2004, Million Worker March, a union movement to communicate our resolution to restore democracy, empower working people and end the promotion of continual war which now dominates the U.S. foreign policy."

The Million Worker March-LA organizing committee was a guest exhibitor during the union's biennial convention.

MWM-LA members and volunteers passed out leaflets and talked with union members. John Parker and Marc Rich, Los Angeles co-chairs of the Million Worker March, addressed a group of postal worker delegates and some local

Why Postal Workers Backed Million Worker March

St. Louis APWU President Speaks Out

[Note: Following is an interview conducted by *The Organizer* newspaper with Roosevelt Stewart, president of the 2,500-member St. Louis Gateway District Area Local of the American Postal Workers Union, AFL-CIO. Stewart is active in both the Coalition of Black Trade Unionists (CBTU) and U.S. Labor Against the War (USLAW). He has been active in the postal workers' union for 25 years. The interview took place in late September 2004.]

"Privatization is going to affect all postal – in fact, all public sector – workers. ... We have to organize the fightback on all fronts."

— Roosevelt Stewart, President, St. Louis Postal Workers Union

Now you can send a letter across the country and it costs the same for everybody. Without uni-

jobs. Their profit comes at our expense.

Already we have what we call

the Wal-Mart model: They want to move the post office into the big Wal-Mart malls.

An antiwar resolution was passed at the June 2004, AFSCME Convention held in Anaheim, Calif., and the Million Worker March, gathered a number of rank-and-file supporters.

Photo: Sharon Black

union presidents in a meeting at the Convention Center.

Also on Aug. 27, United Teachers of Los Angeles, which represents the Los Angeles school district, endorsed the march during its annual leadership conference held in Palm Springs, Ca.

These endorsements came on the heels of Teamsters General Secretary Treasurer C. Thomas Keegel's August 18, announcement that the Teamsters would contribute "a significant amount of money" to the MWM during the 29th annual Conference of the Teamsters National Black Caucus in Orlando, Fl., led by Chris Silvera, secretary-treasurer of Teamsters Local 808.

A large and growing number of unions and their locals have endorsed this historic march on Washington. On July 30, Transport Workers Union Local 100, with 35,000 members in New York City, endorsed the march, and leaders said they will actively mobilize members.

On August 6, the third biggest AFSCME local, Local 1550 from Houston, endorsed the MWM, announcing it will send buses to Washington, D.C. On August. 12, AFSCME Council 92, the second biggest council representing over 30,000 workers, threw its support to the march. Council 92 announced that it will actively mobilize in the Greater Washington, D.C. area, and help to coordinate for the march.

On August 30, the opening day of the Communications Workers convention in Orange County, Ca., MWM-LA members distributed thousands of fliers about the march. MWM-LA will petition the union to endorse the march.

The MWM promises to be a turning point for labor, which has been undermined and marginalized with devastating consequences for working people.

As the Mission of the Million Worker March, posted on its web site (www.millionworkermarch.org), declares: "In our name, a handful of the rich and powerful corporations have usurped our government. A corporate and banking oligarchy changes hats and occupies public office to wage class war on working people. They have captured the State in their own interests. "The vast majority of working Americans are under siege. Social services and essential funding for schools, libraries, affordable housing and health care are slashed and eliminated. "Decent-paying jobs are disappearing through outsourcing and privatization whose real purpose is to break unions and roll back the gains of one hundred years of struggle.

"Sweatshops and starvation wages are imposed on workers across the world and deployed against workers at home to undermine our jobs and our benefits. "The time has come to mobilize working people for our own agenda."

Abridged from WW, Sept. 9, 2004.

The Teamsters contributed $10,000 to the MWM in 2004 and an additional $10,000 to the 10th Anniversary Commemoration of the Million Man March named the Million More Movement.

A Call to Young Workers

Steven Ceci Organizer,
Service Employees Local 500

The state of young workers is desperate and needs to be addressed. You don't need statistics to know that youths, young workers, and students are catching hell. But statistics do give concrete evidence about these poor conditions that youths face.

Jobs and unemployment

According to the Bureau of Labor Statistics, Current Population Survey," the July unemployment rate for white youths 16 to 19 years old was 14.9 percent. For Latin@ youths from 16 to 19 it was 23.8 percent. That's pretty bad, but African Americans 16 to 19 years old had a jobless rate of 40.5 percent.

Black teenagers are two-and-a-half times more likely to be unemployed than white teenagers.

Homelessness, health care and AIDS

Young people make up a big portion of those who are homeless, uninsured and living with AIDS. The National Coalition on Homelessness reports that approximately 39 percent of the homeless population is under the age 18.

The fastest-growing population of HIV positive people is those under the age of 25. The Bush administration has cut funding for AIDS prevention programs that promote condom use.

Education, prisons and the military

Prison spending grew five times as fast as spending for higher education in the past 20 years, according to a report released Aug. 25 by the non-profit Justice Policy Institute, based in Washington, D.C. The study examined prison growth in 17 states considered key to this year's presidential election. In the growing prison and jail population; nearly twice as many Black men in their early 30s have been to prison than have obtained a bache-

On Oct. 17, 2004, hundreds of protesters from the MWM marched to the Hotel Washington near the White House to show support for the workers.

WW photo: Deirdre Griswold

Students march for jobs in Baltimore on August 11, 2011.   Photo: Sharon Black

lor's degree, according to the same report.

In 1999, the last year that national statistics are available from the U.S. Department of Justice, juvenile facilities reported a 50-percent increase of youths locked up compared to 1991. Youths of color account for 35 percent of the U.S. population.

Abridged from WW, Sept. 9, 2004.

Open Letter to women activists

The following letter was distributed to thousands of women at the pro-reproductive rights march on Aug. 28, 2004 in New York City.

New York City on Aug. 28, 2004.
WW photo: Deirdre Griswold

Why do women need to participate in the Million Worker March on October 17 in Washington, D.C.?

Because ... we are workers and we deserve pay equity, health care, child care and more.

Because ... women need to be paid for the value we produce. We continue to be paid less than men (on average 22 percent less in 2002) and face other forms of discrimination on the job. Sexism and racism help the boss get richer at our expense and often keep us divided. We seek to end all forms of discrimination in the work place and in our communities.

Because ... women, especially single mothers and immigrants, need jobs that pay a national living wage, like $15 an hour, so we can adequately support our families and put an end to poverty once and for all. We affirm that a job is a human right.

Because ... women need to organize and belong to unions. Women workers, especially women workers of color, are the largest sector of workers demanding the right to unionize, though their rights are being violated on a daily basis by the bosses who spend millions of dollars to prevent unionization and to bust the unions that exist. We affirm that the right to work, the right to organize, and the right to join unions are human rights.

Because ... women need a national universal single-payer health-care system that guarantees health care is a right of all people from cradle to grave. Women need the full range of reproductive services, including birth control, abortion on demand, and Ob-Gyn coverage.

Because ... women need fully subsidized, community-controlled child care so they can work without worrying about the safety, health and educational needs of their children.

Because ... women need the right to same-sex marriage in every state, unbiased child custody rulings, and the freedom to work and live openly and safely as lesbians, bisexuals, and trans people.

Because ... women need our tax dollars to be spent not on war but on life-affirming quality education and schools, affordable housing and community services that meet the needs of everyone from the very young to the very old. Women, children and the aged are forced to bear the brunt of the budget cuts while the Pentagon feeds off the gravy train. We need to bring all U.S. troops home now, defend the civil rights of all people, especially Arabs, Muslims and immigrants, and stop the fear-mongering and scapegoating.

Because ... women need to make sure our demands are heard loud and clear in the fight-back movement. We need to unite with all workers to send the corporate bosses a strong message: We don't like the way you're running things. We need real power over the decisions that affect our lives.

Women have been playing a crucial, leading role in organizing the Million Worker March. We invite you to join us in Washington, D.C., on October 17. *Abridged from WW, Sept. 9, 2004.*

National Coalition of Blacks for Reparations endorses MWM

Black people of African descent were compelled into forced labor without compensation that produced the enormous wealth of the U.S. This is a crime against humanity for which reparations are due now. The response by the U.S. government remains, in Martin Luther King's words, a "bad check marked insufficient funds." N'COBRA calls on all supporters of Reparations for Black people to join and help build the MWM and to raise Reparations as a central issue of workers' justice and fundamental human rights.

'There is a war at home as well as abroad'

Interview with Clarence Thomas

Clarence Thomas of the ILWU, Local 10 on the West Coast, speaks with Bryan G. Pfeifer in July 2004 about the conditions leading up to the decision to call the MWM. Thomas was in Boston for demonstrations at the Democratic National Convention.

Clarence Thomas: A resolution was passed at the beginning of the year 2004 by the ILWU Local 10 executive board. That resolution was introduced and passed because working people are under unprecedented attack. It's an attack that has not just started with the Bush administration but it's the culmination of decades of policies that basically have been about putting profits before people.

If you look at the Reagan years, you probably could pinpoint that as an era when there was intensification of policies that attacked labor, creating tax breaks for the rich, increasing Social Security taxation on working people.

But, more importantly, it's an era that brings to mind constructive engagement, when the Bush/Reagan administration defined that as the policy of the U.S. with regards to South Africa. The Reagan administration was closely aligned to the apartheid regime.

The anti-apartheid movement of the 1980s was a reflection of the stake that U.S. workers had in the offshoring issue. At that time there were a number of jobs that were being off-shored to South Africa. Auto plants were being shut down here in the United States and they were being opened in South Africa.

The ILWU Local 10 boycotted a ship by the name of the Nedlloyd Kemberley in 1984 for 11 days. And that set into motion the very intense labor solidarity around the Free South Africa movement.

But I bring that up because I think that many people put too much focus on what

is happening with the Bush administration. What's going on right now is not only a neoconservative agenda but it is also an agenda that is supported by both the Republican and Democratic Parties. Congress has been complicit in everything that the Bush administration is doing and all we have to do is look at the record.

To make a long story short, the reason for the Million Worker March is that we are organizing the march in our own name because of the fact that the only time that working people gain any concessions from the system is when we organize independently from the Democratic and Republican Parties. If you look at the Civil Rights movement, it was organized outside the scope of the Democratic and Republican Parties. And Black people did not get to vote by voting. Black people got to vote by organizing in their own name. You look at the anti-war movement of the 1960s as well as the anti-war movement of today. The same thing could be said of that, as well as the women's movement.

Speaking on the Boston Commons on July 25, 2004, Clarence Thomas, ILWU, Local 10 and co-convener of MWM said: "There is a war at home as well as abroad. The Million Worker March is organizing in our own name. The only time that working people gain concessions from the system is when we organize independently from the Democratic and Republican Parties." The rally launched a week of protests against the Democratic National Convention. Brenda Stokely is in the red jacket.

WW photo: Liz Green

So this is long overdue. This is about workers coming together, putting forth an agenda that speaks directly to our needs: national health care, cutting the military budget. There is no way we can have guns and butter. In other words, if there's going to be any change in terms of the domestic policies of the United States government, that military budget has to be cut because that's where the money to pay for the needed social services and the rebuilding of the infrastructure of the United States is going to come from that military budget.

The other thing is no matter what the expectations are of people towards the national elections, we have to hold all elected officials accountable. And that means that this Million Worker March isn't going to stop after the march is over. Those demands mean something and we want action taken on those things. The Democratic Party for a number of years has enjoyed support from the Black community, even though they are not representing the Black community. And so we think that there has to be a decision made on the part of working people to support the status quo or to support those issues and programs that are in their best interests.

There's been a tremendous amount of opposition to the Million Worker March by business unionists throughout the country who believe that the Democratic Party is the party of working people, which it is not. And they also think that there should not be any movement to empower working people before the election.

In my opinion, I think they believe that to be the case even after the election.

So when we look at the elections of Bill Clinton in his first and second terms people who are defined as being liberal said let's give Bill a chance. Well, Bill had his chance, two terms, and what did we get? We got NAFTA. We got GATT. We got welfare reform. We received the WTO and just an endless number of examples that show his actual contempt for working people, even though he was a very able campaigner who, because of his working-class origins, was able to translate that into a great deal of admiration, especially from the Black community. But the reality of the situation is that Bill Clinton's years were years that were very damaging to working people.

If you look at the Carter years, for example, when Carter came into office he increased the military budget. Carter also gave tax breaks for the rich on capital gains and he increased the Social Security tax on working

people. He bailed out Chrysler, which set into motion a whole trend of concessionary bargaining on the part of unions. Not only that, but he invoked Taft-Hartley on the miners, who struck from 1977 to 1978.

So those are just some of the examples from recent history of the kinds of adverse policies that have been implemented during a Democratic administration. So we say the reason for that is because the Democratic Party does not represent the interests of working people. They represent the corporate agenda. The rhetoric may be somewhat different but the policies are the same. ...

I was in Iraq as part of an international labor delegation in October 2003 organized through U.S. Labor Against the War. But I can tell you that there is a war at home as well as the war abroad. When you look at the companies that are benefiting from the war in Iraq, companies such as the Stevedoring Services of America, which is one of our employers, they were one of the most belligerent segments of the Pacific Maritime Association during our contract negotiations and they have received the contract to operate the Port of Umm Qasr.

The kinds of policies that have been enacted upon Iraqi workers since the invasion are such that ... Iraqi workers don't have the right to organize because they're enforcing laws passed by Saddam Hussein which prohibit the organizing of workers in the so-called public sector. Those are the workers that were employed by the state.

But I think that the bottom line is that the war on Iraq and the war on working people in America are connected and it's very important that we come together, the anti-war movement and the labor movement, to oppose the war, bring the troops home now and push for a workers' agenda.

Abridged from WW, Sept. 30, 2004.

Port of Oakland Terminal Shut Down on April 4, 2011.   Photo: Dolores Lemon-Thomas

Mumia Abu-Jamal on the MWM
War against workers

Almost all of us, from wherever we've come, have something of value in common, we are engaged in the world of work. Some of us are members of unions as am I, a proud card carrying member of the National Writers Union which is affiliated with the United Auto Workers.

Some of us, perhaps the majority, are not members of a union and yet as so called contingency workers, as temps, as part timers, as on call workers, as workfare, as day labors, as perma-temps, as immigrant workers, care giving workers, invisible workers, house wife's, and last but not least as prison laborers where people who are workers who add to social good in all of us are catching hell. That's because wherever there is a war against wages that means a war against workers.

If we speak the truth it doesn't matter who wins the white house workers are catching hell that's because the only choices for the American people are corporate choices a thin narrow slice between two quite similar brokerage parties who sell their souls to the highest bidder.

Think of it this way the last president supported by vast labor votes was William Jefferson Clinton. And how did Clinton award labor support? By passing NAFTA and opening the door to the Globalist monster that is sucking the life blood from most working families across the Nation. The drastic loss of U.S. manufacturing jobs and the resultant drop in wages can be traced to the NAFTA Bill.

That is why a Million Worker March Is so necessary to break through the corporate dibble-dabble that now dominates the coming elections. Corporate candidates covered by corporate media for corporate interests. It's no wonder it's so slimy. It's also no wonder that the word workers rarely if ever crosses the lips of the

Left, Gloria Verdieu in San Diego, July 2003.
Photo: Bob McCubbin

corporate candidates. It is no wonder that the word union sounds like profanity when they mention it. It is only workers that can or will defend the interest of workers like Universal Health Care for all people, a national living wage and livable retirement benefits, to bring democracy to the shop floor so that decisions about work are made by those who labor, like taxation that is progressive on corporations and the wealthy and relieves the burdens on the working class and the poor, like an end to wars waged for corporate America like Iraq, like the immediate revocation of all anti-labor packs like NAFTA, FTAA, the WTO, and CAFTA. The repeal of Taft-Hartley, and the repeal of the so-called Patriot Act.

These are but some of the demands motivating the Million Worker March but it can't be all of them. Workers actually built this society. It is they and only they who can rebuild it. This means a resurgence of the labor movement that is truly revolutionary that does not settle for its slice but changes the social order completely or else we will be choosing the same old monkeys to sit over us as they betray us forever. That time must end.

From Death Row
Mumia Abu-Jamal

Prison Radio, prisonradio.org, Oct. 17 , 2004.

The ILWU led a march of 20,000 for Mumia's freedom in San Francisco on April 24, 1999. All the ports on the West Coast were shut down to demand: 'Stop the Execution, Free Mumia Abu-Jamal!' The 300-strong longshore contingent chanted, 'An injury to one is an injury to all! Free Mumia Abu-Jamal!'

San Francisco protest in support of the Charleston dock workers and Mumia Abu-Jamal May 2005.
Photo: Bill Hackwell

Democracy Now! Amy Goodman interviews Brenda Stokely October 14, 2004

We speak with Brenda Stokely, president of AFSCME, DC 1707 and an organizer of the Million Worker March about the grassroots labor movement, the election, unions and much more.

Amy Goodman: Can you respond to the candidates on labor and talk about how you're organizing?

Brenda Stokely: This is definitely a rank-and-file grassroots organizing movement. I'm almost 60, and I haven't seen anything like this since the 1960s in terms of the response. We were organizing the buses. We all got commitments for those who could provide buses to provide seats, but now we have to come up with whole buses. Danny Glover has been very instrumental in helping us do this, as well as other people, because we are responding to immigrant groups which have no money and providing buses for them to get there. We were responding to shelters that have no money; these are displaced workers.

Unfortunately, none of the international unions with the exception of two have come forward to support the March; as a matter of fact, they have done everything to undermine this particular effort. The only three international unions, that have endorsed are the teachers, NEA, the postal workers, APWU and the railroad workers, BMWE.

ILWU, Local 10 out of San Francisco, which we fondly refer to as the anti-apartheid local because they're the ones who refused to unload cargo from South Africa during the anti-apartheid movement. This call came from their local. Their own international is not supporting it.

What they're trying to do lock everybody's hands to the Democratic Party and to Kerry and not independently provide a space for workers to express their own concern and their own agenda.

This is a beginning of a movement to mobilize people, as Howard Zinn was talking about, the kind of movement that's needed. Well, this movement is being built right before our eyes. It raises a lot of questions, both within the anti-war movement and also within organized labor as to why they would actively, not unconsciously, oppose such a movement of rank-and-file members.

This movement includes people that are not in unions. As we all know, less than 12 % of people are in unions. So we're appealing to people that are unorganized as well as people that are organized. And the response is unbelievable. Their view is, why hasn't this happened before?

One person even said to me, an old-time retired fireman in Harlem, "You know, labor should have had something during the RNC" I said, "Dear, labor did have something during the RNC on September 1." He didn't know anything about it because they excluded retirees and people that were not in unions. And they excluded the key issues that were relating to workers."

So we think our demands are very important for national health care for all, for workers' rights, because workers are being battered whether they're in unions or not. And they

talk about the increase of numbers of people in new jobs. Those jobs are mainly temporary jobs, part-time jobs, per diem jobs, fee for service jobs, have no benefits, no union representation. These are not the kind of jobs. We are talking about jobs with a living wage, not a minimum wage. We are talking about housing issues; All of the issues that face working communities every single day.

Juan Gonzalez: I'd also like to ask Brenda, people who want to attend the Million Worker March, how can they contact the organizers and get more information?

BS: Well, in New York City they can call 212-219-0022, We have buses in every borough. And so we welcome people to come and get a seat and go down with us.

AG: People around the country are coming?

BS: Yes, around the country. Also an important aspect of the march is that they're going to be organizing tents so that people will not just be rallying, but they will also leave with an agenda and a plan and connect to national activities, and campaigns. So, we invite everybody to come and participate.

AG: Well, Brenda Stokely, I want to thank you very much. We'll have links on our website at democracynow.org. Brenda Stokely is president of AFSCME, District Council 1707 in New York City, one of the key organizers of the Million Worker March this weekend in Washington, D.C.

Building a movement for democracy:
African Americans, the MWM and beyond!

BLACK WORKERS LEAGUE   Saladin Muhammad

The struggle for democracy is of paramount importance to working class, African Americans, communities' of color and their social movements and organizations in the current political direction and organization of U.S. society from the government to the economy.

In the name of fighting a war on terrorism, the U.S. is targeting global regions like the Middle East, South Asia, Africa and the Caribbean, declaring them bases of international "terrorism."

At home, oppressed nationalities and working class sectors like African Americans, Latino, Native Americans, women, unemployed, immigrants, gays, Muslims and organizations like trade unions are also defined as threats to national security. Race and religious bigotry is a major part of the Bush and U.S. strategy.

The economic and social crises facing working people in the U.S. are intertwined with the imperialist wars waged against Afghanistan, Iraq and in support of Israel's racist and brutal occupation of the Palestine.

Funds for social programs, state budgets, community development, environmental protection and the education of the children of workers are being used to finance unjust wars and occupations that are killing and destroying the lives and futures of millions of people at home and abroad.

Why a Million Worker March?

The call for the MWM is a call for working and oppressed people to build a mass movement for fundamental change of society. It is a call for national and local struggles and organizations to mobilize their collective power around a program for worker's democracy and self-determination in solidarity with the struggles of workers and oppressed people throughout the world.

This call comes at a time when the fragmentation of left and progressive social movements, including the lack of political independence of the trade unions, pose a grave danger for the defense of mass democratic rights that were won through hard fought struggles during the last two centuries.

Progressives and radicals have an important role to play in helping to build for the MWM, as it helps to expose the imperialist programs of both major political parties and further raises the need for independent political action to advance a program for working people.

Political Disenfranchisement

The political disenfranchisement of African Americans in Florida and throughout the country led to the stolen 2000 presidential election of Bush by the forces of the state — the police, the Republican party control of the election process and the U.S. Supreme Court.

This is a betrayal of the Civil Rights Movement, its martyrs and the historical demand for voting rights, present throughout African American's struggle for democracy and self-determination, including the fight to end chattel slavery.

It clearly points out, how all of democracy is threatened when African Americans and all of the oppressed lack power and a voice to enforce their democracy.

This is an important opportunity to make a link between the U.S. racist system of national oppression and worker exploitation. To educate the working class about the importance and fundamental role of African American self-determination in the struggle for workers democracy.

This alienation needs a radical working class and anti-imperialist mass political organization and program to help give it direction. It does not need to be encouraged to realign with the Democratic Party.

The U.S. War on Terror

The 2000 stolen election contributes to the increasing alienation of millions of African Americans and working people from the U.S. electoral system, especially its domination by the corporate controlled Democratic and Republican parties.

In the name of fighting a "war on terrorism" to make the U.S. and world "safe" and "democratic," the U.S. government has unleashed a campaign of repression, attacking democracy abroad and at home.

Preemptive military strikes, wars, occupations, forced regime change, embargoes, torture of war prisoners, refusal to abide by international laws, and increased police and state repression, have become the actions of a 21st Century U.S. domestic and global doctrine of Manifest Destiny.

The so-called instruments of democracy like the press, educational systems, courts, and constitutional provisions are being weakened, gutted, directly controlled by big corporations and forced in some way to eliminate civil liberties and justify the practice of repressive government.

Globalization = Imperialism

The U.S. has forced "free trade agreements" like the FTAA and NAFTA on every country in Central America, South America and the Caribbean, except Cuba.

With "free trade" comes privatization; the process of converting publicly owned resources, into private property and corporate venues. This reduces access to vital public services.

The massive increase in immigration has become source of cheaper labor for the corporations and has intensified the competition among low wage workers. Immigrants, mainly working class and undocumented, are made scapegoats along with African Americans by the corporate owned media and government for the crises facing U.S. workers, creating divisions within the working class.

The criminalization of Black and Latino youth by the main stream media and the courts are part of the scapegoating of these two large nationally oppressed and working class sectors. The racists attacks on Black and Latino rights are aimed at aligning white workers with corporate and government's anti-democratic policies.

The forming of working class based African American-Latino alliances are important for waging a united struggle against racism by workers who are forced to compete with each other for jobs and services.

Business Unionism

The AFL-CIO, a federation of 16 million union members sends a wrong message about the power of labor, when it publicly opposes the call for a MWM, a national mobilization for a working people's agenda. The fear by the national union bureaucracy of waging a challenge against the policies of capital has led many unions to enter into compromises that are eroding hard fought gains. This makes the corporations more arrogant and aggressive.

However, the growing endorsements of the MWM by local unions and working class organizations despite the refusal of support by the AFL-CIO, is an important statement about the increasing dissatisfaction by the rank-and-file with the betrayals of both political parties in addressing the needs of working people. It speaks to their desire for a mass movement and program of independent political action, and also the need for rank-and-file democracy within their national unions.

The MWM mobilization is a very important beginning in the development of a politically independent rank-and-file movement. Its success should not be measured by whether it meets a goal of mobilizing a million workers. The process of organizing the MWM has been an important step toward breaking labor's bureaucratic stranglehold.

It is important for all who oppose racism and want to see a greater involvement by the African Americans and people of color communities in the leadership and national mobilizations opposing the war, to unite with and contribute resources to help mobilize for the MWM.

African American Self-Determination

The African American demand for reparations must be raised as a demand for self-determination empowering the Black working class, and as an anti-racist and anti-imperialist demand challenging the concentration of global wealth by a predominantly white ruling class.

It is important that organizations considering themselves part of the African American liberation movement unite with the MWM. This will help to ensure that the ongoing development of the struggle for a working people's democracy has roots in the struggle for African American self-determination, thereby helping people to understand the strategic interrelationship between the African American liberation and workers movement in bringing about a radical transformation of U.S. society.

A break by the African American masses with the Democratic Party to form an independent working class based political party, would represent a major advance in the direction of self-determination and workers power.

The MWM can be a launching point for a movement for democracy that builds alignments and institutions for mobilizing independent people's power beyond the elections. Workers, People of color, tenants, the disabled, seniors, women, youth, students, immigrants, gays and their organizations and allies in the middle class, can all unite in the MWM and movement for democracy.

The Black Freedom Movement

Like the 1963 March on Washington, leading to the passage of the 1964 Civil Rights Act, Dr. Martin L. King and the civil rights movement made clear that voting is not enough.

King's emphasis was on mobilizing a Poor People's March on Washington. He also lead a campaign in Memphis, Tenn., in support of union rights for sanitation workers.

Labor laws, low unionization and the lack of collective bargaining rights for workers in the Southern states, has led to conditions of under development in terms of adequate water and sewerage, decent housing, paved roads and adequate healthcare. King as expressed in his 1963 "Letter from the Birmingham Jail", "we know through painful experience that freedom is never voluntarily given by the oppressor; it must be demanded by the oppressed ....."

Support the Million Worker March!

Abridged from the Black Workers League Statement 2004, Rocky Mount, N.C.

MILLION WORKER MARCH October 17, 2004

Now is the time to show our strength and to fight for our rights

Ralph Schoenman and Clarence Thomas   Editor Lou Wolf

The MWM organizing committee responds to the directive from the AFL-CIO

On June 23, 2004, John Sweeney, the leadership of the AFL-CIO and the director of the Field Mobilization Department, sent out a Memorandum to "All State Federations and Central Labor Councils of the AFL-CIO" referencing the "Million Worker March," and directing them "not to sponsor or devote resources to the demonstration in Washington, D.C."

This Memorandum was dispatched without any prior communication with the organizers and endorsers of the Million Worker March. These include the entire ILWU Longshore Division, the National Coalition of Black Trade Unionists, S.C. State AFL-CIO, and Labor Councils across the U.S. The leadership of the AFL-CIO has gone over the heads of significant sectors of the labor, antiwar, community and inter-faith organizations in issuing a directive to boycott a labor mobilization in Washington, D.C.

This is unprecedented and requires us to pose the question: Why would the leadership of the AFL-CIO feel threatened by a labor mobilization that confronts the crisis facing working people in the U.S. and seeks to reverse the wholesale attacks on our living standards, social services, housing, health, and education while challenging the diversion of trillions of dollars derived from the labor of working people to fund permanent war over decades and a brutal war for oil and occupation in Iraq?

The MWM is organizing working people to put forth our needs and our agenda independently of politicians and parties. We say that only by acting in our name can we build a movement that advances our needs. The very formation of the union movement was the result of independent organizing of working people. The struggle for industrial unionism, the movement for women's suffrage, the great movements for civil right, all these flowed from the will to mobilize independently in our own name.

Will the defeat of George Bush result in our aims, with which the AFL-CIO leadership purports to agree, universal single-payer healthcare and ending the stranglehold of greedy insurance companies.

Our aims include an end to the corporate trade agreements brought to us by the Democratic Party: NAFTA, MAI and FastTrack, with Disney and J. C. Penny paying Haitian workers 21 cents per hour?

Will the defeat of Bush end privatization and the destruction of unions in the public sector when the Democratic Party privatized and outsourced our jobs under the rubric of "downsizing government?" What were downsized were our social services while corporate profits and the military sucked trillion of dollars taken from the sweat of our collective labor.

Will the defeat of George Bush bring a crash program to restore

our decaying and devastated public schools? Will it result in the rebuilding of our inner cities and an end to homelessness? Will it secure, free mass transit systems? Will it launch a national training program in skills to enlist people in rebuilding the country? Will it end the criminalization of poverty or abolish the prison-industrial complex that has destroyed generations of Black and Latino youth? Will it roll back the bipartisan union-busting and anti-labor legislation, such as Taft-Hartley, that has been on the books for 67 years?

John Kerry, outflanking Bush from the far right, has called for an intensification of the "war on terror" by targeting people "before they act," giving explicit sanction to secret arrests, detention without trial and the labeling of opponents as "terrorists."

Will the removal of George Bush preserve the Bill of Rights, repeal the Patriot Act, Anti-Terrorism Act and the repressive legislation that has set the stage for a Police State in America? John Kerry has demanded a dramatic increase in the number of soldiers in Iraq and the extension of U.S. military control in the Middle East and beyond.

Today, 71% of U.S. corporations pay no taxes but John Kerry's principal economic adviser is Wall Street's Warren Buffett. Does Lee Iacocca of General Motors and Chrysler, who endorsed Kerry, represent the interests of labor and working people?

The leadership of the AFL-CIO, faced with rapidly growing rank-and-file support for a great mobilization of working people, has ordered organized labor to cease and desist in its support for the Million Worker March. The labor movement has been put on notice to boycott the MWM.

Working people are under siege. The corporate and banking oligarchy that has power in this society is waging class war against us all. In the face of attack after attack, the response of the leaders of the AFL-CIO has been silence. They fail to take note that the two parties are financed by the same people and their address is Wall Street. The labor movement is facing a crisis of its own. The number of unionized workers has steadily declined from a high of twenty percent in 1983 to twelve percent in 2004. This is the result of a campaign by the one percent of the population that owns and controls ninety percent of the national wealth.

We are at the point of production. When we mobilize our ranks, we represent a force that no illicit power, however concentrated, can hold back. We have taken the pulse of the rank-and-file and of unorganized labor. The overwhelming majority of working people want an end to permanent war and the hemorrhage of national resources into military production and war. AFSCME and SEIU, two of the largest unions have passed unanimous resolutions calling for an immediate end to the war in Iraq, and a return of all U.S. troops.

That is why the Million Worker March reaches out to labor. We are proud that labor councils across the country have endorsed the March. We are inspired by the knowledge that every ILWU local from San Diego to Anchorage has endorsed.

We are energized by the endorsement of the Coalition of Black Trade Unionists, by the Farm Labor Organizing Committee and by national organizations for immigrant rights. We are organizing and drawing upon the energy of the labor movement wherever people desire change.

Ours is a mobilization for all who say "enough is enough." Infant mortality in Harlem is greater than in Bangladesh. In Bangladesh the same Stevedore Association that sought to break the ILWU is privatizing their ports and imposing starvation wages.

Unemployment in our inner cities has reached catastrophic proportions with over 60% of Black male youth without work while militarized police units are deployed as an occupation army. One out of four children goes to bed hungry but hundreds of millions of dollars of our union dues fund politicians who do nothing about it.

Our labor movement has the opportunity and the obligation to reach out to working people, organized and unorganized. We need not hand politicians a blank check so they can soft soap us at election time and destroy our jobs, benefits and social services. We say to every union member, to every union local and to every labor council, to every State Federation and to the Central Labor Councils, let labor's voice be heard.

Join us in standing up for our rights and advancing our own agenda. Join us in fighting for our communities and our jobs. Support the ILWU workers who shut down the port to protest apartheid and launched a mobilization against Taft-Hartley and repressive anti-labor legislation. Support the one and a quarter million women who marched in Washington D.C. for reproductive rights and equal pay for equal work.

Send a message to all the politicians whoever they are and under whatever banner they parade: "We are not for sale. Let them know that we have our own agenda."

Every gain we have ever made has been won under the banner of labor: we are working people, union strong, fighting for our rights with our own voice and in our own name. Come together, sisters and brothers. Let us tap into our great strength, the desire for change and for social justice. We call on everyone to endorse, build, finance and mobilize the Million Worker March.

Abridged from Covert Action Quarterly, Fall 2004.

Coretta Scott King endorses MWM and
Martin Luther King III to speak

at workers' rights and anti-war rally on the steps of the Lincoln Memorial where Rev. Dr. Martin Luther King Jr stood in 1963

Plans are underway for Martin Luther King III to stand in the footsteps of his father at the Lincoln Memorial on October 17, 2004, and address the mass mobilization. A declaration of support by Coretta Scott King will be presented.

The Million Worker March will also feature presentations by Rev. E. Randel T. Osburn, of the Southern Christian Leadership Foundation, and a close collaborator of Rev. Dr. Martin Luther King Jr., and by Dick Gregory, the noted social activist and associate of Dr. King.

The call for the MWM was initiated by ILWU Local 10. The presence of the family of Dr. King is a fitting expression of historical continuity.

On September 21, 1967, Rev. Dr. Martin Luther King Jr. made a moving presentation at the hall of the ILWU Local 10. *The Dispatcher* reported: "Referring to labor history, King noted that the civil-rights, sit-in movement was actually invented by the labor movement. We have to keep sitting in at factory gates, at the steps of Congress and even in front of the White House."

Rev. Dr. King was made an honorary member of ILWU Local 10. At the presentation Dr. King appeared with William 'Bill' Chester who had become the first major African American labor official of the ILWU as its International Vice President, a direct consequence of the civil rights movement infusion within the labor movement itself.

The linkage of the struggle for civil rights with that of the labor movement and of opposition to devastating war on

Vietnam led Dr. King to march and mobilize on behalf of the sanitation workers on strike in Memphis, Tennessee.

Dr. King announced a Poor People's Campaign that would culminate in a Poor People's March on Washington, D.C. with demands for an Economic Bill of Rights: guaranteeing employment, a living wage, national economic support for those unable to work and decent housing for all.

He was assassinated on April 4, 1968, as he prepared a march in support of sanitation and other municipal employees.

The Mission Statement of the MWM declares: "Thirty-six years ago, Rev. Dr. Martin Luther King Jr. summoned working people across America to a Poor People's March on Washington to inaugurate 'a war on poverty at home.' The U.S. government," he proclaimed, "is one of the greatest purveyors of violence in the world. ... America is at a crossroads in history and it is critically important for us as a nation and a society to choose a new path and move on it with resolution and courage."

Working people are under siege while new wars of devastation are launched at the expense of the poor everywhere. The MWM will revive and expand a great struggle for fundamental change as we forge together a social, economic and political movement for fundamental change.

Press release by the MWM Publicity Committee

Rev. Dr. Martin Luther King Jr, Thomas Berkley, attorney and publisher, and William 'Bill' Chester, International Vice President of the ILWU. It was taken on Sept. 21, 1967 at ILWU Local 10, where Dr. King spoke, and was made an honorary member.

Photo: The Dispatcher

Bush & Kerry: What's the antidote to election-year quagmire?

Greg Butterfield

With the U.S. presidential election less than two months away, both the Democratic and Republican candidates are running to the right, and alienating the left wings of their own respective parties in the process.

On Sept. 9, 2004 the Rev. Jesse Jackson lashed out at Sen. John Kerry, the Democratic nominee, in a CNN interview. Jackson has campaigned on Kerry's behalf, trying to galvanize support among African Americans and labor unions. But he said the Kerry campaign was frustrating his efforts at every step.

Jackson criticized Kerry for "distancing himself from his base," those in the African American community, women's and lesbian/gay/bi/trans movements, labor unions, etc., who traditionally vote for Democratic candidates. He said Kerry's ballyhooed "shakeup" of his nearly all-white campaign staff was inadequate. "It can't be just a vanilla shake," Jackson stated.

Kerry has doggedly sold himself to Big Business as the best candidate to successfully carry out the occupation of Iraq. But recent events have undercut this appeal. As the Iraqi resistance grows ever wider and fiercer, there is less of a basis for Kerry's plan to "internationalize" the occupation.

At the same time, his pro-war stance is alienating anti-Bush, anti-war progressives, like the 500,000 who marched in New York City against the Republican National Convention.

Abridged from WW, Sept. 23, 2004.

Labor Notes supports the Million Worker March

Chris Kutalik

For many union members the presidential election season is known mostly for painfully predictable things: glossy magazine covers from the International featuring the candidate of choice; appeals for COPE money by local officers; repeat calls to come to the union hall and pick up yard signs; speeches at whistle stops; and other familiar activities.

It's not known for putting thousands of people out in the streets to support a labor agenda, but that's exactly what organizers of the MWM are aiming for on October 17.

Evolving from a call put out in Spring 2004 by members of ILWU Local 10 in San Francisco, the march intends to draw attention to positions on issues near and dear to labor activists: promoting universal health care; pushing a national living wage; guaranteeing pensions; canceling free trade agreements; repealing the Taft-Hartley Act; and opposing the war in Iraq — positions that neither presidential candidate supports.

According to spokespeople, "The Million Worker March is organizing working people to put forth our needs and our agenda independently of politicians and parties. We say that only by acting in our name can we build a movement that advances our needs." March backers claim that no politicians will speak from the stage.

AFL-CIO Opposition

This independent spirit may be what has motivated the AFL-CIO to oppose the march. The Director of Field Mobilization, Marilyn Scneiderman, circulated a memo June 23 stating, "We encourage our state federations, area councils, and central labor councils not to sponsor or devote resources to the demonstration in Washington, D.C. but instead to remain focused on the election…"

MWM organizers questioned this decision in an open letter to Schneiderman: "Why would the leadership of the AFL-CIO feel threatened by a labor mobilization that confronts the crisis facing working people ?"

Endorsements for the march are piling up. The NEA, APWU, South Carolina AFL-CIO, Coalition of Black Trade Unionists, ILWU's Longshore Division, Farm Labor Organizing Committee, Teamsters National Black Caucus, SEIU 1199 Joint Delegates Assembly, AFSCME DC Local 37 and 92, and a number of central labor councils, locals, and community organizations have signed on.

As with the antiwar resolutions passed by many unions over the past two years, it's not clear to what degree these endorsements will translate into mobilization for the event, but reports of buses and local committees being organized are starting to surface from many major cities.

Demonstrations like the MWM are just one part of the struggle that goes on every day in the workplace and in the community, tough fights over work conditions, against discrimination, for democratic control of the union.

But marches like the MWM have the potential to bring together workers from different unions, regions, and industries in a show of strength and solidarity. These experiences can keep union members energized for the hard, long-haul fights. *Labor Notes* supports the marchers in this effort.

This article appeared as an editorial in Labor Notes Sept. 30, 2004.

Lesbian, gay, bisexual & transgender workers: Join the Million Worker March!

National call for LGBT participation and mobilization for the MWM

The voices and issues of LGBT workers will be raised at the Million Worker March. We will be there as union members and unorganized employees, unemployed, immigrants and youth, joining hundreds of thousands of other workers and supporters.

We will be there because we need what all workers need: jobs for all, higher wages, shorter hours, and freedom to organize a union if we don't have one.

We will be at the MWM March because we need a movement that is independent of the major parties. The interest of LGBT communities is with other working class people, not corporate greed or with war abroad. We understand that our bosses, the corporate media and the President and Congress work overtime to try to divide us from our co-workers and friends by institutionalized discrimination, harassment and violence, so that all workers suffer by disunity. We understand the long history of racism, sexism, and bigotry in the U.S., and how the corporate divide-and-conquer strategy is designed to hurt all workers.

We demand the dignity, safety, and respect of all peoples, including LGBT people and immigrants. We demand a comprehensive program against hate crimes and discrimination, and assert the right of people to define their own families. This includes the recognition of individuals and families to raise and adopt children without discrimination or deterrence.

We demand an end to the privatization of our jobs and of social security.

Human need should take priority over corporate greed, and we demand affordable housing for all and an end to private profit for health care and drugs. We demand full civil marriage rights, including healthcare benefits for our partners. We demand increased funding for AIDS research and free AIDS medications for the people of Africa and other developing nations. *Join us on October 17th!*

Endorsers as of October 12, 2004: (* for identification only)
Ali Ibreighith, Political Activist, U.A.W., Anaheim, CA
Andre Powell, AFSCME LOCAL 112, Executive Board*
Antonio Salas, Convener, Faith & Socialism Commission of the Socialist Party USA
Benjamin Grunde, Holistic Massage Therapist, Ashland, OR
Bet Power, Dir. Sexual Minorities Archives Bisexual Resource Center, Boston, MA
Bob McCubbin, Author "The Roots of Lesbian & Gay Oppression," San Diego, CA
David Ebony Allen Barkley, Alliance of Black Union Workers, MA*
David Mariner, www.temenos.net, The progressive LGBT community online*
Dian Killian, UAW 1981; Pride at Work (AFL-CIO)*
East Coast FTM Group, Northampton, Massachusetts
Gale Crooks, Co-Chair, Lapeer County Equal Rights Alliance (LCERA), Michigan*
Gerry Scoppettuolo, Co-founder; Gay Men Fight AIDS, Portsmouth, NH*
Gunner Scott, butchdykeboy.com
Henry Millbourne, President, Detroit Black Gay Pride, Inc.*
Holly Richardson, Co-director, Out Now, Springfield, MA*
Imani Henry, Playwright/Performer, National Writers Union (NWU) UAW Local 1981 *

Irish Queers, NYC
Jesse Heiwa, Pacifica Radio*
Joan Healy, Retired, Sunnyvale, CA
LAGAI, Queer Insurrection from the SF Bay Area
Leilani Dowell, Candidate for Congress, Peace & Freedom Party
Leslie Feinberg, Co-chair Nat'l Queer Caucus, NWU/UAW Local 1981
Letta Neely, Writer/activist
Mark Maron, President, Rim & Rotor Repair, Gilsun, N.H.
Martha Grevatt, Northeast Ohio Pride At Work/UAW Local 122*
M'Bwende Anderson, Nat'l Youth Advocacy Coalition, Wash. D.C.*
Metropolitan Community Church of New York City

Leslie Feinberg
March 13, 2004
WW photo: Liz Green

Minnie Bruce Pratt, Lesbian writer, National Writers Union UAW Local 1981*
Noah Sax, Owner, McWheel, Swanzey, N.H.
Patricia Galloway, Eliot, ME.
Queer Caucus, National Writers Union (UAW Local 1981)
Queer People of Color Action
Queers for Peace and Justice
Renita Martin, Playwright and actor
Rev. Pat Bumgardner, The Metropolitan Community Church
Sharon Danann, Secr., NE Ohio Pride at Work, AFGE Local #2089 Cleveland, OH.*
Solidarity Coalition for Equal Marriage Rights & Against All Forms of Discrimination, Bigotry and Racism (www.equalmarriagesolidarity.org)
Steph Simard, Boston area gender queer activist
Stephen Eagle Funk, U.S. military personnel serving time for resisting Iraq War, S.F..
Stonewall Warriors, Boston
Sue Ahern, Portland, OR.
Susan Schnur, Executive Board, ATU Local 268, Amalgamated Transit Union, Cleveland, OH.
Teresa Gutierrez, Vice Presidential Candidate, Workers World Party

July 13, 2004

Mr. Henry C. Graham, President
ILWU Local 10
400 North Point
San Francisco, CA 94133

Dear Brother Graham:

I am in receipt of your letter of June 28th, in which you appeal to the AFL-CIO to endorse an October 17th mobilization in Washington.

While we agree with many of the aims and goals of the march, we are not endorsing this mobilization. This is because our federation and our affiliate unions have made a decision many months ago that we would devote our time, resources and energies into a massive grass roots member education and mobilization effort to defeat George Bush. We need every local union to be working in local communities all across the country in the weeks leading up to the election to carry our message to union households – and to organize registration and turn out of union members and their families in unprecedented numbers.

We respect the long and proud tradition of your union, and look forward to continuing to work with you as we have on so many issues. However, we believe that devoting resources to a protest demonstration a few weeks prior to the Presidential election, is a diversion that our movement cannot afford.

Sincerely,

John J. Sweeney
President

JJS:lah/opeiu#2

cc: James Spinoza, President, ILWU
      William Adams, Secretary-Treasurer, ILWU

President Sweeney's letter is evidence of the AFL-CIO leadership's attempt to block the MWM.

In the letter Sweeney argues that resources are needed to support the Democratic Party candidate, Kerry, while using his position as head of the AFL-CIO to stifle a political mobilization of the union movement.

Another argument used against the MWM was on the timing of the March. In the following year the leadership of the AFL-CIO split over their inability to grow the union movement.

Excerpts from U.S. Labor Against the War (USLAW) letter to the organizers of the MWM

RE: USLAW position on endorsement of MWM August 12, 2004

We wish to inform you of the outcome of a referendum of the Leadership Council on the question of endorsing the MWM. There was broad support for the concept of the MWM and its demands. The reason that affiliates declined to endorse was its timing. While USLAW is not endorsing the MWM demonstration in Washington, D.C., no doubt some of our affiliates will participate.

Shown here is side two, **The USLAW Referendum on the MWM.** Note, the third point of opposition which says: "The AFL-CIO has publicly opposed participation in the MWM. It is not helpful for the USLAW to pick a fight with them over this. It will be seen as 'mischievous' act."

U.S. LABOR AGAINST THE WAR

Leadership Council Referendum

QUESTION: SHOULD USLAW ENDORSE THE MILLION WORKER MARCH ON OCTOBER 17TH IN WASHINGTON, DC?

U.S. Labor Against the War has been asked to endorse and help build the Million Worker March called for October 17 in Washington, DC. The Steering Committee considered this request over the course of two regular monthly conference calls. When a vote was taken, the outcome was 9 in favor and 8 opposed. In light of the evenly divided vote and the desire that USLAW should act, whenever possible by consensus and in accord with the desire of a majority of its affiliates, the Steering Committee decided to poll the Leadership Council on this question.

ARGUMENTS IN FAVOR	ARGUMENTS OPPOSED
• Regardless of the outcome of the elections, the struggle for peace, workers' rights, justice, and human needs will need to continue and escalate. Neither major candidate is committed to a workers' and antiwar agenda.	• Unions are totally involved in mobilizing their members for the elections; all resources and energy will be devoted to getting Bush out of office between now and the election.
• There needs to be an independent voice for a workers' agenda before the election.	• It is not possible to divert energy and resources two weeks before the election to go to DC.
• It is imperative that we demonstrate support for a workers' agenda, peace, justice and democracy to put whichever candidate wins on notice that we will not be silenced.	• Putting the MWM in competition with labor's election work guarantees a small labor turn-out on Oct. 17.
• Another terror attack may be used to suspend constitutional rights and postpone or cancel the election.	• The AFL-CIO has publicly opposed participation in the MWM prior to the election. It is not helpful for USLAW to pick a fight with them over this. It will be seen as 'mischievous' act.
• Endorsements by the NEA and important African American labor groups and individual leaders should not be ignored.	• The program, mission and goals of MWM are laudable but timing is wrong. It should be done after the election to put whoever wins on notice.
• Labor unions are accustomed to working on more than one thing at a time and can do both the MWM and election work.	• If actions are to be held prior to the election, they should be local and regional and tied to mobilizing for get-out-the-vote work.
• The MWM will bring new activists forward and develop new leaders.	• Only a few USLAW affiliates have endorsed the MWM. USLAW should not endorse if its affiliates haven't done so.
• This is an opportunity to mobilize both organized and unorganized workers, labor and community together for joint action.	• Endorsing if we don't intend to really work oh it is tokenism and it diminishes USLAW's credibility. USLAW should only endorse if we are serious.
• This is an opportunity to strengthen labor's ties to youth, community and religious forces that will strengthen our fight in the future.	• USLAW should only endorse if MWM receives endorsement of UFPJ and the broad antiwar movement.

PLEASE REGISTER YOUR ORGANIZATION'S VOTE BY RESPONDING BY EMAIL OR PAPER BALLOT NO LATER THAN WEDNESDAY, AUGUST 11TH AT 8:00 P.M. EDT.

PMB 153, 1718 M Street, N.W., Washington, D.C. 90036
info@uslaboragainstwar.org   www.uslaboragainstwar.net

. . . ◆

October 1, 2004
Clarence Thomas
Co-Chair
Million Worker March

Dear Brother Thomas,

I am writing to let you know that I would like to be listed as an endorser of the Million Worker March, with my title, Co-Convenor of U.S. Labor Against the War for identification purposes only. Although I will be endorsing as an individual I do so with the agreement of the Steering Committee of USLAW on September 28.

We also agreed to send a notice to our list with with an announcement of the MWM and to provide a link to the March on our web page.

If it's possible we would like to participate in the anti-war tent.

Lastly, we hope that a representative of the MWM will be able to attend our Leadership Assembly on December 4 , which is a meeting of our affiliates and invited guest organizations.

We wish you sucess with this important effort. Feel free to call if you have any questions. If I don't see you before the MWM, I will see you there

In Solidarity

Gene Bruskin

Co-convener USLAW

. . . ◆

October 6, 2004

Thanks for the quick response. I look forward to the March and would very much appreciate a chance to speak.

USLAW would love to join the tent discussion and bring literature

We are putting the word out and will continued to do so.

Thanks for being bold in this initiative, it took a lot of guts to take it on.

Let me know if there is any other way I can help.

Gene Bruskin

South Carolina
AFL – CIO

Donna S. Dewitt
President

Michael R. Godfrey
Secretary–Treasurer

Vice Presidents
Kenneth Riley
Jesse Weaver

Board Members
Billy Atkinson
Tom Ayers
Charles Brave, Jr.
Bennie Colclough
Joyce Fields
Charles Hill
Andrew J. Maute
Jack Powers
James Sanderson, Jr.
Helen C. Washington
Bill Wise
Dennis Zimmerman

Marilyn Sneiderman, Director   July 10, 2004
Field Mobilization
AFL-CIO Washington, D.C. 20006-4104

Dear Marilyn:

On June 9th, 2001 approximately 7,000 union supporters marched to the South Carolina State Capital to show their support for the five Longshoremen, who had been indicted by South Carolina Attorney General, Charlie Condon, in his scheme to run for governor. These five men became known as The Charleston 5 .

This campaign brings to the fore basic constitutional issues regarding freedom of speech and association, not to mention the statutory right of all workers to organize. AFL-CIO President, John Sweeney, wrote to union members.

The rally helped to send a strong message of solidarity to the Attorney General and employers that resulted in the exoneration of the five men. The struggle of the Charleston 5 became a struggle for the entire labor movement.

Now, each time a union member or activists tell me this campaign revived the union movement, I remember the excitement, the color, and the power of the hundreds of thousands of union members that marched in Washington on the Day of Solidarity in 1991. This march sent a strong message, too and previewed the change for the White House the following year.

For the last two years the AFL-CIO staff and officers have traveled with IAM affiliates to Washington for their National Day of Action. I am amazed at the excitement and growing empowerment displayed by the members who are attending their first Washington rally.

I revisit these events to relay their significance in mobilizing our members and allies to the urgency of the November elections. The South Carolina AFL-CIO knows that there will be few resources to assist us with our efforts toward this cause. They are excited and confident that the Million Worker March presents the opportunity to repeat history. It presents an opportunity for South Carolina AFL-CIO affiliates to mobilize their members and send a strong message to America that workers demand rights that are being taken away from them.

I know the Million Worker March will mobilize South Carolina union members for the November election and I can t afford to miss this historical opportunity. This is not about resources. This is about rallying workers and supporters to a demand for justice.

Sincerely,

Donna S. Dewitt
President

Excerpted Facsimile of letter

Protest in support the 'Charleston 5' in South Carolina on June 9, 2001.   Photo: Lallan Schoenstein

Green Party proposal:
Presence at Million Worker March

Background

On October 2004, there will be a march on Washington D.C. This mobilization is being proposed by the ILWU Local 10, in response to the attacks upon working families, the illegal war on Iraq, and the millions of jobs lost during the Bush administration with the complicity of Congress.

Local 10, a union with an outstanding history of successful struggle, proposed this march out of a frustration with the major party candidates and an understanding that no matter who was in office working people and their allies would need a social movement to hold the politicians accountable. They wrote: We shall be representing ourselves during this march, independent from all politicians, while putting forward to the entire country, our program for the betterment of the working population.

The demands of the March are Green Party (GP) demands. This march offers an opportunity for the GP to develop relationships with the wings of the labor movement and anti-war movement that prioritizes building street heat over campaigning for "Anybody But Bush," to fight for our needs no matter who wins the election. These are forces in the labor movement who should be GP members and help both leverage trade unions to support the GP and also to help continue transforming the GP into the kind of party we need to be to become a more effective vehicle for the needs and aspirations of working and oppressed communities.

At the same time, in part because of AFL-CIO leadership pressures to devote all resources to electing Kerry and view the March as a distraction, working on the March will provide opportunities for the GP to build relationships with the forces in the trade union movement. It will also be an opportunity to do internal education in the GP about the labor movement.

This March also offers us and the Green presidential campaign, another opportunity to build relations with and provide some leadership to the anti-war movement as some anti-war forces in the East Coast have already oriented towards the MWM as the major anti-war mobilization between the RNC and the election.

When Local 10 member and March organizer, Clarence Thomas, spoke to the GPUS CC, he received a standing ovation and positive feedback. Now, as a Party, we can make it official.

Proposal

The Green Party of the U.S., as well as the Labor Green Network, shall formally sponsor and assist with logistics the Million Worker March and will approve an ad-hoc organizing committee including members of various state Green Parties. We will produce literature to be developed by the Labor Greens solidarizing with the demands of the MWM and labor here and internationally. We will organize a contingent behind the GP banner and attempt to recruit to the Green Party.

Adopted Sept. 5, 2004.

Labor Greens fight to build the Million Worker March

By Michael-David Sasson

Green Party labor activists in the Bay Area have been involved in planning meetings of the Million Worker March from the very beginning. Local 10 leader and March organizer Clarence Thomas spoke at a local "Green Sunday" forum. Thomas stressed the need to build a united front, regardless of people's political party or affiliation, committed to building a movement of working people willing to speak in our own name, and ready to demand a better world that could be built through our united efforts.

Our forum helped inspire Brother Thomas to come to the GP National Convention. There the Labor Green Network introduced Thomas to the national leadership of the Greens, who gave him a standing ovation. There began a dialogue that led to the GP to endorse the March and commit to building a strong contingent to march on October 17.

Labor Greens in North Carolina, Wisconsin, Michigan, and elsewhere are helping to organize buses to D.C. The Houston Organizing Committee for the MWM nominated Henry Cooper, a machinist active in the Latino community and the Harris County Green Party , to speak in D.C. In Minnesota, Jenny Heiser, used her connections as a member of the Steelworkers and the Industrial Workers of the World to mobilize people to make it to Washington, D.C. for this event.

Abridged from Solidarity News, Oct. 2004.

Referendum on Million Worker March
U.S. Labor Against the War August 2, 2004

Dear Sisters and Brothers,

Please read why we are endorsing the Million Worker March. We think there are more reasons than stated in the note for why we need to support it.

Most important we think this historic initiative led by African Americans trade unionists should get the support of the entire labor movement.

So often those of us in the trade union movement try to build multi-racial and multi-national coalitions in defense of workers and their rights. So often we make demands of progressive African American groups that they support labor's struggles and so often they do, even when labor movement is slipshod or worse on raising issues of discrimination, police brutality, the criminalization and militarization of Black youth, racism, etc., issues that are of paramount importance to the African American community.

Here are some of the reasons we need to take a stand in favor if this march in addition to those already put forward:

1. All too often white progressive organizations demand that Black organizations unite with them while refusing to unite with activities initiated and led by those same organizations.

2. This is an attempt to form a "labor left" initiated and led by the African American progressive trade union movement that should be united with.

3. The issue of the difficulty of organizing a million workers is more a question of spin than numbers, we certainly can claim to represent millions of workers and we can work on literature that explains it. If organizations can't spend a lot of time organizing for the MWM the least they can do is show their solidarity by endorsing it.

4. Having a demonstration before the election makes the important point that the people have a right to make a demand of government and even have the right to change leaders in ways that are not necessarily defined by elections.

5. If we want to be able to unite with those who are leading this March in the future, we have to be able to unite with them now for this March. It is not unreasonable and it is a measure of solidarity.

6. It strikes us as interesting that the AFL-CIO chose to put the kibosh on an African American led event, when they rarely or ever try to smash or undermine other similar events led by progressive, pro-labor forces.

7. We need to take a stand against a top-down leadership style in the AFL-CIO that does not leave room for the development of bottom up initiatives from union locals, rank-and-file and constituency groups.

8. This March does not stop people from mobilizing the masses to oppose the current president in the streets and on election day.

In solidarity,

Laura Chenven

Endorsers & Supporters of the MWM in the beginning of September 2004

American Federation of State County & Municipal Employees, AFSCME Council 92, Baltimore, Wash. D.C. Area • AFSCME Local 1550, Houston Texas • AFSCME Local 167 • AFSCME Local 1072 • AFSCME Local 1550, Houston,TX; Kimbal Urrutia Vice Pres. Distr. 3 Texas AFL-CIO Council • AFSCME Local 1881 • AFSCME Local 205 • AFSCME Local 215 • AFSCME Local 253 • AFSCME Local 3506 • AFSCME Local 3800, Minneapolis, MN • AFSCME Local 389 • AFSCME Local 95 • AFSCME Local 1930, D.C.-37, Exec. Brd NY Public Library Guild • Brenda Stokely, Pres. District Council 1707, AFSCME, AFL-CIO • Calif. Building Trades Council • American Postal Workers Union Int'l APWU • Int'l Brotherhood of Teamsters, IBTWU contributes funds • John R. MacArthur, Harpers Magazine • Transport Workers Union Local 100 ATU 100 NYC • Action For Justice, Charlotte, NC • Bring The Troops Home Now • ActionLA • Action LAAFM, Local 1000, Wash., D.C. • AfrikanAm Institute for Policy Studies, Greenville, SC • Albany, NY Labor Council • All People's Congress, Baltimore, Md. • Amalgamated Transit Union 1555 (BART Operators, Station Agents, Fore workers & Transportation Clerks) • American Federation of Musicians, Local 6 • ANSWER, San Francisco • Anti-War Joint Action Committee, Kikuchi Takao • Yippie Global Pastry Uprising • Axis of Logic, Boston, MA • Bay Area Local Socialist Party USA, Oakland, Calif. • Bay Area United Against War • Bethlehem Neighbors for Peace, Delmar, NY • Black Telephone Workers for Justice, Jersey City, NJ • Brigada 21 de Marzo • So. Bay, Calif. Central Labor Council • Calif. Coalition for Fair Trade & Human Rights, Oakland • Calif. State Association of Letter Carriers • Letter Carriers Local 214 • Plumbers Local 393 • Calif. State Pipe Trades Council • Carpenters for a Rank-and-File Union • Casey Kasem, radio personality for Independent Communication • Baldemar Velasquez, Chair, Farm Labor Organizing Committee (FLOC) • Chris Silvera, Chair, Teamsters Nat'l Black Caucus; Secretary-Treasurer, Teamsters Local 808 • Saladin Muhammad, Chairperson, Black Workers For Justice, NC • Charleston, SC Labor Council • Chumbawamba • Coalition for Consumer Justice, Cranston, RI • Coalition of Black Trade Unionists. Atlanta National Convention • Coalition of University Employees Local 3 • Collective Bargaining Congress of the American Assoc. University Professors • College of the Mainland, Texas City, TX • Mike Rubin, CSEA Member • CUE Local 3 • CWA Local 1104, Binghamton, NY • Danny Glover, actor • Daves-DirtyRatBastardsHuntingClub, Columbus, OH • SF Day Laborers' Program • Defenders for Freedom, Justice & Equality, Richmond, VA • Howard Wallace, Delegate S.F. Labor Council, founder of Pride at Work • Industrial Workers of the World IWW • IWW Pensacola, FL • IWW, Philadelphia, PA. • IWW, St. Clair Shores, MI • Detroit IWW • NYC IWW • Socialist Party USA, Detroit affiliate • Dick Gregory, comedian • Jim Houghton, Dir., Harlem Fight Back (Organization of Black Construction Workers frozen out of hiring); Harlem Unemployment League; fmr. Nat'l Organizer, Negro-American Labor Council with A. Philip Randolph; fmr dir., Labor Committee, NAACP • District Council 1707, (AFSCME) • DNC2RNC • Democracy UP-

Continued

rising • nextstep@riseup.net • Donna Dewitt, Pres., S.C. State Federation of Labor, AFL-CIO • Doro Chiba Railroad Workers Union of Japan • Dropkick Murphys • Evan Greer, folk singer • Michael Everett, IATSE, Local 728, Studio Electrical Lighting Technicians; Delegate, L.A. County Federation • Ferran Pedret Santos, Socialist Youth of Barcelona, Spain • Steve Weiner, Exec. Secretary-Treasurer Santa Barbara and San Luis Obispo Counties Building Trades Council • Farm Labor Organizing Committee, AFL-CIO (FLOC) • Jahahara Alkebulan-Ma'at, Foundations For Our Nu Afrikan Millennium (FONAMI) • Jerome Otis, No. Calf. Teamsters Black Caucus • Jose A. Ibarra, Founder, Professional Flight Attendants AFA NWA (North West Airlines) • G7 Welcoming Committee Records (Punk Rock Recording Label, Canada), Participatory Economics at the workplace • Global Coalition for Peace, Chevy Chase, Md. • Global Exchange • Gordon Lafer, professor (Labor Education and Research , Univ. of Oregon) • Graphic Communications Int'l Union.Local 4-N, SF Chapter (GCIU), Local 4N • Green Party, Clovis, Calif. • Greens/Green Party, USA, Eureka, Calif. • Green Party, Raleigh, NC • Guns and Butter, producer, Bonnie Faulkner, KPFA • KPFA - Pacifica Network Station for No. Calif. • Union of Producers & Programming Network, UPPNET • Mya Shone and Ralph Schoenman, co-producers , Taking AIM, WBAI • Guyanese American Workers United • Harlem Fight Back • Harlem Unemployment League • Harvard Social Forum, United Students Against Sweatshops • Howard Zinn, historian, prof. emeritus Boston University* • IAM LL 1145, Troy, NY • IAM Local 1145, Selkirk, NY • IBEW Local 617, San Mateo • IBEW Local 77 + Radical Women & Freedom Socialist Party, Seattle, WA • IFPTE Local 21 • Int'l Longshore Delegates' Caucus • ILWU Local 10 • ILWU Local 34 • ILWU Longshore Division for entire West Coast • Independent Progressive Politics Network (IPPN) • Justice 4 Homeless SF • Justice for Palestinians, San Jose, Calif. • Kansas City Labor Council • La Raza Centro Legal, SF • Labor Action Coalition • Labor Council for Latin American Advancement (Bay Area) • Labor Green Network • LaborNet. org • Labor Tech • Local 1, Labor Action Coalition • Maine Coalition for Peace & Justice, Blue Hill, ME • Michael Franti, singer and Spearhead Vibrations • MidwestUnrest, Chicago, IL • Phil Hutchings • Mike Buck Studios, Wash., D.C. • Minneapolis City Council, Minneapolis, MN • Monterey Bay Central Labor Council, Calif. • Nat'l Assoc. of Letter Carriers Branch 3825 Rockville,

Continued

*We must keep marching . . . before the elections and after the elections . . . until we win justice for the homeless , the unemployed and we must bring the troops home now. . . . Come out on Oct. 17. That's the voice of **Danny Glover** calling you to get on the bus for the Million Worker March.*

– San Francisco Bay View News   September 22, 2004

Pictured here, Leo Robinson speaks at ILWU Local 10 meeting called to discuss the contract settlement for the coast wide longshore workers in 1999.

Photo: David Bacon

***Clarence Thomas** and other organizers say that much of the funds for the event come from rank-and-file workers. One retired longshoreman, **Leo Robinson** from Local 10, has contributed more than $50,000. Thomas said: "He is teaching us and showing us what it is going to take in the future to mount any kind of movement in the name of working people. We're going to have to do it ourselves."*

– Washington Post   October 14, 2004

As the leadership of AFL-CIO continued to distance itself from the MWM, organizers wrote: "Let's end subservience to the power of a privileged few and their monopoly of the political process. We need not hand politicians a blank check so that they can soft soap us at election time. They argued that on issues like poverty, high prison rates for young Black men, anti-union organizing laws and the war in Iraq, a Democratic victory will not usher in significant change.

Many argue that the labor movement has lost touch . . . and point to the continuing decline of union membership. They say that the revitalization of unions can only happen through a broad social movement, uniting progressive activists, community groups and workers.

– The News Standard / People's Networks   August 19, 2004

In 1984, Local 10 staged a boycott of South African apartheid cargo.

Longshore Local 10 which has inspired many by its stand on social and political issues through dock actions against South African apartheid, for freedom for Black political prisoner Mumia Abu-Jamal, in protest against the bloody Pinochet dictatorship in Chile, now is calling for a Million Worker March in Washington, D.C., independent of both Democratic and Republican Parties.

– Counterpunch   May 12, 2004

Coming Soon to Washington D.C. The Million Worker March

Alan Jones, Shop Steward, IUOE

A growing number of workers' organizations are building for a mass workers' demonstration in Washington, D.C. on October 17 to protest the government's anti-labor policies, the occupation of Iraq, the attack on civil liberties, and the budget cuts to desperately needed social programs while Wall Street and the super-rich get tax breaks.

The organizers of the Million Worker March (MWM) model their campaign after the Poor People's March organized by the civil rights movement and Martin Luther King Jr. 36 years ago, to inaugurate a "war on poverty at home." King declared that the vast arsenal of death unleashed by the Pentagon on the people of Vietnam was in reality a war on working people at home and abroad.

The MWM mission statement declares: "The time has come to mobilize working people for our own agenda. Let us end subservience to the power of the privileged few and their monopoly of the political process in America…Let us forge together a social, economic, and political movement for working people. We are the many. The secretive and corrupt who control our lives are the rapacious few."

The opposition of the AFL-CIO leadership to the MWM is the outcome of the "Anybody But Bush" alliance with John Kerry. While no resources will be put towards the MWM, the AFL-CIO will spend over $160 million to help Kerry and the Democrats. This money would go much further in advancing the interests of workers if it went to building the MWM.

Abridged from www.socialistalternative.org

Md. • Ted Glick, Nat'l Coor., Independent Progressive Politics Network • National Education Association, NEA • Nat'l Grassroots Peace Network, Wash., D.C. • Father Lawrence Lucas, Our Lady of Lourdes, Harlem, N.Y. • National Immigrant Solidarity Network • IWW • NY Labor Against the War • Newspaper Guild-CWA Local 32035 Wash., D.C. • Noam Chomsky, linguist; prof. linguistic theory, philosophy of language MA Institute of Technology*· Norman Finkelstein, prof. political science DePaul Univ., Chicago*· No. American Commercial Conference of the GCIU • No. American Newspaper Conference of the GCIU • Public Service Workers Union - UE Local 1, NC • Coalition of Black Trade Unionists, NC Chapter • No. Calif. Committees of Correspondence for Democracy & Socialism • No. Calif., Convention of Plumbers & Steamfitters • Teamsters Black Caucus, No. Calif. • No. Calif. Chapter Coalition of Black Trade Unionists • Open World Conference Continuations Committee • Alan Benjamin and Ed Rosario, Co-Coordinators, OWC Cotinuations Committee • Peace & Freedom Party, Calif. • Philadelphia Committe to Free the Five • Members Local 393 • Members Union, Local 355. San Jose, Calif. • Frank Martin Del Campo, Pres., Labor Council for Latin American Advancement • Raymond Sanders, Pres., NC Public Service Workers Union, UE Local 150 • Mike Keenan, Pres., Troy Area Labor Council • Jon Flanders. Pres. IAM Local 1145 , Troy, NY Labor Council • Pride At Work, San Francisco / SF/LCLAA, Berkeley, Calif. • Propagandhi • Psi Sigma Phi Multicultural Fraternity • Queers For Peace And Justice, NYC • Richmond Coalition for a Living Wage • Rutgers Council of the American Association University Professors AAUP • Arlene Rodriguez, Staff Rep. AAUP, Rutgers • San Francisco Labor Council • San Jose, Calif. Members Union, Local 355 • Santa Barbara & San Luis Obispo Counties Building Trades Council • SDHughes.org, Brooklyn, NY • Al Avants, Secretary-Treasurer, UFCW Local 373R • SEIU Local 535, Altadena, Calif. • Maria Guillen, V.P. Seiu 790 • Simon's Rock College of Bard, Great Barrington, MA • Chris Willmeng • Socialist Alternative, Seattle, WA • The Socialist Party USA • Socialist Party, NYC • Socialist Party, PA • Rich Page, State Chair, Socialist Party, Pennsylvania • Socialist Party NYC • Socialist Youth of Barcelona, Spain • Solano County Peace & Justice Coalition • Solidarity • Solutions for Humanity, Inc. • Student Peace Action Network, Raleigh, NC • Support Network for an Armed Forces Union • Teamsters Local 808, Long Island City. NY • The Psychoanalytic Collective, Louisville, KY • Rail, Maritime & Transport Union of Britain • Tidewater Labor Support Committee, Williamsburg, VA • Transit Workers Union Local 100. NYC • President Roger Toussaint, Transit Workers Union Local 100 NYC • Troy, NY Labor Council • UAW - National Writers Union, Bayonne, NJ • UAW 1981, Chapter 3 • UE Local 160, Williamsburg, VA • Selma Blair, UE 160 Williamsburg, VA • United Food & Commercial Workers Local 328, Providence, RI • United Food & Commercial Workers Local 373R • Steve Gillis, United Steel Workers of America • United Teachers Los Angeles • Pasadena, Calif. • Utah Phillips, folk singer • Ron Dicks, Vice Pres. Legislative & Political Affairs, Professional & Technical Engineers (IFPTE) Local 21 • Maria Guillen, Vice President, SEIU 790 • War Zone Education • We the People of America, Arlington, VA • Women's Economic Agenda Project, WEAP • Workers Solidarity Alliance

CHAPTER 2

The Million Worker March

OCTOBER 17, 2004

LINCOLN MEMORIAL • WASHINGTON D.C.

We salute the MWM!

Monica Moorehead

We extend our heartfelt solidarity to all who are marching in the historic Million Worker March, a beautiful demonstration of class unity. And we especially salute Local 10 of the International Longshore & Warehouse Union in San Francisco, for their tenacity, vision and courage in initiating this March.

Part of the power of the MWM is its strategic timing, coming before the Nov. 2 elections. The choice of Oct. 17 was not primarily based on trying to politically influence either of the big-business candidates, George W. Bush or John Kerry.

While the top leadership of the AFL-CIO is spending tens of millions of dollars in union dues to elect "the lesser evil" candidate, Kerry, the message of the Million Worker March is that a new, dynamic workers' movement is on the horizon, a movement that will speak and fight in its own name for full social justice.

The MWM is a clarion call for unity. The billionaire money class the real rulers of the United States, have grown rich off profits produced by the labor of the multinational working class. These bosses use racism, sexism and lesbian, gay, bi and trans oppression to divide the workers in order to keep them from coming together to organize for union jobs, health care, housing, education and other human needs.

These divisions help profits soar while impoverishment and disfranchisement deepen. The tiny minority of the rich get even richer while the vast majority of the workers become even poorer.

This same ruling class uses its government and the mainstream media to justify its wars for empire abroad by pitting workers here against workers in other countries. The capitalist bosses mask their drive for super-profits under the guise of "fighting terrorism" or "defending national security." This kind of jingoistic frenzy helped to justify the repressive Patriot Act after Sept. 11, 2001, targeting Arabs, South Asians and Muslims.

The initiators of the MWM have taken a clear stand against these dangerous divisions, in word and in action. They have stretched out a hand of solidarity to all currents of the anti-war movement that have been mobilizing in the streets against war and occupation in Iraq, Afghanistan, Haiti, Palestine and elsewhere.

The MWM is a revolutionary concept

The MWM has some similarities to the 1995 Million Man March in Washington, D.C., the 1997 Million Women's March in Philadelphia, the 1998 Million Youth March in Harlem and the 1999 Millions for Mumia demonstration in Philadelphia. These mass demonstrations were not just about bringing out large numbers of people but about building unity based on a political program of fighting repression.

The 1995, 1997 and 1998 Marches brought out predominantly African American masses with implicit demands for long-denied political representation and economic empowerment. Those in the leadership of these Marches were grassroots Black community and political activists.

Monica Moorehead speaking at The Women's Anti-Imperialist League Conference in March 2004 entitled "Uniting Women's Response Against Wars of Aggression and Globalization." Monica Moorehead, a leader of Workers World Party, tied in the struggle of African women to imperialism. The conference was called by the Gabriela Network, a Philippine-U.S. Women's solidarity organization.

Photo: Mathew Barnett

Local 10 is a Black-led union that has fought against apartheid in South Africa and supported a new trial for African American death-row political prisoner Mumia Abu-Jamal. The Black leadership of Local 10 is attempting with the MWM to build an independent, grassroots movement based on broad class-wide solidarity to embrace all nationalities, including immigrant workers, documented or undocumented.

This merging of anti-racist and class issues by the MWM shows the potential of this movement to ignite revolutionary struggle. It is in the interests of the entire U.S. progressive movement to help strengthen this exciting new phase of the workers' upsurge that we are witnessing by providing concrete solidarity.

Abridged from WW, Oct. 21, 2004.

Million Worker March reclaims labor's militant roots

Monica Moorehead

Brenda Stokely

Clarence Thomas

Sharon Black

Larry Holmes

Timely, unifying, forward moving, and most of all, necessary, these adjectives and many more describe the historic Million Worker March that took place at the steps of the Lincoln Memorial in Washington, D.C., on Oct. 17.

For almost eight hours, workers, organized and unorganized, along with anti-war and community activists, heard speeches and cultural presentations that emphasized the tremendous need to build a new independent movement that will fight in the interests of working people.

The MWM was initiated by the Black leadership of Local 10 of the International Longshore and Warehouse Union in San Francisco. Clarence Thomas, a leader of Local 10 and a national co-convener of the MWM, said at the rally: "The majority of working people in America are not doing well. With jobs being offshored, outsourced, privatized, our young people are looking at a much more dismal future."

People came in buses, vans and car caravans as well as by train and airplane from all over the country to get to the MWM. In New York City, from which most buses came, union locals like Transit Workers Local 100, Teamsters Local 808, Service Employees/1199 health care workers and AFSCME District Council 1707 mobilized sizable delegations of workers.

From Pennsylvania, delegations of workers representing Service Employees Local 668, International Electrical Union Local 119, the Federation of Government Employees. Western Massachusetts was represented by Auto Workers Local 2322, the Graduate Employee Organization and Office of ALANA Affairs at UMass Amherst, and a Worcester carpenters' union, along with students from Mt. Holyoke, Smith and Hampshire colleges.

From Virginia, IUE Local 160 from Williamsburg along with the Richmond and Blacksburg Organizing Committees of the MWM were there. The Richmond Coalition for a Living Wage brought its members to MWM.

The Michigan Emergency Committee Against War and Injustice organized welfare rights and environmental activists for the MWM.

Steel Workers Local 8751, school bus drivers and monitors in Boston, mobilized. So did International Longshore Association Local 1422 in Charleston, S.C., and the North Carolina-based Black Workers for Justice. Haitian workers and activists also came.

The police estimate of the crowd was 10,000, although some MWM organizers felt that the participation was as much as twice that number. Organizers reported that police had illegally diverted at least 30 buses to RFK Stadium, located far from the rally site.

Labor and anti-war movements join forces

When the MWM was first conceived in the beginning of 2004, the initiators had hoped the national leadership of the AFL-CIO, headed by John Sweeney, would give full political support and the resources needed to fill buses. Instead, the AFL-CIO leadership refused to help the March, and even undermined it.

To counter the AFL-CIO leadership's negative response, MWM organizers then reached out to the anti-war movement for broad political and concrete support. The International Action Center helped form "Anti-War Committees 4 the MWM" all over the country, to link the anti-war struggle and the workers' movement.

Some of the MWM's main demands

D.C. protest calls for new movement

were to bring the troops home from Iraq and to divert money from Pentagon wars abroad to human needs.

These struggles were linked not just in words but also in deed. For instance, the Central New Jersey Coalition for Peace and Justice shared a bus with Casa Freehold, an outgrowth of the Workers Committee for Progress and Social Welfare and Monmouth County Residents for Immigrants' Rights.

Rally speakers included Clarence Thomas, Leo Robinson and Trent Willis from Local 10; Brenda Stokely, president of AFSCME District Council 1707; International Concerned Family and Friends leader Pam Africa, who introduced an audio-taped message from Mumia Abu-Jamal; Ramsey Clark; Larry Holmes, IAC co-chair and principal anti-war organizer of the MWM; Dick Gregory; Danny Glover; Martin Luther King III; Marlene Jean-Louis of Haiti's Lavalas movement; ANSWER representatives; Chris Silvera of Teamsters Local 808 and many more.

The rally co-chairs included Sharon Black, MWM's Washington regional coordinator, and Ralph Schoenman, MWM's media coordinator.

On-going issue-oriented discussions took place in tents on the Lincoln Memorial grounds during the rally, including youth and student organizing, the environment, political prisoners, reparations, the war on Iraq, women's issues and more.

Hundreds of MWM participants marched to the Hotel Washington near the White House, where hotel workers looking out the window greeted them with waves. UNITE HERE Local 25 Executive Secretary-Treasurer John A. Boardman greeted the primarily youthful marchers. He expressed appreciation to the MWM for much-needed solidarity at a crucial time, when almost 4,000 hotel workers in the D.C. area are in fierce negotiations with greedy hotel bosses for a new contract.

Leading the march to the hotel was Fight Imperialism – Stand Together (FIST), a newly formed militant youth group; Youth United for Change, a predominantly Black group from Philadelphia; and a delegation of anarchist youth.

AFL-CIO leadership and the MWM

On June 23, AFL-CIO President Sweeney had authored a letter regarding the MWM to all state federations and central labor councils of the AFL-CIO. He told them "not to sponsor or devote resources to the demonstration in Washington, D.C."

And Sweeney emphasized in the letter that "the AFL-CIO is NOT a co-sponsor of this effort and we will not be devoting resources toward mobilizing demonstrations this fall," but will work instead to remove "George W. Bush from office."

In the eyes of the top AFL-CIO leadership, not only would they spend tens of millions of dollars of union dues to try to elect John Kerry, but they would prevent the mobilization of millions of workers who might come to Washington, D.C., to fight for universal health care, a living wage, amnesty for undocumented workers, guaranteed pensions, a repeal of anti-labor legislation like the Taft-Hartley Act and much more.

This approach sabotaged and undermined the full potential of the MWM. For instance, SEIU/1199's rank-and-file in New York City voted to endorse the MWM and arrange buses for its members. Instead, the local leadership diverted buses to take their staff and others to canvas for Kerry in Pennsylvania and other "swing" states.

At a Teamsters National Black Caucus meeting held in Florida over the summer, the locals voted overwhelmingly to organize buses to the MWM. Soon afterward, Teamsters President James Hoffa personally ordered the union's locals to abort those plans.

In union after union, from the Postal

Leo Robinson

Trent Willis

Keith Shanklin

Pam Africa WW photos: Arturo Pérez Saad

Danny Glover

Ramsey Clark

Workers to AFSCME to the National Education Association, activists who wanted to devote their time and resources to organizing workers to attend the MWM were pressured to cease building for the MWM, and in some cases in the week before Oct. 17, to canvas for Kerry.

Despite these problems, thousands of workers and union activists came to Washington.

What's next after Oct. 17?

On Oct. 18, regional organizers of the MWM met in the D.C. area to both evaluate the March and brainstorm on proposals to move the MWM movement forward.

Among the ideas that regional coordinators agreed to bring back to their regions for further discussion were setting a national day in solidarity with the hotel workers as well as other low-wage workers struggling for contracts, and identifying International Women's Day and May Day for MWM activities.

Other ideas included setting a "Repeal the Taft-Hartley" day, setting up workers' boards, and setting dates for MWM planning meetings and conferences.

In addition to proposing to the regions that Dec. 3-10 be designated "Stop the War Now Week" for mass actions, the meeting also began discussing its posture toward next summer's AFL-CIO convention in Chicago, as well as setting a date for another MWM day of action during the fall of 2005.

Despite the efforts of those labor leaders who promote the Democratic Party as the primary organization for advancing the cause of workers, the MWM has not only arrived, but its leadership is making exciting plans to build a new movement to push the struggle for workers' rights forward. Workers World newspaper will continue its coverage and assessment of the MWM as more information becomes available in the coming period.

Abridged from WW, Oct. 28, 2004.

Dick Gregory and Martin Luther King III

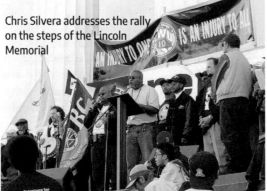

Chris Silvera addresses the rally on the steps of the Lincoln Memorial

Ignacio Menesese and Ray LaForest

Teamsters National Black Caucus, Connecticut chapter. Harvey Jackson and Michael Jackson.

Ralph Schoenman

WW photos: Arturo Pérez Saad

...and the Million Worker March

Joann Wypijewski

History and its symbols having been central in conceptualizing the demonstration for jobs, peace and human needs that took place at the Lincoln Memorial on a crisp afternoon this past October 17, it is worth casting the mind back a bit before proceeding with our story of that event, recalling first the organizational finesse and political discipline of this latest demonstration's most famous forebear, the 1963 March on Washington for Jobs and Freedom.

The 1963 March was called to demonstrate a public demand for action on civil rights legislation then before Congress. The dreams were bigger, of course, freedom, equality, economic and every other kind of justice. But when King proposed the idea, on June 1, 1963, he had particular strategic objectives: to take advantage of mass actions throughout the South; to put heat under the Kennedy administration, to pressure Congress and spark the national conscience by the display of a unified mass meeting the likes of which the country had never seen.

It may seem unfair to juxtapose the Million Worker March with one of the iconic events of modern American history, but the event invited the comparison. Martin Luther King III spoke on the steps of the Lincoln Memorial on October 17. The name, on the other hand, was borrowed from the Nation of Islam's 1995 Million Man March.

The Million Worker March on October 17 was important, for the agenda on the collective action of workers, union and nonunion, against structures that depend on racism, exploitation and war; for the prospect of what one of its organizers, Clarence Thomas, ILWU, called "the civil rights initiative for the 21st century"

The idea for the demo emerged this past January within ILWU Local 10 in Oakland. Throughout the proceedings in Washington, it was referred to as "the historic" Local 10, justifiably given that it was home base for Harry Bridges, founder of the ILWU and leader of the 1934 West Coast Maritime Strike (the San Francisco General Strike), that it pioneered U.S. labor actions against apartheid in the 1980s, that it has played a central role in shutting down the West Coast ports on behalf of everything from contract grievances to international solidarity to Mumia Abu-Jamal.

Local 10 is a militant Black member of the labor movement. Its International donated $1 million to the Southern California grocery strike earlier this year, and some of its members and retirees shelled out thousands, in one case $50,000, of their own money for the MWM. It is a local that has come to see audacity rewarded, so why shouldn't it call for a national mobilization? But it is still a local, and without the endorsement of its International president and executive board, it was clear from the beginning that mounting such a demonstration two weeks before a tooth-and-claw national election would be a mighty, contentious undertaking.

On June 23, the AFL-CIO's director of field mobilization, Marilyn Schneiderman, sent a memo to all state federations and local labor councils encouraging them "not to sponsor or devote resources to the demonstrations in Washington, D.C., but instead to remain focused on the election."

As Thomas notes, there's something badly amiss when mobilizing on behalf of such things as national health care, a living wage, affordable housing, jobs, literacy, Social Security, progressive taxation, democracy and an end to the war in Iraq is considered audacious.

Other demands included cancellation of neoliberal trade agreements, an end to "the criminalization of poverty and the prison-industrial complex," an end to privatization, repeal of Taft-Hartley and other impediments to the right to organize, major investment for neighborhood revitalization, environmental restoration, free mass transit, repeal of the Patriot Act, deep cuts in the military budget, open airing of military and intelligence budgets, enforcement of all civil rights, resistance against all forms of discrimination, development of democratic media and an end to media monopolization.

"These are things workers can agree on, no matter what a person's political persuasion," Thomas says. "We felt it was important to express the urgent demands of workers, organized and unorganized, in the face of assaults on the working class, hardships not seen since the Great Depression, and the failure of either political party to take up a workers' agenda. Fact is, we need to be making demands on all politicians."

Local 10's original resolution for the demonstration spoke of it as a necessary adjunct to "get-out-the-vote" work, a means of motivating people who might reasonably find the candidates lacking. In the world as it might be, this is what organized labor would do: mobilize voters but also organize mass action to buck up the base, build and leverage power; engage closely enough in the electoral process to influence politicians but independently enough to challenge and, as necessary, punish them.

In the days before the demonstration, AFL-CIO HQ was a ghost place, virtually everyone from secretaries to executive vice presidents having gone to "battleground states" to work the phone banks, leaflet communities, get out the vote. In places like Wisconsin, the 5,000-member Teamsters Local 200, committed its all mobilization efforts to the election. Steelworkers were going door-to-door. From Philadelphia, the head of the Central Labor Council, which opposed war in Iraq before it began, told Gene Bruskin, co-convener of U.S. Labor Against the War, that they couldn't spare a single body for the MWM if it were held before the election.

Thomas found it insulting to suggest that unions couldn't do two things at one time. And Bruskin says he heard the same from other member groups.

Along with all those bodies focused on elections flow dollars, millions of them. Donna Dewitt, president of the South Carolina State AFL-CIO, the only State Fed to endorse and organize for the MWM, said she, like all the union people I spoke with, resented the memo. And especially

resented Schneiderman gesturing disapprovingly at her MWM T-shirt at an earlier federation gathering, and snapping, "We have to talk."

"If the AFL had supported and mobilized for the march, even tacitly, even by just encouraging affiliates to do what they could and giving a little money," DeWitt continued, "it would have been a lot bigger. She added, It gave organizations like USLAW and the Labor Party, which depend on state and local union labor bodies for their funding, a reason to be fearful about endorsing. Neither did endorse, though Bruskin did personally, as did individual Labor Party members, like DeWitt and Brenda Stokely, a March organizer who is also president of AFSCME, DC 1707 in New York.

Who defined the March? The activists, but perhaps just for now. Larry Holmes said afterward, "We hit a home run." Because the event was broadcast over CSPAN, Clarence Thomas could justifiably say, "We may not have had a million people but we reached a million households."

The most hopeful note is that the people who did come were not by in large professional activists. From their jackets and T-shirts, flags and caps, they seemed mostly to be workers or organized immigrants. At least half the crowd was Black. Two buses had come from South Carolina (com-

pared with one from Chicago), and the day after, Ken Riley, president of International Longshore Association Local 1422 out of Charleston, said workers who had attended or watched it on TV thanked him for affording them an opportunity, rare in their home state.

As Ron Washington of Black Telephone Workers for Justice out of New Jersey said later, the overall success of the event will be determined by whether it begins to construct a skeletal framework on which people can build, uniting workers who are now fragmented and isolated, articulating the interests of the broad working class through specific fights but also helping those struggling to gain power or even just develop a strong left opposition in their unions. The nature of leadership does, after all, influence the nature of engagement.

There's no rule of politics that says national mobilizations must come only after strong local networks have been built and are active, but it helps. But there's no saying it can't work the other way around, especially if the most serious people behind this effort forge good regional leadership, good coalitions, good communication and define a clear aim and enemy.

Abridged from Counterpunch, Oct. 30, 2004, www.counterpunch.org/ 2004/10/30/and-the-million-worker-march

Photos from video of the event.

Photos taken at a MWM fundraiser in the Martin Luther King Labor Center Auditorium in midtown New York City.

MWM: flexing labor's independent muscle

Heidi Durham

On October 17, the Lincoln Memorial in Washington, D.C. will be the site of a labor demonstration the likes of which hasn't been seen in over 40 years.

The call for a Million Worker March, initiated by ILWU Local 10 from the Bay Area, has captured the imagination of union activists from coast to coast.

Working people, both union members and the unorganized, are urged to carpool, catch a bus, a train, a plane, hitch a ride; just get to Washington and send a thundering, unified call for jobs, housing and healthcare for all, an end to war and privatization, repeal of the USA Patriot Act, and aggressive enforcement of civil rights!

A visionary union takes the lead.

In calling for the march, African American leaders of the longshore workers of Local 10 are continuing an impressive tradition. Its current call for workers to hit the streets with their own agenda has put the local in labor's vanguard once again.

Leo Robinson, a retired Local 10 vice president, recently toured the West Coast to promote the march. At Seattle's Labor Temple he said, "The Million Worker March is going to be the expression of the will of the working class of this country, which has not been expressed since the 1940s, prior to the McCarthy era."

An idea whose time has come.

Local 10 has clearly struck a chord. The march idea is catching fire, with strong leadership coming from African American trade unionists and public employee unions.

Although the march was initiated on the West Coast, MWM committees have sprouted up across the U.S. so that working people will be represented and visible from all points south, north, east and west. MWM banners and contingents captured the interest of protesters in Boston and New York during demonstrations at the Democrat and Republican conventions. The 330,000-strong American Postal Workers Union voted at their annual convention to endorse the march. Their endorsement joins those of the 2.7 million-member National Education Association and the national Coalition of Black Trade Unionists. Meanwhile, Teamsters International is giving a significant donation to the march, encouraged by the Teamsters National Black Caucus.

Other major labor endorsers include the 30,000-member AFSCME, Council 92 (Baltimore/Washington, D.C. area) and NYC's 30,000-strong Transport Workers Union Local 100. Several labor councils and union locals have endorsed; combined, they represent millions of organized workers.

Additionally, a growing number of community organizations, left parties, and prominent individuals, from Black Workers for Justice to Danny Glover, are throwing their weight behind the event. Women labor leaders drummed up support at the August 28 reproductive rights action in New York, and Radical Women is mobilizing feminist participation on both coasts.

Shaking up the workers' movement.

The excitement generated by the march is highlighting a longstanding rift within the AFL-CIO, the largest U.S. labor federation.

At one pole sit AFL-CIO President John Sweeney and other top union officials, who routinely direct millions of dollars of members' money into Democratic Party election efforts. And they want nothing to interfere with their discredited strategy of tying labor's fortunes to the Democrats.

At the other pole from the heads of the AFL-CIO are the people within it who believe labor's power lies in strikes, organizing the unorganized, and independent political action.

March organizers have tapped into a deep reservoir of frustration among rank-and-file union members whose jobs, wages and benefits are evaporating. Phone-banking for fair-weather politicians and putting up yard signs is no way to fight a class war, action is needed.

At the 1963 March on Washington, the great African American labor leader A. Philip Randolph said: "All who deplore our militancy, who exhort patience ... would have social peace at the expense of social and racial justice."

Vote with your feet.

Local MWM organizing committees springing up in cities around the country are drawing unionists who want a fighting labor movement, but have had nowhere to go to help create it.

In Seattle, when members of the longshore union and labor leaders from the Freedom Socialist Party collaborated to start a local MWM committee, the group quickly attracted union stalwarts in the grocery and dairy industries, where heroic battles have been fought, but lost, because of labor's weakened status and timid leadership. Now, these activists are building the MWM committee, with the hope of building a revitalized labor movement.

Abridged from Freedom Socialist October-November, 2004.

A large Haitian contingent participated in the MWM.

WW photo: G. Dunkel

As repression mounts in Haiti
Resistance & solidarity grow

Pat Chin and G. Dunkel

Activists from African American organizations, Venezuela's Bolivarian Circles and their supporters picketed the Haitian Consulate in New York on Oct. 25, 2004, to demand an end to the bloody imperialist occupation of Haiti and the return of exiled Haitian President Jean-Bertrand Aristide.

Endorsers of the "Emergency Rally in Support of the People of Haiti" included the December 12 Movement; Patrice Lumumba Coalition; Africans Helping Africans; People's Organization for Progress; Black Telephone Workers for Justice; Roger Toussaint, president of Transit Workers Local 100; Brenda Stokely, president of AFSCME District Council 1707; the Africa is Home Coalition; and the International Action Center.

White House backed repression in Haiti has expanded so sharply that Haitians weren't able to go out into the streets for planned demonstrations the weekend of Oct. 16-17. But when police and foreign occupation troops raided Bel Air and Martissant, poor neighborhoods of Port-au-Prince where support for Aristide and his Fanmi Lavalas Party is strong, they were met with gunfire and burning barricades.

Chuck Mohan AFSCME DC 1707 and Danny Glover longtime supporter of Haitian solidarity movements at MWM 2004.

Photo: Andrea Mohan

Oct. 17 was the 198th anniversary of Jean-Jacques Dessalines's assassination, and the 10th anniversary of Aristide's return from the first U.S. coup against him in 1991. The second putsch took place earlier this year, on Feb. 29, when U.S. Marines kidnapped Aristide and flew him from the country.

There's been an upsurge in resistance to the U.S. installed puppet regime headed by Interim Prime Minister Gerard Latortue since the Sept. 30 police killing of two anti-coup protesters. As a result, the de facto government is negotiating with the U.S. State Department to purchase new weapons.

A huge contingent of flag-waving Haitians joined the Million Worker March in Washington, D.C. Lavalas activist Marlene Jean-Louis called for continued solidarity with Haiti from the podium.

"More than 8,000 Haitian workers have lost their jobs since Feb. 29 because of their political association," she told the crowd. "The U.S. government along with the French and Canadian governments have taken President Aristide out of Haiti because they want to implement their own neoliberal plans in Haiti, and also because Aristide is the first president in Haiti's history to call for reparations for the Haitian people, the over $21 billion that France had forced us to pay in indemnities after we won our independence.

As the popular resistance continues to grow in Haiti, so too does the solidarity movement in the United States. It's now time to globalize the struggle.

Abridged from WW, Nov. 4, 2004.

Election validates premise of Million Worker March

Larry Holmes

Sometimes it takes a little while for people to appreciate how significant something was. This is very true of the Million Worker March on Oct. 17 in Washington, D.C.

It's no small accomplishment to bring together some 10,000 workers, representing scores of labor unions in every part of the country, along with a slice of the antiwar movement and progressives in Washington, D.C., on any day, under any circumstances.

In all honesty, when one considers what the MWM was up against, the "Anybody but Bush" pressure to do nothing but concentrate on the election, the lack of any serious funds, as well as constant hostility both from wrong-minded leaders in the labor movement who should have known better and from the government, it's almost a miracle that it happened at all.

Now that we are all pondering what to do with the outcome of the presidential election, it's instructive to remember the essential message over riding the MWM: no matter what happens on Nov. 2, the working class is going to be organizing, it's going to be fighting, it's going to be in the face of the bosses, getting stronger, getting more unified, no matter who wins.

MWM was initiated by African American militants in Local 10 of the International Longshore and Warehouse Union. What made it so unique and revolutionary was that even though it came from Black militants, the call was to all workers, regardless of race or nationality. It was a call for workers' unity.

What the MWM leaders understood was that the problem was not just Bush. It's capitalism.

MWM was an effort to respond to this crisis. To push forward the fight to organize workers. To strengthen unions. To make them more independent, more inclusive, more radical, more struggle-oriented, more militant and global in their outlook.

The response of the top leadership of the AFL-CIO to the Million Worker March can politely be called a big mistake. AFL-CIO President John Sweeney issued a statement in response to MWM last summer saying that, while the AFL-CIO leadership agrees with the goals of the March we feel that all of our efforts should be directed to the elections and so we are instructing the members of the AFL-CIO not to participate in it.

In other words, in his view, you couldn't have both. It was impermissible to work on the elections and the Million Worker March at the same time. It was impermissible to have the March at all.

It's an old argument on the left. Whether we should be "dreamers" and organize independent of the two capitalist parties, or whether we should be "practical."

The organized labor movement probably spent several hundred million dollars on the elections. Workers have the right to do that if they believe that it serves their interests. Whether it does or not is subject to argument.

The good news is that now that the elections are finally over, we have a chance to open up the next phase of the struggle against the war and the system responsible for war.

Anyone for a Million Worker March?

Abridged from WW, Nov. 11, 2004.

Larry Holmes speaking at the Million Worker March.

WW photo: Arturo Pérez Saad

Gwen Lucas IBT Local 507.

San Francisco workers force end to hotel lockout

Brenda Sandburg

The timing was perfect.

As hundreds of people gathered at a rally in solidarity with San Francisco's locked-out hotel workers, union officials got the hotel bosses to end the 38-day lockout and accept a 60-day cooling-off period.

Tho Do, secretary-treasurer of UNITE HERE Local 2, the union representing the hotel workers, announced the victory at a Nov. 20, 2004 rally called by the Million Worker March.

"Last night we went into negotiations and because of your support the company began to show signs of ending the lockout," Do said. "Our workers will return to work in the next couple of days."

Do introduced Vedrange Colas, who has worked at the Westin St. Francis Hotel for 16 years. "Thank you for your support," she told the cheering crowd. "We have to get what we need."

The struggle began September when workers at four hotels went on a two week strike to force employers to negotiate a favorable contract. The hotel operators retaliated on Oct. 13, locking out the striking workers as well as those at 10 other hotels.

Since then the 4,300 locked-out workers have held picket lines at the hotels, chanting from early in the morning into the evening. They have had support from other unions and the community, as well.

Many have refused to cross the picket line. According to a Local 2 representative, more than 90 groups canceled meetings at the hotels, costing the owners millions of dollars.

"The members of Local 2 are heroic," Clarence Thomas, a leader of ILWU Local 10 and co-chair of the MWM, said. "They deserve health care. They deserve pensions. They also deserve equal opportunity."

And they need to have a contract that is in sync with hotel workers in other cities, Thomas said. "None of this piecemeal two years here, four years there. Local 2 is trying to stop the union from being busted."

'Time to stand up'

The length of the contract is a key point in the negotiations. The union is pushing for a two-year contract that would expire at the same time as contracts in Boston, New York and other major cities, giving hotel workers more bargaining power.

Local 2 is also fighting to reduce work loads, raise wages and protect health and pension benefits. The owners want workers to pay hundreds of dollars more per month for health-care coverage.

Trent Willis, newly elected president of ILWU Local 10 and co-chair of the MWM Committee, said workers around the country are in similar struggles. The employers "have taken the posture to lower our wages, take away our health care," Willis said.

"No matter what color, nationality, whatever part of the country or whatever other country you're from, it's time to stand up and say we've had enough."

Representatives from several other unions expressed solidarity with the hotel workers. Keith Shanklin,

a member of ILWU Local 34 and secretary-treasurer of the MWM Committee, announced that his local had given $10,000 to the hotel workers. Walter Johnson, former secretary-treasurer of the San Francisco Labor Council, called for a Million Worker March to be held in San Francisco if the hotel workers don't get the contract they want.

Other speakers included a member of Service Employees Local 790, who expressed solidarity on behalf of Bay Area Rapid Transit workers, and Eddie Rosario, of Graphic Communications International Union Local 4N.

Shane Hoff, a member of United Transportation Union Local 1741, said her union's school bus drivers had joined the picket lines three times. Each time, 10 to 20 members drove up in a school bus and disembarked into the picket line.

"We need to build a national fighting movement," Hoff said. "We need to take the offense and build the Million Worker March movement."

After a rally at Union Square, in San Francisco's shopping district, protesters marched to the hotels that had locked out workers: the Four Seasons, Sheraton Palace, Hyatt Regency and the Argent. A band joined the march, adding to the jubilant mood.

Local 2 President Mike Casey arrived at the closing rally to offer his gratitude to the Million Worker March Committee for its solidarity.

"We will remember this day because the MWM rallied and marched for us and this is the day the lockout ended," Casey said.

Abridged from WW, Dec. 2, 2004.

Lessons of MWM and the election
'Labor is at a crossroads'

Milt Neidenberg speaks to the Nov. 13-14, 2004 Workers World Party National Fightback Conference

Our conference salutes, Sister Brenda Stokely, and the other African-American trade union leaders who had a vision and made the Million Worker March in Washington, D.C. a reality.

The MWM brought out thousands of demonstrators who shared the dream of building an independent, class-wide movement of workers and oppressed nationalities to speak in their own names and on their own issues. Under the most difficult conditions, the MWM appealed for unity, sharing the platform with a host of organizations who spoke of the preemptive wars abroad and the war at home as one giant conflict.

In that spirit, I'm reminded of the call, "Dare to struggle, dare to win," made over 40 years ago by the Black Panthers, who fought boldly and courageously to serve the African-American community in the struggle for economic and social justice and self-determination.

The election contest between two factions of billionaires has brought four more years to a right-wing, anti- union, anti-worker, anti-immigrant, anti-lesbian/gay /bi/trans, war mongering and racist administration.

The MWM, with a minimum of resources, proved the correctness of its strategy. Compare its program of an independent class-wide movement to that of the AFL-CIO top leaders, who banked on the anybody-but-Bush strategy.

The AFL-CIO Executive Council tied labor's fortunes to the Kerry leadership and the Democratic Party.

Of course, it was correct to oppose Bush with every resource and with rank-and-file mobilizations in the streets as well as at the ballot box.

Look at his record: He made the rich

richer and the workers poorer. He tore up the rights of the workers and the oppressed whose contracts, civil rights and civil liberties had been won over years of struggle and sacrifice.

The Bush assault, however, drove the AFL-CIO to put all its money and resources behind Kerry — a serious mistake. The Democratic program was molded by its corporate donors. Kerry forces took labor support for granted.

The AFL-CIO mobilized their 13 million members and spent $45 million on Kerry. Other unions spent millions more and sent thousands of members into the field.

The AFL-CIO and its member unions mobilized 5,000 staff members, more than 225,000 volunteers, staffed hundreds of phone banks, knocked on 6 million doors, and distributed 32 million fliers. And they sent 850 monitors to high-risk polling places such as Ohio and Florida.

One percent of what the AFL-CIO spent on Kerry would have made a huge difference to the Million Worker March, whose leaders had to hock their savings and their pensions to bankroll the MWM.

And what did labor get for all this money and resources?

They became foot soldiers for the Kerry leadership and the Democrat-

Brenda Stokely addresses Million Worker March on Oct. 17, 2004.

Photo: Don Williams

Henry Graham Local 10 President.

Photo: CSPAN Video of MWM Rally

ic Party. Kerry's advisors put out their own bourgeois program that buried most of the labor movement's critical issues. They defended occupying Iraq, seeking international support for the war, and expanding the troop levels — which would mean diverting more funds from social programs.

Hitching their wagon to the Kerry wing of the ruling class was a no-win strategy for the AFL-CIO.

The outcome of the election confirmed the correctness of the decision to organize the MWM. This should be acknowledged by the AFL-CIO at their Executive Council meeting. While they didn't allocate a nickel for the march, they admitted early in the MWM organizing drive that they were for the issues raised.

But they were against the timing in the midst of the election. In fact, the timing was exactly right.

Million Worker March Movement meeting in Detroit

Clarence Thomas (left), co-chair MWM with other CBTU members, including Nathan Head (right), at the MWMM National Report back and Networking meeting held in Detroit, May 14 and 15. Subjects of discussion and strategizing ranged from the war on Iraq to immigrant rights and the cutback budgets facing public sector workers in Detroit and other cities.

– Photo and story Cheryl LaBash
Abridged from WW, May 28, 2005.

The AFL-CIO is now in disarray. Bitter factional arguments have broken out on how to proceed.

Two contending factions emerged at the Executive Council meeting that just took place. Andy Stern, head of the 1.6-million Service Employees, speaks for four unions who call themselves the New Unity Partnership (NUP). He proposes accelerating the consolidation of the labor movement into 10 to 15 multi-jurisdictional amalgamated international unions.

The bourgeois media are having a field day agitating for the idea that a split will take place. For Stern and the other male white union leaders in the NUP to split from the AFL-CIO would be suicidal at a time when the Bush administration is on the offensive and is preparing another four years of anti-union attacks, especially on unions whose members are primarily multinational and women workers.

Hotel workers on strike and locked out in San Francisco must have their say in this factional struggle, along with the millions of other members of these unions.

The struggle to build a leadership must and will come from below. History has confirmed that all profound social change comes from the struggles of the rank-and-file. This will win the hearts and minds of the workers and the oppressed nationalities. Will both AFL-CIO leadership factions continue to ignore the development of independent class-consciousness that is pervading the low-paid service workers, many of them women and/or from oppressed nationalities? The labor movement is at a crossroads.

Our party and the many allies that helped build the MWM see progress and growth in the post-Bush period. The workers and the oppressed are moving leftward. Leaders who have learned the lessons of the election will take the high road of independent, class-wide struggle. We hope that the pressure from below will be a wakeup call to the top leaders who are currently floundering in dispute and despair.

MILLION WORKER MARCH MOVEMENT STATEMENT

Racism & Sexism: Major pillars of the crisis in the U.S. trade union movement

Clarence Thomas and Saladin Muhammad

Black workers make up 30 percent of the total union membership in the AFL-CIO. People of color and women workers are a large percentage of the membership of the non-affiliated "independent unions."

Yet, despite the major divisions among workers caused by institutionalized racism and gender discrimination that weaken the unity of workers and the power of the trade unions, the struggles against racism and sexism in the labor movement are not taken up as priorities. Nor are they viewed by either camp reflecting the current major divisions within the AFL-CIO as major sources of labor's crisis.

Racism and sexism have been the two major pillars of business unionism. They are fundamental to the lack of rank-and-file union democracy and to labor's weakness in organizing the unorganized, especially in the U.S. South. Labor's greatest compromises with capital have been around issues of improving conditions of wages, training, promotions and job classifications for Blacks, workers of color and women workers.

The failure to organize the South, a low wage region which has been used historically by the corporations to force billions in concessions from organized workers and tax abatements from cities and states throughout the country by their threat of plant closings and runaway shops to the South, stands out as a major in-

Clarence Thomas is an executive board member of Local 10 and national co-chair of the MWMM.

Photo: Delores Lemon-Thomas

dictment of labor's failure to struggle against racism.

Organizing labor in the South, especially during the 1950s and 1960s, meant taking on the struggle against legal segregation and white supremacy. It meant aligning with the Black civil rights movement and broadening the character of labor organizing and representation from being a narrow economic movement to a movement for social and economic justice.

Today, even with the employer and government offensive against labor, too few labor leaders have been willing to acknowledge the issue of white supremacy, racism and sexism in and outside of the unions. They have not addressed the policies and practices

Saladin Muhammad, national chairperson of Black Workers for Justice based in Raleigh, N.C. and a leader of the MWMM.

WW photo: Liz Green

of organized labor that perpetuate the lingering and crippling effects of institutional racism. How can labor defend against corporate-driven attacks when its ranks can easily be divided against itself?

Blacks, workers of color, women and oppressed groups must have democracy and power to drive and guide labor's structural changes!

The struggles against racism on the job and in the unions had to be pushed forward by organizations of Black workers. This has been true beginning with the formation of the Colored National Labor Union in 1869, which called for the "Unity of workers without regard to color;"

the Brotherhood of Sleeping Car Porters in the 1920s, who led the call for a March on Washington in the 1940s against racism in the defense industries; the National Negro Labor Congress in the 1950s; the League of Revolutionary Black Workers; and DRUM in the Detroit auto plants in the 1960s, who called for Black workers to take the lead; the Coalition of Black Trade Unionists in the 1970s, calling for Black leadership at the highest levels of the unions; and Black Workers For Justice in the 1980s, calling for organizing the South.

These struggles were able to bring about some changes in labor, including the election and appointments of a few Blacks to leadership positions and the recognition by the AFL-CIO of Black and other constituent groups which they sought to control and direct as top-down organizations loyal to labor's bureaucracy.

Today, as the AFL-CIO faces a major split in its ranks, the main proposals for restructuring and solving labor's "crisis" indicate that the organization and representation of Blacks and other worker constituency groups are no longer needed to strengthen the labor movement. This is a direct signal to the bosses that once again labor is willing to sacrifice and compromise around the interests of Blacks, Hispanics (or Latino), women and other workers of color.

Representation of constituency organizations in the AFL-CIO must be defended. However, "diversity" without the empowerment of Black workers and other constituency workers cannot challenge the racism and sexism in the trade unions or be a force to push forward the trade unions in struggling against the racism and sexism of the employers. Black workers and other constituencies must be empowered from the bottom as well as the top to struggle against racism, sexism and all the

other forms of discrimination.

The government and corporate attacks on labor during the Reagan period exposed the tremendous weaknesses in U.S. labor's solidarity. This contributed to business unionism's acceptance of labor-management cooperation and increased support and funding for the Democratic Party as an alternative to a rank-and-file fightback movement based in national and international labor solidarity.

Black workers and the Black led poor people's movements have called on labor to unite with them in a fightback movement against corporate and government attacks. Labor has constantly rejected those calls for unity.

In 1967, Dr. King called on the leadership of the AFL-CIO to support the Poor People's Campaign (PPC). While some local unions and a couple of national unions endorsed the PPC, the AFL-CIO refused to endorse it. King saw the Poor People's Campaign as becoming a focal point of a Black-Labor Alliance linking the struggle of unionized workers with the struggle to organize the unorganized in the South; to help increase the power of Black people to demand enforcement of the right to vote and other civil rights that were won during

the 1960s benefiting women and other sectors of the working class.

In 1995, when close to 2 million Black people, largely working class, came to Washington, D.C. for the Million Man March, labor refused to support Black workers in raising their working class demands at the March.

Today, labor continues its history of trying to solve its crises without a fight-back movement. The AFL-CIO's opposition to support the Million Worker March in 2004, once again sends a message to the corporate rulers, that labor-management cooperation and collaboration with the two corporate parties, including U.S. foreign policy of war and empire, is at the heart of labor's strategy for survival and "growth."

Rank-and-file democracy

The union movement is rooted in the principle that the trade union leaders can only take action based on the mandate from the workers. Trade unionism is about accountability. The proposals outlining the main directions addressing the crisis of labor have not come from the rank-and-file; and certainly not from Black workers and others hardest hit by the demands and conditions of the employers.

Harry Bridges listening to ILWU members in San Francisco's Local 10 hiring hall, about 1960.

The current leadership is in denial as to the importance of confronting racism and acknowledging the important role Blacks have played and continue to play in the trade union movement. When organizing efforts involve a large number of Black workers, history has proven there's a greater likelihood of success. This begs the question, why doesn't labor officialdom utilize Black trade unionists for organizing?

Organized labor needs greater unity, strength and independence at a time when the corporations wield unprecedented power and influence in both political parties. Blacks, workers of color, women and oppressed groups are essential in building the labor movement in the 21st century.

If we want to build a real fightback movement that challenges the abuse of capital and mobilizes the rank-and-file to fully participate in resolving labor's problems, we call on labor to build on the efforts of the Million Worker March.

Million Worker March Mobilization

Union members from across the United States and Haiti, Japan and South Africa gathered at the steps of the Lincoln Memorial on Oct. 17, 2004, making a passionate call for workers' rights. Thousands stood at the foot of the Memorial and alongside of the Reflecting Pool calling for: universal health care; protection of social security and pensions; a right to strike without replacement; an end to the war in Iraq; repealing corporate free trade agreements; a national living wage; stopping the dismantling of public education; stop off-shoring North American jobs; amnesty for all undocumented workers; slashing the military budget; tax release for the working class; preserving and restoring the environment; enforcement of all civil rights; stopping corporate greed, and repealing the Taft-Hartley. The active support and endorsement of Black, Hispanic and Latin@ workers' organizations, from the Coalition of Black Trade Unionists, the Teamsters National Black Caucus, Black Workers For Justice, the Immigrant Rights Association and the Farm Labor Organizing Committee, played a leading role in the mobilization.

The March was initiated by the International Longshore and Ware-

The Sanitation Workers Strike in Memphis, Tenn., where Dr Martin Luther King Jr. was assassinated on April 4, 1968.
Photo: UFCW 324

house Union Local 10 in San Francisco. Local 10 is the most racially diverse Longshore local on the West Coast. It was also the local of the legendary labor leader, ILWU founder and human rights activist, Harry Bridges. Brother Bridges was in the vanguard of all North American trade union leaders of his generation on the question of race.

During the 1934 Maritime Strike, Bridges went to Black churches and implored them to join him on the picket line. He made a commitment to stand for their inclusion in the industry. That way the employers couldn't attempt to use them as scabs.

Brother Bridges said **"discrimination is a tool of the bosses."** He wrote in ILWU's newspaper, *The Dispatcher*, on February 15, 1938, which featured a series of articles on "The Economics of Prejudice:"

"Prejudice means profit for the boss. … For the worker, Black and white, it means lower living standards, humiliation, violence, often death."

This statement was distributed at the "National Summit on Diversity in Our Union Movement: A Voice for Every Worker," sponsored by the AFL-CIO and Labor Coalition for Community Action in July 2005. Thomas presented the statement along with the official MWM rally DVD to AFL-CIO President John Sweeney and Secretary-Treasurer Richard Trumpka.

Above, Washington, D.C., June 1968, the Poor People Campaign mobilizes tens of thousands to demand justice. In 1967, Dr. Martin Luther King Jr. saw the Campaign as a Black-Labor alliance linking the struggle of unionized workers with the struggle to organize the unorganized in the South; to help increase the power of Black people to demand enforcement of the right to vote and other civil rights that were won during the 1960s, benefiting women and other sectors of the working class.

Rank-and-file unity
MWM statement on the AFL-CIO split

The following are excerpts from a Million Worker March Movement statement August 2005

The AFL-CIO has been split almost in two, mainly on the basis of personalities and inter-bureaucratic hair splitting. The differences causing this rupture boil down to two main questions.

First, what share of union resources should go to organizing the unorganized versus what share should go to electoral efforts supporting the Democratic Party?

Second, should diverse unions be reorganized and merged by sector in order to achieve enough density and power to stand up to the current anti-worker corporate offensive?

Left unmentioned in the discussion, were more central questions of concern to the rank-and-file and to the Million Worker March Movement. These include:

- How to transform and make the existing top-down structure business unionism democratic;

- how to end the inequality, injustice and ecocide of a racist capitalism;

- what to do about the endless sellouts of the union-supported Democratic Party;

- and how to stop the war crimes, mass murders and tortures of the U.S. empire and its ongoing imperialism?

If a split of the magnitude that has taken place in the AFL-CIO was going to happen there should have been a great rank-and-file debate on these fundamentals. Instead, the "debate" over the collective future of over 100 million U.S. workers, both organized and unorganized, was confined to a few hundred leaders, with an even smaller group having a decisive role.

The Million Worker March Movement wants an ongoing dialogue among the rank-and-file about the grand issues of our day. This is where we stand, for a large and full discussion of all the issues facing the people.

What we have had so far has been what amounts to a false debate. We believe that the issues we raise in more detail below can provide a basis for a necessary debate on the full restructuring of the national labor movement. We need to have this discussion to move forward toward a positive and forward looking vision of workers power, which is required for our collective survival.

Business Unionism

The labor movement has lost its ability to confront the employer because of the threat of court intervention through injunctions, strikers' replacement and the National Labor Relations Board (NLRB.)

Trade unionism should be a democratic people's movement, not in any way a business run on corporate principles.

Yet business unionism is the dominant perspective in the current leadership of the U.S. labor movement, on both sides of the new split. The major premise of business unionism is that the most labor can ever achieve is to be the junior partners of capitalism, which is seen as an eternal system destined to last forever. Respectability is desired, so that a special relationship with the "enlightened" wing of the capitalists can be fostered.

During and after the Great Depression and World War II, sections of capital did agree to a kind of "social contract" which provided some benefits to workers. They did so to prevent the left from gaining power. But those days ended decades ago, now the bosses are constantly on the offensive to destroy any residual remains of this "social contract," along with wiping out unions and all New Deal type benefits. Their war on the working class, started about 30 years ago, has given a one-sided, severe beating to the working class, a beating that is continuing, with only a very weak response from the AFL-CIO and its unions.

We must deeply understand that dominant sectors of corporate capital no longer want to accommodate the trade union movement; on the contrary, they want to destroy us. Supposed union "leaders" who fail to recognize this reality are totally, even criminally, out of touch.

Much of the labor movement still operates on undemocratic, top down principles, based on business unionism. Yet, if there is to be a future for the labor movement, an educated, active, informed and empowered rank-and-file is fundamental, along with a serious vision of working class power.

To achieve this, the working class must speak in it own name, not as a junior partner of our oppressors. We need to advance the civil rights and economic interests of the working class as a whole, not only union members. These include the demands raised at the MWM such as health care for all, protection of pensions and Social Security, preservation of full funding of public education, and full employment at living wages. For this, union democracy, and rank-and-file control of our unions is central, not business unionism.

Racialized Capitalism

A globalized capitalist market system now dominates the earth, its sole goal is the acquisition of capitalist property. It requires the removal of all political, economic, social and ecological restraints so it can endlessly accumulate more wealth for those already wealthy.

This system can be labeled "hypercapitalism," a cancer-like system in which the privatization and commodification of everything, is accelerating, forcing human activity to conform to market laws so that capital accumulation can expand further.

The resulting competitive market system is a kind of war which excludes millions of people from the material conditions needed to sustain life, while millions are grossly exploited. This system destroys and breaks apart the ecological foundations of life to gain ever greater profits. There is no obligation or desire to sustain life, only to sustain capital.

Capital also takes over the state and makes government its pawn. Democracy is destroyed and military imperialism is used to conquer and force the private market system on other nations.

This modern capitalist system was born together with racism and slavery. White workers' class consciousness was deformed at the same moment the Black worker was enslaved and the Asian, Native or Latin-American worker bonded in a second class status through debt peonage. The U.S. labor movement has been crippled by racism and white supremacy, which divides workers by destroying class solidarity and class consciousness.

Capitalism, which is a dictatorship of the rich, can only be transformed through an end to white supremacy. Class conscious rank-and-file unity, and class solidarity for all working people, can be won with anti-racist theory (education) and practice (an injury to one is an injury to all).

Racist oppression inside and outside the workplace must be confronted and a power base built through assistance to oppressed communities to advance a working class agenda.

The Million Worker March Movement believes that the priorities of capitalism can never be reformed. Massacres are taking place in today's labor market, with Black labor taking the brunt of the cuts.

Black workers, other workers of color, and women workers must have representation built into all level of power, into the structure of the labor and social movements. Social justice unionism must ally and collaborate with community organizations fighting the racist oppression inherent in capitalism, by becoming an organic part of a community-based fight back. We have to fight for working class control of economic development, including control of investment and community development.

The Democratic Party

The Democratic Party is a sellout party increasingly influenced by corporate donations and lobbyists. It is adrift with no clear ideology or mobilizing approach to politics, and represents a weak, "Republican-lite" approach. Largely taken over by the pro-corporate Democratic Leadership Council (DLC), the Democrats are a junior partner and frequent supporter of the current corporate capitalist offensive against the working class.

Key examples of this support, such as NAFTA, the 2000 trade deal with China; the sellout on health care for all in 1992-1994; the theft of the

Social Security surplus; support for corporate tax cuts; "welfare reform;" voting and speaking for war and the "Patriot Act;" They didn't fight Republican election thefts in 2000 and 2004, or the two trillion dollars in tax cuts for the rich during George W. Bush's first term.

By 2004, the Democratic retreat from pro-working class economic positions had created such a vacuum that its former base had become confused and vulnerable to right wing appeals on cultural/social/religious issues.

The overall function of the politically bankrupt Democratic Party is to try to co-opt people's movement and channel it into dead ends controlled by the corporate power structure.

For all these reasons the Million Worker March Movement believes that workers must break with this sellout party and form an independent working class party. This new party must be based on a spirit of service and sacrifice for all the people, not greed and selfishness for a few. We must craft another way of doing politics, one which will be based more on the direct action of the movement than on the electoral corruption of the current system.

History of Support for U.S. Imperialism

AFL-CIO foreign operations, often in cooperation with the CIA and other branches of the U.S. government, has helped to overthrow democratically elected governments in Guatemala, 1954; Brazil, 1964; and Chile, 1973. They subverted and helped repress progressive movements in Guyana, 1964; Dominican Republic, 1965; El Salvador, 1980s; Nicaragua, 1980s and South Africa, prior to 1986. The AFL-CIO has refused to "clear the air" with an honest accounting of their support for the imperialism, support which has led to the murder of hundreds of thousands of progressive people and the repression of even more.

As U.S. imperialism has become more aggressive under both Clinton and the current Bush regime, there has been a continuation of what can only be called "labor imperialism" during the tenure of John Sweeney.

This labor imperialism has helped the U.S. government try to overthrow the popularly elected government of Hugo Chavez in Venezuela.

It is instructive to note in this regard that Sweeney is a member of and has participated in the activities of the Council on Foreign Relations (CFR), a key private ruling class think tank/policy planning and membership organization run by some of the biggest bosses on the planet. What is a supposed "leader" of the working class doing paying dues to the CFR, and mixing and mingling with ruling class corporate leaders like David Rockefeller, Louis Gerstner Jr., Maurice Greenberg and Peter G. Peterson — all of whom are current leaders of this organization, which has been accurately called "the citadel of America's establishment."

We Need an Anti-racist, Class Conscious, Rank-and-File Led Mass Movement

The Million Worker March Movement wants a rank-and-file led mass movement that is the direct action assertion of popular leadership by the people themselves, a real democracy. Only such a mass movement will be able to rapidly transform our society. When our movement becomes large

enough and militant enough it will drag the culture, the politicians, the economy, the courts, the laws and society itself in its wake.

Public outrage combined with the creativity of youth and an aggressive leadership can lead to the successful mass movement we need, which will achieve its core demands through direct struggle.

The labor movement of the 1930s; the Civil Rights Movement of the 1950s and 1960s; and the anti-war movement of the 1960s and 1970s; were all mass movements. We need a rebirth of all of these in a grand coalition to fight for the just, equal and peaceful society we all want.

The supreme task of labor is to challenge corporate America head on as part of a new Civil Rights Movement for all workers. This can only be done with an anti-racist and anti-sexist class conscious mass democratic movement. Unionism must be linked to social transformation, not just collective bargaining. The future demands that we mobilize millions as a part of a cause, the battle for social justice, democracy, solidarity and workers power. Join us as we build a people's movement that can transform the planet.

Million Worker March Movement

The MWMM is the continuation of the mobilization for the Million Worker March which took place on Oct 17, 2004, at the Lincoln Memorial in Washington, D.C. It was conceived by current ILWU Local 10 President, Trent Willis when he was a rank-and-

filer in January 2004. The March was subsequently initiated by ILWU, Local 10.

This was the first time the rank-and-file workers from all across the U.S. as well as from Haiti, Japan and South Africa, from a broad cross section of the labor movement, organized a national workers rally and demonstration that was not under the auspices of the AFL-CIO or the Democratic Party.

The MWM was not only concerned with organizing and mobilizing workers in their own name independent of the two corporate controlled parties; it was also about building rank-and-file unity by "forging the fight back" against the attacks on all working people by governmental policies and the corporations.

Conclusion

"A union is built on its members. The strength, understanding and unity of the membership can determine the union's course and its advancements. The members who work, who make up the union and pay its dues can best determine their own destiny. If the facts are honestly presented to the members in the ranks, they will best judge what should be done and how it should be done. In brief, it is the membership of the union which is the best judge of its own welfare, not the officers, not the employers, not the politicians and the fair weather friends of labor." *

* Quote from one of the **TEN GUIDING PRINCIPLES of the ILWU** from which the union continues to operate.

Abridged statement written by: Larry Shoup, a member of UAW Local 1981 and MWMM, and Clarence Thomas, co-chair MWMM, and a member of Local 10 Executive Board.

Building a broad working-class movement
The Million Worker March Movement

Exerpts from Fred Goldstein book 'Low Wage Capitalism'

The Million Worker March Movement called for the workers to establish their own political identity

I
s the kind of trade union movement that Marx envisaged, when he urged those gathered around the First International to fight for the downtrodden, the low-paid, and the unorganized and to be part of every social and political movement, merely a hypothetical abstraction?

In fact, the embryonic development of such a movement manifested itself, with a clear political vision from an advanced sector of the labor movement, during 2004. The Million Worker March Movement (MWMM) came forward with an independent working-class program during the spring of that year, in an attempt to galvanize sections of the union movement and the entire progressive, radical, and revolutionary movement. The MWMM issued a call to build a movement and unite in a demonstration in Washington in October around the slogan "Organizing in Our Own Name and Putting Forth an Independent Workers' Agenda."

The MWMM coalition was initiated by Black leaders from Local 10 of the International Longshore and Warehouse Union in San Francisco, which has the largest African-American membership on the West Coast. The local is also the most racially diverse in the area, including Blacks, Latino, Asians, and women. It was joined by Black and other progressive unionists from around the country.

Local 10 has a militant history of anti-racism and international solidarity. It has been in the vanguard of the struggle for economic and social justice. It refused to unload cargo from apartheid South Africa begin-

Fred Goldstein   ww photo Liz Green

ning in 1977, including a ten-day boycott of the South African ship in 1984. In 1978, the union refused to load bomb parts going to the fascist dictatorship in Chile, thus exposing U.S. military aid to the Augusto Pinochet regime. In 1981, the ILWU imposed an embargo on military cargo for the U.S.-backed death squad regime in El Salvador and later joined a boycott of Salvadoran coffee.[255]

Local 10 organized solidarity for the world-renowned African-American political prisoner, journalist, and liberation fighter Mumia Abu-Jamal, known as the "voice of the voiceless." He has been on death row since 1982, after being framed up by the Philadelphia police. After Hurricane Katrina, Local 10 organized the shipping of containers of clothing and other supplies to New Orleans, raised funds, and invited survivors to speak in the Bay Area and the Pacific Northwest. On May 1, 2008, Local 10 initiated within the ILWU a one-day general strike of West Coast dockworkers against the war in Iraq.

Local 10's roots were in the historic 1934 San Francisco general strike referred to earlier, led by Harry Bridges. In this sense the MWMM represents a direct historical continuity with the legacy of the 1930s and the high point of the labor movement.

Despite a boycott and sabotage by the AFL-CIO leadership at all levels, the MWMM call reverberated among important Black trade unionists and progressive labor councils. Among its supporters were the Black Workers for Justice, with a twenty-five-year record of organizing in racist right-to-work states of the South, especially North Carolina and South Carolina; the Teamsters National Black Caucus and Teamsters Local 808 out of New York City; AFSCME District Council 1707 representing low-paid social service workers, a majority of them African-American and Caribbean women; the Coalition of Black Trade Unionists; the Charleston (South Carolina) Labor Council; the Farm Labor Organizing Committee; the San Francisco Day Laborers, and many others in the California Bay Area and New York State.

There was also support from a limited number of other areas, including the anti-imperialist wing of the anti-war movement, some peace groups, student groups, academics, religious progressives, and celebrities such as Danny Glover and Dick Gregory.

The MWMM put forward a detailed set of elementary democratic demands. What made their program noteworthy was the fact that it called for the workers to establish their own political identity as workers and that it went far beyond the narrow political horizons of the AFL-CIO leadership. It claimed the right and necessity of the workers to demand a say in all aspects of capitalist politics and economics — from Social Security to war to the struggle over sexual preference, from a living wage for all to an end to global warming and the preservation of the ecosystem.

It called for the repeal of the anti-labor Taft-Hartley Act as well as the repeal of the Patriot Act and the Anti-Terrorism Act. It demanded "universal, single-payer health care from cradle to grave" as "a right of all people." The MWMM demanded amnesty for all undocumented workers, an end to NAFTA, and an end to all racist and discriminatory acts, including those based on sexual orientation or gender in the workplace and in the communities.

The MWMM called for "an end to both the criminalization of poverty and the prison-industrial complex." It called for "guaranteed pensions that sustain a decent life for all working people." It aimed to "slash the military budget and recover trillions of dollars stolen from our labor to enrich the corporations that profit from war." Thus it introduced the important concept that when the capitalist government takes billions from workers' taxes and hands it over to the military-industrial complex, this is just another form, in addition to direct exploitation at the workplace, in which the ruling class steals workers' labor.

This was further elaborated in a subsequent demand to "extend democracy to our economic structure so that all decisions ... are made by working people who produce all value through their labor." This conception has unlimited application in the struggle for jobs, workers' rights on the job, and the right to keep workplaces open.

There were demands to fund "a vast army of teachers," a free mass-transit system, a national living wage, a program for affordable housing and an end to homelessness, and many other demands that affect the lives of all workers.

The program raised democratic political demands against oppression and reaction side-by-side with social and economic demands for the benefit of the broadest masses. No document such as this had emerged from any section of the labor movement in generations. It had a truly liberating aspect to it.

The demonstration itself fell short of expectations and the MWMM was unable to reach the considerable potential inherent in the appeal of its program. But this was largely because the labor leadership and the social democrats in the political movement were fanatically dedicated at the time to the election of John Kerry, the Democratic presidential candidate.

The MWMM demonstration was an implied declaration of independence from the Democrats. In fact, one of the factors that led to the calling of the demonstration was that the labor leaders were pouring hundreds of millions of dollars into the coffers of the Democratic Party at a time when the labor movement desperately needed to expand its organizing and support workers' struggles already in progress.

The labor leaders not only boycotted the march but engaged in sabotage by lobbying against it behind the scenes. Social democrats of all stripes outside the labor movement would have been hard pressed to disagree with any of the specific democratic demands put forward by MWMM. Nevertheless, forces in the peace and "social justice" movements

regarded an independent working-class movement as a challenge to the strategy of relying on the Democratic Party. They tightly withheld all support and stayed away from the march.

The MWMM was a bold affirmation that Black working-class leadership was ready to step forward with a highly progressive, comprehensive program for an independent working-class movement. Its demands were calculated to unite the workers with the community and the entire movement. It fell on deaf ears among the bureaucrats of the AFL-CIO.

Whether or not the MWMM and its program will be revived in its present form, sooner or later a similar current will have to reemerge among advanced forces within the labor movement. The labor leadership is slavishly dependent upon the Democratic Party and is squandering hundreds of millions of dollars of workers' dues in the 2008 presidential campaign. The leaders are throwing it away in the hope that they can get some voice in the future administration, after having been shut out by Bush for eight years.

But when the smoke clears, whoever gets into the White House, the attacks by the bosses on the workers and the oppressed will continue, particularly if the economic crisis deepens further. All the so-called "friends of labor" (if there are any left in the Democratic Party) will not substitute for the independent class struggle. As this becomes apparent after the elections are over, programs of the type initiated by the MWMM for an independent workers' movement will surely resurface.

[255] See www.ilwu19.com/history/the_ilwu_story/contents.htm.

Abridged from "Low Capitalism"
*For more on Goldstein's book "**Low Wage Capitalism,**" published in 2008, visit lowwagecapitalism.com/*

Unionists Mobilize for Work, Benefits

Manny Fernandez and David Nakamura

Union members from across the country gathered at the steps of the Lincoln Memorial yesterday for a rally dubbed the Million Worker March, assembling in smaller-than-expected numbers but making a passionate plea for workers' rights.

Linking their struggle with the Rev. Dr. Martin Luther King Jr. by standing on the same spot where the slain civil rights leader made his famous "I Have a Dream" speech in August 1963, workers from a variety of trades and causes said King's vision of social and economic equality remains more dream than reality.

In the crowd were postal workers and longshoremen, school bus drivers and teachers, department store staff and railway repair crews. They said they came to Washington by car, bus and airplane just days before Election Day to highlight the social, economic and political hardships facing workers at home and on the job.

"I think we need a change," said Ronnie White, 48, a production worker at a food plant in Kansas City, Mo., who stood on the steps above the Reflecting Pool proudly wearing his Teamsters Local 838 jacket. "We need the jobs here, not overseas."

An end to the outsourcing of jobs abroad was just one of the rally's many far-reaching goals. Workers called for health care coverage from "cradle to grave" for all, a national living wage, a repeal of the USA Patriot Act, more funding for public schools and free mass transit, to name a few of their 22 demands.

Antiwar sentiment was also strong. Workers criticized the Bush administration for leading the country into what they called an unjustified war with Iraq, saying that the billions of

Celso Tolman, left, of Seattle was among the estimated 10,000 protesters from across the country at the Mall rally.

dollars paying for the war are needed instead in struggling schools and communities. "We need to employ, not deploy," said Mark Barbour, 51, of Blacksburg, Va., a longtime railway worker and a member of the Brotherhood of Maintenance of Way Employees Local 551.

Steve Burns, 43, a teacher at a Madison, Wis., community college, endured a 14-hour van ride to Washington to have his voice heard and his handmade sign seen. Burns' felt-pen message was "End For Profit Health Care." He said he does not receive health care benefits as an adjunct math instructor and is still paying off a recent $1,200 hospital bill for an infection. "Our health care system is a disaster, and neither candidate wants real reform," Burns said.

Though organizers had planned their protest as nonpartisan, speakers and rally goers were not bashful in showing their disapproval of President Bush.

From a podium on a wide granite landing on the memorial steps, former U.S. attorney general Ramsey Clark called for the impeachment of Bush for war crimes. Activists in the audience carried anti-Bush stickers and signs.

The turnout fell short of the 250,000 who filled the Mall for the labor movement's last major Washington demonstration, an 1991 "Solidarity Day" rally that blamed political leaders, including Bush's father, President George H.W. Bush, for turning their backs on U.S. workers. That rally was sponsored by the AFL-CIO,

Million Worker March
National Mall   C-SPAN

Charlene Thomas traveled to Washington, D.C. from Oakland with her sister Lois Drake. They appear on the middle left side of this C-SPAN image captured by Wendy Carter.

USWA Local 8751 - District 4
Boston School Bus Drivers Union

25 Colgate Rd.• Roslindale, MA 02131
Telephone (617) 524-7073 Fax (617) 524-1691

November 6, 2004
Keith Shanklin
Treasurer, Million Worker March
c/o ILWU Local 10, San Francisco, CA 94133

Dear Shank,

I hope you have had some time to wind down from the first Million Worker March sprint. I want to personally thank you for the gargantuan task you took on as Treasurer, making sure the MWM could happen.

Our Local — having been in a fierce contract battle the entire course of the MWM organizing, with an International that was pounding on the door for months to sell the company's 'final offer' (there ended up being 7 of those) — never got a chance to hold a meeting to officially endorse the MWM, until October 28th. Please accept our belated endorsement, and the modest contribution (enclosed) to help defray your debt. (You can see the outcome of our struggle on the pages of www.bostonschoolbusunion.org.)

Now that the elections are over, it seems clearer than ever — despite a contrary view from the pundits and politicians — that not only has the independent road of the MWM been entirely confirmed by events, but that the workers have moved huge strides away from the Bush program of war and cutbacks. Just 3 years ago. Bush's popularity was 70-80%, and huge sections of the workers from both parties were gung-ho for war in the wake of 9/11. Problem with the pro-war Kerry was, obviously, that he gave even the conservative workers, many of whom are opposed to the Bush wars, no reason to break with Bush and his bankers.

The Million Worker March redux is precisely what is needed. Many are demoralized, but the MWM can give them a vehicle to fight I look forward to hearing your and the MWM committee's, thoughts about how we can re-group and bring people out in the streets again to strengthen our movement.

Please share this with Clarence, Delores and all at Local l0, and let them know we in Boston send our love and solidarity.

With great hope for the future

Steven Gillis
President USWA Local 8751

the nation's largest labor federation. But AFL-CIO leaders refused to officially endorse or help organize yesterday's gathering, saying they were focused instead on mobilizing voters for the presidential election.

Organizers, who said unions representing more than 3.5 million workers backed the demonstration, said the AFL-CIO's decision hurt the turnout, but they expressed pride that their low-budget rally was largely a rank-and-file effort.

Not all were trade unionists. About 100 protesters took part in an 11 a.m. "anarchist march," where Daniel Hall, 20, a student at the University of Maryland, marched with a group of students holding up a large banner that read, "Students and workers unite!" Hall said he hoped the march "gets people thinking about labor and how things are not getting better. It's a system of inequality."

Later in the afternoon, following speeches by King's son, Martin Luther King III, and other civil rights and union leaders, a few hundred marched from the Lincoln Memorial to the Hotel Washington on 15th Street NW in support of District hotel workers.

Negotiators for several major Washington hotels and the union that represents 3,800 hotel employees remain deadlocked on a new contract. Protesters chanted outside the hotel's doors as police looked on. Three hotel workers leaned out a third-floor window, looked down on the crowd and waved in support.

Celso Tolman, left, of Seattle was among the estimated 10,000 protesters from across the country at the Mall rally. Virginia Rodino, a supporter from Baltimore, wears her ambitions: "Living wage now!"

Abridged from the Washington Post on Oct. 18, 2004,

The Way Forward

Million Worker March Statement on the October 17 Mobilization

'Union members from across the country gathered at the steps of the Lincoln Memorial for a rally dubbed the MWM ... making a passionate plea for workers' rights. ... Thousands stood at the foot of the memorial and along the sides of the Reflecting Pool on a chilly October afternoon, calling for more jobs, universal health care and an end to the war in Iraq."

So began the report in the *Washington Post* on Oct. 18, 2004, under the headline "Unionists Mobilize for Work, Benefits, Thousands Drawn to Rally at Lincoln Memorial in Prelude to November Vote."

The MWM Mission Statement described a "crisis facing working people" in which "the vast majority of working Americans are under siege."

Working people need to have a political alternative to the common agenda of the U.S. corporate elite that both the Democrats and the Republicans represent.

The call for the MWM emanated from ILWU Local 10, which has a legacy of providing leadership within the union movement in the fight for economic and social justice. The call for the March was adopted unanimously at the ILWU Longshore Caucus, representing the longshore workers at all 29 ports on the West Coast.

The active support of Black and Latino worker organizations, from the Coalition of Black Trade Unionists, the Teamsters National Black Caucus, Black Workers For Justice, the Immigrant Rights Association and the Farm Labor Organizing Committee, brought to the fore of the MWM the most oppressed sectors of the work force.

The leadership role of Black trade union activists, notably of ILWU its co-chairs Clarence Thomas and Trent Willis, Local 10 and Keith Shanklin, Local 34, was manifested by the national centrality of Black and Latino trade union leaders.

The voices of the most oppressed sector of the working class and of the population at large, Chris Silvera, Chair of the TNBC; Brenda Stokely, President of AFSCME DC 1707; Roger Toussaint, President of TWU Local 100; and Saladin Muhammad of BWJ, were conjoined with immigrant rights' organizations and the FLOC.

This was reflected no less in the role played by renowned actor and activist Danny Glover and civil rights leaders Dick Gregory, Martin Luther King, III and Rev. E. Randel T. Osburn of the Southern Christian Leadership Foundation.

In every part of the U.S., District Councils, County and State Labor Federations and union locals endorsed the March. Support for the mobilization increased after the largest trade unions in the United States, AFSCME and SEIU, called at their national conventions for an end to the war in Iraq, an end to the occupation and the withdrawal of all U.S. troops.

A signal feature of the disaffection among rank-and-file workers was the endorsement of the MWM by trade unions whose conservative leadership had prevented the rank-and-file from organizing in their own name.

Among the first California endorsers were the Santa Barbara and San Luis Obispo Counties Building Trades Council, Building and Construction Trades Councils of Napa and Solano Counties and the Calif.

State Pipe Trades Council. This was followed by the Calif. State Association of Letter Carriers and the Secretary-Treasurer of the Los Angeles County State Federation of Labor.

In New York City, key trade unions endorsed the March: The TWU Local 100 and its President Roger Toussaint joined SEIU Local 1199, Teamsters Local 808 and AFSCME DC 1707 and 37 in organizing for October 17. Twenty-seven AFSCME locals and District Councils in New York, Maryland and Texas endorsed the MWM.

At the national convention of AFSCME, widespread support for a resolution of endorsement was evident at the convention. The AFSCME leadership, however, succeeded in preventing the Resolution from reaching the floor.

The AFL-CIO leadership gave over $100 million to the Democratic Party, embracing of their corporate agenda and conspiring to prevent any worker involvement with October 17.

The memorandum from Marilyn Schneiderman of the AFL-CIO on June 23 directing Labor Councils not to participate in the March, or to give it material support, was timed for the AFSCME convention.

The President of ILWU Local 10 and ILWU leaders of the MWM met with ILWU President James Spinosa and the leadership of the Longshore Division in August.

It was there that we learned of a meeting that took place at Hyannisport, Mass., during the Democratic National Convention where the MWM was discussed. This meeting involved Senator Edward Kennedy, AFL-CIO President John Sweeney, Teamsters President Jimmy Hoffa,

SEIU President Andrew Stern and ILWU President James Spinosa. Spinosa stated that he objected to the timing of the March, and they concurred.

The leadership of the AFL-CIO not only gave vast sums of money to the Democratic Party campaign, they embraced the corporate agenda and the strict framing of the election .

In September, John Kerry appeared before the Detroit Economic Club and presented his chief policy makers, notably Warren Buffett, Lee Iacocca, Bank of America Chairman, Charles Gifford and August A. Busch IV of Anheuser Busch. All are registered Republicans and all were architects of George W. Bush's 2000 Campaign.

On September 30, *The Los Angeles Times*, in a analysis of the campaigns, concluded: "Foreign Policy Divide Is Slim for Bush, Kerry," They might not be in the same ZIP code, but they're in the same area code."

The MWM made clear that the 2004 Presidential election unfolded with two parties whose programs embodied the relentless class war on working people at home and abroad.

The AFL-CIO leadership was directing workers to put their concerns for a workers' agenda on the back-burner and subordinate themselves to the election of Kerry, regardless of the program he represents.

Such a perspective is aimed at aborting the movement for national health care, social security, public education along with slashing the military budget, ending the war and challenging the banks and corporations who control both political parties and the U.S. government itself.

It is a measure of the courage a of a growing number of U.S. workers to organize around their own urgent demands that they defied an all-out

effort to strangle this mobilization.

Endorsements and support by the rank-and-file mushroomed. The American Postal Workers Union, the National Education Association and the Brotherhood of Maintenance of Way Employees, representing over 3 million workers, endorsed at their national conventions.

This was the first time that the rank-and-file organized a workers' rally, mobilizing workers from a broad cross-section of the labor movement, not under the auspices of the AFL-CIO or the Democratic Party.

The composition of the Mobilization represents a historic shift whose consequences will unfold as the movement expands. For the first time, the anti-war coalition was joined by rank-and-file labor. The predominance of African-American, Caribbean, Latino voices both on the stage and in the crowd is a harbinger of struggles to come. The International Action Center played a critical role.

The MWM mobilization held all politicians accountable to a working people's agenda.

Standing in the footsteps of his father, Martin Luther King Ill, recalled the civil rights movement and his father's call for a Poor People's March on Washington, D.C. The speakers at the Lincoln Memorial spoke on behalf of social movements, labor councils, immigrant rights' organizations, welfare mothers, unemployed, part-time workers and youth.

Regional Committees for the MWM, were represented on the platform from New York; Philadelphia; Baltimore; Washington, D.C.; Williamsport, Va.; Charleston and Columbia, S.C.; Atlanta; Cleveland; Chicago; Decatur, Ill.; Minneapolis and St. Paul, Minn.; Houston; Los

Angeles; San Francisco; Portland, Ore., and Seattle, Wash.

The movement that we have launched is international in scope. Simultaneous mobilizations in support of the MWM were held in Seoul, Korea, Madrid, Paris, and Sao Paulo, Brazil, among other cities. There were ten actions in Japan, spearheaded by Doro Chiba, the Japanese Railway Workers Union that has led the fight against privatization.

Leaders of union federations and worker organizations from Venezuela, Brazil, Russia, South Africa, Great Britain, Slovakia, India, Bangladesh, Pakistan, Haiti, South Korea, Japan, Philippines and Hong Kong sent statements of support and plans for coordinated struggles. These messages were sent on behalf of 47 million organized workers across the globe.

The MWMM declared that working people must put forward their own agenda and in their own name.

The emerging Movement will take that agenda to every trade union local and to every location where people work, seek work and struggle to survive.

The energy and vision that infused the Million Worker March and enabled us to surmount the obstacles placed in our path. It will draw upon the legacy of the great organizing drives that gave birth to U.S. industrial unionism, the direct action in the streets that begat the civil rights movement and the historic struggles that gave political voice to the disenfranchised. The historic Million Worker March was not merely an event but the launching of a movement which will be emerge as a defining struggle of the 21st century.

– MWM Organizing Committee

March, March, March

(For MWM and Brother Ray Quan)

Zigi Lowenberg,
Clarence Thomas,
Delores Lemon-Thomas,
and the acclaimed poet
Raymond Nat Turner.

I.

Wizardry tattooing highways
On mountainsides, scooping
Diamonds from Mother Earth's
Inflamed womb, weaving towers
From Chicago wind, Santiago sun,
Bejeweling New York skyline…
Magic conjuring City-sized ships
Gliding smoothly beneath great
White horses, trotting above ports,
Crowning chassis with treasure chests,
Waltzing through traffic to warehouses,
Windows and bellies of the world…yet…

Crippled pallets loiter on loading docks
No longer loaded with dark skins sparkling
Under fresh coats of sweat, and lunch bucket
Language lingering beneath blue plumes
Of forklift fumes, instead dust dances on
Sunbeams streaming through busted eyes
Where ghostly weeds peek through concrete
Once rumbling with machines… 24/7…

Will Work For Food

Reads the crumpled cardboard sign at
The long light, two blocks down and a
World away from corn syrup slogan of
"Recovery's right around the corner,"
Getting out votes for Dems, vetoing resistance…

II.

We flip the burgers and peel the potatoes,
We pick the grapes, lettuce and tomatoes…
We print Bibles, Korans, Euros, pesos, dollars
We stitch britches, shirtsleeves, and collars…
We print newspapers, phone and electric bills,
We press stethoscopes, scalpels, dental drills…
We sweat broke over plows and milk worn cows,
Stitch the belts and shoes, ship rhythm and blues…

March, March, March
Militant rank-and-file

March, March, March
Forward an inch, a mile

March, March, March
We never march alone

March, March, March
With leaders of our own –

Robinson, Willis, Silas, Soto
Thomas, Toussaint, Turra

March, March, March
Militant rank-and-file

March, March, March
Forward an inch, a mile

March, March, March
We never march alone

March, March, March
With leaders of our own –

Romero, Silvera, Stokely,
Stevens, Shanklin, Schoenman

Our sorcery divines water,
Electricity and gas, clarifies
Sewage, transports the mass…

March, March, March
Militant rank-and-file

March, March, March
Forward an inch, a mile

March, March, March
We never march alone

March, March, March
With leaders of our own
Bailey, Montilla, Mabasa,
Masakazu, Nyasha, Quezada

We push the papers
We monitor the screens,
We count the Rand,
The rupees and beans…
March, March, March
Militant rank-and-file

March, March, March
Forward an inch, a mile

March, March, March
We never march alone

March, March, March
With leaders of our own
Graham, Griggs, Griffin,
Gonaceros, Becker, Black

March, March, March
Militant rank-and-file

March, March, March
Forward an inch, a mile

March, March, March
We never march alone

March, March, March
With leaders of our own –

Corbin, Dewitt, Durham,
Gatto, Gillis, Heyman

We scrub gilded toilets and
Mop marble floors, yet kill
Blindly in rich men's wars…

March, March, March
Militant rank-and-file

March, March, March
Forward an inch, a mile

March, March, March
We never march alone

March, March, March
With leaders of our own –

Hillard, Holmes, Lawrence,
Maspero, Miyashiro, Muhammad

March, March, March
Militant rank-and-file
March, March, March
Forward an inch, a mile

March, March, March
We never march alone

March, March, March
With leaders of our own –

Riley, Reyes, Casey, Gilbert,
Quan, Hollie, Zimmerman

March, March, March
Workers on a rise…

March, March, March
October surprise!
March…

Raymond Nat Turner

CHAPTER 3

THE HONORABLE MINISTER LOUIS FARRAKHAN
ACCEPTED AN INVITATION AS KEYNOTE SPEAKER AT THE
30th ANNUAL EDUCATIONAL CONFERENCE & BANQUET

TEAMSTERS NATIONAL BLACK CAUCUS
CHICAGO • ILLINOIS • OCTOBER 2005

MILLIONS MORE MOVEMENT
How it will relate to the working class

Photo: Gloria Verdieu

MILLION MAN MARCH 1995
MILLIONS MORE MOVEMENT 2005
'JUSTICE OR ELSE' MARCH 2015

Bob Simpson a founder of the Teamsters National Black Causcus shakes hands with Minister Louis Farrakhan. Also pictured, from the left, Waymon Stroud, TNBC, M.C. Lewis IBT Local 247, Kenneth Hollowell TNBC, and Chris Silvera TNBC.

Photo of Minister Farrakan, above: Edward G. Downie, Videographer

MWMM worker's group backs upcoming Million More Movement

Call from MWMM leaders: ILWU Local 10 Pres. **Trent Willis***, Local 10 Exec. Brd.* **Clarence Thomas***, Teamsters Nat'l Black Caucus Chair* **Chris Silvera***, AFSCME DC 1707 fmr. Pres.* **Brenda Stokely***, Transport Workers Local 100 Pres.* **Roger Toussaint***, Black Workers for Justice* **Saladin Muhammad** *and anti-war leader* **Larry Holmes.**

In mid-May 2005, the MWMM held a report-back and networking meeting in Detroit, which brought together MWMM organizers and leaders representing various regions of the country.

The consensus of those present expressed support for the MWMM's endorsement of the 10-year commemoration of the Million Man March, which is being organized as the Millions More Movement (MMM). The MMM will seek to mobilize millions to Washington, D.C., on Oct. 14.

Ninety-five percent of all African Americans are workers; 30 percent of African American workers are union members and make up an important segment of the labor movement; nearly 50 percent are women; and 55 percent live in the U.S. South, where right-to-work laws are part of the Southern states' structure as a low-wage region with the lowest percentage of unionized workers.

We see the MMM as an important vehicle for convening a national Black united front to help reunite the fragmented forces of the African American liberation movement and to help facilitate the unity of Black workers.

In 1995, the Million Man March mobilized close to 2 million people to Washington, D.C. Despite some criticisms it helped to propel successive grassroots mobilizations over a 10-year period, as represented by the Million Women's, Million Family, Million Youth, Million Reparations and Million Worker marches, the latter helping to spawn an independent workers' movement.

The majority at the 1995 March were Black workers, organized and unorganized. Many came despite opposition and threats of retaliation from their employers. Most, including those in unions, used their personal resources to attend because most of trade unions did not support the march. This failure to carry out and support struggles against racism inside and outside of the trade unions is a major weakness of the U.S. trade union movement and a key reason for its current crisis of direction. Black workers must continue to struggle to change this reality.

The 1995 March represented an historic event as it was the largest single mobilization of African Americans in U.S. history. However, the organized identity and demands of Black workers, which are at the core of the issues facing all workers, were not strongly represented.

In the words of Minister Louis Farrakhan, the main convener of the MMM, "Millions More," he explained, "means that we are reaching for the millions who carry the rich on their backs." We agree totally with this formulation. We believe this points out the importance of Black workers mobilizing the broadest possible U.S. base and international working class regardless of race or gender to this historic mobilization. The MWMM has demonstrated an ability to advance demands that build international worker solidarity.

The MMM organizers reached out to MWMM to participate in this historical mobilization. Knowing that the MWMM involves workers of all races, nationalities, genders, religions, and sexual orientations indicates the breadth of the mobilization that is being called for by the MMM.

The MMM will be a major mobilization linking the U.S. war at home with the U.S. led and supported wars and occupations abroad. This will send an important message of hope around the world that there is a powerful movement on the horizon.

Now, the attacks on the workers have made the stakes much higher than 1995. No one can afford to sit this one out! We see the main task of the MWMM as organizing and mobilizing the conscious and enthusiastic participation of workers in our own name.

Our demands must include:

- National health care
- Bring the troops home now
- Preserve & protect Social Security
- Family-supporting living wage
- Repeal U.S. Patriot Acts
- Protect worker pensions
- Stop dismantling of public education
- Bring jobs back to the U.S.
- End to privatization
- Affordable housing
- Protection of the environment
- Progressive taxation
- Amnesty for all undocumented workers.

Workers must build a Black and people of color led broad workers' coalition to mobilize for the MMM. We must bring together organizations like Coalition of Black Trade Unionists, A. Philip Randolph Instit., Nat'l African American Caucus-SEIU, Teamsters Nat'l Black Caucus, Black Workers for Justice, Black Telephone Workers for Justice, Harlem Fight Back, Global Women's Strike Cmte., Farm Labor Organizing Cmte., Labor Council for Latin American Advancement, Asian Pacific American Labor Alliance of AFL-CIO, Pride At Work, immigrant rights organizations, and many others.

We call on all the unions, worker groups, anti-war and social-justice activist organizations who are affiliates with or supporters of the MWMM to sign on and help build for the MMM!

Mobilizing in Our Own Name!

Abridged from WW, July 21, 2005.

Clarence Thomas and Leo Robinson wearing the MWM/MMM tee shirts.

Keith Shanklin

Brenda Stokely with daughter Zenzile and granddaughter Kalola Keith

Cheryl LaBash

Michael Hoard and Gabriel Prawl

Photos: Delores Lemon-Thomas

Chryse Glackin

Minister Louis Farrakhan to address Black labor

Chris Silvera   Chair of the Teamsters National Black Caucus

Chris Silvera with Minister Louis Farrakhan.

Photo: O'Neil Nanco

The Teamsters National Black Caucus is an organization of Black trade unionists fighting to defeat discrimination inside and outside of the International Brotherhood of Teamsters. We believe in educating and activating the rank-and-file.

The Honorable Minister Louis Farrakhan, on behalf of the Millions More Movement, will be addressing the delegates attending the Caucus's 30th Annual Educational Conference and Banquet in Chicago, on Aug. 16-21, 2005. Minister Farrakhan will be the Keynote Speaker at our banquet.

In Chicago, we pick up the torch that was carried so valiantly by the late Rev. Dr. Martin Luther King Jr. The clergy, the civil rights warriors, the anti-war movement and Black Labor have joined together to mobilize the working class to "forge a fightback."

The Million Worker March Movement and the Teamsters National Black Caucus have joined with the Millions More Movement to put forward a workers' agenda with a list of demands which includes:

- workers' and human rights,
- the right to a job with a living wage,
- the right to organize,
- the right to strike without being replaced,
- the right to national health care,
- the enforcement of civil rights against all racist and discriminatory acts,
- the right to affordable housing,
- and an end to the war in Iraq,
- We must protect and enhance Social Security and multi-employer pension plans which should be guaranteed for all working people.

Education is a right, not a privilege.

Common cause has brought us together to build a movement powerful enough to affect social and economic justice. This movement must be built and led by the "millions who carry the rich on their backs." We must let Wall Street corporate bosses, who control both political parties and run our government, know that we will not accept the theft of jobs, resources and the future of our children instead of the rebuilding of our cities and the full restoration of vital public services.

The membership of the Teamsters National Black Caucus comprises officers, stewards and rank-and-file labor activists. The organization continues to stretch forth its hands in support of all worthy actions that uplift all workers. TNBC has worked tirelessly to improve the wages, benefits and working condition of all workers.

Besides being chair of the Teamsters National Black Caucus, Silvera is also secretary-treasurer of Teamsters Local 808. The International Brotherhood of Teamsters has 400,000 Black members. Silvera was one of the co-coordinators of the MWM on the East Coast.

Abridged from WW, Aug. 25, 2005.

Black Teamsters Caucus meets
Anti-war fight, MMM, Farrakhan's talk are highlights

Johnnie Stevens

Highlights of the Teamsters National Black Caucus meeting in August 2005, were the group's commitment to the struggle against the war and occupation of Iraq, its plans to participate in the Millions More Movement in October, and a keynote talk by Minister Louis Farrakhan of the Nation of Islam.

MMM leader Farrakhan addressed 500 members and supporters of the TNBC who gathered in Chicago for their annual conference. Minister Farrakhan was invited to speak at the banquet by its current president, Chris Silvera, a Teamsters leader in the New York area and one of the leaders of the Million Worker March Movement.

The invitation to Minister Farrakhan had grown out of discussions within the MWMM about how to highlight Black workers' and Black trade unionists' concerns and their participation in the upcoming MMM march, set for Oct. 15 in Washington, D.C.

Minister Farrakhan slammed the war in Iraq, saying, "Instead of Saddam Hussein, it´s Bush who should be put on trial for war crimes.' The NOI leader noted that this was the first time he had spoken before a gathering of trade unionists.

MWMM co-chair and Local 10 official Clarence Thomas who attended the TNBC event, said, "Having Minister Farrakhan here is a major breakthrough for Black labor participation in the MMM march this fall."

Thomas also noted, "The fact that Farrakhan, in his remarks, called on the labor movement to go back to the table and work out its differences, because the split only serves the interest of greedy corporate executives, is very significant and timely." Recently several major unions, including the Teamsters, UNITE-HERE and the Service Employees, separated from the AFL-CIO.

The five-day-long TNBC conference endorsed the MMM march, the Sept. 24, anti-war march in Washington, D.C., as well as a call for three days of protest against the war, racism and poverty set for Dec. 1-3. These dates coincide with the 50th anniversary of the day Rosa Parks opened the famous Montgomery, Ala., bus boycott when she was arrested for refusing to give her seat to a white man.

Larry Holmes of the Troops Out Now Coalition and the MWMM, said: "The response at the meeting to the protest on the anniversary of Rosa Parks´ defiant stand and the incredible bus boycott that it sparked is really strong. The support of the TNBC will help us get more trade unionists involved in the December protest, and help our ambitious plans to encourage workers to plan job actions during that time."

Trent Willis, MWMM co-chair and president of Local 10, also addressed the meeting, as did other MWMM leaders Brenda Stokely and Leo Robinson. Coalition of Black Trade Unionists President Bill Lucy and Transport Workers Union NYC Local 100 President Roger Toussaint also spoke.

Abridged from WW, Sept. 1, 2005.

Minister Louis Farrakhan addresses meeting of unionists in Chicago. WW photo: Johnnie Stevens

Notes from a conversation with Louis Farrakhan

MWMM talks to MMM about the working class

Clarence Thomas

During Nation of Islam Minister Louis Farrakhan's keynote address on behalf of the Millions More Movement (MMM) at the Teamsters National Black Caucus 30th Annual Educational Conference Banquet on Aug. 20, 2005, he publicly extended an invitation to the TNBC National Chair, Chris Silvera, to have a meeting in order to include MWMM issues with the MMM platform.

The Nation of Islam's (NOI) chief of protocol, Sister Claudette Marie Muhammad, made arrangements with the assistance of Harlem's NOI Minister Kevin Muhammad, to set up the meeting in New York Aug. 27, 2005.

Silvera, an East Coast convener of the MWM, indicated to Kevin Muhammad that he wanted to have two other MWM East Coast conveners, Brenda Stokely, former president of District Council 1707, and Larry Holmes, co-director of the International Action Center, along with myself, at that meeting.

Farrakhan had traveled to New York to meet with various sectors of the community and movement regarding the upcoming Oct. 14-16, MMM events in Washington, D.C., to commemorate the 10th anniversary of the Million Man March.

He greeted the four of us individually with an embrace and a handshake. Despite his hectic schedule, which included a flurry of interviews and other meetings, we were able to have a 45-minute meeting at his hotel.

Many trade union rank-and-filers have a misconception of who Minister Farrakhan is and his importance. While he is certainly an important historical figure in the struggle for Black liberation, we found him to be attentive, humble, full of great wisdom and graciousness.

I presented the Minister with MWM statements on "Rank-and-file unity and the AFL-CIO split" and "Racism and sexism: Major pillars of the crisis inside the U.S. trade union movement," and with an outline of how the MWMM would be doing broad outreach to workers, organized and unorganized, anti-war activists and others for the MMM. I also gave him a copy of the "*War at Home, Economic Class War in America*" a book by Jack Rasmus.

Prior to the Aug. 27 meeting, a MWMM tee shirt, pin and Oct. 17 rally DVD had been presented to Minister Ishmael Muhammad, a Farrakhan assistant, during the July 23 AFL-CIO pre-convention activity at Mosque Maryam in Chicago. Silvera presented the minister with a TNBC embroidered leather shoulder bag, tee shirt and history of the TNBC DVD.

In response to a request made by Silvera, a verbal agreement was made that the MWM will be one of the national co-conveners of the MMM representing labor, and that this agreement will be conveyed to Minister Willie Williams, the national executive director of MMM. Farrakhan told us that each of the local MMM organizing committees should have labor representation. These committees will be made aware of this recommendation along with the MMM executive body that meets regularly to discuss issues. Farrakhan told us that no one can speak for workers like workers themselves and therefore asked us to select a MWMM representative to speak on the issues of labor at the MMM Oct. 15 rally.

There was a mutual agreement on the plight of working people, organized and unorganized. Farrakhan mentioned that even though many of us in the trade union movement are facing this onslaught from not only the corporations but the government, still the plight of those who don't have jobs cannot be lost in all of this.

This includes those who don't have pensions, don't have livable wages and medical benefits, those who want a job and can't have one, and how those of us who do have jobs serve as buffers, superficial divisions, between the unemployed on the one hand and the corporations and the ruling class on the other.

Minister Farrakhan made the point that there is a disconnection in many instances between those of us who are working and those who are not, as well as between those who have jobs that are unionized and jobs that are not unionized.

Stokely mentioned how the MWMM embraces those who don't have jobs, because we call for universal health care, a national livable wage, affordable housing and education, and that a worker, unemployed or displaced is still a worker.

Chris Silvera, Clarence Thomas, Minister Louis Farrakhan, Brenda Stokely, Larry Holmes and Bashiri Silvera holding MWM tee shirt Aug. 27.

Photo: Nation of Islam

Minister Farrakhan reminded us of the forces that we were going up against and about the fear that the government has of retribution from the Black community based on the racism and white supremacy that we still face.

Farrakhan said that the only way that we are going to be able to re-alize livable wages and jobs for the unemployed is to make fundamental changes in the government, including the military-based economy.

He stated that the government has committed wrongdoing to the victims of "American foreign policy," and that government fear created an atti-tude of locking up Black folks before there is some kind of action taken by the Black community to the oppres-sion that we've been under.

I underscored the fact that Farrakhan continues the legacy of the Honorable Elijah Muhammad and the ongoing struggle for economic and social justice. Farrakhan has the moral authority to be able to make Black trade unionists respond and mobilize around the issues raised at the MWMM.

Farrakhan's speech on Aug. 20 with regard to issues of the Black working class was in fact helping to carry forth the work of Dr. Martin Luther King with respect to the Black community, the working class or labor, the inter-faith community around issues of the right to a job,

decent education and health care.

When we mentioned to him the issues of bringing the troops home, repealing anti-labor laws such as the Taft-Hartley Act, upholding workers' critical weapons like having the right to strike without replacement workers, ending all discrimination in the work place, be it based on race or gender, Farrakhan told us that he was not interested in just being able to rattle off statistics, but he wants to develop a perspective of what the working class is facing in order to feel their pain. He wants us to provide him with an additional perspective on issues put forward by the MWMM.

To quote from the MWMM's Letter for a Millions More Movement Resolution: "Oct. 16, 2005, marks the 10th Anniversary of the historic Million Man March. This event was not only the largest gathering of Af-rican American people; it was also the site of the greatest mobilization of workers in a single demonstration in U.S. history. However, there was no specific labor organization that par-ticipated in the MMM responsible for organizing a conscious Black worker presence with clear national working class demands.

"The Million Worker March Movement is issuing the call to Black workers (organized and unorganized) and the entire labor movement to endorse and mobilize for the 10th anniversary of the MMM, called the

Millions More Movement on Oct 14th-16th in Washington, D.C.

"The present attacks on all workers have made the stakes for Black work-ers in particular and the working class in general much higher than they were when nearly 2 million workers elected to attend the MMM and did not go to work on Oct. 16, 1995.

"The MWMM clearly recognizes that the labor movement cannot be absent from this next mobilization. We will be mobilizing workers to participate on Oct. 14th-16th around the demands put forward by the MWM on Oct. 17, at the Lincoln Me-morial in Washington D.C."

Our Aug. 27 meeting was a recon-firmation of what Minister Louis Far-rakhan stated at the kick-off MMM news conference this past May: "Millions More means that we are reaching for the millions who carry the rich on their backs."

Thomas is a member of the ILWU Local 10 executive board and past secretary-treasurer, a member of the executive committee of the Alameda County Central Labor Council, and a member of the Northern California Chapter of the Coalition of Black Trade Unionists. Silvera is secretary-treasurer of Teamsters Local 808 in Long Island City, N.Y. Brenda Stokely and Larry Holmes are members of the Troops Out Now Coalition.

Abridged from WW, August 30, 2005

MILLION WORKER MARCH MOVEMENT

1632 7th Street, Oakland, California 94607   510-4446272, Fax 510-632-6816

Ms. Cheryl L. Johnson
Assistant to the General President
International Brotherhood of Teamsters
Washington, D.C. 20001

Dear Ms. Johnson:

I am Clarence Thomas, Co-Chair of the Million Worker March Movement (MWMM) writing you at the behest of Chris Silvera, Chair of the Teamsters National Black Caucus (TNBC).

Million Worker March Movement's letter for **Millions More Movement Resolution**

October 16, 2005 marks the 10th Anniversary of the historic Million Man March (MMM). This event was not only the largest gathering of African American people; it was also the site of the greatest mobilization of workers in a single demonstration.

However, there was no specific labor organization that participated in the MMM responsible for organizing a conscious Black worker presence with national working class demands.

The MWMM and TNBC are issuing the call to Black workers, organized and unorganized, and the entire labor movement to endorse and mobilize for the 10th Anniversary of the MMM, called the Millions More Movement on October 14-16m 2005 in Washington, D.C.

The present attacks on all workers have made the stakes for Black workers in particular and the working class in general much higher than they were when nearly 2 million workers elected to attend the MMM and did not go to work on October 16, 1995.

The MWMM and the TNBC clearly recognizes that the labor movement can not be absent from this next mobilization. We will be mobilizing workers to participate on October 14 – 16 around the demands put forward by the Million Worker March on Oct. 17, 2004 at the Lincoln Memorial in Washington D.C. These demands include but are not limited to:

- National Health Care
- Bring the Troops Home Now
- Full Employment with a Living Wage
- Repeal of all Free Trade Agreements

- Repeal of U.S. Patriot Act
- Repeal of Taft Hartley
- Right to strike without replacements
- Protection of Social Security and Pensions

This event is too important for Labor not to demonstrate its leadership as well as to forge new alliances as we address the crisis facing workers today.

In solidarity,

Clarence Thomas,
Co-Chair, Million Worker March Movement
Past-Secretary Treasurer, ILWU, Local 10   Member, ILWU Local 10 Executive Board
Executive Committee Member, Alameda County Central Labor Council
Member, Northern California Coalition of Black Trade Unionists

INTERNATIONAL BROTHERHOOD OF TEAMSTERS

JAMES P. HOFFA
General President

25 Louisiana Avenue, NW
Washington, DC 20001

C. THOMAS KEEGEL
General Secretary-Treasurer

202.624.6800
www. teamster.org

September 19, 2005

Dear Brothers and Sisters,

The Teamster Union is fully supporting the Million Worker March Movement and their upcoming events in the Nation's Capital. We are making a financial contribution and encouraging members to attend the Millions More Movement from October 14-16 in Washington, D.C.

The Million Worker March Movement and the Teamsters Union share many goals, including reforming health care and the pension system, as well as fighting for living wages for all Americans.

The current attacks on workers have made the stakes for black workers in particular, and the working class in general, much higher than in years past. Events like this allow the Teamsters Union to forge new alliances as we address the crisis facing workers today.

We encourage you to participate in these worthy events.

Fraternally,

James P. Hoffa
James P. Hoffa
General President

C. Thomas Keegel
C. Thomas Keegel
General Secretary-Treasurer

JPH/CTK/tw

'We need a movement of millions'

**Long live John Africa.
On a move!**

I want to thank Minister Louis Farrakhan and the Millions More Movement for the kind invitation to join y'all here. As we gather, in person or electronically, we do so in a time of peril.

We do so in the aftermath of Hurricane Katrina, when the state showed us all that they don't give a damn about Black life. But every day of our lives we see smaller but no less lethal Hurricane Katrinas'. Every year in public schools, millions of Black, Latin@, and poor kids are miseducated, thereby destroying, as surely as any hurricane, their life hopes and chances.

In our communities, our taxes pay for our own oppression, as racist and brutal cops make our lives hell daily. We are consumers of a media that is as dangerous as any hurricane, for it poisons our minds and the minds of millions of others by wholesale lies designed to demean and denigrate us.

Look at the tale of horrors that came out of Katrina: The horror stories of mass rapes and mass murders, told by Black politicians and Black cops to deflect attention from the armed, roving gangs of New Orleans cops, who stole everything that they could get their hands on. By putting out these lies, they turned hearts and minds from their betrayal of their own constituency, Black and poor New Orleanians, who needed transport, food, clean water, toilet facilities, and medical care and safety.

What's the point? That they represent, not the interests of those who voted for them, but the wealthy and well-to-do. If you doubt me, ask yourself what percentage of the tens of thousands of people in the Superdome or the convention center, those people the government left to starve, in the dark, thirsty, deathly afraid, were registered Democrat?

If we're honest, we'll agree over 90 percent. What did it matter? It did not. Their loyalty was rewarded with betrayal. Did it matter that there was a Democratic governor? Kathleen Blanco's first order was to send National Guard into the streets, where she authorized them to shoot to kill to protect property. Did any of you, in a week, see such governmental passion displayed to protect human life? Did you see any interest in protecting Black life?

I did not think so.

What we saw then was what we have always seen, the government as adversary, not ally. In prisons across America, in police stations, and in courthouses, we experience daily hurricanes of hatred and indifference. These institutions, just like other government branches, are threats to our welfare, not tools of our will. They are tools of white supremacy, even and sometimes especially when their leaders have Black faces.

We have Black politicians with virtually no political power which means, once again, we pay for our own oppression. Our taxes pay for them, but they do not serve our people's interests. They serve the state of white supremacy. They serve the will of capital.

We need a movement of millions to build true social power. To free our minds and our bodies from the mud that we languish in.

We need a movement of millions to transform our current social reality of repression and destitution. We need a movement of millions to bring back light to the eyes of our people. To engage in a struggle for freedom, for justice, and for liberation.

We need a movement of millions of the poor, of workers, of women, of youth, of students, of prisoners, of all those dedicated to change to build independent organizations that can't be bought or sold and will do the work necessary to be free.

We need a movement of millions to bring freedom to the brothers and sisters of the Move 9, to bring freedom to Sundiata Acoli, to bring freedom to Mutulu Shakur, to Russell Maroon Shoats, and hundreds of other Black prisoners of war and political prisoners.

We need a movement of millions to resist the state oppression that has brought us Patriot Acts, but not patriotic actions, wars for empire and countless attacks on the poor. We need a movement of millions to make common cause with oppressed people the world over, in Cuba, yes in Iraq, in Venezuela, in the Congo, in Haiti, in the Philippines.

We need a movement of millions that is anti-imperialist, that is anti-racist, and that unites us, not divides us. We need a movement of millions and let us begin right here.

Thank you, on a move! Long live John Africa. Free the Move 9.

**From death row, this is
Mumia Abu-Jamal**
Oct 13, 2005.

MWM: Fight for independent Black and working-class political action

Alan Benjamin

On Oct. 14, 2005, the day before the Millions More Movement, the MWMM organized a conference at the hall of Teamsters Local 639 in Washington, D.C. The purpose of the gathering, which brought together MWMM activists and supporters from across the country, was to educate around, and build support for, the platform demands and independent orientation.

Conference speakers included Saladin Muhammad, a leader of Black Workers For Justice; Gene Bruskin, co-convener of US Labor Against the War; Colia Clark, a civil rights activist; Jack Rasmus, author and organizer of the National Writers Union; Brenda Stokely, coordinator of MWMM, East Coast; Chris Silvera, chair of the Teamsters National Black Caucus; Clarence Thomas, co-chair of the MWMM; Alan Benjamin, editor of The Organizer newspaper; Larry Holmes, organizer of the International Action Center, among others.

In October 2004, the MWMM brought together rank-and-file workers, unorganized workers, immigrants, youth and activists to raise their own independent voices. Central to this agenda were the demands for national single-payer healthcare, quality public education for all, repeal of Taft Hartley, repeal of all exploitative "free trade" agreements, protection of social security and pensions, repeal of the Patriot Act, full employment with a living wage, the immediate return of U.S. troops from Iraq and other countries, and the right to strike without replacements.

These demands were featured in a leaflet produced by the MWMM Eastern Region for mass distribution at the October 15th mobilization. The leaflet also put forward an independent perspective for winning these demands, stating, we must build a powerful and united movement that is capable of:

"Taking to task a criminal government that only serves the interests of the wealthy few;"

"Substantially supporting those organizing a powerful fightback in the Gulf Region, including the right to return, right to determine the rebuilding plan, freezing contracts to the Halliburton, reinstatement of wage protection, i.e., Davis-Bacon Act; and "Maintaining its allegiance only to the poor and workers, rejecting any attempts to subordinate their interests."

This last point, refusal to subordinate the interests of Blacks and working people to the political machinations of the ruling rich and the political parties in their pay, was the subject of considerable discussion at the MWMM Conference.

Clarence Thomas said it was necessary to bring a class perspective into the MMM, something only the MWMM could do, and to put a halt to the endless sellouts of the Democratic Party. "We need an empowered rank-and-file along with a serious vision of working-class power, Thomas said. "To achieve this, the working class must speak in its own

Larry Holmes, Trent Willis, Brenda Stokely, Clarence Thomas, Lybon Mabasa, past president of the Socialist Party of Azania/South Africa and Alan Benjamin.   PVN photo: Johnnie Stevens

name, not as a junior partner of the oppressors."

Jack Rasmus, explained in great detail, using data published in his book, *The War at Home: The Corporate Offensive from Ronald Reagan to George W. Bush,*" how the corporate offensive has been implemented both by Democrats and Republicans over at least the past 30 years.

Chris Silvera noted that working people need their own political party. "Both parties are conspiring against the working class," Silvera said. "Clinton was a wolf in sheep's clothing. At least Bush is a straight-up wolf."

This writer explained that the Democrats have never been the party of working people and that more than ever, Blacks and all working people must break with the Democrats and build their own independent political party. This writer further noted: "The MWMM has a unique role to play in the Millions More Movement. It has a program that defends the interests of Blacks and all working people .... The Democrats aren't going to give us national single payer healthcare, the repeal of Taft-Hartley or the repeal of NAFTA, CAFTA and the FTAA. The Democratic Party, in fact, is a major proponent of corporate healthcare and corporate 'free trade.'

"The independent MWMM program must become the program of a mobilized working-class movement. It is a fightback program that must be fought for in the streets and in the political arena by independent Black and labor community slates in the 2006 and 2008 elections. We cannot count on the Congressional Black Caucus or anyone else beholden to a party of the ruling class to speak in our own

Naeema Muhammad, Organizing Co-Director of the North Carolina Environmental Justice Network with her spouse, Saladin Muhammad.
Photo: Delores Lemon-Thomas

name. We must speak in our own name and not subordinate the interests of Black and the poor to the Democratic Party and its agenda." Other speakers echoed these basic themes of the Million Worker March Movement.

Not a Cry in the Wilderness

The call for Black workers and their organizations to run independent Black candidates for political office in 2006 and 2008, is not a cry in the wilderness.

While the most prominent figures in the Black struggle today have not broken with their perspective of reforming the Democratic Party and making it "more answerable" to the demands of working people, the failure of the Democrats to heed even the most limited demands of Blacks and poor people, combined with the growing rage of millions of Blacks and oppressed workers

across the country, have compelled these leaders to give voice publicly to the deep aspirations for independent political action.

A few months later, in the August 23 issue of "*The Final Call*" Farrakhan asked the following question: "So why do Black people and Latino people, Native American and white people themselves need the Millions More Movement?" He answered his own question: "You no longer have representative government. How can these rich speak for the poor?" Farrakhan went on to talk about the need to build "a party of the poor."

Clearly, the Million Worker March Movement has a major role to play in taking the discussion "to build a party of the poor" to the hundreds of thousands of Black and working class activists who have been inspired by the October 15th MM and who are looking for solutions to their most pressing problems. Building that movement is the task of the Million Worker March Movement.

Abridged from Unity & Independence, October 2005.

10TH ANNIVERSARY October 14, 15, 16, 2005
MILLION MAN MARCH
ORGANIZING COMMITTEE

MMM, Oct. 15, 2005

On 'Day of Absence' MWMM to host town hall meeting

Monica Moorehead

The Million Worker March Movement will be holding an important town hall meeting on Oct. 14, 2005 in Washington, D.C. It is being held on the **"Day of Absence"** called by the Millions More Movement, which is urging people not to go to work or school to protests all forms of injustice.

The Millions More Movement will be holding a mass rally the next day at the National Mall to mark the 10th anniversary of the Million Man March, which attracted more than 1 million, predominantly Black, men in 1995. The principal spokesperson for the MMM is Nation of Islam leader Minister Louis Farrakhan.

The MWMM, one of the official national co-conveners of the MMM, is calling upon activists who represent labor, organized and unorganized, working class issues and anti-war groups to attend the town hall meeting in order to strategize to help build a powerful, united movement against government-sponsored wars against the workers and poor at home and abroad.

Fighting against the racism and poverty that Hurricane Katrina helped to expose will be a focus of this meeting. Some of the issues to be addressed are: taking to task a criminal government that serves the interests of only a wealthy few; supporting the right to return to the Gulf Coast region of thousands of mainly Black and poor people displaced by Katrina; fighting so they can determine how their communities should be restored; the freezing of all Halliburton type contracts to rebuild for profit; reinstating the prevailing wage under the Davis-Bacon Act; stopping the military recruitment of people of color and other poor youth to fight in wars for profits, like in Iraq.

Speakers at the town hall meeting will include Clarence Thomas, Brenda Stokely, Chris Silvera and Saladin Muhammad, all national leaders of the Million Worker March Movement; Nellie Bailey, Harlem Tenants Council organizer; author Jack Rasmus; Larry Holmes, Troops Out Now Coalition representative; and John Parker, International Action Center-Los Angeles.

The MWMM, founding national D.C. rally a year ago, brought together thousands of rank-and-file workers, the unemployed, immigrants, women, youth, antiwar activists and LGBT people in a call for an independent workers' movement to demand universal health care, repeal of the U.S. Patriot Act, bring U.S. troops home now, the protection of Social Security and pensions and much more. The MWMM is based on the principle of workers speaking in their own name.

Abridged from WW, Oct. 15, 2005.

Colia Clark
Civil Rights Activist

Clarence Thomas
Million Worker March Co-chair
ILWU Local 10 Exec. Brd. Mbr.

Alan Benjamin
San Francisco Labor Council
Editor 'The Organizer'

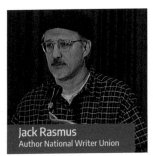
Jack Rasmus
Author National Writer Union

Nellie Bailey
Harlem Tenants Council

Saladin Muhammad
Black Workers for Justice

Chris Silvera
Teamsters National Black Caucus
Chair and Secr. Treas. of Teamsters Local 208

Photos taken from video 'MWM & TNBC Speak Out at Local 639 IBT"

Black trade unionist address the Millions More Movement

Alan Benjamin

On Oct. 15, 2005 an estimated 600,000 to 700,000 people rallied in Washington, D.C., at the Millions More Movement in response to the call by Nation of Islam Minister Louis Farrakhan. Built as a "United Front" of Black working people, the MMM included a broad spectrum of speakers, including three leading Black trade unionists who presented a labor perspective to the crowd. Following are major excerpts from these three presentations.

Patricia Ann Ford, Representative, Metro Washington, D.C. Labor Council

On behalf of my President, Joslyn Williams of the D.C. Labor Council, I bring you greetings. But more important, I'm going to bring you my feelings. I'm going to quote one of our well-known, famous civil rights sisters, Fannie Lou Hamer: 'I am sick and tired of people trying to tell us who our leaders are.'

I am sick and tired of them trying to tear up the labor movement, when we have done more to lift people out of poverty than anybody on Capitol Hill or the White House has. I am sick and tired of the racism in this country.

America got undressed with Katrina. We now know; the world now knows. So we just shouldn't be talking about globalism from an economic perspective, we should be talking about globalism from a community perspective.

So, let us join with out brothers and sisters around the world. Let's join with each other and act like this is our country and demand what we want and tell them who's going to speak for us, not allow them to tell us when and how and who can speak.

"Millions More Movement"
U.S. Capitol

From a video of Patricia A. Ford with Clarence Thomas and Chris Silvera.

Chris Silvera, Chair; Teamsters National Black Caucus

We're here on behalf of the labor movement. Ninety-five percent of Black people work. Of that 95 percent, 30 percent are members of the labor movement, organized labor.

I'm here this afternoon with my brother, Clarence Thomas of ILWU Local 10, and I'm here representing the Teamsters. We want to bring greetings to all working people here. We're making a call for a more militant labor movement.

The labor movement has empowered workers, bringing us the eight-hour day, vacations, pensions, and an end to child labor laws. Today we mobilize in our own name, and as Black trade unionists we make a call for workers to galvanize to protect the gains of the labor movement.

We make a call to mobilize to protect Davis-Bacon Act, to protect the prevailing wage laws for the re-building of the Gulf Coast region. We demand a living wage for all workers, we demand protection for all multi-employer pension plans, we make a demand for the immediate repeal of the anti-union Taft-Hartley Act, we

make a demand for the right to strike without being replaced.

"These are the demands of workers. It is immediate, we can achieve it now. We must mobilize, we must march, we must blockade the Gulf Coast region to ensure that workers will not work for poverty wages.

Clarence Thomas, Co-Chair, Million Worker March Movement; Exec. Bd., ILWU Local 10

This is a defining moment, for not only the labor movement, but for all of us. Workers need to speak in their own name. It's time for us to start forging new alliances. There needs to be a stronger alliance between organized labor, unorganized labor, the interfaith community and progressives.

We need to take a stand right now with respect to what's going on in the Gulf Coast. We need to take a stand by mobilizing with the people in the Gulf area and saying that we will have prevailing wages, that there will be the right of return for those who live in the Gulf area.

No matter how great this particular event must be and is, we have to understand that we have to build a movement. We have to begin to build a united front, to come together around common-ground issues, putting our differences aside. Because we don't have much time to do what's necessary. And I say to you right now: Seize the time! Long live the Millions More Movement! Long live the spirit of the Million Worker March!

Abridged from Unity & Independence, Fall 2005.

Millions More Rally calls for organizing a Black United Front Coalition

Angaza Laughinghouse

We knew the Millions More Movement Rally was going to be a special day … Oct. 15, 2005! By 9 am hundreds of thousands of African Americans had gathered on the Washington, D.C. mall and on steps of the U.S. Capitol.

A range of issues including: The wars in Iraq and Afghan that are killing our youth; The U.S. government's deadly response to Hurricane Katrina, that is building political energy and awareness like a Category 5 Hurricane. As a result, many African Americans came out to demonstrate their outrage at the government's and big business response to the crisis.

The Millions More Movement was more than a commemoration of the 1995 march which drew 1.2 million participants. This broad coalition of our diverse Black community, of workers, youth, revolutionaries, entrepreneurs, business, students, womens' organizations, cultural nationalists, etc.; spoke to several major issues that unite us.

Black workers must speak in our own name!

Million Worker March Movement co-leader Chris Silvera, president of the Teamsters National Black Caucus, spoke to the lively crowd reminding them: "90% of our community consist of Black workers, unemployed and employed, retired and young. Our youth must struggle with all labor for a living wage, universal health care, retirement security, workers' right to organize and collectively bargain for better wages and conditions."

Another MWMM leader, Sister Brenda Stokely, from the northeast,

stated that: "We must organize Black workers and caucuses in our unions and labor organizations for more democracy, to better fight the bosses/government's sexist/racist practices and policies."

Farrakhan: U.S. gov't handling of Katrina was 'criminal neglect'

Minister Louis Farrakhan of the Nation of Islam addressed the issues of Katrina: "When a parent leaves a baby in a hot car during a hot steamy summer day, the parent is leaving that child at risk of harm! This is called criminal neglect. Although there may not be an intent to harm."

The U.S., the state, and the local governments, knowing the lack of financial and material resources, capability limited by poverty, the powerlessness of the poor oppressed class (mostly Blacks) left in the path of Hurricane Katrina, should be brought to justice for their crime of criminal neglect. Our society, our community and the world community should move to hold the U.S. Government accountable for "Criminal Neglect!"

We need to hold them accountable for using Gulf Coast relief money for corporate "No Bid" give aways, while they refuse to give "clean-up relief workers" the prevailing living wages to rebuild their lives!

Go home and build the Black United Front

Farrakhan charged the crowd to, 'build broad unity' in our community as we return home from the rally; to do the hard work of organizing our people to win on the issues that confront us; and be prepared for

Angaza Laughinghouse

opposition from 'within' as well as 'without by the ruling powers that are vested in keeping us oppressed and exploited.'

The MMM Rally, is a new start to organize a unified, broad, independent Black United Front coalition. As we move towards a March 2006, "Second National Black Political Convention" in Gary, Indiana, the last took place in 1972, we must learn the valuable lessons of the 1960s through the 1990s.

Build a broad "Black People Congress in Gary" that will operate on fundamental social democratic principles, that will smash opportunistic deal-making with Democratic and Republican Parties. Do the necessary organizing to make certain that Black workers have a voice and a greater presence with an organized agenda.

Organize "Gulf Coast Survivors Solidarity and Support Committees" to build a national movement to support justice and reconstruction for Hurricane Katrina and Rita survivors from New Orleans and the Gulf Coast of the U.S. south.

Abridged from the December 2005 "Justice Speaks," Black Workers for Justice

Longshore workers:
'Shut It Down May Day 2016'

Cheryl LaBash

The Baltimore Workers World Party meeting on Oct. 11, 2015, featured veteran African-American longshore workers Clarence Thomas and A.J. Mitchell. Both had attended the "Justice or Else" commemoration of the 20th anniversary of the 1995 Million Man March in Washington, D.C. a day earlier.

Thomas and a delegation of ILWU members only a month ago attended the Charleston, S.C., "Days of Grace" Labor Day march, and conference, in the aftermath of the racist murder of nine women and men at the Mother Emanuel African Methodist Episcopal Church, as well as the videoed police killing of Walter Scott. The longshore workers traveled from the West Coast to demonstrate solidarity with International Longshore Association Local 1422, whose membership lost family in the church murders.

So it was in Charleston that an ILWU Local 10 resolution calling for a "National Day of Mourning" on May 1, 2016, International Workers'

Day, was announced. And it was news that broke the night before on Oct. 10 of reports justifying the police slaying of 12 year-old Tamir Rice in Cleveland that focused Thomas' reflections on the MMM, and the "Justice or Else" march.

Thomas recalled that the 1995 MMM was on a work day, yet huge crowds of working-class Black men traveled to Washington, D.C., instead of reporting to their jobs. Although the call was from Nation of Islam (NOI) leader Minister Louis Farrakhan, most of the attendees were not Muslims or adherents of the NOI. Thomas appreciated the difficulty of organizing such a huge outpouring during a work day based on his activist experiences in the Northern California labor movement and in organizing the MWM in October 2004.

MWM organizers Brenda Stokely, Charles Jenkins and Clarence Thomas at the 2005 Millions More Movement.
Photo: Delores Lemon-Thomas

Organized labor had a voice at the 2005 MMM. Speakers included Pat Ford from the Service Employees union, Chris Silvera from the Teamsters National Black Caucus and Thomas. Farrakhan spoke at an earlier TNBC Educational Conference.

In his talk Silvera challenged the Bush administration for suspending prevailing wage requirements, opening the door to substandard wages for the cleanup of the devastation from hurricanes Katrina and Rita. Facing such wide opposition from the labor movement, the Bush administration later reversed itself.

Referring to the just-released report laying groundwork for the exoneration of the cops who killed Rice, Thomas thought that if the police were not held responsible there might be a large response to a "National Day of Mourning" on May Day in ports across the U.S. "That could be the spark," said Thomas.

To be heard, labor must Shut It Down, Thomas asserted: "That is the only leverage we have. All of this talk means absolutely nothing. We have

Jerome Johnson and John Krusuki, Local 19, Anthony Lemon, Local 52, Clarence Thomas, Local 10, Chris Silvera, IBT and Gabriel Prawl Local 52 at the 2015 'Justice or Else March' on the 20th Anniversary of MMM in Washington, D.C.

had discussions about cameras on dashboards, cop's body cameras, and they still are killing us.

"If we can get longshore workers across the country to shut down for eight hours on International Workers' Day 2016, and it is on a Sunday, I think we may be able to get some real serious discussion about income inequality and structural racism."

In response to a question about organizing a general strike when most workers, especially young Black workers most directly affected by police brutality, are non-union, Thomas clarified that the proposal was for the ILWU and the ILA longshore workers to take action. But he also pointed out that some of the most effective mass actions have been by unorganized workers, including the 2006 Great American Boycott of Latino workers when 90% the Port at Los Angeles and Long Beach were shut down by the immigrant port truckers.

"We are not suggesting that you go out on the same day," Thomas said. "It is important for the longshore workers to do it. We could have rolling strikes. The day before May Day for fast food workers. We don't have one general strike. We could have a whole bunch of strikes on different days.

"Longshore workers are in a very strategic position. There are no other workers like them anywhere in the world because they are responsible for the movement and documentation of maritime cargo and passengers.

"If people are wondering what they can do after the Justice or Else gathering, this is something workers can do. Shut it down on May Day all over the country. Let's get it going."

Abridged from WW, Nov. 5, 2015.

Clockwise, Phillip Alley, Frank Jefferson, Clarence Thomas, David Stewart, Andrew Dulaney, Leo Robinson and Howard Secrease, attended the Million Man March in Washington, D.C., 1995.

ILWU members find spiritual renewal and brotherhood on pilgrimage to the Capitol

Clarence Thomas *The Dispatcher* Nov. 20, 1995

On October 16, 1995, one of the most significant events in the history of our nation took place. More than one million Black men gathered at the nation's Capitol for the Million Man March. ILWU members were there.

During the ILWU Longshore Division Caucus Sept. 27-30, a resolution was passed by the delegates to endorse and support the intent and purpose of the Million Man March, heeding a call for atonement, spiritual renewal, solidarity and political action. ILWU members traveled 3,000 miles to participate in an event

the magnitude of which is yet to be determined. I am proud and honored to say that I was among them.

Why a million man march?

The march was needed to bring attention to the conservative right-wing forces in America that are fomenting an increasingly hostile climate for the aspirations of poor and working people in general and the Black community in particular. These forces have succeeded in eliminating many gains achieved in the civil rights struggles of the 50s and 60s.

New Orleans in the aftermath of Hurricane Katrina, August 2005.

CHAPTER 4

Katrina Survivors demand Reparations

Katrina survivors, marched in New Orleans on Aug. 29, 2006, on the first anniversary of the hurricane from the site where the levees were breached in New Orleans' Ninth Ward to a rally at Congo Square. They demanded: 'Justice for Katrina Survivors,' including the right to return and full reconstruction of the Gulf Coast. Pictured here a memorial in Congo Square with the names of those who perished.

WW photo: Monica Moorehead

Union leaders see hurricane survivors' conditions as
'21st century slave ship'

Clarence Thomas and Chris Silvera

Hurricane Katrina forces us to deal with the whole question of self-determination and how national oppression pertains to the issue of the class struggle. There is a sentiment among the Millions More Movement leadership that the devastation and catastrophe will create an environment to bring various organizations together in building a national movement.

Representing the Million Worker March Movement (MWMM), we were invited by the Nation of Islam's, Millions More Movement delegation to visit the George R. Brown Convention Center, where thousands of Gulf Coast evacuees were being warehoused. The delegation included: the Honorable Minister Louis Farrakhan, along with his Chief of Staff Leonard Farrakhan Muhammad; Minister Robert Muhammad, Southwest regional representative of the NOI; Ben Chavis, CEO of the Hip-Hop Summit Action Network; economist and syndicated columnist Julianne Malveaux; and others. After our visit to the convention center we attended a Town Hall meeting for victims to share their hurricane experiences. Texas has become the "home" to over 250,000 displaced victims of Hurricane Katrina.

'21st-century slave ship'

We did not visit the Astrodome, but we were told that it's like Motel 6 and the Brown Convention Center is like the Hilton Hotel in terms of the quality of life there. To us, the situation at the convention center is nothing more than a slave ship for the 21st century. People have no privacy. They are not being treated with dignity. People cannot come in and out without going through security measures like you would experience at a prison. For people going through such deep-seated trauma, you want to put them in the best possible situation.

'A wake-up call for Black America'

Following the Brown Convention Center visit, approximately one thousand evacuees were taken by bus to the town hall meeting, at the Power Center, in Houston. Erykah Badu, the hip-hop artist, was there and spoke. The meeting was dedicated to the hurricane victims. For the first time, people had the chance to collectively share their experiences and ordeals before the world.

People stepped up to the microphone to tell their stories; some shouted in anger about how they were neglected by authorities as they tried to escape to safety. Others cried as they described their fear and frustration about having lost everything, going days without food and water and some even contemplating suicide.

There was also a sense of hope expressed by some of the speakers including Farrakhan, that despite the neglect from governmental agencies, material things are replaceable and that this experience can be used to come together to build a movement to deal with racism, class divisions and poverty in the U.S.

Chris Silvera, Maria Farrakhan (Louis Farrakhan's daughter), and Clarence Thomas in Houston, Sept. 11, 2005.
Photo: Nation of Islam

The MWMM has a plan!

One of the most important accomplishments of our visit was that the MWMM came up with a list of demands for the Gulf Coast survivors along with Saladin Muhammad's Sept. 5, 2005, statement on "Hurricane Katrina: The Black Nation's 9/11!" See page 206.

Hurricane Katrina forces us to deal with the whole question of self-determination and how national oppression pertains to the whole question of the class struggle. Because it's very clear from the images of what was seen on television, Black people are economically exploited and politically oppressed.

Labor must be at the table!

Organized labor has been silent on all of this. They have not been saying, "This is an outrage!" They're not calling on their elected officials that they've endorsed to say, "This is an attack on labor!"

Once again, it is absolutely clear from the manner in which labor has responded, in terms of the officialdom of labor, that they're primarily concerned with business unionism and not with how trade unions should be

At the Houston Convention Center with Dr. Ben Chavis.

fighting for economic and social justice on behalf of the entire working class. That's the failure.

There were discussions today involving the NOI and MWMM leadership regarding having Gulf Coast survivors speak at the October 15, Million More Movement rally and making it an event that launches a united front movement dealing with the hurricane crisis and beyond.

The Million Worker March calls for labor to be at the table with the community, and with Katrina survivors. As African American trade unionists, who organized the MWM, we understand that labor needs to be part of the struggle of that legacy of fighting for economic and social justice for the working class.

Clarence Thomas is an executive board member of ILWU Local 10, co-chair of the Million Worker March Movement, and executive committee member of the Alameda County Central Labor Council. Chris Silvera is secretary-treasurer of Teamsters Local 808, chairman of the Teamsters National Black Caucus, and a Million Worker March Movement Eastern Regional co-convener.

Excerpts from the book **"Marxism and Reparations, The Black Freedom Struggle"** *edited by Monica Moorehead Sept. 19, 2005.*

MILLION WORKER MARCH MOVEMENT

1632 7th Street, Oakland, California 94607   510-4446272, Fax 510-632-6816

The Million Worker March Movement issues an urgent call
No More Lives Destroyed at Home or Abroad!

This call is to all committed activists, their organizations and communities. We must Build a Powerful and United Movement that is capable of:

• Taking to task a criminal government that only serves the interest of the wealthy few.
• Substantially supporting those organizing a powerful fight back in the Gulf Region, including the right to return, right to determine the rebuilding plan, freezing contracts to "Halliburton," reinstatement of wage protection, i.e., Davis-Bacon Act.
• Maintaining its allegiance only to the poor and workers and reject any attempt to subordinate their interest.
• Stopping the War profiteers from sending our children to kill others as a means to control the world's resources.
• Mobilizing the majority to STOP the Government and corporations from conducting business as usual

October 2004, the Million Worker March Movement brought together rank-and-file workers of organized labor, the unorganized, the unemployed, immigrants, women liberationist, youth, anti-war activists and other activists committed to freedom and justice. They raised their own voices to state their Agenda:

• National Health Care
• Repeal of Taft Hartley (Anti-worker laws)
• Repeal of exploitive trade agreements
• Protection Social Security and Pensions
• Repeal of the U.S. Patriot Act
• Full Employment with a living wage
• Bring The Troops Home Now
• The right to strike without replacements

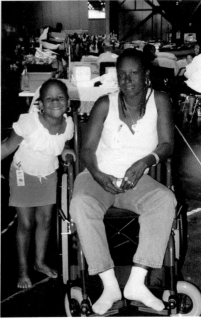

Katrina survivors at R. Brown Convention Center in Houston on Sept. 11, 2005.

Photos: Chris Silvera

Hurricane Katrina:
The Black Nation's 9/11!

Saladin Muhammad

The magnitude of the destruction and human suffering caused by Hurricane Katrina to the people and communities of the Gulf Coast region, while not the result of an act of "terror," is directly the result of a profit-driven system of capitalist exploitation reinforced by the national oppression of African American people in the U.S. South, a region where the majority of Black people live and where the conditions of oppression, poverty and underdevelopment are most concentrated.

As anti-imperialists and progressives engage in work to build support for the Gulf Coast survivors, we must have an analysis and political context for properly understanding the reasons for this crisis and the contradictions surrounding its aftermath.

The response to this human tragedy must be more than a humanitarian response in order to deal with the magnitude and complexity of issues, and the various levels of local, national and international network mobilizing that must take place to build a powerful movement for social justice.

It is important to define the race and class character of the crisis and to call on the larger working class to unite with its most oppressed section, the African-American working class, which is also the predominant basis of an oppressed nation, historically denied real democratic rights and subjugated by U.S. imperialism.

The government's failure to correct this impending danger, known far in advance, that led to the unfolding massive human tragedy, helps all to see the racist nature of the U.S. capitalist system and how the system of African American national oppression is guilty of crimes against humanity.

The demand for self-determination is both a national democratic demand for African American people's power as well as a demand for working class and women's power. Thus, national, working class and gender democracy are essential pillars of the politics of a Black working-class led African American liberation struggle.

African American National Oppression

African American national oppression was/is definitely a major factor contributing to the magnitude of the disaster caused by Katrina. National oppression takes on more factors than race. It includes where people live and work and has a working class character represented by the most exploited strata of the U.S. working class. Thus African American national oppression is at the deepest point of the intersection of race, class and gender oppression and exploitation of the U.S. working class.

As more than 90 percent of Black people throughout the U.S. are workers, African American national oppression places its primary emphasis on the exploitation and oppression of Black workers and their communities. More than two-thirds of New Orleans' inhabitants were African American. In the Lower Ninth Ward, a neighborhood that was one of the hardest hit, more than 98 percent were Black.

The slow U.S. federal and state government responses to natural disasters like Hurricanes Katrina and Floyd in North Carolina in 1999, made clear that the value of Black and working class life is subordinate to capitalist property and profits.

The racist economic, social and political policies of the U.S. government and capitalist system shape society's attitudes. They seek to isolate, criminalize and scapegoat African Americans as social pariahs holding back the progress of society.

The characterization of the Black working class in this way is a part of the continuous ideological shaping of white supremacy that gives white workers a sense of being part of another working class, different from that of the Black working class. This often leads many white workers to act against their class interests, discouraging them from uniting with the Black working class in struggling to seek common, equal and socially transformative resolutions. However, on the ground in New Orleans, the working class regardless of race forged a level of unity as survivors, led by the African American working class that the system wants to hide.

The media's different descriptions of acts of desperation and survival by Blacks and whites in obtaining food and supplies following Katrina, "looting" versus "finders," is an example. The police and National Guard were ordered to stop looking for survivors and to stop "lawlessness."

Bush's statements about getting tough on "looters," along with that of Louisiana Gov. Kathleen Blanco when she said, "These troops are battle-tested, have M-16s that are locked and loaded, know how to shoot and kill and I expect they will," made clear that New Orleans and the

Gulf Coast were becoming areas of military occupation.

White supremacists like David Duke and others have utilized this disaster and repressive racist climate to promote hatred for African Americans and Latinos and have encouraged the formation of racist vigilante bands roaming areas of New Orleans, attacking Black and Brown people.

The refusal by thousands of mainly Black people to leave their homes was initially described by the media as the main problem related to the slow evacuation efforts. Nothing was mentioned about the low wages, poverty and high rates of unemployment preventing people from leaving.

After it took almost a week for the government evacuation effort to begin, leaving people to fend for themselves without electricity, food and water, it became shamefully clear and impossible for the media to hide that the government had made no provisions for a major evacuation.

The acts of heroism by the people themselves in rescuing their neighbors, although not emphasized by the media, could be seen throughout the coverage. These acts have no doubt reduced the numbers expected to die resulting from the slow "emergency" rescue response of the government.

The so-called "looting" and "lawlessness" must be addressed and placed in proper context. When it became clear that there was no emergency evacuation plan in place, people waiting up to a week before any major evacuation effort began – people were forced to take desperate actions for survival, both until they got "rescued" and for their uncertain future as refugees with no resources and sources of income. TVs, appliances, etc., become a form of capital and a means for trade during a crisis.

Some survivors were forced to "steal" cars and buses to get their families out of the areas. Should this be considered a crime? NO! Also, when people are oppressed, neglected and left to die, they often engage in spontaneous acts of rebellion, striking out against those who control wealth and power.

This is why the term "racism" without the context of national oppression and imperialism is grossly inadequate in describing the scope and depth of the impact of the U.S. oppression of African American people. It fails to point out the impact that African American national oppression has on influencing the standard of living and social conditions of the general working class, regardless of race, especially in areas where Black workers make up a majority or large minority of the population.

U.S. Imperialism on the Domestic Front

Not only did the U.S. federal and state government place the working class of the Gulf Coast in impending danger, including failing to develop a planned emergency response, it has also refused the aid of other countries like Cuba and Venezuela, which have offered to send doctors, medical supplies and fuel to help the people.

U.S. imperialism has decided that it has the sole right to decide whether the majority African American and working class people and communities in the Gulf Coast region have the right to survive. This is an international human rights question where the demand for self-determination must be part of the resolution.

Though food, water and transportation trickled in, the government made sure the oil industry was taken care of fast. Over 10 major refineries were knocked out of commission in the Gulf region, but many of them were back operating within the week.

Bush released federal oil reserves, but oil companies jacked up gas prices to a criminal level anyhow. Environmental safeguards were loosened for gasoline producers to allow more pollution. All this while the four largest oil companies made profits of nearly $100 billion over the last 18 months. Why isn't this labeled as corporate "lawlessness"?

Many of the African American working class of New Orleans and the Gulf Coast have been "evacuated" in some cases thousands, of miles away from their communities. More than 1,800 children are still separated from their families almost two weeks after the flood. Many feel that their communities will never be restored and that they won't be returned home.

They have good reason to feel this way, as some majority African American communities have begun to experience gentrification, the moving of Black and poor people out of the inner cities and replacing them with more affluent and predominantly middle and upper class whites.

Many reports have warned that profit-driven development along the coast had done away with millions of acres of wetlands that buffered coastal communities from storms. Thus, this disaster and the racist and capitalist circumstances surrounding its occurrence and aftermath raise the issue of "ethnic cleansing."

The media in cities receiving the "evacuees," are describing them as "the worst of New Orleans' now-notorious lawlessness: looters, carjackers and rapists." This sounds like the racist labels placed on working class and poor refugees from Latin America and the Caribbean, who have been forced to leave their countries and come to the U.S. for economic and political reasons. Many African Americans experienced these labels when they were forced to migrate out of the South in the first half of the 20th century.

Many African Americans in particular will experience problems related to the loss of identification documents in the flood, and fall into a similar status as undocumented and immigrant workers. Their residential and citizenship status will be challenged,when it comes time to get disaster relief subsistence. The racist nature of U.S. capitalism often makes being a refugee and undocumented worker within one's "own" country a unique reality for African Americans and other oppressed nationalities, especially during times crises.

We should expect the U.S. to use this disaster to increase restrictions on forced economic immigration. It is important that African Americans and Latinos unite in challenging the refusal of survivors' assistance on the basis of the lack of documentation and to point out that countries in Latin America have offered aid to all, without regard for citizenship status or nationality, even though the U.S. seeks to overthrow their governments.

Forging unity between African Americans, Latinos and working class ethnic groups throughout the U.S. and especially within the Gulf Coast region in responding to this disaster is an important part of a larger, more difficult and absolutely essential process of building U.S. multinational working class unity and international solidarity against U.S. imperialism.

The future of New Orleans and the Gulf Coast in terms of the reconstruction of the historical communities, but at a higher quality of social conditions and standard of living, will be decided by the U.S. corporate class, the white power structure, unless there is an organized and combined African American and working class struggle led by the African American working class. Such a struggle must take the popular form of a combined struggle for African American self-determination and workers' power, and must have an international component. Emphasizing the majority African Amer-

ican working class character of the Katrina-U.S. imperialist disaster is important to exposing its unmistakably racist character.

The Katrina disaster exposes how U.S. imperialist war in Iraq and throughout the Middle East, including billions of dollars of support for Israel's occupation of Palestine, is directly connected to the human tragedy in the Gulf Coast region.

Vital resources, which had been allocated to fix the substandard levees in New Orleans and the erosion of marshlands along the coast that caused the enormous flooding and massive loss of lives, were cut and shifted to the war budget.

Both Republican and Democratic administrations have refused to maintain the levees that protect New Orleans. Hurricane and flood control has received the steepest federal funding reductions in New Orleans history, down 44.2 percent since 2001.

The emergency management chief for Jefferson Parish, La., told *The Times-Picayune*" in June 2004: "The money has been moved in the President's budget to handle homeland security and the war in Iraq." Requests for an additional $250 million for Army Corps of Engineers levee work in the delta went unmet.

There are close to 15,000 National Guard from the Gulf Coast region in Afghanistan and Iraq fighting unjust wars. Their equipment, including generators, water purification systems and other needed life support and disaster preparedness supplies were overseas as well.

As was the case during every war engaged in by this country, African Americans and working people were sent to fight, kill and die to bring about so-called "freedom" while they and their communities are denied freedom from hunger, imminent dangers, racial violence, gender oppression and state repression.

Now the U.S. military has the audacity to start recruiting at the Gulf Coast Survivors evacuation shelters in various parts of the country. This is outrageous, as it was the U.S. war in Iraq that was responsible for diverting funds away from repairing the levees in New Orleans.

It is very important to draw the trade unions into this movement, the Gulf Coast wide coalition and national support network. They should be encouraged to contribute directly to a survivors and people-driven support coalition in the region.

It is important that workers see that trade unions have a broader concern and commitment to the needs of the working class and not just to their immediate members.

Trade unions can play an important role in supporting those evacuated to their cities, especially outside of the South. The unions can help in adopting families and shelters in their areas. They must also play a leading role in helping to combat the racist attempts by the media, white supremacists, the religious right and others to alienate and scapegoat survivors evacuated to their cities by educating their members and getting them actively involved in support efforts.

The movement in the Gulf Coast region requires the organization, and leadership of the African American liberation struggle to help unite a broad, multi-national, multi-racial and international campaign for social justice and reconstruction. A Right of Return Committee should be organized and headed by a prominent African American activist figure to begin promoting a campaign for the right of a speedy return.

Saladin Muhammad is National Chair of Black Workers For Justice and a co-convener of the Million Worker March Movement in the South.

To read the entire article go to: workers.org/2005/us/hurricane-0922/

MILLION WORKER MARCH MOVEMENT

1632 7th Street, Oakland, California 94607   510-4446272, Fax 510-632-6816

The Million Worker March Movement's Proposed Initiatives for the Survivors of Hurricane Katrina

The crisis that continues to unfold from Hurricane Katrina demands bold, massive and comprehensive programs and initiatives. It's time for the billions that have been given to bailout corporations, funding the war in Iraq, and tax cuts for the rich be spent on the displaced survivors of the Gulf Coast Region.

An immediate freeze and moratorium on awarding of an contracts until survivors of the Gulf Coast have input in those decisions.

- All people especially those from New Orleans have the right to return to the Gulf Coast Region.

- Extended unemployment and emergency financial relief based on a living wage until people are returned to their homes and jobs.

- A People's Referendum on all decisions affecting the political and residential issues of the Gulf Coast survivors.

- Establish a public works program funded by the federal government and the big corporations to rebuild New Orleans and the affected Gulf Coast Region.

- Employ the survivors at a living wage as required by the Davis-Bacon Act (1931) to work on clean-up and reconstruction of New Orleans and the Gulf Coast, with the right to organize unions.

- The list of priorities regarding reconstruction and cleanup up should hospitals, schools and other public service oriented infrastructure

- It is critical that affordable housing be constructed with the participation of those displaced using "Habitat for Humanity" as a model or a facsimile thereof utilizing journeymen tradesmen for on the job training.

- All displaced survivors nor matter where they are, be able to register and receive an absentee ballot for all elections.

- U.S. Post Offices be utilized as the site of a National Registry where displaced survivors can be located.

- Issue massive bankruptcy executive order for Gulf Coast survivors forgiving all debts of property lost or damaged by the disaster.

- Major contracts for clean up and reconstruction of New Orleans Black and working class communities be awarded to Black contractors

- The U.S. immediately allow other countries to provide aid to the survivors where needed.

- Exemption for the payment of taxes for displaced survivors for 2 years.

The magnitude of the destruction and human suffering caused by Hurricane Katrina to the people and communities of the Gulf Region requires these and other initiatives be implemented without exceptions.

'This is criminal'

Malik Rahim reports from New Orleans

If you ain't got no money in the U.S., you're on your own. People were told to go to the Superdome, but they have no food, no water there. And before they could get in, people had to stand in line for 4-5 hours in the rain because everybody was being searched one by one at the entrance.

I can understand the chaos that happened ofter the tsunami because they had no warning, but here there was plenty of warning. In the three days before the hurricane hit, we knew it was coming and everyone could have been evacuated.

The hurricane hit at the end of the month, the time when poor people are most vulnerable. Food stamps don't buy enough but for about three weeks of the month, and by the end of the month everyone runs out. Now they have no way to get their food stamps or any money, so they just have to take what they can to survive.

This is criminal. These people are dying for no other reason than the lack of organization.

Excerpts from Rahim's report.

Katrina survivors deserve reparations

Monica Moorehead

The Oct. 15, 2005 rally of the Millions More Movement, with its focus on the Gulf Coast crisis, could not have come at a more opportune time in the U.S. This mass gathering will, no doubt, help to shine a humongous spotlight on the central issues of racism, national oppression, and poverty, especially in light of Hurricane Katrina.

The winds and flooding caused by Hurricane Katrina did more than physically destroy countless lives and homes throughout the Delta region, including in Biloxi, Miss., Mobile, Ala., and especially New Orleans. Millions of people here and worldwide were deeply horrified to see the insensitive manner in which the Bush administration as well as local and state officials left tens of thousands of poor people, the vast majority of them Black, to suffer and die needlessly during and after Katrina hit, especially in New Orleans.

No other single event in recent U.S. history has more forcefully unmasked the heinous reality that national oppression, a devastating combination of white supremacy and poverty that impacts people of color disproportionately, does exist inside the wealthiest, most powerful, imperialist country in the world. This is what really lies beneath the collective negligence of those in power.

The Katrina crisis helped to expose for so many just who are the haves and have-nots in society. Katrina showed that the have-nots are not just individuals in the ones or twos, or even in the hundreds or thousands, but in the millions. Not only are the have-nots the poor, officially 37 million people who live in poverty and extreme poverty, but many are African American, Latin@, Arab, Asian and Indigenous, out of proportion to their numbers in the overall population.

And sitting on top of the have-nots are those who own and control everything in society, those consumed with capitalist greed, the ruling class. They are the Fortune 500 CEOs, an exclusive club of multi-millionaires and billionaires, mostly white, straight males who worship making profits, not serving human needs. And those who occupy the White House, the U.S. military hierarchy and other seats of power are willing servants for the ruling class.

For African-Americans, Latin@s and other people of color, enduring racist oppression in its overt and covert forms has become a fact of life for many generations. The videotaped brutal beating of Robert Davis, a 64-year-old African American retired teacher, by racist New Orleans cops is an all too familiar reminder that racism is, as the old saying goes, "as American as apple pie."

The White House and the profit-hungry corporations they represent have made it clear through their actions that Black people, immigrants and the poor, including whites, will not be welcome back to New Orleans. Thanks to their hostility towards the poor and Black people, they want to use the Katrina tragedy to transform New Orleans into a playground for mainly affluent whites. That can not be allowed to happen. In fact, many Black activists from around the country, especially in the South, have

Dianne Mathiowetz, Aloyd Edinburgh Jr., Monica Moorehead, and Aloyd Edinburgh Sr. Clarence Thomas met with survivors, including the Edinburghs, from 9th Ward of New Orleans in August 2006.

Photo: Delores Lemon-Thomas

quickly come together to say no to this racist gentrification plan.

Grassroots redevelopment plan

These Black activists, including leaders of Black Workers for Justice, MWMM, Community Labor United, Millions More Movement, Malcolm X Grassroots Movement, December 12th Movement and many others have collectively set up the People's Hurricane Relief Fund as a vehicle for establishing solidarity committees nationwide to build a united front to win real justice for the Katrina survivors.

What kind of justice for the survivors? Justice that includes the right of Black Katrina survivors to return to their respective homes and to rebuild their communities in any fashion that they want; the right to a decent and guaranteed income provided by state and federal governments; the right to a living wage including upholding the prevailing wage laws under the 1931 Davis-Bacon Act; the right to decent housing, not the substandard housing that many of the Katrina survivors had before the hurricane even hit; the right to control reconstruction funds to rebuild their communities, not for no-bid Hallibur-

Congo Square on Dec. 10, 2005.
Photo: Gloria Verdieu

9th Ward signs. WW photo: Monica Moorehead

Brenda Stokely and Jaribu Hill at an anti-war rally in Washinton, D.C., Sept. 24, 2005. Photo: Julia LaRiva

ton contracts; the end to martial law including police terror and the right to decent health care and education.

All these demands and more encompass the fundamental right to self-determination and reparations that have been systematically denied to African Americans since the days of slavery and the overthrow of Reconstruction following the Civil War. Some of these organizers and their supporters have called for a national conference of Katrina survivors on Dec. 9 in Jackson, Miss., and a national march in New Orleans to raise the right of return for these evacuees.

All of these demands would be justified even if it weren't for the Katrina crisis but this crisis has helped to galvanize the Black movement in a such way not seen since the 1960s. But these Black forces need and deserve the full support and solidarity of broader progressive forces and are starting to get it.

The Troops Out Now Coalition, along with some of these Black forces, has helped to initiate a Dec. 1 nationwide day of absence, a day of no school, no work and no shopping, to shut down war, racism and poverty. That day marks the 50th anniversary of the arrest of Black seamstress Rosa Parks, who in 1955 refused to give up

her seat to a white man on a segregated bus in Montgomery, Ala. Her heroic action not only sparked the Montgomery bus boycott but launched the modern-day civil rights movement.

Already, there are many hundreds of endorsers for this day of nationally coordinated protests.

Anti-war activists can play a strategic role in supporting the demands of the Black led People's Hurricane Relief Fund by demanding that the hundreds of billions of dollars being spent on brutal wars and occupations against Iraq and Afghanistan instead go to provide human needs at home.

There is no better way to show concrete anti-racist, working class solidarity with the Katrina survivors than to support the efforts of the People's Hurricane Relief Fund and the actions planned for Dec. 1, 9 and 10.

Abridged from WW, Oct. 20, 2005

Saladin Muhammad
WW photos: Monica Moorehead

Delores Lemon-Thomas, Clarence Thomas and Dianne Mathiowetz at Katrina Memorial in Ninth Ward, New Orleans, Aug. 29, 2006.

Police run wild in New Orleans

Larry Hales

The state repression in New Orleans, especially against African American people, continues to intensify in the aftermath of the Katrina catastrophe. For instance, reminiscent of the videotaping of the 1992 brutal beating of Rodney King at the hands of four white Los Angeles cops, a similar incident has now occurred in New Orleans.

On Oct. 9, 2005, an Associated Press television producer captured on videotape two white cops beating 64 year-old Black retired schoolteacher, Robert Davis. A third cop shoved the producer and tried to seize the tape from him. The tape has been made available for the whole world to see. Davis was arrested for public intoxication, assault and resisting arrest. Davis stated that all the charges against him were false and that he will be seeking compensation.

The racist cops who attacked him have been put on leave without pay. The police have announced an "investigation" into the incident, which will most likely amount to a slap on the wrist for the cops.

Even though the big business media could not ignore what the tape showed, they are clearly trying to whip up sympathy for these cops in general to offset the terror that the police have unleashed on the Black and poor population. The media are excusing police brutality by dwelling on the alleged post-traumatic stress they are suffering. But what about the real post-traumatic stress that the survivors of Katrina have had to endure, including the on-going demonetization by the New Orleans Police Department and the mainstream media?

In the days following Hurricane Katrina, as the misery of the tens of thousands of New Orleanians who were left to bear the brunt of the devastating storm began to compound, salt was heaped on the wounds of the residents of the city and the poor and people of color that went beyond the borders of the Gulf Coast.

The corporate media began to paint horrific pictures of a New Orleans descending into chaos, where the inhabitants of the city were killing, raping and torturing one another. This false, racist coverage was broadcast everywhere, all to divert ire away from the true criminals and the gross criminal neglect that led to close to a thousand reported deaths, with more left unaccounted for.

Recently, the superintendent of the racist police department resigned, amid reports of these gross distorts by local officials and the media. People at the Superdome died while waiting for help; one person committed suicide.

Wherever these reports came from, local officials worsened the situation by using them to depict Black people and the poor of New Orleans as subhuman. State and national officials followed suit, and the media ran the reports hourly, often embellishing, but with no actual footage to substantiate the rumors.

Chaos of the unnatural kind

There was chaos. But the chaos was of a capitalist nature. The only emergency planning consisted of ordering those who "have the means" to evacuate, quartering thousands more in facilities with no food or water, and asking millions of others to "pray down the hurricane," as Governor Kathleen Blanco of Louisiana suggested.

Further injustice came as the horrors of New Orleans revealed that the levees began to fail and millions of gallons of water poured into the city. The media denigrated the poor, overwhelmingly Black inhabitants of the city, labeling people searching for food as "looters."

There was at least one caption that depicted two sets of people differently, one Black, the other white. One caption showed a Black couple with food and labeled them "looters." Another caption from the same news source showed a white couple with food and described them as "finding" food.

Whatever footage existed of so-called "looters" showed people taking food and clothes, not fighting over the items, but helping one another. Yet none of this was widely shown. There are images that exist of great individual heroism, like strangers pulling next-door neighbors on inflatable mattresses, and of a young man who was able to confiscate a bus, fill it with evacuees and drive them to Houston.

Over 15,000 people waited at the New Orleans Convention Center, starving and thirsty, withering in the blistering heat and humidity, even as fetid water was permeating the New Orleans atmosphere. This was broadcast all over the world, but the head of FEMA at the time, Michael Brown, claimed to not be aware. Yet he was not above relating fictional stories of mass rapes, murders and "looters."

The National Guard was let loose, along with local police who have a history of brutality and corruption, and they were given the go-ahead to shoot to kill. One television interviewer was able to capture the sentiments of so many. The reporter, wading in waist-deep water, ran into

National mainstream media depicted two sets of people, one Black, the other white. A caption showed a Black couple with food and labeled them 'looters.' Another caption from the same news source showed a white couple with food and described them as 'finding' food.

a group of three young Black men. When the young men heard that police and the National Guard were allowed to kill, they lifted their bare feet out of the water and said, "Why would they shoot us when we don't have shoes? People lost everything and we don't have shoes, so we went to get us some shoes."

It was people like these young men who were being targeted, who were left behind and being hunted for trying to meet basic needs. The stores would be declared a total loss and recoup their losses from insurance companies. Not to mention that these very stores had robbed the people of New Orleans of their labor, paying meager wages and little to no benefits.

This is to be expected, as the media is hardly anything else other than the bull-horn for the rulers and their aims. It is not to be expected that the media would report on killings that could be attributed to the police and National Guard, as they rolled into the city prepared to protect property and shore up the French Quarter. In fact, in the days after the hurricane hit, New Orleans looked more like a militarily occupied zone than an area devastated by a powerful storm.

Instead of resembling an area organized to help the people, New Orleans looked like an occupied area in Iraq.

One thing that the media could never gloss over is the great outrage at the racist coverage, and that outrage will grow this fall with the Black led Millions More Movement and the Dec. 1, 2005 strike to shut down the war, racism and poverty. No amount of praying, or obfuscation coming from the corporate media, will pray down this coming storm of righteous anger.

Abridged from WW, Oct. 20, 2005.

Malcolm Suber
Katrina survivor from New Orleans; People's Hurricane Relief Fund

'I have been in New Orleans for 27 years, leading many, many struggles of the working-class, oppressed African American nation there. I compare what happened to us in New Orleans to what happened to my ancestors when we were kidnapped and stolen from Africa.

The method and means that they got us out was like us on the auction block once again. Men and women, mothers and children, sisters and brothers were split up. When you got on the bus, you didn't know where you were going.

They had officers with guns and soldiers with guns on the bus. You couldn't get off the bus.

Many of us who have been active in New Orleans decided to pull together as a united front all of those who had been active in fighting on behalf of the working class and poor people of New Orleans. And we had a meeting a week after the storm, in Baton Rouge, where we began to talk about the necessity of building a movement with supporters around the country to allow our people to get back on their feet and to return home.

We have to build an action to take on the inaction of the government which has exposed itself."

*Excerpts from the book "**Marxism & Reparations, The Black Freedom Struggle**" edited by Monica Moorehead Sept. 2005.*

In the days after the hurricane hit, New Orleans looked more like a militarily occupied zone than an area devastated by a powerful storm.

March on New Orleans

Lead banner in New Orleans on December 10, 2005

Photo: Gloria Verdieu

'We Shall Not Be Moved'

Leilani Dowell

The streets of New Orleans were filled with angry and determined protesters, survivors of Hurricane Katrina and their supporters, on Dec. 10, 2005, International Human Rights Day. Chanting: "We're back to take it back" and "No justice, no peace!" a crowd estimated at 5,000 marched from the historic Congo Square, also known as Louis Armstrong Park and described by Reuters as "a centuries-old meeting place where African slaves once gathered to trade, play music and dance," to City Hall for a rally, where they demanded "Justice after Katrina."

The march was a vibrant display of the culture and resistance of the people of New Orleans. Babies were pushed in strollers alongside marching youth and elders. Groups represented on the march included Community Labor United; Common Ground Collective; Million Worker March Movement; Millions More Movement; Troops Out Now Coalition; Fight Imperialism, Stand Together; New Black Panther Party; ANSWER and

others. African drums accompanied the chants, and the march was led by the Soul Rebels, a New Orleans brass band.

Survivors traveled from as far away as Texas and California to speak their minds and lend their voices and feet to the effort. The march and rally were organized by the People's Hurricane Rights Fund and Oversight Coalition, which raised money to bring survivors home for the day. The PHRF announced a list of demands to be presented to the office of Mayor Ray Nagin that included an end to evictions, the right to return for evacuees, and a halt to Mardi Gras festivities in the midst of the devastation of the Black community.

The rally at City Hall was chaired by New Orleans resident and activist Malcolm Suber, who told the cheering crowd: "We want our voices heard. We're here standing tall, ready to fight. The government promises everything and gives you nothing. This government don't give a damn about poor people, the working class, and especially don't give a damn about Black people."

New Orleans activists with 'Mama D' at podium.   Chokwe Lumumba, left, Malik Rahim, above.   Malcolm Suber.   Photos: Monica Moorehead

Speaker after speaker pressed their demands and told horror stories of the travails they had to endure at the hands of the government, both local and federal. One protester noted, "They could get troops over to Iraq overnight, but couldn't get anyone here to save our people." Another young man told about being beaten, along with his pregnant sister and another female friend, at the hands of the police.

An environmental justice activist led the crowd in a chant: "We have the right to healthy and safe neighborhoods." She spoke about the high levels of toxic arsenic that have been found in every area where flooding occurred, and how the federal government has consistently done nothing about it. The toxicity in the wake of the hurricane was exacerbated by the environmental racism that allowed housing for the poor to be built on top of a landfill. When the hurricane hit, these toxics leached out into the rest of the area.

'Mama D,' a New Orleans resident who opened her own home early in the wake of Katrina for relief efforts, described the

poverty and neglect that Black people in the region had suffered long before Katrina struck. She demanded, "Come clean, New Orleans! Enough of my babies are dead, and it didn't start with Katrina!"

Abridged from WW, Dec. 22, 2005.

Left, Micheal Hoard, ILWU Local 52, Gabriel Prawl, ILWU Local 19, Dyan French Cole 'Mama D' and Clarence Thomas, ILWU Local 10 in New Orleans, September 2006.

Photo: Delores Lemon-Thomas.

Condemned home in the 9th Ward. The meaning in the X: on top date inspected; left, signed by task team; right - NE - no entry; F/W - food and water left; gas off etc., Bottom, how many bodies found in house.   WW photo: Monica Moorehead

Brenda Stokely and Chris Silvera gather signatures during a petition campaign in New York City.

WW photos: John Catalinotto

Survivors of Hurricane Katrina and supporters rallied nationally in January, 2008, to demand the right to return to their homes.

INTERNATIONAL TRIBUNAL ON KATRINA & RITA:

We charge genocide

Monica Moorehead

Aug. 29, 2007, marked the second anniversary of when Hurricane Katrina began its reign of devastation along the Gulf Coast, especially Louisiana, Mississippi, and Alabama. Before many residents could recover from Katrina, Hurricane Rita quickly followed, deepening the mass destruction and the suffering.

While George W. Bush and Democratic presidential candidates Hillary Clinton and Barack Obama were in New Orleans taking their photo-ops on the anniversary, two other significant events were taking place.

One was a march in the morning of about 1,000 people from the Industrial Canal, site of the broken levee in the lower 9th Ward, to Congo Square. The other was the opening session of the International Tribunal on Katrina and Rita, which was boycotted by the national mainstream media.

The tribunal, initiated by the People's Hurricane Relief Fund (PHRF), was supported by national and international organizations, and attended by hundreds of survivors of both hurricanes along with political and community activists from around the country and the world.

The purpose of the people's tribunal was to expose to the world a multitude of crimes against humanity amounting to genocide carried out by the U.S. government on a local, statewide and federal level against the survivors, then and now.

It has already been documented that it wasn't Hurricane Katrina that destroyed 80 percent of New Orleans; it was the flooding from the broken levees, especially in the largely African-American and poor Lower 9th Ward,

that resulted in the highest numbers of deaths, unimaginable repression and massive forced displacement.

While billions of dollars have rapidly been directed to restoring the economy of New Orleans, notably the industries related to tourism, the Lower 9th Ward still resembles a weed-infested ghost town, as thousands of residents struggle to rebuild and to return home.

The goals of the tribunal were to fully expose the human rights abuses committed by the U.S. government and its agencies and operatives in the aftermath of Hurricanes Katrina and Rita; to attain national and international recognition as Internally Displaced Persons (IDPs) for all the survivors of Hurricanes Katrina and Rita; to attain comprehensive reparations for all Gulf Coast IDPs (including migrant workers and communities); to strengthen the Gulf Coast Reconstruction Movement and build a broad national and international movement in support of its aims and demands; and to hold the rogue U.S. government accountable for its human rights abuses and crimes.

Bush, along with Louisiana Governor Kathleen Blanco, Mississippi Governor Haley Barbour and New Orleans Mayor Ray Nagin, were sent letters by the tribunal's prosecution team requesting their presence at the tribunal to face various charges. Not only did they not show up for the tribunal; they never responded.

The tribunal judges came from Brazil, Venezuela, Mexico, France, Guadeloupe, Martinique and the U.S. The conveners traveled from Algeria, Brazil, South Africa and U.S. cities.

Opening the 'casket' on human rights violations

Nkechi Taifa, a tribunal prosecutor from the Legacy Empowerment Center, officially opened up proceedings. She spoke eloquently about how "the spirit of Emmett Till" was being felt at the tribunal. It was almost 50 years ago to the day that Till, a 14-year-old African American youth from Chicago, was tortured and shot to death in Money, Miss., by racists for allegedly whistling at a white woman.

Emmett's mother, the late Mamie Till Mobley, demanded in 1955 that the casket of her murdered son be opened for the world to see his horribly disfigured body. Taifa stated that the tribunal is about "opening the casket," the casket in this case being the racist, anti-poor treatment that hurricane survivors still face today.

The ten charges that the prosecuting team would present at the tribunal with evidence and testimony were gross violation of the human rights:

1. to be free from racial discrimination, including discrimination based upon perceived immigration status;
2. to return, including the resettlement and reintegration of internally displaced persons;
3. to life, human dignity, and recognition as a person;
4. to be free from torture and other cruel, inhuman and degrading treatment or punishment;
5. to freedom of association and assembly and freedom of movement;
6. to work, to adequate health care and adequate housing;
7. to an adequate standard of living, freedom from poverty and right to education;

The August 29, 2007 International Tribunal on Katrina and Rita. Wearing black cap is MWMM leader Clarence Thomas.

GREAT FLOOD COMMEMORATION

One Year later...

Honor and remember our loved ones who have passed.

Fight for the right to return for all those still displaced.

DAY, AUGUST 29TH, 2006

8. to vote, including electoral rights and right to participate in governance;
9. to a fair trial, to liberty, security and equal protection under the law; and
10. to privacy, family life, and missing relatives.

Roderick Dean testified on prisoners' rights abuses. His voice filled with emotion, Dean, who was falsely arrested in New Orleans before Katrina, talked about the subhuman treatment that he and other prisoners suffered when Katrina hit. Prisoners were not allowed to leave their cells and had to wade through feces-contaminated water; he and other prisoners were denied their medications; and prisoners had to endure languishing on a bridge in 105-degree heat for days without food, water or toilet facilities. Dean was released from jail in early December 2005 with no charges.

Charlene Smith, a child nutritionist, was arrested and jailed for writing a bad check in Walmart because her mother and children needed items to survive after Katrina. Some of her experiences in jail included being housed with 19 other women in one cell, hearing a prisoner scream while being beaten by a guard and denied sanitary napkins and medications.

Under the police brutality session, Romell Madison, a Black dentist, spoke on how his brother Ronald was shot five times in the back by white cops with assault rifles on the Danziger Bridge. Last December, white cops were indicted for killing several members of the

Bartholomew family, including children, trying to flee the flood waters across the same bridge.

Impact of Katrina on women

Mayaba Levanthal, from the group Incite! Women of Color against Violence, gave testimony on how poor women, especially single mothers, were unlikely to be evacuated during a hurricane because they don't have the means to do so. She also spoke on the failure to reopen public schools; the lack of shelters in the midst of a rise of domestic violence and sexual assault; and how stress disproportionately impacted Black and poor women. An estimated 187,000 workers lost their jobs

New Orleans resident Myrna Merricks at Katrina Memorial, August 2006.

WW photos: Monica Moorehead

in New Orleans post-Katrina, and 50 percent of those jobs belonged to women.

Stephanie Mingo, from the St. Bernard section, gave testimony on her struggle to survive as a single mother of four and a grandmother. Her 89 year-old mother died on a bridge waiting to be rescued. A food service technician, Mingo stated that she still couldn't get home because "she is not one of the rich folks." She stated that 90 percent of those living in public housing before Katrina were women. Mingo said: 'My rent is higher than my income. I am discriminated against because I am a woman." She kept repeating, "I want to go home."

Military occupation

Malik Rahim, executive director of Common Ground Collective in New Orleans (CGC), gave testimony on the racist military occupation of New Orleans post-Katrina. The occupation included the National Guard, state and local police, Blackwater mercenaries and local armed white vigilantes, all working in concert with each other. Many of the National Guard

had just returned from Iraq.

CGC is a grassroots, multinational organization that provides free health care, clothing, tools and much more to Katrina survivors. Rahim spoke on seeing dead bodies, of Black men shot to death in the streets. He saw military personnel driving by survivors, rather than rescuing them.

Portions of a documentary called "Welcome to New Orleans," directed by a Danish filmmaker, were shown at the tribunal. White vigilantes, with their guns drawn, "jokingly" spoke on how they were "protecting their neighborhoods and their city from Black men." Rahim reminded the tribunal that this reign of racist terror in New Orleans was sanctioned by Gov. Blanco, who publicly gave orders to the National Guard to "shoot to kill" to restore "order."

Dale Warren testified on the horror that she witnessed when the police forced her to stay in the Convention Center with thousands of others. Lights and air conditioning were shut off. Dead bodies were found in the freezer instead of food. Toilets were overflowing. She witnessed a man

The U.S. government blocked entry to a Cuban medical team experienced in hurricane relief and was prepared to aid survivors. Cuba is known all over the world for its record of protection and medical care.

shot in the head by a national guardsman after he jumped on his jeep. The man had told her that he wanted to commit suicide. The guardsman kept driving after the shooting.

Sobukwe Shukura, an Atlanta representative of the National Network on Cuba, gave testimony on how the U.S. government denied Cuba's gesture to provide humanitarian aid to Katrina survivors. This aid included close to 1,600 disaster-trained physicians along with medicines and equipment. The U.S. also denied relief aid from Venezuela. The snubbing of this aid is further proof of how the U.S. government put politics before saving the lives of poor people, especially if they are African Americans.

Other tribunal sessions focused on gentrification and housing rights, children's rights, forced dispersal, environmental racism, health care, cultural rights, Indigenous rights, voting rights, labor and migrant rights, misappropriation of relief, education rights and more.

Chokwe Lumumba, a lawyer from Mississippi and a Republic of New Afrika member, gave a powerful talk summarizing the findings and putting the testimonies in a historical framework of resisting racist repression. He asked the judges to consider all the testimonies presented over the three days as nothing more than genocide.

Abridged from WW, Sept. 13, 2007.

Thousands rallied in Times Square, N.Y., and then marched to the U.N. to demand an end to the U.S. occupation of Iraq, no war on Iran, and the right of Katrina and Rita evacuees to return to the devastated areas of the U.S. Gulf Coast, March 2006.   Photo: Roberto J. Mercado

Delores Lemon-Thomas with her aunt Ms. Elmer Decquir, who transitioned in May 2020 at 99 and 9 months old. She lived in the 9th Ward, evacuated to Atlanta before returning to her home in NOLA.

MILLION WORKER MARCH MOVEMENT

1632 7th Street, Oakland, California 94607   510-4446272, Fax 510-632-6816

November 29, 2005

Brother Curtis Muhammad,

It was great seeing you at the recent National Conference to Reclaim Our Cities in Detroit, November 12-13th.

I would like to formally acknowledge the work of the People's Hurricane Relief Fund and Community Labor United regarding the relief effort for residents of the Gulf Coast.

As you know the Million Worker March Movement and the International Longshore and Warehouse Union Local 10 in San Francisco were able to secure 10 forty feet containers from various employers of ILWU Local 10 to send much needed supplies to survivors of Hurricane Katrina.

Thank you for all your assistance in facilitating our efforts to get the items our union members and community volunteers sent to the Gulf Coast.

You should be aware that additional containers will be coming from an ILWU Local in the Pacific Northwest in a few weeks. We will once again be relying on your help.

I look forward to seeing you in Jackson, Mississippi on December 9th and New Orleans on Dec 10th.

In Solidarity,

Clarence Thomas
National Co-chair MWMM
ILWU Local 10
Executive Board Member

Delores Lemon-Thomas on the porch of her uncle Shep Davis' house 350 yards from the levee. The signs say: 'Please don't bulldoze' and includes contact information. The house was rebuilt using bricks after Hurricanes Betsey in 1965 and Camille in 1969.

Photos: Clarence Thomas

I AM COMING HOME!
I WILL REBUILD!
I AM NEW ORLEANS!

WW photos: Monica Moorehead

Puget Sound Coalition aids in relief – reconstruction – return

Gabriel Prawl

The Puget Sound Katrina Relief and Reconstruction Committee (PSKRRC) is a coalition of unions and community groups established after the Gulf Coast devastation left by Hurricane Katrina.

PSKRRC is a part of a nationwide network that has been formed to support relief efforts and political organizing led by Louisiana based Community Labor United (CLU).

The CLU network has responded to the crisis by launching the People's Hurricane Relief Fund and Oversight Coalition to ensure hurricane survivors aren't stripped of their homes, land, jobs and rights by the Bush administration rebuilding process. This effort by the labor movement and its allies is rapidly gaining recognition and momentum nationally. The joint effort is demanding:

- The right to return for all displaced people;
- People's participation in all aspect of the reconstruction process;
- Affordable housing, living wage jobs, quality healthcare and education; and
- Justice for people neglected or abused by the government.

In Seattle, dock workers from the ILWU, African American Longshore Coalition (AALC), MWMM with members of ILWU Local 19 and 52 have joined forces with the CLU, ILA Local 3033 in Baton Rouge, the Martin Luther King Jr. County Labor Council and the Port of Seattle to set up the Burt Nelson Memorial Katrina Relief Warehouse. The warehouse is named after a Seattle dockworker who organized in solidarity with African American Longshore workers to fight

racism and corruption on the New Orleans waterfront during the 1930's.

Unions like the Teamsters Local 174, the Teachers' Union and others have contributed supplies and labor.

In the spirit of the MWM, we are mobilizing in our own name. We're working as a grassroots labor-to-labor, community-to-community effort to directly aid other working class people and help to build an independent national movement to compel government officials and politicians to meet the needs of people most impacted by Katrina.

The PSKRRC raised over $10,000 in donations that was used in shipping and operation expenses of two containers full of building supplies to help with the reconstruction. In one container, there is estimated to be $19,000 in donated materials and close to $50,000 in the other.

ILWU Local 19 members donated $11,000 dollars in the form of a Lowes account to 'Mama D,' an activist in New Orleans who is working to rebuild her community. Also, the ILWU Coast Committee donated $3,261 to help in the shipment of the container. PSKRRC contributed $4,478.

Rank-and-file members donated tools and money. Shoreline Community College donated a generator and building supplies. Community organizations like LELO and FSP, a part of the PSKRRC played a role in public relations, organizing, and fund raising. Black community organizations like Woman for Police Accountability, Paul Robeson Peace and Justice, and A. Philip Randolph Institute (APRI) are working with others in the ongoing relief effort.

Change Agent

R. V. Murphy

GABRIEL PRAWL saw his share of poverty and prejudice while growing up in Panama. The plight of the Gulf Coast and the city of New Orleans in the aftermath of Hurricane Katrina resonated with Prawl, who's one of the founders of the Puget Sound Katrina Relief & Reconstruction effort. "There's always been poverty in that area, but the hurricane exposed it," he says. "And the racism is heavy."

A longshore worker in ILWU Local 19, Prawl hopes to load 10 cargo containers with hand tools, power tools, and various other items including flashlights, first aid kits, and bottled water. The containers are currently stored at the Burt Nelson Memorial Katrina Relief Warehouse at Terminal 106, but will eventually be transported to an open port in Baton Rouge. The local Community Labor United (CLU) will then deliver it to neighborhood-based distribution points.

Abridged from "Real Change Issues," Dec 2005 - Jan. 2006.

The committee was under the impression that the railroad was going to ship the containers for free. In the end, the ILWU Local 52 was unable to negotiate with the railroad. **It is shameful when large national companies refuse to help, allowing those in need, to be neglected and forgotten.**

It only takes each person involved to be a humanitarian to achieve the goal of the people of New Orleans: **'Relief-Reconstruction-Return!'**

Abridged from document by Gabriel Prawl, ILWU/AALC September 15, 2006.

ILWU mobilizes relief for Katrina victims

John Showalter

Kris Hillyer ran into her daughter's bedroom and began packing clothes when she first saw the devastating images of Hurricane Katrina victims flashing across her television screen after the Category Five storm crashed into New Orleans. Hillyer, an ILWU Local 52 marine clerk works as an on-dock rail supervisor at the Port of Seattle.

Hillyer's actions are mirrored in the cash and material donations given by many ILWU local members Coastwise. The Coast Committee and the International have, together, donated $10,000 to the AFL-CIO's hurricane relief fund.

Local 19's Jack Block, Jr., is coordinating hurricane relief donations and their shipment south with Hillyer, Gabriel Prawl of Local 19 and others from ILWU Puget Sound locals, and member organizations of the Million Worker March. Tacoma Local 23 members paid $2,900 for Teamsters Local 174 drivers to transport items to a distribution center in San Antonio, Texas.

Members at other locals in California and the Colombia River region are giving through the AFL-CIO fund and coordinating with local churches, donors' companies and distribution centers for evacuees in cities around the country.

At Local 10 in San Francisco Bay Area, just days after Hurricane Katrina struck, retired longshoreman Reverend Joe Noble, Local 10 President Trent Willis, and Executive Board member Clarence Thomas met with U.S. Representative Barbara Lee (D-CA), member organizations of the Million Worker March and local NAACP officials to plan material donation efforts to the Gulf Coast. Mountains of community donations piled up in front of the Grand Lake Theater in Oakland were then loaded into containers. On Sept. 8, longshore workers began packing the first San Francisco

Hurricane relief donations — water, blankets and other necessities were packed in containers. Eight containers shipped out from Oakland, two from San Leandro and one from San Francisco.

Local 10 members load a container with Katrina relief supplies outside their dispatch hall.

Photo: John Showalter

Leith Kahl of Local 19 In Seattle and his brother Silas, a Local 19 casual, load hurricane relief donations headed for a distribution center in San Antonio, Texas.

Photo: Amber Trillo

Local 10 passed a resolution opposing Bush's repeal of the Davis-Bacon Act for the rebuilding of New Orleans. That Act requires contractors receiving federal money pay their workers at the prevailing wage. The resolution supports the right of New Orleans residents to rebuild their own communities.

container in the Local 10 hiring hall parking lot with water, blankets and other necessities. Eight containers in Oakland and two in San Leandro and one in San Francisco were shipped out.

Local 10 also passed a resolution opposing Bush's repealing of the Davis-Bacon Act for the clean-up and rebuilding of New Orleans. That Act requires contractors receiving federal money for construction projects to pay their workers at least the area prevailing wage. The resolution also supports the rights of New Orleans and Gulf community residents/victims to rebuild their own communities as part of a federally funded public works program, and not have outside contractors awarded the work.

In Southern California, volunteers from ILWU Local 13, building trades unions and other unions within the L.A. County Federation of Labor are working to convert warehouse space into a one-stop relief center that will house 100 families displaced by Katrina.

The Inlandboatmen's Union, the ILWU's Marine Division, has set up an "IBU Hurricane Relief Fund, …donating to help the dozen IBU members in the Gulf who have been affected by Katrina.

Abridged from The Dispatcher, September 2005.

Frank Taylor, a retired ILA longshore crane operator and a Katrina survivor in New Orleans, holds hooks that he used when he began to work on ships 50 years ago.

Photo: Clarence Thomas

MWMM contingent wearing tee shirts made for the 2005 Million More Movement March at the New Orleans 'Justice after Katrina' march in December of the same year.   WW photo: Monica Moorehead

CHAPTER 5

MAY DAY
INTERNATIONAL WORKERS' DAY

2005 to 2018

MAY 1   NEW YORK CITY 2005   WW photo: Deirdre Griswold

CUBA   BOLIVIA   VENEZUELA

Anti-war coalition looks to March 19 & May Day

David Hoskins

Protesters will hit the streets on the weekend of March 19, 2005, to mark the second anniversary of the U.S.-led invasion of Iraq. The March 19 'Troops Out Now' demonstration in New York City will be at the center of these protests.

Protesters will march to billionaire Mayor Michael Bloomberg's house to demand money to rebuild cities instead of for imperialist occupation. They will be joined by demonstrators marching from a rally at Harlem's Marcus Garvey Park.

The Troops Out Now Coalition, has worked hard to linking opposition to the war against Iraq to the struggle for jobs, health care and education.

The combined cost of the Iraqi and Afghani occupations is almost $6 billion a month. Meanwhile, poverty and homelessness are skyrocketing. Most of the 40 million impoverished people are women and their children. (CBS News, "Victims of Minimum Wage," March 13)

The Bush administration's agenda has intensified the conflict between the working class and the ruling class, whose interests are represented by the government.

As the Troops Out Now Coalition looks beyond the weekend's demonstrations it will continue the struggle to integrate the class war at home within the context of the war abroad. Black, Latin@, Asian, Arab, Native and white people, members of the multinational working class, make up the leadership of this anti-war coalition and contribute to its progressive character.

The Million Worker March has made reviving May Day one of its principal aims. The MWM-NYC, a key member of the anti-war coalition, is already working on May Day here. There is much discussion about how to revive May Day as a revolutionary day of resistance for workers. During its March 9 coalition meeting, the Troops Out Now Coalition decided to join this effort to revive May Day.

Origins of May Day

Many workers in this country do not know about the origins of May Day. This is because of the capitalists' largely successful effort to erase working-class history and disassociate today's workers from their legacy of militant struggle.

May Day has its origins in the struggle for better working conditions in the U.S. The first May Day protests took place in 1886, when the American Federation of Labor called for a national strike to demand an eight-hour workday. Over 350,000 workers answered the call and participated in the strike.

Cities around the country were paralyzed as railroads and manufacturing plants were forced to close. Chicago was particularly affected by the strike. After two days of protest,

police attacked striking workers, killing six. When workers protested in Chicago's Haymarket Square on May 4, 1886, and 180 cops attacked, a bomb was thrown. One cop was killed. Police then fired on the crowd. Two hundred people were wounded and seven cops later died, probably from friendly fire.

Eight radical labor leaders were rounded up and framed on charges of conspiracy. All were found guilty. Seven were sentenced to death.

Albert Parsons, August Spies, George Engle and Adolph Fischer were executed. One defendant committed suicide and three others were eventually pardoned.

In 1889, the communist Second International declared May 1 an international working-class holiday in commemoration of the Haymarket martyrs. May Day has lived on for more than a century as an international day of protest for the most class-conscious workers around the world.

What better way to call attention to the international class struggle and demand that U.S. imperialism stop its assault on workers at home and abroad than to use this year's May Day to highlight the connection between domestic class struggle and foreign occupation?

As protesters around the country gear up for the March 19 actions, anti-war organizers are saying it is important to look ahead. They say the struggle to reinvigorate May Day will help the working class get back in touch with its militant history, and strengthen it for the struggles to come.

Abridged from WW, March 16, 2005.

JOBS NOT WAR:
Bring the troops home now
SOLIDARITY MAKES US STRONGER
End the occupation of Iraq, Stop endless war

Unite Against Racism
And Political Repression

- We demand jobs at decent wages, health care, housing, & education for all

- Solidarity with immigrant workers — we will not be divided

- Hands off Social Security

- Stop the reinstatement of the draft

- Solidarity with the peoples of the Middle East, Asia, Africa, Latin America and the Caribbean

NEW YORK CITY · MARCH 19, 2005
Million Worker March Movement and the Troops Out Now Coalition

Endorsers of May Day include: NYC Labor Against the War; Int'l Action Center; Nat'l Immigrant Solidarity Network; Artists & Activists United for Peace; Brenda Stokely, President District Council 1707 AFSCME; NYC Council Member Charles Barron; Chris Silvera, Secretary Treasurer. of Local 808 IBT, Chairperson of Nati'l Black Teamsters Caucus; Pam Africa, International Concerned Family and Friends of Mumia Abu-Jamal; NYC AIDS Housing Network; NY Coalition to Free Mumia Abu-Jamal; NJ Solidarity- Activists for the Liberation of Palestine; Harlem Tenants Council; Korea Truth Commission; Network in Solidarity with the People of the Philippines; Haiti Support Network; Queers For Peace & Justice; NY Committee to Free the Cuban 5; NY Committee for Human Rights in the Philippines; Al-Awda NY, Palestine Right to Return Coalition; BAYAN-USA; Workers World Party; Homeless Action for Necessary Development; DAMAYAN Migrant Workers Assoc.; Int'l Socialist Organization; FIST; Jersey City Peace Movement; Monterey County Peace Coalition; New England Human Rights Organization for Haiti; People's Solidarity for Social Progress; Iraq Solidarity Campaign (Brit.); No Draft No Way; Boston Stonewall Warriors; Women's Fightback Network, Boston; Central NJ Coalition for Peace & Justice; Casa Freehold; Baltimore All Peoples Congress; People Judge Bush; Movement in Motion; SNAFU- Support Network for an Armed Forces Union; Steve Gillis, Pres., USWA Local 8751 Boston School Bus Union.

The March 19, 2005 march from Harlem to Central Park.   WW photo: G. Dunkel

Resolution by ILWU Local 10 to Reclaim May Day

WHEREAS in 1884 the Federation of Organized Trades and Labor Unions passed a Resolution in Chicago stating that eight hours would constitute a legal day's work from and after May 1, 1886 ...

WHEREAS this Resolution of 1886 summoned workers in the U.S. to carry out a General Strike to achieve the goal since all legislative methods had failed ...

WHEREAS ILWU Local 10 hereby calls upon the ILWU Longshore Division, all trade unions and working people, both organized and unorganized, to Reclaim May Day, to acknowledge May Day as a central and pivotal part of our history, and to recapture the spirit of struggle that it represents ...

WHEREAS the government, the corporations that dominate it and the officialdom of labor in the past have sought to conceal and deny the true history of May Day, seeking to erase the memory of May Day and to suppress the class struggle that it embodies ...

WHEREAS they have replaced May Day with "Labor Day," a date devoid of any historical or class struggle significance ...

WHEREAS by seeking to eradicate the history of May Day, the powers that be have sought to break our ties to our own militant past and to separate labor from its historic role in the ongoing fight for social justice ...

WHEREAS May Day is celebrated by labor and working people the world over with the exception of the United States whose working class gave birth to May Day ...

WHEREAS each May Day workers in every country joined together to unite against the growing global corporate onslaught which pits workers against each other, a global attack that has intensified ...

WHEREAS the suppression of May Day was intended to isolate U.S. workers and prevent an international workers' response to the ever increasing global nature of the attack upon us ...

WHEREAS by Reclaiming May Day at a time when privatization, outsourcing and the mad race to the bottom pit workers against each other everywhere, making ever more critical the need for international unity in struggle among working people ...

WHEREAS by Reclaiming May Day as an International Day of struggle and unity we take a decisive step in reversing the attempts to isolate U.S. workers and to build international labor solidarity ...

WHEREAS in Reclaiming May Day we pay homage to the historic mobilization of 1886 that won us the eight hour day and prepared us for the battles ahead ...

THEREFORE BE IT RESOLVED that the U.S. Labor Movement in the interests of working people the world over, reclaims May Day as an International Workers' Day of Struggle and applies to the present the lessons of the historic mobilization of 1886 that galvanized the workers of the world ...

THEREFORE BE IT RESOLVED that, in Reclaiming May Day, the U.S. Labor Movement will launch a united struggle to reverse the brazen attacks upon the gains of the past and advance the interests of working people, with specific campaigns that will become the driving force behind Reclaiming May Day today:

a) National health care with community control over delivery of health care services;

b) Preserve Social Security and the protections it provides to all workers, including the elderly, disabled and the beneficiaries of workers who have died by increasing the taxation on corporations and the rich by the small amount necessary to sustain the Social Security safety net for working people;

c) Protect, restore and increase pensions to guarantee a decent living standard for all retirees;

d) Overturn and restore the vicious cuts in social services at the federal, state and municipal levels that are gutting health, education, housing, libraries, food stamps and vital public programs that benefit working people;

e) Stop the destruction of public education for our children and adults throughout the nation and demand a crash program to fund the rapidly decaying public school systems;

f) Guarantee every worker a living wage and increase the minimum wage to levels that allow all workers to provide decent housing, adequate food, basic transportation and proper education for themselves and their dependents;

g) Protect the right to strike and end the use of scabs (replacement workers) as a strike-breaking tool sanctioned by corporate controlled government;

h) End the forced march to part time and precarious work and guarantee full time work with decent wages that rise with the cost of living, provide secure pensions, health care and full wage retirement for working people;

i) Fight for a crash program to rebuild our cities and provide decent, spacious and affordable housing for all;

j) Slash the military budget and the subordination of government to the warfare state that menaces working people abroad and sends our youth abroad to defend corporate exploitation and profits;

k) Stop the unbridled attack on public sector workers and the attempts to undermine and destroy our public sector unions, notably SEIU and AFSCME I) End the privatization of public services at federal, state, county and municipal levels that replace government services with price gouging, profiteering and union busting;

m) Bring the full force of a united labor movement to defend all workers under attack and stop the corporate use of salami tactics that seek to isolate and pick off one sector of labor at a time, notably hotel workers, airline workers and grocery workers.

THEREFORE BE IT RESOLVED that our union will mobilize our membership to **Reclaim May Day** and join with our brothers and sisters from unions across the U.S. and internationally in demonstrating on May Day 2005 and

THEREFORE BE IT FURTHER RESOLVED that we call upon Central Labor Councils, State Labor Federations and the AFL-CIO to join in the decision to restore May Day to its rightful place in the consciousness of U.S. workers.

– Submitted by Clarence Thomas
ILWU Local 10 in 2005

YES! Time to revive May Day

Fred Goldstein

The most significant thing about this year's attempt to revive May Day as a day of international working class solidarity is that it comes from a segment of the working class itself, particularly from the Black working-class leadership of the Million Worker March, along with others.

May Day has historically been a day for the working class to declare itself as a class against the bosses and to raise its particular demands in each country and its international solidarity with the struggles going on around the world. May Day began as a struggle for the eight hour work day in the United States in 1886. It became international in 1890. From then on throughout the world, including the United States, workers marched under the slogans of the day, against imperialist war, colonial oppression, racism and lynching, freedom for political prisoners, universal suffrage and other demands.

May Day 2005, to be held in Union Square in New York as well as San Francisco, Los Angeles and other cities, is in that tradition.

This 2005 May Day call signed by working class, community and movement leaders, concludes with such demands as: end the occupation; bring the troops home now; jobs at a living wage; housing, health care, education for all; fight against racism and political repression; hands off Social Security; no draft; workers' right to organize; solidarity with immigrant workers; solidarity with lesbian, gay, bisexual and trans people; and solidarity with the peoples of the Middle East, Asia, Africa, Latin America and the Caribbean who are resisting U.S. imperialism's drive to own and exploit them.

The demands end with a clarion call for the rebirth of worldwide solidarity.

Ruling class tried to erase May Day

In the post-World War II era, when U.S. imperialism launched its anti-communist Cold War from a position of hegemony, one of the important tasks of the ruling class, along with witch-hunting communists, socialists, progressives and militant trade unionists of any type, was the suppression of May Day as a working-class holiday. Reactionary elements were rallied to launch physical attacks on May Day parades as the Cold War ratcheted up in the late 1940s.

As far back as 1949, the Americanism Department of the Veterans of Foreign Wars began a campaign to have May Day declared Loyalty Day.

A decade later, after May Day had been suppressed by the witch hunt, Congress passed Public Law 529 designating May 1 as Loyalty Day in an attempt to make sure that it was not revived. In 1961, a joint resolution of Congress revised this and declared May 1 as Law Day USA.

The capitalist bosses were extremely conscious of May Day as a day for the political manifestation of class consciousness and internation-

Clarence Thomas speaking in Union Square, New York.

WW photo: Liz Green

Multi-lingual banners, placards, posters, leaflets and stickers, making the May Day demands were produced in major cities around the country.

alism among the workers and were thoroughgoing in their attempt to wipe it off the calendar of the working class.

Not just a ceremonial May Day

What is distinctive about the attempt to revive May Day as a militant, working class day of political struggle in 2005, is that it emanates from advanced leaders in the workers' movement who have fought the workers' battles and who have watched working-class rights being torn away.

These are the leaders of the Million Worker March. And they want to strike out on an independent political path.

The MWM leaders have watched in anger and frustration as the AFL-CIO leadership has continued along the path of support for the war; ignored racism and the myriad of social and economic issues of the workers; engaged in lackluster, top-down organizing or no organizing at all; and placed much of its reliance, to the tune of hundreds of millions of dollars in workers' dues in the Democratic Party politicians.

The May Day 2005 development does not come out of the blue.

Melissa Roxas from HabiArts/BAYAN-USA and John Parker from the Los Angeles IAC, speak from the bed of a truck in a Los Angeles May Day caravan.
Photo: Julia La Riva

The MWM leaders announced their determination to open up an independent road by coming out on Oct. 17, 2004, on the steps of the Lincoln Monument, in the midst of the presidential election campaign, and declaring that the workers should organize "in our own name."

They linked opposition to the war with struggle for workers' rights at home. In doing so, they had to fight the upper crust of the AFL-CIO leadership, which was committed to the pro-war Democratic Party candidate John Kerry and which was deeply opposed to the independent class politics advocated by the MWM.

Brenda Stokely speaking at the 'Reclaim May Day Rally' in Union Square, New York City.
WW photo: Liz Green

Additionally, the MWM had to contend with various currents in the anti-war movement and radical movement that were panicked by any attempt to divert resources or attention from the Kerry campaign and turned their backs on the ground-breaking effort to chart an independent course.

MWM leaders refused to bow down, and came out publicly for the 2005 revival of May Day from the steps of the Lincoln Monument.

Then they took another historic step forward by uniting with student, youth and community activists and the Troops Home Now Coalition on March 19, 2005, for a joint anti-war, anti-imperialist, pro-working class rally and march on the second anniversary of the Iraq War. This rally, which boldly brought together the workers' struggle and the militant antiwar struggle, was additionally significant because it began in Harlem.

May Day must again become rooted in the working class. Once it does, the connection between May Day, imperialist war and the class struggle becomes a material factor in the struggle that is powerful and truly profound.

Abridged from WW, May 5, 2005.

Berta Joubert-Ceci with Gerardo Cajamarca, Colombian SINALTRAINAL union and Charles Jenkins, TWU Local 100, CBTU in New York City.   WW photo: Liz Green

Revive May Day International Workers' Day
Unite with working and poor people all over the world

The Million Worker March Movement, the Troops Out Now Coalition and other progressive groups are calling for a rally and march in Union Square on May 1, 2005.

Reclaiming May Day reflects a growing consensus that the movement can only move forward by uniting the anti-war movement with the workers' movement and with those communities which suffer the most from war, cutbacks, poverty and repression.

The empire has demonstrated that if allowed it will rule the world by military force, and pit worker against worker on a global scale in its quest for profits. Our challenge is to work harder and act boldly in linking our struggle against the war abroad to our struggle against the war at home.

We cannot depend on the system's elections, its politicians, or any other force but the united power of working and poor people all over the world to accomplish this urgent task.

May Day is about solidarity, standing together. It is about uniting against all that imperialism would use to divide us. May Day is about reaffirming that the future belongs to the people in the world and not a handful of billionaires. May Day belongs to the working class.

The MWMM set the reclaiming of May Day 2005, as one of its principal goals at a meeting of regional representatives the day after its historic Oct. 17, 2004, rally. The Troops Out Now Coalition, which organized the March 19

Contingent of CBTU New York Coalition in Union Square.
Photo: NY CBTU Chapter

march from Harlem to Central Park, has joined MWMM's call. One of the reasons that the March 19 demonstration began in Harlem was to say: "The struggle against the war in Iraq is also the struggle against the war at home."

International Workers' Day grew out of the struggle of working people in this country more than 100 years ago for an 8-hour work day with a full day's pay.

The system has sought to bury the history of May Day in this country.

The government sought to silence and crush radicals and radical ideas in the labor movement, particularly during the infamous 'witch hunt' period of the 1950s and in response to the progressive and revolutionary movements of the 1960s. Their war on radicals, and radical ideas like international solidarity, continues today.

Our interest in reviving May Day does not come from nostalgia for times past, but from the need to nurture a higher political consciousness about how important solidarity and political independence are to the strength of our movement.

We don't need to have a million workers in Union Square on May Day 2005, enough of us can be there to help set the direction for the movement.

Abridged from a call by the Coalition organizing the May Day rally at Union Square in New York April 2005.
WW photo: Deirdre Griswold

Chris Silvera's son Bashiri leads March out of Union Square on May 1, 2005.

Across the U.S. militant labor leaders join with anti-war forces

Deirdre Griswold

New York City is known around the world as the home of Wall Street and of thousands of giant banks and corporations whose glass encased steel towers scrape the sky. Its stock exchanges are linked to investors across the globe through an intricate web of communications.

But on May 1, 2005, another New York reached out to a different world.

For the first time in many years, leaders of working class struggles joined antiwar forces to reclaim May Day, the International Workers' Day that is honored by millions of workers from Asia, Europe to the Middle East, Africa and Latin America. Yet it had been effectively suppressed in the United States even though it originated here with the struggle for the eight-hour day in 1886.

This year's revived May Day started with a rally in Union Square. One thousand people of many different nationalities marched through a working class shopping district to the East Side. They paused at hospitals threatened with closing while chanting, "Money for health care, not for war."

This and other demonstrations to revive May Day in this country were an outgrowth of last October's Million Worker March in Washington, which called for militant working-class action independent of the big business political parties. The largely Black led MWM Movement has teamed up in New York with the Troops Out Now Coalition (TONC), a group of community, labor and anti-war forces that met weekly for several months shaping and building the May Day event.

Almost until the last day, they had to wrestle with police and picket City Hall for the right to march. And when the sound permit for Union Square expired during the final rally, cops marched up and pulled the plug in the middle of remarks by Charles Jenkins, a Transit Workers Union activist and member of the MWMM.

MWMM leaders Clarence Thomas, Brenda Stokely and Chris Silvera had revved up the crowd earlier with strong speeches urging a revival of labor militancy in the U.S.

Thomas had flown in from San Francisco, where he is a well-known militant in the ILWU. His political roots, he told the crowd, go back to the 1960s and the Black Panther Party. Thomas reviewed the glorious history of his union, which has many times walked off the docks in support of workers' liberation struggles, like the anti- apartheid movement in South Africa. It was putting into action labor's great slogan, "An injury to one is an injury to all," he explained.

Brenda Stokely represents thousands of NYC day care workers and is president of AFSCME DC 1707. She urged the union members present to organize to make their leaders fight, and if they won't, "then change your leaders." Going over the struggles of workers today for jobs, health care and other necessities of life that are becoming increasingly hard to get, she was optimistic. "We can win these things," she said. "It's not just in my imagination. Look at Cuba. They have won these rights and we can, too."

Chris Silvera is chair of the Teamsters National Black Caucus and a leader of Teamsters Local 808. He asked, "Why does a $400 billion war budget pass without debate while health care and education are stalled in Congress?" He asked, "Why won't the AFL-CIO organize a national strike to fight for them?"

Gerardo Cajamarca of the Sinaltrainal food industry union in Colombia, whose members include Coca-Cola bottling plant workers, talked of the violence against unionists there that has spurred the union to launch its 'Killer Coke' boycott.

Nellie Bailey of the Harlem Tenants Council, Larry Holmes and Sara Flounders of the International Action Center, and Dustin Langley of No Draft No Way, spoke about the connection between the attacks on workers at home and the colonial occupations of Iraq and Afghanistan.

Teresa Gutierrez explained the importance of the struggle to free the Cuban 5, who are held in U.S. jails for trying to protect their homeland from U.S.-sponsored terrorism.

Leilani Dowell of Fight Imperialism, Stand Together spoke for young people who are demanding jobs and education instead of an economic draft that has forced so many youth into the military.

A taped message from political prisoner Mumia Abu-Jamal had opened the rally. He called on everyone to begin organizing now to make May Day 2006, the 120th anniversary of Haymarket in Chicago, a major event in the rebirth of independent working-class struggle in the United States.

Abridged from WW, May 12, 2005.

May Day celebration draws labor activists

Brenda Sandburg

The spirit of labor leader Harry Bridges could be felt in San Francisco May 1, 2005, as members of his union celebrated International Workers' Day with a call for renewed resistance to exploitation, racism and war.

The International Longshore and Warehouse Union Locals 10 and 34 and the Million Worker March Movement held a rally at a plaza named after Bridges, the renowned ILWU leader who led the militant labor strike of 1934. About 150 labor activists and supporters gathered to reclaim May Day.

Trent Willis, Local 10 president and one of the founders of the Million Worker March Movement, remembered the workers who were killed demonstrating at Chicago's Haymarket Square and the labor leaders who were hung by the government afterwards.

"Working people saw the need for the eight-hour work day so they could come home to their families instead of being worked to death," Willis said. "We pay homage to those who sacrificed their lives, just as those who sacrificed fighting for the Local 10 union hall down the street."

"May Day is about organizing," said Local 34 President Richard Cavalli. "That's the way we put pressure on the government, the way we keep Social Security in place. The only way workers of this world can get the job done is to organize."

Willis and MWMM organizer Keith Shanklin of Local 34 chaired the rally. Others who spoke included Harold Brown, president of Amalgamated Transit Union Local 1555; Alan Hollie, community liaison of ATU Local 1555; Alan Benjamin, San Francisco Labor Council delegate, AFL-CIO; Ralph Schoenman, UAW 1981; and Dick Becker, Answer. The ILWU Drill Team also marched in formation.

Keith Shanklin of ILWU Local 34

Shane Hoff of the San Francisco Bus Drivers United Transportation Union Local 1741 and the International Action Center praised the MWMM, which organized thousands of people to march in Washington, D.C., last October.

"The leaders of the MWM stood up and walked up a steep hill of threats, backstabbing and attacks to do what needed to be done," Hoff said. "They have earned the right to give leadership because nothing important in the liberation of masses has ever been achieved without taking risks and being brave."

Hoff thanked the MWMM for making the reclaiming of May Day a priority.
Abridged from WW, May 5, 2005.

Trent Willis, ILWU Local 10 president speaking at May Day 2005 Rally.

'The leaders of the MWM stood up and walked up a steep hill of threats, and attacks to do what needed to be done,' Hoff said. 'They have earned the right to give leadership because nothing important in the liberation of masses has ever been achieved without taking risks and being brave."

Shane Hoff of the San Francisco Bus Drivers Union Local 1741 and the International Action Center.

WW photos: Brenda Ryan

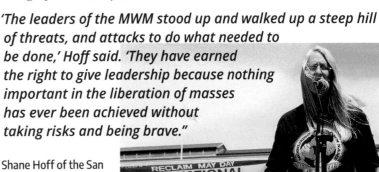

May 1 'Great American Boycott' for immigrant rights gathers momentum

Sharon Black

The national call for a May 1 "Great American Boycott of 2006: No Shopping, No School, No Work" to demand full rights for immigrant workers and their families is gathering momentum. This call, initiated by the March 25th Coalition Against HR4437, a grassroots coalition that grew out of the Los Angeles action that brought hundreds of thousands of immigrant workers into the street, has likened the May action to the Montgomery, Ala., bus boycott of 1955.

The call has struck a chord in many immigrant communities. For many immigrant workers May 1 is celebrated in their home countries as a day to commemorate the working class struggle and is marked with marches and rallies worldwide.

In Los Angeles, taxi drivers have vowed to shut down LAX airport and trogueros (truck drivers) will be closing the harbor. Demonstrations are being planned in cities throughout the country, including Los Angeles, San Francisco, Dallas, Chicago and New York. Wherever possible, students and workers are planning both individual and group action. Many small businesses, particularly in the Mexican community, will be closing.

On April 22, organizers will meet in Chicago to form a national network. Following the meeting, there will be a press conference in Washington, D.C., when Congress reconvenes.

In New York City, the Million Worker March Movement and the Troops Out Now Coalition, plan a May 1 rally in Union Square. They voted to support the immigrant rights movement and the 'Great American Boycott' action. The coalitions held a march and rally last year to revive May Day and were making plans to march again this year.

Chris Silvera, secretary treasurer of Teamsters Local 808 and president of the Teamsters National Black Caucus, said, "We embrace this movement." His union local is hosting the May 1 Great American Boycott 2006 Coalition, which is composed of New York immigrants including Latin@, Filipin@, South Asian, African, and Caribbean communities.

National organizers are making plans to politically and legally support any worker or student who is retaliated against for their participation in activities.

Abridged WW, April 22, 2006.

Chicago

Long Island, NY   Photo: Workplace Project

In May 2006 a Paris street was named for an honorary citizen : 'Rue Mumia Abu-Jamal.'

Boston   WW photo: Liz Green   **Fidel Castro speaks in Cuba.**

San Juan, Puerto Rico   WW Photo: Tom Soto

No business as usual: Millions demand immigrant rights
Super-exploited workers revive May Day

Leilani Dowell

On May 1, 2006 a "Day Without Immigrants," May Day, International Workers' Day, was revived in the U.S. In every state, businesses closed, workers took the day off, students walked out of schools, and a multinational sea of humanity rallied to demand full rights for all.

The impact of the boycott was felt in the streets as well as in the pocketbooks of businesses that profit from super-exploited immigrant labor.

The demonstration in **Chicago** was the biggest protest in the city's history. Organizers estimated the turnout at 700,000.

Tens of thousands marched from schools. There were feeder marches, one from Benito Juarez High School, and another organized by the Coalition of African, Arab, Asian, European and Latino Immigrants of Illinois. Colorful tee shirts distinguished union members from UNITE-HERE and SEIU.

Organizers estimated that between half a million and a million people overfilled **Union Square in NYC** and then marched down to Federal Plaza. The diverse immigrant communities were reflected, with contingents from virtually every Latin American and Caribbean country; from China, Korea and the Philippines; from Senegal; from Pakistan and South Asia; from Poland and Ireland. Celebrities like Susan Sarandon joined speakers representing Latin America, Africa, Asia and the Pacific Islands.

The Revs. Jesse Jackson and Al Sharpton and Councilmember Charles Barron made clear that the Black struggle is in solidarity with immigrants, and would have no part of the attempt to 'divide and rule' Blacks and Latino. "It's the big corporations that take jobs away, not the immigrants," said Jackson.

Transport Workers Union Local 100 President Roger Toussaint, who is from Trinidad, (was released from jail after five days for leading the December transit strike) and Teamsters National Black Caucus leader Chris Silvera, who offered his union's office as the May Day Coalition headquarters, applauded the immigrant struggle.

Anti-war organizers like Larry Holmes of the Troops Out Now Coalition, Brenda Stokely of the MWM, Berna Ellorin of BAYAN USA, Nellie Bailey of the Harlem Tenants Council and International Action Center's Teresa Gutierrez also spoke.

Before imposing court buildings, thousands gathered to listen to the closing rally at Federal Plaza. Along with demanding legalization of immigrants, speakers explained how neoliberalism had driven so many from their homelands to seek work at the center of world imperialism.

A sea of protesters, tens of thousands, continued marching in well after the rally ended. Traffic was forced to a standstill on the Brooklyn Bridge until police violently attacked the crowd.

Lauren Giaccone reports: "The cops then started pushing. We pushed back. A

Bernadette Ellorin with the Justice for Immigrants/Filipin@ Coalition speaks at a April 13, 2006 press conference on the steps of New York City Hall in support of the May Day protests for the rights of immigrant workers.

Ellorin said, "Immigrant rights are workers' rights."

Brenda Stokely a leader of the MWMM stated, "We are not separate from people because they speak a different language or come from a different land mass. People should have the freedom of movement to go wherever they need to go to take care of their families. It's a working person's issue. These are issues that tie us together against forces that deny people their humanity. Come out on May 1 to defend human rights for everybody."

WW photo: Heather Cottin

New York City

cop punched a girl, she went down and that started a huge fight between the cops and the people. The people fought back against the brutality. The cops threw people to the ground, so hard that a metal post fastened to the ground outside of the subway station went flying. As people were on the ground, cops still beat them. ...

"We continued to march ... when scooter cops hooked around us and jumped on the sidewalk, cornering us. We had no choice but to run across the street into oncoming traffic, to avoid the brutality we just witnessed. We were at the other side ... when they drove across the street and rode up onto the sidewalk yet again.

"This time, however, they revved their engines and pinned several of us against the wall." (nyc.indymedia.org)

When Workplace Project organizer Carlos Canales asked the mayor of **Hempstead, on Long Island**, for a rally permit for 800 people, he never expected that 5,000 would show. "Labor and immigrants changed history today," he said. "Immigrants have brought back May Day."

Organizers convinced businesses to close. And they sent five busloads of people to the NYC rally. Participants cheered when organizers called for 'Primero de Mayo 2007.'

In the **San Francisco Bay Area**, despite attempts by the big-business media to downplay May 1, businesses stood idle as more than one million people took to the streets. The day began with an **East Oakland** march to the downtown Federal Building; community contingents of unions, churches and student groups marched through **San Francisco**'s financial district; more than a thousand people rallied at the University of California, **Berkeley**; demonstrators blocked the on-ramp to Route 80, a major thoroughfare and in **San Jose**, tens of thousands marched.

In **Los Angeles** the May 1 boycott and march was initiated by the Mexican American Political Association and Hermandad Mexicana Latino American. Organizers estimate the City Hall demonstration at up to one million marchers. Reportedly 72,000 students missed school. Ninety per-

cent of Los Angeles and **Long Beach** port truckers did not work. Boycott participants bolstered the numbers at a demonstration in McArthur Park.

The City Hall march showed more unity than ever. The Nation of Islam provided security. Speakers included Minister Tony Muhammad of the NOI, and Pastor Louis Logan of the large AME Bethel Baptist church, as well as leaders of the Southern California District Council of Laborers, Grupo Parlamentario PRI and other Mexican-American organizations.

The streets of south **San Diego** overflowed. There was no business as usual. Events were held in downtown San Diego as well as **San Ysidro, Escondido** and **Vista**.

In a show of solidarity, protesters in **Tijuana** shut down the U.S./Mexico border on the Mexican side. After a 500-person march in San Ysidro, youths shut down the border again— this time on the U.S. side.

By evening, crowds had more than doubled as people gathered in Balboa Park, where a candlelight vigil was scheduled. However, instead of stand-

Clarence Thomas, Dick Becker, Federico Chavez and Gloria La Riva in San Francisco.

Local 10 was present in solidarity on May Day 2006. Photo: Charles Slay

San Diego

Photo: Gloria Verdieu

Chicago   Photo: Lou Paulsen

Los Angeles   Photo: Julie La Riva

ing still, folks broke police barriers and took to the streets in an impromptu march that surrounded the mall.

In **Denver**, over 75,000 began their march across the street from Escuela Tlatelolco, the school founded by the Chicano activist Corky Gonzales.

The Latino working class shut down the agriculture and service industries across **Washington state**. Sixty-five thousand workers poured into downtown **Seattle**. Marchers carried flags of countries from Somalia to Honduras. In the agricultural town of **Yakima, Wash.**, 15,000 marchers paraded. Thousands more demonstrated in **Wenatchee**, which is apple country.

The country's biggest beef processor was forced to give workers the day off in **Colorado, Kansas, Iowa, Illinois, Texas** and **Nebraska**.

Tens of thousands honored the boycott in **Georgia**. Not one worker showed up at the Vidalia onion farms in southern Georgia. Thousands, including families with small children, rallied in **Atlanta**. A theme of speeches was that immigrants are struggling for their children to have education, health care and opportunity.

In **Athens, Ga.**, some 2,000 grade school and high school students, young workers assembled near the University of Georgia campus. One activist said, "It was the biggest protest Athens had ever seen."

During the rally, the emcee, Pedro, discussed the origin of May Day and how immigrant workers struggled for the eight-hour day in Chicago. He said it was historic that immigrants are taking to the streets for justice.

Some 10,000 people marched in **Charlotte, N.C.** Over 800 students were absent from the Charlotte-Mecklenburg school system. Student Amanda Medina said, "It made me feel proud of who I am and where I come from, and that so many people support us." (wcnc.com)

African American high school student Nigel Hood said, "I just couldn't help thinking back to my ancestors and predecessors who were in the Civil-Rights Movement. It made me feel very special." (wcnc.com)

Protesters also marched though downtown **Lumberton, N.C.** They were joined by workers from Smithfield Foods Inc.'s plant in **Tar Heel**. Gene Bruskin, with the Food and Commercial Workers union, said, "We're in the middle of absolutely nowhere, pig farms, and you've got 5,000 workers marching." (wbt.com)

In **Raleigh, N.C.**, people surrounded the state capitol. (wbt.com)

Thousands rallied in **Washington, D.C.** demanding an end to government attacks on undocumented workers. Signs said, "There are no borders in the workers' struggle." Construction workers at Dulles International Airport boycotted work. (AP) Businesses from downtown D.C. to Georgetown closed because of absent workers.

Hundreds of residents, workers, students and professors rallied at the University at **Buffalo, N.Y.** They demanded an end to anti-immigrant racism and U.S.-sponsored apartheid. Police attacked and beat two students, one a Bolivian, while protesters shouted, "Let them go!" The march continued despite the police presence.

Across **Massachusetts**, tens of thousands demonstrated in over 30 cities. In **Boston**, a delegation from Steel Workers Local 8751, the School Bus Drivers' Union followed a banner hoisted by mostly youths of color.

Service Employees union leaders led chants with Local 8571 Boston School Bus Drivers, including the local's chief stewards, its newly elected Haitian President Frantz Mendes, and Vice President Steve Gillis.

The militant protesters filed past the Federal Building to an anti-imperialist speak-out and to support a pro-immigrant news conference, where Rosa Parks Human Rights Day Committee member Bishop Filipe Teixeira was speaking. They then marched to Boston Common rally.

Speaking from the stage, Cassandra Clark Mazariegos of the Young Revolutionaries, of the RPHRDC, said: "The young people are here to support our parents. They left their countries because of hardships due to the things this country did."

Fight Imperialism, Stand Together organizer Ruth Vela summed up the historic May Day activities: "Today showed that the so-called 'sleeping giant' was not asleep. If workers are not given the respect, dignity and justice demanded, then they will take it."
Abridged from WW, May 4, 2006.

Longshore workers say: 'All Out on May Day!'
Support immigrant rights

Judy Greenspan

Longshore workers on the West Coast have passed a resolution supporting national May Day 2007 actions for immigrant and workers' rights. The ILWU took solidarity a step further by announcing a work stoppage in major West Coast ports on May 1 to support and participate in the "Great American Boycott II."

Longshore workers will stop all work in the California ports of Oakland, San Francisco, Richmond, Benicia and Redwood City, as well as in Seattle, Wash. Locally, the ILWU Local 10 Drill Team will perform at the May Day protest.

Clarence Thomas, of Local 10 and coordinator of its Saving Lives Campaign, told this reporter, "Last year, we not only supported all of the demands of the immigrant workers' movement but we fought for the defense of longshore jobs against a similar right-wing attack."

Last year, with the passage of the Maritime Transportation Security Act, under the guise of "national security" longshore workers found themselves being questioned about past felony convictions, medical conditions and political affiliations.

The union was able to remove some of the worst elements of the government witch hunt. However, longshore workers still have to face scrutiny from Homeland Security before being issued a Transportation Worker Identification Credential, which is needed to work on the docks.

"We strongly oppose the criminalization of immigrant workers and see the similarity with government attempts to criminalize our union members," Thomas added.

The resolution passed by ILWU Local 10 in San Francisco and ILWU Local 19 in Seattle reads:

WHEREAS, Local 10 adopted a resolution for our April 2005 Longshore Caucus reclaiming May Day which commemorates the struggle for the 8 (eight) hour work day;

WHEREAS, Local 10 endorsed May 1st, 2006, to protest the criminalization of immigrant workers by legislation such as HR4437 and the MTS Acts criminal background checks on dock workers;

WHEREAS, On May 1st, 2006, 90 percent of the container cargo at the Ports of Los Angeles and Long Beach was halted as the result of immigrant truckers not going to work;

WHEREAS, Agribusinesses such as Tyson Foods and Cargill closed several plants in anticipation of workers not going to work on May 1, 2006, in support of immigrant rights;

WHEREAS, Our own Harry Bridges, an Australian immigrant worker, faced four prosecutions by the U.S. government, was wrongfully convicted, illegally imprisoned, fraudulently stripped of his citizenship, and his attorneys sent to jail for defending him;

WHEREAS, ILWU in 2008, will start difficult contract negotiations with the employer which requires we start to mobilize our members and build coalitions; and

WHEREAS, Hornblower Cruises has yet to hire experienced ILWU and other union ferry workers as well as to negotiate a fair contract;

THEREFORE BE IT RESOLVED, that the membership instruct Local 10's president to convey our intentions of having our stop work meeting on Tuesday, May 1st, 2007, at 9 a.m. to Pacific Maritime Association;

THEREFORE BE IT FURTHER RESOLVED, that Local 10 participates in the Great American Boycott II, in support of workers and immigrant rights, including the workers of Hornblower Cruises, on May Day, 2007, and that the ILWU Local 10 Drill Team perform; and

THEREFORE BE IT FINALLY RESOLVED, that a copy of this Resolution be sent to all ILWU locals, the International, and affiliated central labor councils.

The longshore workers have a long history of support in working class struggles. "Seven decades of ILWU militant unionism shows that we understand the significance of international labor solidarity," Thomas said.

It was the first union to oppose U.S. intervention in Vietnam in 1964. The longshore workers took a stand against apartheid and refused to handle South African cargo. It refused to load bombs or military cargo destined for Chile and El Salvador.

"The ILWU was founded by Harry Bridges, an immigrant worker from Australia, who was hounded by the U.S. government because of his militant trade unionism and political beliefs," Thomas explained. "We will always continue to embrace the aspirations of all workers, organized or unorganized." As coordinator of the ILWU's 'Saving Lives Campaign', Thomas leads union efforts to reduce diesel fuel emissions at 29 ports on the West Coast.

Abridged from WW, April 8, 2007.

From anti-war protest to resistance
West Coast Ports Shut Down

Clarence Thomas

The ILWU, known for its militant and democratic traditions as well as its economic and social justice activism, has written a new chapter in its glorious labor history by shutting down all 29 ports on the West Coast for eight hours on May Day 2008.

This historic and courageous action on the part of the ILWU came about as the result of a "No Peace No Work Holiday" resolution adopted by the Longshore Division Caucus, its highest ruling body, in February. The caucus passed the resolution by an overwhelming majority of the 100 longshore delegates representing all locals on the West Coast.

This resolution demanded "an immediate end to the war and occupation in Iraq and Afghanistan and the withdrawal of U.S. troops from the Middle East."

It also asked the AFL-CIO and Change to Win to issue "an urgent appeal for unity and action" to end the war. The resolution included a request for a May 1 Coastwide 'Stop Work' union meeting to accommodate the closure of the ports. Contractually, the ILWU is entitled to one stop-work meeting a month to address union business.

The Pacific Maritime Association (PMA), which represents shippers, stevedoring companies, terminal operators, and negotiates labor contracts on their behalf, denied the request for a Coastwide union meeting for May 1. Such requests have been honored with advance notice. PMA received nearly three months advanced notice and still denied the request.

The rank-and-file proceeded with plans for a stop work shut down even though the International leadership withdrew its request to the PMA for the May 1 Coastwide meeting.

PMA then insisted that the union leadership notify its members of the withdrawal of the request for May Day. The PMA even went to an arbitrator to force the union leaders to do this. The arbitrator ruled that the union is obligated to notify members that the union's request had been withdrawn.

None of this pressure weakened the resolve of the rank-and-file, who organized marches, rallies and other demonstrations in San Francisco and the Pacific Northwest. Union locals continued to prepare for the May Day action.

In San Francisco, Local 10 members organized the Port Workers' May Day Organizing Committee, made up of union members, immigrant rights, and anti-war and social justice groups. In the Pacific Northwest, May Day organizing groups were headed up by rank-and-filers: Gabriel Prawl of Local 19 Executive Board in Seattle; and in Portland Local 8 members Jerry Lawrence, member of the Executive Board, and Debbie Stringfellow.

There were numerous solidarity statements not just from trade unionists but from around the world in support of ILWU's unprecedented planned action. The first was called by the National Association of Letter Carriers locals observing two minutes of silence in all carrier stations on May 1 in solidarity with the ILWU action. Independent port truckers on the West Coast took solidarity actions in support of the ILWU. In the ports of Newark and Elizabeth, N.J., as well as the Port of Houston, independent truckers protested against higher gas prices and in support of the ILWU May

The iconic Local 10 rank-and-file Drill Team.

Rep. Cynthia McKinney from Georgia and Clarence Thomas Local 10 Executive Board member; Co-chair, Port Workers' May Day Organizing Committee; and National Co-chair, Million Worker March Movement.

Danny Glover and Cindy Sheehan.

Photos: Delores Lemon-Thomas

LeRoy King and Phillip Alley Local 34 with Danny Glover, Leo Robinson and Cythnia McKinney.

Trent Willis Local 10 president.
Photo: Delores Lemon-Thomas

The marquee of one of the oldest movie theaters in Oakland, Calif., the Grand Lake, displayed how much ILWU action resonated in the community. It had the following message on its marquee for a week leading up to May Day: "We Salute the Longshoremen's May Day Strike to Protest the Criminal Occupation of Iraq." Due to its location near the central city thoroughfare, thousands of people could see the marquee.

Photo: Steve Zeltzer

Day action. Students at the Universities of Seattle, of Washington, and Seattle Community College left their campuses to join the march and rally of ILWU Local 19.

The most significant solidarity action of all came from Longshoremen in Iraq. Members of the Port Workers Union of Iraq shut down the Ports of Umn Qasr and Khor Alzubair for one hour on May Day in solidarity with the ILWU shutdown of West Coast ports in opposition to the occupation of Iraq.

The General Union of Port Workers in Iraq sent this message to the ILWU: "The courageous decision you made to carry out a strike on May Day to protest against the war and occupation of Iraq advances our struggle to bring a better future for us and for the rest of the world as well."

A second solidarity message received from the Iraqi Labor Movement, a cross section of union leaders from different unions and labor federations in Iraq. The message read in part, "On this day of international labor solidarity we call on fellow trade unionists and those worldwide who have stood against war and occupation to increase support for our struggle for freedom from occupation, both military and economic."

Jack Heyman, Local 10 Executive Board member and Co-Chair, Port Workers May Day Organizing Committee, was interviewed by Amy Goodman of Democracy Now! about the significance of the May Day action. He responded: "We're really proud here on the West Coast as longshoremen. The ILWU is making a stand because it's part of our legacy,standing up on principled issues.

"This is the first work stoppage ever where workers were withholding their labor and demanding an end to the war and the immediate withdrawal of the troops. Not only did we defy the arbitrator, but in a certain sense we defied our own union officials who did not want to have the actions we organized up and down the Coast despite the arbitrator's decision. Simply, we don't take our orders from the arbitrator don't take it from judges. The rank-and-file goes out and does what it has to do.

"We did that in 1984, during our struggle against apartheid when Local 10 members, refused to work a South African ship for 10 days. That was in defiance of what the arbitrator said and what our union officials were telling us. So, we've got strong traditions in the ILWU, rank-and-file democracy where we implement what we decide in a democratic fashion."

In San Francisco, more than a thousand people marched from Local 10's union hall, led by the Local 10 Drill Team, along the Embarcadero where the 1934 General Strike took place, to a noon rally at Justin Herman Plaza: actor activist Danny Glover; Rep. Cynthia McKinney, former congresswoman from Georgia; Cindy Sheehan, whose son was killed in Iraq; and many others spoke to the crowd.

Local 10 was the local of the legendary labor leader and founding member of the ILWU, Harry Bridges. Local 10 initiated the Million Worker March (MWM), which took place on Oct. 17, 2004, at the Lincoln Memorial. The MWM movement calls upon the rank-and-file of the labor movement, organized and unorganized, to wage a fight-back movement for the working class. One of its aims following the 2004 mobilization was to reclaim May Day by reclaiming our proud history of struggle and social gains which International Workers' Day stands for.

Rallies, marches and resolutions play an important role in terms of organizing, but the ILWU's May Day action of shutting down all 29 ports on the West Coast is an example of how workers can exercise their power in the workplace and move from protest to resistance.

ILWU strikes for peace

Mumia Abu-Jamal

It should surprise no one that the mighty ILWU (International Longshore and Warehouse Union) is in the forefront of this eight-hour dock shutdown for peace. The ILWU's proud and illustrious history is one of supporting people's movements for life, freedom, and workers' solidarity, and also immigration rights, worldwide.

They remember the stirring words of Eugene Debs, who said, almost a century ago, "It is the master class that declares war, it is the subject class that fights the battles." For these words and his antiwar sentiments, Debs was cast into prison. That the ILWU is echoing his words today is proof of their power and truth, 100 years later.

It also proves how little we have moved, from the dawn of the 20th century to the dawn of the 21st, for war is still a tool of imperial power, to fuel corporate wealth and global domination. Who can deny that this is a war for oil? Who can deny that this is an illegal occupation, more concerned with what's under the earth than for the millions living in dread upon it?

For Iraq may not have been a barrel of laughs before the invasion and occupation but it is surely hell now. And Congress, like Nero amidst the fires of Rome, does little more than twiddle its thumbs. It is labor power that makes the wheels go round, and this powerful demonstration of the denial of labor, for May Day, for peace and an end to occupation in Iraq, is workers' solidarity made real.

Kudos to the ILWU. For labor power, peace, and anti-imperialism, I thank you.

Ona Move.
Long live John Africa.
From Death Row, this is Mumia Abu-Jamal.

April 25, 2008.

Free Mumia Abu-Jamal

Pam Africa leader of the International Concerned Family and Friends of Mumia Abu-Jamal called for the Freedom of Mumia at the May Day rally. "Free them All!" said Africa.

Bay Area.   Photo: Internationalist

New York City on May Day 2008. Walter Sinche and Charles Jenkins in TWU safety vest on the speakers' truck. After the rally Jenkins led the march into NYC Police Plaza to demand justice for Sean Bell.

Photos: Lallan Schoenstein

INTERNATIONAL LONGSHORE & WAREHOUSE UNION
AFL-CIO

1188 FRANKLIN STREET
SAN FRANCISCO
CALIFORNIA 94109
(415) 775-0533
(415) 775-1302 FAX
www.ILWU.org

ROBERT McELLRATH
President

JOSEPH R. RADISICH
Vice President

WESLEY FURTADO
Vice President

WILLIAM E. ADAMS
Secretary-Treasurer

February 22, 2008

John J. Sweeney, President
AFL-CIO
Washington, DC 20006

President Sweeney,

ILWU delegates recently concluded a two-week caucus where we reached agreement on our approach for bargaining a new Pacific Coast Longshore Contract that expires on July 1, 2008. We expect talks to begin sometime in March and will keep you informed of developments.

One of the resolutions adopted by caucus delegates called on longshore workers to stop work during the day shift on May 1, 2008, to express their opposition to the war in Iraq.

We're writing to inform you of this action, and inquire if other AFL-CIO affiliates are also planning to participate in similar events on May 1 to honor labor history and express support for the troops by bringing them home safely.

We would appreciate your assistance with spreading word about this May 1 action.

In solidarity,

Robert McEllrath
International President

RMcE/lk
cwa39521

HOUSE OF COMMONS
LONDON SW1A 0AA

International Longshore Workers Union
1188 Franklin Street, 4th Floor
San Francisco
CA 94109-6800
USA

Saturday 28th June 2008

Dear Brothers and Sisters of the International Longshore Workers Union,

We the undersigned wish to congratulate our comrades in the International Longshore and Warehouse Union (ILWU), for the brave and principled actions you have taken in opposition to the wars in Iraq and Afghanistan.

The ILWU has a proud history of internationalism, and of active opposition to the wars in Iraq and Afghanistan – which have been led by our two countries, and led to hundreds of thousands of innocent deaths.

Your actions have been an example to all trade unionists and peace activists in the US and the UK – and around the world – in opposing the imperialist wars of the US and UK, and we will do all we can in solidarity with you to defend your union's right to take such actions.

In solidarity,

John McDonnell MP
Chair, Socialist Campaign
Group & LRC

Maria Exall
Vice Chair, LRC

Jeremy Corbyn MP
Vice Chair, Socialist Campaign
Group

Neil Gerrard MP
Socialist Campaign Group

Simeon Andrews
LRC Secretary

Kelvin Hopkins MP
Socialist Campaign Group

**House of Common Early Day Motion 1452
International Longshore and Warehouse Union's Action for Peace Campaign**

That this House commends the decision of the International Longshore and Warehouse Union (ILWU) to stop work for eight hours in all West Coast ports in the United States of America on 1st May to call for an end to the wars in Iraq and Afghanistan; recognises the proud history of the San Francisco Longshore Union of internationalism and active opposition to the wars in Iraq and Afghanistan; is concerned that the US maritime companies are pursuing legal attempts to prevent the Longshore Union's right to demonstrate; and calls upon workers in the US, United Kingdom and around the world to join in solidarity with the ILWU in support of this courageous action in the struggle for peace.

San Francisco Chronicle
Saturday, April 26, 2008

BUSINESS

Longshore workers taking off

Members plan to shut ports while holding war protest

By George Raine
CHRONICLE STAFF WRITER

Members of the International Longshore & Warehouse Union are proceeding with plans for a work stoppage at 29 West Coast ports on May 1 to protest the wars in Iraq and Afghanistan, despite the fact that union leadership has withdrawn its request to waterfront employers that they accommodate closure of the ports.

Planning for the protest began in February when the Longshore Caucus, the highest decision-making body for the 25,000 members of the longshore division within the ILWU, overwhelmingly approved a resolution in support of a day of protest.

According to its contract, the ILWU is entitled to schedule a "stop-work meeting" each month to discuss union business. It must give adequate advance notice to employers, who are represented by the Pacific Maritime Association, a group of shipowners, stevedore companies and terminal operators that negotiates labor contracts on their behalf.

The PMA routinely grants these requests, but only for meetings that are to be held during the second work shift, beginning in the evening. For the war protest, the ILWU said it wanted stop-work time during the day, 8 a.m. to 5 p.m., the busiest cargo-handling shift of the day.

After the matter was approved by the caucus, ILWU President Bob McEllrath said on the ILWU Web site, "The caucus has spoken on this important issue, and I've notified the employers about our plans for stop-work meetings on May 1."

However, in March, the president of PMA, James McKenna, said he would not agree to the request. Employers do not want the ports to be shut during the first, or day shift, as it would be disruptive to the flow of cargo. The PMA said Friday that about 10,000 containers are loaded and unloaded coast-wide during an eight-hour day.

On April 8, the union leadership withdrew the stop-work request for May 1.

The employers wanted the union to convey the withdrawal to its members, but management sources said it was unclear whether that had happened. So the PMA took the issue to an arbitrator. On Thursday, he issued an opinion that the union is obligated to inform members that the request has been withdrawn. There was no mention of the matter on the ILWU Web site on Friday.

Craig Merrilees, a spokesman for the ILWU, issued a statement seemingly supportive of a war protest: "The Longshore Caucus resolution calling on all locals to honor May 1 by taking action to end the war and bring the troops home safely from Iraq continues to move forward. Various voluntary rallies and public demonstrations are scheduled for May Day."

The protest was advanced by Jack Heyman, a longshore worker who is a member of the Local 10 Executive Board. He said Friday he expects the ports to be shut down May 1. He added, "I have never seen our membership so resolute on a given issue."

He said it was Vietnam War veterans in the caucus who drove the discussion.

Steve Getzug, a spokesman for the PMA, said, "They informed us they had dropped their demand for a stop-work meeting May 1. An arbitrator has ruled they inform their members, and in light of that we hope the day (May 1) will come and go without disruption."

Heyman and other organizers said there will be a rally at noon May 1 at Justin Herman Plaza in San Francisco. Speakers will include activists Danny Glover, Cindy Sheehan and Daniel Ellsberg.

In the meantime, the PMA and ILWU are negotiating a labor contract. The current contract expires July 1.

Canadian Peace Alliance   Report – June 10, 2008

Clarence Thomas,
ILWU Local 10 Executive Board Member

The Canadian Peace Alliance, the largest peace organization with 150 member groups across Canada, organized a "Labour Against War" forum at the Canadian Labor Congress Convention in Toronto, Canada on May 27, 2008. The forum included an "eye witness report" on the May Day coast wide shut-down.

The Alliance congratulated the ILWU for its historic action on May Day. I spent two days at the Convention speaking and meeting with of Canadian trade unionists and activists including several ILWU leaders from Canada. The U.S. Steel Workers Union was well represented at the Convention. It is important to note that they are quite active in the anti-war movement in Canada.

The U.S. Steel Workers Union strongly acknowledged ILWU Local 10 for launching the May Day action. I was presented with an U.S. Steel Workers jacket as a gesture of solidarity.

The ILWU longshore attendees included: Tom Dufresne, the Canadian president of the ILWU, Gordie Westrand, president ILWU Local 500; Chad O'Neill, president Local 502; Frank Scigliano, president, ILWU Ship and Dock Foremen, Local 514; and rank-and-file members. They were present at the anti-war forum where I spoke before a standing room only crowd. All ILWU members were introduced before my remarks as keynote speaker. I presented an ILWU hook pin and a MWM tee shirt to Sid Lacombe, coordinator of the Canadian Peace Alliance. ILWU hook pins were also given to U.S. Steel Workers Union leaders.

This was the first major report back to trade unionists and activists in North America. My attendance at this convention afforded me the opportunity to meet with trade union activists from Zimbabwe, Namibia, and Somalia.

I was introduced at the International Solidarity Forum at the Convention by Tom Dufresne who is a member of the executive committee of the Canadian Labor Congress which is equivalent to the AFL-CIO. The speech was well received as shown in the reaction by the delegates at the Convention including the ovation I received the following day at the International Solidarity Forum.

The Canadian visit was productive and it established international ties amongst trade union activists against the war. The Canadians have 2,000 troops in Afghanistan. As much as the government of Canada tries to define its role in the Middle East as a peacekeeping force, they part of the problem and not the solution.

The impact of this action is still resonating.

Vancouver ILWU leaders Frank Scigliano, president, Ship and Dock Foremen, Terry Engler president Local 400, Clarence Thomas, Gordie Westrand president Local 500 and Tom Dufresne, Canadian ILWU president.
Photo: Mike Eisenger

ILWU locals honor May Day organizer
Vancouver, British Columbia

The shutdown of West Coast ports on May 1 continues to resonate internationally. On Nov. 10, 2008, in Vancouver, Longshore Workers Union Local 400 Maritime Division and Longshore Local 500 sponsored a dinner for Clarence Thomas. Thomas is co-chair, along with Jack Heyman, of the Portworkers May Day Organizing Committee. The dinner, held at the Maritime Labor Centre auditorium, was attended by officers, rank-and-file members, pensioners and their families.

Terry Engler, president of Vancouver's Local 400 said: "It is unfortunate that there was virtually no reporting of the May Day shutdown in our media. . ... I believe that union members would benefit from Thomas' experience regarding rank-and-file solidarity of the ILWU."

During his talk Thomas explained the May Day "No Peace, No War" mobilization, initiated by ILWU Local 10 rank-and-file in San Francisco, called for an end to the war and occupation of Iraq and Afghanistan and the withdrawal of U.S. troops from the Middle East.

Thomas stated that this was the first time in the U.S. that workers withheld their labor to oppose U.S. imperialism. The action took place despite the fact that their union leadership withdrew its request to waterfront employers that close the ports on May 1, 2008.

Local 500 presented Brother Thomas with "*Bluesprint*", a comprehensive collection of literature and spoken word of Blacks in British Columbia. He also received the video "Betrayed" from Local 400. This documentary captures the history of the Canadian Seaman's Union, which brought the eight-hour day, sick leave and pay increases to an industry known for low wages and brutal working conditions.

Abridged from WW Dec 7, 2008.

LABOUR AGAINST WAR

EYEWITNESS REPORT
25,000 longshore workers strike against the Iraq war on May 1

TUESDAY, MAY 27, 5:30pm
Metro Toronto Convention Centre, 255 Front Street West, North Building, Room 103A
TTC: Union (walk west along Front Street)

Featuring
CLARENCE THOMAS Member, International Longshore and Warehouse Union (US)

Other guests
HAMID OSMAN Member, Toronto Coalition to Stop the War, Afghan caucus
CATHY CROWE Member, Housing Not War Campaign
SUSAN SPRATT (moderator) National representative, Canadian Auto Workers

On May 1, 2008, 25,000 members of the International Longshore and Warehouse Union (ILWU) in the US took strike action against the Iraq war – the first time that an American union has ever taken strike action against a US war. Over 30 ports were shut down on the west coast of the US as dockworkers declared May Day a "no peace, no work" holiday. Please join us to hear an eyewitness report by Clarence Thomas, an executive member of ILWU and a central organizer in the strike. Discussion to follow.

Organized by the Canadian Peace Alliance
www.acp-cpa.ca | cpa@web.ca | 416-588-5555

Canadian Peace Alliance
L'Alliance canadienne pour la paix

International delegations stand with Cuba on May Day

Cheryl LaBash　Havana, Cuba

First-time visitors from the U.S. were unsure what the day would hold as they watched dawn break in Revolution Square on May Day morning.

The international delegations, more than 2,000 in all from 70 countries, including union leaders and revolutionaries, often both in the same person, and representing 200 union and solidarity organizations streamed off buses and into the reviewing area at the foot of the José Martí statue.

They chatted, chanted and taped their banners to the walls displaying the international demand to free the five Cuban heroes imprisoned in the U.S. as they waited for the program and march to begin. It was a global echo of the message President Barack Obama received at the recent Summit of the Americas: End the blockade! Cuba is not alone, and U.S. imperialism is not invincible!

"Why are there so few people in the Plaza?" one queried, before the Cuban workers marched in, wave after wave, for hours. "Will Cuban President Raul Castro speak?" A cheer greeted Castro when he appeared, but it was the Confederation of Cuban Workers (Central de Trabajadores de Cuba, CTC) General-Secretary Salvador Valdés Mesa who addressed the International Workers' Day event in Havana, as is customary on May Day.

This May Day was the 50th since the 1959 Revolution broke free of the colonial past and charted a path of development to meet peoples' needs instead of profit and exploitation. It also marked the 70th anniversary of the founding of the CTC, which has been instrumental, side-by-side with the Communist Party of Cuba, in developing workers' power.

And it was the workers and youth who marched in Havana with the theme of unity, combativeness, productivity and efficiency. They carried representations of their workplaces such as a huge cigar from the La Corona Factory, a taxi, housing construction brigades with tools, and pictures of rebuilding the 500,000 dwellings destroyed by the three hurricanes suffered in 2008.

Gigantic Cuban and Venezuelan flags, supported by hundreds of youth, undulated like ocean waves. Multiple massive delegations from the UJC Communist Youth Union (Unión de Jóvenes Comunistas) marched with the message: "The youth will not fail. All for the revolution!" Gymnasts and professional dancers, entered the square. Handmade signs demanded freedom for the Cuban Five, saluted and supported Cuban leaders Fidel and Raul, and saluted socialism.

Delores Lemon-Thomas, visiting from Richmond, Calif., recalled protesting at the White House against the U.S. invasions of Iraq and Afghanistan and seeing heavily armed troops burdened with body armor along with rooftop snipers, as well as police phalanxes controlling San Francisco protests. She noted she was only a few hundred feet away from the Cuban president and that, with hundreds of thousands marching in the street, only unarmed youth gently encouraged the marchers not to stop to take pictures at the José Martí monument.

Another example of the contrast

Left, Magali Llort, mother of Cuban 5, U.S. political prisoner Fernando Gonzalez.

between life witnessed in Cuba and experienced in the U.S. was expressed on May Day by CTC leader Salvador Valdés Mesa, who spoke of the global economic crisis and supported the Cuban government's efforts "to protect people from the effects of the crisis.

"Even more so, at a time when humanity is immersed in a global economic crisis making the political, economic and social situation more complex globally, this impacts on the people, and workers face bleak prospects from which no country can escape.

"In our case, this is compounded by the effects of the ironclad economic blockade that the U.S. government has maintained for almost half a century, with the obsessive and failed object of destroying the Revolution.

"The unity and resistance in the face of any obstacle, which Fidel has formed within us, are pillars on which the Cuban Revolution is triumphantly erected and have become the central and constant battle flags. We will continue supporting with determination the measures that our government adopts to reduce the effects of the crisis on the population."

And that is the profound difference between a social system based on capitalism, with its profits for banks and corporations, and socialism.
Reprinted from WW May 21, 2009

J. Menéndez Museum curator with C. Thomas and D. Arian with ILWU donated documents delivered by Jack Heyman in 2001.

Cuban heart transplant patient 25 years later

Maximiliano Velázquez Montesino, right, a 76-year-old former long- shore worker in the Mariel Harbor for over three decades, won awards as a 'Cuban Hero' for a lifetime of intense hard work. Some 25 years after a heart transplant, Montesino, called Malanga by his friends, thanked the medical team for his free health care: 'If it wasn´t for the Cuban revolution I wouldn´t be here alive at the moment. I never thought that I would survive such a long time.

Abridged from Cuban radio 2009
web@radiorebelde.icrt.cu

Right, delegation leaving J. Menéndez Museum after reviewing documents and discussing ILWU's participation in organizing the Cuban 'Int'l Sugar Workers Committee' in Hawaii 1947.

Photos: Delores Lemon-Thomas

ILWU, ILA and U.S. labor delegation with translators.

David Arian past ILWU Int'l Pres., led delegation to the 'CTC Interna- tional Meeting of Solidarity' with Cuba on May 2, 2009.

Immigrants, labor unite on May Day

John Catalinotto

The workers' movement took a significant step forward on May Day 2011 when New York City labor and immigrant organizations came together under the banner "May Day Is Workers' Day."

There was a groundswell of sentiment from rank-and-file union members for unity on May Day. Organizers worked out a joint message with an exchange of speakers at two of the big rallies. The May 1st Coalition gathered at Union Square and marched to Foley Square, uniting workers at both actions.

Thousands of workers, from the various immigrant communities as well as from unions, and from neighborhood, anti-war, women's, lesbian-gay-bi-trans-queer and other organizations marched along Broadway.

May Day is celebrated all over the world as a workers' holiday, with roots in the socialist movement.

Despite originating in the U.S., until 2005, when the Million Worker March Movement revived it, May Day's role as a workers' holiday had been usurped by Labor Day.

This was the sixth straight year that the May 1st Coalition organized a Union Square action. As has been its tradition, the march had representation not only from many Latin American communities but from virtually all nations around the world.

Organizers gave a national character to the action by inviting two African-American labor leaders whose union struggles are showing the direction in which the labor movement must move to counter the relentless attack by the bosses and bankers.

Gilbert Johnson, president of Federation of State, County and Municipal

MAY DAY
Labor Rights, Immigrant Rights, Jobs for All!

Employees Local 82 at the University of Wisconsin-Milwaukee, talked about the struggle in Wisconsin. Since Gov. Scott Walker used alleged budget shortfalls as a pretext to break the public sector unions, a mass response has reverberated. "If the state and the politicians are broke," said Johnson, "then we workers have to fix it."

Clarence Thomas, a leader of ILWU Local 10, told how the workers voluntarily shut down the ports of Oakland, Calif., and San Francisco in solidarity with the workers in Wisconsin. Thomas pointed out that while "marches and rallies and vigils are good, the bosses can ignore them, but if we workers withhold our labor, that's the real power."

Despite the attacks on immigrants leaving a million people deported since 2008, the march was militant and upbeat. Day laborers, street vendors, domestic workers and unionists marched behind the banners. The crowd included members of Vamos Unidos, a Latino vendors' association, plus groups like Domestic Workers United, Jornaleros Unidos de Woodside, BAYAN USA, Dominican Women Development Center, Desis Rising Up and Moving, 1199 SEIU Healthcare Workers, the Committee Against Anti-Asian Violence, Teamsters Local 808, Workers World Party, Las Buenas Amigas and the

Pictured at the podium are Chris Silvera, Teamsters Local 808, Teresa Gutierrez, May 1st Coalition, Julia Camagong, National Alliance for Filipino Concerns, Clarence Thomas, ILWU Local 10, and Gilbert Johnson, FSC&ME Local 82.

Other speakers were: Roberto Meneses, Day Laborers United, Rhadames Rivera, 1199 SEIU Healthcare Workers, Victor Toro, La Peña del Bronx, Larry Hales, NYs Against the Budget Cuts, Joe Lombardo, United National Antiwar Comm., Charles Jenkins, TWU Local 100, Michelle Keller-Ng, AFCSME DC 37, Lucy Pagoada, Honduras USA Resistencia, Marina Diaz, Centro Tecuman, Hanalei Ramos, BAYAN USA, Jocelyn Campbell, Domestic Workers United, Wilfredo Larancuent, Labor and Immigrant Rights, Jobs for All and Laundry Workers Joint Board, Workers United.

WW photo: G. Dunkel

Independent Workers Movement.

At Foley Square, thousands rallied chanting, "The workers united will never be defeated." There were trade unionists from the Laborers' union, Teamsters Local 210, Service Employees 32B-J, Food & Commercial Workers, Professional Staff Congress at CUNY, Transport Workers Union Local 100, and AFSCME DC 37.

"Immigrant workers once again defied threats of deportation in order to demand legalization, an end to raids and the right to organize," said May 1st Coalition for Worker and Immigrant Rights co-coordinator Teresa Gutierrez. "Today thousands rallied against cutbacks and for jobs. In New York, Los Angeles, Milwaukee, Buffalo and other cities, the movement is confronting increased attacks on the working class. By uniting the forces have strengthened the movement against layoffs and foreclosures.

Abridged from WW, May 12, 2011.

May Day protests begin with Port Shut Down

Darwin Bond Graham

ILWU Local 10 who handle cargo at the Port of Oakland, one of the busiest U.S seaports, stopped work across the Bay Area May 1, 2015, to protest against police brutality. Rallying near the gate of an idle port terminal, Bay Area longshore workers were joined by labor leaders representing BART train operators, city and county workers, port workers from Los Angeles, and community members.

"There is an epidemic of police terror," said Jack Heyman, a retired Oakland port worker. "We in the longshore union are here to let them know it's got to stop!" Heyman said the Port Shut Down was part of the movement to disrupt business as usual and force the system to change.

Longshore workers have idled West Coast ports in the past to fight South African Apartheid, and oppose the invasions of Iraq and Afghanistan. Longshore workers also shut down Bay Area ports in 2010, to demand charges be pressed against the BART police officer who shot and killed Oscar Grant.

Stacey Rodgers, a rank-and-file port worker who sits on ILWU Local 10's executive board, said Bay Area longshore workers felt it was time to take action.

"Walter Scott was a relative of some South Carolina longshore workers," Rodgers said. On April 4 Scott was shot in the back and killed by a North Charleston police officer as he fled on foot. "We had been talking about his murder, and about other people getting shot by the police. I felt that we needed to do something."

Family members of those killed by the police climbed into the bed of a truck to speak at a port terminal gate.

"I'm the sister of Jeremiah Moore. He was killed in his front yard by the Vallejo police," Rebecca Moore said. Jeremiah Moore, 29, was shot on Oct. 21, 2012. The family disputes the police department's account of the incident. "He was an autistic young man who was shot and killed while he had his hands up," said Moore.

Signs naming those shot and killed by Bay Area police, including Richard Perez, Kenneth Harding, Jr., and Yuvette Henderson, bobbed over a sea of heads.

Mollie Costello of the 'Alan Blueford Center for Justice', told the rally that after Blueford was killed by an Oakland police officer in 2012, one of the first groups to support the family was the port workers union. "This is how we are going to win, through solidarity and love," she said. "We are united to say, end state-sponsored police terror."

Devon Thomas, another Oakland longshore worker, stood in the truck with his son, a young Black man. "The kids being targeted these days are his age," said Thomas. "It's a shame when I have to worry about my son from what the police might do to him."

After leaving the port the protesters marched through West Oakland chanting: "Don't fear the revolution, Black freedom is the solution!" A heavy police presence followed the march.

Abridged from "East Bay Express", May 1, 2015.

Stacey Rodgers Local 10 chaired the 2015 rally with Jack Heyman.

Mollie Costello of the 'Alan Blueford Center for Justice.'
Photos: Bert Johnson

Longshore workers:
'Shut It Down May Day 2016'

Cheryl LaBash

Brother A.J. Mitchell, ILWU Local 10 pensioner was amongst the hundreds of thousands who attended 'Justice or Else,' the 20th anniversary of the Million Man March on Oct. 10, 2015. He also attended the 10th Anniversary of the MMM in 2005 and the MMM in 1995.

A Baltimore meeting on Oct. 11, 2015, featured African American longshore workers Clarence Thomas and A.J. Mitchell. Other ILWU members that were in attendance included Local 19 members Jerome Johnson, John Krusuki and Anthony Lemon; Gabriel Prawl of Local 52.

Thomas and a delegation of ILWU members from various locals had only a month ago attended the Charleston, S.C., "Days of Grace" march, in the aftermath of the racist murder of nine women and men at the historic Mother Emanuel African Methodist Episcopal Church, as well as the police killing of Walter Scott. The longshore workers traveled from the West Coast in solidarity with ILA Local 1422, whose membership lost family in the church murders.

So it was in Charleston that an ILWU Local 10 resolution calling for a "National Day of Mourning" on May 1, 2016, International Workers' Day, was announced. And it was news that broke the night before on Oct. 10 of reports justifying the police slaying of 12 year-old Tamir Rice in Cleveland that focused Thomas' reflections on the MWM, the 10th Anniversary of the MMM and 'Justice or Else.'

Thomas recalled that the 1995 MMM was on a work day, yet huge crowds of working-class Black men traveled to Washington, D.C., instead

ILWU Local 10 retiree A.J. Mitchell at the 2015 MMM.

Photo: Rochelle Mitchell

of reporting to their jobs. Although the call was from Minister Louis Farrakhan, most of the attendees were not Muslims. Thomas appreciated the difficulty of organizing such a huge outpouring during a work day based on his more than 30 years of activist experiences in the Northern California labor movement and in organizing the MWM.

Yet organized labor did not have a voice at these events, except at the 2005 10th Anniversary MMM. Pat Ford from the Service Employees union, Chris Silvera from the Teamsters National Black Caucus and Thomas all spoke from the platform after Farrakhan had spoken at an earlier TNBC Educational Conference. In his talk Silvera challenged the Bush administration for suspending prevailing wage requirements, opening the door to substandard wages for the cleanup of the devastation from Hurricanes Katrina and Rita. Facing wide opposition from the labor movement, the Bush administration reversed itself. But not the least was the voice representing 400,000 Black Teamsters on that stage.

Referring to the report laying groundwork for the exoneration of the cops who killed Rice, Thomas thought that if the police were not held responsible there might be a large response to a "National Day of Mourning" on May Day in ports across the U.S. "That could be the spark," said Thomas.

To be heard, labor must shut it down, Thomas asserted: "That is the only leverage we have. All of this talk means absolutely nothing. We have had discussions about cameras on dashboards, cop's body cameras, and they still are killing us.

"If we can get longshore workers across the country to shut down for eight hours on May Day 2016. I think we may be able to get some real serious discussion about income inequality and structural racism."

In response to a question about organizing a general strike when many young Black workers directly affected by police brutality — are non-union, Thomas clarified that the proposal was for the longshore workers. He also pointed out that some of the most effective mass actions have been by unorganized workers, including the 2006 Boycott of Latino workers. In Los Angeles and Long Beach, 90 percent of the ports were shut down because the immigrant port truckers didn't come to work.

"We are not suggesting that you go out on the same day," Thomas said. "We could have rolling strikes. The day before May Day for fast food workers. That would light them up. We don't have one general strike. We could have a whole bunch of strikes.

"Longshore workers are in a unique position because they are responsible for maritime cargo and passengers. We are in a strategic position.

"If people are wondering what they can do after the 'Justice or Else' gathering, this is something workers can do. Shut it down on May Day all over the country. Let's get it going."

Abridged from WW, Oct. 22, 2015.

May Day 2016 'National Day of Mourning'

Solidarity Greetings to the Rank-and-File of the ILA Local 1422

As stated on Local 1422's Labor Day tee shirts, 'Labor Must Lead.' The ILA and the ILWU along with United Electrical Workers Local 150, Black Workers for Justice and the Southern Workers Assembly contributed in bringing working class unity to the 'Days of Grace' mobilization.

Organized labor has played a leading role historically in the struggle for economic and social justice for the working class. Black trade unionists have been in the forefront of the civil rights movement.

Longshore workers have boycotted South African cargo during apartheid, organized international solidarity campaigns such as the Charleston 5, and shut down ports in acts of resistance to the killings of unarmed Black men by police as in the case of Oscar Grant and Walter Scott by ILWU Local 10.

The membership of Local 10 passed a resolution for a no work 'National Day of Mourning' to take place on May 1, 2016, International Workers Day in memory of Walter Scott, shot by Michael Slager, a South Carolina police officer on April 4, 2015, and the nine members of Mother Emanuel Church, who were murdered by a white supremacist June 17, 2015.

The resolution put forward the following demands from the 'Days of Grace':
• End to racist policing
• $15-per-hour minimum wage and collective bargaining rights for all workers
• Expanding voting rights
• Medicaid expansion; healthcare for all
• Quality education is a human right.

The five demands are the issues that were supported by Rev. Clementa Pinckney, church pastor and state senator and one of the Emanuel 9.

The support of your Local's rank-and-file will be critical in mobilizing for a 'National Day of Mourning' because Charleston is where Walter Scott and the Mother Emanuel 9 lives were taken.

One of labor's greatest strengths is the withholding of its labor. That is how we achieved the eight hour work day, collective bargaining, the right to have a workers' controlled hiring hall, and democracy at work.

With ILA and ILWU rank-and-file unity we can make May Day, National Day of Mourning a reality.
Let's make it happen!

If the working class is to be heard then Labor Must Shut It Down!
– Clarence Thomas

Clarence Thomas speaking as a rank-and-file member of the ILWU Local 10 talks about the importance of being part of the 'Days of Grace,' a demonstration and conference against racism and for economic justice called by ILA Local 1422 in September 2015.

The gathering which honored the nine members of Mother Emanuel Church as well as Walter Scott killed by police in North Charleston provided the opportunity for unions to take the lead in the battle against structural racism and income inequality.

International Dockworkers Council
Consejo Internacional de Estibadores

Coordination Office ■ Oficina de Coordinación
C/Mar, 97 · 4° · 08003 Barcelona · Spain ■ Ph: +34 93 225 25 28
coordination@idcdockworkers.org

ILWU Local 10
Oakland, California, USA

IDC statement in solidarity with ILWU Local 10 on May Day 2016

BLACK LIVES MATTER

Barcleona, April 11, 2016

Brothers and Sisters; San Francisco Bay Area Dockworkers,

On behalf of the IDC and the +90.000 affiliates we represent around the world, we express our solidarity with the ILWU Local 10 in Oakland and all Bay Area dockworkers who on May Day this year will stand united against racism and police violence in the United States, shutting down the port and marching to protest the recent wave of police violence against black Latino, and immigrant communities in the Bay Area and many other U.S. cities.

ILWU Local 10's brave steps speak to a long tradition of struggle and protest towards social justice and economic reform from Bay area dockworkers in Local 10, who mobilized against apartheid in South Africa, dictatorships in Latin America, the Iraq and Afghanistan wars, and other cases of racial injustice such as Oscar Grant in 2009. We stand with you now in your fight for a $15 an hour minimum wage, healthcare and quality education for all.

Such a determined stand against outrageous social injustices serves as an example for all of us, and for labor movements worldwide-- for all dockers around the world to mobilize and fight for a better world, to fight against discrimination and to fight for social justice. We have received the 2016 Caucus Resolution and we stand behind you in your fight. The labor movement has been a key part in changing history; let us be at the forefront of social changes again.

WE WILL NEVER WALK ALONE AGAIN! SOLIDARITY FOREVER!

Fraternally,

Jordi Aragunde Miguens
Coordinador General IDC

OSCAR GRANT ALAN BLUEFORD
ANDY LOPEZ ANTONIO GUZMAN-LOPEZ
CHARLES BURNS JAMES RIVERA JR.
MARIO ROMERO CAESAR CRUZ ALEX NIETO
PEDIE PEREZ NATE GREER KELLY THOMAS
DIANA SHOWMAN AMILCAR PEREZ LOPEZ

May Day International Workers Day
**If Labor Is To Be Heard
Then Shut It Down !**
International Longshore and Warehouse Union Local 10

Oakland SIN FRONTERAS

MAY 1 INTERNATIONAL WORKERS' DAY 2018

10 am RALLY outside Matson Terminal
Berth 63 1579 Middle Harbor Rd (near end of Adeline viaduct)
11 am MARCH to Rally at Little Bobby Hutton (DeFremery) Park
march to
3 pm RALLY & MARCH Oscar Grant Plaza, Oakland, Calif.
for Immigrant & Worker Rights

ILWU To honor May 1st · MAY DAY · the International Longshore and Warehouse Union Longshore Division, will stop work for eight hours at all 29 ports on the West Coast. Join dockworkers Local 10 & 34 for a day of solidarity & resistance.

For more information: maydayilwulocal10@gmail.com

JUSTICE for STEPHON CLARK
JUSTICE for SAHLEEM TINDLE

**STOP police repression!
WORKERS RIGHTS FOR ALL!**
If the working class is to be heard then *Labor must Shut it Down*

**Shut Down the West Coast Ports!
Support** *the* **Longview, WA Longshore Workers**
Committee to Defend the I.L.W.U.

The Fight Against White Supremacy

1934 – 2019

Johnnie Stevens, left, leads march at July 2004
Democratic Convention in Boston with a banner calling
for the Oct. 17, 2004, MWM in Washington, D.C.
Protesters made their demands in the street.

WW photo: Liz Green

C.L. Dellums, Brotherhood of Sleeping Car Porters.

Clarence Thomas, speaks on the fight against white supremacy

Monica Moorehead

Clarence Thomas, a retired rank-and-file member of International Longshore and Warehouse Union Local 10 in the Bay Area, Calif., spoke at an Oct. 10, 2017 Workers World Party political discussion in New York on **'Why workers must fight white supremacy.'**

Thomas was a founding member of the MWM, a coalition of Black trade unionists from around the country who called for workers to speak in "our own name" and not as an appendage to the Democratic and Republican parties during the 2004 presidential election.

The MWM public call to action stated: "The time has come to mobilize working people for our own agenda. Let us end subservience to the power of the privileged few and their monopoly of the political process in America."

At the Oct. 10 meeting, Thomas' presentation focused on the struggle against white supremacy during the Great Depression of the 1930s, especially the heroic efforts made to bring Black workers into the ILWU, led by Harry Bridges, an Australian immigrant unionist. This was a revolutionary act since at the time most Black workers were forced to scab during strikes or else languish in low-wage jobs while locked out of all-white, closed-shop, skilled crafts unions.

Thomas also spoke about the heroic shutting down of West Coast docks since the 1980s, mainly on May Day, International Workers' Day, in political solidarity with oppressed peoples' struggles around the world. These work stoppages include against the apartheid regime of South Africa, the Zionist regime of Israel, police brutality and for the freedom of political prisoner Mumia Abu-Jamal.

Thomas stated that global capitalism exploits all workers, be they dock workers, prisoners, migrants or NFL players. That is precisely why, he emphasized, that all workers must unite and resist a system that relies on white supremacy for its very existence.

Abridged from WW, Oct. 16, 2017.

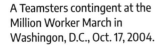

A Teamsters contingent at the Million Worker March in Washington, D.C., Oct. 17, 2004.

Why workers must fight white supremacy

Special presentation by Clarence Thomas

Since the election of Donald Trump in 2016, ILWU Local 10 has seen various displays of racist graffiti and symbols of racial terror on the docks, in the form of racist graffiti and nooses.

After 911, Homeland Security swooped in their security technology, placing high-tech cameras all around. The employers use it for their benefit. They can't come to grips with using it for the benefit of the workers. I wanted to get that out there, because I want to tie it in.

Few occupations better illustrate the class struggle, working-class consciousness and the complexity of ethnic racial conflict and accommodation in the U.S. than the men and women who labor along the shore. That's where the name longshoreman derived from because years ago when the clipper ships arrived along the shore men would congregate to discharge the cargo.

Why must workers fight white supremacy? The short answer is because it's in our class interest.

To not do so allows the ruling class and others to divide the working class by race, color, national origin, gender, sexual orientation, religion, and so forth.

Can you have capitalism without racism? Edward Baptist's book, ***"The Half Has Never Been Told,"*** provides an answer to that question. The kidnapping and enslavement of Africans was truthfully the bloody foundation of capitalism. The major commodities in the world were cotton, sugar, and tobacco. That was the foundation for capitalism. It's

perpetuation is exemplified through racism, exploitation, oppression and white privilege.

Now, let's get to what it is that longshore workers do because it's important to understand that they are some of the most critical workers in the global economy. The reason is because of the cargo that comes off of these vessels. It is the electronic devices that most of us in this room have: computers, athletic shoes, the food we eat, the cars we drive and many other things that we hardly ever think comes off a ship.

As a member of the International Longshore and Warehouse Union, (ILWU) we represent 29 ports on the West Coast, Hawaii and Vancouver, Canada. The International Longshore Association (ILA) represents the East Coast, the Gulf States, also the Great Lakes, and the Midwest.

The ILWU, ILA and the Teamsters are three of the strongest industrial unions in the U.S. If we don't go to work the supply chain is disrupted. That is the global power of the working class.

The ILWU was born, actually in 1937, after we broke away from the ILA.

What's critical to understand is the 1934 West Coast Maritime Strike. The 'Shock Troops' of U.S. capitalism, the shipping companies said, "that they were in a fight against Bolsheviks and that this was a revolution." The reason why was because of the demands that the workers were making: Coastwide collective bargaining and an end

Clarence Thomas spoke at an Oct. 10, 2017, Workers World Party political discussion. Thomas was joined at the event by Brenda Stokely and Chris Silvera, all leaders of the Million Worker March Movement.
Photo: Peoples Video Network

to working around the clock. They were demanding a six-hour work day.

The most revolutionary demand of all was the right of workers to control the hiring hall. Before that we had what was called a shape-up, a very demeaning, undemocratic and divisive system of providing jobs.

What would happen is that the boss representing the company would select the men to go to work for the day. They would make the selection of those workers based upon nepotism, kickbacks, selecting folks on the basis of their ethnic group. The shape-up system was dehumanizing.

When the union demanded that workers have the right to democratically distribute those jobs we were challenging the power of the boss. That was unheard of and they weren't going to give that up.

Now, coincidentally in May of 1934, the Teamsters in Minneapolis, Minnesota had a trucker's strike. That wasn't a coincidence. No, that was based upon the external conditions of 1934, in the Depression.

It was also a time when the influence of the left was most evident. The unions that had the most credibility were those that were led and influenced by the left. They challenged the company unions.

The longshore strike paralyzed all of the ports on the West Coast. San Francisco was the number one port city in the world.

There was an immigrant from Australia, of all places, named Harry Bridges. He was a rank-and-file leader. He had an uncle who had gone to sea. Harry's father was a well-to-do real estate broker who thought Harry was going to go into the business.

Harry Bridges wanted to be a seaman. He had read Jack London and Karl Marx. He understood the class struggle. He had traveled to many ports and seen the condition of the working class and how terribly the men who worked on ships were treated and how dangerous the work was.

July 5, 1934, is an important day in our history that is called 'Bloody Thursday.' On that occasion two maritime strikers were killed, shot in the back by the San Francisco Police Department. That led to a four-day San Francisco General Strike where the entire city was paralyzed.

During the strike, black longshoremen are recruited into the ILA for the first time. Racial unity is key to the strike's success and becomes a guiding principle of the union. After the strike, Bridges states that if only two longshore workers are left on the docks, one would be black and the other white.

Cop and a worker during the 1934 San Francisco General Strike.

Photo: ILWU archive

All of the capitalist forces were lined up as well as the state, the newspapers, the National Guard, the police department, the city, the mayor and the governor. They were determined to keep the ports open.

It's unfortunate that this history isn't available to our young people. I didn't learn any of this in school. I learned about it when I became an ILWU member. I'm a third generation longshoreman. The first time that I ever heard of Harry Bridges was at my grandfather's kitchen table, when he brought longshoremen home for lunch. It was also the first time I heard Paul Robeson's name. He became an honorary member of the ILWU in 1943.

To connect the narrative to the issue of white supremacy and how it was challenged during the 1934 Strike, let me explain.

Do you know who did the work when the unions were on strike? It was Blacks because it was one of the few times that we had an opportunity to work. There's a book called: "Divided We Stand," by Bruce Nelson and he wrote, "In the nineteen century, immigrants from Ireland and Germany competed for employment on the docks with northern free Blacks and southern slaves."

It's critical to understand how white supremacy works. Black folks were used as scabs during the 1934 Strike. That's how many of them got on the waterfront. They were kept on in certain instances. However, Bridges and the other leftists in the union realized that they could not win the Strike with Black folks working. What do we do?

Bridges in his wisdom along with other leftists, and radicals, went to the Black community and spoke with leading pastors in San Francisco and Oakland. They appealed to them to allow them to speak in the churches. It would be what we call today: "Labor

in the pulpit." I've been a part of those important actions. I tell people who are close to the church that I belong to the secular church, the union that allows members to make their tithings.

All the ministers understood that this was a revolutionary action on the part of the white working class: "How are we going to win the Strike Harry when the Black people are working?"

The only reason why is because they're not members of the union. What vested interest do they have in supporting the strike? Bridges went to the churches and made a strong plea for the community to support the 1934 Strike. It didn't happen overnight, but it did happen.

We can make the connection between the 1934 Strike and point out what W.E.B. Du Bois wrote in his book, "The Souls of Black Folk," where he describes how enslaved Black people were the determining factor in the victory of the North in the Civil War.

Enslaved Africans were fleeing plantations going to union encampments. Union soldiers returned them to the plantations. But, when the enslaved Africans stopped doing the work on the plantations, that impacted the confederate supply chain.

We can draw an analogy between that and when Black folks started supporting the Strike. The longshoremen could not have won that 1934 struggle without the support of the Black community.

This action on the part of the Black community was a blow against white supremacy. The employer used Black people to generate the profits during the Strike because Black people were out of the union; unlike the ILA where you had segregated unions, Black and white.

Let me just deviate for a quick second to show you how even in the South, white supremacy was challenged from 1899 to 1920. In New Orleans, they had what they called 'screw men' workers who worked on the docks. They used a jackscrew to handle giant bales of cotton.

The Black union and white union dock workers competed for work. Whites (German and Irish immigrants) were not going to remove Blacks from the riverfront who had been working there as enslaved and freed men. Employers believed the wages of white labor would increase with the removal of African American dock workers. Instead of competing for work, the Black and white workers decided to share the work equally. The decision was based upon mutual interest. This unity remained in place until the 1920s.

In the North, Blacks were not represented in unions and they worked as scabs to get work; in the South, workers were in segregated unions but were paid less.

The reason for "right to work" is because the Southern bosses said to poor whites in the working class, 'you won't work with Blacks.' By keeping white workers from uniting with Black workers and from forming integrated unions, they had a cheaper labor market in the South. That drove the whole issue of "right to work for less." They used it as a race measure and it is still working.

UAW has been attempting for many years to organize workers at the Nissan Plant in Canton, Miss. After years of anti-union propaganda and threats of job losses from "right to work" state elected officials the workers voted in August 2017 to reject the UAW.

Black workers at Nissan believe white workers' resentment of African American in leadership positions is a primary reason for the anti-union vote. It also happened in Tennessee with Volkswagen. The race measure is still working! That's why the working class needs to fight against white

Clarence Thomas speaking on struggle against racism at a Rosa Parks Commemoration in New York City December, 2005.

WW Photo : Deirdre Griswold

supremacy. Our Constitution opposes racial and all forms of discrimination.

Now I want to talk about some solidarity actions that made the ILWU world renowned.

In 1935, when Mussolini invaded Ethiopia, there was a community action. It was a blockade to stop the shipment of nickel and zinc to Mussolini. In 1939, we refused to load scrap iron destined for Japan after it invaded Manchuria. If we were brought into the war then this material could be used on U.S. soldiers. When we took that action FDR sent a letter to Bridges saying, "Harry you need to stay out of matters of foreign policy." Harry's response was, "That's our right as citizens."

One could see where our anti-fascist roots started.

During the military juntas in El Salvador and other Latin American countries, ILWU members refused to handle cargo. We shipped ambulances to Nicaragua with the assistance of veterans of the Abraham Lincoln Brigade. That's the kind of union I come from.

We refused to handle the grapes that Cesar Chavez's workers were

boycotting. 'We're not gonna handle those grapes!' The ILWU participated in the first march that Cesar Chavez had in San Francisco in the mid-1960s.

International solidarity is not an empty slogan. The ILWU believes that international solidarity and economic and social justice for the working class is the key to a peaceful world. We opposed the Korean War, the war in Vietnam, the war in Iraq, and the war in Afghanistan. Now, workers won't unload Israeli cargo.

Local 10 shut down ports for 24 hours on the anniversary Dr. Martin Luther King's assassination to support the campaign of the workers in Wisconsin. The public sector workers were defending their right to collective bargaining.

The ILWU was part of the West Coast Occupy action. The ILWU said, "Stop Wall Street on the Waterfront." It was not an empty slogan about how we were going to disrupt Wall Street. No, we shut down commerce on the waterfront. We had to fight our own international leadership on this question.

And on May Day in 2015, 2016, and 2017, Local 10 dock workers 'Shut It Down' to protest police killings.

On the question of the struggle against apartheid in South Africa, I'd like to talk about a comrade to many people in this room.

Leo Robinson, is one of the most important rank-and-file leaders of the ILWU in its modern era.

In 1962, community people in San Francisco came to the port terminals to call attention to apartheid and to setup a picket line. Our members didn't go to work.

Our union was very familiar with the issue of apartheid. In the mid-1970s, Brother Robinson was moved by the killing of the South African youth who didn't want to speak the Africana language. He wrote a resolution calling for the boycott of South African cargo.

What makes our union unique is that we have democracy where the rank-and-file can write a resolution. They can submit the resolution to the Executive Board and then have

As early as December 28, 1962, San Francisco members of the International Longshore and Warehouse Union (ILWU) staged a boycott of South African apartheid cargo.

membership vote on it. After that it goes to the Longshore Caucus or to the International Convention. We're a bottom-up and not top-down union.

Robinson made a bold move calling for the boycott of South African cargo. Immediately following that, the ship Nedlloyd Kemberley arrived in San Francisco.

I'm going to show you how real socialism on the job happens when you have a hiring hall and the workers control the jobs. We live in a capitalist society where the means of production is controlled by the ruling class. In our industry it is not the shippers, but the workers control the production, which means we can stop it or we can change it. We can speed it up. We can slow it down. We have that power, if we use it.

We got word that there was going to be a picket line formed against the Nedlloyd Kemberley. We learned of it before dispatch at the hall before the ship came in.

Leo Robinson and others, who were in support of the anti-apartheid struggle met with the job dispatchers. They said listen there's going to be an action when the Nedlloyd Kemberley comes in. We want certain members to take that job who can stand not getting a full day's pay.

See, that's what happens when you control the dispatch. You see things that are happening behind the scenes, where the workers control the work that the world doesn't know about.

Our employers had no knowledge of what was going to happen. They just knew that there was a demonstration but they didn't know that we had done our part to facilitate the action. The employers were upset because there was a picket line. They know if there's a picket line on the job we don't go to work. Even if you haven't worked in a week, if there's a picket line you 'stand by.' The police cannot escort us across a picket line. Why, because the police shot our members in the back in 1934.

This is why we understand the relationship between Black Lives

No. Calif. CTBU founder Geraldine Johnson and Leo Robinson with South African medical student David Ndaba. Photo: Daily Worker/Daily World

Matter and the labor movement. Because we understand that the police
represent the bosses. Those members
went out there to insure that ship was
stopped. That was the first shot across
the bow in our fight against apartheid
in the 1970s.

We didn't work South African
cargo for 11 days in 1984. But you
have to understand that didn't happen
overnight. We had a lot of struggle in
the meantime with many of our Black
and white members who questioned
Robinson and others. "Brother Leo,
what does this South Africa 'BS'
have to do with our pork chops?
We're concerned about our contract."

We showed videos and brought
members of the ANC to speak to
our union. We organized a Southern
Africa Liberation Support Committee
which was one of the first unionized
anti-apartheid groups in the country.
We were able to explain how Ronald
Reagan was lying about the issue of
constructive engagement by saying:
"Conducting business as usual in
South Africa and muting criticism of
apartheid was preferable to economic
sanctions." You have to explain it to
the rank-and-file.

We didn't work the South African
cargo. We collected humanitarian
supplies and sent containers to Tanzania where there was an ANC base.
Those supplies made their way into
the hands of the freedom fighters.

We were able to secure containers
from our employers who would say:
"Well yeah, you can have that old container it's rusted." That's where our
class consciousness comes into play.

The working class can make these
kinds of demands. Leaders of the
MWM secured and filled containers
with humanitarian supplies for
Hurricane Katrina survivors in
New Orleans.

We secured and filled containers
with humanitarian supplies and sent

In the mid-1970s Leo Robinson was moved by the killing of the South African youth who didn't want to speak the Africana language. He wrote a resolution calling for the boycott of South African cargo.

South African ship Nedlloyd Kimberley arrives in the Bay Area.

them to Mozambique and Angola.
When we loaded those containers for
free the employer said they'd give us
space on the ship.

Leo Robinson, told me that one
day he was listening to KPFA. He
heard two Black women describing how they were being harassed
and terrorized by the Ku Klux Klan
and neo-Nazis in a little town called
Oroville, California. Robinson invited them to a membership meeting,
being the rank-and-file leader that he
was. We invited members of the community to share their issues and concerns when such opportunities may
not have been open to them in other
forums. The women from Oroville
came to tell us their story.

After the sisters spoke at the Local
10 meeting, a motion was made to
have our next monthly membership
meeting in Oroville. We took hundreds of rank-and file members to
Oroville and we marched down that
thoroughfare and met with city officials demanding an end to the harassment. Johnny Stevens was a part of
an organizing committee that brought
thousands of people demanding an
end to the racist attacks. That was a
show of working-class power. The
harassment ceased.

Ku Klux Klan gatherings in the
Bay Area in Alameda and Contra

Costa Counties were frequent in the
1920s, and later. Malcolm X once
said, "Any time that you're south of
the Canadian border you're South."

In 1981, Local 10 member Roosevelt Presley and his family lived
in the city of Richmond in Contra
Costa County. His family had to
endure sniping and cross burning at
his home. When brothers and sisters
found out about how Presley was
being assaulted by the Klan, they
went out to his home armed to the
gills to protect his family. We hired
a security company to protect that
brother. The union also organized a
Civil Rights committee made up of
labor and the inter-faith community
to address systematic racism in that
community. This is another example of ILWU Local 10 fighting white
supremacy.

The Justice for Oscar Grant Movement has a special meaning for me.
My nephew, Ryan Coogler, directed
a movie called "Fruitvale Station,"
which captures Oscar's last day alive
and his graphic murder. When Oscar
Grant was killed in 2009, the membership invited his "Uncle Bobby,"
Cephus X Johnson and Jack Bryson,
whose sons witnessed Oscar being
murdered, to Local 10 for a Black
History Month gathering. There was
a great community outrage to the

death of Oscar Grant and the county district attorney was dragging her feet in handling the case. Local 10 decided to fight and mobilize for 'Justice for Oscar Grant.'

I'm going to tell you what a revolutionary movement looks like; it is when you have a diverse coalition such as Blacks, Latinos, Native Americans, whites, anarchists, clergy, LGBTQ, Marxist-Leninist, Nation of Islam, ILWU Local 10 and other labor unions, all in one room uniting for 'Justice for Oscar Grant and Jail for Killer Cops,' and not allowing their differences to get in the way.

This is what it's going to take to stop white supremacy!

We had a rally on October 23, 2010, at what now is called Oscar Grant Plaza. We shut down five Bay Area ports calling for 'Justice for Oscar Grant.' Johannes Mehserle's (killer cop who killed Oscar), attorney posed a question on the nightly Bay Area news. What does longshore workers shutting down the ports have to do with Oscar Grant? Simple answer, labor is responding to the murder of unarmed Black people by the police.

Not just any labor organization, but one that is involved with the movement of international cargo. We have comrades, brothers and sisters, that are members of the International Dockers Council, a progressive coalition of dockworkers from around the world. When we bring up issues like this, they can do important solidarity actions. It was the first time in U.S. history that labor had taken an action at the point of production on the question of police brutality and the murder of Blacks by the police.

On Saturday, August 26, 2017, the Patriot Prayer group, a right-wing organization with a history of inciting racial violence from Portland, Oregon, held a rally in San Francisco. Local 10 passed a motion to: "Stop the Fascists in San Francisco," expressing opposition to the rally and its plans to organize. The motion called for all unions and anti-racist and anti-fascist organizations to join in defending unions, people of color, immigrants, LGBTQ people, women and all oppressed people.

Thousands of anti-racists and progressives turned out at a counter demonstration at their rally site out

numbering the few fascist that showed up. These actions on the part of ILWU Local 10 further demonstrates its leadership in the labor movement in the struggle against white supremacy.

In conclusion, the white working class must understand the relationship between race and class in this country. Brother Saladin Muhammad, chair of Black Workers for Justice and co-convener for the MWMM Southern Region, writes about it very eloquently in "Hurricane Katrina, The Black Nation's 9/11!" "The racist economic, social and political policies and practices of the U.S. government and capitalist system shape society's attitudes about the reasons for the historical oppression of African Americans. It seeks to isolate, criminalize and scapegoat African Americans as social pariahs holding back the progress of society.

"The characterization of the Black working class in this way is a part of the continuous ideological shaping of white supremacy that gives white workers a sense of being part of another working class, different from that of the Black working class. This often leads many white workers to act against their own class interests, discouraging them from uniting with the Black working class in struggling to seek common, equal and socially transformative resolutions to their class issues." See "Hurricane Katrina: The Black Nation's 9/11!" on page 84.

Why should workers fight white supremacy? If we don't we could be facing fascism or a civil war.

Workers must fight white supremacy!

To see Clarence Thomas' entire presentation on YouTube go to: tinyurl.com/y55unmz9

Above, ILWU Local 10 members gather to denounce white supremacy. Patriot Prayer a right-wing organization with a history of inciting racist violence, declared it would rally in San Francisco in August, 2017. Local 10 took a lead role in organizing counter-protests that contributed to the event being canceled.

"Dockworkers Show Labor Movement How to Stop Fascists," by Peter Cole, Aug. 29, 2017, *In These Times.*

'Fight or be Slaves'
Black workers take the lead

Pamphlet written by Clarence Thomas written in response to receiving the prestigious C.L. Dellums Award

From the time of the formation of the first U.S. trade unions in the 1790s to the early 1930s, a major plight of the Black worker has been one of trying to build a unified, democratic and powerful national trade union movement where the struggles of Black workers and the African American people were recognized in the spirit of the principle of, "An injury to one is an injury to all."

This has required Black workers to not only be good trade unionists, but also freedom fighters both inside and outside of our unions. When Black workers were excluded from joining the national unions, we built unions of our own like the Colored National Labor Union and the Brotherhood of Sleeping Car Porters which continued to call for the unity of all workers.

The struggles by Black workers continued to be a struggle against super profits made from corporate racism not only off Black labor but on every aspect of African American oppression, the underfunding of our schools, the inadequate but high cost of housing, the prison industrial complex which profits from the disproportionate jailing of African Americans and Latinos.

Because of this challenge to corporate greed, Black workers who spoke out against racism that divided workers within the unions and in the larger society were demonized or written out of history. The true history of the role of Black workers not just as laborers, but as leaders in the fight for democracy and radical change of the system that denies democracy, has not been taught to our children in the schools. When they are taught about Frederick Douglass, he is never described as a union leader, as the first vice president of the Colored National Labor Union.

They never teach of Douglass' speeches demanding that "white employers give Black workers the opportunity to become apprentices and to work in the trades" [1] held exclusively by whites; or his plea for "labor unions and labor papers to educate white workers on the value of unity in the struggle for a decent livelihood, regardless of race or color." [2]

"Fight or be Slaves!" These were the words of our brother C.L. Dellums, a leader, vice president and president of the Brotherhood of Sleeping Car Porters and a leader of the March on Washington Movement (MWM) that was initiated by African American workers and leaders like A. Philip Randolph. The MWM in the 1940s was the launching point of the Civil Rights movement of the 1950s. In fact, one of the members and organizers of the Brotherhood of Sleeping Car Porters and the MWM, E.D. Nixon was a major organizer of the 1955 Montgomery, Alabama Bus Boycott centered on Sister Rosa Parks and led by Dr. Martin L. King.

C.L. Dellums and other Black workers like Moranda Smith, the regional director of the Winston-Salem, N.C.'s FTA Local 22 food, tobacco, agricultural workers, were pioneers. They advanced the cause of all workers and fought for African American democracy as the two essential struggles of their time to improve the conditions of life for working and oppressed peoples.

I am proud to list among these great working class fighters for workers rights and social justice Harry Bridges the founder of the ILWU, my union. Bridges, while not a Black worker, understood the importance of the struggle against racism and the need for anti-racist working class

Moranda Smith, a rank-and-file union organizer and leader of N.C. tobacco workers who throughout the 1930s and 1940s initiated a challenge to the racist discrimination, disfranchisement, and economic exploitation of workers in the South. She was first African American to sit on FTA international executive board.

Smith was born in Dunbar, S.C. to a sharecropping family.

C.L. Dellums, a rank-and-file leader and vice president of the Brotherhood of Sleeping Car Porters.

Dellums was also a leader of the 1940s March on Washington that was initiated by African American union leader A. Philip Randolph, founder of Brotherhood of Sleeping Car Porters.

COMMEMORATOR

Published by the Commemoration Committee for the Black Panther Party

Volume 15, Number 1   Suggested Donation $2.00   March 2005

Million Worker March Demands Fundamental Change

Newly elected President of Local 10, ILWU, Trent Willis (left), co-chair of the Million Worker March, and David Hilliard, BPP Founding Member and Executive Director of The Huey P. Newton Foundation.

By Melvin Dickson

Editor's note: On October 17, 2004, ten thousand people converged at the Washington Monument in Washington, D.C. under the banner of the Million Worker March to voice their demands to the federal government about health care, living wage jobs, education, US aggression in other countries killing working people around the world, including the US war in Iraq, and much more. The Million Worker March (MWM) demonstrated the anger of workers and unemployed

people, union members and non-union members, organizers and activists from across the country who came together to fight for change. The organizers of the march declared that no matter who was elected President of the United States, working people would have to organize to fight for the power to accomplish their goals and force the government to meet their demands.

Representatives of the MWM denounced the policies and political positions of both Kerry and Bush because both men represent the forces of US imperialism, doing the bidding of international monopoly capitalism led by the US-controlled World Bank and International Monetary Fund.

The rally consisted of speakers who addressed a multiplicity of issues, denouncing the US based corporations outsourcing of jobs that once employed US tax-paying citizens, the general lack of living wage jobs throughout the world, and the fight

inside the US for affordable health-care, housing and education. Some speakers addressed the need for the American people to demand the federal government revoke the Patriot Act, as well as the imperialist policies that have led the US government to criminally occupy Iraq and Haiti.

The Million Worker March incorporated not only an advanced sector of the labor movement, but also unemployed workers, professionals and students, as well as representatives from organizations of the homeless and of temporary workers, independent contractors, part-time and seasonal workers, service and farm workers.

Melvin Dickson, Commemorator editor, conducted the following interview with Trent Willis, who, along with Clarence Thomas, organized the Million Worker March. An emerging labor leader, Mr. Willis was recently elected President of International Longshore and Warehouse Union

Continued on page 10

The Commemorator newspaper was a newspaper printed in South Berkeley from 1990-2013 by the Commemoration Committee for the Black Panther Party.
The newspaper collection consists of 54 issues of Commemorator newspaper printed from 1990-2012.

Melvin Dickson, publisher of *The Commemorator* wrote about the significance of the MWM for the Black Liberation Movement.

---

unity for democratic trade unions. These views were fostered and established as policy during union organizing on the San Francisco waterfront in the early 30s. [3]

In 1942, his "On the Beam" column in *The Dispatcher,* Bridges "called for an end to discrimination against Blacks and women. He was among the first in the labor movement to condemn the internment of Japanese Americans during World War II. And in the early 60s, he was strongly critical of the government's lackluster investigation into the bombing of Black churches and the deaths of civil rights activists in the South." [4]

As I think about the words of Brother C.L. Dellums: "Fight or Be Slaves," it rings of the true spirit and dedication of the Black worker activists, trade unionists and Freedom fighters. It sounds similar to the slogan of the Million Worker March "Mobilizing in Our Own Name!" We were trying to make clear that workers of all races, nationalities

and genders and especially African Americans should not be slaves for the Democratic or Republican Parties or the system of corporate greed.

The Million Worker March had similar pressures as the March on Washington Movement to call off the demonstration in Washington, D.C. on October 17, 2004, but we understood our history of calling off demonstrations in exchange for broken promises, betrayal and disappointment.

The challenges facing African Americans and all workers in the U.S. and internationally today, are magnified by this unjust war of corporate greed and global domination; the same greed that created the system of slavery and its racist justification which has been institutionalized within the U.S. and global economy. The greed and stereotypes promoted by the corporate owned media to divide workers and people's of different nationalities and a major driving force promoting anti-Iraqi, anti-Arab

and anti-Islamic hatred. Unless this war is ended immediately by bringing the troops home now, not only will tens of thousands of Iraqi children, women and men and thousands of U.S. troops die for U.S. corporate greed, but this war will have long term affects on the culture and sense of humanity for future generations.

African American workers and all working people must let the world know where we stand on this unjust war. They must know and be shown by our actions of resistance, that the U.S. is making war at home on working and oppressed peoples as it makes war abroad. Thus, the Million Worker March believes that the movement against the war abroad and at home must expand from protest to action.

Thank you for this prestigious award. Again, in the words of Brother C.L. Dellums: "Fight or be Slaves!"

1 *Organized Labor and the Black Worker, pg 7, by Philip Foner*
2 *Ibid*
3 *Harry Bridges Institute for International Education and Organization*
4 *Ibid*

Black Workers for Justice launch Southern campaign for union rights

Monica Moorehead

A significant pro-labor, anti-racist event occurred in Raleigh on April 2, 2005. It was the 22nd annual Martin Luther King Jr. Support for Labor Banquet hosted by the Black Workers for Justice (BWFJ).

About 200 union, community, student and political activists and supporters from the local area, as well as from other parts of the South and the U.S., filled a hall at the North Carolina Association of Educators building. Among the invited delegations were the Raleigh FIST (Fight Imperialism, Stand Together) youth group, International Action Center and Workers World Party.

BWFJ, founded in 1981, played a national role in helping to build the Oct. 17, 2004 Million Worker March rally in Washington, D.C. It mobilized workers from the South to heed the call to build an independent workers' movement free from the shackles of the pro-big business Democratic and Republican parties.

Musical numbers were performed by the Fruit of Labor Singing Ensemble, the cultural component of BWFJ, along with Washington, D.C., vocalists Pam Parker and Lucy Murphy.

Saladin Muhammad, BWFJ's national chairperson, introduced the keynote speaker: Clarence Thomas, co-chair of the Million Worker March and a leader of Local 10 of the International Longshore and Warehouse Union in San Francisco.

Thomas recalled that a similar call for a March on Washington was made in 1941 by the Brotherhood of Sleeping Car Porters, led by A. Philip Randolph and C.L. Dellums. These two Black union leaders wanted to bring 100,000 Black workers to Washington, D.C., to demand an end to racist discrimination in hiring practices. The plans for the march forced President

Left to right, BWFJ leader Angaza Laughinghouse, Clarence Thomas, UE 150 member Larsene Taylor, Larry Holmes, Saladin Muhammad and Monica Moorehead.
WW photo: Sue Kelly

Million Worker March leader honored

Clarence Thomas, co-chair of the Oct. 17 Million Worker March and a leader of the ILWU Local 10 in San Francisco, gives the keynote address at the Black Workers for Justice Banquet (BWFJ) in N.C. Association of Educators Building on April 2, 2005. In this photo, Ashaki Binta hands Thomas the microphone.

BWFJ played a leadership role in building and supporting the MWM rally held last fall at the Lincoln Memorial, which called for creating an independent workers' movement. The BWFJ organizes campaigns alongside United Electrical Local 150 to win long-denied collective-bargaining rights for all workers in North Carolina.
WW photo: Monica Moorehead

Ashaki Binta, the BWFJ's director of organization, said the banquet was the expression of our unity in the fight to 'Organize the South' with a new trade union movement.

Musical numbers were performed by the Fruit of Labor Singing Emsemble, the cultural component of BWFJ, along with Washington, D.C., vocalists Pam Parker and Lucy Murphy.

WW photos: Monica Moorehead

Franklin D. Roosevelt to sign an executive order prohibiting discrimination in the hiring of people of color in the federal government and by federal contractors.

Thomas praised the first president of the ILWU, Australian-born Harry Bridges, who practiced what he preached when it came to building anti-racist class solidarity. Bridges, whom Thomas referred to as a Marxist, made a conscious effort to bring unorganized Black workers into the ILWU back in 1934. At that time, the majority-white trade unions still maintained an openly racist policy of shutting their doors to Black and other oppressed workers. This meant that Black workers, through no fault of their own, were forced to cross picket lines during strikes to put food on the table. Thomas ended his talk with a resounding, urgent call to revive May Day, or International Workers' Day, which grew out of the struggle in this country for the eight-hour day.

A group of Latino workers associated with the Farm Labor Organizing Committee received one of the self-determination awards at the banquet. FLOC won a hard-fought historic union contract for 8,000 immigrant farm workers last year, the first of its kind in North Carolina, with the growers.

Larry Holmes, co-director of the International Action Center, gave a solidarity message in which he praised the BWJF and ILWU Local 10 in their ongoing efforts to build the MWM movement. He, along with other members of the New York committee of the MWM, accepted a self-determination award on behalf of Brenda Stokely, AFSCME District Council 1707 president and MWM leader, who was unable to attend the banquet.

Ashaki Binta, the BWFJ's director of organization, focused her remarks on a very important campaign that BWFJ, along with the North Carolina Public Service Workers Union, UE Local 150, initiated last August. It is called the International Worker Justice Campaign for Collective Bargaining Rights.

Binta said the banquet was "the expression of our ongoing unity in the fight to 'Organize the South'; to build the new trade union movement in the South; to support the building of UE Local 150, UE Local 160, the Carolina Auto, Aerospace and Metal Workers Union (CAAMWU), and the non-majority union movement.

Abridged from WW, April 12, 2005.

Honoring Black History
Longshore union unites past, current struggles

Joan Marquardt

Several hundred people gathered in the ILWU's historic San Francisco union hall on Feb. 14, 2009, for a Black History Month rally, entitled "Racism, Repression and Rebellion: The Lessons of Labor Defense."

Local 10 rally chair Clarence Thomas recounted the history of the ILWU, a predominantly African American union in the Bay Area. He reminded the crowd: "Racism is pervasive in our society and affects the labor movement, like all other areas of society." Despite the history making election of the first African-American president, Barack Obama, Racism is still alive and well in this country."

Thomas noted a news story of juvenile court judges who accepted kickbacks from racists to convict Black youths accused of petty crimes. He added that the police killing of Oscar Grant, a 22 year-old Black father by a white transit cop, would not have become known if it had not been recorded on several passengers' cell phones and made public.

The Local 10's 1984, historic refusal to unload cargo from apartheid South Africa was later recognized by Nelson Mandela himself. This past week the Congress of South African

Portable memorial of people killed by police.

Clarence Thomas and Martina Davis-Correia, Troy Davis' sister, Feb 14, 2009.

Photo: Delores Lemon-Thomas

Trade Unions held a national week of action, entitled "Free Palestine, Isolate Israel," where Durban dockworkers refused to offload cargo from a ship from Israel. Thomas called this action a strong testament to the power of international labor solidarity.

Tayo Aluko, a Nigerian actor, performed a cultural piece, written, spoken and sung by the great African American, Paul Robeson. Thomas stated that, "The ILWU made Paul Robeson an honorary member of the union because he was a revolutionary artist who put his career on the line to defend the oppressed."

Cristina Gutierrez, a longtime supporter of Mumia Abu-Jamal and community activist, told the rally that immigrants are tired of being used against striking workers, often striking Black workers, because immigrant workers are part of the working class. She lead the chant, "Free Mumia! Workers of the world, Unite!"

Haiti Action Committee member Pierre LaBossiere spoke of the historic uprisings of Haitians against foreign exploitation. LaBossiere explained that President Aristide's

attempt to raise the minimum wage of Haitian workers triggered the U.S. Marine invasion that forcibly removed Aristide from office and out of Haiti.

Martina Davis-Correia, sister of death row prisoner Troy Davis, spoke about his wrongful conviction for killing a man he was actually attempting to protect, and the years since 1991 he spent in prison. The crowd chanted, "Free Troy Davis!"

JR Valrey, Minister of Information of Prisoners of Conscience, spoke about Oscar Grant and called on everyone to support freedom for the Oakland 100, those arrested for participating in a spontaneous rebellion following Grant's killing.

Richard Brown, one of the San Francisco 8 and a former member of the Black Panther Party, demanded that charges be dropped against the community activists. Rev. Cecil Williams spoke on racial profiling and commended the ILWU for promoting action to empower Black youth to overcome racist oppression.

Jack Heyman of Local 10 recalled the heroic ILWU shutdown of West Coast ports in 1999, demanding that renowned political prisoner Mumia Abu-Jamal be set free. Robert Bryan, attorney for Abu-Jamal's defense, talked about the struggle to get Abu-Jamal released from prison, where he is still on death row.

Clarence Thomas closed the rally by recognizing the women responsible for much of the organizing of the rally, stating that "These young ILWU members are the future of the ILWU."

Abridged from WW, Feb.26, 2009.

Dock workers shut down Bay Area ports as
Strike, rally demand justice for Oscar Grant

Judy Greenspan

The stage and steps of Frank Ogawa Plaza in downtown Oakland shook and trembled with the strong unifying cry of "We are all Oscar Grant!" as over 1,000 people, Black, Brown, Native, Asian and white, came out despite rain to attend a rally that followed the dramatic

Bobby Seale, Chairman of the Black Panther Party, and Clarence Thomas spoke at the Oct. 23, 2010 rally pictured below.

Photo: Delores Lemon-Thomas

shut down of Bay Area ports by workers of the Local 10.

The Local 10 Drill Team opened the Oct. 23, 2010, program in full uniform, marching to the beat of "What time is it? Union time!" and "We are the union, the mighty, mighty union!"

Clarence Thomas, long-time ILWU Local 10 member and labor activist who co-chaired the rally with Jack Heyman, another Local 10 dock worker, proudly announced, "All of the Bay Area ports are shut down today in honor of the fight for justice for Oscar Grant."

This rally comes just two weeks before the sentencing of Johannes Mehserle, the Bay Area Rapid Transit cop who shot and killed 22 year-old Grant, an unarmed Black man, as he was tightly restrained face down on a BART platform on Jan. 1, 2009. The labor and community protest was held to send a message to the court demanding the harshest possible sentence for Mehserle.

Mehserle was charged with second-degree murder but was convicted of only involuntary man-slaughter. Grant's mother, Wanda Johnson, said immediately after the verdict, "My son was murdered. He was murdered and the law has not held the officer accountable." (San Francisco Chronicle, July 9, 2010)

Many speakers noted the incredible role played by the ILWU in supporting today's rally. The union has a long history of supporting anti- racist and progressive causes with work stoppages. The dock and warehouse workers union has also, since its 1934 General Strike, developed a strong relationship with the Black community in West Oakland and other parts of the Bay Area.

Power of the working class

Richard Mead, president of ILWU Local 10, recalled that the shooting of two workers sparked the 1934 General Strike led by the dock and maritime workers in San Francisco. "Oscar Grant's death was also murder," Mead said. "A general strike, that's where we need to go now."

Thomas put Grant's killing in a larger perspective. "The war on the Black community, particularly on the youth of color, always intensifies during times of economic crisis. Oscar Grant could have been any one of our sons, nephews or grandsons.

"We stopped international commerce today. We shut down all of the ports. That's the power of the working class," Thomas announced.

Cristina Gutierrez, an activist representing Barrio Unido, a San Francisco-based organization for general and unconditional amnesty for immigrants, delivered a moving statement on the strength of the unity of all people against oppression. "Yo soy Oscar Grant, I am Oscar Grant, I am Mumia, I am Lynne Stewart, I am Black, I am Brown, I am Chinese, I am a worker," Gutierrez exclaimed.

"I am the one who came to this country to seek work. Unless we work hand in hand with our Black brothers and sisters, we cannot win," said Gutierrez.

BART workers from the Amalgamated Transit Union Local 1555, led by past president Harold Brown, stood together on stage and delivered a moving statement in support of justice for Oscar Grant. Brown, a train operator on the BART line which passes through the Fruitvale Station, the site of Grant's killing, noted, "There's not a day that goes by that I don't think of Oscar Grant. This should never have happened."

The impetus for the justice rally came from members of Oscar Grant's family, who went to the Local 10 seeking their support. The highpoint of the event came when a large group of Grant's family and friends took the stage.

The atmosphere on the plaza became electrified when Grant's 6 year-old daughter Tatiana was introduced to the crowd. A moving letter to the sentencing judge demanding the maximum sentence for Grant's killer was read by Tatiana's aunt.

Other speakers at today's gathering included Bobby Seale and Elaine Brown, former leaders of the Black Panther Party, and representatives from several unions including the Service Employees and the Oakland Education Association/California Teachers Association.

Throughout the afternoon, rally organizers reminded the crowd, "We cannot let this movement end today." Plans are underway to keep the momentum of this coalition going, including a mass meeting of the Justice for Oscar Grant Community Outreach Committee on Oct. 26 in Oakland.

Abridged from WW, Nov. 4, 2010

Tatiana, Oscar Grant's six-year-old daughter.

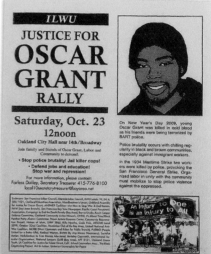

Oct, 23, 2010, rally two weeks before the sentencing of Johannes Mehserle, the Bay Area Rapid Transit cop who killed 22-year-old Grant, an unarmed Black man, as he was tightly restrained face down on a BART platform. Clarence Thomas, co-chaired the rally announced: "All of the Bay Area ports are shut down today in honor of the fight for justice for Oscar Grant." WW photo: Judy Greenspan

BART ATU 1555 past president
Harold Brown speaks at Oscar Grant Rally

Labor Video Project

Harold Brown, past president of BART ATU Local 1555 spoke at the Oscar Grant rally for justice in Oakland on October 23, 2010. Also joining him was a delegation of BART drivers and station agents.

Grant was killed by BART policeman Johannes Mehserle at the BART Fruitville station in Oakland. Brown was joined by a delegation of rank-and-file ATU 1555 BART drivers and station agent workers. The rally was sponsored by ILWU Local 10, San Francisco Labor Council, Alameda Labor Council, Oakland Education Association and SEIU 1021.

Photo by Kazmi Torri, Labor Video Project
www.laborvideo.org

A delegation of ATU 1555 BART workers joined past union president Harold Brown at the Oakland Justice for Oscar Grant rally.

Oscar Grant rally Oct 23, 2010, from the left, Ed Henderson, Jack Heyman, 'Uncle Bobby' Cephus X Johnson and Clarence Thomas.

The San Francisco Labor Council passed a resolution commending ILWU Locals 10 and 34 for shutting down all Bay Area ports on Oct. 23 to demand justice for Oscar Grant, and in calling the powerful Justice for Oscar Grant Rally in Oakland on the same day, "In the spirit of Harry Bridges, this is an example of a union looking beyond narrow economic self interest to support the broader struggle for social justice and support for communities of color. This kind of stand can strengthen the labor movement as a whole by building ties with broader communities outside the organized labor movement. Thank you for this progressive move."   Photo: Delores Lemon-Thomas

Rallies were held in several cities, including Oakland, San Francisco, Los Angeles and Houston, above, following the sentencing of Johannes Mehserle, the Rapid Transit cop who killed an unarmed Oscar Grant on Jan. 1, 2009. Although the killing was videotaped and Mehserle fled the state after the shooting, the Court last July 2010 found him guilty not of murder, but of involuntary manslaughter.

WW photo: Gloria Rubac

Alameda Central Labor Council resolution:

APRIL 2013

Justice for Alan Blueford

The Alameda Central Labor Council (ACLC) passed the following resolution in support of Justice for Alan Blueford unanimously at its monthly delegates meeting Feb. 4, 2013. This followed unanimous approval by the council's executive committee. Four member locals had passed the same resolution by their own bodies, prior to bringing it to the ACLC: Service Employees Local 1021, ILWU Local 10, the Oakland Education Association, and UNITE HERE 2850.

Alan Blueford was killed on May 6, 2012, by Oakland police officer Miguel Masso. It was racial profiling, with Blueford "guilty" of standing on a corner while Black. The Blueford family and the Justice for Alan Blueford Coalition have been waging a battle to publicize the truth about what happened and to have Officer Masso prosecuted for murder.

Alan Blueford's Family demands justice at a rally in 2012.

Whereas a Black person is killed by law enforcement once every 36 hours, per the Malcolm X Grass Roots Movement's study;

Whereas the federal report monitoring the Oakland Police Department (OPD) states that the Oakland Police Department pulls guns on Black and Latino people disproportionately to the number of times guns are pulled on whites;

Whereas two new reports by a federal monitor criticized the OPD's handling of officer-involved shootings and Occupy Oakland protests;

Whereas Alan Blueford, an 18-year-old Black youth, who was about to graduate from Skyline High School, was killed by OPD Officer Masso on May 6;

Whereas OPD has provided at least four versions of what happened the night Alan Blueford was killed, including the claim that Officer Masso was shot in a gun battle with Alan Blueford, when he later admitted that he shot himself in the foot;

Whereas the OPD:

A. Engaged in racial profiling and violated numerous OPD policies;

B. Engaged in a cover-up (made numerous false statements and repeatedly changed their story);

C. Showed complete disregard for the life of Alan Blueford and the dignity of the family;

D. Had the coroner's report withheld from the family for three months and the police report for five months;

Whereas the coroner's report reveals that Alan Blueford had no gun residue on his hands, no alcohol or drugs in his system, and implies that Alan Blueford was shot while lying on his back;

Whereas Alameda County District Attorney Nancy O'Malley declared she will not charge Officer Masso for the killing of Alan Blueford. Her report shows strong bias as, for example, relying on Masso's statement that Alan was standing when he shot him, despite 11 out of 12 witness statements to the contrary;

Therefore, be it resolved that the Alameda Labor Council pass a resolution seeking Justice for Alan Blueford and demand that the Federal Monitor and Compliance Director appointed by Judge Henderson take strong action against OPD including:

1. Stopping the OPD from racial and ethnic profiling and violence against people of color;

2. Instituting stricter background checks, training, apprehension and gun use policies within the OPD;

3. The firing of Officer Masso;

Further be it resolved, that the Alameda Labor Council demand that the Alameda County District Attorney immediately charge Officer Masso with murder;

Finally be it resolved, that the Alameda Labor Council send this resolution to U.S. District Court Judge Thelton Henderson, D.A. O'Malley, ALC affiliates, the California Federation of Labor, and the AFL-CIO, for concurrence and action.

Performers, artists hold #JusticeforFlint event

Cheryl LaBash

In the tradition of Black actors and artists like Harry Belafonte who used their celebrity to help advance the Civil Rights Movement, Blackout for Human Rights organized a free public event, #JusticeforFlint, at Flint's Whiting Auditorium on Feb. 28, 2016. A surprise appearance by Michigan-born Motown music legend Stevie Wonder capped the performances .

Onstage testimony by Flint residents and young organizers highlighted a spirit of resilience and struggle, but also the personal cost imposed on them by the state government. A high school student who was told that water at her private school was unsafe said students had originally been directed to buy water from vending machines. Elementary school students talked about skin eruptions and other illnesses from washing with lead laden water and of bathing with baby wipes.

Dr. Mona Hanna-Attisha, the Flint pediatrician who sounded the lead poisoning alarm, pointed out that Flint families have been fighting for justice for almost two years, but no

Delores Lemon-Thomas, Brenda Harmon, Clarence Thomas and Stacey Rodgers.

Photo: Cheryl LaBash

one heard their voices. "They needed evidence that our kids were being poisoned. And our water is still not safe. The 18 months of corrosive untreated water damaged our infrastructure, and we still cannot drink from our taps. That is not justice. Lead, is an environmental injustice. Our Flint kids have higher lead levels than the kids in the suburbs.

"They already have too many obstacles for success." She cited Flint's 40% poverty rate and lack of nutrition sources. "Our work is just beginning. It will continue for decades to come." She thanked the performers for providing the best medicine, laughter and enjoyment.

Latino/a community representatives sat on stage with actor and author Hill Harper and explained that without Spanish language information many Latin American families attempted to make the water safe by boiling it, which only concentrated the lead levels. Undocumented residents are fearful of having their children tested because of the climate of repression. Harper called for Black-Brown unity against common oppression.

Fighting for human rights

Filmmaker Ryan Coogler, the founder of Blackout for Human Rights, is from Oakland, Calif., the home of militant ILWU Local 10. A delegation from Local 10 came to Flint, including Clarence Thomas and Stacey Rodgers, who authored a resolution "For Labor Action to Stop Flint's Poisoned Water Crisis and Hold Michigan's Governor Snyder Accountable." It was passed

unanimously by the San Francisco Labor Council. Read the resolution at tinyurl.com/j6gx2ao.

Coogler's first film, "Fruitvale Station" (2013), followed by the critically acclaimed "Creed" in 2015, was made to expose and stop blatant police killing like that which took Oscar Grant's life in 2009, captured for all to see on cellphone video. As the videoed killings of Black and Brown men, women and children have continued and accelerated, Coogler and his colleagues founded Blackout to use their considerable creativity and talent for the same purpose.

According to a press release for the event, Blackout for Human Rights is a collective of filmmakers, artists and activists, "devoting their resources to address the staggering number of human rights violations in the U.S." The collective includes Michael B. Jordan, Ava DuVernay, David Oyelowo and many others. In January 2016, Blackout hosted #MLKNOW at Riverside Church in Harlem. That event didn't shy away from the revolutionary words of slain Black Panther leader Fred Hampton, which were also heard in video clips shown on the Flint screen.

As of Feb. 29, #JusticeforFlint raised more than $145,000 in donations to help Flint organizations. A Flint People's Hearing is planned, sponsored by Flint Rising, Flint Democracy Defense League and Michigan Faith in Action.

Abridged from WW, March 10, 2016.

'Fruitvale Station' Oscar Grant's story

Cheryl LaBash

African-American writer/director Ryan Coogler graduated from the University of Southern California School of Cinematic Arts only two years ago, but his life and times prepared him to make the dramatic story "Fruitvale Station," which won both Audience Award and Grand Jury Prize at the Sundance Film Festival in Utah on, Jan. 26, 2013.

At the first showing on Jan. 19, 2013, tears flowed in the audience, relatives of Oscar Grant reported in excited phone calls. By Jan. 21, the show business daily Variety announced the forthcoming "theatrical release" of this true story of the 2009 New Year's Eve police killing of young Grant in the Fruitvale Bay Area Rapid Transit Station. The New York Times suggests a future Oscar nomination.

Michael B. Jordan portrays a multi-faceted Oscar Grant during his last day alive. Oscar-winner Octavia Spencer plays Wanda Johnson, his mother. Melonie Diaz plays the mother of Grant's young child; Tristan Wilds is his best friend. The killer cop, Johannes Mehserle along with his partner are played by Chad Murray and Kevin Durand. Oscar-winner Forest Whitaker and Nina Yang, his Significant Productions partner, produced the film.

In a Jan. 25, 'Democracy Now!' interview, Coogler explained choosing Jordan for the dramatic lead, still a rare opportunity for African-American actors, especially in corporate Hollywood. "He was in a few feature films that were very successful, but I'd never seen him in that lead role. It was funny, because every time I watched him, I would want the camera to stay on him, as opposed to going to whoever the lead was in whatever movie it was." Jordan's compelling screen presence can be felt even through the short clips available at this time.

Coogler, now 26, is the same age that Oscar Grant would have been. They are both from the Bay Area, where outrage erupted immediately after the cold-blooded killing that was witnessed and recorded by so many others on the BART platform. Coogler, who was at home from film school on that day, remembers the killing, the outrage, the protests. In the grainy video Coogler said, "All you could tell, that he was a Black guy wearing a certain kind of clothes, with a certain group of friends, and he looked like he could have been any one of us. Like, he dressed like all of us, you know what I mean? His friends look like my friends. … It was horrifying. It was frustrating, these things happen so often." (Democracy Now!, Jan. 25, 2013)

"Fruitvale Station" ends just before the ongoing struggle for justice for Grant began. A mini rebellion and outraged protest, including rallies by the International Longshore and Warehouse Union Local 10, forced the rare murder indictment of a killer cop. However, Mehserle was convicted only of involuntary manslaughter by a Los Angeles jury that excluded all African Americans. He served only 18 months of a 2-year sentence, a slap on the hand for what Oscar Grant's mother, Wanda Johnson, calls murder, which was witnessed again and again in cell phone

videos like the one that opens "Fruitvale Station." Read more about the trial online at: bit.ly/14lB1cz.

The movement against police killings and against the incarceration epidemic of youth, especially youth of color, is growing nationwide. Demanding that "Fruitvale Station" be shown in your area is another way to call for justice.

Abridged from WW, March 10, 2013.

National convergence in St. Louis, Ferguson:
People resist police terror

Monica Moorehead

An unprecedented weekend of mass resistance took place in St. Louis, Ferguson, Clayton and other parts of Missouri on Oct. 10-13, 2014. The actions demanded an end to police terror and justice for Michael Brown, John Crawford III, Vonderrit Myers Jr, and countless others who have lost their young lives at the hands of the police.

Initiated by local activists united under the theme of Ferguson October, the extremely organized, creative, disciplined and inspiring actions, some planned, some spontaneous, reminded Missouri, the U.S. and the world that the police murder of 18-year-old African-American Michael Brown on Aug. 9 will continue to be a major catalyst for building a national movement against police abuse and occupation.

The four days of resistance included marches, rallies, civil disobedience, forums, picket lines, assemblies and cultural events that erupted throughout St. Louis County.

One of the first protests took place in Clayton at the office of Robert McCullough, the county district attorney. McCullough comes from a cop family and is currently conducting the Grand Jury investigation to determine whether police officer Darren Wilson will be indicted for Brown's murder. Brown's family and their supporters have been demanding that McCullough recuse himself from this investigation, due to his well-documented bias against Black people and be replaced by an independent special prosecutor.

One of the culminating activities was the dramatic unfurling of a banner in the stands during the pro-football game between the St. Louis Rams and the San Francisco 49ers. The banner read: "Rams fans know that Black Lives Matter on and off the field."

"No justice, no peace," "Stop killing our people" and "Arrest Darren Wilson" were demands for many of the protests. The largest action took place on Oct. 11 when 3,000 people took to the streets of St. Louis in a "Justice for All" march. Delegations representing labor, youth and students, community groups and the political movement all came together with a common sentiment: Enough is enough, as the racist war against youth of color worsens. The march ended in a park in front of the famous St. Louis Gateway Arch, which ironically is the exact site where at one time kidnapped Africans were sold during slave auctions.

Speakers, many of them young and African American, stated that they have spent more time in jail for protesting than Darren Wilson has for killing Brown. Links were made between police brutality, the need for union jobs and a decent education.

Solidarity between the Palestinian people in Israeli-occupied territories and Black communities being occupied by police was echoed by several speakers. It was publicly acknowledged that #FergusonOctober was the most retweeted site in the world that day, numbering over 91,000 tweets.

The families representing Brown and Myers thanked the marchers for their support.

John Crawford was fatally shot at a Walmart store outside Dayton, Ohio, on Aug. 5, 2014. A student activist from Ohio stated to cheers that in response to the grand jury not indicting the cop who fatally shot Crawford, the Beavercreek Police Station was recently shut down by activists. On Oct. 13, three Walmart stores were shut down in St. Louis and Ferguson by activists chanting, "I am John Crawford/We are John Crawford." The action, mobilized by the Organization for Black Struggle, resulted in arrests inside and outside the stores.

Brown family led Ferguson march

Just hours after the march in St. Louis, an estimated 1,000 people gathered in Ferguson for a brief vigil at a memorial set up at the exact place where Michael Brown had been gunned down in the Canfield Gardens apartment complex. Brown's mother, Leslie McSpadden, and other family members helped lead a militant march down West Florissant Avenue, a flashpoint for the Aug. 10 uprising, to the Ferguson Police Department located on South Florissant Road.

As we were marching in the streets, a multitude of drivers honked, their fists outside their car windows, to express solidarity. Residents came out of their houses to give the "Hands up, don't shoot" salute, which has become a clarion call for this struggle.

The protesters were met by armed police blocking the entrance to their fortress. But no amount of force could intimidate the marchers from getting right in the faces of the majority-white police force, chanting "Arrest Darren Wilson!" and "Hands up, don't shoot!" They then sat in the street for several minutes in an act of civil disobedience.

Wearing glasses, center, Leslie McSpadden, Michael Brown's mother, led Ferguson march. Ferguson police station on Oct. 11, 2014

WW photos: Monica Moorehead

Following the march, hundreds of the same protesters went back to St. Louis to express their outrage at the killing of 18 year-old Vonderrit Myers Jr. by an off-duty police officer on Oct. 8, 2014. Myers was shot at 17 times and was hit at least six times. Countering the account by the police that Myers had a gun, eyewitnesses say he had just bought a turkey sandwich. The protest ended at the Quik Trip gas station in the Grove section. When an estimated 50 protesters held a sit-in there, they were attacked with pepper spray and other forms of violence by the police. At least 10 people were arrested.

Moral Monday: No business as usual

Progressive clergy and faith-based people started day-long actions of civil disobedience in the tradition of Moral Monday protests that took place in North Carolina. There, hundreds were arrested over the past year challenging the ultra-right-wing, racist, anti-worker policies of the state government.

In addition to the shutdown of the three Walmart stores, 400 people marched to the Ferguson Police Department, where 10 people, mainly clergy, were arrested. Individuals took turns lying down on a symbolic chalked outline

of Brown's body. The police allowed his body to remain in the street for at least four hours after the murder in August.

Participants from Missourians Organizing for Reform and Empowerment and Ferguson October protested outside a fundraiser for Steve Stenger, the County Executive candidate known for close ties to supporters of Darren Wilson and DA McCulloch.

Despite a downpour, a coalition of labor and community members were arrested after blocking the street in front of Emerson Electric. This Fortune 500 company, based in St. Louis, had revenues of $24.6 billion in 2013, while the average per capita income in Ferguson last year was $21,000.

"We are calling attention to the economic injustice we live with in Ferguson," said Jermaine Arms of 'Show Me $15.' Justice for Mike Brown means justice for all of us. This should be a moment where we all take responsibility for the conditions that his death exposed. Businesses and corporations based in Ferguson and St. Louis should promote fair employment and contribute to the well-being of our community."

Millennial Activists United, a youth group,

occupied two floors of Plaza Frontenac, an upscale shopping center in St. Louis, where they engaged in a call-and-response choir demanding justice for Michael Brown.

Brittany Ferrell, a spokesperson for MAU, stated: "Young people are being killed by police in the streets of Ferguson. We came here today because we cannot continue with business as usual in the face of such injustice. Whether it's the elected officials, the local police or places like Plaza Frontenac, we will continue to sound the alarm and demand justice for the family of Mike Brown.

Youth Activists United protested at St. Louis City Hall to demand that Mayor Francis Slay and Police Chief Sam Dotson make sweeping police reforms. Protesters were arrested attempting to unfurl banners.

Youth Activists United are demanding: Body cameras must be worn by ALL police officers who have any interaction with the public; a civilian review board be chosen by the citizens, not by mayoral/police-approved appointees; removal of the St. Louis Metropolitan Police Department from the 1033 Program, a federal law that allows for the militarization of local police; and independent investigations of all police shootings resulting in fatalities, starting with Vonderrit Myers.

Abridged from WW, Oct 13, 2014.

WW forum links Ferguson, Palestine

Terri Kay

WW photo: Monica Moorehead

Photo: Sharon Black

'What's happening in Ferguson isn't rioting, it's rebellion. And this isn't the first time in our history we've rebelled," declared Clarence Thomas, a rank-and-file member of the ILWU and co-chair of the Million Worker March. Thomas was speaking at a Workers World Forum held at Laney College in Oakland, Calif., on Sept. 29, and co-sponsored by the Laney Black Student Union.

The forum's theme, "Occupation Is a Crime from Ferguson to Palestine," linked these struggles with talks by Nadia Gaber from the Block the Boat Coalition and family members of young Black men killed by the police: Jeralynn Blueford, mother of Alan Blueford, who was slain by Oakland police, and Cephus "Uncle Bobby" Johnson, uncle of Oscar Grant, slain by the BART transit police. They talked about the connections between militarization and police repression, from Oakland to Ferguson, Mo., to Palestine. Thomas declared at one point: "I'm not afraid of ISIS. I'm afraid of the police."

Abridged from WW, Oct. 16, 2014.

12-year-old Tamir Elijah Rice was killed by Cleveland police officer Timothy Loehmann on Nov. 22, 2014.
In December 2015, a grand jury declined to indict the police officers involved.
On Dec. 29, 2020 The U.S. Justice Department declined to bring federal criminal charges against the police officers in the 2014 killing of 12-year-old Tamir Rice

Dock workers to 'Shut It Down'

Clarence Thomas and Cheryl Labash

On May 1, 2015, International Workers' Day, the cranes for loading cargo at the San Francisco and Oakland ports will be still.

The April meetings of both the Executive Board and membership of the ILWU Local 10 unanimously endorsed a call for "Union Action to Stop Police Killings of Black and Brown People." A unanimously approved amendment called for the monthly union membership meeting to be held on the May 1 shift and conclude with a march and a rally at Oakland City Hall, to demonstrate that the rampant killings by police are an urgent labor issue.

The killing of young Michael Brown by Ferguson, Mo., police on Aug. 9, 2014, and the cell phone videoed killing of Eric Garner by New York police on Staten Island galvanized a rainbow movement, led by Black and Brown youth.

Creative and determined protests have interrupted business as usual in streets, highways, shopping malls, restaurants, everywhere. Protesters have faced tear gas and militarized SWAT units while chanting, "Hands up! Don't shoot!" Union banners and "Fight for $15 and a union" militants hit the streets in St. Louis, but organized labor action has been missing until now, even though the police killings continue.

Labor protests Walter Scott's murder

The New York Times printed pictures on its April 8 front page from video footage capturing the moment when 50 year-old Walter Scott was shot in the back and killed, murdered, by a white cop in South Carolina. But the article didn't mention the Scott's family relationship with the International Longshore Association (ILA) Local 1422 in Charleston, or that the local's union hall became a center for organizing the protests that followed.

Ken Riley, ILA International Vice President and ILA Local 1422 President explained in a condolence statement issued by the ILA: "Walter Scott's brother, Rodney Scott, joined our workforce two years ago. One of Local 1422's dispatchers, Marion Green, and James Gibbs, a foreman, are all close relatives. The Scott family and the Riley family worshiped together for many years … and remain close.

"Local 1422 recognizes that we have a social responsibility to our community and we take that responsibility very seriously. That is why Leonard Riley Jr. took the lead and arranged the organizational meeting for the protest at the North Charleston City Hall. He and other members also participated in the rally. Local 1422 will continue to stand up and speak out against injustice in any form, whether it is racial profiling, racial discrimination or, as in this case, racial homicide." tinyurl.com/yx92ytbs

The South Carolina AFL-CIO thanked ILWU Local 10 for their demonstration of solidarity: "You supply courage to the members of the SC AFL-CIO as we continue to address the unwarranted killing of Walter Scott. We will share your message of solidarity and reach out to workers around the country to join with us on May 1st in actions to protest the continuing unjustified killings."

ILWU forged in fighting racism, police killings

Local 10 actions, including rescheduled union meetings, are deep in the union's tradition of fighting racism and injustice. The resolution included some examples.

Every year the ILWU shuts down all West Coast ports to remember 'Bloody Thursday:' July 5, 1934. That day, the

Ken Riley speaking at the Million Worker March Rally on the steps of the Lincoln memorial on Oct. 17, 2004.

WW photo: Arturo Pérez Saad

Walter Scott

Video footage captured moment when police killed Walter Scott.

San Francisco port bosses had unleashed a torrent of vigilantes, mounted police and tear gas to beat back maritime strikers and reopen the ports. Cops shot two union members, Nick Bordoise and Howard Sperry, in the back, killing them near the union hall. Tens of thousands marched in their funeral, sparking the 1934 General Strike.

That massive labor solidarity won union control of the hiring hall and the Coast contract uniting all 29 ports. It ended the racist "shape-up system" on the docks that had pitted worker against worker based on race, national origin, kickbacks or other favors, all to the bosses' benefit.

Strike leader Harry Bridges said: "The owners have only one objective, the destruction of labor unions. … If we can't control the hiring hall, then the right of longshore workers to organize is just a farce. … The unions will be destroyed by discrimination and blacklisting."

Local 10's recent resolution notes that, "the ILWU has a proud history of standing up against racial injustice, like the 1984 anti-apartheid action and the 2010 Shut Down for justice for Oscar Grant." Oscar Grant was killed by a transit cop at the Bay Area Rapid Transit's Fruitvale station on Jan. 1, 2009. It was one of the first killings captured on camera phone.

Local 10's Oct. 23, 2010, Port Shut Down of the type planned for the May 1 rally at Oakland City Hall demanded: Stop police brutality! Jail killer cops! Defend jobs and public education! Stop the wars and repression!

In 1984, South African cargo sat in the harbor for 11 days. The courts sided with apartheid, ordering the ILWU to unload the ship, but community pickets blocked the entrance to Pier 80, refusing to allow business as usual with the racist apartheid South African regime.

When racists attacked the homes of Black families in Contra Costa County, Calif., including the home of ILWU Local 10 member Roosevelt Presley, the Bay Area Longshore Memorial Association hired a private guard to protect the Presley family. The newly formed ILWU Bay Area Civil Rights Committee included Local 10 members Lawrence Thibeaux and the late Leo Robinson. They united other labor and religious groups in Richmond, Calif., to rally against Klan violence that also marked the Rev. Dr. Martin Luther King Jr.'s birthday in 1981. (ILWU Dispatcher, Jan. 1981)

Just prior to that, Leo Robinson had invited two sisters from Oroville, Calif., to come to the Local 10 meeting to tell the membership about harassment they were suffering from the Ku Klux Klan and others. Robinson wrote: "The rank-and-file wanted to give support. I wrote a resolution to have our next membership meeting in Oroville, a 'stop work meeting' with Pacific Maritime Association's approval. On the morning of the meeting, we loaded buses and cars to Oroville and marched through the main thoroughfare of the town to deliver a message to the police chief — stop the harassment, cross burnings, graffiti, etc. against the single mothers."

The ILWU's 1971 Convention "voiced strong support for the defense of Angela Davis and pledged a renewed battle against racism." The ILWU's policy statement outlined the role of labor: "Because unions must be spokespeople for all the people who work for a living, and because we must be in advance of all social and economic programs for progress, we have no choice but to take the lead in eliminating the scourge of racism from our land." (*The Dispatcher*, April 1971)

Abridged from WW, April 30, 2015.

ILWU Local 10 shut down the San Francisco and Oakland, California ports on May 1, 2015.   Photo: Terri Kay

Bay Area ports closed in protest over police killing of Oscar Grant

Jamo Muhammad

Despite the rainy weather, more than 1,000 peaceful demonstrators rallied at the Frank Ogawa Plaza on Oct. 23, 2010, to support the family of Oscar Grant III and to echo its request that the former transit cop who shot him be sent to prison.

ILWU Local 10 led by executive board members Clarence Thomas and Jack Heyman, shut down the Ports of San Francisco, Oakland, Richmond, Benicia, and Redwood City.

Members of other labor unions that supported the Shut Down attended the rally in Oakland's City Hall Plaza during the eight-hour work stoppage. BART employees came to support the Grant family. Harold Brown represented engineers at BART who opposed the unjust killing.

"The killing of Oscar Grant connects us to an historical moment as longshoremen," Mr. Thomas said. In 1934, San Francisco Police fatally shot two longshoremen in the back.

According to Jack Heyman, labor must defend minorities against racist police attacks. He detailed the link between labor and the police killing of Oscar Grant. The longshoremen were murdered on 'Bloody Thursday' on July 5, 1934, during a strike over "the favoritism and racism of the 'shape-up' hiring system."

Since then, every July 5, all ports on the West Coast are shut down in their honor. A mural in remembrance of the slain workers rests in front of the ILWU Hall in San Francisco.

Johannes Mehserle was a Bay Area Rapid Transit cop that shot Mr. Grant in the back on a station platform, before dozens of witnesses on New Year's Eve, 2009. A year later, after the case was moved from Alameda County to Los Angeles, a jury consisting of no Blacks convicted Mehserle of involuntary manslaughter.

The Alameda County DA argued for prison, but to the disappointment of Mr. Grant's family and supporters, he failed to specify a term.

Student Minister Keith Muhammad of Muhammad Mosque 26B in Oakland said the case is of great historical significance. "We want justice applied fairly under the law. Not one way for Blacks and another for whites. "Judge Robert Perry needs to know he has a shared duty along with the people and God. The case of Oscar Grant is being heard in the real 'Supreme Court,' which is the court of God, Himself," the Minister said.

Supporters traveled from as far away as Georgia for the rally. The host of speakers included spoken word and musical artists. Elaine Brown, the only woman to ever chair the Black Panther Party, was among the guest speakers, as well as a longshoreman who came from Tacoma, Washington to show solidarity.

With her child by her side, Sophia Mesa, Mr. Grant's partner and mother of their daughter, read a letter they plan to read at the sentencing hearing.

Mr. Thomas called politicians to task for ignoring the concerns and

ILWU Local 10 marching against police terror on May Day 2015 in Oakland California.

Counter-protest against a 2010 police rally in Walnut Creek, Calif. The cops were rallying to defend the cop who killed Oscar Grant. The ILWU protest outnumbered police rally three to one.

needs of the community and feigning interest only during election time.

"The Tea Party, Democrat and Republican Parties are encouraging us to get out the vote, yet our concerns go unheard. None of them speak to this epidemic of police brutality, so you won't see any politicians on this stage today," he said.

The rally also heard from Jack Bryson, the father of Mr. Grant's friends, who were on the platform the night he was murdered, and who charged they were also victimized by BART Police. "It's been quite an experience," he told *The Final Call*. "I didn't know after the verdict was read, we would make a phone call and organize like this to bring everyone out. Imagine if we had the sun, how many more would have showed? We have hundreds out here in the rain."

"The support has brought a smile to my sister's face," Cephus "Uncle Bobby" Johnson told *The Final Call* about Mr. Grant's mother, Wanda Johnson. He said his family was comforted by the support they have

received and in knowing they were not alone in their struggle. According to Mr. Johnson, they have received international letters of support from French dock workers, the Japan Railway Union Workers, and even the British Parliament.

Other supporters present included Rutie Corpuz of the United Playaz and Richard Brown of the San Francisco 8, former Black Panther members who were rounded up and charged with killing a San Francisco policeman four decades ago.

Mr. Brown said he was joyous to see the coalition between labor and the masses and added, "I'm even happy to see the rain, because it will let the oppressor know we will wither this storm!"

Abridged from the Final Call, Nov. 8, 2010.

Hundreds of people rallied for justice for Oscar Grant and all victims of police brutality on Jan. 1. 2012. Organizers from Occupy Oakland, on foot and on bicycle, directed the crowd through the streets.

Speakers at the rally included Grant's mother, Wanda Johnson, and her brother, 'Uncle Bobby,' Cephus Johnson who thanked everyone for attending the protest.

He reminded everyone that before Occupy Oakland, the Local 10 had shut down the Port of Oakland to demand justice for Oscar Grant. "We have to tie together both movements and keep working together," Johnson said.

WW photo and abridged caption: Judy Greenspan

March on Mississippi

Clarence Thomas

On March 4, 2017, Delores Lemon-Thomas and I accompanied Danny Glover, actor and humanitarian, to attend the **March On Mississippi**, for the rights of workers employed by Nissan in Canton. Senator Bernie Sanders, Nina Turner of Ohio, Jaribu Hill, Executive Director of the Southern Workers Center in Greenville, Mississippi, were also in attendance. Thousands of people including union members, civil rights, and social justice activists, attended to protect workers civil and human rights at the Nissan plant.

The theme of the march was 'Workers Rights = Civil Rights.' The purpose was to call on Nissan to respect workers' right to a union election free from fear and intimidation. Nissan has union representation at 42 of 45 plants globally, the American south is the exception.

Danny Glover said, "Nissan spends hundreds of millions of dollars a year marketing itself as a socially respon-

Senator Bernie Sanders, Clarence Thomas and Danny Glover traveled to the Nissan plant to protect the auto worker's rights.

Photos: Delores Lemon-Thomas

sible car maker, even going so far as to brag about its appeal to African American car buyers. Yet, behind the scenes is violating rights of African Americans workforce that makes these cars."

ILWU Local 10 halts work to fight racism

Minnie Bruce Pratt

In a stunning worker action against racism, about 100 members of ILWU Local 10 walked out May 25, 2017, at one of the largest and busiest terminals in the Port of Oakland. They suspended all operations there and brought international container traffic to a complete standstill for hours. Container trucks were backed up all around the port and on Interstate 880.

Local 10 called the Shut Down to protest blatant racist acts at the job site, including the discovery that morning of a noose, a despicable symbol of white supremacy and lynching, inside a truck used by Local 10 members. According to Derrick Muhammad, the union's secretary-treasurer, about 60% of Local 10 is African American. (KPIX 5)

Muhammad noted that an unspecified number of nooses have been found at the terminal in recent weeks. They have been left on a fence, on the ground and on trucks. Another noose was found as recently as May 15. In late 2015, someone had spray painted a piece of equipment with a racist slur against African Americans. (*East Bay Times,* May 25, 2017)

Muhammad said that longshore work is already inherently dangerous, and all workers need to know that their co-workers, "have their backs." He stressed that, "every worker has the right to work in a safe environment." He pointed out that this fact makes the racist acts, "a bonafide health and safety issue because of the history behind the noose and what it means for Black people in America." A health and safety issue is an acceptable reason to stop work under the ILWU standard union contract.

The East Bay Times reported that ILWU International President Robert McEllrath issued a statement that, "the ILWU is a progressive and diverse union, and we reject in the strongest possible terms racism in all its forms. The display of a hangman's noose for the second time in two weeks at the work site is inexcusable and expressly prohibited conduct under the terms of the ILWU-PMA collective bargaining agreement. The union is committed to securing a non-discriminatory work environment for all individuals working at the ports."

ILWU Local 10 has a long and militant history of progressive work actions, from its leadership in the 1934 San Francisco General Strike under Marxist Harry Bridges to its boycotts of South African apartheid cargo, starting in 1962.

More recently, in 2010, the local shut down the port to protest the murder of Oscar Grant, an African-American man killed by cops at Oakland's nearby Fruitvale Station. Last year the local affirmed its support for Indigenous sovereignty at Standing Rock, N.D., and this year refused to work on Jan. 20, Inauguration Day, to protest the election of Trump and the ramping up of attacks on working and oppressed people, especially unions.

Every racist act or symbol at a workplace is significant because racism is always an attack on the solidarity and unity of workers. The recent action by Local 10, is a call to all workers to fight against racism and for solidarity at their jobs with creative and militant actions.

Abridged from WW, June 1, 2017.

The ILWU called the Shut Down to protest blatant racist acts at the job site, including the discovery of a noose, a despicable symbol of white supremacy and lynching.

Oscar Grant's family holds a vigil on Jan. 1, 2011, 'Uncle Bobby,' Cephus Johnson, supports his sister, Oscar's mother, Wanda Johnson, at the very difficult time for them both and for Oscar's young daughter.

Photo: Judy Greenspan

#DoItLikeDurham in smashing white supremacy

Deirdre Griswold

A public meeting on Oct. 14, 2017, on the theme "Do It Like Durham" lived up to its promise of bringing the revolutionary spirit of the struggle against white supremacy to New York.

The two main speakers Takiyah Thompson and Loan Tran, had come from North Carolina with other activists to explain the significance of the movement there that is shaking the foundations of racism implanted in this country through the capture and enslavement of millions of African people to be super-exploited by rich Southern plantation owners.

Thompson is the iconic figure in videos viewed around the world. She climbed up a tall ladder on Aug. 14, 2017, and placed a rope around a statue of a Confederate soldier that stood in front of the old Durham County courthouse.

At a New York City meeting on Oct. 14, 2017 speaker Takiyah Thompson (front row, second from right with a fist) is wearing #DoItLikeDurham baseball cap.

WW photo: Brenda Ryan

A crowd of anti-racists then toppled this symbol of the Confederacy and the war to preserve slavery, the bloodiest war in U.S. history. Thompson and 14 others were arrested within days and given serious charges, including felonies.

Thompson received a standing ovation as she explained how talking about the struggle is therapeutic and enhanced her "desire to learn and understand the pathways to freedom and the pitfalls."

"I always fall back on friends and comrades," said Thompson. "Revolutionary love is for the liberation of others and oneself. It's all the same." Her modesty in not talking about her own courageous conduct was deeply felt by the audience.

Loan Tran, another person arrested after the symbolic act against slavery and its virulent heritage in the U.S., emphasized that those arrested are proud of this struggle and "have done nothing wrong."

Tran, who had been asked by many journalists why so many of those arrested are queer and/or trans people of color, said: "What I know, as a queer and gender nonconforming person of color, is that many of us fight because materially, we have much to lose if we don't fight: our safety, our jobs, our homes, our lives because of capitalist oppression and exploitation."

Tran added: "Another key lesson from Durham is that while we must never underestimate the power of state repression, the answer is not paranoia or fear but to get organized. During the first week following the statue toppling, as organizers were targeted, arrested, getting their homes raided, not to mention being followed, doxed and threatened by white supremacists while the state turned its

Confederate statue pulled off its base.

August 14, 2017, confederate monument toppled and crumpled.

back on us, we had to make sure we were getting organized broader and deeper.

"One strong example of this was an action on Aug. 17, which called for anti-racist fighters in our city to show up at the jail to turn themselves in, to say: 'If you target some of us for tearing down white supremacy, then arrest us, too!'

"Hundreds showed up for this action, with over 70 people turning themselves in. One after another, they were turned away by the sheriffs." Tran's entire talk is online at workers.org.

The meeting blended in reports from New York on related struggles. Imani Henry spoke about the struggle in Brooklyn for affordable housing led by Equality for Flatbush. Teresa Gutierrez announced efforts underway to send a brigade to Puerto Rico to support the people there battling the Trump administration's criminal neglect and insults after the devastation of Hurricane Irma.

William Camacaro gave a brief update on the new threats by the U.S. against Venezuela. John Steffin reported on a struggle at Columbia University to cancel speaking invitations to far-right ideologues.

The program was further enlivened by a powerful rap and hip-hop number delivered by Vijou Bryant of Gabriela New York, a Filipina women's group. Bryant is also co-coordinator of the International Working Women's Day Coalition and is of both Philippine and African-American heritage.

Abridged from WW, Oct. 19, 2017.

November 14, rally on the courthouse step. Heavy charges were filed aganist the miltant heros.

In Durham on August 18, 2017, many anti-racist fighters said: "If you target some of us for tearing down white supremacy, then arrest us, too!'

ILWU shuts it down and leads the way!
25,000 March for Mumia Abu-Jamal in San Francisco May 1, 1999

The ILWU shut down the West Coast ports in 1999 to 'Stop the Execution of Mumia.'
Photo: Bill Hackwell

Howard Keylor speaking at a May Day 2008, anti-war shut down of all West Coast ports. Keylor joined the longshore union in Stockton, Calif. in 1953. During his decades on the waterfront he initiated, organized and participated in labor actions, including the longshore strike of 1971-1972, the 1984 boycott of South African cargo and the 1999 coast-wide shut down to demand freedom for Mumia Abu-Jamal.

occupyoakland.org/event/ilwu-10-tribute-to-howard-keylor-120918/

Jack Heyman

At the head of a sea of protesters defending Black political prisoner Mumia Abu-Jamal on Pennsylvania's death row was the 300 strong ILWU contingent, from longshore, warehouse, IBU and even some pensioners, chanting, "An injury to one is an injury to all, Free Mumia Abu-Jamal!" Joining San Francisco members in the militant march were workers from the ports of Sacramento, Los Angeles, Port Hueneme, and as far away as Seattle. The Longshore Clerks and Walking Bosses' Caucus voted overwhelmingly to shutdown the Coast on April 24, 1999, to demand: "Stop the Execution and Free Mumia!"

Vice President Jim Spinosa, who headed up ILWU contract negotiations, and the Coast Committeemen made it clear that the rank-and-file of the Longshore Division had spoken through the vote of its elected Caucus delegates. Every port on the West Coast was shut down from 8 am to 6 pm. The unity of action couldn't have happened for a better cause, using collective muscle to save the life of an innocent man and at a better time, just weeks before critical contract negotiations.

Defend Mumia! Stop The Execution! Free Mumia!

Free Em All! Free Mumia!
On the 45th anniversary of the assassination of Malcolm X, support for Mumia Abu-Jamal's defense was raised in a packed hall in Oakland. Carol Seligman, Pam Africa, Fred Hampton Jr., Ramona Africa, Jack Heyman, Richard Brown, Noelle Hanrahan spoke at the event. Pictured here, Adimu Madyun, Jack Bryson and JR Valrey, also spoke. The event sponsored by Prison Radio, the Labor Action Committee to Free Mumia Abu-Jamal, and Prisoners of Conscience Committee (POCC).

Photo: Dave Id, www.indybay.org/newsitems/2010/02/28/18639038.php

CHAPTER 7

INTERNATIONAL SOLIDARITY

2003 ➤ 2017

SOUTH AFRICA

JAPAN

VENEZUELA

INDUSTRIA VENEZOLANA ENDOGENA DEL PAPEL
INVEPAL

AQUI CONVERTIMOS EL POTENCIAL DEL EN PODER POPULAR

U.S. OUT OF HAITI

CUBA

MOBILIZING IN OUR OWN NAME
MILLION WORKER MARCH

PALESTINE

Longshore workers say:
STOP THE WAR IN IRAQ!
END THE OCCUPATION!
WITHDRAW THE TROOPS NOW!
International Longshore and Warehouse Union Local 10

MONEY FOR SCHOOLS, JOBS
HEALTHCARE AND HOUSING
NO WAR FOR OIL AND EMPIRE
International Longshore and Warehouse Union Local 10

International endorsers of the Million Worker March send solidarity messages

Paris, International Liaison Committee
Daniel Gluckstein, Coordinator

On behalf of the ILC and its affiliated unions and organizations in 72 countries, I extend our solidarity with MWM and wish it great success. We in the ILC are honored that Brother Clarence Thomas has been able to represent his union in the various antiwar and workers' rights activities we have hosted or supported over the past two years.

Workers in Japan rally in solidarity with Million Worker March

Kikuchi Takao writes that on Oct. 17, in solidarity with the MWM, more than 600 workers and students held a rally in Tokyo, Hundreds also came out in Hiroshima and Osaka. At the Tokyo rally Hiroshi Ashitomi, made a special appeal about the struggle in Henoko, Okinawa. The solidarity message of the MWM was read to the participants.

Yasuhiro Tanaka, president of Nat'l Railway Locomotive Power Union, said, "We see a new age in which Japanese workers and workers in the U.S. truly struggle together." His union sent a delegation to the MWM in Washington.

Russia, V. G. Gamov, Defense of Labor Union Atomic Center of the Russian Federation

"Workers here join hands with our comrades in solidarity, as if we are marching together through Washington in defense of the oppressed workers of the world! 'Socialism is our goal and the solution for the catastrophe the world is facing! 'Victory to the MWM'

Slovak workers support MWM

U.S. Steel, has eliminated tens of thousands of jobs in the U.S., destroying whole communities. While the same time, it acquired the East Slovak Metal Works in Kosice, Slovakia. Since then, conditions for the mill's 16,000 workers have become hell. Zuzana Cingelova, a crane operator and a union activist sent the following message to the MWM:
"We fully support your efforts to organize a workers' march on Oct. 17.

New Delhi, India
H Mahadevan Dy, General Secretary
All India Trade Union Congress (AITUC)

The MWM wil revive and expand a great struggle for fundamental changes and forge together a social economic and political movement. We, in India and other developing countries attach great value to the linkage of the struggles for civil rights with the labour movement. We fondly recall the historic March in opposition to the devastative war on Vietnam led by Martin Luther King Jr.

Labor rights and trade unions rights cannot be achieved in the absence of civil rights. We believe that the trade unions are the powerful weapons in the hands of the working class to change the social order.

Caracas, Venezuela
Saludo a la Marcha de Trabajadores
Por la Coordinacion Nacional de la UNT

From The National Union of Workers (UNT), event "No to the FTAA and the Free Trade Agreements," 500 union leaders and militants of the workers' and anti-imperialist movement of Venezuela, from 23 regions throughout the country, address greetings to our fellow unionists in the MWM.

We express our support for the demand for universal health coverage, for the defense of public education and the withdrawal of the occupation troops from Iraq. The UNT and participants in our event consider that our struggle against the FTAA is the same as yours against war and overexploitation.

In Venezuela, in the recent battle in defense of national sovereignty, we benefited from the solidarity support of U.S. labor organizations. Now it is our turn to support the demonstration on October 17. This is the golden rule of internationalism and class solidarity among workers. Wishing full success to the MWM receive our class greetings from the Bolivarian Republic of Venezuela.

India
C. K. Sanyal, National Federation Of Sales Representatives, Unions (NFSRU)

We are with you at the MWM in the fight against war, poverty, unemployment and the devastations thrust upon the working class by the imperialist globalization and their ruling collaborators all over the world. Everyday is becoming more dangerous with new wars, nuclear proliferation, enormous defense budgets at the cost of basic human needs. The "New World Order" has brought the working class to a point of rampant joblessness and insecurity. The vast majority of mankind is being plunged further into abject misery – in Russia, in Africa, in Asia, in Europe, even the U.S.

The never-ending greed of imperialism has trampled humanity. The pretext for war is a ploy of world capital to destabilize the peace and prosperity of regions enriched with natural resources - be it oil, water, minerals or human labor. In the dictionary of imperialism: anti-terrorism means killing of millions and millions of innocent people!

Afghanistan
Nasir Loyand, Left Radical of Afghanistan (LRA)

We strongly support your struggle for the defense of workers rights. The workers and oppressed of Afghanistan have suffered the disasters of war more than any class of society. Due to non-democratic regimes the Afghan workers have had no chance to organize independent unions. We ask you to help Afghan workers to fight for their basic rights. The working class needs your solidarity in their particular weak situation in Afghanistan.

All Pakistan Trade Union Federation
Gulzar Ahmed Chaudhary, General Secretary

Brazil, The National Executive Board of the Unified Workers Federation
Joao Antonio Felicio, Secretary General

Bangladesh. Chittagong Port Workers Union, M. Shariat Ullah, General Secretary
Tafazzul Hussain, President
Bangladesh National Workers Federation

Korea, Jung Sik Hwa, Vice president
Korea Metal Worker's Federation

Philippines, Edgar P. Bilayon, Chairman
Philippine Railway Workers Union
Deputy General Secretary
Philippine Workers Party

Hong Kong, Chan Ka Wai, Associate Director
Hong Kong Christian Industrial Committee

Venezuela, Julio Turra, Repeat of Caracas

Great Britain, Charlie Charalambous
Chair, TGWU. President, Torbay & District Trades Union Council

Peru, Erwin Salazar Vasquez
President De LA CGTP

Equador, Jose Limaico Vela, President 'SAIP'

Mexico, Dr. Victor Hugo Zavaleta SNTSA

Mexicali, Mexico, Liliana Plumeda

Mexicali, Baja California
Dr. Carlos Maya Quevedo

Madrid, Fdo. Francisco Javier Lupez Martin
Secretario General, CCOO-Madrid

Barcelona, International Dockworkers Council
Consejo Internacional de Estibadores
Jordi Aragunde Miguens
Coordinador Geneneral, IDC

On behalf of the IDC and the +90.000 affiliates we represent around the world, we express solidarity with ILWU Local 10, who on May Day 2016, will stand united against racism in the U.S., shutting down the port and marching to protest the police violence against Black, Latino, and immigrant communities in the Bay Area and other U.S. cities.

ILWU Local 10 has a long tradition of struggle, mobilizing against apartheid in South Africa, Latin Amercian dictatorships, the Iraq and Afghanistan wars, and other cases of racial injustice such as Oscar Grant in 2009 . We stand with you now in your fight for a $15 an hour minimum wage, healthcare and quality education for all.

Such a determined stand against social injustice serves as an example for labor movements worldwide – dock workers to fight for a better world. We stand behind you in your fight. The labor movement has been a key part in changing history; let us be at the forefront of social changes again.

Report on International Labor Delegation to Iraq

Brother Clarence Thomas, Local 10 Executive Board Member

On Oct. 6, 2003, an international labor delegation of five union activists traveled to Iraq for a six-day visit to investigate the conditions and violations experienced by workers and unions under U.S. occupation.

Bay Area labor activist David Bacon, a widely published labor journalist and labor news host on KPFA in Berkeley, and this writer joined the delegation organized by USLAW. The other delegation members came from the Paris-based International Liaison Committee: a member from the French teachers' union, a Iraqi trade unionist and a human rights advocate.

I was chosen to participate in the delegation because of my ILWU Local 10 efforts to build international labor solidarity and labor rights, as well as opposing Bush's war on working people at home and abroad.

OccupationWatch, a non-governmental organization, affiliated with Global Exchange, handled the delegation's logistics. It monitors the role of foreign companies in Iraq, and advocates for the Iraqis' right to control their own resources, especially, oil. It monitors the relationship between U.S. corporations/subcontractors and Iraqi workers, and supports the formation of independent trade unions.

In Baghdad, we met with primary trade union organizations, the Workers Democratic Trade Union Movement (WDTUM), and the Worker's Unions and Councils (WUC). The delegation was fortunate to meet with members of the Executive Council, representing workers from transportation, oil, manufacturing, and other sectors of the Iraqi industry. They informed us of the Iraqi's significant history of labor and radical activity; first organizing the oil industry,

then the railroads and then the docks.

We were introduced to Muhsin Mull Ali, a longshore worker since 1949, who spent half a century on the piers and in the harbor building unions for dockworkers. Although retired, he was still active in the WDTUM and politically active to ensure workers have a say in their destiny. (October 2003 *The Dispatcher*, "Organizing on the Iraqi docks" by David Bacon.)

The following is a summary of what we learned from our visit:

Since George W. Bush declared an end to the war on Iraq in April, 2003, unemployment among Iraqi workers has reached 70%, causing many families to face hunger and dislocation.

Since then, the U.S. occupying authority has frozen Iraqi wages for most workers at $60 a month, while at the same time eliminating bonuses profit sharing and subsidies for food and housing, causing a sharp cut in the income of those Iraqi workers.

Some $87 billion was appropriated by Congress for the reconstruction of Iraq, yet not a dime is set to raise Iraqi wages or unemployment benefits. These extraordinary expenditures will come at the expense of services and jobs in the U.S.

Since April 2003, Iraqi workers have begun to reorganize their trade union movement, seeking a better standard of living and to preserve their jobs and workplaces.

The U.S. occupation authority has continued to enforce a 1987 law issued by Saddam Hussein prohibiting unions and collective bargaining in the public sector and state enterprises where most Iraqis work.

Muhsin Mull Ali

The U.S. occupation authority has announced it intends to sell off the factories, refineries, mines and state enterprises despite the fact that they belong to the Iraqi people. The U.S. has issued Public Order 39, allowing 100% foreign ownership of Iraqi business and repatriation of profits, barring resistance to privation for Iraqi unions and preventing workers from having a voice in the future of their own jobs.

The privatization of the Iraqi workplace would result in massive layoffs to Iraqi workers when unemployment is already at crisis levels.

Iraqi unions are seeking to organize despite having no resources, while the U.S. occupying authority withholds welfare funds, as well as union buildings and other assets.

Workers in the U.S. have experienced an erosion of our right to organize and collectively bargain in defense of our jobs and working conditions and thus understand what the loss of these rights mean.

Iraqi trade unionists want an immediate end to the U.S. occupation so that they can be governed by their own people.

The USLAW delegation was able to achieve its objectives by making contact with trade union leaders and workers.

We demonstrated it is possible to go to Iraq and meet with people who invited us. I would like to thank the executive board and the membership of Local 10 for making my participation possible.

'We can rebuild our country ourselves'
Iraqi labor leader speaks to longshore workers

Clarence Thomas

On June 16, 2005, Iraqi trade unionist Faleh Abbood Umara, General Secretary of the General Union of Oil Workers (GUOW) in Basrah spoke to hundreds of dock workers in San Francisco. The ILWU Locals 10 and 34 invited him to address their membership meetings.

The 46-year-old trade unionist is a founding member of the oil workers union and worked for the Southern Oil Company in Basrah for 28 years. In 1998, he was detained by the Hussein Regime for his activities on behalf of his co-workers. He has served on the union's negotiating team with both the Oil Ministry and British Occupation authorities to defend the rights and interest of oil industry workers in the post Saddam era.

GUOW has 23,000 members and is a federation of oil unions representing members in the nine separate Iraqi companies which make up the oil sector in Basrah, Amara and Assyria.

ILWU Local 10 President Trent Willis, an emerging African American trade union leader and the originator of the Million Worker March, introduced Umara.

Brother Faleh Umara proved to be a charismatic and dynamic speaker whose speech was punctuated by thunderous applause in the historic Local 10 union hall.

Brother Umara opened his remarks by expressing his solidarity with ILWU longshore workers that were arrested in Whittier Alaska protesting the outsourcing of longshore jobs by Carnival Cruise Lines. "I declare my struggle and support that the oil labor union in Iraq is in support of your struggle in Alaska. Our struggle and yours are the same," said the Umara.

Brother Umara represents one of the most militant unions in Iraq which has challenged the former Coalition Provisional Authority (CPA) and current anti-labor laws on the books by engaging in strikes which are prohibited.

"The labor movement in Iraq is a fighting movement," said David Bacon, an independent journalist and photographer, who was recently in Basrah.

Bacon also explained how the GUOW was organized. He described how three months into the occupation, British troops came out to the gates of the refinery where the workers were in protest because of the withdrawal of a wage increase.

"Workers put a crane across the road and stopped all the movement in and out of the refinery. When the troops arrived at the gate there were 100 workers there. Ten of those workers got under trucks behind the crane full of gasoline and fuel oil.

"They held up their cigarette lighters under those tanks and told the troops, 'if you want to shoot at us, we will light our cigarette lighters.' That is how they got their union organized and recognized by the Basrah oil refinery and that's the spirit of Iraqi trade unionism" stated the journalist.

"My country suffers from occupation. The workers are being oppressed every day" said the Iraqi trade union leader, and he called for the immediate withdrawal of all U.S. troops and urged international labor solidarity to make it a reality.

Clarence Thomas, Faleh Abbood Umara, general secretary, General Union of Oil Workers and Trent Willis.   Photo: Luis Ochoa

He reported that Kellog, Brown and Root (KBR) an oil drilling company and subsidiary of Halliburton had been kicked out of the oil fields of Southern Iraq by the GUOW.

The U.S. has handed KBR a no-bid contract to rebuild the oil industry infrastructure. The GUOW successfully stopped KBR from bringing in 1,400 foreign workers insisting that if the Iraqi oil infrastructure was to be rebuilt it would be done by Iraqis.

Brother Umara explained "We had to go on strike and stop the flow of oil for 3 days, and then the dock workers supported us by not loading and unloading the ships.

"We are capable of rebuilding our country by ourselves. We are not only oil workers, we also provide security with arms and we put our lives on the line in protecting our jobs."

The general secretary's national tour was organized by the U.S. Labor

Jean Pierre Barrios a translator who accompanied Thomas to Iraq in 2003.

Against the War. (USLAW) Six Iraqi trade unionists toured two dozen cities, providing the opportunity for thousands of U.S. trade unionists, to meet and talk with representatives of the Iraqi labor movement. The tour will also build the USLAW network to oppose the war and occupation. The ILWU Local 10 Drill Team accompanied the officers of the GUOW during their Bay Area Visit.

Labor under occupation

The Iraqi workers are currently fighting U.S. and multinational corporations' efforts to privatize the Iraqi economy. In 1987, trade unions were dissolved by Saddam Hussein and all workers were declared to be civil servants.

The Coalition Provisional Authority (CPA) has continued to enforce Hussein's 1987 decree. Although the CPA has been disbanded, the 1987 law is still on the books.

The GUOW in Basrah is still an "illegal" union as it has not been officially recognized by the government. "We take our legitimacy from the workers and not from the government," states GUOW President Hassan Juma'a Awad Al Asade, who was also a part of the Iraq trade unionists' tour of the West Coast.

Abridged from the San Francisco Bay View National Black Newspaper, July 6, 2005. www.sfbayview.com

U.S. LABOR AGAINST THE WAR   January 13, 2004

Henry Graham, President and Executive Board Members
ILWU Local 10, San Francisco, Calif.

Dear Brother Henry Graham and officers of ILWU Local 10:

We are writing this letter to express our deepest thanks for the support you have given USLAW. We are particularly appreciative of the role Clarence Thomas, the past secretary treasurer of your local has been able to play in the broadly sponsored Campaign for Labor Rights in Iraq.

Trade unionist across the country have read with interest the coverage in the *The Dispatcher* of the fact-finding trip to Iraq in which David Bacon and Brother Thomas participated. As a result of this trip and the support its conclusions have received within the labor movement nationwide, USLAW is organizing an East Coast speaking tour featuring Brothers Bacon and Thomas. They will be traveling to Washington, D.C., Philadelphia, New York City, Detroit, Boston and Hartford, Conn. The tour has been sponsored by leading AFL-CIO bodies, including the Maryland Federation of Labor, the Philadelphia and Washington, D.C. Labor Councils, among others.

In Washington, Brothers Thomas and Bacon will be meeting with the Congressional Black Caucus and the Progressive Caucus to inform them of the violations of basic labor rights under the U.S.-led occupation of Iraq, including an enforcement of laws banning the right to organize and strike for public sector workers. An objective of the East Coast tour is to help launch Congressional hearings into the Bush administration's violations of basic universally recognized labor rights.

One of the tour events, will be held at the headquarters of the AFL-CIO in Washington, D.C. It will be co-sponsored by the AFL-CIO International Affairs Department.

This tour comes at an opportune moment. Bush is vulnerable on the issue of the war in Iraq, particularly on the claim that his administration is establishing a democracy in Iraq. The bitter reality is that Bush wants to privatize Iraq's economy on behalf of his corporate cronies.

The case of the SSA takeover of the Port of Umm Qasr is an example of this. SSA wants a non-union port in Iraq, just as it wants to smash the union port workers in Chittagong, Bangladesh and everywhere else. Brother Thomas' interview with the leader of the dockworkers' union in Umm Qasr brought this issue to the attention of working people everywhere.

Iraq is a laboratory for Bush's "New World Order." It is meant to be a totally privatized economy, with no unions, no labor and democratic rights – all functioning under the U.S. government in the interests of the large U.S. corporations. USLAW and a number of unions, as well as state and local AFL-CIO bodies, have understood the threat to our own democratic rights and working conditions posed by Bush. We are as much the target of these attacks as are the working people of Iraq. The "order" they impose on Iraq will become the model imposed workers across the globe.

The USLAW initiated East Coast tour is therefore part of a larger effort to change the political climate and discussions in this country toward the impact of Bush's war against working people, both at home and in Iraq.

Thanks to the groundbreaking effort of Brother Thomas and ILWU Local 10, the campaign for labor rights in Iraq is gaining international attention. The East Coast speaking tour is an important part of the campaign. ILWU Local 10's support to the mission to Iraq and its affiliation with USLAW have enabled this work to get off the ground. We thank you for your ongoing support and look forward to working with you on this campaign in the weeks and months to come.

In solidarity,

Amy Newell USLAW National Organizer & Tour Coordinator
Michael Eisenscher USLAW Organizer/Website Coordinator

Conference calls for united march to end occupation

A call for a united effort of antiwar forces came from the Dec. 4, 2004, Emergency Antiwar Conference in New York City. It was greeted with a renewed determination to be in the streets to fight the illegal occupation of Iraq.

The conference, called by the International Action Center, was supported by: NYLAW, Haiti Support Network, N.Y., MWMM, Korea Truth Commission, N.J. Solidarity-Activists for the Liberation of Palestine, New School Graduate Program in International Affairs Human Rights Group, International Concerned Family and Friends of Mumia Abu-Jamal, The Association of Mexican American Workers, FIST, Queers for Peace and Justice, Democratic Palestine, the No Draft No Way Campaign, PeopleJudgeBush.org, and more.

The following points are submitted as points of discussion that merit the movement's wide attention:

- We need to demand the immediate and unconditional withdrawal of all U.S. occupation troops from Iraq.

The occupation's sole purpose is to control the natural resources of Iraq and render the Iraqi people and their institutions subservient to U.S. corporate interest by military force.

- We must support politically, morally and organizationally members of the U.S. armed services who are resisting the war. Moreover, we must encourage this resistance.

- We must organize to fight any attempt by the Bush administration to reinstate the draft, and prepare to support resistance if it returns.

- It is time for the anti-war movement to acknowledge the right of the Iraqi people to resist the occupation of their country without passing judgment on their resistance. The founding charter of the U.N. affirms the right of an occupied people to resist by force of arms.

- There must no longer be any hesitation on the part of our movement regarding our support of the struggle of the Palestinian people to free themselves from occupation.

- We must work to facilitate the widest unity between all of the forces that are seriously organizing against the war and occupation.

- It is up to us to revitalize the mass struggle against the war and to insure that it is uncompromising, and supportive of a wide array of tactics, from the mass marches to the militant tactics of the youth, to the tactics that are effective for the inclusion of workers, labor unions and people of color.

- One way of accomplishing a fusion between the anti-war movement and the working class and the poor is through linking the issues that affect the mass of the people with the struggle against the war.

- We propose to reach out to other forces with this perspective. The Million Worker March Movement has issued a call for all of the various anti-war organizations and workers' struggles to unite on the weekend of March 19-20, 2005. We endorse this call for broad unity.

Abridged from WW, Dec. 16, 2004.

Members of MWMM delegation, Clarence Thomas and Larry Holmes, at USLAW conference in Chicago.

U.S. Labor Against the War attracts trade unionists, antiwar activists

Nearly 200 gathered in Chicago Dec. 4, 2004 for the National Leadership Assembly of USLAW. They represent workers from unions and anti-war groups from coast to coast.

Acknowledging his disappointment over USLAW's failure to support the Million Worker March in Washington, D.C., MWMM leader Clarence Thomas urged in his address that trade unionists put the past behind them and look toward the future. Thomas called on USLAW to issue a joint call with the MWMM organizers and others to build for mobilizations against the U.S. war on Iraq on the weekend of March 19-20, 2005, the second anniversary of the U.S. war on Iraq.

— Dave Sole

Unite the anti-war movement
Oppose the occupation of Iraq and Palestine!

Black Workers League statement on the Sept. 24, 2005, anti-war demonstrations

The anti-war movement is at the center of world politics. It confronts preemptive war and occupation of oppressed nations by imperialist forces. The lies and deceptions leading to the war, the slaughter of the Iraqi people, the suppression of labor rights, the increased oppression of Iraqi women, and the use of U.S. working class women and men as cannon fodder and torturers demands that African American people, the multi-national working class, and all honest and progressive people turn out to the anti-war demonstrations in Washington, D.C., on Sept. 24.

Opposition to the war in Iraq must be seen as part of the anti-war struggle against the endless war of plunder and occupation in the Middle East and throughout the world being carried out in the name of the "war on terror." This means supporting an end to all occupations and the right of self-determination for all the nations in the region, especially Palestine, including their right of return.

The U.S. anti-war movement embraces forces fighting for peace and those opposing imperialist domination. While there may be differences within the anti-war movement in terms of long-and short-term goals and tactics, it is important that this movement and its demands be guided by anti-racist, anti-sexist, democratic and human rights principles.

While the primary demand of the anti-war movement centers around ending the U.S. led war and occupation in Iraq, it must also include demands that expose and put pressure the U.S. imperialist strategy of using wars and occupation for empire building throughout the Middle East.

Israel's occupation of Palestine and its role as an outpost of U.S. imperialism is a central component of the U.S. strategy to dominate the Middle East, the most energy-rich region of the world and the gateway to both Africa and Asia.

In addition to its cruel oppression of the Palestinian people, Israel's

occupation of Palestine has served as a base for Zionist expansion and U.S. military aggression throughout the Middle East.

Israel has carried out 'preemptive' strikes against Iraq in the 1980s and Syria more recently. It is planning to do the same in Iran. Its arsenal of nuclear weapons makes it the greatest threat to peace.

The refusal to build a unified U.S. anti-war demonstration on Sept. 24 that includes a demand to end Israel's occupation of Palestine as part of the struggle for peace and democracy in the Middle East is a refusal to oppose white supremacy and the racist character of the war in that region, and amounts to defending Zionism.

For the African American community, this points to similar arguments used by progressives against supporting demands opposing racism and for Black power, claiming they are divisive to building 'broad' campaigns.

Progressive forces should be in the forefront of promoting democracy and in opposition to racism and human rights violations. Yet, there is hesitation to oppose Israel's occupation of Palestine, which is a clear violation of human rights any way one cuts it.

The Israeli occupation of Palestine has been central to shaping U.S. and European racism against the Arab peoples. The occupation of Palestine and Iraq has led not only to racist profiling against Arab peoples, but

Jack Heyman, Trent Willis, Adele Yafia, Clarence Thomas from Local 10 at a 2003 anti-war rally in Oakland.

Photo: Delores Lemon-Thomas

Solidarity Message from Million Worker March to Africa Tribunal Follow-Up Session in Algeria

Pride at Work National Co-chair Nancy Wohlforth and MWM Co-Chair Clarence Thomas address ILC World Conference in Madrid. Thomas also participated in Africa Tribunal in Madrid.

Attention: Louisa Hanoune, Parliamentary Group of the Workers Party of Algeria

On behalf of the Million Worker March Movement, I send greetings and our expression of solidarity to your important May 14 conference in Algeria titled, "The Deadly Evolution that

Threaten the African Continent: What are the Causes and What Can Be Done?"

We hope that your conference will be successful and will contribute in providing the much needed leadership in marshalling forces to cancel the debt.

This weekend (May 14-15) the Million Worker March Movement is convening its "National Reportback and Networking meeting: Building the Movement!" in Detroit, Michigan.

The Million Worker March will be taking up the international debt in relation to Africa and the rest of the world as well as internally within the United States. This is a vital issue for workers everywhere.

In solidarity,

Clarence Thomas,
Co-Chair Million Worker March Movement

also Muslims, the largest number in the U.S. being African Americans.

The unity of the U.S. anti-war movement for a united demonstration must not be obstructed by sectarianism, or by bowing to racism, chauvinism and Zionism. All are enemies to the struggle for peace and against imperialism.

It's essential that we build a united front of the anti-war coalitions against U.S. war in the Middle East, centered on ending the war in Iraq and opposing the occupations in Palestine.

If there are two demonstrations in D.C. on Sept. 24, we urge people to mobilize and raise demands opposing U.S. war and occupation in Iraq, Palestine and throughout the Middle East. Troops out now!

Abridged from WW, Sept.1, 2005.

HAITI ACTION ALERT

Haitian grassroots woman activist and labor leader arrested, harassed by police

The situation in Haiti continues to be critical. Since the U.S.-backed coup of Feb. 29, 2004, followed by the occupation of Haiti first by U.S. Marines and then by UN forces, approximately 10,000 Haitians have been killed and over one thousand jailed.

Grassroots leaders and other supporters of President Aristide are under constant threat. Your help is urgently needed to oppose the most recent arrest and harassment of grassroots labor leaders. an attack clearly aimed at undermining and silencing grassroots resistance to the occupation, attempting to halt the right to travel outside of Haiti, as well as stifling international solidarity. This harassment violates the protections of the right to organize workers contained in the Haitian Constitution and numerous international instruments to which Haiti is a party.

Ginette Apollon, President of the National Commission of Women Workers (CNFT) was arrested on April 19, 2005, at the Port-au-Prince airport upon her return from the Encuentro Mundial de Solidaridad Con la Revolucion Bolivariana in Venezuela. Ms. Apollon, a member of the Confederation des Travailleurs Ha'tiens (CTH), a mother and an activist working with grassroots women, was invited to Venezuela by INAMUJER, a Venezuelan women's rights organization, where she met with Central Latino-Americana de los Trabajadores (CLAT) with whom CTH is affiliated. Apollon was

Paul Loulou Chery and Ginette Apollon, a speaker at the MWM, before their arrest in Haiti. Photo: Steve Gillis

questioned by police about the purpose of her trip to Venezuela, who she met with and more.

Also arrested at the airport were Paul Loulou Chery, a prominent labor leader who is General Coordinator of the Confederation of Haitian Workers (CTH) who was at the airport to greet Ms. Apollon. The police interrogated them about their work as labor leaders, supporting the return of democracy to Haiti. Authorities confiscated the cell phones of the arrestees and videos belonging to Apollon. Ginette Apollon, who suffers from high blood pressure, had to be hospitalized during the ordeal. The interim regime has raided union offices and arrested activists on the basis of vague charges.

Photo and text from a leaflet circulated in 2004.

Venezuelans declare Bolivarian revolution is moving forward

International delegates meet with workers at historic gathering

Berta Joubert-Ceci reporting from Caracas, Venezuela

International delegations visiting Venezuela for the Third Gathering in Solidarity with the Bolivarian Revolution in April 2005, had a chance to see how the working people are participating in the transformation of this country.

This event commemorates the failed coup d'etat in April 2002, when President Hugo Chávez was kidnapped by the oligarchy with instructions and in collaboration from Washington. By the thousands, the people marched from the hills and neighborhoods to the Presidential Palace, a ceaseless tide of outrage and determination to liberate their president.

They returned him to office in less than 48 hours, with the help of a progressive sector of the armed forces.

It can be clearly seen that this commitment to the Bolivarian Revolution, which finally has included the people and elevated their standard of living and dignity, is even firmer today. Last year's gathering illustrated the firm decision by Chávez to elevate the quality of life of the people, particularly the poorest, through special Misiones, or alternative projects of health, education and employment.

Revolution at critical juncture

The gathering this year had exceptional significance. The revolution is at a crucial juncture. It has tremendously increased its base of support, having been ratified by nine election processes. It has survived innumerable destabilization campaigns directed by the U.S. government, both inside the country and worldwide through a hostile media campaign.

The time has come when the advancement of the process has led to a confrontation with the Venezuelan bourgeoisie and the property relations that support its enormous privileges.

Contradictions are so sharp that only two roads are possible, go back or go forward. The dynamism of the revolution does not allow for anything to stand still.

Since they achieved their goal of freeing Chávez, the masses have learned much in a short time. Their political awareness has developed as they tasted the flavor of empowerment. How can they go back?

The road forward has been defined by Chávez himself. The Bolivarian Revolution will take the glorious road of socialism. He first announced it in January in a press conference during the World Social Forum in Brazil, and has repeated it many times since.

During the opening of this event in the Teresa Carreño Theatre, Chávez said that "After much thinking, and reading about the world, I have turned into a socialist." This was received warmly by Venezuelans and their international guests, judging by the prolonged applause.

This statement, which closed the inauguration ceremony, was preceded by the phrase "and if this was not enough ...." Chávez was referring to the progress made by the revolution, developments that are making the U.S. government and corporations, particularly oil companies, nervous.

Ready to defend the revolution

The developments mentioned were many. They include activating a 200,000 strong Military Reserve of both women and men, of all ages, to defend the country. This will be increased to 2 million in the coming months. Venezuela is keenly aware of being a Pentagon target and thus is preparing the reserve army in every corner of the country, from the Apure region where reservists patrol on horseback to Indigenous people in the Amazon jungle. As Chávez said, "The revolution is advancing, and as it advances, the threats increase."

"Venezuela has the largest oil reserves in the world," Chávez said, "and they are the first interest of the U.S." The oil today is being managed by the revolution for the benefit and advantage of the people and not for the profit of U.S. oil companies, as it was during previous governments. Taxes are finally being imposed and enforced on foreign companies. Stealing of oil and its derivatives will no longer be permitted in Venezuela.

Companies used to pay a ludicrous amount of rent for the land they occupied, just pennies per year. The royalties on oil ran as low as 1% on heavy crude. That has been raised to 16%, and under a new law, the royalty on regular crude is raised to 30% and could be increased further. Thorough investigation by the Bolivarian government discovered that the foreign companies were not paying rent for their land. Now this robbery will stop.

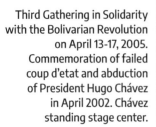

Third Gathering in Solidarity with the Bolivarian Revolution on April 13-17, 2005. Commemoration of failed coup d'etat and abduction of President Hugo Chávez in April 2002. Chávez standing stage center.

WW photo: Betsey Piette

Chávez also mentioned trade relations with other countries. Venezuela will supply nearby Argentina with oil for the first time in 100 years. It will exchange 8 million barrels of fuel oil for pregnant cows, nuclear medical equipment for cancer treatment and agricultural machinery. This avoids having to use hard currencies.

"Similar treaties have been established with Cuba, Jamaica, Uruguay, Paraguay and many other countries of the Caribbean and Central America," said Chávez. "Now we have a strategic agreement with China, to supply oil, and with India."

He explained that Venezuela, together with Brazil, "will form Petro-America, a grouping of oil and related companies. Soon Petro-Caribe will be born in the Caribbean."

He also mentioned the new initiative of Telesur, a television network based in Caracas and other South American countries. Venezuela is also proposing a 'Bank of the South' to break the oppressive chains of economic imperialism of the IMF and World Bank.

Needless to say, the U.S. CIA is operating 24 hours a day to break the revolution. The political will of the masses is progressing in spite of this.

Participatory and protagonist democracy, the cornerstone of the Venezuelan revolution, was palpable in the sessions where a six-person delegation from the U.S. organized by the International Action Center participated. They were Steve Gillis and Frantz Mendes, president and vice president, respectively, of the Boston School Bus Drivers Union; Julie Fry from Fight Imperialism, Stand Together; Lourdes Bela of the Alberto Lovera Bolivarian Circle; Betsey Piette and this writer.

Workers are taking over plants

These delegates attended different working sessions held during the gathering. They covered: "Farmers facing the challenge of making the agrarian reform irreversible;" "The role of workers in the management of companies;" and "Education for social transformation. ..."

Betsey Piette said that over 500 Venezuelan workers gathered for the workshops, which focused on Bolivarian co-management and alternative economic models. They were joined by international delegates from Latin American countries, Canada and the U.S. The program was organized and facilitated by the National Workers Union of Venezuela (UNT).

Among the program participants were the head of the UNT; representatives of the Bolivarian Workers Force; the president of the Invepal workers' union; Venezuela's minister of labor; labor leaders of the transport sector; Cuban representatives, and representatives of workers' struggles in Brazil and Argentina. Among those attending were workers from the oil, aluminum, transport, education and electric industries.

The national director of the UNT and a representative from Invepal described the three-year struggle of the workers to stop the shut down of a paper plant through the development of a union, occupation of the plant, and a takeover of the facility with government support in 2005.

The workers will reopen the plant, producing books for use in Venezuela's literacy program. An alternative example of co-management at the electrical plant CADAFE was presented. The facility includes a recreation area for workers and their families and a cooperative cafeteria. Conference participants were able to visit CADAFE and also tour the Invepal plant.

Speakers received resounding applause when they raised that co-management is not about Venezuelan workers becoming "shareholders who own capital," but about overturning capitalist property relations and replacing them with workers' control over all the industry through socialism.

Abridged from WW, April 28, 2005.

Workers are taking control in Venezuela

Betsey Piette Caracas, Venezuela

Everywhere in Venezuela today workers are forging ahead with formations of workers' organizations. They are taking over factories and experimenting with co-management. Workers are challenging the old class relationships and coming to a collective realization of their historic role in the struggle for socialism.

The problems faced by the Venezuelan working class are massive: 80% live in poverty, millions are in need of better housing, education, higher wages and benefits. As the workers of Venezuela begin to flex their muscles and to exercise their rights under the Bolivarian Constitution, there appears to be a growing recognition that their collective power should stop at nothing short of state control. It is a struggle that holds out hope for the world's working class.

Throughout the process of the Bolivarian Revolution, the role of the workers has gone through a transformation. In April 2002, workers particiated in massive demonstrations that turned back an attempted coup d'etat against President Hugo Chávez. Progressives within organized labor played a key role in defeating employers' lockouts starting in December 2002. Today the momentum of the class struggle is propelling workers into a leadership role.

To understand how the change is taking place in Venezuela's working class today, we need to look at the history of organized labor in this oil-rich Latin American country. For over 30 years prior to the U.S.-backed attempt to overthrow Chávez, the workers' struggle against neoliberalism was held in check by the leadership of the Confederation of Venezuelan Workers (CTV), the country's labor council who subordinated the interests of the workers to big business political parties that opposed Chávez. It is reported that the CTV received financial aid from a conduit for the CIA, the National Endowment for Democracy, disbursed through the AFL-CIO by Alberto Ruizin his article: "What is the AFL-CIO doing in Venezuela?" (March 2, 2004)

In 2001, the CTV was forced to hold its' first leadership election. It was so corrupt that 50 to 70 % of the workers refused to participate, and Venezuela's Supreme Court refused to recognize the results.

During the CTV-backed lockout by the business opposition, workers responded by occupying factories and running them as cooperatives. When owners threatened to shut down factories, workers took over plants, including a Pepsi-Cola facility owned by an active supporter of the coup.

Venezuelan workers, fed up with the CTV's corporate unionism, gave up attempts at reform. In May 2003, at a gathering in Caracas, workers from nearly every sector of the country's labor force joined together to form a new confederation, the National Union of Workers (UNT).

Within two years 76.5% of collective bargaining agreements were with UNT-affiliated unions, compared to 20.2% with the CTV.

The UNT has been at the forefront as workers exercise their rights under Venezuela's new constitution to form parallel unions to replace the old corporate unionism. This constitution contains many provisions that guarantee workers' rights. The UNT has pushed for regular, open elections and supports workers' co-management

Betsey Piette with Lenin and Franz Mendes, president of the Boston School Bus Drivers Union, in Carabobo, Venezuela.

or self-management in workplaces. With an increased say over what gets raised at the bargaining table, the new unions have excited workers about their prospects for improving working conditions, wages and benefits.

The UNT has adopted the slogans "No to globalization, yes to worker-management." They are taking the struggle beyond the economic confines of traditional trade unionism, from a fight merely to improve wages, benefits and working conditions to one prepared to challenge capitalist control over these conditions.

The massive popular demonstrations that turned back an attempted coup in 2002, opened the floodgates for revolutionary change and swept the working class of Venezuela onto center stage. They face many problems. The forces of counter revolution, while temporarily set back, nevertheless remain poised in the wings.

The workers, however, are making it clear that they will not be satisfied with a simple change in plant management to workers' control. They want workers' control over the state; they want socialism. They know that in the struggle ahead they have nothing to lose but their chains.

Abridged from WW, May 5, 2005.

Workers made Venepal paper factory more productive than the bosses ever had. They received broad support from other workers and food was provided by local fishers and farmers. Now they are producing books for the literacy campaign.

Bus drivers union solidarity

Ruben Linares, a national director of the UNT and President of the National Transportation Workers' Union, being interviewed by Steve Gillis, President of the Boston School Bus Union. Linares told a moving history of how the Caracas taxi and bus drivers refused to participate in the April 11, 2002 "strike" called by the CTV and the Venezuelan Chamber of Commerce in an attempt at a coup de etat against the Bolivarian government. Instead, the drivers shuttled workers from the poor neighborhoods to the city center, where a mass uprising of workers, supported by rank-and-file soldiers, lead to the restoration of the democratically elected president, Hugo Chavez, on April 13, 2003.

WW photos: Betsey Piette

MILLION WORKER MARCH MOVEMENT
April 12, 2005

Solidarity letter from MWM to Venepal workers

The Million Worker March stands in solidarity with the workers at the Venepal paper plant in Venezuela. Your three-year-long struggle, not only to save your jobs, but to exert workers control over the plant production, is an inspiration for workers around the world who are fighting against layoffs, cutbacks and plant closings.

The world-wide crisis facing workers is felt here in the U.S. as well. Union jobs are being lost in record numbers, with African American workers taking the hardest hit — 55 percent of the 300,000 union jobs lost in 2004 were held by Black workers who have lost not only paychecks, but health and retirement benefits as well.

We recommend the action of the San Francisco Labor Council (SFLC, AFL-CIO) defending Venezuelan workers through the unanimous passage of a resolution opposing the complaint initiated by the Venezuelan employers association, FEDECAMARAS, before the International Labor Organization (ILO). This complaint has been endorsed and supported by employers' associations in 23 countries, including the United States.

The San Francisco resolution views the convening of the ILO Commission of Inquiry as another attempt to undermine the UNT, the new progressive Venezuelan labor federation. It further opposes the funding by the national AFL-CIO of programs that support U.S. government policy in Venezuela.

The SFLC resolution noted, "Opposition to the ILO Commission of Inquiry on Venezuela by the U.S. Labor movement is part of the same struggle to promote a new foreign policy by labor that is independent from U.S. State Department objectives." Long Live the struggle of the Venezuelan workers to build a workers movement and a nation in your own name!

Trent Willis
Trent Willis
President of ILWU Local 10

Clarence Thomas
Clarence Thomas
Executive Board, ILWU Local 10
Co-coordinators of the Million Worker March Movement

Venezuelan models of co-management

Betsey Piette   Carabobo, Venezuela

Experiments with workers' control were discussed in April 2005, during an conference on the role of workers in the Bolivarian Revolution, facilitated by the National Union of Workers (UNT) in the Venezuelan state of Carabobo.

The models of co-management being promoted by the UNT have nothing in common with the top-down versions promoted by bosses in the U.S. attempting to break unions by circumventing contracts. Joaquin

Osorio, representing the Bolivarian Workers Force, told the gathering, "We are not talking about the Toyota model of quality control."

Alexis Onero, a national director of the UNT and a leader of the workers now controlling the Invepal (formerly Venepal) paper plant, was a keynote speaker. Venepal

had employed 1,600 workers. In 2003, the plant's owners, supporters of the attempted anti-Chavez coup, announced plans to sell off the company's assets.

Workers at Venepal responded by occupying the plant. When no bosses showed up, the workers occupied the plant. Becoming aware of their

Columbia's workers, Venezuela's revolution

Frank Neisser

A meeting in solidarity with the peoples' struggles in Colombia and Venezuela took place in Boston on April 23, 2005, at the union hall of the Boston School Bus Drivers Union, USWA Local 8751, It was co-chaired by Jorge Marin of the Martin Luther King Bolivarian Circle and Berta Joubert-Ceci.

The featured speaker was Gerardo Cajamarca, a leader of the SINAL-TRAINAL union in Colombia that is leading the struggle of Coca-Cola workers and the international Boycott Killer Coke campaign. A city council member in Facatativa, Cundinamarca, he was elected with the support of the unions and social movements.

Cajamarca and his family are political refugee due to threats they faced from Colombian paramilitaries because of his work as a human rights defender and community leader.

Cajamarca showed photos of trade union leaders in Colombia assassinated by the Uribe government death

squads whose killings have escalated in recent months. In the world, nine out of 10 trade union leaders killed over the last year were Colombian.

Steve Gillis, president of the Boston School Bus Drivers Union, who attended the conference in solidarity with the Bolivarian Revolution in Venezuela, described meeting with paper workers and seeing a revolutionary process that is moving toward socialism and putting the resources in the hands of the people.

Jorge Marin and Berta Joubert-Ceci, who also attended the conference, spoke of the international solidarity. Joubert-Ceci described the Bolivarian history of Colombia and Venezuela, which had originally been one country.

Dario Zapata of the Permanent Committee for Colombian Peace, spoke of the struggle of democratic forces against the Uribe government.

Rhode Island Colombian activist Elvira Bustamante, explained how the Free Trade Area of the Americas

Berta Joubert-Ceci and Gerardo Cajamarca leader of the SINALTRAINAL union in Colombia, speaking in the union hall of the Boston School Bus Drivers Union, USWA Local 8751 on April 23, 2005.
WW photo: Liz Green

destroys the livelihood of people in Latin America and the sovereignty of countries subordinated to the IMF and the World Bank.

In a subsequent meeting, Cajamarca was enthused to hear about the struggle of maintenance workers at the Bromley Heath Housing Project, who attended the meeting, as well as the MWMM.

Abridged from WW, April 28, 2005.

collective power the workers proceeded to take on the tasks of running the plant, creating committees for sales, production schedules and procuring raw materials.

When the workers opened the books they learned how much the owners had lied to them about profits and benefits. Onero, emphasizing that "unity was the key to our success."

President Hugo Chavez opened the way for a Venepal co-management arrangement between the government and workers. The plant will produce books for a literacy campaign.

Another model of co-management was the CADAFE electric company, Planta Centro in Carabobo, Venezue-

la's largest power plant, producing 80% of Venezuela's electricity. Now workers elect plant managers who are subject to recall. Angel Navas, president of Fetraelec, a UNT affiliated union representing 34,000 workers, sits on the CADAFE board. Benefits have been improved and working conditions are safer. Workers more say over production, but it has stopped short of workers' control.

Speakers and participants talked about the need for the unions; how co-management would affect relationships between workers-own-

Venezuela Labor Minister María Cristina Iglesias.

ers; and consumers who would "own" Venezuela's resources.

Maria Cristina Iglesius, Venezuela's minister of labor, cautioned, "It's not possible to succeed by having capitalism with a more humane face. The idea of co-management is not for the unions to give up power, but for the workers to gain power. We have to change labor relations, we have the power to make the extreme change in the productive apparatus to bring us revolutionary socialism."

Abridged from WW, May 5, 2005.

ILWU, MWMM activists attend rally in Japan

A delegation of U.S. trade unionists led by the ILWU and Million Worker March Movement activists participated in a National Workers' Rally in Tokyo's Hibiya Amphitheatre which 4,900 trade union workers and other activists attended on Nov. 5, 2006.

The rally and march was organized by Kan-Nama/ Solidarity Union of Japan, Minato-Godo/Metal and Machinery Workers' Union in Osaka, and DORO-CHIBA (National Railway Motive Power Union of Chiba).

The purpose of the rally was to build solidarity among Japanese trade unionists to fight against privatization, union busting, war and a Japanese Constitution revision.

A statement issued by rally organizers explains that, "A large number of workers have been deprived of their right to organize, fired from jobs, and been made irregular (part-time) workers."

The rate of poverty in Japan, second only to the United States, is growing, as work forces are being

The international delegation speakers included Joseph Prisco, Ted Ludig, Keith Shanklin and Clarence Thomas.
Photo: Hiroyuki Yamamoto

Photos: Delores Lemon-Thomas

downsized, wages lowered and working families forced to work harder while earning less.

According to Hiroyuki Yamamoto, the Secretary-Treasurer of the DORO-CHIBA International Labor Solidarity Committee, "Each year this rally has succeeded in forging solidarity of the working class and has contributed to the workers' movement of each participating country."

The international delegation attending the rally included representatives from the Korean Confederation of Trade Unions (KCTU) of the Seoul Regional Council; Aircraft Mechanics Fraternal Association (AMFA) Locals 9 and 33; the ILWU Locals 10, 19, 34, 52 and the Inland-boatmen's Union; and Brotherhood of Locomotive Engineers and Trainmen (BLE&T), an affiliate of the Teamsters.

Several African-American trade union activists representing the ILWU and the Million Worker March Movement have visited Japan several times since the MWM in 2004.

ILWU delegates included Clarence Thomas Local 10 and co-chair of the MWMM; Juan Del Pozo, Keith Shanklin Local 34 executive board member; John Griffin and Todd R. Weeks Local 19; Michael Hoard Local 52 and member of the African American Longshore Coalition and the MWMM; and Joel Schor, member of Inlandboatmen's Union.

AMFA delegates included Joseph Prisco, president Local 9; Ted Ludwig, president Local 33; Douglas Butz, national treasurer and Paul Jensen, member of BLE&T.

Clarence Thomas led the 16-member U.S. delegation.

The DORO-CHIBA invited the U.S. delegation to Japan. It has a history much like the ILWU of being militant, democratic, an advocate of international solidarity and a fighter for social justice causes.

Its leadership has been in the vanguard of trade union activism. Its founder, Hiroshi Nakano, has been

Joel Schor Local 10.
Photos: Delores Lemon-Thomas

Johnny Griffin Local 19 and Paul Jensen BLE&T Local 582.

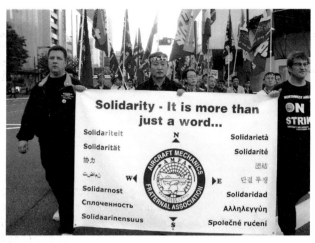

AMFA, Joseph Prisco, President Local 9, Douglas Butz, National Treasurer and John Renner Local 33, with Hiroyuki Yamamoto.

Douglas Butz and a rally host carries the AMFA banner with John Renner. Photos: Delores Lemon-Thomas

called the Harry Bridges of the DORO-CHIBA. (Bridges was a founder of the ILWU.) Like Bridges, Nakano understands the nature of class struggle. He led his union in breaking away from its affiliate, the Dora National Leadership, to establish an independent progressive union.

The ILWU had its origin as part of the International Longshore Association (ILA) in 1934. In 1937, it broke away and formed the ILWU, a more militant and democratic union independent of the ILA and representing all dock workers on the West Coast. DORO-CHIBA led the railway struggle against privatization of the Japan National Railways (JNR)

In July 2000, DORO-CHIBA executive board member Kawasaki Masahiro came to San Francisco to develop a friendly relationship with U.S. trade union militants when 40 workers of the DORO-CHIBA were dismissed for waging strikes to stop jet fuel transportation to the Narita airport and also to oppose the division and privatization of the JNR.

The DORO-CHIBA rail workers sent a large delegation to the MWM in October 2004. The DORO-CHIBA union has embraced the MWMM and has been inviting ILWU and MWM organizers to Japan since 2004. Hundreds of Japanese workers wear the

classic blue MWM tee shirt at rallies and marches sponsored by DORO-CHIBA.

International labor discussion

On Nov. 6, there was a briefing involving Yasuhiro Tanaka, president of DORO-CHIBA; Hiroyuki Yamamoto, secretary-treasurer of their International Labor Solidarity Committee; Kim Chang-Sedo, vice president of the KCTU Seoul Regime Council; Han Hyuk director of Foreign Cooperation Seoul Regional Council (KCTU); with Joe Prisco and Clarence Thomas. The discussion focused on building international labor solidarity between Japan and the U.S.

The Korean workers are fighting massive repression. The Korean government is seeking to destroy the Korean Government Employees Union (KGEU) and the Korean Confederation of Construction Industry Trade Union. There will be actions worldwide to demand justice for Korean workers. At the Korean Consulate in San Francisco, a solidarity picket and rally was held on Nov. 15 as part of an international solidarity action. ILWU activists Michael Hoard, John Griffin and Todd Weeks participated in a four-hour warning strike in Seoul, Korea, on Nov. 12. A full-fledged general strike is planned for Nov. 22, 2007.
Abridged from WW, Dec. 7, 2006.

Clarence Thomas and Keith Shanklin, in the foreground, spoke at the National Workers' Rally in Tokyo's Hibiya Amphitheatre attended by 4,900 trade union workers and other activists.

Longshore worker at Tokyo rally:
'An injury to one is an injury to all'

Clarence Thomas addresses workers' rally in Tokyo, Japan, on Nov. 5, 2006

Joseph Prisco, Maria Arevalo and John Renner with Clarence Thomas at the mike. Delores Lemon-Thomas, Juan Del Pozo, Todd Weeks, Johnny Griffin, Michael Hoard and Joel Schor.

I bring you greetings and solidarity on behalf of the ILWU, Local 10, in San Francisco and the Million Worker March Movement.

One of our recent labor struggles was over the destruction of the Gulf Coast. Hurricane Katrina was a 21st century snapshot of the genocidal policies of the U.S. government. Katrina exposed the conditions faced by working class African Americans and people of color under U.S. style democracy.

Today, the upsurge by Latino workers throughout the U.S. against criminalization and repression should be viewed as very important in building a rank-and-file workers' fightback movement.

The Immigrant Rights Mobilization and Boycott on May Day, 2006, represented one of the most successful general strikes in recent U.S. history. This was accomplished by workers that do not belong to unions, have no benefits, and without the support of organized labor.

Ninety percent of the cargo shipment at the Port of Los Angeles and Long Beach was halted as the result of immigrant truck drivers not going to work. Several large businesses shut down their plants for the day

Workers today need to build a rank-and-file global fight back movement. The labor movement must embrace grassroots formations to unite Yellow, Red, Black, Brown and white workers into a militant international force for progress on behalf of the working class. Workers must be able to follow their work as it traverses the globe.

Workers must be able to take their collective bargaining agreements and their unions to any country to which their work has been relocated.

Like the immigrant struggle, international workers must hit the streets and demand full protection for all eligible workers. We must have an international progressive program tied in to a workers' agenda.

ILWU dock workers, trade unionists, workers, and anti-war and social justice activists from around the world, including DORO-CHIBA workers, gathered at the steps of the Lincoln Memorial on Oct. 17, 2004, at the Million Worker March.

Thousands stood demanding an end to the war at home, the war abroad, international workers rights and an end to privatization.

It is occasions such as this that make it possible for workers to build real international rank-and-file unity.

Todd Weeks and Johnny Griffin ILWU Local 19, Delores Lemon-Thomas, Clarence Thomas, Michael Hoard and DORO-CHIBA hosts Takao Saito and Eriko Seikojima.
Photos: Hiroyuki Yamamoto

Join us in the MWM
Michael Hoard ILWU Local 52

I'm here today with my Brother Todd Weeks from ILWU Local 19 Seattle, Washington to show solidarity with my sisters and brothers in Japan and also the rest of the world.

On October 17, 2004 brothers from Japan told me that they were having a rally and I said I'd be there because you guys are like the ILWU, you are strong in unity. I believe in people from all over the world coming together in one voice.

Michael Hoard Local 52.
Photo: DORA-CHIBA.

Johnny 'Cat' Griffin with a host from the Japanese rally, and Todd Weeks. Photo: Delores Lemon-Thomas

My dream
Gabriel Prawl ILWU Local 19

It is a great honor to be part of an International Labor Movement. I thank my brothers and sisters in Japan for the invitation to your International Rally.

I regret not being able to attend but I am with you in spirit, fighting to expand our labor movement keeping in mind that your fight is our fight. The ILWU believes "An Injury to One is An Injury to All."

We have reached the era where organized and unorganized labor must be unified to survive the international oppression of the corporate bosses and their attempt to destroy the organization of labor with selfish greed.

The MWMM has taken the first step to call on workers nationally and internationally. It's time corporations become aware of the fact that the workers are the rank-and-file of the world.

We keep the globe circulating. When our labor movement reaches the goal of international solidarity, I have a dream that workers around the world will be united and celebrate a day free from oppression.

The MWMM has clearly marked that first step of a new tide. So let's keep expanding our struggle of rank-and-file labor movement to gather power. Power to the working class!

I close with special thanks for keeping the faith strong and alive.

Photos: Delores Lemon Thomas

Yasuhiro Tanaka President of DORO-CHIBA leads march in Tokyo, on Nov. 5, 2006.

Bordeaux

Lille

March 21, 2006

Hand of solidarity
Black unionist
to French workers

The Million Worker March Movement is hereby expressing its solidarity to the French youth and workers who have organized and mobilized in their own name. You are courageously protesting in the streets against the policy of allowing employers the right to fire young workers without cause within the first two years of employment.

The "First Employment Contract" law is clearly an attack not only on French youth but the entire working class. In fact, many of the French youth protesting are workers already, while the others represent the future French working class.

There are similarities with how the argument is framed in France, that this law will aid companies to bring down unemployment, and the argument in the U.S. regarding not raising the minimum wage: "We'll hire more of you if we can exploit you more."

In the U.S., an employer must show cause before firing a union worker only. Other workers must be able to prove discrimination to keep from being fired.

If this new law is permitted to stand, French workers can expect the further erosion of hard-fought worker rights.

I was a student activist at San Francisco State College in 1968, and participated in one of the longest student strikes in U.S. history to establish a Black Studies Department and a School of Ethnic Studies, which still exist today.

The current struggle of the youth of France reminds me of the student activism at the Sorbonne in 1968. It is wonderful to see that the youth of France have not forgotten the history of activism and struggle of French youth and workers.

An injury to one is an injury to all,

Clarence Thomas
Past Secretary-Treasurer, ILWU Local 10
National Co-Chair, Million Worker March Movement

Paris

Marseille

Building Global Solidarity
MWMM travels to Brazil

Clarence Thomas   **An eyewitness report**

The First National Coordination of Struggles (Conlutas) Congress took place in July 2008, in Betim, Minas Gerais, Brazil. Conlutas' purpose was the coordination of struggles of the working class, involving unions, Brazilians of African descent, popular movements and youth organizations, including peasants, women and the LGBT communities.

Conlutas is an emerging political movement that is committed to putting forward a rank-and-file, democratic agenda. More than 4,000 delegates throughout Brazil and international observers from 22 countries attended the Congress. The Conlutas movement opposes the policies of the World Bank and International Monetary Fund.

Following the Conlutas Congress, there was a Latin American and Caribbean Workers conference. More than 500 delegates representing countries, including Argentina, Bolivia, Brazil, Colombia, Costa Rica, El Salvador, Haiti, Paraguay, Peru, Uruguay and Venezuela. Also present were participants from Ireland, Portugal, Spain, Sweden and the United States.

The aim of this meeting was to develop Latin America and Caribbean solidarity actions to meet the challenge of global capital looting their material resources at the expense of the poor and working class. Discussions focused on privatization, outsourcing, the Central America Free Trade Agreement (CAFTA), and opposing the use of casual labor to supplant union workers.

I participated in a transportation workers workshop where we discussed issues of longshore workers. One important topic was how employers attempt to criminalize trade union activists by framing and then imprisoning them in order to marginalize the trade union movement. Another topic was building working class rank-and-file democracy.

When given an opportunity to address the delegates, I spoke about the decades of militant and democratic trade union activism of the ILWU. The delegates were thrilled to hear a U.S. trade unionist representing an organization that has a history of struggle in the fight for social justice. I emphasized that independent rank and file action is critical in being able to carry out a working class agenda.

One of the cornerstones of the ILWU is international solidarity. Rank-and-filers visit workers in other countries, to learn more about our mutual interests as a class, and in some instances our mutual employers. The ILWU has routinely shared information about collective bargaining and working conditions with foreign unions and labor federations.

Abridged from WW, July 31, 2008.

Clarence Thomas with Didi Travesso the leader of Conlutas in Brazil 2008.

Thomas with another Conlutas participant and Ahmed Shawki, the founder of Haymarket Books. Haymarket aims, 'to be a socialist workplace in a capitalist world.'

Clarence Thomas, center, met with Latin Amercian dock workers. Photos: Delores Lemon-Thomas

Tariq Ali and Clarence Thomas speak at World Peace Forum

Nov. 11, 2008. The World Peace Forum used the 90th anniversary of the end of the First World War to hold a Teach-In, in Vancouver, British Columbia. During three days activists, academicians and artists gathered to discuss what is currently happening in the struggle to stop war and start mobilizing for a sustainable "just and peaceful future."

Participants included Tariq Ali, author, activist, and filmmaker; Denis Lemelin, National President Canadian Union of Postal Workers; activists Sunera Thobani and Dahlia Wasfi, M.D.; and Clarence Thomas, ILWU Local 10 executive board member and national co-chair of the MWMM.

Renowned intellectual and writer Tariq Ali, was the keynote speaker. He discussed how the anti-war movement is as old as war itself. How the 20th century perfected the art of killing. He explained how rulers have the capacity to pump up the working class through propaganda and manipulation to support war. Tariq also talked about how wars provoke revolutions and break up world empires. He reminded the audience that the only country to use weapons of mass destruction was the US when it bombed civilians in Hiroshima and Nagasaki during World War II. He explained that current economic crisis is a mega collapse of the free market ideology.

Tariq Ali and Clarence Thomas, during the plenary session spoke on international perspectives concerning the building of the peace movement.

As co-chair of the Portworkers May Day Organizing Committee, along with Jack Heyman, Thomas had provided rank-and-file leadership for the courageous and historic shut down of 29 ports on the West Coast on May Day 2008. For the first time in U.S. history, workers withheld their labor for 8 hours to strike against a U.S. foreign policy decision.

Thomas gave a brief history of the ILWU and its formation, an overview of a chronology of historic actions in support of international labor solidarity and world peace. He laid out how, "ILWU policies and actions on foreign affairs have always been built on the belief that international labor solidarity and world peace are the cornerstones of social and economic justice for all workers including the membership of the ILWU." He described how during the 30s, the union blocked the shipment of scrap iron to Japan and fascist movements in Europe.

An overview was provided as to how the ILWU during the early 60s opposed the escalation of the arms race and the Cold War and how the union was the first labor union to oppose the Vietnam War.

Also included was how Local 10 rank-and-file, independent of the union leadership authorization, repeatedly refused to handle South African cargo as an act of international solidarity. Such actions included boycotting cargo for military dictatorships in Chile and El Salvador.

Thomas reported how the Million Worker March mobiliza-

Tariq Ali, Dahli Wasfi, M.D. and Clarence Thomas.
Photo: Delores Lemon Thomas

tion withstood the attacks from the Democratic Party. Undermining by the AFL-CIO leadership proved to be a sound preparation leading to the May Day 'No Peace No Work' eight-hour strike of longshore workers on the West Coast.

The lessons prepared the rank-and-file leadership to overcome opposition from the Pacific Maritime Association and a coastwide arbitrator's ruling against the May Day action.

The May Day West Coast Port Shut Down was an act of resistance against U.S. imperialism. He closed his remarks by speaking of the importance of the peace movement in the U.S. having working class radical leadership, and how the movement must move from protest to resistance. The ILWU set an example of labor taking an action at the point of production that the government and the military industrial complex could not ignore.

World Peace Forum Teach In

A workshop was conducted on the theme, "Solidarity Forum, labor strategies for peace activism." This workshop was co-led by Denis Lemelin, Canadian Union of Postal Workers, Ottawa, Ontario, a union that has been very involved with the peace movement in Canada.

The workshop commenced with the showing of a video of Thomas' six day visit to Baghdad to meet with Iraqi workers and trade union leaders which was organized by USLAW in 2003.

The video captures Iraqi workers speaking in their own name about life under the occupation, conducting demonstrations in opposition to the Coalition Provisional Authority.

When discussing May Day, Thomas explained how the most meaningful solidarity action came from the Port Workers Union of Iraq, who shut down the Ports of Umn Qasr and Khor Alzubair for one hour on May Day in opposition to the occupation of Iraq. This action was taken in defiance of Baathist party legislation of 1987, which occupation forces used to ban trade unions in the public sector and public enterprise.

One of the key organizers of this Forum was Canadian trade unionist Mabel Elmore of the British Columbia Labour Against the War (BCLAW). According to Ms. Elmore, BCLAW was formed after the World Peace Forum in June 2006. BCLAW has membership from locals, district councils, provincial and national affiliates. BCLAW has an education program and are invited to deliver workshops and speak at rallies and events.

BCLAW organized a May 1, 2008, event to reclaim May Day and express support and solidarity for the ILWU action. The Forum was held at the ILWU Maritime Labour Centre.

Submitted by,

Clarence Thomas

May Day 2008: Dock workers Shut Down West Coast ports in an anti-war protest

Amy Goodman - Democracy Now!
Protests took place on May Day in the largest labor strike since the invasion of Iraq, ports along the West Coast, all 29 of them, were shut down as some 25,000 dock workers went on a one-day strike to protest the war. The ILWU strike, brought port operations to a halt from Long Beach to Seattle in defiance of employers and arbitrators.

Jack Heyman - ILWU officer: We are proud of the longshore union making this stand, because it's part of our legacy. This is the first strike ever of workers withholding their labor and demanding an end to the war and withdrawal of the troops.

An arbitrator said that the longshoremen should not go out on strike. Our own union officials did not want the actions that we organized up and down the coast. We don't take our orders from above.

The rank-and-file goes out and does what it has to do. We did that in 1984, we refused to work a ship from South Africa for eleven days in defiance of an arbitrator and what our union officials were telling us.

We've got a strong tradition in the ILWU of rank-and-file democracy. And our action took place based on a motion that came out of our Caucus, which is like a convention of all longshore workers represented up and down the coast. We decided to stop work to stop this war, and that's what was carried out.

We appealed for solidarity actions. The most stunning solidarity came from the port workers in Iraq, who struck in solidarity with us. That was really a very courageous move, because they're literally under the gun of a military occupation.

Democracy Now!
May 2 2008: tinyurl.com/y2z7drlw

Iraqi declaration of support for dock workers exemplary show of workers international solidarity

On May Day, 25,000 dock workers in the U.S. went on strike to protest the continuing U.S. war in Iraq and to show their support for their fellow workers in Iraq.

Dock workers in the ports of Basra in Iraq stopped the work for one hour on the same day to show their solidarity with their U.S. comrades. The Left worker-Communist Party of Iraq (LWPI), appreciates this solidarity and expresses its support for their demand to end war.

The bonds between dock workers in the U.S. and Iraq is a wonderful example of workers' international solidarity. It is a blow in the face to the bourgeoisie the U.S. and Iraq, the class which has not spared any effort to destroy Iraq's society and turned it into a battlefield, for their own domination, at the expense of the lives, security and rights of millions of people.

Our party stresses that the bourgeois class is incapable of resolving the disastrous situation in Iraq. The solution lies in the hands of the working class and socialists who have an interest in putting an end to the situation and to building a free, equal, and prosperous society.

Our party confirms that the urgent solution requires the immediate expulsion of U.S. forces from Iraq and the disarming of Islamic and nationalist militias. We call for U.S. dockworkers to rally around these demands. It is the only way to end the terrible humanitarian crisis for millions of workers, toilers and the deprived, and to bring security and peace to Iraq.

Long Live Solidarity of dock workers in the USA and Iraq!
Long Live Workers' International Solidarity! Long live the Socialist Republic!
The Left worker-Communist Party of Iraq   May 2, 2008, abridged message

West Coast activists block Zionist ships

Terri Kay

Thomas with Lara Kiswani executive director of of Arab Resource and Organizing Center (AROC) at their 10 Anniversary dinner.   Photo: Delores Lemon-Thomas

Los Angeles activists continue battle against Israeli ships at the entrance to SSA Terminal in Long Beach, Calif.

Photo: Mike Chicky

The action to stop the Israeli ship Zim from unloading at the Port of Oakland, initially planned as a one-day event, became a movement. Originally organized by Block the Boat for Gaza, a coalition of about 70 organizations led by the Arab Resource and Organizing Center (AROC), the Aug. 16, 2014, action kept growing. The movement included independent activists and, most significantly, the ranks of the ILWU.

During four days of demonstrations and picket lines, with the support of the Local 10 rank-and-file the ship was not unloaded. On the last day, some cargo was unloaded, though much of it remained on the ship. This was only after the Zim pulled out of its berth at the SSA terminal in Oakland, left the San Francisco Bay, passed under the Golden Gate Bridge, only to return to Ports of America, a different terminal operator later on.

Lara Kiswani executive director of AROC said, "Our call for a West Coast action was extremely successful, as people around the world are thinking of doing similar actions. People in Palestine are applauding our efforts here and see this as part of Boycott, Divestment, Sanctions (BDS) in action. This has caused real economic damage to the state of Israel."

Monadel Herzallah national organizer of the U.S. Palestinian Community Network and a protest organizer said: "The overwhelming support for our action has been amazing. We were prepared and organized to go one day, but the energy was there to continue . ....

"The port workers had a history of standing up against injustice, and they were respectful of our cause and picket lines. They have worked in the past against injustice in South Africa and before that against the fascists and the Nazis. The community and the activists continued the protest through the fourth day. I think that the Block the Boat action in Oakland started a momentum that energized the BDS movement globally, including the workers and community across the West Coast.

"People in Palestine and Gaza were aware and recognized the support from the Oakland community, and it helped them to know that they are not alone in fighting the brutal Israeli aggression."

Clarence Thomas said, "We affect the global economy." He said, "It was the longest action taken against an Israeli vessel using community blockades and the second time at the Port of Oakland. The first was in response to the killing of unarmed people in international waters on board the ship Mavi Marmara, which was attempting to bring humanitarian aid to the Palestinian people in 2010."

Thomas discussed the role of the union in this struggle in solidarity with Palestine. "There was a great deal of outreach to the ILWU rank-and-file which allowed them to get familiar with the Local 10 history, from the struggle against apartheid in South African to what happened in Ferguson allowing them to relate to that with respect to an occupying army.

"Having seen videos of police actions, from a Black woman being beaten up by a highway patrolman to a Black professor being beaten up, it's not difficult or a stretch to empathize with people in Gaza.

"When I learned there are 1.1 million people in Gaza who were 18 and younger and about the displacement of Palestinian families, the relation to the conditions in the Black community is apparent."

Thomas said of his union, "The rank-and-file responded in a splendid way. The longer the struggle went on, people were identifying with the struggle. They were following the Zim, watching its movement live on their cell phones.

"I've told members that we've respected community picket lines since 1935, when Local 10 workers refused to load metal that was bound for the war machines of fascist Italy and Japan, to 1984, when Local 10 longshore workers refused to unload South African cargo from the Ned Lloyd Kimberley, during the height of the anti-apartheid struggle. It was the first time many of them had been involved in anything like that.

"They learned that if they don't load a vessel, it affects the global economy. The action brought the local together, petty differences were pushed aside, as we united in struggle. They knew the response from Palestine to what we've done. It was very, very meaningful.

"The 1993 Oslo Accord announced a program for the establishment of a Gaza Sea Port. Part of self-determination means to be able to have shipping and air ports, to be able to conduct international trade."

Other cities block Zionist ships

Jefferson Azevedo, of the Los Angeles International Action Center, described how the Block the Boat movement won a victory in southern California against another Zim ship. Two hundred people arrived on August 23, at the Port of Long Beach. They were organized by groups, including Al-Awda, BDS-LA, IJAN (International Jewish Anti-Zionist Network), Answer Coalition, Global Women's Strike, IAC and Workers Voice.

Around 7:30 a.m. the police made an attempt to stop picketers. Youth of color joined hands, led by Palestinian youth, to prevent the workers' cars from crossing." Azevedo continued: "Some workers came

through and then backed out. Some of the workers cheered and applauded, and some made a U-turn and left. Another demo was set for the afternoon shift, but the union called the shift off for the day."

Ed Mast, of the Palestine Solidarity Committee, said of the delay of the Zim Chicago at the Port of Tacoma, Wash. "On Aug. 23 the two gates that Washington United Terminal used for their workers were blocked. However, they opened another gate. It felt like a defeat, but then we found that we had delayed the starting of their shift, costing them money.

"They called for more workers for the Zim ship in the afternoon. We set up the blockade, using bikes and roving pickets, delaying entry of workers into the gates. Using police presence the workers went in, but some chose not to show up."

A press release issued by Block the Boat NW states, "The Block the Boat campaign is preparing more blockades for the Zim Chicago ship's arrival in Seattle. It is not yet clear whether similar factors as before are causing apparent delays in docking and unloading in the Port of Seattle. Blockade actions are being planned for as soon as Aug. 25."

Updates are being posted at blocktheboatnw.wordpress.com/

Abridged from WW, Sept. 4, 2014.

Herb Mills, in the white cap, at protest blocking the Zim ship. Mills, Local 10 led efforts in the refusal to ship military cargo to Chile and to the El Salvador military junta in 1974.

Block the Boat march in Oakland. On August 16, 2014 thousands of Palestinian solidarity activists convened at the Port of Oakland.

Photo: Bob Ristelhueber

'Block the Boat,' Oakland keeps ship away

Terri Kay

More than 200 pro-Palestinian protesters marched from the West Oakland Bay Area Rapid Transit station to the Stevedoring Services of America terminal at the Port of Oakland on Oct. 26, 2014. They were celebrating the failure of the Zim Beijing container ship to arrive at the port for unloading and, in the words of organizers, "...showing Zim what they can expect if they try to come back. Let's show the world that the Bay Area says no to Zionism."

The Block the Boat coalition had led the effort that kept the Zim Piraeus from unloading the bulk of its cargo in Oakland over the course of four days starting on Aug. 16. They declared the new target was the Zim Beijing, originally scheduled to arrive at the Port of Oakland on Oct. 25.

After 'Block the Boat' declared its plans, the Zim website dropped Oakland from the ship's schedule. However, MarineTraffic.com, reported that the ship never changed its Oakland destination. As of this writing, the Beijing continues to head West and is more than 1,100 nautical miles away from U.S. shores.

According to JWeekly.com, a Jewish Bay Area newsletter, "While the Zim Integrated Shipping Services website lists the vessel for an Oct. 25 arrival, the schedule shows no more Zim dockings in Oakland beyond that date, and a report on TheJewishPress.com noted that, 'Zim may not call Oakland home again.' "

The 'Block the Boat' call states that, "The military assault on Gaza, which killed more than 2,200 Palestinians and left more than 100,000 homeless, has halted, thanks to the Palestinian resistance, but our struggle is not over. With the full support of the U.S. government, Israel continues to carry out its brutal occupation, confiscate more land and build more settlements, imprison thousands of Palestinians and maintain the siege on Gaza as part of its policy of ethnic cleansing.

"The apartheid state of Israel not only impacts Palestinians, but also plays a role in the oppression of communities all across the globe. The Zim shipping line is instrumental in upholding this system of global repression. There are direct ties, training, weapons and surveillance, between Israel's occupation of Palestine and the increasingly militarized occupation of Black and Brown communities in the U.S. It is now a well-known fact that police departments in and around Ferguson, Mo., have received training from Israel."

Solidarity actions were held in conjunction with the Oakland action at the Israeli Embassy in New York City and in Baltimore. Last week, 'Block the Boat' Los Angeles held off the unloading of the Zim Savannah for two-and-a-half days.

Abridged from WW, Nov. 5, 2014.

Cephus X Johnson, Beatrice X Johnson, Clarence Thomas and Mphunzi Maqundgo.   Photo: Jack Heyman

In August 2012, workers at the Marikana, English-owned mine in South Africa went on strike for better wages and living conditions, 33 workers were killed by the police.

From Marikana, South Africa to San Francisco

Mphunzi Maqundgo, National Treasurer of NUMSA and past chair NUMSA, the South African Miners Union, spoke at Local 10 on the struggle for workers' power on May 1, 2014.

Political prisoner Mumia Abu-Jamal sent a recorded message to Local 10 and Brother Maqundgo. Mumia recalled the Marikana massacre of miners by South African security forces in 2012.

FREE, FREE PALESTINE! DON'T CROSS THE PICKET LINE!

From Ferguson to Palestine: Occupation is a crime!

Good evening sisters and brothers, friends and comrades,

On behalf of the ILWU Local 10, I want to thank the Arab Resource and Organizing Center (AROC) for having Local 10 and I as honorees at its 10th Anniversary Dinner Celebrating Community Defense, Movement Building and Resistance.

Four years ago, I met sister Lara Kiswani through Tova Fry. Kiswani asked for a meeting with officers of Local 10 to discuss AROC's plans for 'Block the Boat' at the Port of Oakland in response to the ongoing Israeli siege of Gaza and the Palestinian people.

At the time, the ILWU was in the midst of contract negotiation, working without a contract and under attack with major give-back demands. Local 10 president invited Kiswani to attend the executive board meeting. This got complicated because a motion had been made not to entertain any outside motions from the community while we were in contract negotiations.

One of ILWU's **TEN GUIDING PRINCIPLES** states, "To help any worker in distress. Labor solidarity means just that. Every picket line must be respected as though it were our own."

In 2009, dock workers in Durban, South African refused to unload the Israeli ship Johanna Russ to protest what they called, "Apartheid Israel's massacres in Gaza." The South African Transport and Allied Workers Union cited as their inspiration the 1984 San Francisco longshore 11-day boycott action against a ship from apartheid South Africa.

Delores Lemon-Thomas, Clarence Thomas and Angela Davis on Sept 9, 2018.

Monadel H. presents Thomas with an AROC award at AROC Anniversary dinner.

In June 2010, a Freedom Flotilla was attacked by Israeli commandos in international waters while attempting to take humanitarian supplies to Gaza. The raid resulted in the deaths of nine activists. Hundreds of Bay Area community and labor activists successfully blocked an Israeli Zim ship from being unloaded for 24 hours, the first time in U.S. history an Israeli ship was blocked.

AROC and the Arab Youth Organizing immediately went to work handing out flyers to explain the struggle of the Palestinian people and asking Local 10 members, to stand as an earlier generation of Local 10 members stood in 1984 against apartheid in South Africa.

I'm proud to say the Local 10 answered the call of the people of Palestine, and the Palestinian General Federation Trade Union. The 'Block the Boat' action lasted not just one day as planned, it lasted a total of 4 days. Local 10 members not only honored the picket line, but they refused to take jobs out of the dispatch window to work the Israeli vessel. It prompted other 'Block the Boat' actions by the Stop Zim Action Committee. In Long Beach, an Israeli vessel was delayed by Palestinian

Solidarity activists for 34 hours.

That action followed weeks of communication with Local 13 members, educating workers about Israel's brutal occupation of Palestine, as well as the group's reasons for targeting Zim, an Israeli shipping line. This cost Zim Shipping a significant amount of money as well as disrupting the supply chain of Israeli commerce.

Solidarity is not an empty slogan!

For workers it means contributing time, resources, strategic action, and money. In Local 10's case, it has cost the union jobs because no Zim ship has come back to the Port of Oakland since 'Block the Boat.' They are afraid of the solidarity of labor and the community. That is a small price to pay when we know our Palestinian brothers and sisters are putting their lives on the line each and every day.

**Stop the Siege on Gaza!
End the Colonial Occupation of Palestine!
Right of Return for All Palestinian Refugees!
Free All Political Prisoners!
Boycott, Divest, and Sanction Now!**
Thank you!
Clarence Thomas
An injury to one is an injury to all!

Oppose NAFTA, immigrant bashing and war
Cuban unionists meet with U.S. and Mexican workers

Sako Sefiani   Tijuana, Mexico

After repeatedly being denied U.S. visas, five leaders of the Confederation of Cuban Workers (CTC) traveled to Tijuana, Mexico, to meet with trade unionists from the U.S. and Mexico on Dec. 10, 2004. They discussed issues affecting workers of all the Americas, such as immigration, the Free Trade Agreement of the Americas (FTAA) and U.S.-Cuba relations.

U.S. and Mexican trade unionists and community activists listened Cuban labor leaders and were able to discuss issues affecting workers on both sides of the U.S.-Mexican border, such as the maquiladora factories and immigration policies.

Leonel Gonzalez Gonzalez, head of the Cuban delegation, provided data on how the FTAA and neoliberal policies have contributed to poverty throughout Latin America while accelerating the transfer of wealth from the South to the North, $29 billion in 2003, alone. "Four billionaires in the U.S. now have a fortune equal to the annual budget of 42 nations combined, with an aggregate population of 600 million people," he said.

While 70% of Coca-Cola sales and more than 50% of McDonalds restaurants are outside the U.S., U.S. corporations still need more markets for their products. Mexico has turned from an exporter of corn to an importer of corn from the U.S. "Does anyone believe," Gonzalez asked, "that the U.S. will open its doors to Latin American products?"

But neoliberal policies hurt U.S. workers, too. When U.S. transnational corporations set up maquiladoras in

special zones on the border to take advantage of cheap labor, U.S. workers lose jobs. Cuba, he added, has been playing a role in the struggle against neoliberal policies.

Jose Antonio Almazan Gonzalez of Mexico's Electrical Workers Union (SME) summed up the results of the North American Free Trade Agreement (NAFTA) after 10 years: poverty for 50% of the people in Latin America and 90% living on less than $8 a day. Farming, he said, has been ruined. The SME is fighting to stop the privatization of electricity and oil and revisions of the Mexican labor law.

"This is imperialism," he said. "We must talk about an alternative for Latin America to counter this devastation. We must accomplish what Venezuelans have accomplished."

Manuel Montero Bistilleiro, director of the Department of Foreign Relations of the CTC, told how the U.S. economic embargo has affected Cuba. They cannot get raw materials for its industries or medical supplies.

"In 2003," said Montero, "the U.S. dedicated $59 million to destabilizing the government of Cuba. Another $23 million was given to nongovernmental groups for the same purpose. When Cuba reacted by arresting these mercenaries, the U.S. cried foul."

Montero admonished labor leaders in the U.S., specifically the AFL-CIO, not to align themselves with the profiteers of finance capital against the workers of Cuba and Venezuela.

He reminded the audience that

John Parker, second from left addressed plenary in Tijuana.
Photo: Gloria Verdieu

although President Hugo Chavez of Venezuela has won seven elections, U.S. policy makers talk of lack of democracy in Venezuela. It is the fifth-largest producer of oil in the world and is located in the strategically important Amazonian Region.

The Chavez government is using the oil revenue to address poverty. It has enacted laws guaranteeing living wages, education and affordable housing and is proposing laws defending the right of women to abortion and the defense of the rights of gay people and Venezuelans of African heritage.

Support for Cuban Five

The conference unanimously called for freedom for the Five Cuban heroes held in U.S. prisons. Maria Del Carmen Machado, from the Department of Education, Communication and Culture of the CTC, explained the Five were not trying to destabilize the U.S. government or engaging in acts of terrorism, as CIA backed mercenaries have done. They were in Miami gathering information to stop the terrorist acts of right-wing Cuban groups there.

Rene Gonzalez, one of the Cuban Five, sent a letter to the conference that contrasted two worlds, one based on greed and profiteering, the other based on meeting human needs.

FREE THE CUBAN FIVE
HEROIC FIGHTERS OF U.S. SPONSORED TERRORISM ON CUBA

Fernando González, Ramón Labañino, Antonio Guerrero, René González and Gerardo Hernández, unjustly imprisoned in U.S. jails for up to 15 years.

Paul Teitelbaum, Bill Hackwell, Alicia Jrapko, Antonio Guerrero, Nancy Kohn, Joelle Deloison, in back, Amanda Bloom and Cheryl LaBash.

Clarence Thomas presents book on ILWU's militant history to Gerardo Hernández while Cheryl LaBash looks on.

Graphic from Cuban 5 banner. Photo, left: Bill Hackwell; right: Delores Lemon-Thomas

International Longshore and Warehouse Union
Local 10 400 NORTH POINT, SAN FRANCISCO, CA 94133

PRESIDENT. **Melvin Mackay**   **Adam Mendez**
VICE PRESIDENT. **Harold Brinkley**   SECRETARY TREASURER

January 15, 2009

President Barack Obama
The White House
1600 Pennsylvania Avenue NW
Washington, DC 20500

Dear President Obama:

On behalf of all members of the **International Longshore and Warehouse Union Local 10**, we urge you to look into the case of the internationally known **Cuban Five**, and immediately free them so they can return to their families in Cuba.

Rene González, Ramón Labañino, Antonio Guerrero, Fernando González and Gerardo Hernández were arrested in 1998 and accused of conspiracy and other charges. After a highly politically motivated trial in Miami, the only city in the US where five men accused of being agents of the Cuban government could not have a fair trial; they were sentenced collectively to 4 life sentences plus 75 years.

Why were the Cuban Five in Miami? Because of the unwillingness from past US administrations to act and put an end to terrorist actions emanating from Miami that has resulted in the death of more than 3,400 Cubans. The Cuban government, because of no other recourse sent these men to be the eyes and ears of the Cuban people to protect them against future terrorist actions. The mission of the Five was never to obtain US military secrets, but to infiltrate and monitor the activities of these criminal groups in Miami and to report their planned threats back to Cuba.

Gloria La Riva of the National Committee to Free the Five, praised their courage in pretending to be defectors in the interest of defending the Cuban Revolution.

Andrés Gómez leader of the Antonio Maceo Brigade in the U.S., discussed Washington's immigration policies towards Cuba. The Cuban Adjustment Act encourages Cubans to risk their lives to get to the U.S.

Clarence Thomas co-chair of the MWM and member of ILWU Local 10 in San Francisco, spoke about the need to build an independent workers' movement that will speak for U.S. workers, rather than put their hopes in the Democratic Party, which does nothing for workers and everything for multinational corporations.

John Parker of the International Action Center, spoke about the genocide taking place in Iraq and the atrocities in Afghanistan, Haiti and Palestine. He also pointed out the U.S. role in terrorism against Venezuela, where Danilo Anderson, the lead prosecutor in charge of investigating pro-coup mercenaries hired by the CIA, was just assassinated.

Parker said, "The U.S. government is afraid to let people see Cuba. But all actions have reactions. It backfires on them. We must create unity between labor and the anti-war movement. We must set aside differences and unite for the sake of the movement."

Juan Jose Gutierrez of Latino Movement USA said, "Capital creates borders to divide us. Tijuana is where our struggles will be united."

Leaders of Mexico's National Workers Union (UNT), Federation of Electrical Workers and Aluminum Workers Union and United Force of Teachers of Mexico also spoke, urging unity. Workers' struggles outside of unions included representatives from the Maclovia Rojas community in Tijuana and veterans of the Bracero 'guest worker' program.

Cristina Vazquez regional director of UNITE HERE, gave an update on her union's battle against hotel chains.

The conference ended by adopting resolutions, summarized here:

- Send letters to U.S. authorities demanding visas for the families of the Cuban Five.
- Support the travel challenge to Cuba in July 2005.
- Send a delegation to Cuba for the Fourth Hemispheric Conference on Neo-liberal Globalization and FTAA to be held on April 26-30.
- General amnesty for undocumented workers. Endorse a National March for amnesty for all immigrants.
- Demand the U.S. end its military occupation of Iraq, call for troops out now. Endorse international days of action on March 19 and 20 against the war in Iraq called by the Million Worker March.
- Support reclaiming May Day demonstrations in the U.S.
- Demand an end to the occupation of Haiti by all foreign troops.
- Support the Bolivarian government of Venezuela.

Abridged from WW, April 28, 2005.

International delegations stand with Cuba on May Day

Cheryl LaBash   Havana, Cuba 2009

First-time visitors from the U.S. were unsure what the day would hold as they watched dawn break in Revolution Square on May Day morning.

The international delegations, more than 2,000 in all from 70 countries, including union leaders and revolutionaries, often both in the same person, and representing 200 union and solidarity organizations, streamed off buses and into the reviewing area at the foot of the José Martí statue.

They chatted, chanted and taped their banners to the walls displaying the international demand to Free the Five Cuban heroes imprisoned in the U.S. as they waited for the program and march to begin. It was a global echo of the message President Barack Obama received at the recent Summit of the Americas: End the blockade! Cuba is not alone, and U.S. imperialism is not invincible!

"Why are there so few people in the Plaza?" one queried, before the Cuban workers marched in, wave after wave, for hours. "Will Cuban President Raul Castro speak?" A cheer greeted Castro when he appeared, but it was the Confederation of Cuban Workers, Central de Trabajadores de Cuba (CTC) General-Secretary Salvador Valdés Mesa who addressed the International Workers' Day event in Havana, as is customary on May Day.

This May Day was the 50th since the 1959 Revolution broke free of the colonial past and charted a path of development to meet peoples' needs instead of profit and exploitation. It also marked the 70th anniversary of the founding of the CTC, which has

Cuban First Vice President, past General-Secretary CTC, Salvador Valdés Mesa, Clarence Thomas, Ernesto Freire Cazaña, the Nat'l Council, the Department of International Relations at a May Day 2015 gathering on the beach.   Photo: Delores Lemon-Thomas

been instrumental, side-by-side with the Communist Party of Cuba, in developing workers' power.

And it was the workers and youth who marched in Havana with the theme of 'Unity, Combativeness, Productivity and Efficiency.' They carried representations of their workplaces such as a huge cigar from the La Corona factory, a taxi, housing construction brigades with tools, and pictures of rebuilding the 500,000 dwellings destroyed by the three hurricanes suffered in 2008.

Gigantic Cuban and Venezuelan flags, supported by hundreds of youth, undulated like ocean waves. Multiple massive delegations from the UJC Communist Youth Union, Unión de Jóvenes Comunistas, marched with the message: "The youth will not fail. All for the Revolution!" Gymnasts and professional dancers, entered the square. Handmade signs demanded freedom for the Cuban Five, saluted and supported Cuban leaders Fidel and Raul, and saluted socialism.

Another example of the contrast between life witnessed in Cuba and experienced in the U.S. was expressed on May Day by CTC leader Salvador Valdés Mesa, who spoke of the global

economic crisis and supported the Cuban government's efforts to protect people from the effects of the crisis:

"Even more so, at a time when humanity is immersed in a global economic crisis making the political, economic and social situation more complex globally, this impacts on the people, and workers face bleak prospects from which no country can escape.

"In our case, this is compounded by the effects of the ironclad economic blockade that the U.S. government has maintained for almost half a century, with the obsessive and failed object of destroying the Revolution.

"The unity and resistance in the face of any obstacle, which Fidel has formed within us, are pillars on which the Cuban Revolution is triumphantly erected and have become the central and constant battle flags. We will continue supporting with determination the measures that our government adopts to reduce the effects of the crisis on the population."

And that is the profound difference between a social system based on capitalism, with its profits for banks and corporations, and socialism.
Abridged from WW, May 21, 2009.

ILWU's history filled with international solidarity

Clarence Thomas   **Havana, Cuba**

The largest 2009 May Day celebration in the world, according to CNN, took place at the Plaza de la Revolución in Havana, Cuba. Past ILWU International President David Arian and Clarence Thomas were part of a U.S. delegation, which also included ILA members.

The ILWU has been guided by the principle that solidarity with workers of all lands is sound union policy. To demonstrate this ILWU has sponsored overseas delegations of rank-and-file members and has hosted trade union visitors from every continent. Long ago the union came to the conclusion that if it was to know the labor movement on a global scale it would have to obtain this information first hand.

ILWU-CTC history of solidarity

Our delegation did just that during our 12-day visit in Cuba. It is also something that is deep in ILWU's history of solidarity. This was not the first time longshore workers met with their Cuban counterparts. The ILWU-Cuban solidarity work started in the years leading up to the 1959 socialist revolution. After World War II, ILWU members visited the Philippines, Cuba, Mexico and Puerto Rico to strategize on how to strengthen labor solidarity with sugar workers.

In 1947, ILWU participated in the organizing of the International Sugar Workers Committee. The initial meeting took place in Havana. ILWU's Louis Goldblatt was elected chairman. Jesús Menéndez, head of the Cuban Sugar Workers representing 350,000 workers, was elected vice-chair. A plan of action was adopted to stop the exploitation of workers by the international sugar cartel.

The following year Menéndez, who was a member of Cuban Congress and the Communist Party, was assassinated while on an inspection tour of sugar mills with which his union had contracts. In *The Dispatcher*, February 1948, Secretary-Treasurer Louis Goldblatt said the killing was the outcome of the U.S. Department of State policies, which were subservient to U.S. based sugar companies.

Goldblatt added, "The murder was part and parcel of the colonial Cuban government, U.S. sugar interests, and the U.S. State Department's plan to destroy the unions and eliminate any vestige of democracy in Cuba."

This history came alive when the delegation visited the Menéndez home, now a museum. The curator showed documents that were donated by the ILWU library and presented to the museum by Local 10 member Jack Heyman during his visit in 2001. While there, ILWU members recounted the history of ILWU and the Cuban sugar workers solidarity. They discussed how the ILWU organized a concert tour for famed singer and humanitarian Paul Robeson in Hawaii. Money from the tour was donated to Menéndez's surviving family.

U.S. port workers say 'Free the Five'

In more recent solidarity, Local 10 sent a letter to President Barack Obama urging him to look into the case of the Cuban Five and free them and also grant visas for Olga Salanueva and Adriana Pérez, who have been cruelly prevented from visiting their spouses, René González and Gerardo

At the Jesus Menéndez Museum, ILWU past International President Dave Arian and Clarence Thomas Local 10 hold copies of 1947 issues of *The Dispatcher* featuring Cuban Sugar Workers Union leader Menéndez.

Photo: Delores Lemon-Thomas

Hernández. Local 10's letter is an important part of the growing international labor struggle to free the Cuban Five, who also include Ramón Labañino, Antonio Guerrero and Fernando González.

The letter and resolution were inspired when unionists met Magali Llort, mother of Fernando González, at the Fifth International Cuba/Latin America/North America/Mexico Labor Conference in Tijuana, Mexico, sponsored by the U.S./Cuba Labor Exchange. While in Cuba, the longshore workers and labor delegations from Ireland, Australia, Britain and the U.S. met with the families of these five heroic Cuban brothers.

At the recent Summit of the Americas in Trinidad and Tobago, Latin American and Caribbean nations called for an end to the U.S. blockade against Cuba. The ILWU has opposed trade sanctions against Cuba, policies that punish workers and their families and ultimately aggravate international peace. It is good for workers to meet with workers.

Abridged from WW, June 11, 2009.

Code Pink delegation at May Day 2015, Havana, Cuba.

Delegate Deborah Washington with Madea Benjamin, political activist and co-founder of Code Pink.

Photos: Delores Lemon-Thomas

Lara Kiswani Executive Director of Arab Resource and Organizing Center (AROC) with Clarence Thomas on May Day 2015, in Havana, Cuba.

Clarence Thomas and Delores Lemon-Thomas with Royce Adams, ILA Local 1291 Philadelphia long-shore worker in Havana, Cuba, May Day 2015.

They presented Adams with the book '*The Men Along the Shore and the Legacy of 1934*' based on an ILWU historical exhibit.

Photo: Deborah Washington

United National Antiwar Coalition Conference, May 2015 in New Jersey. Boston School Bus Drivers Union USW Local 8751. Georgia Scott, Nora Broggs, Claude 'TouTou' St Gremain, Bobby Trayham, Chantal Cashmir and Union President Andre François. Pam Africa with Mumia tee shirt.

Left, Ralph Poynter, Clarence Thomas and Lynne Stewart.

Photos: Delores Lemon-Thomas

Unions, communities in U.S. embrace Cuban labor leader

Minnie Bruce Pratt

Secty-treas. Derrick Muhammad, Lemagne Sánchez and President Ed Ferris Local 10.

Victor Manuel Lemagne Sánchez, secretary general of Cuba's hotel and tourism union and elected delegate to Cuba's National Assembly, recently completed a triumphant two-week tour of 11 U.S. cities. After landing in northern California on June 27, 2017, Lemagne Sánchez concluded his travels in the Baltimore/Washington, D.C., area on July 11.

A public event in Berkeley featured Lemagne Sánchez and Clarence Thomas, union militant and past Local 10 secretary-treasurer, retired. The event was sponsored by the International Committee for Peace, Justice and Dignity, and supported by many Cuba solidarity organizations.

That meeting, held at the hall of the University Professional and Technical Employees, Communication Workers Local 9119, highlighted the support for Cuban workers by the ILWU over the last 70 years.

Lemagne Sánchez also addressed the ILWU's 'Bloody Thursday' commemoration at Local 10 on July 5. This annual event honors two dock workers killed by police in 1934. Their deaths unleashed the historic San Francisco General Strike. Lemagne Sánchez's tribute was documented, available at Facebook, com/2017CTC, along with photographs and other video highlights of the tour.

Abridged from WW, July 18, 2017

Clarence Thomas, Delores Lemon-Thomas, Alicia Jrapko and Lemagne Sánchez, attended an Oakland A's baseball game. Upon seeing that the tickets for the game were $40 each, he said that sports and culture are free in Cuba.

Photo: Bill Hackwell

Victor Manuel Lemagne Sánchez, with tranlator Lisa Milos and Local 10 officers during 'Bloody Thursday' on July 5, 2017, visit to the Bay Area.

Lawrence Thibeaux with Lemagne Sánchez Secretary General of Cuba's National Assembly.

Hosts Bernie Houdin and Alicia Sanchez from Santa Rosa, Calif.

Photos: Delores Lemon-Thomas

CHAPTER 8

¡Trabajador@s de todas nacionalidades, Únanse!
En Nuestra Lucha no Hay Fronteras

Están invitad@s a una

CONFERENCIA

Preparándonos para el
RENACIMIENTO
de la
lucha
mundial
por el
SOCIALISMO

Workers of all nationalities unite
There are no borders in our struggle

You are invited to a

CONFERENCE

Preparing for the
REBIRTH
of the
World
Struggle
for
SOCIALISM

NEW YORK CITY · MAY 2006

Importance of Katrina struggle

Monica Moorehead   Secretariat, Workers World Party

In his document, "Build a Black-Brown Alliance for Justice and Human Rights," Saladin Muhammad writes: "Hurricane Katrina was a 21st century snapshot of the genocidal direction of the U.S. government. It exposed the reality of conditions faced by working-class African Americans and people of color under U.S. style democracy. There has yet to be a massive upsurge that expresses the deep outrage of the African American masses against the U.S. government for this crime against humanity."

If the greedy capitalist developers and the corrupt politicians can carry out a racist gentrification of New Orleans without defiant resistance from a mass movement, then this would prove to be a historical blow to the African American struggle for the right to self-determination in the South with huge ramifications.

The struggle to rebuild the Gulf Coast should be viewed as an unfinished stage of a revolutionary process that began with the first Reconstruction after the Civil War. That first stage was drowned in a bloody betrayal with a full-blown counter-revolution when the federal government abandoned the newly freed Black people, fighting for full democratic rights, leaving them defenseless and powerless when it came to KKK terror and semi-slavery conditions in the South. Black people became isolated after slavery just as

they were isolated during Katrina. So what we are seeing today are Katrina survivors who have had their right to self-determination once again trampled upon by this racist government.

Even the right to vote, is being taken away from the Black population in New Orleans, a city that used to be at least 70 percent Black. When the municipal elections took place in New Orleans last month, a reported 31 percent of the Black registered voters took part in the elections, which resulted in a run-off election. This percentage is down from 45 percent of Black voters who participated in the 2002 elections, according to the Associated Press. There were no polling places set up for dispersed Orleanians in Houston, Atlanta and other cities with large numbers of Katrina survivors.

The bigger question is what kind of commitment the rest of the movement will make in order to elevate the struggle of the Katrina survivors. This is tantamount to elevating the struggle against racism and national oppression and will help forge class unity with all workers, including white workers.

Why isn't the anti-war movement finding a way to support Katrina survivors with all its resources? Where is the trade union movement and others who support the broad solidarity of the super-exploited, super-oppressed sector of our class?

Where was the support

from the anti-war movement for the immigrant rights struggle? If the leaders of these movements do not support the rights of the Katrina evacuees and immigrant workers, then how can we expect large numbers of their followers to come out?

No class realizes the potential of a united working class more than the capitalists. Their repressive state apparatus rules over society with divide and conquer tactics, as we witness how the ruling class is trying to pit the interests of the oppressed nationalities against each other where African Americans and immigrants are concerned.

Real class unity is more than words. It's about deeds, including building consciousness and making sacrifices. As Karl Marx and Frederick Engels stated in the "Communist Manifesto," the capitalists will create their own grave diggers. What happened on May Day 2006 is a glimpse of great struggles to come.

Abridged from WW, May 26, 2006.

No future without struggle for socialism

Larry Holmes　Secretariat, Workers World Party; Troops Out Now Coalition leader

We must be clear about what is historically necessary and how our role will be decisive

We must convince this generation of revolutionaries, potential revolutionaries and all those who once were dedicated to the good fight for a new world, that there is no future without the struggle for socialism. We must have this vision, and we cannot put it off.

In Hugo Chavez's speech to the World Social Forum late last year, he urged that Earth is in danger. If we do not get to socialism soon, we may lose the planet.

We do not have our head in the clouds. We are for every gain the workers can win, the right to a coffee break, a union, a street lamp. These things are important. But we never forget the vision to take back the world from the imperialists.

We did not decide to put Che Guevara on the conference banner just to be in vogue. He is the most important internationalist of the last half-century.

The best thing for us to be concerned with is the development of the working class in the U.S. That is what people of the Middle East, Asia, Latin American and Africa are waiting for.

May Day was welcome news to them. In this country was a huge de-

feat for U.S. imperialism. For decades they have done everything possible to smash May Day, International Workers' Day, in the country of its origin. Uh oh, it's back. They tried to stop this May Day too.

Some labor leaders went against it, and they should be ashamed. Hopefully, they will think and say, "This helps workers, doesn't hurt them. What am I thinking?"

It is important to point out that while the struggle against racist legislation was the impetus behind this, this was not just the undocumented working class. This was their families who are workers, predominantly Latin@ but also Asian and African, this reflected what the working class looks like.

Imperialist globalization has brought workers together. It has brought May Day back to the U.S. It has brought back class consciousness and militant traditions. Consider it a wake-up call. If you have doubted that there could be any qualitative political change, look at May Day.

It just goes to show that you do not have to depend on the bourgeois parties. Imagine if we had a general strike over what they are trying to do to Delphi workers, or around national health insurance, or to stop the war. All those things suddenly

are less nutty because look what the immigrants did. Yes, it will. But the struggle of the undocumented for their rights must be unconditionally supported. We must fight the racism, the fear, the chauvinism.

This struggle cannot reach its maximum potential without the decisive participation of workers of all nationalities, and trade unionists.

Black and Brown unity is decisive. We know that because the bourgeois mouthpieces are trying to create tension between Latin@ and African American workers.

We live in the prison house of nations. This is the center of oppression, racism, sexism, homophobia, of every kind of ugly division that imperialism spawns. We would be naïve to think that it does not have its impact in the movement.

We must fight it every day.

Abridged from WW, May 26, 2006.

Strategic role of Black labor

Saladin Muhammad   National Chairperson Black Workers for Justice;
Coordinator MWMM Southern region

The system of national oppression is anchored by African American national oppression; not because it was the first experience of national oppression in what became the U.S., we know that the Native peoples were the first. It is because of the role that Black labor has played in the historical development of U.S. capitalism, as the economic base for the institutionalized racist political superstructure, and for the consolidation of white supremacy as an expression of white national social consciousness.

There can be no real revolutionary working-class unity without a consistent struggle against African American national oppression. However, the African American liberation movement must have an internationalist character, so that it helps the African American masses to see immigrant workers as their allies in a struggle against the same system of national oppression.

White workers whose political consciousness is also shaped by bourgeois democracy and white supremacy, which is further encouraged by the trade unions, see these voting blocks of oppressed nationalities as a threat to white skin privilege, and associate its diminishing character with the increased immigration of Latinos and the social programs won by the African American

struggles of the 1960s and 1970s, which racists claim is the reason for the U.S. government debt crisis.

The Latino communities' call and massive mobilization for a general strike and boycott on May Day was significant. It made the issue of mobilizing working class power a central component of the Latino struggle against national oppression. This can help set the tone for other struggles against national oppression and the trade union movement, which has become weakened by its failure to exercise power as a working class, as was shown during the PATCO (Professional Air Traffic Controllers) strike in 1981 and more recently in the New York transit-workers strike.

How to unite the masses into revolutionary anti-imperialist movement is a continuing question facing the revolutionary struggle in this country. Should it take the form of a multi-national struggle of workers and oppressed nations against U.S. imperialism, or as a multi-racial working-class struggle? The failure to support the right of self-determination of oppressed nationalities has been a major impediment to building revolutionary working-class unity.

This raises the question about the role of conscious political forces, revolutionaries, in the spontaneous national movements. Too often, there

has been a practice of mainly trying to recruit from the spontaneous movements into the revolutionary organizations, with little or no effort to help organize the working-class leadership and organizing capacity of the national movements.

The working class of the oppressed nationalities must be organized to popularize the slogan of self-determination within the national movements.

The strategic alliance between African American and Latino national movements must be concrete and built around real struggles that are able to help both communities and the broad movements for social justice see the strategic importance. That is why it is so important to focus this alliance today around the struggle for Reconstruction in the Gulf Coast and the struggle for immigrant rights.

Abridged from WW, May 26, 2006.

A space for frank discussion

Brenda Stokely   President AFCSME DC 1707; East Coast Million Worker March

I was with one of the Katrina survivors here in New York City in court when she was rearrested because of alleged fraud, because they claim she is stealing money from taxpayers. And by the same token, Halliburton and other contractors who have gotten billions of dollars have not been arrested and would not be arrested.

I'm raising this because I think that you should be applauded for having this discussion, because we don't have the discussions about the beast that we're dealing with, or how we're not organized well enough to deal with it, and what the dictatorship of the bourgeoisie really means. Because it was so frustrating and apparent that the court system, as we know, and the injustice system, as we know, are ill equipped to free our people, and that we are ill equipped to do it ourselves. We were in a system and a building that was built by working people but used by the ruling class to screw us and keep us divided.

We have to find a serious space to have a true, honest discussion on all the details involved in dealing with this bastard imperialism, in dealing with all of its leaders, in dealing with the government, in dealing with all of the traitors that are in the movement pretending to be about freeing people, in dealing with the racism and sexism that keeps us divided.

How do we identify the revolutionary leaders of the immigrant rights movement, of the oppressed nations here in this country? How do we deal with the international struggle? Why are we compartmentalizing all the different struggles when, as a working person, I do not have the luxury to do that? I must be on the forefront of the anti-war movement, because it's my nephews, and when my granddaughter gets older and the shit isn't resolved, it will be her, sent to die over in another country defending an imperialist beast.

It is my children, and me, and other workers who must go to work and not be paid right. It is us that are being told that we cannot organize. So, it's a no-brainer to those who truly understand who the enemy is, that we would automatically, without hesitation, be involved in the struggle around Katrina, in the immigrant rights struggle.

It was automatic for the Million Worker March Movement to say hell no, we're not going to have a separate activity on May 1. We must have an activity that galvanizes all the people who are currently under attack, and combine the struggle.

So when we gave homage to those that were killed crossing the border, we said, don't leave it at that, you must give homage to the brothers and sisters who are dying in Iraq, and you must give homage to the Katrina brothers and sisters who have families who were left with their dead bodies floating in the water. Those people are the same people. And that's how revolutionaries must think. That is how they must act, and that's what they have to put into practice.

Abridged from WW, May 26, 2006.

Building revolutionary consciousness

Prof. Tony Van Der Meer Co-chair Boston Rosa Parks Human Rights Day Cmte.

How do we build mass revolutionary consciousness among oppressed nationalities and working people in this nation? How do we get working people to become conscious of themselves as an exploited and oppressed class while also taking into consideration the deeper divisions that are centered on race and gender?

If white workers cannot see how institutional racism and cultural imperialism has created internalized white supremacy on their part, how can they see how racism, be it personal, systemic, covert or overt, not only dehumanizes non-whites, but divides the very class of people whose lives are smothered by the political, cultural and economic elite of this nation?

While there are many different movements, the Black liberation movement, the undocumented worker movement, and the antiwar movement are three that have greater potential for building the class solidarity critical in forging an anti-imperialist movement.

Katrina is not an isolated political act; it is an extreme example of a form of gentrification that is happening to African Americans and other oppressed nationalities throughout this country.

This development was centered more around the historical bases of the Chicano national movement fighting for self-determination in the Southwest, which played a major role in this important political upsurge, than getting Democrats to replace Republicans in November.

As a result of the call for a national day of absence on the 50th anniversary of Rosa Parks' arrest, Boston developed the Boston Rosa Parks Human Rights Day Committee. In many ways the committee is an example of forging class solidarity; unity with the oppressed and overcoming fragmentation in the movement. The BRPHRDC was an alliance of the Black liberation movement, labor and the anti-war movement connecting Katrina, immigration, violence, workers' rights and jobs, healthcare, and housing to the billions being spent on the Iraq war.
Abridged from WW, May 26, 2006.

Unity will be engine for liberation

John Parker   Los Angeles MWMM; West Coast International Action Center

For most of our experience here in this country, people of African ethnicity born here were denied citizenship rights in the Constitution, from voting, to organizing in unions, to drinking from a damn water fountain, to being allowed to live with your children and loved ones, denied during slavery.

And after the unnatural disaster of Katrina, we are even more familiar with being forced from our homes to cities that appear and feel like foreign lands. Like our immigrant sisters and brothers, the Katrina survivors are victims of U.S. policies that lay bare their cities to natural and unnatural disasters, from hurricanes to real estate and Wall Street thieves acting like the IMF, stealing livelihoods and homes.

But our history also has great examples of solidarity. The annexation of Mexico and the issue of slavery in the United States were intertwined. And it was our Mexican sisters and brothers who provided us African slaves refuge when we escaped south

across the border. It was our Mexican sisters and brothers who brought us in like family and refused, even under the threat of U.S. war, to throw us

Defeat the guest-worker program

Chris Silvera   Secty.-treas. Teamsters Local 808; Chair Teamsters National Black Caucus; East Coast MWMM;

This is the 130th anniversary of Haymarket, which was mostly immigrant workers. The labor movement and immigrant rights movement have always been one, in which the boss seeks to create divisions to weaken that movement. So, I do not really believe that we created something new on May 1; I think we struck a chord that made people get up and risk everything to be on the front line of change.

I believe that labor needs to make some of the same demands that capital has made. Capital has said that it wants to tear down borders and have unfettered freedom to surge the globe looking for profit. If that is true, labor must have the same unfettered right in looking for work.

What we have to do here is to build and make this movement significant, so we have got to tie in mainstream labor, and we have to make sure the mainstream labor movement has a focus that is purely in the interest of workers from a global perspective.

So where is the labor movement in this struggle? What is the demand of labor and is it different from the Democratic Party, and does the Democratic Party have a demand that is even worth listening to? The Democratic Party is a failure, certainly for working people. I suspect that if you are on the upper side of a quarter million dollars a year, then the Democratic Party is as favorable to you as the Republican Party.

I cannot tell you what the significance of the immigrant rights movement is, but what I can tell you is that we have positioned ourselves to become an important part of this resolution. But Congress is running with a group of people who you did not see in the march. Most are on the payroll, and those people are going to be the ones to say yes to guest worker programs.

In enslavement time you had slaves and indentured servants. The indentured servant is the original guest worker, and their situation was so bad that at many times, they banded with enslaved people to seek freedom. So,

the guest worker is an absolute no-starter in trying to resolve this issue. It has got to be defeated up front.

If the unions properly got on board with this solution, I believe we would have three, four million members quick. We have an opportunity that we have not had since 1886.

The eight-hour day did not just come in one day because of Haymarket. Haymarket was one day in years of building what is known as "Eight-Hour Leagues." So, we are going to have to continue to fight. We must build a series of actions that are coordinated and effective, because we have proven we have the numbers and the power.

Abridged from WW, May 26, 2006.

back into that bondage of hell.

We remember that solidarity and will respond in kind, be it legal or illegal. Divide and conquer has been practiced and refined since the ruling class first stole this land; and when poor whites and Native people and African slaves were collaborating to fight their rich oppressors, the rulers developed methods to keep us all from uniting.

And more and more of our Asian, African, Native and Arab sisters and brothers are joining and coming into the leadership of this struggle, providing more basis for unity amongst

our working class.

Like the Civil Rights Movement lifted all working-class struggles for justice, this unity will become a major engine for the movement against war, poverty and racism and the liberation of our entire working class.

All we must do is unite. The chains may have been physical for African slaves, yet economic for our immigrant sisters and brothers, but the chains still make us bleed. And we have nothing to lose but them, and a world to gain. All workers and oppressed people of the world unite.

Abridged from WW, May 26, 2006.

Dr. Martin Luther King Day in Los Angeles 2006.   Photo: Sekou Parker

Immigrants revive the class struggle

Teresa Gutierrez   Secretariat, Workers World Party

Immigrants and their supporters have revived the class struggle in the U.S.! They have reminded the powers that be that the irreconcilable struggle between the ruling class and the working class is far from dead.

This struggle may at times be dormant or hidden, but if there are bosses and workers, if there are exploiters and exploited, the class struggle will not end.

Even if this was not their aim, immigrant workers revived in the U.S. a historical date that the ruling class fears very much: May Day, a day for workers that is a clarion call for struggle.

Our party, like many other immigrant activists and others, knew that this day would come, that it was inevitable.

Why? Just listen to the horrors of immigrants, the accounts of those who travel here in perilous seas from other parts of the world. Remember the plight of those who have died from the heat of deserts ablaze or in the backs of stifling sealed truck beds.

Many families will spend the rest of their lives never really knowing the fate of their loved ones. They may have died at sea or on the border or maybe in some agricultural field somewhere in the U.S.

And there is a whole generation of children whose mothers were torn by indecision, should they stay so their child at least has a mother by their side, but watch them go to bed hungry every night, or should they go to the other side of the border?

Many are ultimately forced to abandon their children. This decision has left a tear in their children's heart that will never be healed. The culprit of those children's pain must be put squarely on the shoulders of imperialism.

So, is it any wonder that millions risked jobs and deportation to take to the streets? Is it any wonder that millions defiantly declared: 'aqui estamos y no nos vamos, here we are and we are not leaving.'

The oppression is exactly why we knew this day would come. The decades of capitalist exploitation would become a specter that would haunt the bosses. That day has come.

We must do everything to show our unconditional support of the immigrant rights struggle. It is they who must lead.

But it was the Communist Manifesto that gave me the tools to understand that the oppression of Chicanos was part of the oppression of all workers. And it was Lenin who explained that even within class oppression there was the special oppression of certain people, a particular oppression that required the most utmost thought in order to build solidarity.

Lenin's view on national oppression could not be timelier as Latin@s take center stage in this period.

Abridged from WW, May 26, 2006.

The Americas reject neoliberalism

Berta Joubert-Ceci   Editor, Workers World / Mundo Obrero

By the hundreds of thousands, undocumented workers, their families and their allies have courageously filled the streets of dozens of cities, including right here in New York. Their demands might have been different from their comrades' demands south of the border, but their defiance and their challenge, and above all, the origin of their struggles are the same.

And that origin is neoliberalism, that imperialist straitjacket that through the International Monetary Fund and World Bank has choked the possibility of oppressed nations to develop on behalf of their peoples; that imposes fiscal austerity when it comes to provide health, education, affordable housing and social benefits like pensions and child care but on the other hand promotes the so-called free trade agreements that are nothing but a road for the transfer of the national wealth and the natural resources to the coffers of transnational corporations on Wall Street. Trade agreements like NAFTA forced millions of Mexican peasants and workers, who had no other choice but to risk their lives, into crossing the border in order to find jobs in the United States so they could survive and feed their families.

But what the capitalists were not expecting, since they always underestimate the power of the working class, is the enormous wave of resistance to their neocolonial plans throughout the whole hemisphere.

The masses have responded with a sweeping upsurge of opposition, trying to take back their countries away from capitalism. Even the capitalist press worldwide, including in the U.S., constantly refers to the "tilt to the left" of Latin America. This is where neoliberalism is collapsing

Abridged from WW, May 26, 2006.

Cuba's battle of ideas

Ignacio Meneses   National Network on Cuba; U.S. Cuba Labor Exchange

In what the Cubans call the "battle of ideas," it is clearer for working people that U.S. imperialism can only offer war, destruction and exploitation, from the extermination of Native people to taking 40% of Mexico, move the border, then call Mexicans living there suddenly immigrants.

In the richest country of the world, they want to cut the wages of Delphi workers from $27 to $12.50 per hour. I worked for 28 years on the floor. I am an auto worker. My co-workers don't know if they'll have a pension or health care for them and their families.

Cuba calls the other side, 'another world is possible.' Cuba deepened the roots of the workers' state. In the veins and blood of the revolution are workers. Everything is for the workers. Eighty percent of the population owns their house. There is free health care, free education, sports and culture. There is no malnutrition in Cuba. Cuba has the highest life expectancy in Latin America and the highest literacy rate. In 2000, the U.S. had 270 doctors per 10,000 inhabitants; Cuba had 582.

Another characteristic of Cuba is the international role Cuba plays. In Angola after helping defeat the racist South African Army Cuba asked for nothing in return, took not one diamond. Three Points about Cuba:

• Cuban workers explained the neoliberal policy: everything for corporations, for workers nothing.

• After the collapse of the Soviet Union: Cuba kept improving education and health care, in the worst times
• Cuba works with the social movements.

The answer to the FTAA is ALBA, the Bolivarian Alternative for Latin America, integration of Cuba, Venezuela and Bolivia based on solidarity and cooperation for literacy, health care and education.

We have a revolutionary obligation to defend Cuba and Venezuela.

Abridged from WW, May 26, 2006.

Resistance is globalized

Sara Flounders   Secretariat, Workers World Party

Today there are more than 200 million migrant workers globally. The largest number is in the U.S., where there are more than 34 million immigrants with papers and 12 million undocumented.

Every industrialized capitalist country is dependent on super-exploited, low paid workers with no benefits, no protection, and no rights.

Consider the rebellions against racism that swept France this spring. Millions of workers and the children of the second generation from North and West Africa rose in rebellion against the relentless racism of imperialist French society.

In Saudi Arabia, where more than half the population is migrant workers, there is rising instability.

Hundreds of millions of other peasants and small farmers are daily being forced off their lands and into the cities of the developing world. .

There are cartels that deal in human trafficking, a modern-day slave trade. The trade in women for the sex industry is organized on a global basis.

Many developing countries' primary source of revenue is the remittances workers send home to their families.

Capitalism has no solutions to the chaos it causes. The giant transnational corporations must maximize profit, not just over the long term, but every minute in order to survive, without regard for human life or the life of the planet itself. This drives them into a frantic race literally around the world to find the lowest possible wage rate.

Due to the cycle of disruption, U.S. imperialism is increasingly the target of rage on a global scale. Ruthless globalization has not only vastly expanded the working class. Technology has connected the working class. Communication is instantaneous. The workers are not only more numerous but far more educated and technically skilled. They are increasingly conscious of their own potential.

The U.S. ruling class is determined to use its military and economic power to shape events and dominate the world. U.S. imperialism is determined that no area remain outside its control, regardless of how small, poor or underdeveloped, from Sudan to Nepal, Haiti to Albania.

But with all that power and enormous weaponry, what the bourgeoisie fears most is a powerful mass movement that can overwhelm them and sweep them aside. Once resistance begins, resistance changes consciousness. It changes the view of what is possible.

The spirit of internationalism and resistance of millions of new workers provides a material basis for the revival of socialism. It will push the whole class struggle forward.

Abridged from WW, May 26, 2006.

Trends in imperialism bring struggle home

Fred Goldstein   Secretariat, Workers World Party

Now who would have thought six months or a year ago, even if you were in Los Angeles, even if you were in the center of the immigrants' rights movement, that there would have been several million people on the streets across this country, in this reactionary heartland, in the "belly of the beast," in a general political strike, demanding their rights?

This momentous development was touched off by a reactionary attack in the legislature on 12 million people and all their friends, families, and supporters.

The stage for the demonstration was set long ago. It was set when the Reagan administration together with the bankers initiated the campaign of neoliberal aggression, and they sent the International Monetary Fund to every capital of every country in the oppressed world to tell them that the day of austerity is here, you have to cut all subsidies to the masses, you have to privatize everything and you have to lower your tariffs and let us in to do as we please in your country. That's when it began in Mexico, in Central America, in Africa, in Asia.

And this continued under Clinton with NAFTA, and under Bush with CAFTA. And it created a huge wave of impoverished people who were assaulted by imperialist finance capital and were driven toward the rich capitalist countries to find a living for themselves and their families.

This is when the material for this demonstration was created. This May 1, demonstration was the climax of the process.

This tolerance of immigration by the imperialists fits with their long-term

intention to take the U.S. from being a high-wage country, as it was after World War II for a section of the white workers who predominated in the labor movement, to a low-wage country. They are in a capitalist crisis which forces them to sell more and more goods flowing from their vast means of production to make their profits.

This began in the 1970s and the 1980s, when they took technology to try to dismantle much of the manufacturing industry and weaken and destroy the unions. They have taken this technology and expanded into a vast reserve army of low paid labor and have forced the working class in this country into a competition with this vast, global network of labor in low-wage countries.

They want to destroy the social wage the workers are entitled to, whether it be welfare, Medicaid, Medicare, or food stamps. This is neoliberalism in the United States. This is what the IMF does in oppressed countries. Only they do not need the IMF here. They are the IMF. They have the capitalist government, the Treasury Department, the Federal Reserve Bank.

Clinton destroyed welfare. Fifty years of social gains were destroyed by Clinton at the behest of the bankers. That is neoliberalism in the U.S.

We do not have a crystal ball. But what we do see is the laws of capitalism, as understood by Marx, operating in the social and economic sphere, and politically. And they cannot get out of this, the imperialists. They cannot go on the way they are.

Abridged from WW, May 26, 2006.

Sam Marcy on
The party and the national question

Deirdre Griswold   Editor, WW Newspaper; Secretariat, Workers World Party

When we talk about building a revolutionary party in this country, the question immediately rises: Where does such a party stand in relation to the liberation organizations of the oppressed that already exist or may arise in the future?

The need of the workers to organize themselves into a revolutionary Marxist-Leninist Party and to unite them in the struggle against capitalism is an indispensable necessity for a victorious proletarian revolution. ...

Some say that each nation within the confines of the U.S. should build their own Party and that since the workers of the oppressing nation and the workers of the oppressed nation have different problems arising from the nature of the oppression, it is impossible, at least for now, to have a single united Party.

The logical conclusion of this thinking is that the whites should have one organization, Blacks another, Puerto Ricans another, etc. Assume that political evolution in this country favored such a development. The result then would be that we would have several Marxist-Leninist organizations. And if each had a generally Marxist-Leninist program, it would evolve from a loose alliance of these Marxist-Leninist organizations into a federation and finally, into a unified multi-national political Party. ...

The working class cannot emancipate itself without at the same time destroying, root and branch, every form of national oppression.

Nor can there be any unity between the workers of the oppressed and oppressing nations as long as the workers of the oppressing nation do not recognize and do not advocate the right of the oppressed nations to self-determination. The right of self-determination can take the form of secession, federation, a variety of forms of amalgamation, or any other form, depending on concrete historical circumstances...

The right to self-determination is a political right which oppressed nations may use in whatever form they may ultimately decide as a nation. We must advocate and support that right. But we do not advocate separation, secession, federation, or amalgamation. That is for the oppressed nation to decide. ...

The heavy repression against liberation organizations in this country, splits within the organizations and considerable confusion resulting from all this has made such a desirable prospect more remote. Nevertheless, it remains a hopeful variant of development.

This conference has been a milestone for us because it represents the development of an honest dialog with serious leaders from organizations of the oppressed, many of them Marxists, on a wide variety of subjects having to do with where the struggle is at today and what needs to be done. They have raised issues and posed questions that will enrich the Party's discussion and political education.

This dialog with other leaders and organizations would be impossible without the excellent leadership of the Black and Latin@ comrades in our Party. They have taken the initiative in moving us from the concept of a truly multinational revolutionary party at all levels into an actual work in progress.

Abridged from WW, May 26, 2006

CHAPTER 9

Oppressed genders say: 'Enough is Enough'

Brenda Stokely, a leading organizer of the Million Worker March Movement, with granddaughter Kalola at the August 26, 2007, 'Women's Equality Day' Speak Out. The event was organized by the National Women's Fightback Network. On her left is cultural worker Nana Soul and on her right is Sue Davis, an activist for reproductive rights. Stokely called for reparations for Katrina and Rita Hurricane survivors.

WW photo: Deirdre Griswold

Photo: Sharon Black, 2015

Victoria Pickering March 2017

Unity Statement

**A. Philip Randolph Institute · Asian Pacific American Labor Alliance
Coalition of Black Trade Unionists · Coalition of Labor Union Women
Labor Council for Latin American Advancement · Pride At Work**

The constituency organizations of the AFL-CIO met on January 15, 2005, in Los Angeles during the annual Martin Luther King Jr. Conference. We are working with the AFL-CIO to convene a Full Participation Conference in July 2005, in Chicago, immediately before the AFL-CIO National Convention.

We wish to express our collective views about the future of the U.S. labor movement and to voice the concerns of organizations representing people of color, women and lesbian, gay, bisexual and transgender (LGBT) workers within the labor movement, the groups who represent the new majority within the American workforce.

We are united in our commitment to build a strong, democratic labor movement, one that represents the hopes and aspirations of all working people for social and economic justice. We believe that there is a crisis within the U.S. labor movement. Declining union density, intensified government and corporate attacks on workers and on our standard of living, policies of free trade, outsourcing, privatization, attacks on social programs, and union busting threaten workers of all colors.

We reject the policies of discrimination, racism, sexism, and homophobia that are being perpetrated by the right-wing and by conservative political leaders. We support multiracial unity, working-class solidarity, and the full democratic participation of all in the pursuit of progress and prosperity.

1. Full Participation

The leadership of the U.S. labor movement at all levels must represent the rich diversity of the workforce. While there has been some progress over the years, the leadership within most unions, especially at the highest decision-making levels, does not reflect the diversity of its membership. This presents a problem as unions attempt to represent the interests of all of their members. We are concerned about the continuing lack of diversity among various leadership bodies within the AFL-CIO, affiliated unions, state federations, central labor councils, and local unions.

We are also concerned about the proposals to drastically reduce the size of the AFL-CIO executive council without a strong commitment to maintain and increase diversity. Representation of constituency groups must be ensured.

4. Civil, Human, & Women's Rights

The U.S. labor movement must defend and expand a comprehensive agenda for civil, human, and women's rights. While we support the focus on organizing and political action, these cannot be separated from a strong civil, human, and women's rights agenda. The civil, human, and women's rights agenda must include:

- An end to all racial discrimination at the workplace and defense of affirmative action;

- An end to all gender discrimination at work, support for pay equity, and an end to violence against women;

- Full labor rights, legalization, and comprehensive immigration reform for all immigrants and a repeal of employer sanctions;

- Access to all rights and protections of civil society for lesbian, gay, bisexual and transgender workers.

5. Globalization

We demand an end to policies of free trade and corporate-dominated globalization. These policies have exacerbated economic inequality and promoted a race to the bottom. Economic inequality has had a particularly devastating impact on the developing world, especially in Asia, Africa, and Latin America.

We oppose global exploitation and global racism. We support the expansion of global labor solidarity. We support freedom of association and the right to collective bargaining, the elimination of forced labor, the abolition of child labor, and the elimination of discrimination in the work place.

In conclusion, we believe that 'Full Participation' is more than a worthwhile slogan. In order to achieve the potential of a strong, unified labor movement, we must fully participate in governance and the development of labor's agenda. The constituency organizations of the AFL-CIO are eager to work side by side with union leaders to organize, educate, and empower all workers. Building a more powerful and more inclusive labor movement requires labor's commitment to diversity, and active implementation of full participation.

Million Worker March Movement holds IWWD event

Leilani Dowell

A March 8, 2006, meeting celebrating International Working Women's Day (IWWD), sponsored by the MWMM, showed the strength of diverse women fighting oppression of all kinds.

Chryse Glackin, of MWMM chaired the meeting. She explained the need to celebrate IWWD: "The MWMM knows that working people are on the run, and we want to turn that around, and build a movement."

The all-woman panel included a member of the youth group FIST-Fight Imperialism, Stand Together; a member of the Transit Workers Union who works for the Metropolitan Transit Authority; members of the New York Solidarity Coalition for Gulf Coast Survivors, including a Katrina evacuee from New Orleans; unionists with the Industrial Workers of the World (IWW) who have been trying to organize Starbucks Coffee; and a performance by a youth group.

The event, held at a Teamsters hall in Long Island City, began with a screening of "Harlan County USA," a documentary by Barbara Kopple on the 1973 coal miners' strike. The film highlights women's extraordinary participation in the struggle against the Brookside Mine of the Eastover Mining Company in Harlan County, Ky.

The audience celebrated the victory of the IWW organizers in a labor struggle against Starbucks. One of the speakers had been fired from her job for union activity. The National Labor Relations Board ruled against Starbucks, however, and the workers' jobs were reinstated the day before the IWWD event. The Labor Board also ruled that Starbucks cannot deny workers the right to wear union buttons while at work.

Brenda Stokely from the New York Solidarity Coalition for Gulf Coast Survivors encouraged the audience, saying: "An upsurge is developing in this country. There is a coalescing of all brothers and sisters of all nationalities This is what imperialism has always feared the most, us coming together and putting aside our differences, whether we speak a different language or were born someplace else, and this is what's developing. It's in its embryonic form, but you can feel the rush and development of it and everyone who's been doing that work should be honored and applauded."

Abridged from WW, March 23, 2006.

Chryse Glackin, Brenda Stokely and granddaughter Kalola at the March 8, 2006 meeting held in a teamster hall in Long Island City, New York.

The International Working Women's Day panel is below.

Photos: People's Video Network

'Our war for equality is right here!'

A Speak Out Aug. 26, 2007, 'Women's Equality Day' was called in several cities by the National Women's Fightback Network to demand full equality for all women. On that day, 87 years ago, women got the right to vote in the U.S.

'African-American women have to be like Fannie Lou Hamer who fought to end segregation. We must be like Harriet Tubman who led our people out of slavery. We must raise our youth so they will not fight in imperialist wars," said Amina Baraka, freedom fighter and poet speaking at a rally in New York City.

Viola Plummer of the December 12th Movement declared, "If we women get the absolute determination of a Harriet Tubman, we can do what we want."

Performer and long-time activist, Vinie Burrows, took the mike: "Poor people are disposable. We must fight back. After 9/11, people began looking for terrorists in the wrong places. We need to look in the White House, in the Pentagon, in the corporations. If I cannot feed my children, that's terrorism. We must stop the war on women and on the poor. The 'weapon of mass destruction' is poverty."

Black attorney Evelyn Warren said she used to leave public speaking to her husband, civil rights attorney Michael Tarif Warren, but not after they were recently brutalized by racist cops. "That happens in New York City every day. We have to demand a change."

Among the speakers were Nieves Ayres and Alba of the May 1st Immigrant Rights Coalition, who called for amnesty for all immigrant workers.

Brenda Stokely of TONC and Katrina survivor Christine Gavin-

Fannie Lou Hamer, Eleanor Holmes Norton and Ella Baker in a Student Non-violent Coordinating Committee delegation outside the Democartic National Convention in 1964.

Photo: Take Stock/Matt Herron

Latham denounced the despicable conditions Katrina and Rita survivors have been forced to endure and called for reparations.

Valerie Francisco from FIRE (Filipinas for Rights and Empowerment) talked about the terrible working conditions in the U.S.-dominated Philippines that force many young women to seek work in this country.

Cultural worker Nana Soul emphasized that Black women endure both national and gender oppression.

Joyce Chediac, an Arab-American, exposed how the U.S. war and occupation of Iraq has drastically worsened life for women who once enjoyed the highest standard of living in the Middle East.

Rachel Duell, a professor of nursing and researcher on HIV prevention in women, spoke about women with AIDS and the need for universal health care.

Leading off the Detroit Action, the Network for Reproductive Rights (DANFORR) held a picket line that many young women joined, received a positive response from passing cars.

Chris Cardenas, president of Wayne State University Students for

Choice, Katey Aquilina and Dessa Cosma, organizers with Planned Parenthood, addressed the need for reproductive rights. Andrea Egypt with Michigan Emergency Committee Against War and Injustice drew parallels between the war in Iraq and the one at home.

"We organized DANFORR in Detroit to have an organization fighting in the interests of African-American women," Debbie Johnson said, "We needed to have that voice for choice in our community. We have to make a difference in the lives of African-American women."

Also on Aug. 24, members of the International Action Center held a demonstration in Buffalo calling for an end to the Iraq war as well as the war on women.

In Boston, the NWFN contingent marched with TONC to protest the war. The women handed out leaflets and carried signs that read "No to sexism and war" and "Money for health care, housing and AIDS."

"We got a good response when we talked about poverty, racism, lack of access to reproductive services, and made links to Katrina survivors," said Maureen Skehan.

"From the Lower 9th Ward to Roxbury, we're coming out in solidarity with the survivors of Rita and Katrina and to speak out against the Katrinalization of our communities," said NWFN organizer Mia Campbell. "This war is costing us billions of dollars. These funds need to be returned to our communities."

Abridged from WW, Sept. 6, 2007.

'ENOUGH IS ENOUGH!'
All Women's March makes history

Gloria Verdieu

Women and men from all over San Diego County gathered at the Tubman/Chavez Center on June 29, 2013, for San Diego's 'First All Women's March.' Marchers called for peace, unity, justice and an end to violence in our communities.

This call to action was organized by Rashida Hameed, a community activist, and founder of Epiphany Women of Focus.

The march began at the Tubman/Chavez Center across the street from the Malcolm X Library, on the corner of Euclid Avenue and Market Street. The cops who pretty much stopped auto traffic, told marchers to stay on the sidewalk.

Family members of victims who had been killed spoke at a ceremony after the march which honored women who are involved in actions aimed at ending the violence. Among those honored were Beatrice X Johnson, Oscar Grant's aunt. Johnson, an organizer for the Justice for Oscar Grant, recently returned from Florida, where she was supporting the family of Trayvon Martin in preparation for the trial of George Zimmerman.

Johnson said that the conviction of Officer Johannes Mehserle, Oscar Grant's killer, was the result of his family speaking out and taking the struggle to the streets. Johnson also spoke about the film, "Fruitvale Station." This film won the Grand Jury Prize and the Audience Award for U.S. Dramatic Film at the Sundance Film Festival (2013) and the Best First Film Award at the Cannes Film Festival (2013). Johnson encouraged everyone to see this film because it shows the true human character of Oscar Grant.

Oscar Grant's mother, Wanda Johnson, spoke from a cell phone. She said that every life is precious and that we must work together to stop the violence. This was the same message offered by the mother of Billye Venable at a meeting to support the family of Victor Ortega earlier. Venable was killed by San Diego Police Officer James Hunter in October 2003. Victor Ortega was killed by San Diego Police Officer Jonathan McCarthy in July 2012.

The message from all the families and supporters is that the pain of losing a loved one from violence is constant because in many cases there is no closure, no answers, no reasons. Police officers who kill are not held accountable.

"Women are the ones left to pick up the pieces after these murders take place," said Hameed. "It is time for the women in our community to speak out."

The flyer given out at the event read, "We are tired of violence in our community and we will not wait for men to lead us. A people can rise only as high as our women. … Women it's time to rise!"

The march was supported by many community organizations, including the NAACP, 100 Men Strong, the Black Contractors, Overcoming Gangs and Beyond, Project New Village and the Chicano Prison Project.

This All Women's March is a first step in bringing this community together to begin the discussion on ending violence in our communities.

Abridged from WW, July 18, 2013.

Cephus X 'Uncle Bobby' Johnson and Beatrice X Johnson at the All Women's March in San Diego on June 29, 2013.

Photo: Gloria Verdieu

'Every issue is a women's issue'

The following came from a brochure prepared for an International Working Women's Day march in New York City on March 8, 2014.

Today, we commemorate International Women's Day declared at the 1910 International Socialist Women's Congress in Copenhagen, Denmark, as proposed by Clara Zetkin.

We honor the women who fought for our liberation by continuing the fight for freedom. Attacks on working women, especially Black, Latina, Asian, Indigenous, Arab as well as women who live in Africa, Latin America, the Caribbean, Asia, the Middle East, Pacific Islands.

In the U.S., there are attacks on public sector workers' union rights; sexual assaults; violence toward lesbian, bisexual and transgender women; and the detention and deportation of immigrant women.

Right-wing millionaire politicians, and their media mouthpieces, spout racist, anti-poor, homophobic and sexist vitriol. State legislatures cut women's reproductive and health care services.

Attacks on living standards and the war budget

The economic crisis, intensified by Wall Street's greed for profits, is affecting women, as income inequality grows. Women are hit by job loss, low-wage and part

time jobs; foreclosures and evictions; dismantling of public housing; and cuts in unemployment benefits, food stamps and other government programs. Social Security, Medicare and Medicaid benefits are endangered.

More women, especially poor and of color, are imprisoned than ever. The war continues on working-class youth and youth of color, with racist police brutality and militarization of schools. Tuition hikes and funding cuts for education and social programs worsen their quality of life. The 'economic draft' takes lives in illegal U.S. wars.

The conditions for women worldwide have deteriorated due to war and occupation costing trillions of dollars. In Iraq and Afghanistan families are assaulted by U.S/NATO bombs and troops and the same forces have devastated Libya. Now, threats imperil Iran and Syria.

The Palestinians, denied any rights, suffer but resist the U.S.-funded Israeli occupation in the West Bank and Gaza, while Israel continues aerial and ground attacks.

U.S. drones hit Pakistan, Yemen and Somalia. Women in Sudan and other African countries are dying from U.S. sanctions and war. Philippine women face brutal reprisals for protesting the U.S.-backed regime.

Haitian women, devastated by the earthquake, cholera and sexual violence brought by U.N. troops, need reparations, not military occupation. Despite severe repression, Honduran women are active in the popular resistance to the U.S.-backed regime.

Bolivian and Venezuelan women celebrate their gains under progressive governments, and so do their sisters in socialist Cuba. Indigenous women face repression for reclaiming their original lands in the Americas.

Corporate globalization is impoverishing women worldwide, destroying local economies, creating sweatshops, low-wage jobs and unemployment. Millions must leave their homelands to find jobs, only to face racism and abuse. Of the world's poorest 70% are women and children. Conditions of imperialist globalization are pushing, women and children into sex trafficking.

What women are doing to resist

The U.S. right-wing onslaught on the rights of women, workers, people of color, immigrants, low-income communities, youth, seniors and people with disabilities requires a strong, united struggle to push back.

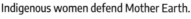

Domestic workers rally for rights.   Indigenous women defend Mother Earth.

The good news is that resistance is growing! Fast food and other low-wage workers, are demanding a $15 an hour minimum wage, the right to unionize and better working conditions, some walking off the job. Women are 65% of minimum wage (or less) earners. New union members, largely women, are demanding work place justice.

Hotel, restaurant, domestic and immigrant workers are leading the way. Public sector workers, Black and Latina, are fighting anti-union assaults.

With students, they occupied Wisconsin's Capitol in 2011 to defend their union rights. Teachers and nurses are standing up.

Meanwhile, women are challenging the right-wing war on their health care services and reproductive rights.

Young women in Texas and at 'North Carolina Moral Monday' protests bravely occupied capitols, facing mass arrests.

The racist murder of Trayvon Martin in Florida, and his killer's acquittal, sparked mass protests demanding justice. Since that outrage, a Florida vigilante fatally shot Jordan Davis, another Black youth. Police slayings of youth of color, including Alan Blueford, in Oakland, Calif., have brought protesters into the streets to show solidarity with Black and Latinx youth who daily face racist police and vigilantes.

We defend survivors of domestic and anti-trans violence like Marissa Alexander and CeCe McDonald who have been unjustly imprisoned.

We show solidarity with our sisters Jeralynn Blueford, Sybrina Fulton,

Lucia McBath and all mothers, sisters, spouses and daughters of those felled by bigots' bullets. Opposing racist violence is a woman's issue.

Every issue is a woman's issue!

Everywhere there are struggles, women are in the lead and organize ceaselessly. Our mission is to empower women and to affirm the need to challenge our wealthy oppressors' divisive tactics: racism, sexism, homophobia and xenophobia, all rooted in the for-profit, capitalist system.

This call is for all of us to honor and uphold the great traditions of women warriors who continue to display courage, strength, wisdom and the will to resist against great odds. Organize, resist and build our movements for victory!

Abridged from WW, March 6, 2014.

HANDS OFF
ASSATA SHAKUR

IWD 2013

LOW-COST HOUSING! STOP Evictions!

No War on Women
at Home or Abroad
No Occupation
Unite to Win Our Liberation
International Working Women's Day Coalition

WOMEN WORKERS FOR PEACE
MUJERES TRABAJADORAS POR LA PAZ

WW photo Brenda Ryan

'Build a Women's Fightback Movement!'

The 'Can We Live!' Campaign is a struggle oriented program aimed to bring women together and to organize initiatives on economic and political issues year around. Its 10-point program calls for:

- Healthy, toxic-free food. Restore/expand food stamps and all nutrition programs.
- Jobs for all, not jails. Promote union rights; defend public workers and Social Security; demand $15/hour minimum wage and/or guaranteed income; extend unemployment benefits; pay equity; paid family leave. End discrimination based on age, nationality, pregnancy, disability. Cancel credit card and student debt.
- Healthcare for all. Preserve/expand Medicaid, Medicare and all social programs. Reproductive justice now.
- Free quality education from cradle to grave.

- Housing is a human right. No foreclosures, evictions, utility shut offs; end homelessness. Affordable housing for all.
- A healthy planet and clean environment.
- Legalization, not deportation. Unite families; end ICE raids and detentions.
- No domestic and state violence against women. Stop sexual exploitation, trafficking and racist police brutality; restore safe houses.
- No imperialist war. Stop violence against women in the military and in occupied lands. Bring all troops home.
- Full rights for lesbian, gay, bisexual, transgender and queer people.

Benton Harbor, Michigan
Black community takes on Whirlpool

Margaret Prescod Women of Color in the Global Women's Strike for Peace

Margaret Prescod originally from Barbados is now living in Los Angeles where she's the producer of a radio show called 'Sojourner Truth' on Pacifica Radio. Prescod is also the author of "A Black Women: Bringing It All Back Home."

I will be reporting on a struggle in Benton Harbor, Michigan, not far from Detroit. Many of you are familiar with Motown music that came out of Detroit. A lot of organizing happens in Detroit. It is the home of the auto workers, who struggled so hard, and are now facing a lot of takeaways.

Black people fleeing sharecropping, which is a little bit above slavery in the U.S., went to places like Detroit to make a way for themselves. People in Benton Harbor are living under apartheid-like conditions that we're familiar with because of South Africa.

The city is 94% Black and has an average income of $8,000 a year. Across the river is a city called St. Joseph's that is mainly white with an average income of $41,000 a year.

In Benton Harbor, people are confronted by racist police, a corrupt criminal justice system, corrupt elected officials, and cross burnings.

The recent story of police killing of yet another Black man began a rebellion that lasted for three days. There were cross burnings that were used in the Deep South and other places by the Ku Klux Klan to terrorize Black people. It represents Jim Crow racism within the U.S.

I'm here to tell you that a cross burning happened last year in Benton Harbor outside the home of an elderly woman who dared to say that Black people have to stick together. That's all she said. As a result a cross was burned outside her home.

The women of Benton Harbor mobilized, started to picket against the police harassment of their children and the fact that the majority of those going through the prisons were their children.

Dorothy Pinkney became active in that group of women. She was married to a Baptist minister the Reverend Edward Pinkney. She encouraged him to join the movement and he became one of the grassroots spokespeople.

When it comes to struggling for justice, it is often the mothers, aunts and grandmothers that do that justice work. But women are rarely recognized for justice work and it is not seen as part of the women's movement because racism hides the fact.

Margaret Prescod speaking in London, Feb. 7, 2009.

The women's movement is instead promoted as those feminists that are interested in self-promotion, but have very little interest in justice.

Mrs. Dorothy Pinkney is part of the women's movement.

Benton Harbor is the international headquarters of the multinational corporation Whirlpool who controls a lot of the political power and the resources of the city.

Whirlpool, in conjunction with land developers decided they wanted to take over 400 acres of Benton Harbor property bordering Lake Michigan to build an exclusive Jack Nicklaus golf course and very expensive homes.

The Black Autonomy Network Community Organization, Reverend Pinkney and Dorothy Pinkney protested loudly. They did something that Whirlpool and the power structure in Benton Harbor thought was totally unacceptable. They organized a recall of an elected city official who was in the pockets of Whirlpool and the developers, whose vote they needed to go through with this project.

They mobilized a grassroots recall of the election defeating the most powerful people in the county.
Excerpts from radio transcript.

Dorothy Pinkney leads a protest against the imprisonment of Rev. Pinkney who was convicted on five felony counts in 2014 involving the purported changing of dates on recall petitions designed to remove Benton Harbor Mayor James Hightower. Rev. Edward Pinkney was finally released 2017.

Photo: Abayomi Azikiwe

Black Trans Lives Matter!
CeCe McDonald: the right to self-defense

Leslie Feinberg

At certain moments in history, the struggle of individuals to survive and organize against fascist attacks, police and prison terror reveals the societal relationship of forces, between oppressor and oppressed, exploiter and exploited. These battles inspire unity of action that define political eras, like the demands to free the Scottsboro Brothers, Lolita Lebron, Leonard Peltier, George Jackson, Joann Little, Mumia Abu-Jamal.

The struggle to 'Free CeCe!' is sparking a broad united front against white supremacy and anti-trans violence. CeCe McDonald's courage and consciousness, and the tireless and tenacious solidarity work by supporters in Minneapolis and the region, led by those who are oppressed, has widened and deepened the demand to "Free CeCe!" in cities across the U.S. and around the world.

Hundreds of thousands of people in the U.S. and internationally now know more facts about the attack on CeCe McDonald than the judge and prosecutor allowed a jury to know during her trial.

CeCe McDonald and her friends were assaulted in Minneapolis on June 5, 2011, by a group that announced its ideology as racist and fascist in words and action. The attackers shouted white-supremacist Klan language, transmisogynist epithets and a slur against same-sex love.

CeCe replied that, "Her crew would not tolerate hate speech." One of the attackers then assaulted CeCe McDonald, smashing her face with a bar glass that deeply punctured her cheek. In the fight that ensued, an attacker died. He had a swastika tattoo.

CeCe McDonald was the only person arrested by the police that night.

CeCe McDonald and Leslie Feinberg, Hennepin County jail, Minneapolis, May 1, 2012. Due to the powerful campaign for CeCe's freedom, she was finally freed on Jan. 13, 2014.
WW photo: Leslie Feinberg

McDonald has been punished ever since as the "aggressor" for defending her life and the lives of her friends. Police, jailers, prosecutor, judge and prison administration have arrested her, locked her up and held her in solitary confinement for long periods.

Stop the war on trans women of color!
Abridged from WW, Dec. 13, 2012.

Pro-trans* is not anti-woman or anti-child

Minnie Bruce Pratt

LGBTQ people continue to be under assault in the U.S. by right-wingers are seeking to divide oppressed people and workers by pushing 'wedge issues' aimed at people of color; women; immigrants; disabled people; and lesbian, gay, bisexual and trans* and queer people. (Trans* is currently used with an asterisk to indicate the spectrum of all the different sexes and genders of people who do not conform to the either/or of male/female or masculine/feminine.)

In February 2016, the Republican National Committee called for the Department of Education to cancel its interpretation that facility use by transgender students was covered by Title IX, U.S. legislation prohibiting sex discrimination in education. The RNC also directed state legislatures to enact laws to "limit the use of

SAG-AFTRA members and ILWU union members at the Pride Parade on June 2016, in downtown Seattle.

restrooms, locker rooms and similar facilities to members of the sex to whom the facility is designated."

The bigots' attempt to reduce human complexity to a simple 'M' or 'F' flies in the face of scientific facts. These show that all creatures, including human beings, live on a vast spectrum of sex and gender, "Evolution's Rainbow: Diversity, Gender, and Sexuality in Nature and People" by Joan Roughgarden

Given these facts, a basic human right should be access to bathroom facilities under safe conditions for every person.
Abridged from WW, March 17, 2016.

INTERNATIONAL WOMEN'S DAY
Women workers rising

Minnie Bruce Pratt

Calls for a Women's Strike ignited International Women's Day (IWD) in the U.S. on March 8, 2017. Organizers were following up on the massive Jan. 21 women's protests, held on all seven continents, against the inauguration of Donald Trump.

According to womenstrikeus.org, 50 U.S. actions were part of a "new international feminist movement" to defend "women who have been marginalized by decades of neoliberalism directed towards working women, women of color, Native women, disabled women, immigrants, Muslims, lesbian, queer and trans women." They condemned the "decades-long economic inequality, racial and sexual violence, and imperial wars."

Also organizing for March 8, were the sponsors of "A Day Without a Woman," to recognize "the enormous value that women add to our socio-economic system, while receiving lower wages and experiencing inequities, discrimination, sexual harassment, and job insecurity."

'One Billion Rising,' a campaign to end the exploitation of women, demonstrated at the U.S. Department of Labor under the banner "Women Workers Rising." The protest was called in solidarity with women around the world fighting to end sexual harassment and violence. (womenworkersrising on Facebook)

The One Billion coalition included: the African American Policy Forum; the AFT teachers union; Family Values @ Work; Int'l Labor Rights Forum; Jobs with Justice; Nat'l Domestic Workers Alliance; NNU nurses union; NOW and the ROC United. Also present were OUR Walmart members.

Schools in both Alexandria, Va., and Chapel Hill-Carrboro, N.C., were closed due to the strike. Organizers in Ithaca, N.Y., and Tompkins County came together in a March for Incarcerated Women. Under the slogan #SayHerName, they reached out to supporters: "We ask you to remember our sisters who are behind bars."

This March 8 was "feminism of the 99%" with stay-homes from work; rallies and marches; organizing workshops; the history of women's labor; performances; and a cry of "Resist!"

But most significant was the call for women to strike, an appeal at a mass level of organizing. This class-conscious rallying cry connected women's struggle for liberation with workers' power to withhold labor as a weapon against capitalism.

The call "Women Strike!" reconnected IWD to its revolutionary socialist origins and promoted the hope that a new movement for women's liberation is emerging, rooted in class struggle. Plans are already underway for the May 1 Global Strike.

In **New York City,** the International Working Women's Day Coalition held an intergenerational, multiracial "Women Rise and Organize!" roundtable. In keeping with the coalition's perspective that 'every issue is a woman's issue,' panelists discussed a wide array of struggles. See page 203.

When the coalition meets again in early April, they'll discuss the Global May Day Strike.
— **Monica Moorehead**

Hundreds of protesters gathered at Logan Square in **Philadelphia**, to protest economic and political inequality as part of the global call for a "Day Without a Woman." Teachers stayed out of work to lobby the City Council on educational issues.

Signs and chants called for the inclusion of Black, Brown, immigrant, LGBTQ+ and Muslim concerns. Speakers demanded solidarity with sex workers, as well as low-wage workers fighting for the right to unionize. Others voiced outrage over the murders of women of color and transgender people.
— **Betsey Piette**

Close to 400 people took to the streets in **Baltimore** to protest on IWD. Called by the newly formed Women's Fightback Network, the march attracted a diverse crowd of mostly young Black, Latinx and white

International Working Women's Day Coalition held a 'Women Rise and Organize!' roundtable discussion in New York.

WW photo: Brenda Ryan

women. The 77-year-old Rev. Annie Chambers, a veteran housing organizer, led from her wheelchair despite harassment from police who threatened to arrest the protesters.

Stopping at the women's jail, protesters demanded an end to mass incarceration, and then marched to the Douglass Homes housing development for a speak-out on how women are exploited in public housing..

Along with major issues facing women, including trans women, LGBTQ+ and gender-nonconforming women, the event addressed ICE violence against immigrant communities. Many chants and speeches were called out in Spanish.

The next step is to organize for the Global May Day Strike.

— Sharon Black

Along with several marches throughout **Chicago** more than 300 women and supporters rallied at the offices of the Chicago Teachers Union where the speakers were predominantly women of color. The program was chaired by Christel Williams, of the CTU, representing the movement to create true sanctuary in Chicago Public Schools, protecting children from ICE deportations and from the school-to-prison pipeline. Adriana Alvarez, a McDonald's worker from Fight for $15 co-chaired. Other union struggles addressed were those of day care and transit workers.

A woman from Black Youth Project 100 highlighted the struggles of Black, queer, trans and gender-nonconforming people against recent violence and murder.

Rasmea Odeh, the Palestinian leader of Arab American Action Network, spoke on the U.S. government's case against her. Nerissa Allegretti, from GABRIELA USA, talked of the growing movement for solidarity and justice for women around the world.

— Jill White

In **Houston** the IWD celebration, organized by Freedom Road Socialist Organization, educated and motivated activists, students and some new to the struggle. Kinsey Tamsin, a trans woman and FRSO activist, spoke about daily obstacles trans people face. She praised Cuba for the progress made through CENESEX, the Cuban National Center for Sex Education, on LGBTQ+ rights. Nikki Luellen spoke about the struggle for justice by the spouse of Alva Braziel, who was killed by Houston cops.

Gloria Rubac's talk focused on revolutionaries: Emma Tenayuca, a San Antonio union organizer; Marsha P. Johnson and Sylvia Rivera, African-American and Latinx trans women, who fought back in the 1969 Stonewall Rebellion; Assata Shakur, Black Liberation Army, who was imprisoned and escaped to Cuba; Leslie Feinberg, wrote Marxist analysis of trans liberation including, "Rainbow Solidarity with Cuba," "Transgender Warriors" and "Stone Butch Blues."

— Joanne Gavin

Several thousand women and supporters rallied in **San Francisco** and Oakland on IWD. The demonstration, titled "Gender Strike, Bay Area," started at Chelsea Manning Plaza and then marched to the ICE Detention Center. A strong chant was "No borders, no deportations."

Another large rally gathered at Oscar Grant Plaza in **Oakland**. Organized by the Oakland Women's Strike Organizing Collective, protesters marched to Sheriff Gregory Ahern's office who has announced he will continue to cooperate with ICE.

On March 11, a multinational rally and march of hundreds in San Francisco was led by GABRIELA SF, with the theme "Rise Against Fear, Resist Attacks on Our Communities and Unite for Self-Determination."

— Terri Kay

Lynne Stewart
People's lawyer, freedom fighter ¡presente!

Mumia Abu-Jamal

Lynne Stewart, after 78 winters in America, has died after battling for years against breast cancer.

But that was just some of her battles, and like most of us, she won some and lost some. But she never stopped fighting!

For decades, she and her husband Ralph fought for New York's political activists and revolutionaries, like the Black Panthers and the Young Lords, a Puerto Rican socialist collective. But mostly, they fought for the freedom of the poor and dispossessed of New York's Black and Brown ghettos.

She, they, fought often and fought well in the city's courts.

Her husband Ralph was a stalwart of the Black Panther Party and her most committed defender.

When Lynne was targeted by the U.S. Justice Department, and she was tried and convicted for putting out a press release for her client, the blind Egyptian Sheikh Omar Abdul Rahman, Ralph stood in the hot Washington, D.C., sun, with a sign in front of the White House, demanding his wife's release.

Her defense of her client was in the best tradition of criminal defense lawyers, and she received significant support from a broad swath of the bar, from lawyers, yes; judges, no.

Initially sentenced to 28 months, the Second Circuit sent her case back for resentencing, and she got 10 years!

Her support only grew. The late activist lawyer Bill Kunstler once opined that defense lawyers should be officers of their clients, instead of officers of the court.

Lynne Stewart was an officer of her clients; a People's Lawyer, beloved and respected.

May she ever be so.

Prison Radio Broadcast. March 9, 2017.

Interview with Naeema Muhammad and Don Webb on Democracy Now!
Fighting for environmental Justice

Naeema Muhammad is organizing co-director of the North Carolina Environmental Justice Network. The Network promotes health and environmental equality for all people of N.C. through community action for clean industry, safe workplaces, and fair access to all human and natural resources.

In eastern North Carolina, residents are battling with one of the state's largest industries, hog farms. The billion dollar industry is primarily clustered in the eastern part of the state, where hog farms collect billions of gallons of untreated pig feces and urine in what are essentially cesspools, then dispose of the waste by spraying it into the air. Residents living in the area of the spray complain of adverse health effects and odor so bad that it limits their ability to be outdoors. For more, we speak with Naeema Muhammad

Amy Goodman: Naeema, can you tell us where you live and what you're dealing with today?

Naeema Muhammad: I live in Rocky Mount, N.C., which is in the eastern part of the state. I live away from where these animals are, but I work with communities that's living

Naeema Muhammad has worked tirelessly to hold the hog industry accountable for the pollution it produces that disproportionately impacts the lives of African Americans living in rural North Carolina counties.

with these animals, and I've been working with them since 1999. I'm constantly going into the communities where these animals are. I smell what the people living there are smelling. I see the spraying going on. I see the hog houses and the open-air lagoons that's just sitting out there. As you travel through those communities, you can't help but see these houses that the animals are kept in, as well as the lagoon and the spray fields.

AG: And I want to turn to former pig factory farm owner Don Webb.

Don Webb: I shut my hog operation down, and I got out of it. I couldn't, I just couldn't do another person that way, to make them smell that. It is a cesspool that you put feces and urine in, a hole in the ground that you dump toxic waste in. I've seen dead hogs in them and stuff like that. I've seen it. I've talked to the people. I've seen the little children that say, "Mom and daddy, why do we got to smell this stuff?" You get stories like "I can't hang my clothes out. Feces and urine odor comes by and attaches itself to your clothes." And then people will say, "We're scared to invite neighbors."

AG: Naeema, explain exactly what is in the spray that people are inhaling and getting on their clothes, the residents in east North Carolina?

NM: The spray is the animal waste that comes out of the hogs who are kept in tin metal housing. They have slats in the floor where whatever, whenever they go to the bathroom or abort baby piglets or whatever happens with them, it falls through the slats in the floor, and it's piped out. There are pipes running underneath the ground. And the waste is piped out into the open-air lagoon. And there are all kinds of chemicals. And this urine and fecal matter produces methane, ammonia gases, and so you can smell it. And what people say, it smells like rotten eggs, sometimes rotten collard greens or, it's just a terrible smell. And they have been forced off of their wells, because they were seeing remnants of the waste in their well

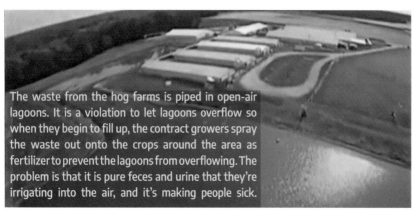

The waste from the hog farms is piped in open-air lagoons. It is a violation to let lagoons overflow so when they begin to fill up, the contract growers spray the waste out onto the crops around the area as fertilizer to prevent the lagoons from overflowing. The problem is that it is pure feces and urine that they're irrigating into the air, and it's making people sick.

waters by the coloring and the odors coming out of their well water.

AG: Naeema Muhammad, I wanted to ask you if you can talk more about the class action suit against Smithfield by those affected by the farms, and your organization also filing a Title VI complaint with the EPA. Explain what that means.

NM: The North Carolina Environmental Justice Network, Waterkeeper Alliance and REACH, which is Rural Empowerment Association for Community Help, we joined together and filed a Title VI complaint, which is an act under the Civil Rights Act of 1964. And under the Title VI, it states that governmental agencies cannot do business in a way that intentionally or unintentionally have a disproportionate impact on low-income communities., In March of 2013, DEQ, which is the Department of Environmental Quality, at that time, it was called the Department of Environment and Natural Resources, renewed all of those contract rules, permits, without putting any protective measures in place for communities living with these animals, even though they had been well informed of the health impacts, the environmental impacts, by the research that was done by Dr. Steve Wing, and also citizens going up, you know, talking with them. They attended the North Carolina Environmental Justice Network. We have an annual summit every year, the third weekend in October. And DENR always had a representative sitting on our government listening panel. So they were in the room. ...

AG: Naeema, we're going to have to leave it there, as the show wraps up, but we are going to continue to follow this issue. Naeema Muhammad, organizing co-director for the North Carolina Environmental Justice Network.

For more go to: tinyurl.com/n43j3fs

Ralph Poynter, Royce Adams, Larry Hamm, Clarence Thomas, Raymond Nat Turner, Pam Africa, Madea Benjamin, Ashaki Binta and Lynne Stewart at a May 2015 UNAC Coalition Conference in New Jersey, May 2015. Sister Lynne Stewart, ¡Presente!
Photo: Delores Lemon-Thomas

'*If indeed all lives mattered, we would not need to emphatically proclaim that "Black Lives Matter."*

'*Or, as we discover on the BLM website: Black Women Matter, Black Girls Matter, Black Gay Lives Matter, Black Bi Lives Matter, Black Boys Matter, Black Queer Lives Matter, Black Men Matter, Black Lesbians Matter, Black Trans Lives Matter, Black Immigrants Matter, Black Incarcerated Lives Matter. Black Differently Abled Lives Matter. Yes, Black Lives Matter, Latino/Asian American/ Native American/Muslim/Poor and Working-Class White Peoples Lives Matter. There are many more specific instances we would have to name before we can ethically and comfortably claim that All Lives Matter.*'

— Angela Y. Davis, "Freedom Is a Constant Struggle, Ferguson, Palestine, and the Foundations of a Movement"
haymarketbooks.org/books/780-freedom-is-a-constant-struggle

Case Studies in Oppression
Lessons from the Sufferers

*Jaribu Hill, was born to south-
ern parents, dad from Deeson, MS
and mother from Memphis, TN. She
went to MS to practice law in the
Dred Scott system of exclusion and
injustice, to use her voice and newly
found legal skills to expose the brutal
reality of contemporary forms of
slavery and worker mistreatment.
The firm and indelible roots of the
Delta, brought her to this place and
time, Aug. 1995. She is a human rights
defender, founder of the Mississippi
Workers' Center for Human Rights
and the Southern Human Rights
Organizers' Conference.*

Terror on the plant floor

In the nineties, when Lazy Boy
International workers from Leland,
Mississippi came to our office, they
spent hours sharing their accounts of
racial hostility, employment discrimination and retaliation. They had witnessed a co-worker being subjected to
humiliation, insults and abuse. They
witnessed this co-worker, a Black
man, being pushed into an equipment
cage, where white employees threw
peanuts at him, called him a monkey
and shouted racial epithets. Infuriated
and horrified, they demanded that the
cage be unlocked and their co-worker
emerged from captivity. Traumatized,
the victim, who feared he would lose
his job, declined to take action.

"To challenge the maintenance of
racially hostile workplaces across the
state, the Mississippi Workers' Center
for Human Rights, launched its 'Terror
on the Plant Floor Campaign.' Popular education, mass messaging and on
-the-ground organizing are the primary components of this campaign.
Mass messaging strategies, including

billboard launches, provide 'Know
Your Rights' information for victims
of workplace hate, violence against
workers and the general public."

Nooses on ship decks

For more than 40 years, Black
workers at Northrup Grumman Ship
Systems endured the indignities and
terror of racial hatred at the largest
employer in the state. They built ships
for the U.S. Navy. For their service,
they were taunted, harassed and
threatened with nooses and lynchings.
They witnessed co-workers who were
victims of attempted lynchings.

These Black workers organized
against human rights abuses and racist violence. With the legal advocacy
and organizing support of Black
Workers for Justice, Employment
Law Center of San Francisco and
the Mississippi Workers' Center for
Human Rights, workers took on the
all-powerful Northrup Grumman
Shipyard, formerly known as Ingalls
Shipbuilding company. These workers, who were steeled in struggle,
organized Ingalls Workers for Justice
(IWFJ). As a united show of force,
they reached thousands of shipyard
workers at NGSS. Their message of
solidarity and victory traveled far
beyond the local plant gate to international worker struggles. Representatives of IWFJ testified before the
International Labor Organization
(ILO), during the 2001 World Conference Against Racism in Durban,
South Africa; United Nations World
Conference Against Racism Prepa-
ratory meeting in Geneva, Switzer-
land and the Southern Human Rights
Organizers' Conference (SHROC) in
Atlanta, Georgia.

*'Town hall meetings, picket lines,
rallies, leafletting, radio interviews,
tv interviews, community speak
outs, and billboards help spread
the word about workers who
dare to struggle.'*

– Jaribu Hill

Photo: Delores Lemon-Thomas

The resolve of the Black shipyard
workers at NGSS led to many victories. The legal action, led by these
workers, was a success because of
their courage. The Zero Tolerance
policies implemented at Northrup
Grumman served as a model for other
employers to follow. Today, Black
workers can claim this victory!

This is the only lawyering that is
worthwhile. I learned how to boldly
stand in the halls of injustice. I learned
to take leadership from the sufferers.
I learned that silence will not save us!
Years later, the struggle against terror
on the plant floor continues; but, workers at NGSS set the example for other
victims of hostile work environments
to follow as they work to abolish all
forms of discrimination."

Note: The lawsuit filed against NGSS
was a Human Rights Action, which cited to the International Convention on
the Elimination of all Forms of Racial
Discrimination (ICERD) in the actual
complaint!!! The preamble contains
ICERD language. In defiance of the
rigid, racist federal court system, I
was proud to include this language
and advocate for the human rights of
these and other courageous workers. It is worth noting that during the
course of this struggle, several white
workers expressed their solidarity!

Tarana Burke activist and sexual assault survivor who started the hashtag #MeToo a decade ago. She's now a program director at Girls for Gender Equity.

Alicia Garza, one of the founders of the #BlackLivesMatter movement and fellow activists.

Photo: Kristin Little

#MeToo Founder Tarana Burke, Alicia Garza of Black Lives Matter on Democracy Now!

Amy Goodman: We asked Tarana Burke about how she started the #MeToo hashtag. We also spoke with Alicia Garza, co-founder of Black Lives Matter.

Tarana Burke:. As a survivor of sexual violence who was struggling trying to figure out what healing looked like, I saw young people, particularly young women of color, struggling with the same issues and trying to find a succinct way to show empathy. "Me Too" is so powerful. Somebody said it to me and it changed the trajectory of my healing process.

"Me Too" was bringing messages to survivors of sexual violence where other people wouldn't talk about it.

Alicia Garza: First I have to say a deep thank you to Tarana for creating this space for survivors like myself.

Lots of people are asking themselves, "What do we do about this epidemic of violence — against women, against women of color, against black women, queer people, trans people? And even, what do we do about violence against men?" Right? Cis men, trans men.

This kind of patriarchal violence really functions off of shame and silence. This requires different types of responses to deal with how systemic the problem actually is.

Excerpts from Democracy Now! Nov. 24, 2017.

Demanding Water

I didn't know when the deluge came. I was in bed up north
where the rain that fell all night pattered about its safe routine,

making a bigger room for me to sleep in. But the levees broke
in New Orleans. People hacked through the ceiling to the roof
if they had an axe. If they didn't, they drowned standing up.
Who knows how many died, mostly Black women and children,
the poor, the old. The government saw it coming. Every summer,
ten times or more, the giant arms will uncurl and start to spin
as weather men guess which city might be hit. They call it Mother
Nature – No. My mother could plan. So I call it a government
unfit to rule, no longer compatible with you and me, *incompetent
to assure an existence to those trapped inside* its earthenware dam,
the river on one side, the lake on the other, the muddy-fingered
water pulling down an ill-built foundation, cracking the concrete
poured on top of flimsy sheet metal while the stop-gap money
is dropped in bombs on Baghdad, blasting open a street corner
where broken pipelines gush not oil, but water into dusty gutters.

The people stand by their dead and look at us. They demand: *Where
is the food? When will we have water?* The radio offers
more tragedy and says the government has a plan. Yes, there is
a plan. But it's not ours. The problem is, the plan is not ours.

– Minnie Bruce Pratt

"Inside the Money Machine," published 2011
Carolina Wren Press Poetry, Series 3.

Harry Bridges
ILWU President 1934-1977

The closer rank-and-file workers get to the public, the more support the public will give to organized labor. For such close communication will make it apparent to those outside our ranks that a community of interests lie between them.

Every effort to split the ranks of labor, and to split the public, the majority of whom are workers themselves, workers way from their organized brothers and sisters — must fail when people realize that what hurts organized workers hurts the unorganized and is dangerous to small business as well.

We must work at all times to place our case before the people — how we live, what we earn, what we aspire to for our children — for those are also the aspirations and lives of the people.

'An Injury to One is an Injury to All'
– Harry Bridges

Taken from 1952 Yearbook ILWU Local 37

INTERNATIONAL LONGSHORE AND WAREHOUSE UNION

Paul Robeson an honorary member of the International Longshore and Warehouse Union at the Moore Shipyard.

ILWU leader Leo Robinson and other rank-and-filers helped shut down apartheid in South Africa and freed Nelson Mandela.

Still photo from video: "ILWU member and anti-apartheid activist Leo Robinson: A Life in Struggle."

1934 ILWU march in San Francisco.

Longshore stalwarts of Bridges Defense Committee in 1949: Rear, Albert James, Howard Bodine, Bill Chester, Bill Goldblatt. In front, Johnny Walker, Harry Bridges and Claude Saunders.

Black-white solidarity key to San Francisco's 1934 General Strike

Cheryl LaBash

Workers call it "Bloody Thursday." On July 5, 1934, San Francisco port bosses pulled out all stops trying to break a two-month West Coast dock strike. The workers fought back.

Police that day killed Nick Bordoise and Howard Sperry, two of seven workers killed between May 15 and July 20. The capitalist class assault on the longshore strikers angered rank-and-file workers from 100 unions in the Bay Area. They voted to strike in support of the port workers, overruling conservative union leaders. On July 16, 1934, the four-day San Francisco General Strike began as strikers and National Guard battled for control of the shut-down city.

What is not so well-known in labor history is the concerted outreach to the African American community by longshore strike leader Harry Bridges, which for the first time brought Black workers into the longshore union.

Thomas C. Fleming, co-founder of San Francisco's African American weekly, *The Sun-Reporter*, wrote about his experiences. "In 1934, one of the low years of the Depression, Blacks could only work on two piers in San Francisco, the Panama Pacific and the Luckenbach Line. If you went to any other pier down there, you might get beaten up by the hoodlums. ...

"The system on the docks then was called the shape-up, in which the bosses on all piers selected whom they wished to hire on a daily basis. They held absolute power. No one had a guarantee of a daily job, unless he was a pet of the dock boss, or paid a sum of his daily earning. ...

The April 21, 1961, issue of *The Dispatcher* showed delegates from Local 10 at the ILWU 14th Biennial Convention held in Hawaii. At left is Henry Schmidt, Bill Chester, Tommy J. Silas, Jr, Reino Erkkila and Albert Bertani. Photo: Archives of Tommy J. Silas, Jr. Local 10

"Before this time, I clung to views that the trade union movement was just formed to continue racial discrimination. But Bridges ... felt that by keeping the unions lily-white, there would be a steady reservoir of Black potential strikebreakers whenever strikes were called, which would weaken the unions when negotiations broke down.

"Bridges went to Black churches on both sides of San Francisco Bay and asked the ministers if he could say a few words during the Sunday services? He begged the congregation to join the strikers on the picket line, and promised that when the strike ended, Blacks would work on every dock on the West Coast. ...

"The waterfront strike ended on July 31 when the International Longshoremen's Association, now the ILWU, was recognized by the ship owners. Bridges kept his word. All piers were opened to Blacks. They began to get the same work as everyone else, and later became union officers.

As part of the agreement, the union got its own hiring hall, a minimum 30-hour week and a raise to $1 an hour."

On April 4, 2011, the rank-and-file of Harry Bridges' ILWU Local 10 honored the labor movement's call for "no business as usual" in solidarity with Wisconsin public workers. The union's motto, "An injury to one is an injury to all," and Bridges' working-class solidarity and unity pledge echoed through the 77 years. They did not report for work.

No cargo moved at the international ports of Oakland and San Francisco for 24 hours, respecting the Rev. Dr. Martin Luther King Jr., who was assassinated on that date in 1968 while supporting African-American sanitation workers in Memphis, Tenn., who were striking for collective bargaining rights. Dr. King was an honorary member of Local 10 and spoke to workers there only six months before he was assassinated in Memphis. *Abridged from WW, July 9, 2011.*

War on the water front

Mumia Abu-Jamal   September 1, 2002

Local 10 member Anna Wills, protests outside the PMA offices in San Francisco, on July 24, 2002.

In times of war, even one so nebulous as the "War On Terrorism," there are wars within wars. Wars not merely fought abroad, but little, internal wars of interests battling for dominance.

With the elevation of George W. Bush to the nation's highest office by the Supreme Court, business interests know they have "their guy" in the White House, and they are now trying to change the rules of the game, using government muscle, and federal power, to threaten labor into compliance with their bosses' interests.

This can be seen clearest in the struggle between the Pacific Maritime Association (PMA), the waterfront employers and the International Longshore and Warehouse Union (ILWU), the unionized workers.

The PMA allowed the labor contract to expire on July 1, 2002, and has issued harsh demands to the unions that would seriously undermine long-standing, and hard-fought labor rights. The PMA wants to introduce new technology into the shipping industry, which the ILWU has agreed to; but the PMA wants to use these technologies to circumvent the time-honored union hiring hall, a move that cuts into pivotal union power.

The union hiring hall didn't always exist; it came into being as a result of long, hard, deadly struggles, organized not by union leaders, but by everyday rank-and-file ILWU members, who pushed the Great Maritime Strike of 1934 into labor history.

Historian Howard Zinn writes: "… Longshoremen on the West Coast, in a rank-and-file insurrection … held a convention, demanded the abolition of the shape-up (a kind of early-morning slave market where work gangs were chosen for the day), and went out on strike. Two thousand miles of coastline were quickly tied up.

"The teamsters cooperated, refusing to truck cargo to the piers, and maritime workers joined the strike. When the police moved in to open the piers, the strikers resisted en masse, and two were killed by police gunfire. A mass funeral procession for the strikers brought together tens of thousands of supporters. And then a general strike was called in San Francisco, with 130,000 workers out, the city immobilized." ("A Peoples History of the United States," pp. 386-7.)

While union organizers recall it was six strikers killed by cops, the point remains that the hiring hall wasn't a gift bestowed by the bosses, but a right won by blood and death. The PMA wants to computerize it away, to distant points like Utah, Arizona, and even overseas!

Another tool of the wealthy owners has been the corporate press, which has falsely portrayed the longshoremen as if they were pro baseball players, making over $100,000 a year, when, in fact, their average wage is closer to half that. While the ILWU quite rightly takes pride in the fact that it has fought for decent wages for its members (over 70% of whom are African American or Latino in the San Francisco/Oakland ports.) The PMA's tactic is designed to stir up labor envy in the midst of a falling, and faltering economy.

Into this simmering labor conflict now comes "Unconstitutional Tom" Ridge, the stone-faced Homeland Security Czar, and guess on whose side? Czar Ridge placed a less-than-veiled threatening call to Jim Spinosa, ILWU president. The message? A breakdown in talks (not to mention a strike!) threatens "national security."

Why isn't it ever that when a worker, or even thousands of workers, faces job loss, that is a "national security" threat? Why isn't job security "national security"? How is it in the "interests" of a nation to abolish a hard-fought right that labor won through terrible battle?

Despite the whines of the wealthy and the bloats of the corporate press, the ILWU has every right to hold firm in the face of this state-managerial assault on their glorious traditions.

The radical writer Randolph Bourne once observed, "War is the health of the state." By this, he meant that governments accrue tremendous powers during war, and rarely, if ever, return power to the people.

The ILWU should fight, and fight hard, in its noble tradition, against this new-age "shape-up" scheme pushed at them by management, and threatened by the Bush regime. The ILWU, with the aid and assistance of sister unions, can once again teach an historic lesson, that "Labor security is national security."

© Copyright MAJ 2002

Local 10 members Keith Shanklin, Byron Moore, and his son, at the 'Battle in Seattle' during Ministerial Conference of the World Trade Organization, WTO in November 1999.

The ILWU fights for a contract in 2002

Photos by David Bacon
unless otherwise credited.

At the Port of Oakland during ILWU protest against the PMA lockout in 2002.

Alex Bagwell Local 34 and Harriet Bagwell are members of the South African Vukani Mawethu Choir. They sing South African Freedom songs. Pictured in 2002. Photos: David Bacon ©2017

Protest in front of the State Building in Oakland, California on August 12, 2002.
Photo: Bill Hackwell

Cliff Murray with his daughter, Philip Taylor, Trent Willis with his daughter, Carlos Austin, Jahn Overstreet and William Cherry, after being sworn in as A-members of Local 10.

At the Port of Oakland Local 10 members Shundra Broomfield and Clyde Hanes protest against the PMA lock out in 2002. Photos: David Bacon.

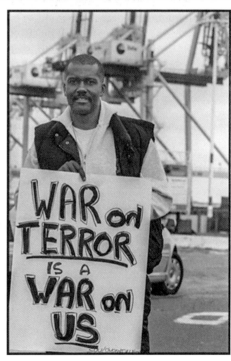

Gary Noble Local 10 in 2002: 'The war on terror is a contract war on us.'

ILWU rejects the recognition of the African American Longshore Coalition

Clarence Thomas   June 26, 2006

The ILWU held its 33rd International Convention May 13-20, 2006, in Vancouver, Canada. The International Convention has the authority to adopt resolutions and statements of policy on political, economic and other issues, and amend the Constitution. The highest governing body of the entire ILWU, it is made up of delegates elected by direct rank-and-file vote in each local or affiliate of the union.

During the Convention, a resolution regarding the African American Longshore Coalition (AALC) was put forward by ILWU Local 10. The AALC, a rank-and-file organization, has been recognized by the International union for its contributions to remedy racism within the ILWU since March 1992. The intent of the resolution was to provide the AALC with the same status as the ILWU Pensioners and Women Auxiliaries with 'voice but no vote.' However, the resolution recognizing AALC was defeated at the Convention and the Longshore Caucus.

Rejecting the resolution is absolutely ironic when reviewing the progressive history of the ILWU. It must also be noted that international unions such as the International Brotherhood of Teamsters, the Service Employees International Union, and the American Federation of State, County, and Municipal Employees to name a few, recognize the formation of Black Caucuses within their respective unions because they recognize that discrimination does exist.

Segregation and White Supremacy in the Longshore Division

The roots of segregation and white supremacy in the Longshore Division are very deep. It is the Port of San Francisco where the world renowned progressive and workers solidarity history was established, not the Pacific Northwest where problems regarding racism, sexism and all forms of discrimination is pervasive today.

The ILWU Story: Six Decades of Militant Unionism, which provides the history of the union from its origins to the present, describes in detail the internal contradictions of racism, within the ILWU. **The ILWU Story** explains how during the Civil Rights Movement:

> ... there were longshore locals that steadfastly refused to integrate their membership. As an indication of the paradoxes of prejudice, these locals, mainly in the Northwest, but also early on in Southern California, agreed with the International policies supporting the civil rights movement and affirmative action programs, and contributed generously to early ILWU support for sit-in demonstrations and marches for equality in the Southern United States beginning in 1955. Yet an unofficial color line held fast in these locals, despite constant efforts by the International leadership and other longshore locals, notably Local 10 in San Francisco. ...

For the Convention to reject the resolution and for it not even to reach the floor is indicative of where the consciousness of ILWU members are on the issue of diversity and democracy. And, it clearly shows that the ILWU is not in line with other international unions who have long recognized the importance and necessity of Black Caucuses.

The reasons put forward in rejecting the recognition of the AALC is in this writer's opinion disingenuous. In my opinion, the real reason is that delegates are in denial of racism and discrimination in all its forms within the ILWU.

The AALC was formed in March 1992, to address the racism, sexism and other forms of discrimination up and down the West Coast of the Longshore Division for the purpose of resolving such problems internally. Its predecessor was the United Coalition of Black and Minority Longshoremen organized in the late 60s to address the discrimination in Local 8 in Portland, Oregon. The organization developed chapters in Seattle and Tacoma to confront discrimination in those locals.

In the February 1992, issue of the *The Dispatcher*, past President David Arian wrote in his column, "For the ILWU in particular, Black History Month also means that we must take a close look at ourselves. We must examine whether we are holding true to the democratic principles upon which this union was founded. We must eliminate any and all barriers that divide us. We must eradicate discrimination wherever and whenever it exists."

At the 1994, Longshore, Clerk and Walking Boss Caucus, the **Report of** the AALC minutes includes Brother Leo Robinson, Local 10 retired, and a founding member of the AALC speaking regarding the pervasive discrimination in the Pacific Northwest. Robinson said:

> "I wrote a very simple resolution that has in the history its genesis that goes back some years when Local 10 refused to pay part of the lawsuit that Local 8 had lost which was a discrimination case. It is the position that I take now... that as a person of color, that the ILWU founded on the principles of democracy and fairness for all should not have to bear the burden of those who choose to step outside of that framework for asserting some illusionary superiority over their fellow workers, and then when they're taken to task for that, they turn around and say to me, 'I want you to pay for my privilege.' The brothers and sisters of this union, whether they be of color or of the majority population of this society, have one thing in common, a threat to one from our enemy which is a class enemy, is a threat to us all and we will respond accordingly."

With this said of 1992, here it is 2020, and the AALC still does not have a 'voice and no vote' at the Convention or Longshore Caucus.

In Jan. 19, 1994, President David Arian wrote to Local 8 Vice President Lynell Hill, regarding the relationship of between the AALC and the ILWU:

> "The International Executive Board and the International officers **support** the activities of the AALC as long as it stays within the confines of the democratic procedures of the Constitution of the ILWU."

In a letter dated Feb. 14, 2006, addressed to all Longshore, Clerk, and Walking Boss Locals, acknowledgments of the important contributions of the AALC was noted by International President James Spinosa and members of the Coast Committee Labor Relations Committee.

The letter addressed **the problems of racism, discrimination, sexism in all of its forms which are more prevalent amongst the Longshore Division in the Pacific Northwest.**

The letter reads in part:

> "At the last Longshore Division Caucus held in April 2005, the AALC presented concerns regarding racial and diversity issues in certain parts of the Longshore Division, including the Pacific Northwest. The Coast Committee along with local officers pledged our commitment to address these problems effectively. To this end, we have had several meetings and discussions with the AALC and other concerned Union members.

> "We are pleased to say that considerable progress has been made in working to correct several individual cases raised by the AALC. However, we also recognize that much more needs to be done to improve solidarity among all ILWU members across racial and gender lines. The ILWU remains committed to its long standing policies against discrimination, harassment and retaliation of all types."

The recognition by Pres. James Spinosa of the efforts of the AALC to remedy racism in the ILWU **begs the question of why he was silent on the resolution recognizing the AALC at the Longshore Caucus!**

Tacoma Washington AALC member
Photo: Kelley Kane

ILWU Local 8 and AALC member Debbie Stringfellow speaking in an interview at the MWM.
Photo: MWM video

While certainly not documented in any precise matter of record, the AALC has been responsible for saving the union potentially millions of dollars in law suits involving racism, sexism, and other forms of discrimination. The impact of the work of the AALC has not been limited to just Blacks and other workers of color. White males and females have been beneficiaries as well. The role of the AALC was to inform the members of Local 23 of the union's grievance procedures and their rights and responsibilities under this longshore contract according to AALC organizer, Leo Robinson.

Local 10 has been referred to on more than one occasion as the "conscience of ILWU." Past International President David Arian, during the historic Longshore Caucus of April 20, 1994, in the **Report of the AALC**, paid tribute to the leading role of Local 10 in setting up the agenda for the whole question of discrimination, democracy, and fairness in the ILWU. Arian said, "I think it is testimony to the fact and to the democracy that exists within Local 10 and their struggle for social equality that has been a conscience to this entire union."

Harry Bridges was in the vanguard of all North American trade union leaders of his generation on the question of race. Brother Bridges said, "Discrimination is a tool of the bosses." He wrote in *The Dispatcher* on Feb, 15, 1938, which featured a series of articles on *The Economics of Prejudice...* : "Prejudice means profit for the boss … for the worker, Black and white, it means lower living standards, humiliations, violence, and often death."

At the Longshore Caucus in 1994, in the **Report of the AALC**, on the question of African American representation in the Longshore locals, Brother Leo Robinson is quoted saying the following:

"On the question of registration, it is obvious that our registration process differs from that of the other locals. And it's historic in terms of how it was done and why it was done. It was at the insistence of our first International president, the late Harry Bridges that Blacks came into Local 10 in numbers."

Local 10 is recognized nationally and internationally as one of the most progressive labor organizations in the world. In the Feb. 14, 2006, letter written by President Spinosa addressed to all Longshore, Clerk, and Walking Boss Locals, he said in the third paragraph:

"Having an open discussion within the Union on issues of race, gender and diversity is key to overcoming these problems and building union solidarity. In order to improve the lines of communication, we ask that each local establish a Diversity Committee that includes rank-and-file union members, including AALC members, to work on issues of diversity, tolerance and solidarity across racial and gender lines, and to make recommendations to the local officers, executive board and membership."

Actions initiated by Local 10 have created greater attention by the Longshore Division but the issues are still out there and much work is still to be done.

The action taken by the ILWU regarding the AALC must be viewed in the national context of the political disenfranchisement of African Americans. In the Longshore Division, Blacks have historically looked toward Local 10 to represent their interest at the Caucus and Convention.

The rejection of Local 10's resolution recognizing the AALC to have a 'voice but no vote' was a betrayal to African Americans and other

progressive ILWU members, past and present, who have been in the forefront contributing to the progressive history of the union. If Harry Bridges, Bill Chester, Paul Robeson or Dr. King, were alive today I'm certain they would support the AALC having a voice in the ILWU. This doesn't take much conjecture based upon their commitment to the struggle to end racism and their fight for social justice. These warriors for peace and justice took an uncompromising position regarding democracy for all and not just the privilege few.

The institutional racism and other forms of discrimination within the ILWU will require institutional change. Blacks, people of color, women, and other oppressed workers must be empowered from the bottom as well as the top to eradicate racism, sexism, and all the other forms of discrimination. The recognition of the AALC initially with 'voice but no vote' will be an important step in bringing about that change. After all, this is about democracy and fairness for all of the rank-and-file of the ILWU. It is for these reasons that the resolution recognizing the AACL was put forward by Local 10.

The San Francisco ILWU hiring hall, which was new when this photo was taken on March 11, 1949.

At the end of World War II Harry Bridges was confronted with questions concerning the racist competition for jobs. He replied that he wished we had a system where there was full employment for everybody, but when things reached the point where only two workers were left on the waterfront, if he was the one to make the decision, **one would be a Black man**. Bridges wrote in his monthly union column that **racist discrimination is anti-labor and that it hurts all workers**.

Ports shut in solidarity with Wisconsin and anniversary of Dr. King assassination

Leilani Dowell

On April 4, 2011, the anniversary of the assassination of the Rev. Dr. Martin Luther King Jr., workers shut down the ports of San Francisco and Oakland, Calif., as part of a national day of solidarity with Wisconsin workers and workers who are fighting union busting.

According to Clarence Thomas, dock workers unanimously agreed to honor a national call for a "no business as usual" day on April 4 in support of public sector workers in Wisconsin and their fight for collective bargaining rights. More than 1,000 actions were held throughout the country, with at least one in every state.

With only one ship in the Oakland Port on April 4, perhaps because the Port bosses got wind of the planned work stoppage, not enough workers reported to work to even unload that ship. "This was a voluntary rank-and-file action, an organized act of resistance," said Thomas. "It is significant that the action by Local 10 was taken in solidarity with Wisconsin public sector workers who are facing the loss of collective bargaining."

Management had suggested that Local 10 use its monthly meeting on April 4 to honor Dr. King, but Local 10 members rejected the proposal, preferring to voluntarily lose a day's pay. King, who was killed in Memphis while demanding collective bargaining for sanitation workers, had been named an honorary member of Local 10 six months before his death.

"So we've come full circle," Thomas concluded. The Memphis public workers got their union recognition with raises, after a two-month strike. Now 40 years later their Wisconsin counterparts are threatened with losing theirs. But it is Wisconsin's "fierce resistance that is inspiring all of us today." In addition to the actions on the docks, thousands of workers took to the streets in the Bay Area on April 4 to support the struggle in Wisconsin and to commemorate King's assassination.

Members of the Oakland Education Association attempted to occupy the lobby of the downtown Oakland Wells Fargo Bank to protest bank bailouts in the face of education cuts. The bank locked its doors before the OEA members could enter. At a spirited rally that effectively shut down the bank for three hours, OEA President Betty Olson-Jones said, "We are one with Wisconsin, Ohio and the workers and poor across the country."

"We Are One" with Wisconsin workers was also the theme of a noon rally called by the Alameda County AFL-CIO Labor Council. More than 1,000 union members representing nurses, teachers, painters, engineers, domestic workers, janitors and others attended. Speakers demanded that the banks and the rich be held responsible for the economic crisis, not the workers.

In the late afternoon, several thousand union members marched through San Francisco's financial district, stopping at all of the major banks and demanding an end to their massive bailouts at the expense of poor and working people. A final rally was held in front of the Federal Reserve Bank's San Francisco office.

Abridged from WW, April 14, 2011.

Workers from all over Wisconsin descended upon the state Capitol in Madison on Feb. 15, 2011 to protest against a bill that attacked the rights of public-sector workers, especially the right to collective bargaining. Not only were the workers outside, but workers inside the Capitol took four floors. Firefighters and teachers organized strong delegations along with youth and students.

– Bryan G. Pfeifer

Idle cranes and trucks in Oakland on April 4, 2011.

Photo: Delores Lemon-Thomas

Hands off ILWU Local 10!
Labor defends dock workers' solidarity with Wisconsin

Cheryl LaBash

MOBILIZE! That is the way the San Francisco Labor Council is answering the Pacific Maritime Association's (PMA) attack on the ILWU Local 10. In a unanimous resolution, the SFLC called for mass action at the PMA's San Francisco headquarters on April 25, 2011, and established a broad defense committee for the union and its members.

The PMA is seeking to punish ILWU Local 10 for its members' rank-and-file job action on April 4. The AFL-CIO had called for a National Day of Action in support of Wisconsin workers. ILWU Local 10 volunteered not to go to work. Without labor power, nothing moved in the ports of San Francisco and Oakland.

ILWU Local 10's job action is part of a bigger fight for all workers, and it's an important issue for the labor movement. By dragging this strong union before an arbitrator and a federal court judge, the PMA is trying to send a message to all workers to stay in line.

The PMA says that it is OK to have rallies, demonstrations and prayer vigils. It is OK to lobby, recall and vote. The PMA even told the union local that it is OK to shut down ports, but that type of action must be planned with them in order to suit the bosses.

The wheels of capitalism routinely roll on, squeezing the workers and unemployed even harder to make up for the bosses' losses from the global capitalist economic collapse. However, when the pain of the working class results in a united job action that pinches the profit stream, it really gets attention.

ILWU Local 10 opened up a second front in solidarity with Wisconsin workers, and California's labor movement is saying that the resulting intimidation by the bosses won't work and is taking action to prove it, starting on April 25.

As a first step for workers beyond California's Bay Area, the Bail Out the People Movement (BOPM) began an letter campaign to PMA president, James C. McKenna. It demands that the "PMA drop all retaliatory actions including its suit against Local 10 or exercising their right to show support for Wisconsin's public workers and to commemorate Rev. Dr. King Jr.'s assassination on the AFL-CIO's National Day of Action on April 4.

"We commend the brave longshore workers who showed the way by acting with conscience on April 4. We believe that 'An injury to one is an injury to all!' "

The BOPM web site asks that community members, students and other activists take their petition to protests against school closings and budget cuts. They ask union members to take the SFLC resolution to union meetings, and supporters to take it to their churches, block clubs or other organizations and ask for a letter of support to stand with ILWU Local 10 on April 25.

Although the anti-working-class offensive focuses on public workers in Wisconsin, Michigan and other states, the rights of every worker, and all union and broader social benefits for the working class, are in the bosses and bankers' cross hairs right now.

On April 12, ILWU members and supporters occupied the PMA office in Oakland, Calif., for several hours. They held a sit-in in the boardroom to highlight the PMA's refusal to negotiate with the union. That bosses' association aims to destroy the solidarity of the coast-wide contract in order to weaken the West Coast dockworkers' union. According to the Labor Video Project, the PMA even brought nonunion crews into the San Diego port as part of their anti-union campaign.

Abridged from WW, April 20, 2011.

ILWU Local 10 members protested at the Pacific Maritime Association headquarters on April 25, 2011 demanding that the employers' group drop its lawsuit against the union. The suit was in retaliation for the dock workers' solidarity action on April 4 in defense of Wisconsin public workers and in commemoration of Dr. M.L. King's assassination.

Photo: Randall White

Bosses target ILWU Local 10
Rank-and-file workers stand with Wisconsin struggle

Cheryl LaBash

Clarence Thomas, called out to the crowd from the podium at the San Francisco anti-war march on April 10 2011, "Everyone within earshot of my voice should understand this. ILWU Local 10 needs your support. We cannot be intimidated and silenced."

Thomas was calling on everyone there to defend his union local against a vicious attack by the Pacific Maritime Association following a dock workers' job action on April 4.

On that day, labor and civil rights movements coordinated national actions to defend collective bargaining and workers' rights. The events honored the Rev. Dr. Martin Luther King Jr. who was assassinated on that date 43 years ago while supporting bargaining rights for sanitation workers in Memphis, Tenn.

In answer to the AFL-CIO's call for "no business as usual," ILWU Local 10 members engaged in rank-and file resistance to the anti-worker offensive symbolized by events in Wisconsin. They stayed home from work on April 4. For 24 hours, no shipping moved through the Ports of San Francisco and Oakland, Calif.

The PMA hit back with a cease-and-desist arbitration award and is now suing the union in federal court. According to Thomas, the PMA has desecrated the memory of Dr. King, and is now attempting to squelch the most basic right and self-expression of any worker in a capitalist economy, the right to withhold labor power.

However, the San Francisco Labor Council quickly called for "a mass mobilization of all Bay Area Labor Councils and the California AFL-CIO

to rally in front of PMA headquarters in San Francisco on Monday, April 25, to demand that the court suit be dropped and that the vindictive lynch-mob procedures against the union in the arbitration be halted immediately."

On April 4th, this writer interviewed Thomas, a former ILWU Local 10 secretary-treasurer and current executive board member, about the historical and special relationship of his local with Dr. King

Cheryl LaBash: Why were Local 10 members moved to take this rank-and-file resistance?

Clarence Thomas: What a lot of young trade unionists do not know is that Dr. King was in Memphis to support sanitation workers; 90% were African American and the union wasn't recognized. They were making rock-bottom salaries, and the workers were arbitrarily sent home, losing pay. The equipment was antiquated and poorly maintained. In 1968 two sanitation workers were killed, swallowed up by packers. There was no workers' compensation. Each family got a month's pay and $500 toward burial costs.

It is ironic that we are facing the same conditions as public sector and private sector workers today.

On Sept. 21, 1967, Dr. King was made an honorary member of ILWU Local 10. He was in the Bay Area to launch a concert headlined by Harry Belafonte and Joan Baez to raise funds for the Southern Christian Leadership Conference. Dr. King spoke at our union meeting, and that connection with Dr. King is incredibly significant for our local.

ILWU Local 10 has responded to

the attacks on collective bargaining and on public workers in the state of Wisconsin by volunteering not to go to work today. Ours is the most militant rank-and-file, bottom-up union in the country. Local 10 is the social conscience of the ILWU.

We have a responsibility to step forward and take action to have a strong union and continue the tradition of Harry Bridges and other founders of the ILWU who believed the union has a commitment to the fight for social justice and the survival of the working class. Or should I say the emancipation of the working class.

This writer also interviewed Local 10 member and former president, Trent Willis, who explained the April 4 action by his local's members.

Trent Willis: We understand the attack on Local 10 and how serious it is. We face an all-out assault on unions in this country where union membership is down to 10% or fewer of organized workers. The effects are starting to show.

Dr. Martin Luther King is a hero. He showed the connection between the union movement and the social movement. When the brothers and sisters start putting it together, we are stronger. Working and unemployed, everyone is a worker. We need to make them not be unemployed, but to have jobs.

I am proud I stood by in honor of the Wisconsin workers. I am glad my brothers and sisters stood with me. The fight is not over. This is either a new beginning or an end of the labor movement, as we know it.

Abridged from WW, April 21, 2011.

Defend Solidarity Actions
Defend ILWU Local 10 against boss' attacks

Letter from Jack Heyman, for the Committee to Defend ILWU Local 10

Brothers and Sisters,

Maritime employers are attempting to intimidate ILWU Local 10 whose solidarity actions time and again have proven it to be the moral compass of the U.S. labor movement. The Pacific Maritime Association filed a court suit demanding "damages" citing the anti-labor Taft-Hartley Act of 1947, which bans solidarity actions by unions. If employers can victimize Local 10, it will have a chilling effect on solidarity actions in the labor movement.

Robert B. Reich, former Secretary of Labor: "In my view, the SF Longshore Union's action in support of Wisconsin state workers was entirely consistent with the basic principle of union solidarity." (April 29, 2011)

Jim Cavanaugh, President of South Central Federation of Labor, consisting of 95 labor unions representing some 45,000 union members in the greater Madison, Wisconsin, area: "At our monthly meeting, the delegates by unanimous vote, directed me to convey to Local 10 our heartfelt thank you for the solidarity your members showed on April 4.

Whether it's racist apartheid in South Africa, imperialist war in Iraq, or fascist plutocracy in Wisconsin, Local 10, over and over again, shows us "What a Union [should] look like!! Please convey our appreciation to your members and kick some PMA ass on April 25."

ILWU Local 10's history

A video made by Kazmi Torri of the Labor Video Project (lvpsf@igc.org) "ILWU Struggles:1984-2010"

chronicles the history of ILWU Local 10's solidarity actions beginning with the 1984 San Francisco anti-apartheid boycott of the Nedlloyd Kemberley, a ship loaded with cargo from South Africa. Nelson Mandela credited this action by ILWU Local 10, with sparking the anti-apartheid movement in the U.S. The video shows longshoremen Leo Robinson, Larry Wright, Howard Keylor and then-boatman Jack Heyman addressing the mass picket of anti-apartheid activists at Pier 80, SF.

It contains dramatic footage of ILWU's Inlandboatmen's Union 1987 strike against Crowley Maritime and the march by boatmen and longshoremen, despite armed police, to chase scabs off a barge unloading scab cargo in Redwood City, California. The SF Chronicle reported that this one-day Bay Area port shutdown and picket reflected shades of the militant 1934 maritime strike for the union hiring hall.

Bonnie Weiss and Bill Doggett, center, celebrate the 111th Birthday of the honorary ILWU member Paul Robeson in 2009.
Photo: Bill Doggett Archive on Race and Performing Arts

The global nature of trade and the power of international labor solidarity is shown in the 1999 anti-WTO protests in Seattle; and the Neptune Jade ship boycott action in the Port of Oakland in solidarity with the Liverpool dockers' dispute of 1996-98.

The ILWU closed all West Coast ports as Local 10 led a march of 25,000 protesters to demand freedom for political prisoner Mumia Abu-Jamal on Penn.'s death row in 1999. This action along with ILWU's defense of Angela Davis in the 1970s, was the first stop work action for a U.S. political prisoner since the International Labor campaign for Italian anarchists Sacco and Vanzetti in the 1920s.

In the 2000-2001 Charleston, S.C. longshore struggle, Local 10 was the first union to come to their defense. Facing state riot police, Black longshoremen defended their picket lines demanding a union contract with Nordana Lines, which had attempted to go non-union after 25 years.

In 2002, Pacific Maritime Association, locked out longshore workers in all West Coast ports during contract talks. Militant longshore picketlines in the Ports of Seattle was led by Rudy Finney and in Oakland by Trent Willis. Then, President Bush invoked the Taft-Hartley Act, at the behest of Democrat Senator Feinstein, forcing longshoremen back to work under the employers' conditions.

In 2003, anti-war protesters and longshoremen were shot by Oakland police. The UN Human Rights Commission characterized this police attack approved by Mayor Jerry

Brown of Oakland, later California Governor, as the most violent police repression since the start of the war. Nine longshoremen and scores of protesters were seriously injured.

The City of Oakland paid out settlements of over $2,000,000 for police brutality. ILWU attorneys cited a history of police violence against longshore workers going back to the '34 strike and won a first-ever police brutality claim for a union, awarding $10,000 in the suit for Local 10.

Courthouse protests in 2007, against port security and the police assault on two Black Local 10 longshore brothers, Jason Ruffin and Aaron Harrison, are well documented in, Tori's video. ILWU Local 54 of Stockton joined Local 10 and Local 34 at the rally. President Ken Riley of the Charleston longshore union, no stranger to police attacks addressed the rally. Leo Robinson proudly called ILWU a rank-and-file, "bottom up" not a "top down" union. He questioned why the International officers weren't present at the rally to defend ILWU members against police attacks.

On May Day 2008, the "No Peace, No Work" action initiated by Local 10 demanded an end to the imperialist wars in Afghanistan and Iraq. Vietnam veterans Rudy Finney of Seattle and Steve Fyten of San Francisco spoke passionately for Local 10's Caucus resolution for a 24 hour stoppage. All West Coast ports were shutdown in defiance of Taft-Hartley as maritime employers impotently decryed this historic action as "illegal" . The May Day march was led by longshore Local 10's Drill Team, along the Embarcadero, site of the Big Strike of '34. marching to the tune of "The Internationale" in the first-ever strike against a U.S. imperialist war.

In 2010, the anti-Israeli protest in which Local 10 longshoremen honored a picket line against a Zim Lines ship, protesting the Israeli army slaughter of 9 aid workers aboard the Mavi Marmara was another first in U.S. labor struggles.

Retired longshoreman Howard Keylor compared this anti-Zionist action to the anti-apartheid ship boycott in 1984. It was Durban, South Africa dock workers who organized the first strike to protest the Israeli killings in Gaza a year earlier.

At the rally for the 24 hour work stoppage Local 10's Clarence Thomas exclaimed, "Today, what you witnessed was the current young membership of ILWU Local 10 answering the call. We claim no easy victory and tell no lies! Solidarity with the Palestinian people! Solidarity with the working class of the world!"

The video ends with the 2010 Oscar Grant rally to protest the police killing of the young Black butchers apprentice shot in the back by transit cops in Oakland. Clarence Thomas proclaims to the 1,000 strong rally in the rain, "This is not just a rally to protest! It's rally of resistance!"

Missing from the tape are two key actions: First, Local 10's refusal, in 1978, to load bombs to the military dictatorship of General Pinochet in Chile which had crushed the workers movement in a bloody military coup. Although no film footage could be found for the video, Herb Mills, then Local 10's business agent is the acknowledged organizer of that courageous action.

And secondly, after the video was made, the April 4, 2011, solidarity actions with Wisconsin workers called by the AFL-CIO which organized workers in 1,000 demonstrations across the country to protest government attacks against public sector workers. Local 10 longshoremen were the only workers that did not work for 24 hours that day, shutting down Port of Oakland. In San Francisco, construction workers walked off the job before the end of the day shift.

The Committee to Defend ILWU Local 10 has been formed by the San Francisco Labor Council and Local 10 to build a united front defense campaign of trade unions, labor organizations, civil liberties groups, antiwar organizations, immigrant rights groups and community organizations. Defend union solidarity, Defend Local 10!

Jack Heyman, for the Committee to Defend ILWU Local 10
April 20, 2011

On Oct. 4, 2007, upwards of 250 demonstrators rallied outside the Yolo County Courthouse in Woodland, California to protest the vicious police assault on two Black dock workers from San Francisco who were working in the Port of Sacramento in August. Workers came from Bay Area Local 10 while others traveled from every ILWU Local in northern California and Portland, Oregon. Ken Riley International Vice President of the ILA, from Charleston, South Carolina, joined the protest. They were joined by local community activists denouncing the brutal actions of the West Sacramento police .

Caption abridged from the October, 2007 Internationalist . Photo: Indymedia

ILWU will Shut Down all Bay Area ports

Jack Heyman

Emotions ran high when longshoremen at their July membership meeting were addressed by Cephus Johnson, the uncle of Oscar Grant, the young Black man who was killed by a cop at the Fruitvale BART station in Oakland on New Year's Day, 2009. Recounting the sidewalk mural in the front of the hiring hall near Fisherman's Wharf that depicts two strikers lying face down with the inscription:

"POLICE MURDER. MEN KILLED – SHOT IN BACK. POLICE MURDER"

He appealed to the union to support justice for his slain nephew. He said, "That mural shook me because that's exactly what happened to Oscar."

It got even hotter in the union hall when Jack Bryson took the mike. He is the father of two of Oscar Grant's friends terrorized by police at the train station as they sat handcuffed and helpless watching their friend die and hearing him moan. Bryson reported that police were calling for a rally the following Monday in the lily-white suburb of Walnut Creek demanding that Johannes Mehserle the convicted killer cop go free. He asked the union members to join Oscar Grant supporters to protest the cop rally and they did; outnumbering the 100 or so pro-Mehserle demonstrators by three to one.

The New Year's Day horror scene was videotaped by other young train passengers and broadcast on YouTube and TV news across the country. Grant, the father of a four year-old girl worked as a butcher apprentice at Farmer Joe's Supermarket nearby on Fruitvale Avenue. The litany of police killings of innocent

young Black and Latino men has evoked a public outcry in California. Yet, when it comes to killer cops, especially around election time, with both the Democratic and Republican parties espousing law and order, the mainstream media either expunges or whitewashes the issue.

Angered by the pro-police rallies and news coverage calling for killer cop Mehserle's freedom, Local 10 of the International Longshore and Warehouse Union has called for a labor and community rally October 23rd in Oakland to demand justice for Oscar Grant and the jailing of killer cops. Bay Area ports will Shut Down that day to stand with the Black community and others against the scourge of police brutality.

Anthony Leviege, a longshore union rally organizer said, "Many unions, including the San Francisco and Alameda Labor Councils, have endorsed and are mobilizing for the rally. They see the need in the current economic crisis to build unity with the community to defend jobs, public education, health care and housing for all. And unions defending Black and Brown youth against police brutality is fundamental to that unity.

In this race-caste society there's nothing more controversial than a white cop convicted of killing a young Black man like Oscar Grant…

or of a Black man like Mumia Abu-Jamal, framed by a corrupt and racist judicial system, accused of killing a white police officer when the opposite was the case. Jamal was nearly murdered by the police. His "crime" was that he didn't die on the spot, as Oscar Grant did. Mumia, the Frederick Douglass of our time, exposes the hypocrisy of democracy in America while fighting for his life on death row in Pennsylvania. His possibly final hearing is set for November 9th. Killer cops belong in jail, their victims (those who survive like Mumia) should go free. But that's not how justice in capitalist America works. The racist heritage of slavery is still with us.

Labor must defend minorities against racist police attacks

The police murder of two strikers provoked the 1934 San Francisco General Strike. Seven maritime workers in all were killed by police in West Coast ports during strike for the union hiring hall. Every July 5, Bloody Thursday, all ports on the West Coast are Shut Down to honor the labor martyrs. It's a living legacy that burns deep in the hearts of longshore and other maritime workers.

Some have asked, what's the connection between unions and the killing of a young Black man? Plenty, according to Richard Washington, an Oakland longshoreman. He recalled the history of the longshore union and its struggle against the favoritism and racism of the "shape-up" hiring system that preceded the union hiring hall. At start of the 1934 S.F. Mari-

General Strike community march at Port of Oakland Nov. 2, 2011.

Anthony Leviege of Local 10 speaks out during the Occupy Shut Down of the Port of Oakland on Dec. 12, 2011: 'People came out here at 5 a.m. There are all kinds of working people. Remember it's Monday not Saturday. People gave up a day's pay. Occupy didn't start this, the longshore workers didn't start this. The situation came about because

people are losing homes and losing jobs millions of people are angry and fed up.'

Photo: Labor Video
tinyurl.com/46ygn7b

time Strike, Harry Bridges, head of the militant Strike Committee, he said, appealed to the Black community. Strikers implored Blacks to support the strike and vowed to share work on the waterfront after their victory in the midst of the Great Depression when jobs were scarce, not unlike today. Blacks were integrated on the docks, a shining example being set by the San Francisco longshore local, and the union has been fighting against racist attacks and for working class unity since then.

ILWU longshoremen have given up a day's wages time and again to show solidarity with dock workers in Liverpool, England, Charleston, South Carolina and Australia and to protest with dock actions on moral issues of the day like apartheid in South Africa, the wars in Iraq and Afghanistan, in defense of innocent death row prisoner Mumia Abu-Jamal and recently the Israeli military killing of civilians bringing aid to Gaza by boat.

Now, the ILWU is calling on unions to link up with community organizations under their banner, "An Injury to One is an Injury to All." From all accounts it's a clarion call that will muster thousands fed up with the economic crisis and the scapegoating of minorities.

Abridged CounterPunch, Oct. 18, 2010.

Stop Police Terror

Disrupt Global Trade

May Day
Port of Oakland

Labor Against Police Terror

May Day celebrates uniting the struggles of workers and all oppressed people fighting for justice

Rally and march with Oakland's Longshoremen as they stop work and shut down the Port of Oakland against police killings!

The labor force has played an integral part in social justice movements throughout United States history and beyond. ILWU Local 10 in particular, has been at the forefront of many monumental events including, but not imited to the Big Strike of 1934, the 1984 Anti-Apartheid action against South Africa, and the 2010 Oscar Grant rally and port shut down.

Police terrorism in the United States is out of control. We have witnessed an endless onslaught of police brutality and police killings of innocent and unarmed people. These assaults have been mainly directed towards the Black community. We as union and non-union workers alike cannot standby and become desensitized to these great injustices.

9AM RALLY at the Port of Oakland
Middle Harbor Road APL Berth 62
* Parking & Shuttles from Middle Harbor Shoreline Park: 2777 Middle Harbor Road

10AM MARCH to Oscar Grant Plaza

12 NOON RALLY at Oscar Grant Plaza
Oakland City Hall at 14th & Broadway

Sponsoring community organizations include:

Onyx Organizing Committee, The Alan Blueford Center For Justice, Anti Police-Terror Project, Community Ready Corps Black Power Network, A.N.S.W.E.R. Coalition Bay Area, AROC: Arab Resource & Organizing Center, Oakland Sin Fronteras, Workers World, Stop Mass Incarceration Network, Transport Workers Solidarity, Love Not Blood Campaign, Oscar Grant Committee, Oakland Socialist, International Socialist Organization - Northern California

Longshore workers call for anti-racist unity in their ranks

Cheryl LaBash

Early on Sept. 8, 2011, hundreds of longshore workers charged through the gates of the new, contested grain export terminal at Longview, Wash., and dumped corn from a 107 car train attempting a first shipment. This struggle in the Pacific Northwest has brewed since the multinational conglomerate EGT began constructing the $200 million facility two years ago. It only became "newsworthy" when the corporate media bashed workers as "violent."

The bosses' challenge to the ILWU Coastwide agreement with the Port of Longview endangers the union itself. In January EGT sued the Port of Longview. Its suit charged that EGT is not bound by the Port agreement in effect since 1934, recognizing the ILWU on Port property.

The hearing on the suit is not scheduled until Spring 2012. Nevertheless, EGT had the grain terminal and two facilities in Montana built to transport the 2011 fall harvest. EGT intends to use the port without waiting for the court's judgment and, if it can, without the ILWU.

In the Spring the union held rallies and actions, which included 100 union civil-disobedience arrests inside the terminal on July 11. Negotiations with EGT failed. In July longshore workers turned back a train. By massing on the tracks, the workers successfully rerouted the corn shipment to an ILWU-worked terminal in Vancouver, Wash.

The Burlington Northern Santa Fe railroad company suspended further shipments until Sept. 7, citing safety reasons. Then longshore women and men again stood on the tracks

blocking the train, first in downtown Vancouver and then on Longview port property.

This time, armed with a temporary restraining order against ILWU locals in Vancouver and Longview, the courts and police weighed in for EGT. A federal judge had issued the order the week before the corporate offensive to get the terminal operational. On Sept. 7 riot-geared cops routed the workers, arresting 19, including at least three women, for trespass.

On Sept. 8 rank-and-file longshore workers refused to stand back when so much was at stake for their union and the entire working class. The corn was dumped, and ILWU members up and down the Washington state coast walked off the job, halting shipping for eight hours.

The ILWU's work is international trade. For the union to succeed, two things are required: international working-class solidarity with workers around the globe and not buying into anti-foreign, big-business propaganda. Capitalism is global.

The driving force behind EGT is a U.S.-based giant international corporation, Bunge Limited, that partnered with global specialists to create a profitable, direct, high-tech export line from the wheat fields of the upper Midwest through Longview and then by ship to India, China and the vast markets in Asia.

PRNewswire, Dec. 10 reports, "EGT's partners are all leaders in the international grain trade and include Bunge; ... ITOCHU, which is a large marketer of grain and food products in Japan; and STX Pan Ocean, which is one of the world's leading shipping

companies of agricultural products."

News media cite the St. Louis-based "majority partner" Bunge NA, the "North American Free Trade" subsidiary in Canada, U.S. and Mexico. But they don't reveal that Bunge Limited "is a leading agribusiness and food company with integrated operations that circle the globe, stretching from the farm field to the retail shelf." Bunge Limited reported $2.4 billion in profits in 2010.

In 1999, Bunge moved its world headquarters to N.Y., to be "closer to world financial centers" in Wall Street. (www.bunge.com)

To supply the 8 million metric ton annual capacity of the Longview grain terminal, EGT simultaneously built two grain-loading facilities in Montana, all to be up and running in time for this fall's harvest.

According to the PRNewswire release, "These state-of-the-art facilities will be built on the BNSF train mainline, ensuring efficient movement from farmers in Montana to vessels and finally to the consumer.

"Each high-speed shuttle loader is capable of loading 110-car unit train in under ten hours. The facilities are also designed to provide farmers with fast weighing, grading and dumping, offering best-in-class cycle times. In addition, the facilities will be able to store about 800,000 bushels apiece." Anticipated jobs: only four to six workers at each facility!

Rank-and-file ILWU sources estimate that a grain train that currently requires two and a half days to unload can be processed in less than half a day in the new Longview terminal. The Billings Gazette reports, "EGT hopes to fill shuttles, get the rail cars rolling to Longview and then get STX freighters loaded and sailing, all in four days or less." (Aug. 17)

EGT wants to eliminate more than the 50 jobs at Longview. Its management yearns to make all port jobs high-tech, low-pay, non-union and under corporate control.

To sidestep charges of union-busting, EGT recently signed an operating agreement with a company that employs subcontracted workers represented by a smaller, different union.

Many small unions are not as strong as one big industry wide union, especially one like the ILWU, which has rank-and-file initiative.

If EGT successfully eliminates the ILWU from the 50 jobs at Longview, this will increase the pressure at other facilities and processes, automated or not, to bring in and exploit workers without union pay, benefits and protection. All the corporations will race to get that extra-profit edge over their competitors, just as other grain terminals are upgrading to compete with Longview or face losing market share if they don't.

The ILA, which represents longshore workers on the East Coast, and the International Transportation Federation, a worldwide confederation of transport unions, have sent strong statements of support to the ILWU about the Longview struggle. Washington and Oregon state AFL-CIOs have sent resolutions supporting the ILWU in the jurisdictional dispute.

The ILWU is uniquely positioned at this time to resist the assault because its members handle all the goods and materials shipped into or out of the West Coast. The key to its strength is the ILWU's history of

The Nov. 2, 2011, Occupy Wall Street Port Shut Down in Oakland, called EGT: 'Wall Street West.'   WW photo: Bill Bowers

internationalism and working-class solidarity based on its slogan: An injury to one is an injury to all.

The 1934 San Francisco General Strike forged this Coastwide union. At that time ILWU leader Harry Bridges personally promised the African American community that in return for their support for the strike, Black workers would no longer be excluded from work on the docks.

The union tradition is bottom-up leadership and initiative from the rank-and-file. Local 10 members exhibited this initiative by putting down their tools for 24 hours last April 4 to stand with public workers under attack in Wisconsin and other states as they remembered the Rev. Dr. Martin Luther King Jr., an honorary member of Local 10, had been assassinated while standing in solidarity with the striking Memphis sanitation workers.

Unfortunately, Harry Bridges' anti-racist example was not embraced in the Pacific Northwest. In Oregon a history of racism and exclusion laws not only discouraged Black workers from coming to the region, but tried to make sure those who toiled in the World War II shipyards didn't stay.

Black workers came into the ILWU local in Portland under court order in 1964, 30 years after the ILWU won control of hiring and working conditions in the ports up and down the West Coast. Portland's metropolitan area includes the port in Vancouver, Wash., Longview, 50 miles away.

A rank-and-file Pacific Northwest ILWU member characterized the Longview struggle as a "major battle." The worker said that in this industry, "We have no other choice than to fight together for our jobs. But we still have issues we need to resolve in-house. ... "It is a must-win battle for the ILWU, from my perspective. If not, it shows a sign of weakness in this area. I think that the ILWU leadership is not fighting as aggressively as we need to. We should be more engaged in our fight. Put on pressure and don't wait until it gets worse.

"When we look at history, the ILWU victory has always been possible once we have the community and other organizations involved. Stick to the strategic system that has been victorious with the ILWU.

"In the Pacific Northwest the union needs some dialogue about opening opportunity for people in the community so we can get support from the community."

As recently as 2006, the issues faced by African American and women workers in the Pacific Northwest were so pressing that ILWU Local 10, based in the Oakland/San Francisco area, withheld its pro-rata payment to the International Union in protest. This resulted in the establishment of Diversity Committees in all locals "to work on the issues of diversity, tolerance and solidarity across racial and gender lines and to make recommendations to the local officers, executive board and membership."

Abridged from WW, Sept. 22, 2011.

Occupy Oakland supports movement for jobs, shutting ports

Solidarity statement written by Clarence Thomas, ILWU Local 10 member and MWM leader, for the People's Assembly meeting held at Hostos Community College in the Bronx, N.Y., on Nov. 5, 2011

Thomas in the financial district of San Francisco with Jake Whiteside and Bryon Jacobs from Local 21 in Longview, Washington.

Occupy's solidarity action in support of the ILWU at EGT in Longview, Washington, on Dec. 12, 2011.   WW photo: Bill Bowers

Greetings and solidarity,

I am exhilarated from the recent historical events here in Oakland. This has been one of the strongest examples of the power of the people in the U.S. and the 21st century. It is difficult to imagine that in one week's time a call for a general strike, **A Day of Action** by the Occupy Oakland General Assembly, could have generated the overwhelming response from the people of Oakland.

They say a picture is worth a thousand words and most certainly the thousands that marched through the fifth largest port in the country speak volumes while ... organized labor, which only makes up 7.2% of the private sector workers, has been incapable of calling for a general strike in response to the unrelenting war on the working class by the ruling class. It is indeed remarkable how rank-and-file union members in the City of Oakland responded so positively to the call.

The city administrator of Oakland, on Oct. 28, 2011, issued a statement that SEIU Local 1021 had been authorized to utilize various types of leave to participate in the stop work action on Nov. 2. This offer was extended to other city workers. It is an example of how this call made by the General Assembly of Occupy Oakland Movement resonated with workers in the City of Oakland.

Although Nov. 2, 2011, fell short of being a full general strike in the truest sense of the word, the City of Oakland and the fifth largest port in the U.S. were SHUT DOWN! Only essential services continued to be provided.

In conclusion, I hope that the action of the Occupy Oakland movement can be duplicated in cities around the country and that issues such as jobs and the Occupy 4 Jobs movement can be put front and center at the Occupy movement.

'Solidarity of labor above all else'

Interview with longshore workers Clarence Thomas and Leo Robinson

As pressure builds for the Dec. 12, 2011, West Coast Port Shut down, the capitalist owners and their media began a battle of ideas to blunt this powerful threat to their profits and control, even for a day.

Two ILWU members, Clarence Thomas, who is a third-generation longshoreman in Oakland, and Leo Robinson, who is now retired, spoke to Cheryl LaBash. Both men have held elected office in ILWU Local 10 and have been key labor activists during their years of work in the ports.

Cheryl LaBash: The Nov. 21, ILWU Longshore Coast Committee memorandum states, "Any public demonstration is not a 'picket line' under the Pacific Coast Longshore and Clerk's Agreement. ...

Remember, public demonstrations are public demonstrations, not 'picket lines.' Only labor unions picket as referenced in the contract." What is your reaction?

Clarence Thomas: A picket line is a public demonstration, whether called by organized labor or not. It is legitimate. There are established protocols in these situations. To suggest to longshoremen that they shouldn't follow them demands clarification. It is one thing to state for the record that the union is not involved, but another thing to erase the historical memory of ILWU's traditions and practices included in the Ten Guiding Principles of the ILWU adopted at the 1953 biennial convention in San Francisco.

Leo Robinson: The International has taken the position somehow that the contract is more important than not only defending our interest in terms of this EGT, grain terminal jurisdictional dispute, but having a

connection to the Occupy Wall Street (OWS) movement in that when you go through the Ten Guiding Principles of the ILWU, we're talking about labor unity. Does that include the teachers? Does that include state, county and municipal workers? Those questions need to be analyzed as to who supports whom. The Occupy movement is not separate and apart from the labor movement.

CT: Labor is now officially part of the Occupy movement. That has happened. The recent *New York Times* article done by Steven Greenhouse on Nov. 9, 2011 is called 'Standing arm in arm."

The Teamsters have been supported by the OWS against Sotheby's auction house. OWS has been supportive of Communication Workers in its struggle with Verizon. Mary Kay Henry, International President of the Service Employees, has called for expanding the Occupy movement by taking workers to Washington, D.C., to occupy Washington particularly Congress and congressional hearings demanding 15 million jobs by Jan. 1.

LR: There was the occupation in Madison, Wis. That was labor led. People are trying to confuse the issue by saying we are somehow separated from the Occupy movement. More than anything else the Occupy movement is a direct challenge or raises the question of the rights of capital as opposed to the rights of the worker. I don't understand that the contract supersedes the just demands of the labor movement. It says so right here in the **TEN GUIDING PRINCIPLES** of the ILWU. See page 253.

Number 4 is very clear. Very clear. **"To help any worker in distress**

must be a daily guide in the life of every trade union and its individual members. Labor solidarity means just that. Unions have to accept the fact that solidarity of labor stands above all else, including even the so-called sanctity of the contract. We cannot adopt for ourselves the policies of union leaders who insist that because they have a contract, their members are compelled to perform work, even behind a picket line. Every picket line must be respected as if it is our own." It says picket line. It doesn't say union picket line. It says picket line.

CT: Only 7.2% of private sector workers have union representation today, the lowest since 1900. Facing a critical moment, the labor movement has been re-energized by the Occupy Wall Street movement.

LR: Any number of times this Local 10 has observed picket lines, including Easter Sunday 1977, when the community put up a picket line at Pier 27 to picket South African cargo. Longshoremen observed that picket line for two days. So, I don't understand how all of a sudden, the sanctity of the contract outweighs the need to demonstrate solidarity. It just does not compute. It doesn't make sense.

CL: What were the similarities between that event and what is going on now with the Occupy movement?

CT: The first action against South African apartheid was a community picket line. It was not authorized by the union. It was a community picket line from start to finish.

LR: It was about 5,000 people out on the Embarcadero, eastern waterfront and roadway of the Port of San Francisco, for two days running a community picket line opposing

December 2011.

South African apartheid. Local 10 officers took the position that it was an unsafe situation and members were not going to cross that picket line. It was ruled as such by the arbitrator.

CL: Who determines whether a situation is safe or unsafe?

LR: We have never waited for the employer to declare what is safe or unsafe. It is always the union that moves first. We don't ask the employers what is safe or unsafe. They wouldn't give a damn one way or the other as long as they got their ship worked. If the police have to escort you in or out, that is patently saying it is unsafe. What if someone decides to throw a rock while you're being escorted in by the police? Does it make it hurt any less? A longshore worker determines what is safe for him or her, on the job and off.

CT: Our members have been hurt by the police and so has the OWS movement. In 2003, when we were standing by at a picket, police shot our members with wooden bullets. In Longview, Wash., at the EGT Grain Terminal, ILWU members and their families have been hurt by the police.

We don't want the police to do anything for us.

CL: What is happening at the grain terminal in Longview?

CT: Our union is at an historical juncture. Our jurisdiction is being challenged up and down the coast, the issue of logs and Local 10 and use of 'robotics.' There has been nothing like this since 1934. If ILWU members don't honor the community picket lines, it will cause an irreparable breach with the community. If the ILWU can't support the community, why should the community support the ILWU in 2014 contract negotiations or when the new grain agreement is up next year? Who knows what the employer has up their sleeve when they demanded only a one-year contract?

LR: Grain work provides 30% of our welfare contributions. Who knows … let us say that EGT is successful? It will open the door for other grain operators to try to work anybody.

CL: Aren't the ports private?

CT: These ports are the people's ports. Ports belong to the people of the Pacific Coast. The money came from the taxpayers in California, Oregon and Washington. EGT was subsidized by the Port of Longview. So the people have the right to go down there and protest how their tax dollars have been ripped off.

CL: Wall Street is in New York City. What do the West Coast ports have to do with that?

LR: To show you the link, last year in *The Dispatcher,* a sister from Local 10 was foreclosed on. I am certain she's not the only one.

CT: Fifty-one percent of Stevedoring Services of America is owned by Goldman Sachs. EGT is a multinational conglomerate trying to control the distribution of food products around the world. The face of Wall Street is in the ports.

CL: Any closing comments?

CT: The ILWU is not some special interest group. We are a rank-and-file militant, democratic union that has a long history of being in the vanguard of the social justice and labor movement.

We don't cross community picket lines. When people begin to do so they have completely turned their backs on the ILWU Ten Guiding Principles. Is it coincidental that Harry Bridges' name has not been asserted in relation to the OWS movement and the history of militancy? Is it an accident? How can we not talk about Harry Bridges? That is how we got what we have today.

Clarence Thomas is past secretary-treasurer of Local 10 and co-chair of MWMM, which was initiated by Local 10 and supported by the ILWU Longshore Caucus.

Leo Robinson is retired and co-founder of African American Longshore Coalition. He is a former member of the Local 10 executive board, a national convener of the MWMM and its major benefactor.

Abridged from WW, Dec. 6, 2011.

Solidarity caravan fights for ILWU

Terri Kay

ILWU rank-and-file members and the Occupy movements in Longview, Wash.; Portland, Ore.; Seattle; Oakland; Los Angeles and other West Coast cities are organizing to blockade a grain ship arriving in Longview sometime in January. This ship is supposed to be loaded by a non-ILWU crew with cargo from the new EGT export terminal. The date won't be known until three to four days in advance.

There is a war going on against dockworkers and their families in Longview, Wash. Members of ILWU Local 21 have been arrested, beaten and their homes raided. They are fighting to protect their union jobs against EGT, which is trying to break the ILWU's coastwide contract, established after the 1934 West Coast Maritime Strike and the San Francisco General Strike.

EGT and its majority partner, Bunge NA, want to bust the ILWU, one of the most militant, progressive unions in the U.S. EGT has broken the union's contract with the Port of Longview and is using scab labor at its export grain terminal. On Sept. 8, hundreds of angry Longshore workers charged through the gates, and EGT claims that grain was dumped from a 107 car train and a cyclone fence was torn down.

This struggle is occurring at a time when national union membership has dropped to a 70 year low of 11.9%, with 6.9% of private sector workers in unions. EGT's actions are part of the ruling-class attack to drive us all to the bottom. Even with low union membership rates, national median weekly wages for union members are $917, compared to $717 for workers not in unions.

The 1% not only wants to take away that extra $200 from the remaining 14.7 million unionized workers, but wants to destroy all unions, especially the militant ILWU, to keep us from organizing to take back what is rightfully ours.

EGT, a joint venture between U.S.-based Bunge NA, Japanese-based Itochu and Korean-based STX Pan Ocean, is part of the 1%. If EGT is successful in its attack on the ILWU in Longview, that will have a ripple effect on all port workers on the West Coast.

The ILWU is a democratic, bottom-up union with an activist rank-and-file. It has a strong history of support for community issues, standing up against apartheid South Africa, against the war in Iraq, and for the Wisconsin workers' struggle against union busting. Bay Area ILWU Local 10 backed community protests after the police killing of Oscar Grant in 2009. They honored picket lines in Occupy Oakland's Nov. 2, 2011 General Strike and the Dec. 12 West Coast Port Shut Down.

Caravans and support actions are being organized up and down the West Coast, nationally and internationally, to greet the STX ship coming to be loaded with scab grain. ILWU Local 10 has pledged support for Local 21's struggle against EGT and their union-busting drive and has funded a bus to Longview. The San Francisco Labor Council has endorsed the solidarity caravan.

Individuals and organizations are asked to support this critical working-class struggle by joining the caravan or other solidarity actions.

Bunge NA, one of EGT's parent companies, is headquartered in St. Louis, Mo., with offices in Washington, D.C. and White Plains, N.Y. If you are in these areas, ask your local Occupy group to organize solidarity actions in conjunction with the ship's arrival in Longview. EGT also has facilities in Chester and Kintyre Flats, Mont. EGT is also building a high-capacity shuttle train loader in Carter, Mont. Bunge has locations all over the Midwest and South.

Abridged from WW, Jan. 4 2012.

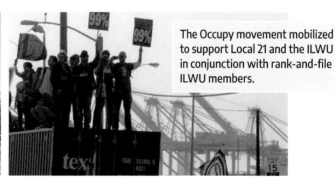

The Occupy movement mobilized to support Local 21 and the ILWU in conjunction with rank-and-file ILWU members.

Support builds for longshore workers

Cheryl LaBash

The San Francisco Labor Council on Jan. 9, 2012, unanimously condemned military escort for the union-busting international grain and food cartel EGT, headed by Bunge Ltd. at the Port of Longview, Wash.

In a Jan. 2 resolution, the executive board of the Cowlitz-Wahkiakum Central Labor Council unanimously called on "friends of labor and the 99% everywhere to come to the aid of ILWU Local 21 ... and participate in a community and labor protest in Longview, Wash. of the first EGT grain ship."

International grain cartel EGT is attempting to break a Coastwide grain terminal agreement, held by the ILWU, that was won after years of militant struggle by the union.

Occupy movements up and down the Pacific Coast, including a caravan from Oakland, Calif., nearly 700 miles to the south, are already organizing a quick-response mobilization to "meet and greet" this latest provocation, supported by the San Francisco Labor Council. The exact date of the ship's arrival is being kept secret by EGT in an attempt to deter protest.

Labor for Palestine has also issued a statement supporting the ILWU.

Supporters are undaunted by ILWU International President Bob McEllrath's report, in a Jan. 3 letter to members, that EGT has enlisted an "armed" U.S. Coast Guard escort, using small vessels and helicopters, for that anticipated ship. This act of intimidation violates the Coast Guard's public procedures: "Under no circumstances will the Coast Guard exercise its authority for the purpose of favoring any party to a maritime labor controversy."

EGT is using the police, the courts, which have levied fines exceeding $300,000 on the union, the commercial media and now a Coast Guard armed escort to craft a false perception that EGT is the victim of militant longshore workers and their allies from the Occupy movement. In the background looms the threat of the 1947 Taft-Hartley Act, a tool of the 1% that tries to strip away any effective tool for unions to fight for justice.

In reality, it is the ILWU and the working class as a whole that are under attack in Longview. The same

conditions as in Longview spurred the state Capitol occupation and mass struggle in Wisconsin, which echoed the mass rebellions in Tunisia and Egypt's Tahrir Square.

EGT has sued the Port of Longview in federal court to resolve its issues. Although workers are told to file grievances, National Labor Relations Board complaints and lawsuits to "let the system" work, EGT isn't waiting for a court ruling in its favor. EGT aims to go to court with the ILWU's Coastwide agreement already shattered, clearing the path for the other international grain profiteers to oust the union when an unusually short, one-year contract ends later this year.

EGT is pushing the trains and now a ship to realize the profit from its $200 million investment in the port terminal, on public land and with public tax breaks. A equally massive EGT construction in Montana is to supply the terminal with the agribusiness giant's grain.

The labor movement in the Pacific Northwest continues to fight the anti-worker and blatantly anti-ILWU thrust of EGT at every step, from massive rallies protesting the construction of the terminal by low-wage workers to blocking the trains supplying grain. A joint leaflet by ILWU Locals 10 and 21 commends Longview sisters and brothers for "doing their part. Under a police reign of terror Local 21, with only 225 members, has 220 arrests for defending ILWU jurisdiction."

Juries acquitted defendants in the first two cases that came to trial.

Occupy Oakland General Strike march to the Port of Oakland on Nov. 2, 2011.
WW photo: Bill Bowers

On Dec. 19, ILWU member Shelly Ann Porter was found not guilty of fourth-degree assault against EGT manager Gerry Gibson. Porter had slapped Gibson's hand to prevent him from snapping an unwanted photo of her. On Dec. 30, ILWU member Kelly Palmer was acquitted of disorderly conduct in only 12 minutes. That same day, trespass charges were also dropped in nine cases resulting from protests on the train tracks.

But it was the Occupy Wall Street movement that lasered attention on this crucial West Coast labor battle and the port truckers' organizing efforts, as Goldman Sachs and EGT/Bunge Ltd., representatives of the 1%, waged war on these port workers. Occupy movements organized the massive community pickets that Shut Down and disrupted terminals up and down the West Coast on Dec. 12, as well as earlier actions interrupting the just-in-time profit stream at the Port of Oakland. The call from Occupy Oakland spoke plainly: "We want to disrupt the profits of the 1% and to show solidarity with those in the 99% who are under direct attack by corporate tyranny."

In the Longview call to action, Kyle Mackey, secretary-treasurer of the Cowlitz-Wahkiakum Counties Central Labor Council, quotes Harry Bridges, the leader of the 1934 San Francisco General Strike: "The most important word in the language of the working class is solidarity."

This is precisely what the 1947 Taft-Hartley Act tries to outlaw: The right of workers to join together for mutual aide against the capitalists.

Taft-Hartley leaves corporations free from any of the harsh penalties threatened and used against unions, including injunctions, jail, fines and "cooling off" periods, to let the bosses reorganize during a strike. It allows the bosses to get mutual aid from the banks and other corporations while unions are prohibited from mass picketing, sympathy strikes or secondary boycotts, for example, boycotting EGT parent company's oil products or other consumer goods. "It acts to frighten conservative leaders and also to restrain militants." See Chapter 15 on "Low Wage Capitalism" on lowwagecapitalism.com. However, the Occupy movement is a powerful working-class ally that is busting through the encrustation of laws and rulings that tip the class struggle scale overwhelmingly in favor of the rule of the 1%.

The ILWU's motto is "An injury to one is an injury to all." This unity underlies the strength of the ILWU, a rank-and-file, bottom up, democratic union, and its Coastwide contract. It is the strength of the historic Local 10, where Bridges won the 1934 San Francisco General Strike by bringing African American workers into the union as equals.

Local 10, the conscience of the ILWU and the labor movement, acts on the understanding that the issues of apartheid in South Africa, military dictatorships in Latin America, the U.S. wars of conquest in Iraq and Afghanistan, the killing of Gaza flotilla participants by the Israeli military, and the constant battle against racism and discrimination are working-class issues and must be addressed by the labor movement.

Abridged from WW, Jan. 11, 2012.

Struggle continues at Longview

Jack Heyman, Clarence Thomas Local 10 and Mike Fuqua Local 21 in Longview, Washington.

Terri Kay

As of Jan. 30, 2012, negotiations are still in process between the ILWU and the union-busting grain and food cartel, EGT. Rank-and-file workers from various ILWU locals on the West Coast, including Local 10 in the Bay Area, plus Occupy organizations, remain mobilized to defend the longshore workers in Longview, Wash. EGT had tried to break a Coastwide agreement with the ILWU, originally won after years of militant struggle.

ILWU Local 21 in Longview is under gag orders from the International not to talk about the pending agreement. Supporters remain on alert to mobilize quickly, should the negotiations go sour. For now, EGT's plan to load a ship using scab labor is on hold. It was the strength and militancy of Local 21, and the company's fear of an impending mobilization of thousands in the small town of Longview, that forced EGT to the table. The Occupy movements in Oakland, Calif.; Portland, Ore.; Seattle, Tacoma, Bellingham, and Olympia, Wash.; and many others, plus Local 10 and rank-and-file from many other ILWU locals, stand ready to give support if needed.

Abridged from WW, Feb. 4, 2012.

ILWU recognized at EGT grain terminal

Cheryl LaBash

On Feb. 1, 2012, ILWU Local 21 was officially recognized as the representative of workers at the state-of- the-art EGT, Export Grain Terminal, in Longview, Wash. According to an ILWU news release, "EGT and ILWU representatives signed a recognition agreement and committed to negotiate a collective bargaining agreement for all landside and shipside operations." Workers hired by EGT through the Local 21, Pacific Maritime Association hiring hall voted in a card-check process, affirming the ILWU.

A joint ILWU/EGT press statement announced the first ship will dock at the terminal on Feb. 7. ILWU members will work it. This ship is key to readying the terminal for full production which had been scheduled for the 2011 harvest.

The ship has been anchored four hours away from Longview for weeks, held back by the threat of a massive protest. ILWU rank-and-file members, the Occupy movement and workers across the country vowed to

Police attack ILWU pickets in Longview, Washington, Sept. 7, 2011, as they block grain train to the EGT facility. Byron Jacobs, in green cap, was arrested, along with 18 ILWU members. Despite federal injunction, the next day 800 union supporters seized the terminal.

Photo: Dawn Des Brisay/Flickr

block the massive carrier if there was any attempt to load the ship without ILWU workers.

Even the announcement that armed Coast Guard vessels would escort the ship failed to dampen the mobilization. Resolutions from the San Francisco Labor Council and N.C.'s United Electrical Local 150 and picket lines around the country condemned the threatened military intervention. Vivid memories of the militant demonstrations in Seattle at the 1999 World Trade Organization meeting no doubt helped spur the Washington governor to find a

solution to the standoff.

In November 2010, the international grain consortium EGT told the union it had "no need" of its services. The company prepared to open the facility, declaring war on the ILWU. This anti-labor challenge to the right of port workers to be represented by the ILWU, won in the 1934 longshore workers strike that led to the San Francisco General Strike, launched a mighty struggle.

Three months after EGT calculated it could shove the ILWU aside, the workers of Wisconsin occupied the State Capitol on Feb. 14, 2011.

Corine Thornton

Corine Thornton is the widow of Nate Thornton Local 34. She was a member of School of the Americas Watch. Currently, she is a member ILWU Bay Area Pensioner's Club. In 2018, when she was 96 years-old, Corine Thornton attended the Fort Point Gang's May Day celebration.

The Fort Point Gang was formed in 1978. It was organized by seaman Bill Bailey, former vice president Local 10, to honor labor leaders on the Left.

Nate Thornton was a veteran of the Abraham Lincoln Brigade made up of anti-fascist volunteers from different countries who fought against fascist forces in the Spanish Civil War, 1936-1938.

"Corine Thornton continues to fight for a better life."
–*The Dispatcher, Jan. 7, 2011.*　Photo: Clarence Thomas

In September, Occupy Wall Street encampments erupted, including all the port cities on the West Coast. The Occupy movement mobilized to support Local 21 in conjunction with rank-and-file ILWU members.

Washington Gov. Chris Gregoire, brokered the Jan. 27 agreement among EGT, the Port of Longview and the ILWU, that resulted in recognition of the ILWU. It specifies that the ILWU issue a statement urging "the public, including the Occupy movement … to cease and desist from any actions … directed against EGT."

During the pickets in Longview over the last six months, state and local police made at least 200 arrests. Four women arrested on Sept. 21 for

Byron Jacobs, a courageous young union leader and an officer of ILWU Local 21, was killed while doing a dangerous job on a EGT dock in June 2018. tinyurl.com/59kr6ta7

Read a story about Jacob's family's history, "Battle of Hayes Pond: The Lumbee and other American Indians ousted the KKK from Maxton, N.C., Jan. 18, 1958." tinyurl.com/ybclawlz

blocking a train loaded with grain bound for the EGT terminal were found not guilty. Others were acquitted, and 12 misdemeanor charges were dropped. The ILWU has called for all charges to be dropped.

Additional issues remain to be resolved in contract negotiations. More than $300,000 in fines against the union have not yet been lifted. *Abridged from WW, Feb 11, 2012.*

The day before the 2020 U.S. presidential election, I called Sadie Williams. The nation seemed to be at loose ends, but 96 year-old Sadie Williams, still quick-witted and with a voice as warm and forgiving as the waters of her native Galveston Bay, was reassuring me that things were good.

"I'm so happy," she said repeatedly, "that white people and Black people are talking to each other about these things. It's so important." But first, she wanted to talk about Cleophas' interest in golf.

"Cleophas was part of the Western States Golf Association. That opened up the sport for many Black people. You see, in his teens, he'd worked as a caddy back in Texarkana, where was able to observe much about the game."

"As a caddy, Cleophas was able to observe local white men interacting, who probably had a certain amount of wealth and power? He was observing the game of how men with power negotiated and made deals." Yes! He really studied it. You know,

Sadie Williams

Sadie Williams, Board of Directors ILWU Bay Area Pensioner's Club.

Black people are invisible to white people. But we are always watching, watching and learning."

After they married, Sadie Williams had accompanied Cleophas nearly everywhere, in part, it seems, to keep him safe when racial tensions

ran high "I've been Black for 96 years," she chortled, "so you can feel free to ask me any questions about Black people. Any questions at all!"

Mrs. Williams had her disappointments, but none of them were with her husband or the ILWU, which is famous for supporting its family members. She was disappointed that young people didn't understand what the union could do for them that unions were losing power.

By November 6, we still had no answer about the election. I wanted her to know young people were working together toward the goals her husband worked for. They were even winning elections. She seemed heartened by the thought.

She said it in a way that deeply moved me, "Meeting people, talking with people, working it out in a democratic union that sometimes disappoints you, was the essence of what Cleophas and his peers had worked so hard to achieve."

Abridged, Marin Post, posted by Eva Chrysanthe, Nov. 12, 2020.

The Honorable Ron V. Dellums Legacy Celebration

It is an honor and privilege to be at this important occasion to honor the legacy of a person who has made significant historical contribution to the global Black Freedom Struggle, the oppressed and the working class while serving his congressional district for nearly 30 years. His support and service to labor and to the working class was unwavering.

He is a man who comes out of the Black radical tradition like W.E.B. Du Bois, Paul Robeson, and William L. Patterson. He was born into radicalism because his father Verney Dellums registration #2283 was a member of the most democratic and radical union in the country; the ILWU led by the leading 20th century labor leader, Harry Bridges.

Just 10 years before Ron's dad became a ILWU member, Bridges led a West Coast waterfront strike culminating in the 4-day San Francisco General Strike of 1934. Bridges believed that discrimination was a tool of the bosses to divide the working class.

Ron Dellums' uncle the legendary C.L. Dellums was a labor and Civil Rights leader. He was a founding member along with A. Philip Randolph of the Brotherhood of Sleeping Car Porters. "Fight or be Slaves" were the words of C.L. Dellums as the porters were organizing. It became his credo for the rest of his life.

It is clear where the foundation of Ron Dellums' commitment to struggle came from.

In 1968, when serving on the Berkeley City Council, Dellums joined the Black Students at San Francisco State College in the longest student strike in history. The struggle succeeded in achieving a Black Studies Department and a School of Ethnic Studies.

There he courageously confronted the San Francisco Police Tactical Squad in their attempts to arrest and break up student protests.

On February 17, 1968, Ron delivered the key note address at a benefit birthday party for Huey P. Newton, Minister of Defense for the Black Panther Party. H. Rap Brown also spoke and Curtis Mayfield and The Impressions performed.

Upon becoming a member of Congress, Ron worked with Rep. Charles Diggs, organizer of Congressional Black Caucus and Rep. John Conyers of Michigan. Together they took on the responsibility of bringing to national attention not only the issues of their urban constituents but also the concerns of Blacks globally.

On March 10-12 in 1972, several thousand African Americans gathered in Gary, Indiana for the National Black Political Convention. The purpose of the convention was to develop a unified political strategy for African Americans. Congressman Dellums was a delegate to that Convention.

In the early 70s, Ron joined the Democratic Socialist Organizing Committee. He went on to join Democratic Socialists of America. Its strategy was to function openly as a socialist group inside the Democratic Party.

In 1972, Ron was part of a congressional committee that sponsored seminars to spearhead a drive to establish a fresh policy on Cuba.

In 1977, Barbara Lee and Dellums were part of a delegation to Cuba, which met with Fidel Castro to discuss health care.

Clarence Thomas with Ron Dellums in March, 2006.   Photo: Melvin Dickson

In 1971, a group of workers from a Polaroid plant in New England came to Washington for the purpose of meeting with members of Congress to discuss their concerns regarding the company's commercial engagement with South Africa. Congressional Black Caucus (CBC) chairman Charles C. Diggs, Jr. from Michigan asked Dellums to meet with workers and report back on their concerns.

The CBC received their petition and agreed to take up case within Congress. They promised to use their offices to bring their case for sanctions against South Africa inside the system and any other way they could. By February 1972, they had introduced a disinvestment resolution for consideration by the House.

In fact it would be more than a decade before Congress would come to grips with ending U.S. complicity in the perpetuation of the apartheid regime. But the resolution provided a vehicle for the people to build pressure on Congress for legislative action.

Meanwhile in 1976, a resolution to boycott South African cargo by the ILWU was adopted by ILWU Local 10. Leo Robinson, a classmate of Dellums' at Oakland Tech High School, wrote the resolution to refuse to handle the cargo to oppose the apartheid system. During that time, the corporate media refused to cover the anti-apartheid actions of the ILWU. Congressman Dellums extended the use of his staff to prepare press releases and briefings regarding the boycott of South African cargo by Local 10.

Members received congressional recognition of ILWU's contribution in the struggle against apartheid. Ron played a critical role in the ultimate passage of legislation and in ending the regime.

In his memoir, published in 2000, Dellums dedicated a chapter to the years of campaigning on apartheid. In his words, "the liberation of South Africa from the yoke of apartheid is one of the most important political and human rights events of my lifetime and I consider having played some role in it to be my greatest legislative and personal achievement."

Ron Dellums is a towering figure of the African American left in this country. He fought against racism, sexism, and homophobia, income inequality, war and imperialism. Were he not a congressman, it is likely that he would not be given a security clearance today. He would be deemed a security risk.

The ILWU wishes to acknowledge your contributions in the struggle for social transformation at home and abroad and your courage of conviction. Your legacy will serve as an example for future generations.

RIP Leo Robinson, Soul of the Longshore

David Bacon

LEO ROBINSON was a leader of the longshore union in San Francisco. For many of us, he was an example of what being an internationalist and a working-class activist was all about. Robinson, a self-described 'Red,' helped organize one of the earliest anti-apartheid boycotts of South Africa in 1984.

Photo: David Bacon

Leo Robinson came into the ILWU because of a deal made by Harry Bridges and the Communists who led the waterfront strike of 1934. That strike spread into three-day general strike after cops killed two strikers on what became known as "Bloody Thursday." It was the birth of the ILWU and changed the politics of the West Coast for decades to come.

At the time, longshoremen were considered bums; every morning, they had to assemble in a "shape-up" and beg a job from the bosses.

The radical leaders on the docks were both Black and white. But the bosses always showed preference for the white gangs. Black crews got the worst jobs if they were hired at all. Every worker on the dock was hungry, poor and desperate for work. Black dockers were the hungriest of all.

As the strike went on, bosses began looking for men who would cross the picket lines and take cargo off the waiting ships. To keep them from recruiting Black workers, the strike leaders went into the neighborhoods

of Black workers and made a promise. The union, they said, was fighting to break the bosses' control over jobs by demanding a hiring hall run by workers. If Black workers would support the strike, African Americans would get jobs like anyone else, and the color lines would come down.

The union won the strike and the promise was kept. The ILWU in the Bay Area became an integrated union with powerful, articulate Black leaders. Some of them became heavyweights in San Francisco politics, where they broke the color line as well. In the city's African-American neighborhoods, longshoremen, and eventually long-shore women, were respected, raised families, sent their kids to college.

That was quite a step up. From waterfront bums, dockworkers became crane drivers, some of the best-paid workers in the Bay Area. The union held real political power.

Eventually Local 10, the longshore union for northern California, became a union with a mostly Black membership. It was more than a source

of good jobs, it brought power to the community. And as waterfront work went across the bay, to the Port of Oakland, the longshore workers of the Black community had those same good jobs, ones their children and neighbors aspired to.

That is where Leo lived, on the border between north and west Oakland. That is where I grew up. I didn't know Leo as a kid, but I knew the schools his children went to, the streets where they hung out, and the language they spoke.

I got to know Leo when he became a leader of the Coalition of Black Trade Unionists. With Geraldine Johnson and David Stewart, they used the CBTU to try to reach into other Bay Area unions and encourage the same kind of progressive politics they knew in Local 10.

This was the 1970s, in an era when apartheid rode high South Africa, the years of the Sharpeville Massacre, passbook laws, and the banning of the African National Congress (ANC), the South African Communist Party (SACP) and the South African Congress of Trade Unions (SACTU). But it was also the era of the Cold War. The ANC, the SACP and the SACTU were all called terrorist organizations by our government and accused of taking help from the Soviet Union.

Red-baiting didn't stop Leo, David and Geraldine. They saw a connection between Oakland and Johannesburg.

They believed that Black people would not be free in the U.S. if they were not free in South Africa. They were determined to end the support given by the U.S. government that kept the apartheid régime alive.

Leo knew that workers in both countries had the potential to break that tie. If longshoremen in San Francisco could find a way to support Black workers in South Africa, it would help the liberation movement there survive, win, and change the conditions for Black workers here at home.

Their work began when the anti-apartheid movement was still small.

Together with other labor activists they brought leaders of SACTU to the Bay Area when the hierarchy of the AFL-CIO, then still under the influence of the cold warriors, refused to support them.

One of the first things I learned about Leo was that he was not afraid of being called a Red. He took pride in it. "When some people insult you and call you a Red," he said, "that's when you know you're really doing good work. When you are hurting the racists, that's their weapon of choice."

He was a tremendous speaker. The best photograph I ever took of Leo was while he was talking in a union meeting about safety conditions on the docks. He had the full attention of every union member in Local 10's cavernous waterfront union hall. Leo was an agitator, but people listened to him because what he said made sense. He knew how to speak their language.

In 1984, Local 10, the Marine Clerks Union Local 34, and members of the Inlandboatmen's Union, together refused to unload the Nedlloyd Kemberley, a ship from South Africa docked in San Francisco Bay. For eleven days, they defied the threats of the ship owners. They didn't just take advantage of a technicality in their contract allowing them to respect outside picket lines. They used the power

Soweto, June 1976, students marching against the forced instruction of Afrikaans language were gunned down.   Photo: Sam Nzima

they won in the hiring hall, dispatching members to unload the ship who would refuse to do the work when they arrived on the pier. Local 10 members risked their union for a principle, something the ship owners here have never forgotten, or forgiven.

Leo was a leader of that action. The ship boycott was ended under the threat of a federal injunction. But then the hundreds of union and community activists moved their picket line to Oakland. There they demonstrated against the Pacific Maritime Association, the shipowners, every day for two years.

That was the real birth of the anti-apartheid movement in northern California. Eventually the shipowners could no longer bring South African cargo into any port on the West Coast. Cities like Oakland and San Francisco divested from companies with South African operations. And when apartheid fell, Nelson Mandela came to Oakland and acknowledged what Leo, CBTU, the ILWU, and our Free South Africa Movement had fought for through the years.

I was chair of the Bay Area Free South Africa Labor Committee for many of those years. I worked with Leo and helped build a relationship between the ILWU and South African unions. Those ties, and that international perspective, is part of the life of the ILWU today and part of the legacy Leo leaves behind him.

Leo's political commitments extended beyond South Africa. He worked for an end to the wars in Iraq and Afghanistan. He protested police brutality in Oakland. He defended the union he loved, and unions and workers everywhere.

Most important, Robinson believed that immediate changes were important because they are steps to a more just world. He once spoke in a packed church in West Oakland to the ones he called the "young comrades." He described his vision of a more just society, in which working people were not exploited for private gain, one that would abolish racism and sexism. He gave that vision a name, socialism, at a time when the media claimed that socialism was dead, and capitalism was the best humankind could hope for.

"I know that's a lie," he shouted out. "The world depends on us, on our labor. And we have the right to decide what kind of world it's going to be."
In These Times, Jan. 9, 2013.

Southern Africa Liberation Support Committee activists and other longshoremen who volunteered to load donations into two shipping containers to be sent to freedom fighters from Mozambique, South Africa, and Zimbabwe. From left to right: Larry Wright, Clarence C. Cooper, Jr., Alton Harris, Leo Robinson, Bill Proctor with his son, Bailey M. Buffin, Charles Jones, Amile Ashley, and David Stewart.

Telling my story in celebration of my life

I Leo L. Robinson was born on May 26, 1937, to the proud parents Arthur Robinson, Jr. and Pearl Lee Young, third oldest of five children, in Shreveport, LA. My mother moved to the West Coast in 1942, to work in the shipyards and to prepare a place for our family. My siblings and I moved with my father to Oakland in 1943. I attended public schools in both Los Angeles and Oakland. At George Washington Carver Junior High School, the school motto struck with me all my life. I'll never forget! I remember it as, "A man educated is easy to lead but impossible to enslave."

I asked my mother could I join the Navy after finishing the eleventh grade. I knew with the running around I was doing with my hoodlum friends that I wouldn't graduate from twelfth grade. With my mother's permission, I enlisted into the Navy in 1954, and spent 3 years, 11 months, 22 days, 11 hours, and 45 minutes of wasted time. I briefly worked for ILWU Local 2 as a ship scaler and for General Motors on the assembly line.

I am a second generation longshoreman. My father worked as a longshoreman beginning in 1944, for 36 years. Before that, he was a sharecropper, railroad worker, rail splitter, otherwise a jack of all trades. I became a member of ILWU Local 10 #6461 in 1963, as a B-Man and moved to A-Man in 1966.

I retired on July 1, 1999, at 12:01 am after 34 years on the waterfront.

One of my earliest memories of ILWU Local 10 and Harry Bridges is when I attended a "stop work" meeting in the late 50s or early 60s before

Leo Robinson and Steve Nakana at an African Diaspora Dialogue meeting in Berkeley, Calif., 2006. Nakana said that when he was a ANC student in exile in Tanzania, they received packages from the ILWU which included chewing gum, candy and dollar bills in the pockets of the clothes. 'Opening the packages felt like Christmas.'

Photo: Nunu Kidane

becoming a longshoreman. It was the first time I ever laid eyes on Harry and he was arguing with a rank-and file-member. Harry said, "Far be it for me to call my Brother a liar, but the record speaks for itself."

When I came on the waterfront I wasn't that political. My issues were all local and it was only later that it occurred to me that everything that's local is also national and international.

During the Vietnam War, a question by a young longshore brother changed my political outlook for life and led me into activism. He said, "I want to ask you a question and you don't have to answer it now, but I want you to answer this question. Of what kind of a threat do the Vietnamese pose to you?"

To me the new trade unionist leadership is more interested in electoral politics than that of rank-and-file. I was a Local 10 executive board member for 20 years. I only campaigned for office one year. My forte was hardball politics, messing with the president. I don't care who you are or what you are, the waterfront will definitely change you. Nobody comes off the waterfront unscathed in terms

of their life, the way they look at the world, or the way they look at society. The waterfront is a culture unto itself.

Along with Sister Geraldine Johnson and several others, I am a founding member of the Northern Calif. Chapter Coalition of Black Trade Unionists (CBTU). Sister Geraldine Johnson, my mentor, my sister, and my teacher, was one of the most dynamic women I have ever laid eyes on. When Geraldine Johnson gave you your marching orders you didn't deviate, you didn't equivocate, you just did it even if you didn't know how. In 1977, I was sent to represent the CBTU in Washington, D.C. to help establish the Women's Commission which was adopted by the National Executive Council. I fought against all forms of discrimination. In later years, I supported the first female secretary-treasurer in Local 10's history, Jolita Lewis.

I wrote a resolution in 1976, calling for the boycotting of all South African cargo in response to the Soweto Massacre of students. A community picket line was formed in protest to apartheid in South Africa and ILWU longshoremen refused to go through the gates to work the cargo. I was appointed by Local 10 to speak at rallies regarding anti-apartheid and the South African Liberation movements.

Along with CTBU and other community organizations, I organized the first trade union conference on apartheid at San Francisco State College and brought high officials from the African National Congress (ANC) to San Francisco. ILWU sponsored many events to bring ANC and other Southern Africans trade unionists involved in liberation movements to the West Coast and beyond to speak on their struggles. We did so much, like nightly meetings, radio interviews, traveling to other cities, raising funds and working with coalitions that raised money to build a clinic in Mozambique.

During the early 1980s, I along with Dave Stewart and Local 10 members of the CBTU, brought a contract resolution, passed at the CBTU convention, to Local 10 calling for all international unions to make Dr. Martin Luther King's Birthday a paid holiday. Local 10 adopted the contract demand for the Longshore Caucus. The Longshore Division gained Dr. Martin Luther King's Birthday as a paid holiday. This is an example of the power of rank-and-file workers.

One day on KPFA, I heard about two sisters who were being harassed by the KKK and other racists in Oroville, Calif. I invited them to come to speak to the membership. The rank-and-file wanted to give support to their plight. I wrote a resolution to have our next membership meeting in Oroville, a "stop work meeting" with Pacific Maritime Association's approval. On the morning of the meeting we loaded buses and cars to the city and marched through the main thoroughfare of the town to deliver a message to the police chief. Our message was to stop the harassment (cross burning, graffiti, etc.) of the single mothers.

A little later, a cross burning at the home of a Local 10 rank-and-file member occurred in El Sobrante, Contra Costa County. Again, Local 10 rank-and-file handled the situation by providing security to our brother.

As part of the CBTU leadership, I was part of the first official Black trade unionist delegation to go to Cuba in 1983, and I was a member of the first official trade unionist delegation to travel to Nicaragua.

In 1986, I was selected as an ILWU International rank-and-file representative to attend the 11th World Congress of the World Federation of Trade Unions, held in Berlin, Germany. I delivered the remarks from the largest country delegation out of the 75 countries in attendance.

In 1992, I along with other rank-and-filers organized the African American Longshore Coalition (AALC) to address racism, sexism, gender and other forms of discrimination up and down the Coast of the Longshore Division, for the purpose of resolving such problems internally. I felt the question of racism, sexism, white privilege and all other forms of discrimination will ultimately lead to the demise of ILWU, if not addressed.

In 1994, while teaching middle school children in Berkeley the history of the ILWU, a former UC Berkeley professor listened in the audience. We had worked together before sending books to students in South Africa. The professor wanted to move his African Studies library to Tanzania and asked if ILWU could help. Local 10 stored the books and obtained a shipping container. A total of 10,000 books were sent. It was said by many, "This is a very unusual act of solidarity." People called from both continents to find out how we did it.

I wrote the ILWU position paper on the Israeli-Palestine question calling for the recognition of the Palestine Liberation Organization as the sole representative of the Palestinian People and calling for the establishment of peace talks for the Palestinian and Israeli governments.

In 2004, I collaborated with rank-and-file members in writing the Local 10 resolution calling for a Million Worker March (MWM) in Washington, D.C. on the steps of the Lincoln Memorial. I had but one stipulation, that there be no elected officials speaking from the podium.

On October 17, the March drew thousands. I have always believed that working people should be able to organize and mobilize in their own names independently of any existing political party. It's for that reason that I wholeheartedly supported MWM. I feel labor is not monolithic. They are Democrats, Republicans, independents, and others. There are workers on both sides of various issues, but there are certain things on which all workers do agree: Universal health care; protection and enhancement of social security; pensions; a national living wage to replace the minimum wage; funding for public education and affordable housing.

On Nov. 2, 2011, I was a part of the tens of thousands that marched to the Port of Oakland in support of the Occupy Oakland movement and the longshore workers in their struggle against Export Grain Terminal. The Occupy movement is not separate and apart from the labor movement. People are trying to confuse the issue by saying that we are somehow separated from the Occupy movement. More then anything else, the Occupy movement is a direct challenge or raises the question of the rights of capital as opposed to the rights of the worker.

Let me say in closing, my interest in the affairs of the ILWU shall remain eternal.

Leo Lythel Robinson   1937-2013

Leo Robinson
rank-and-file, internationalist fighter

Cheryl LaBash

Leo Robinson, a working-class fighter on the West Coast docks and in the community, and an internationalist, succumbed to cancer on Jan. 14, 2013, at the age of 75. He is survived by his spouse and partner, Johnnie, six children and by militant rank-and-file longshore workers who learned how to fight from the bottom up from Leo's example.

The ILWU was established when the port bosses were forced to recognize the union after the 1934 San Francisco General Strike and the famous pledge by strike leader Harry Bridges ensuring that Black workers would have an equal place in the union and for waterfront jobs.

In his 20 years on the Local 10 Executive Board and throughout a lifetime of union activism, Leo Robinson lived and breathed internationalism and class struggle.

In the 1970s and 1980s, Leo's leadership exercised the power of the U.S. working class on the side of the South African liberation struggle and against the racist apartheid regime. In July 1976, after the Soweto youth uprising was massacred, Leo introduced a resolution to Local 10 for a boycott of goods to and from South Africa.

In April 1977, he put that resolution into action. A 5,000 person strong community picket was honored by ILWU Local 10 members stalling South African cargo at San Francisco's Pier 27 for two days, at a

Photo from Memorial brochure.

time when then imprisoned Nelson Mandela and the African National Congress were slandered as terrorists by the U.S. government. South African cargo sat on the Dutch ship, Nedlloyd Kemberley, for 11 days in 1984, when longshore workers from Locals 10, 34 and others honored the community protest. Mandela recognized the pivotal role of the ILWU when he spoke at the Oakland Coliseum on his 1990 U.S. tour. What started as a union resolution became global struggle that helped to change U.S. policy.

Leo used his experience and these precedents to politically defend the Occupy movement's Dec. 12, 2011, West Coast port shut down that began shaping a new way for the working class to fight in the high-tech age.

In Oct. 17, 2004, at the Lincoln Memorial just a couple of months before the U.S. elections, the Million Worker March called on labor to mobilize in its own name. The MWM pulled against the capitalist election frenzy. Robinson, a convener and the largest benefactor, drafted the iconic teeshirt with the MWM program that stands as a working-class agenda today: Bring the troops home now; Universal health care; Enforce all civil rights; Stop dismantling public education; Slash the military budget; National living wage; Hands off Social Security; Workers' right to organize; Repeal Taft-Hartley; Stop corporate greed and offshoring jobs; Repeal free trade agreements;

Amnesty for all undocumented workers; Truth in media; Preserve the environment; and Tax relief for the working class.

Although his concern was international, writing the ILWU position paper on Palestine calling for recognition of the Palestine Liberation Organization, opposing the Colombia free trade agreement, leading CBTU delegations to Cuba and a labor delegation to Nicaragua, and national with the MWM and pushing forward the ILWU to be the first union to recognize the Martin Luther King Jr. holiday, and founding the Northern California CBTU, he also strengthened the union. He was one of the founders the African American Longshore Coalition in March 1992, to address the racism, sexism and other forms of discrimination of the Longshore Division up and down the West Coast for the purpose of resolving such problems internally.

Brenda Stokely, MWMM Northeast co-organizer, said: "My first recollection of Leo Robinson was during a Coalition of Black Trade Unionists convention. He was a force that was able to move progressive resolutions through the CBTU process and garner support despite strong opposition.

"He embodied courage and commitment to his class and stood unwaveringly on the side of the aspirations of that class. His skills as an effective working-class strategist, and organizer encouraged others to never falter in the face of opposition.

"He was vigilant in ensuring that Local 10 ILWU maintained its revolutionary character; remained capable of stopping their employers' attacks

Leo Robinson, ruthlessly committed to being a fighter for the working class, active in community as well as being an internationalist.

WW photos: Arturo J. Pérez Saad

'Leo Robinson embodied courage and commitment to his class . . . stood unwaveringly on the side of the aspirations of that class. His skills as an effective working-class strategist, and organizer encouraged others to never falter in the face of opposition.'
– Brenda Stokely

to weaken their contracts; and was able to exercise their right to carry out both political and economic strikes.

"He led a Local 10 delegation to the Labor Party's founding convention. … Leo will forever be an inspiring model of revolutionary leadership ."

"Leo was an extraordinary person, worker, intellectual, trade union activist, freedom fighter, thinker, organizer, orator, movement builder and teacher, and a superior domino player, ruthlessly committed to being a fighter for the working class, active in community as well as being an internationalist. He gave generously of his time and money in the fight for economic and social justice for the oppressed and working class," said Clarence Thomas, fellow ILWU Local 10 member and MWM co-chair.
Abridged from WW, Jan. 23, 2013.

Leo Robinson speaking on the steps the Lincoln Memorial on Oct, 17, 2004.

My Reflections of Leo Robinson

Looking back at 2004, when I started organizing for the Million Worker March (MWM), I asked the executive board of ILWU Local 19 for money to help organize the call for rank-and-file workers to join MWM in the Nation's capital. A motion was made to give me $500. I was embarrassed to call the organizers of the MWM to tell them that all my Local was willing to give was $500 to organize for a massive gathering of workers and communities from around the world .

At that time brother Leo Robinson, a retired Local 10 member, had put up $50,000 from his retirement money for MWM tee shirts.

Brother Leo Robinson was an organizer of MWM and a revolutionary leader in the Black trade union movement. He who became a mentor to me. Brother Michael Hoard and I started selling tee shirts and spreading the word to rank-and-file members. We needed to raise more funds to help MWM become a reality in our state. I was the chair of the African American Longshore Coalition (AALC) and brother Hoard was the co-chair in Local 19 Seattle.

Leo Robinson put the AALC together in 1994, with support from Local 10 to help Black and Brown workers in the Northwest who were disenfranchised from advancement in the ILWU. He was an extraordinary speaker who spoke truth to power.

As the chair of the Local 19 Education Committee, I invited brother Robinson to speak at our meeting, We saw history in the making when brother Robinson delivered his message. You could hear a pin drop in the room as he got the full attention of the membership saying, "Even if I wanted to stop this I could not, it's growing and moving fast." When he was done, a motion was put on the floor by brother Jeff Vigna to donate $5,000 to the MWM.

The March became an inspiration that lifted and moved rank-and-file members as well as Seattle community organizations. Workers speaking in their own name, independent from all parties.

I want to be clear, there were still labor leaders that did not want this to happen, they were more focused on getting a Democrat into the Oval Office, but it did not happen. Today, I could confidently say the MWM did happen in 2004, in spite of opposition.

It was a success seen by millions of people! There were workers who traveled across the country and from around the world who shared the same struggle, oppression and solidarity with the list of demands brought forward by the organizers of the MWM who are still on the forefront of the labor movement.

Gabriel Prawl
Past president ILWU Local 52.

South African Ambassador Ebrahim Rasool honors Leo Robinson and ILWU Local 10

Introduction by Clarence Thomas

'I would like to say a few quick words about South African Ambassador Ebrahim Rasool. He is a man of struggle like Brother Leo Robinson. While fighting against apartheid he was held under house arrest. He is indeed a freedom fighter. Lets give the Honorable Ebrahim Rasool a warm welcome.'

Thank you Clarence Thomas. I want to say to Mrs. Johnnie Robinson, the Robinson family and the comrades of Leo Robinson who supported him, who fought with him and who were led by him, I want to say to the ILWU leadership, especially to Local 10, that on behalf of the people of South Africa, on behalf of the African National Congress, on behalf of Nelson Mandela, that our hearts go out to you when we express our condolences for the loss of a great human being, a great leader and a visionary.

We come here to express gratitude for without the ILWU, under the leadership of Robinson, the end of apartheid may not have come as quickly in South Africa. Nelson Mandela would not have been freed as early.

There was a union with a leader on the U.S. West Coast, an entire ocean and an entire continent away from the southern tip of Africa where we were not free. In the greatest tradition of workers across the world and of the ILWU, Leo Robinson said, "An injury to one is an injury to all."

Your commemoration of Leo Robinson cannot be more poignant because it comes near the 21st of March when South Africans commemorate that event that fired Solidarity in Leo Robinson. On March 21, 1960, police gunned down 69 people in Sharpeville for protesting the wearing of passes.

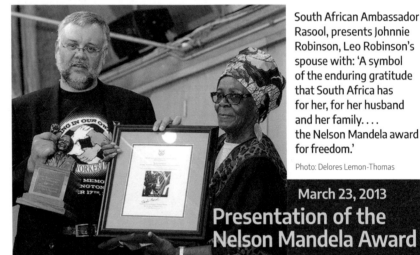

South African Ambassador Rasool, presents Johnnie Robinson, Leo Robinson's spouse with: 'A symbol of the enduring gratitude that South Africa has for her, for her husband and her family.... the Nelson Mandela award for freedom.'

Photo: Delores Lemon-Thomas

March 23, 2013
Presentation of the Nelson Mandela Award

Whatever I may say today on behalf of South Africa, cannot be a higher attribute than the one Mandela paid to Leo Robinson, to the ILWU, to the people of Oakland and the solidarity community on the West Coast. Soon after he was released from prison, Mandela came to Oakland to address your union and your community, to say thank you very much for his freedom.

Our hearts are full of gratitude for what Leo Robinson has given us. We thank the ILWU Local 10 and Local 34, the Inlandboatmen's Union, the Coalition of Black Trade Unionists and the Free South African Movement for fighting to end apartheid.

Your actions came at a crucial time when apartheid thought it had destroyed the African National Congress and the entire movement. Nelson Mandela and the comrades were in jail for 20 years or more. Oliver Tambo and his comrades were exiled in places like Zambia, Tanzania and Angola. The people of Sharpeville had been massacred in the streets, the youth of Soweto were massacred in the streets of Africa.

They thought apartheid could reign forever. They did not reckon with

the solidarity led by Leo Robinson and that was decisive. They thought apartheid would survive another few decades when Margaret Thatcher and Ronald Reagan came into office. They did not reckon with a union in San Francisco and Leo Robinson, who would fire the emotion of hundreds of thousands.

It was in 1976, that Leo Robinson and the ILWU signaled their intention to launch a boycott of South Africa. That lit the spark that would meld the passion in all of you to put an end to apartheid.

However it was in 1984, after Ronald Reagan won the election for a second term and announced a policy of constructive engagement. It was when the ship the Kimberley entered the Port of San Francisco laden with goods from apartheid South Africa. For 11 days Leo Robinson, the ILWU, the Clerk's Union and the people of Oakland and San Francisco decided they're going to be the Waterloo for apartheid.

Never before had the U.S. government seen in the will of the workers, seen the solidarity and fury of the communities, of people who suffer by virtue of the color of their skin. The solidarity that held a ship in the harbor without the goods being offloaded.

That was the end of South African apartheid ships coming anywhere on the West Coast, anywhere where the ILWU are strong, anywhere where Leo Robinson's phone reaches out.

I end up by saying that moment when we commemorate the death of Leo Robinson and celebrate his life much of what he stood for is under attack all over the world. This working class champion, this activist and leader would find that the rights he gained for workers are being rolled back all over the world.

The human solidarity that he embodied is being rolled back. We need to protect the gains that he has made. Most importantly, we must defend his vision that workers had the right to decide what kind of world it is going to be. All the people, workers, Blacks, people all over the world on the poor side of the poverty scale, have to have a say in what kind of world it is going to be in honor of Leo Robinson.

We need to say that we want the world to be a gentler place, a more equal place, a place where poverty is abolished and where obscene wealth is shared far more equitably. Leo Robinson fought for us. We need to run with his vision.

I come here to hand over to Mrs. Johnnie Robinson, a symbol of the enduring gratitude that South Africa has for her, for her husband and her family. I come here to award the Nelson Mandela Award for Freedom.

— Honorable Ebrahim Rasool
  South Africa Ambassador

From the left is ILWU Secretary-Treasurer Willie Adams, Honorable Ebrahim Rasool, Clarence Thomas, Mrs. Johnnie Robinson, Consul-General Cyril Ndaba and Local 10 President Michael Villeggiante.
Photo: Delores Lemon-Thomas

Hunny Powell

Jerry Lawrence
Photos: Kelley Kane

Saladin Muhammad and David Bacon

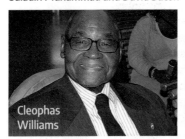

Cleophas Williams

Leo Robinson and Johnnie Robinson at the Millions More Movement in 2005.

Photo: Delores Lemon-Thomas

Consul-General Cyril Ndaba, James Curtis Local 10, Ambassador Ebrahim Rasool, Clarence Thomas, Delores Lemon-Thomas and Chris Silvera IBT.

Photo: Malaika H. Kambon

Larry Wright, Local 10 member and South Africa anti-apartheid activist in 1984.

Photo taken from a video recording

Clarence Thomas with Bill Proctor Local 19 who helped organize the Southern Africa Liberation Support Committee.

A few significant quotes by Leo Robinson

'*You have to understand, a lot of people, you know, they have a job right, and that's all they have. In some ways, to be a longshoreman, it becomes a state of mind, and a state of being. So that, you don't look at it as a job that I work for X Company or Y Company. You're a longshoreman and you get your job out of the Hall, and the bosses are incidental to your employment. I mean, I work for Matson tonight; I work for APL the next night; or whoever; and I'm through with them; but I'm never through with that Hall. That's my life blood. That's the place, it's my second family, it's my second home.*'

Excerpted from a YouTube recorded in Jan. 27, 2015 titled: **Harry Bridges: A Man and His Union**

On the 5th Anniversary of the MWMM:

'*The MWM is not the exclusive purview of the trade union movement. It is made up of trade unionists, community people, the clergy, students, the unemployed, and the employed. We are not an adjunct of any political party. We are the nucleus of a mass movement. Today's labor movement is part and parcel of the Democratic Party machinery and is subservient to the Democratic Party. That is the state of the trade union movement. ...*

'*Concessionary bargaining in part is the strategy of the leadership of labor. They are more comfortable out on the golf course with the employer than they are at a local union meeting with the people who pay their salaries. Rank-and-file members should introduce resolutions that say if workers take a cut in wages that the leadership take a cut in their wages as well. ..*

The trade union movement as a whole, is the most undemocratic institution in the United States. That is one of the goals of our movement, to bring more democracy to the labor movement. ...

'*Only in unity is there strength. You will either organize or you will starve. It is as simple as that.*'

Excerpted from a presentation Robinson gave at the Teamsters Local 808 in Long Island City, New York, October 2009.

International Longshore and Warehouse Union
TEN GUIDING PRINCIPLES

1. **A union is built on its members.** The strength, understanding and unity of membership can determine the union's course and its advancements. The members who work, who make up the union and pay dues, can best determine their own destiny. If the facts are honestly presented to the members in the ranks, they will best judge what should be done and how it should be done. In brief, it is the membership of the union which is the best judge of its own welfare; not the officers, not the employers, not politicians and fair weather friends of labor. Above all, this approach is based on the conviction that given the truth and the opportunity to determine their own course of action, the rank-and-file in 99 cases out of 100 will take the right path in their interests of all the people.

2. **Labor unity is at all times the key for a successful economic advancement**. Anything that detracts from labor unity hurts all labor. Any group of workers through craft unionism or through cozy deals at the expense of others will in the long run gain but little and inevitably lose both its substance and its friends. No matter how difficult the going, a union must fight in every possible way to advance the principles of labor unity.

3. **Workers are indivisible.** There can be no discrimination because of race, color, creed, national origin, religious or political belief. Any division among the workers can help no one but the employers. Discrimination is a weapon of the boss. Its entire history is proof that it has served no other purpose than to pit worker against worker to their own destruction.

4. **To help any worker in distress** must be a daily guide in the life of every trade union and its individual members. Labor solidarity means just that. Unions have to accept the fact that solidarity of labor stands above all else, including even the so-called sanctity of contract. We cannot adopt for ourselves the policies of union leaders who insist that because they have a contract, their members are compelled to perform work, even behind a picket line. Every picket line must be respected as if it were our own.

5. **Any union, if it is to fulfill its appointed task, must put aside all internal differences and issues to combine for the common cause of advancing the welfare of the membership.** No union can successfully fulfill its purpose in life if it allows itself to be distracted by any issue which causes division in its ranks and undermines the unity which all labor must have in the face of the employer.

6. **The days are long gone when a union can consider dealing with single employers.** The powerful financial interests of the country are bound together in every conceivable type of united organization to promote their own welfare and to resist the demands of labor. Labor can no longer win with the ancient weapons of taking on a single employer in an industry any more than it can hope to win through the worn-out dream of withholding its skill until an employer sues for peace. The employers of this country are part of a well organized, carefully coordinated, effective fighting machine. They can be met only on equal terms, which requires industry-wide bargaining and the most extensive economic strength of organized labor.

7. **Just as water flows to its lowest level, so do wages if the bulk of the workers are left unorganized.** The day of craft unionism – the aristocracy of labor – was over when mass production was introduced. To organize the unorganized must be the cardinal principle of any union worth its salt; and to accomplish this is not merely in the interest of the unorganized, it is for the benefits of the organized as well.

8. **The basic aspirations and desires of the workers throughout the world are the same.** Workers are workers the world over. International solidarity, particularly among maritime workers, is essential to their protection and a guarantee of reserve economic power in times of strife.

9. **A new type of unionism is called for which does not confine its ambitions and demands only to wages.** Conditions of work, security of employment and adequate provisions for the workers and their families in times of need are of equal, if not greater importance, than the hourly wage.

10. **Jurisdictional warfare and jurisdictional raiding must be outlawed by labor itself.** Nothing can do as much damage to the ranks of labor and the principle of labor unity and solidarity as jurisdictional bickering and raiding among unions. **Both public support and strike victories are jeopardized by jurisdictional warfare.**

The Ten Guiding Principles are from the ILWU Local 13 website, at www.ilwu-local13.org/history-guiding-principles.html.

Harry Bridges (center) with striking waterfront workers in a mass demonstration at Fort Mason Sept. 15, 1948.

The San Francisco Chronicle headlined its Nov. 5, 2011, editorial:

'Harry Bridges, honoring the original occupier'

HARRY BRIDGES, in his words

Program for the Future

"The basic perspective of our union remains the same as they were the day it was founded. The primary job continues to be the building and cementing of unity within the ILWU based upon its democratic structure and its full autonomous rights. Our union will continue the fight for these principles and will resist in every possible way and with any action deemed necessary, all attempts to divide or split our union.

"We will work, as we always have, for national labor unity and world trade solidarity."

Trying days are ahead

"We believe that the membership of the International Longshoremen's and Warehousemen's Union is proud of its record. And it has good reason to be proud. Never have we ducked a fight where the interests of the membership could be served or advanced. This union has earned for itself a real place in the history of American labor and of the world. As a union, we have tried our best to live up to the best traditions of the American labor. We haven't been ashamed of the great battles of the American workers and of their wonderful heritage. We recognize, appreciate and are grateful for the contributions that have been made by the great old Western Federation of Miners, and the old IWW; and we see their leaders as one-time labor heroes who did more to advance the cause of America than many so called respectable 'labor statesmen.

"We will never forget that American history has always been marked by the jailing and persecution of those who dared to challenge the powers that be: The Haymarket victims when they fought for the eight-hour day, Eugene V. Debs, Big Bill Haywood, Sacco and Vanzetti, Tom Mooney – they fought, and when they fought they were singled out for victimization. ...."

We're left-wing

"In the past few years, to be called a 'left-wing' union seemingly or apparently is to be called something that is bad. Gosh! I can remember here in this City a few years ago when to be called a 'right-winger' practically invited you to a battle. We have forgotten a few things. ... And if this Convention does nothing else and if the press does nothing else, please, by no manner of means associate the National leadership of the Union with the right-wing. We're left-wing. We are left-wing and proud of it, and there is nothing wrong with it. ...

"We are a democratic organization, more so than any organization in the country. Our membership can talk back. If they think the President is a bum, I ask anyone here when in any union meetings anyone has been stopped from getting up and saying so, for any reason. ...

"We fight for and adopt militant policies. I have told you some of them. ..."

People respect union

"We're left-wing. I hope we continue that way and not worry about people trying to make distinctions. If we ever get to be right-wing around here,

I will wonder what is with us. Any time you catch any of your National officers being called 'right-wingers,' start the recalls going, fellows! They have sold you out. Any time you read anything good about your National officers in these newspapers, start the recalls going! They sold you out. Now, that's true. And that's the way I think you should operate."

No Plots

"...We have no revolutionary plots or programs. We are not dedicated to a program of Communism. No. But every one of our members has the right to be a Communist and to preach Communism, if he or she desires, without being expelled from this Union. And all the other political beliefs, too. All we say is that they do it in accordance with the democratic rules of our organization. And when they get through, the people who disagree with them have the right to get upon the floor and say, "You don't mean anything for my dough. You don't talk any sense at all.

"That is the way our Union functions; and as long as we keep it functioning like that and as long as we stand for those things, there is room within it to settle our differences without tearing each other's hair off. That is what has kept us strong all these years, and it was that type of philosophy and program that enabled us to stand up against almost prohibitive odds."

Excerpts from the Proceedings of the ILWU Biennial Convention, 1949. Taken from archives of Jack Mulcahy Local 8.

CHAPTER 11

OCCUPY OAKLAND
'SHUT IT DOWN'

November 2, 2011, Occupy Oakland marches to the waterfront.

Photo: Luke Hauser/DirectAction.org

MWMM supports Occupy Wall Street

Statement was issued by the Million Worker March Movement on Oct. 17, 2011

The Million Worker March Movement (MWMM) organizers and activists call upon all workers, organized and unorganized, and the unemployed to join and defend the Occupy Wall Street (OWS) movement. We extend the call to anti-war, immigration rights, environmental and social justice activists to join this movement, which could replicate the Arab Spring here at home.

The MWMM, initiated by Local 10 in October 2004, advanced the slogan "mobilizing in our own name," independent of the two Wall Street controlled political parties to address the economic crisis of working people in which the vast majority are under siege financially.

All important social movements that have occurred in this country were started from the bottom up, rank-and-file and grassroots, not from the top down.

The MWMM's mission statement speaks to how: "A handful of the rich and powerful corporations have usurped our government. A corporate and banking oligarchy changes hats and occupies public office to wage class war on working people. They have captured the State in their own interests." They represent what the OWS activists call the 1%. otherwise known as the ruling class.

Like the MWMM, the OWS has emerged at a time when the corporate controlled political parties are preparing for the presidential election, a smokescreen where billions are spent to promote a top-down and false ceremony of democracy.

Like the MWMM, the OWS will be criticized for having demands that are too broad. We have endured more than 50 years of corporate assault on working people, social services, jobs, wages, pensions, health care, public education and housing. The pursuit of endless wars, the lack of a compre-hensive immigration policy and the erosion of the environment in pursuit of corporate greed makes it impossible to address all of these issues in a soundbite.

Yet one thing is crystal clear: OWS conveys a definite anti-capitalist message. It is being expressed to the entire world at the temple of U.S. capitalism, Wall Street. The OWS, while now a major protest movement against the capitalist elites, must continue to deepen, expand and become a direct challenge to corporate power. Class warfare demands fighting on multiple fronts, and it all leads back to Wall Street. While the officialdom of labor has given verbal support to OWS, the rank-and-file possesses the real power of the labor movement. It is only through rank-and-file unity that labor's true power can be realized in this OWS movement. Workers can take action at the point of production and service, as well as put people in the streets.

We must be mindful of attempts to co-opt this movement. Let us not forget the action of the Democratic Party and its surrogates within the AFL-CIO to pressure Wisconsin unions not to initiate any general strike actions in opposition to Gov. Scott Walker's plans to eliminate collective bargaining for state workers. Wisconsin workers were limited to circulating petitions to recall targeted state Republican elected officials. This took away labor's only real power, the ability to withhold its labor in defense of collective bargaining.

Local 10's executive board has adopted a resolution to join and defend the OWS and called for other longshore locals to do the same. More

Stan Woods Local 6, Clarence Thomas Local 10, Byron Jacobs Local 21, Jack Heyman Local 10, in the front Jake Whiteside Local 21 at Occupy protest in San Francisco's Financial District in 2011.   Photo: Delores Lemon-Thomas

importantly, Local 10 is connecting the OWS movement with the Pacific Northwest dockers' struggle with EGT in Longview, Wash. (EGT is an international grain exporter that is attempting to rupture longshore jurisdiction.) The driving force behind EGT is Bunge Ltd., a leading agribusiness and food company that reported $2.4 billion in profits in 2010. This company has strong ties to Wall Street. This is but one example of Wall Street's corporate attack on union workers.

On Oct. 12, the vice-president and secretary-treasurer of Local 21 in Longview … were allowed to speak by the organizers of Foreclose on Wall Street West. They explained their struggle to several hundred people attending the rally, which took place in the San Francisco financial district. This is an important and strategic show of solidarity between labor and OWS.

It was Black trade unionists that conceived and launched the MWMM. Black workers and other workers of color should play an integral role in expanding the power and influence of OWS. The Black unemployment rate is 24 percent and growing. This needs to be a part of the discussion of the people's assemblies, as it concerns empowering this people's movement.

Working people need to have a political expression of our own that

Photo: Luke Hauser/DirectAction.org

is an alternative to the U.S. corporate sector that both the Democrats and the Republicans represent. The timing of the MWMM in Washington was to prepare for the beginning of a fightback precisely because of the agendas of two political parties, acting as one, the corporate agenda of permanent war, destruction of all social services, Jim Crow and a relentless assault upon working people.

This is an opportune moment for rank-and-file working people to forge a mass movement for fundamental change. Rarely has the importance of unity in struggle been more compelling along an axis of class independence.

Only by our own independent mobilization of working people, the

99%, across America can we open the way to addressing a people's agenda. The MWM and OWS are both about building grassroots and rank-and-file, anti-racist unity, forging the fightback on all governmental and corporate policies influenced and or directed by Wall Street.

Lets take it to the corporate state; let the 1% take the weight.

WW photo: Bill Bowers

Oakland, Calf. November 19, 2011.

Photo: Delores Lemon-Thomas

Reflections on the Oakland General Strike

Dave Welsh

When the masses of people are in motion, watch out. They may just be chipping away at the foundations of the old established order, while you aren't looking!

Take, for example, the Oakland General Strike on Nov. 2, 2011, which was an all-day festival of people taking power into their own hands. First, many thousands surged through downtown, sidewalk-to-sidewalk, and shut down the four major downtown banks (with many trillions of dollars in assets). Then, when the crowd had grown to 30,000 plus, they poured into the Port of Oakland in three giant waves and Shut Down the entire Port, the fifth-busiest in the country. When is the last time something like that happened in the U.S.?

Okay, maybe it wasn't a 'traditional general strike,' like 1934 in San Francisco, or 1946 in Oakland, or like the general strikes today that regularly paralyze Greece, where the labor

Local 10 members applaud as David Welsh reads a letter of solidarity on April 25, 2011 at the Pacific Maritime Association headquarters to demand that the employers' group drop its lawsuit against the union. The suit was in retaliation for the dock workers' solidarity action on April 4 in defense of Wisconsin public workers and in commemoration of Rev. Dr. Martin Luther King Jr's assassination.   Photo: Randall White

movement is strong and militant.

But every general strike is different. And in a country where only 7.2 % of the private-sector work force even belongs to a union, 12% including public workers, where organized labor has been on the defensive for the last 30 years, absorbing bruising concessions, two-tier wage scales, runaway shops and now Wisconsin-style union-busting, for us, the Nov. 2 Oakland General Strike was like a breath of fresh air.

The November 2 General Strike not only had pretty good support from the city's major unions, 350 unionized Oakland teachers reported to the streets that day, not to work! But it brought into the streets thousands of low-wage workers and their families, youth and students, the unemployed and the foreclosed upon of all races and nationalities, mostly not in unions because there are no longer or not yet any unions there for them, an outpouring of the many faces of today's suffering U.S. working class, and a sign that this sleeping giant may just be awakening from its slumber.

You could say it was a general strike "of a new type," reflecting not only the temporarily diminished power of the unions, but also the changed character of the working class in the U.S., and one that is starting to make common cause with oppressed communities, that is beginning to take bold collective action to defy our adversaries in the 1%.

Abridged from WW, Nov. 22, 2011.

Photo: Luke Hauser/DirectAction.org

Police attacks spur resistance
Occupy Oakland says, 'Shut It Down!'

Deirdre Griswold

Like a force of nature that astonishes everyone with its power, Occupy Oakland has inspired bold actions by youth and workers across the United States, electrifying the political climate and forcing city officials and police authorities to constantly revise their plans for dealing with this broad-based people's movement.

Just a week ago, before dawn on Oct. 25, 2011, a massive police raid on the encampment in downtown Oakland, Calif., was supposed to put an end to it. The cops arrested more than 100 people, trashing their tents and other belongings in Oscar Grant Plaza. It was meant to send a signal to other occupations all across the United States.

By that evening, however, thousands had gone back downtown to reclaim the plaza. This time the police were even more vicious. Driving armored vehicles and encased in Robo Cop riot gear, they fired tear gas, stun grenades known as "flashbangs," and projectiles they euphemistically called "bean bags" at the protesters. A 24-year-old member of Iraq Veterans Against the War, Scott Olsen, was hit in the head with one of these projectiles and hospitalized with severe injuries. Others required first aid. Again, there were massive arrests.

An article by Steven Argue on the indybay.org website pointed out: "Police forces across the country have been carrying out repression against the Occupy protesters with brutality and arrests in New York, Denver, Boston, Chicago, Oakland and elsewhere. Unarmed protesters have been repeatedly beaten, maced, tear gassed and arrested for exercising their right to free speech. Meanwhile, armed Tea Party protesters who have pushed an extreme right-wing agenda of austerity for the working class have showed up at protests armed, but are not touched by the police."

Even with this brutal offensive against the movement, the surge of people who have been suffering in a thousand different ways from a capitalist system gone berserk could not be turned back. It grew as those who watched the videos and heard the reports of the Oakland police riots reacted with revulsion and anger.

The next night, under enormous pressure from an inflamed public, the city allowed about 2,000 people to occupy the plaza for a General Assembly. The mood was exuberant. At one point a solidarity statement was read from Cairo saying that Egyptians were marching in support, chanting "We are Oakland!" Loud cheers replied, "We are Tahrir Square!"

It was announced to more cheers that Occupy Wall Street was sending $20,000 to support Occupy Oakland.

'Strike, strike, strike!'

A proposal was introduced that called for a general strike on Nov. 2. In short but succinct language, it said, "Instead of workers going to work and students going to school, the people will converge on downtown Oakland to Shut Down the city. All banks and corporations should close down for the day or we will march on them."

The proposal ended with: "The whole world is watching Oakland. Let's show them what is possible."

The proposal passed with 96.9 % in favor. At that point, a participant told WW, "The whole crowd erupted in chanting 'Strike, strike, strike!'"

This bold call for a general strike has energized the labor movement, which had been pronounced moribund by the capitalist media. Support for the Occupy Oakland strike has been pouring in from all over. While anti- union laws threaten huge fines and decertification for officially striking, rank-and-file committees are calling on their sisters and brothers to swarm downtown Oakland on Nov. 2.

Some union locals, like Service Employees Local 1021 of Oakland, have called for their members to be there. Their statement called on members "to join a day long 'Peaceful Day of Action' in support of Occupy Oakland and against the banking industry and police brutality against the Occupy encampment." The Carpenters' union issued a similar statement.

The movement intends to march to the Port of Oakland, where longshore workers sympathize with their demands. A leaflet from rank-and-file-members of Local 10 read: "Occupy Oakland protesters have called for a General Strike on November 2. Whether this actually means real strike action by workers depends in large part on union participation. Local 10 has always been in the lead in the labor movement and all eyes are on us. As a first step, in defending our union and others against economic and political repression, we need to mobilize our members to participate in the rally and occupation Nov. 2 in Oscar Grant Plaza. "Shut It Down!"
Abridged from WW, Nov 2, 2011.

Notes from Occupy Oakland

Dave Welsh

On Oct. 25, 2011, a pre-dawn police raid tore up and destroyed the Occupy Oakland camp. It was a war zone. Over 500 police from 17 jurisdictions took part in the paramilitary operation, arresting over 130 by day's end, beating many and sending one Iraq War vet to the hospital in critical condition.

But the people had the last word, fighting to re-establish their liberated area. Many hundreds of militants marched for hours through the downtown war zone, thick with cops, to reclaim the streets.

By Thursday someone had torn down the police fence, and tents sprouted up again on Oscar Grant Plaza. Soon a new camp kitchen was up and running, dishing out plates of hot food. The mayor and police, stung by the ferocity of public outrage at Tuesday's police riot, were in retreat. The initiative was once again with the people.

Every day since then, mass meetings of 1,000 to 3,000 people have packed the open-air amphitheater in front of Oakland's City Hall, building for a one day General Strike and Mass Day of Action on Nov. 2, to converge on downtown and 'Shut Down the 1%.' This is a movement with legs.

The encampment began on Oct. 10, Indigenous People's Day. I brought my sleeping bag and started camping out there about 10 days later. The large plaza was a sea of tents. There were maybe 300 people camping, with many more coming by for rallies, a bite to eat or some sharp conversation about the burning issues facing us.

There was a medical tent, with help from California Nurses Asso-

Oakland Oct. 26, 2011.
WW photo: Judi Greenspan

ciation, child care tent, media tent, kitchen, supply tent, and porta-potties courtesy of the Oakland's teachers, city workers and Everett & Jones BBQ. Teamsters brought the water. Donations flowed in from a supportive community.

The big banner at the entrance said, "Oakland Commune, Oscar Grant Plaza." and it's true that the camp became a real community. During my four nights in the camp, African Americans made up about 30-35% of those who were eating and sleeping there, making the food or taking on other camp responsibilities. On Friday night musicians and dancers took over the amphitheater with some politically-charged reggae music. On Saturday it was hip-hop night. Sunday was movie night, showing the powerful film 'Viva Mexico' on a big screen.

At midnight following camp rules, the sound was turned off so people could sleep. But a lot of people weren't ready for bed and gathered in groups around the plaza to debate everything from the U.S.-NATO assault on Libya, the attacks on migrant workers, New Jim Crow, prisons, or how to deal with sexism and homophobia inside the camp. It was like a People's Free University on the streets of Oakland. You got a glimpse of what a society based on real equality might look like.

The outpouring of support following the police raid was something to behold:

- **Vigil** 3,000 rallied in the amphitheater at Oscar Grant Plaza in a moving candlelight vigil for Scott Olsen, the Iraq war vet who was in the hospital with a concussion and brain injury from a police projectile. His comrades from Iraq Veterans against the War and Steve Morse, a Vietnam vet, spoke simply, powerfully about the wars overseas and the war at home that had just struck down their friend.

- **General Strike** The General Assembly of Occupy Oakland, which meets at 7 p.m. every day, voted by 97% to hold a General Strike and Mass Day of Action on Nov. 2, 1,484 voted for, 46 against, with 77 abstentions. The Strike Committee meets every day at 5 p.m. A first run of 12,000 flyers is being distributed, saying: "Everyone to the streets! No work! No school! Converge on downtown Oakland." Demands are:

1. Solidarity with the worldwide Occupy Movement;

2. End police attacks on our communities;

3. Defend Oakland schools and libraries;

4. Oppose an economic system built on inequality and corporate power that perpetuates racism, sexism and destruction of the environment.

- **Blockade the Port of Oakland** On a proposal from Boots Riley, Oakland based hip hop artist of The Coup, the Occupy Oakland strike assembly voted unanimously to march on Nov. 2 to Shut Down the Port of Oakland. The resolution stated: "As part of the Occupy Oakland General Strike, we will march on the Port of Oakland and Shut It Down. … We are doing this in order to blockade the flow of capital," as well as show solidarity with longshore workers in their struggle against EGT in Longview Washington. EGT is a grain exporter, backed by major Wall Street interests, trying to break ILWU jurisdiction over longshore work so they can hire cheaper labor. The resolution said: "This is but one example of Wall Street's corporate attack on workers…. The entire world is fed up with the huge disparity of wealth caused by the present system. … The Occupy Oakland General Strike is a warning shot to the 1%. Their wealth only exists because the 99% creates it for them."

• **Labor support** Many unions and labor councils have condemned the police raid and endorsed the Nov. 2 General Strike. Without specifically calling for strike action by their members, they are nevertheless actively encouraging their members to participate in a mass Shut Down of business as usual in Oakland. Union staff and members came to the plaza to take part. Rank-and-file members of the Local 10 issued a statement titled, "Defend Occupy Oakland with the muscle of organized labor," which urges support for the General Strike. Other cities are mobilizing to support the Nov. 2 call from Occupy Oakland. One flyer in Philadelphia called on workers to strike for 99 minutes on that day in solidarity with the 99 %

Note: This author was one of those arrested by Oakland police at Oscar Grant Plaza in the wee hours on the morning of Oct. 25, 2011.

Abridged from WW, Nov. 10, 2011.

Dave Welsh, a retired postal worker and member of the San Francisco Labor Council, sub@sonic.net.

The Occupy Oakland encampment in October 2011.

Photos above: Luke Hauser/DirectAction.org

Arial view of the encampment.

Occupy Oakland prepares for strike

Clarence Thomas and Boots Riley started the day with an interview on Democracy Now!

Clarence Thomas: The Nov. 2, 2011 General Strike is a call to working people, not only throughout the U.S., but throughout the world, to retract their labor.

The only time that working people can gain the attention of the bosses or the ruling class is when we withhold our labor. It's the greatest action that we can take against capital. It is difficult to organize a general strike within a week's time. This is a response to the brutal attack on the Occupy Oakland activists, and the serious injury of Brother Scott Olsen, The attention of the world is on this movement.

It was not labor who made this call. It was the General Assembly of the Occupy Oakland movement. The majority of the people in this country do not belong to a union. Only 7.2% are members of a union in the private sector, 12% overall.

Young people, who are the driving force behind this movement, are looking at an uncertain future. Students are facing $1 trillion in student debt. A society that does not care for its young people has no future.

Amy Goodman: What is the involvement of the longshore workers in this strike?

CT: We are in support of the Occupy Wall Street movement and the Occupy Oakland movement. We are a democratic, rank-and-file union. We have not had an opportunity to vote on a general strike. Having said that, if there is a picket line today, longshore workers will not cross that picket line. We also have free will. I am not working today. There will be other members of the ILWU who will not be working, because we understand the importance of strikes.

It was 1934, in San Francisco where two maritime workers were killed, which led to the General Strike in San Francisco, culminating in us being able to have a Coastwide agreement.

Today, when young people in the community march to the Port of Oakland, they are doing so in solidarity with longshore workers in Longview, Washington, who are fighting the face of Wall Street in the workplace.

EGT, an international grain conglomerate received subsidies from the Port of Longview, then turned around and double-crossed the community and the longshore workers.

For 77 years, longshoremen have handled grain in the Pacific Northwest. The driving force behind this betrayal is Bunge Limited, an international agribusiness, that trades on Wall Street. It is the face of Wall Street on the waterfront, adding focus to this emerging movement.

AG: Boots Riley, What do you expect to see happening today in Oakland? Why is a hip-hop artist involved with Occupy Oakland?

Boots Riley: This General Strike puts some teeth to the slogan that we are the 99%. It's not only that we are the 99% it's that the 1% gets all of their wealth by exploiting us. We want to show people that they can take it back.

I visited OWS early on. Earlier in the year, visited Syntagma Square in Athens and Barcelona, where OWS gets its inspiration from. I performed for Occupy Oakland a couple times. When they were evicted, I helped put out the word for people to show up for the march to take back the plaza. Somebody handed me a bullhorn while we were marching. I've been

involved since then.

The other day we had 3,000 people at a General Assembly, meaning 3,000 organizers to start with. So, if you see that those organizers were working overtime to make this happen, and on top of that, we're gaining momentum.

SEIU has jumped in, encouraging their workers to take the day off. As a matter of fact, to do phone banking and job visits to get their workers to take the day off. All the unions, the Oakland Education Association is taking the day off and informing parents that they're not going to be at work. High schools are walking out. Community groups and churches are involved. There are going to be a lot of people.

So, I would say, we start with the 3,000 that are organizing it, so they will be there, and we will probably have multitudes more than that, tens of thousands of people out.

CT: If I may add, Black labor is also in support of this. The Coalition of Black Trade Unionists, Northern California Chapter, will be involved. There will be demonstrations at banks and financial institutions today.

There are three things that distinguish the Occupy Oakland Movement:

1. No politicians;
2. No political parties;
3. The absence of police presence at the occupation camp.

This is very significant, because I know that the similarity we find between the MWMM and the Occupy Oakland movement is mobilizing and organizing in our own name, independent of the two Wall Street political parties.

Amy Goodman interviewed Clarence Thomas and Boots Riley on Democracy Now! Nov. 2, 2011.

BR: This is a significant for the OWS movement, because of criticisms that their message is unclear. We're sure that with the millions of dollars and the profit that's lost from closing the Port in this General Strike, will sent a message to the 1%. This is a warning shot. There is no contract to negotiate right now. What we are saying is, is that the working class is about to get more militant and more organized.

AG: I want to get your response to Oakland Mayor Jean Quan. She attempted to speak at Occupy Oakland encampment outside City Hall.

BR: Mayor Quan ordered the police to evict the Occupy Oakland encampment. It was violent and with tear gas and rubber bullets.

The only reason that the city is saying that there will be no retaliation against workers is because we have momentum and the unions are behind us. The community sees what's going on. It's not a favor.

The point is, is that when you elect a politician, it has nothing to do with their personality. Politicians perform a function, a role in government. And the role of city government is not one that serves the people, unless the people make it do what they want.

AG: Police Chief Howard Jordan, defended the use of force to break up the camp. He said, "The decision was based on public health and safety, fire hazards, violent behaviors, and denial of access of medical aid."

CT: The reasons for the police taking the actions that they have are somewhat analogous to the weapons of mass destruction that was the rationale for going to war in Iraq. These allegations are unfounded. If there was a question concerning health and safety, the camp is open to having conversations with department heads.

Let's say that those reasons were in fact true. Was it the appropriate response to come down in a shock and awe, using 'non-lethal weapons' that have put an Iraqi veteran in a trauma center? People have a right to peaceably assemble and they have a right to free speech. That's exactly what is being exercised and what is being challenged.

Schools will be closing and teachers will be walking out. There will be teach-ins dealing with such issues as social justice and the purpose of general strikes.

BR: Everywhere you go people are talking about the General Strike. It's news all over the world, everyone ready to take part in history.

There are convergences and marches to go and take over the Port, We are going to Shut It Down.

AG: Clarence Thomas, do you see this as representing a turning point in this movement with the people at Occupy Oakland working with unions?

CT: Yes, because if nothing else, there will be a new discussion about the issue of working people withholding their labor, working people

becoming proactive. It is a watershed moment. We're seeing the emergence of new coalitions that are very important in terms of building the movement. For too long, the labor movement has not embraced the social justice movement. They're too concerned about business unionism.

Now international presidents, such as Bob McEllrath of the ILWU and James Hoffa of the IBT, have sent statements of solidarity supporting the OWS movement. This is a breakthrough. The rank-and-file of their respective unions are turning out.

BR: Most of the working class is not unionized. The ILWU is probably the most militant union out there. But many people feel that unions aren't militant and don't do anything.

The OWS movement, by putting out the idea that the 1% is leeching off the 99%, opens a new discussion, people are figuring out how to withhold their labor, to put their issues on the table. This marks a new day in direct action organizing. We're doing something which can stop the mechanisms of industry long enough so we can negotiate a different deal.

CT: This is a fight-back movement, Amy, in the true sense of the word.

AG: I want to thank you both for being with us, Boots Riley of The Coup, Clarence Thomas past secretary-treasurer of the Local 10, now a spokesperson for the MWMM.

tinyurl.com/yxne8rq6

Victory in Oakland buoys Occupy Movement

Larry Hales

The call by Occupy Oakland for a General Strike on Nov. 2, 2011, came after police from Alameda County brutally assaulted people trying to return to their encampment on Oct. 25 at Oscar Grant Plaza after police had ousted them and ransacked their belongings.

Videos show what resembled a war zone as police attacked demonstrators with pepper gas, 'flash-bang' grenades and disabling projectiles. A 24 year-old Marine veteran, Scott Olsen, was severely injured when a projectile launched by police hit him in the face. Dozens of people were arrested and injured and more than 500 cops from 12 different police agencies were involved. The call for a General Strike on Nov. 2 was a bold move.

The attempt to crack down on the occupation in Oakland was not an isolated event. Similar actions by police have occurred in the States of Colorado, Georgia, Washington and elsewhere.

Each time the state has stepped in, the movement has grown larger and attracted more attention. Its primary target, as evidenced by Occupy Wall Street, has been the banks and financial institutions and the wealthy. Each attack has made it ever clearer that the fundamental function of the state apparatus is to protect the interests of the ruling elite.

The Occupy Oakland General Strike came at this juncture. Even four months earlier, it would have seemed impossible to launch a large action in a week's time. When the South Central Federation of Labor in Wisconsin, which represented 45,000 workers, endorsed a call for a General Strike last winter in response to Gov. Scott Walker's bill to curtail collective bargaining, labor, progressives and revolutionaries held their breath. A tremendous uprising was underway in Wisconsin, but labor leaders did not heed the call.

But in Oakland, the occupation movement, spurred by the police attack and the lies emanating from city politicians, wasted no time. The proposal for a General Strike, made by Marxist and cultural artist Boots Riley of the rap group The Coup, was supported by more than 90% of the General Assembly in Oakland. Support poured in from around the country. A national call was put out by BAYAN USA, Bail Out the People Movement, and other groups and individuals.

The call was ultimately supported by the Oakland Education Association, California Nurses Association, members of Local 10, Service Employees Local 1021, United Auto Workers Local 2865, United Brotherhood of Carpenters Local 713 and the ILWU Inlandboatmen's Union.

City workers were allowed to take the day off. Starting at 9 a.m. people began amassing at Oscar Grant Plaza and from there marched to downtown banks. They forced Wells Fargo, Bank of America and Chase to close. Young people tied a banner that read 'Death to Capitalism' between two lamp poles.

Though police across Alameda County, were put on alert and fully mobilized, they were not a visual presence as young people took streets, sealed off bank doors with caution tape, taped eviction posters to their doors and banged on the windows while chanting.

The noise was deafening. It is estimated that at least 30,000 people took part in numerous protests that wound through the streets of downtown Oakland. The activists directed traffic and ultimately ended up at the Port of Oakland. Several bus loads of people were also driven the two-plus miles to the port. Earlier in the day, the port operated at 50% capacity, with at least one-third of the jobs unclaimed. Because many high-skilled positions weren't filled, whole crews were idled. The march to the port began to assemble at 4 p.m.

Three groups of marchers left from downtown Oakland between 4:30 p.m. and 6 p.m. Still there was no visible police presence other than helicopters. It was later revealed that there were plainclothes police in the crowd, but no cruisers or uniform cops on motorcycles, bikes, horses or foot could be seen.

As the march neared the docks, it became clear how large it was. No trucks could leave. Barricades were erected and protesters blocked trucks with their bodies, asking the drivers for solidarity. In every case the trucks turned back.

Protesters blocked every gate and waited until nightfall, when an arbitrator was supposed to come and determine whether the workers could "safely" cross the picket lines at each gate. The thousands who marched on the port remained, sitting on cold concrete, or standing, talking politics, getting acquainted with one another. The mood was electric.

ILWU Local 10 has a history of dynamic action, going back to one of its founders and leaders, Harry Bridges, who helped lead the San Francisco General Strike of 1934, that ended with all the ports on the West Coast being unionized. ILWU Local 10 has led solidarity actions against the wars in Iraq and Afghanistan, against apartheid in South Africa and in solidarity with the Palestinian struggle. ILWU Local 21 is currently leading a valiant effort against EGT grain terminal in Longview, Washington.

Demonstrators waited as the start of the shift was moved from 7 p.m. to 8 p.m. Finally, word of the shift being canceled was greeted by cheers. The marching band that had participated in the day's actions continued to play, energizing the crowd.

Marchers began leaving the port, stopping to talk to people at the barricades. It was under an overpass, just off the docks, that the first police cars were spotted: Rows of them from California Highway Patrol and other agencies.

Some people remained to make sure no trucks left to deliver their cargo. Later in the evening a group of a few hundred tried to take over a building and were met with police violence. Again, a thick cloud of pepper gas wafted over downtown as cops battled the protesters who had chosen a more confrontational action.

The day was a success and has inspired other calls for General Strikes around the country. The crisis is not going away. Now is a time for boldness and action. The Occupy Oakland General Strike proves that much is possible and can be achieved.

This is a time when revolutionary ideology is needed more than ever. The fundamental contradiction is between the oppressed and working class, on the one hand, and the ruling wealthy class and their system, on the other. The only way to end the increasing misery is to do away with this capitalist system and build socialism.

Downtown Oakland on Nov. 2, 2011.
WW photo: Bill Bowers

May Day Rallies Celebrate Unity; Labor Unions & Immigrants Plan to March Side by Side
tinyurl.com/ygujpcln

Chris Silvera, Juan González and Clarence Thomas, on April 29, 2011, at the Democracy Now! studio.

Photo: Tamara Choi (DN! Volunteer)

Longshore workers applaud Occupy Oakland's Port Shut Down

Clarence Thomas

The eyes of the world were on the City of Oakland and the massive people's march to the nation's fifth-largest container port on Nov. 2, 2011, for the General Strike and Day of Mass Action called by Occupy Oakland. Not only has the Occupy movement gone global, Occupy Oakland has become the focal point of the movement. In fact, on Oct. 28, Egyptian pro-democracy protesters marched from Tahrir Square to the U.S. Embassy in support of Occupy Oakland and against police brutality witnessed in Oakland on Oct. 25, and commonly experienced in Egypt.

The unprecedented outpouring of a broad cross section of the community numbering in the tens of thousands is the most significant independent people's mobilization in the U.S. thus far.

This call for a General Strike was in response to the coordinated military-style attack by 18 police agencies in the Bay Area that attempted to evict the encampment of Occupy Oakland at Oscar Grant Plaza, where U.S. veteran Scott Olsen, was critically wounded by a tear gas canister shot to his head by Oakland police.

This call for a General Strike was not called by labor, and perhaps rightfully so, because only 12.9% of the overall workforce is unionized. This is the lowest percentage since 1900.

While it is true that it would take more

than a week to organize a General Strike in this country, the fact of the matter is that organized labor would not get the blessing of their Democratic Party masters to take such an action. Remember, the Republican and Democratic parties are controlled by Wall Street and the 1%.

The rank-and-file of labor is ready to take militant action at the point of production or service. SEIU Local 1021 was able to get their city workers the day off to either participate in the "stop work" action or not to be required to come to work for health and safety reasons.

The Port of Oakland's last two Shut Downs came as the result of Local 10 members taking solidarity action. The first was the Justice for Oscar Grant, "Stop Police Brutality, Jail Killer Cops," action, where longshore workers closed five Bay Area ports on Oct. 23, 2010.

The second Port of Oakland Shut Down was the April 4, 2011, rank-and-file action to shut down the Port of Oakland for 24 hours on the anniversary of the assassination of Rev. Dr. Martin Luther King Jr. in solidarity with the Wisconsin public sector workers' fight for collective bargaining.

The resolution by the Occupy Oakland Strike Assembly states on its website www.occupy oakland.org the reason for shutting down the Port of Oakland:

"We are doing this in order to blockade

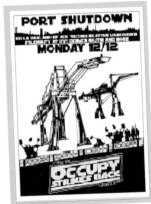

the flow of capital on the day of the General Strike, as well as to show our commitment to solidarity with Longshore workers in their struggle against EGT in Longview, Wash. EGT is an international grain exporter which is attempting to rupture longshore jurisdiction. The driving force behind EGT is Bunge LTD, a leading agribusiness and food company which reported $2.4 billion in profit in 2010; this company has strong ties to Wall Street.

This is but one example of Wall Street's corporate attack on workers. The Oakland General Strike will demonstrate the wide-reaching implications of the OWS movement. The entire world is fed up with the huge disparity of wealth caused by the present system. Now is time for the people to do something about it. The Oakland General Strike is a warning shot to the 1%. Their wealth only exists because the 99% creates it for them."

The importance of the Port of Oakland Shut Down was that it linked up labor, the community and Occupy Oakland in a strategic action at the point of production. Not only was the Port of Oakland Shut Down impacting the movement of cargo in the Pacific Rim, it also disrupted rail schedules, trucking scheduling and 'just in time delivery' services for companies such as Walmart, on Nov. 2, 2011.

The labor movement must take a leading role in building a broad-based, working-class movement that challenges corporate rule and power by putting forward a people's agenda, such as the one put forward by the

OAKLAND IS OCCUPIED OHLONE LAND

DECOLONIZE THE 99%
DEFEND MOTHER EARTH

MWM in 2004, which includes the following:

- Stop corporate greed!
- Hands off Social Security!
- Slash the military budget!
- Universal health care!
- Stop dismantling public education!
- Bring the troops home now!
- Tax relief for the working class!
- Repeal corporate free trade agreements!
- Amnesty for all undocumented workers!
- Stop off shoring American jobs!
- Preserve and restore the environment!
- Workers right to organize!
- Tax the rich!
- National living wage!
- Truth in media!
- End to police brutality!
- Repeal Taft-Hartley!
- Enforce all civil rights!
- Guaranteed pensions!
- Repeal Patriot Act!

The Nov. 2 General Strike and Day of Mass Action in Occupy Oakland was more than just a day of protest against corporate rule, power and police repression. It was a day of resistance interrupting the flow of commerce, and the closure of banks and the Port of Oakland. It sets the example for other Occupy movements throughout the country to follow.

Abridged WW, from Nov. 24, 2011.

Estibadores aplauden cierre del puerto por Ocupar Oakland

Clarence Thomas

El 2 de noviembre los ojos del mundo estaban puestos en la ciudad de Oakland y la masiva marcha del pueblo al quinto puerto de buques portacontenedores más grande del país. Ese era el día de la Huelga General y Día de Acción Masiva convocadas por Ocupar Oakland. No sólo el movimiento de Ocupaciones se ha vuelto global, sino que Ocupar Oakland se ha convertido en el centro del movimiento. De hecho, el 28 de octubre manifestantes egipcios en pro de la democracia marcharon desde la Plaza Tahrir a la embajada de Estados Unidos en apoyo de Ocupar Oakland y en contra de la brutalidad policíaca que fue exhibida en Oakland el 25 de octubre y que comúnmente se experimenta en Egipto.

La sin precedente marea humana de decenas de miles de personas provenientes de una amplia sección de la comunidad, es la movilización popular independiente más importante en los Estados Unidos en lo que va del siglo XXI.

Esta convocatoria de huelga general fue en respuesta al ataque de estilo militar coordinado por 18 agencias de la policía en el Área de la Bahía que intentaron desalojar el campamento de Ocupar Oakland en la Plaza Oscar Grant, donde el veterano militar estadounidense Scott Olsen, quien sirvió dos períodos de servicio en Irak, fue herido por una bomba de gases lacrimógenos que fue disparada directamente a su cabeza por la policía de Oakland.

Esta convocatoria de una Huelga General no fue llamada por el movimiento sindical y quizás con razón, porque sólo el 12,9 por ciento de la fuerza laboral está sindicalizada. De hecho, en el sector privado sólo el 7,2 por ciento de los/as trabajadores/as está sindicalizado. Este es el porcentaje más bajo desde 1900.

Si bien es cierto que tardaría poco más de una semana para organizar una Huelga General en este país, el hecho es que el sector sindical no recibiría la bendición de sus amos del Partido Demócrata para tomar tal acción. Recordemos, los partidos Republicano y Demócrata están controlados por Wall Street y el 1 por ciento.

Las bases de los sindicatos sin embargo, están preparadas para tomar acciones militantes en su punto de producción o de servicios. El Local 1021 del sindicato SEIU fue capaz de obtener el día libre para sus trabajadores/as de la ciudad para que participaran en la acción de "dejar de trabajar" o para que no fueran requeridos/as a ir al trabajo por razones de salud ó seguridad.

Los dos últimos paros del puerto de Oakland sucedieron como resultado de la acción solidaria tomada por miembros del Local 10. La primera fue por la justicia para Oscar Grant, la acción – "Alto a la brutalidad policial, a la cárcel los policías asesinos" – donde los estibadores cerraron cinco puertos de la zona de la bahía el 23 de octubre de 2010.

El segundo cierre del puerto de Oakland fue la acción voluntaria de miembros de base del sindicato el 4 de abril de 2011 para cerrar el puerto de Oakland durante 24 horas en el aniversario del asesinato del Dr. Martin Luther King Jr. en solidaridad con la lucha de los trabajadores/as públicos/as de Wisconsin sobre la negociación colectiva.

El acuerdo de la Asamblea de Huelga de Ocupar Oakland afirma en su sitio Web www.occupyoakland.org la razón para cerrar el puerto de Oakland:

"Estamos haciendo esto para bloquear el flujo de capital el día de la Huelga General, y también para mostrar nuestro compromiso de solidaridad con los trabajadores estibadores en su lucha contra la EGT en Longview, Wash. EGT es una exportadora internacional de granos que está tratando de romper la jurisdicción de los estibadores. La fuerza propulsora detrás de la EGT es Bunge LTD, una destacada compañía de la industria agropecuaria y de alimentos que reportó ganancias de $2,4 mil millones en 2010; y esta compañía tiene conexiones fuertes con Wall Street. Éste es solamente un ejemplo del ataque corporativo de Wall Street contra los/as trabajadores/as. La Huelga

General de Oakland mostrará las implicaciones del gran alcance que tiene el movimiento Ocupar Wall Street. El mundo entero está harto de la enorme disparidad en riquezas provocada por el sistema actual. Ahora es el momento cuando el pueblo está haciendo algo para cambiar la situación. La Huelga General es una señal de advertencia al 1 por ciento – que su riqueza solamente existe porque el 99 por ciento la crea para ellos".

La importancia del paro en el Puerto de Oakland fue que conectó los sindicatos, la comunidad y el Ocupar Oakland en una acción estratégica en el punto de producción. El cierre del puerto de Oakland no solamente tuvo un impacto en la transporte de cargamentos en el Pacífico, sino que también interrumpió los horarios de los ferrocarriles, de camiones y de los servicios de "entregar a tiempo" para compañías como

Wal-Mart el 2 de noviembre.

El movimiento sindical debe desempeñar un papel de liderazgo para construir un amplio movimiento basado en la clase trabajadora que desafíe la dominación y el poder corporativo al avanzar una agenda del pueblo, como la que fue promulgada por el Movimiento Marcha de un Millón de Trabajadores/as en 2004.

La Huelga General y Día de Acción Masiva en Oakland el 2 de noviembre fue más que un solo día de protesta contra la dominación corporativa, el poder y la represión policíaca. Fue un día de resistencia que interrumpió el flujo del comercio y el cierre de los bancos y el Puerto. Fue un ejemplo para otros movimientos de Ocupaciones para que continúen por todo el país. La Asamblea General de Ocupar Dallas ya ha llamado a una Huelga General de Dallas que tendrá lugar el 30 de noviembre de 2011.

ILWU Local 21 Longview president:
Dan Coffman at Occupy Oakland

We represent all the working people of the world. When Occupy Oakland called for a general strike on Nov. 2, 2011, you cannot believe what you did for the inspiration of the union members in ILWU Local 21 who have been on the picket line against EGT for six months.

This is what we're talking about,

it is the corporate greed. EGT consists of three multinational corporations with tentacles that extend around the whole world, including Bunge, North America. It's part of a grain cartell which controls the world's food supply. These people are part of the one percent that is trying to dictate to the ILWU how we're going to work. We don't want any part of it. The ILWU will fight these people until the bitter end.

Occupy Oakland and Occupy Wall Street, you are the core of this whole thing. You'll shed light in Portland Oregon, in Seattle, Washington and Eugene, Oregon. This movement is growing. The workers of the world, the poor of the world,

Dan Coffman speaks at a Occupy Oakland rally on Nov. 11, 2011 about their struggle against EGT and the support by Occupy Oakland . See the YouTube video at: tinyurl.com/y3bn9w3n

the students of the world have to lead this. We're not going to stop until we change the last 30 years of what's been happening to this country

Once again speaking for ILWU Local 21: "We love you. Thank you Occupy Oakland from the bottom of our hearts!"

Oakland on Nov. 19, 2011
Photo: Terri Kay

West Coast Occupy Wall Street:
'Shut Docks Dec. 12!'

Terri Kay

Battle lines have formed as the West Coast Occupy movements, from San Diego to Alaska, flex their collective muscle against the federally coordinated, brutal attacks targeting the pro-Occupy Wall Street movements across the country. They are organizing for blockades of West Coast ports on Dec. 12, 2011, in San Diego; Los Angeles/Long Beach; Port Hueneme, Calif.; Oakland; Portland, Ore.; Seattle; Tacoma, Wash.; and possibly more. Solidarity actions have been called by OWS in New York and inland locations, as well.

The pro-OWS movement is aligning itself with labor and the working class, as the West Coast Occupy movements organize to support the struggle of the ILWU in Longview, Wash. Longshore workers there are waging a battle against transnational EGT, controlled by Bunge Ltd., of the grain cartel that controls most of the world's trade in food products. EGT is trying to break the ILWU in an attempt to drive down wages and destroy the union.

The West Coast Occupy movements are also aligning with the struggle of port truckers, who are fighting for the right to union representation. Twenty-six of them were fired in Los Angeles for wearing Teamsters jackets to work. Occupy LA and Long Beach are targeting SSA, an anti-union terminal operator, majority owned by Goldman Sachs, the notorious Wall Street investment bank. Teamsters president, Jimmy Hoffa Jr., has expressed support for the Occupy movement.

Michael Novick of Anti-Racist Action, one of the main organizers at Occupy LA working on the port shutdown action in Los Angeles, said that the strategy will be to shut down three main targets. Novick states, "When we put the resolution through at the General Assembly in support of the Port shut down, it was tied to building a General Strike on May 1, 2012, and building relations to the migrant rights movement."

Finally, the West Coast Occupy movements are targeting the ports as major commercial centers, showing that they can strike at the institutions which help to aggregate the wealth of the 1% by disrupting Wall Street on the waterfront. It's the history of the militant ILWU which enables this attack to have teeth. The ILWU rank-and-file have supported struggles such as the anti-apartheid movement, the anti-war movement, in defense of Palestine, in support of the Wisconsin struggle against union busting, etc.

The 1%, under the banner of the Port of Oakland, launched their assault on Dec. 4, with full-page ads in the San Francisco Chronicle and Oakland Tribune against the Occupy Port Blockade. They know how powerful this movement has become, evidenced by the historic General Strike call at the Port of Oakland on Nov. 2, the Occupy movement, with the support of the ILWU rank-and-file and port truckers, shut down the entire Port.

The battle is just beginning. EGT is planning to bring a huge grain ship to the Port of Longview, some time January, to unload the grain piled up there, with the use of scab labor. That isn't going to happen without a major fight. Plans are in the works for phase two of this struggle. Caravans will be heading up to Longview to support the ILWU's fight to keep their jobs and maintain their union. Port truckers in Oakland have also had teach-ins to help their ranks understand what this struggle means to them. The battle is on!

Abridged from WW, Dec. 15, 2011.

Barucha Peller, Clarence Thomas and Tova Fry on Dr. Martin Luther King Day 2015. Thomas is wearing a hat from the April 4, 2011 port shut down.

The revolutionary socialist vision
Our debt to the Occupy Wall Street Movement

Larry Holmes

We are in the opening stages of a wholly new epoch. This epoch in all likelihood will be protracted and long. It will be uneven, it will be explosive, it will be fraught with dangers, all of it necessary to that which we have been waiting so long for: the awakening of our global proletariat, and especially the awakening of that section of the proletariat whose development we are responsible for, the U.S. working class.

The epoch I am referring to is the beginning of the end of capitalism. The epoch will end with the destruction of capitalism and the expropriation of the capitalist class.

Of course, it is possible that at the opportune time, when the system is at its weakest and the capitalist bourgeoisie is the weakest, our class and its leadership might not be prepared to carry through the revolution.

In that case, capitalism might get another short lease on life, the way a parasite does if it is not stomped out. It is axiomatic for revolutionary Marxists that no matter how much it seems that capitalism will fall apart of its own dead weight and decay, it will not simply fall apart. It will need to be buried. And that process can only be completed by the working class. But that is a caveat.

The important point is that anti-capitalist consciousness is growing on a global basis. It is actually surging. Some of it is incipient, not well articulated; some of it is better articulated; some of it is articulated by those who are not real revolutionaries and who have another agenda

with whom we have differences. All of that will be part of the terrain that we are developing and fighting.

The revolutionary movement and all who are moving in a revolutionary direction should not underestimate the depth of the radicalization of sections of the working class, especially the youth but not only the youth. Because radicalization, especially when it abets the struggle, becomes contagious.

And so, if the revolutionary movement is ultimately going to play its role in helping our class to move toward what is sometimes called the maximum program, socialist revolution, it will be necessary for us to be very conscious, very meticulous and serious in how we go about it.

There are sections of the world capitalist class that are more aware than even the most militant sections of the working-class movement of the reality that this capitalist crisis is no "garden variety" crisis; but rather something infinitely more profound than all previous crises and more importantly, a crisis from which there is no way out.

This is no small matter because our class and its organizations cannot fight that which it does not fully understand. It goes without saying that we communists must assist the working class and the oppressed in defending all the gains, be they significant or meager gains, that are under relentless attack. However let there be no illusions, the epochal class struggle that is in the making on a global level will not be resolved on the basis of concessions or re-

forms, or a return to some semblance of 'capitalist stability.' Those days are over.

It is important, henceforth, for us to see the possibility of socialist revolution, no not tomorrow, but neither as merely some idea that has no relevance to the class struggle today. To truly understand how unprecedented and irreversible the present world capitalist crisis is, is to understand that the question of the need for world socialist revolution is not something that can be postponed.

Whatever other work the revolutionary movement undertakes in the day-to-day class struggle, we will not be of help to our class and only cause more confusion, if we fail to illuminate the road to the socialist revolution.

Significance of Occupy Wall Street movement

The Occupy Wall Street development is symptomatic of this. We have debated inside the Party and in the movement whether or not OWS should have been anticipated. Let's take a look at that. If you just say in the narrowest sense that no one knew how significant Sept. 17 was going to be and what would happen, I suppose you could make a case for that.

In a larger sense, a truer sense, the Occupy movement should have come as no surprise. Why? The OWS development is wholly unique to the unprecedented character of the current global capitalist crisis. And if we had been paying attention, we would have known that it was in the making. For example, at our last plenum, some of you may recall, we took note of an article that appeared in Forbes magazine shortly after the rebellions in the United Kingdom in the mid-summer, mid-August.

Forbes magazine, not some radical publication, had an article titled: "UK riot means global class war is coming." This was several weeks before Sept. 17, 2011.

The article is significant because it reflected the thinking of at least some within the world capitalist establishment. The article mostly talked about how high unemployment is, particularly among youth, both oppressed and working-class youth, as well as youth who previously considered themselves somewhat more privileged, how devastating unemployment is and how they are all saddled with enormous college-related debt.

One of the most intriguing, astonishing and gratifying aspects of OWS is that it reflected, at least to some extent, that this is a critical social stratum that by virtue of education and other factors is usually promised a place in capitalism. But now, those days are over. And now, this social stratum in the working class and the middle class that capitalism and imperialism have usually depended on for support is beginning to defect.

This must be a cause for great alarm within the bourgeoisie.

We understood right away that there would be tension between some of this stratum and the oppressed sectors of the working class. Most of the young, white participants in the Occupy uprising knew nothing about racism and the national question because it hasn't been an issue for them.

In the final analysis, however, the rebellion of this heretofore more privileged stratum in the working class and the middle class will ultimately be of help to all the workers and the oppressed of the world.

OWS has sharpened the crisis for the revolutionary movement. It is a crisis for us and our friends and allies. Why? Because even though we are ideologically ahead and can teach the best elements in the Occupy movement things they need to learn about imperialism, about the national question, about the woman question and on and on, in some ways they are ahead of us.

I am talking in general about a phenomenon that is hard to avoid. It is what happens when the revolutionary movement contracts as a result of an extended and painfully long reactionary period.

Even when you survive such a period, it can't help but affect your thinking. It may make your thinking more conservative, your expectations more conservative, more narrow. In which case you can be surprised by something that signals a break from that period.

I think this is a process the entire working-class movement is going through.

The Occupy Wall Street movement should serve as a wake up call to all who remain committed to a revolutionary Marxist-Leninist direction. The collapse of the Soviet Union, and the developments that led up to it, are easier to understand today as we can more fully appreciate the devastating toll of more than 30 years of worldwide counterrevolution. Part of that devastating toll has been the degeneration and weakening of the revolutionary socialist orientation.

Degeneration does not happen all at once, overnight, but rather incrementally, almost unconsciously, over an extended period of time and under the pressure of disappointments and

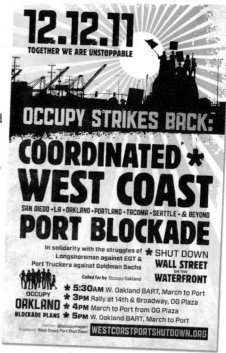

frustrations, the causes for which in large part can be traced to stagnation in the working-class movement, demoralization, contraction and fragmentation in the revolutionary movement, and the seemingly endless prevalence of bourgeois triumphalism, a prevalence that has clearly now come to an end.

In some ways, the young, inexperienced and ideologically eclectic makers of the Occupy movement, precisely because they are not burdened by the baggage of past defeats, understand the gravity of the global capitalist crisis and the revolutionary potential that it has opened better than many of us seasoned veteran revolutionary Marxists.

We will not be able to help the OWS movement advance until and unless we catch up to it.

Presentation to the WWP meeting Dec. 17, 2012 in New York City. Holmes' position as First Secretary of WWP was officially ratified at this meeting. Abridged from WW, Jan. 8, 2012.

General Strike leads to a new call for Dec. 12

Dave Welsh

When the masses of people are in motion, watch out. They may just be chipping away at the foundations of the old established order, while you ain't looking!

For example, the Occupy Oakland General Strike on Nov. 2, 2011, which was an all day festival of people taking power into their own hands. First, many thousands surged through downtown, sidewalk-to-sidewalk, and shut down the four major downtown banks (with many trillions of dollars in assets). Then, when the crowd had grown to 30,000 plus, they poured into the Port of Oakland in three giant waves and shut down the entire port, the fifth busiest in the country. When is the last time something like that happened here in the United States?

Okay, maybe it wasn't a 'traditional' general strike, like 1934 in San Francisco or 1946 in Oakland, or like the general strikes today that regularly paralyze Greece, where the labor movement is strong and militant.

But every general strike is different. And in a country where only 12% of the work force even belong to a union, where organized labor has been on the defensive for the last 30 years, absorbing bruising concessions, two-tier wage scales, runaway shops and Wisconsin-style union-busting, for us, the Occupy Oakland's General Strike was a breath of fresh air.

The Nov. 2 General Strike not only had pretty good support from the city's major unions, 350 unionized Oakland teachers reported to the streets that day, not to work! But it brought into the streets thousands of low-wage workers and their families, youth and students, the unemployed and the foreclosed upon of all races and nationalities, mostly not in unions because there are no longer or not yet any unions there for them, an outpouring of the many faces of today's suffering U.S. working class, and a sign that this sleeping giant may just be awakening from its slumber.

You could say it was a general strike "of a new type," reflecting not only the temporarily diminished power of the unions, but also the changed character of the working class in the U.S., and one that is starting to make common cause with oppressed communities, that is beginning to take bold collective action to defy our adversaries in the 1%.

Now, Occupy Oakland has called for a coordinated West Coast Port Shut Down on Dec. 12, 2011, in solidarity with longshore workers in Longview, Wash., who are fighting to preserve the union there. The call is for Occupy movements in each port city and port truckers to participate in the Coast-wide action.

The first leaflet conveyed the fighting spirit of this young movement: "Together we are unstoppable."

The writer is a retired union letter carrier and longtime activist in the Bay Area.

Abridged from WW, Dec. 1, 2011.

OCCUPY OAKLAND

Police continue attacks; activists continue resistance

Dan Coffman, president of Local 21 in Longview, Wash., spoke at the Nov. 19, 2011, rally in Oakland, Calif. Their local is in support of a call for a West Coast Port Shut Down on Dec. 12. Meanwhile, school children at Lakeview Elementary, one of five Oakland schools scheduled to be closed, also rallied on Nov. 19.

A new Occupy Oakland encampment was destroyed by Oakland police on the morning of Nov. 20. Undaunted, an emergency General Assembly was held at Oscar Grant Plaza that evening, focusing on both the most recent attack and the Port Shut Down. Some are urging the re-occupation of Oscar Grant Plaza, which Occupy Oakland renamed in honor of the young Black man killed by Oakland transit police in 2009.

— **Bill Bowers and Terri Kay**

WW photo: Bill Bowers

Oakland police repression intensifies

Terri Kay

The brutal attack on Occupy Oakland on Jan. 28, 2012, by the Oakland Police Department (OPD) is part of a nationally coordinated attack against the Occupy movement, which includes the Feb. 4 eviction of Occupy D.C. from McPherson Square in the U.S. capital by riot-clad cops.

The Jan. 28 march was an attempt to take over an abandoned public building and convert it into a community center, a place to feed and shelter the homeless, and an operations center for General Assemblies and other meetings and activities. Occupy Oakland has faced increasing police harassment at Oscar Grant Plaza, where it continues a 24/7 vigil ever since the last encampment was broken up.

According to the National Lawyers Guild, at least 284 people were arrested Jan. 28, with many reports of assaults on protesters by the OPD. This included one person who had their teeth knocked out from a strike to the face by a police baton, others thrown through a glass door and down a flight of stairs, and the clubbing of a videographer by the OPD. Once in Alameda County Sheriff's custody, the brutality continued.

Significantly, Occupy Oakland has been intensively engaged in building solidarity with workers' struggles, and demands. It inspired activists around the U.S. with the Nov. 2 General Strike and Port Shut Down, organized in just one week, after the Oct. 25 vicious police raid on their camp.

In addition to shutting down downtown Oakland and focusing on the banks, which have destroyed the economy and stolen peoples' homes, Occupy Oakland, with the support of the ranks of the Locals 10 and 34,

Occupiers wanted to turn vacant building into a community center.   Photo: Terri Kay

shut down Oakland's ports. They raised demands to support Local 21 in Longview, Wash., which was engaged in a militant struggle against international grain cartel EGT.

Then, Occupy Oakland led other Occupy groups in organizing an entire West Coast Port Shut Down on Dec. 12, with the major demands being support for the Local 21 struggle in Longview and support for port truckers in Los Angeles fighting to get union recognition. Ports were shut down in Oakland; Portland, Ore.; Seattle; and Longview, Wash., with port slow downs and solidarity actions in other cities.

Occupy Oakland then took on a campaign to organize a caravan to Longview to blockade the loading of scab grain onto a ship in response to a call by Occupy Longview and the Cowlitz-Wahkiakum County, Washington Central Labor Council. Support was organized up and down the Coast and EGT was forced back to the bargaining table under threat of thousands of protesters descending on the small town.

The government wants to discredit these organizers and keep them from being able to continue building solidarity between the community and labor. "Stay away" injunctions have been issued to at least 12 of the Jan. 28 arrestees, who are not allowed to go

near Oscar Grant Plaza. Felony burglary charges were leveled against at least 50 people who ran into the open YMCA to get away from the police.

The Oakland City Council is pursuing a resolution on Feb. 7 to basically use any "legal" means at their disposal to prevent any future shut downs at the Port of Oakland. The resolution was originally raised as an emergency resolution after the Dec. 12 Port Shut Down. Occupiers filled the council chambers in protest.

Calif. Gov. Jerry Brown has offered up the National Guard to aid the OPD in the event of another port shut down attempt. Meanwhile, hundreds of port truckers have walked off the job in Seattle, in protest of unsafe conditions, effectively shutting the Port of Seattle for days.

At the same time that the City of Oakland has spent millions of dollars repressing Occupy Oakland, they are planning major layoffs of city workers and related service cutbacks to the community. When the Council planned a vote in January on the proposed layoffs, 100 occupiers marched right into the council chambers in support of the Service Employees Union, disrupting the meeting with chants against the layoffs and demanding that payments to the banks be withheld instead.

Abridged from WW, Feb. 16, 2012.

ILWU's Northwest Export Grain Terminal conflict:

Business unionism or fighting class-struggle unionism

Jack Heyman

When Wisconsin state workers were courageously occupying the state capitol to protest Governor Scott Walker's attack on their unions' right to bargain, AFL-CIO president Richard Trumka trumpeted a call for solidarity actions throughout the labor movement on April 4, 2011, the anniversary of the assassination of Martin Luther King, killed during the Memphis sanitation workers' strike.

International Longshore and Warehouse Union (ILWU) president Robert McEllrath reiterated the call to mobilize labor. It was to be a day of 'no business as usual,' proclaimed the labor media. Yet, only one union, ILWU Local 10, organized a solidarity job action that day shutting down the Port of Oakland and sending their Drill Team to march with their sisters and brothers in the Wisconsin battleground.

When the employers' Pacific Maritime Association (PMA) threatened a Taft-Hartley lawsuit against the local for an illegal sympathy strike, neither Trumka nor McEllrath came to their defense. But the labor federations of South Central Wisconsin, San Francisco, South Bay, and Alameda passed resolutions defending ILWU Local 10 as labor's moral compass.

As the Wisconsin labor federation messaged to a rally in front of PMA headquarters in San Francisco: "Whether it's racist apartheid in South Africa, imperialist war in Iraq, or fascist plutocracy in Wisconsin, Local 10, over and over again, shows us 'What a Union should look like!'

(See sites.google.com/site/defendilwulocal10).

ILWU vs. The Grain Monopolies

Now the ILWU is under attack from the grain monopolies, "ABCD," Archer Daniels Midland, Bunge, Cargill, and Dreyfus who control 75-90% of the world's grain trade. According to Oxfam their profits are rooted in the world's hunger and poverty, not to mention ecological devastation and attacks on unions. ILWU longshore workers are locked out and scabs are doing their work in Vancouver, Washington, and across the Columbia River in Portland, Oregon.

The union has only put up token informational picket lines, while scabs continue to taunt them provocatively. Picket lines mean 'DON'T CROSS!' ILWU's militant history shows mass labor mobilizations can stop scabbing.

What's at stake here is the future of the ILWU and of the entire labor movement. If employers can attack what historically has been the most militant trade union in the U.S. without any unified response from organized labor, then the obvious question is: Where is the trade union movement heading?

If unions like the Operating Engineers and now the Masters, Mates and Pilots Union (MMP) can waltz across union-sanctioned picket lines without a qualm and the head of the AFL-CIO remains silent, then what kind of labor movement do we have? Worse still, according to an ILWU document, not only has the MMP

crossed a picket line, they're renting office space to Gettier (strikebreakers' services) in the MMP's building less than a mile from the Portland docks. And both MMP and ILWU are members of the newly formed Maritime Labor Alliance!

Longshoremen led the struggle, But then . . .

In 2011, U.S.-based Bunge began an employers' feeding frenzy, by hiring another union Operating Engineers Local 701 to scab on ILWU at its new grain facility in Longview, Washington, the Export Grain Terminal (EGT). Then, EGT demanded and got cataclysmic concessions. Bunge is the dominant consortium partner of EGT with Japanese-owned grain trader Itochu and Korean owned STX Pan Ocean Shipping.

Initially, rank-and-file longshore workers in the Northwest mounted a bold defense blocking grain trains, twice occupying the EGT facility, and on September 8, 2011, shutting down major ports including Portland, Seattle, and Tacoma. Longshore workers were linking up with other unions and the Occupy movement for a planned mass mobilization in January 2012, in Longview to 'meet and greet' EGT's first scab grain ship.

However, fearing threats from Democratic Party 'friends of labor' like President Obama, his Coast Guard and Homeland Security, as well as Washington Governor Gregoire's mustering of police forces and the mounting fines, union tops capitulated. To mollify angry members, ILWU officers claimed they had a 'secret plan' which was neither divulged nor implemented.

Following his members in blocking a train, McEllrath was jailed last year for a day. Rather than shutting down ports in protest for the day, as they'd done in 1980, for Inlandboatmen's Union president Don Liddle jailed in Seattle for leading a ferry boat strike, officials just gave a nod, as longshore workers walked off the job for barely an hour at the end of the day. This was a sign of weakness rather than a demonstration of strength. Other members were arrested several times and jailed for weeks, like Byron Jacobs, former Secretary-Treasurer of Longview Local 21. Yet, nothing was done to protest their jailing or support their families.

EGT management won their demands: cutting out job dispatch through the union hiring hall, the basis of ILWU's power won in the militant 1934 West Coast Maritime Strike; elimination of all ship clerks' jobs, now done by management; a minimum of 12-hour shifts; removal of the union operator from the grain loading console, this, too, done by management; no grievance machinery or work stoppages for safety; allowing work to continue behind union picket lines with scabs and managers.

McEllrath and ILWU Coast Committeeman Leal Sundet, who heads up grain negotiations and was formerly a PMA honcho in the Columbia River, claimed a jurisdiction 'victory.' With more 'victories' like this, the future of the ILWU is in jeopardy!

Steps down the road to defeat

'Big Bob,' as McEllrath's cohorts call him, and Coast Committeeman Leal Sundet, now the leadership of the union, have turned the once militant ILWU around 180 degrees on a course toward business union-

ILWU President Bob McEllrath was arrested Sept. 7, 2011, following his members in blocking a shipment of grain to a non-ILWU terminal.

Photo: Dawn DesBrisay

ism. They want to collaborate with management, but the grain monopolies are giving them a cold shoulder. Their actions endanger the union. Let's count some of the ways:

There's a crying need to stop the scabbing and end the lockout in Vancouver and Portland through a mass mobilization of labor. That's the ILWU's militant legacy. Yet, when Sundet and McEllrath organized a flag-waving rally at United Grain, owned by Mitsui, patriotic, anti-Japanese venom was spewed. Rather than linking up with unions here and internationally, especially in Japan, they led workers not through the gates of United Grain to chase out the Gettier Security scabs but to Mitsui headquarters demanding they sign the 'good' concessionary interim contract signed by 'an American company,' Cargill/TEMCO. ILWU arbitrations show they have one of the worst anti-union records.

McEllrath and Sundet opposed the ILWU's 'bottom-up, not top-down' union democracy. They denied Longview longshore workers the right to read, discuss, and vote on the EGT grain contract as guaranteed in the ILWU Constitution. They refused to call a Longshore Caucus (Convention) at the start of the EGT dispute for delegates to hammer out a program of action to stop the scabbing at EGT. They undermined any rank-and-file longshore action, opposing rank-and-file rallies to stop the scabbing. To

enforce their policies of capitulation they give virtually no information to the membership on the Coast about the Northwest grain conflict.

'Big Bob' McEllrath and his partner, Pacific Maritime Association head James McKenna, in a gesture of ultimate class collaboration, together received the Connie Award from the maritime employers' Containerization and Intermodal Institute for signing a six-year contract in 2008, without a strike. Yet the contract included a robotics clause which is already devastating longshore jobs in Los Angeles and other major ports. It also included a clause to allow employers to negotiate a change in the medical benefit administrator, something the ranks have always opposed.

When the populist Occupy Wall Street movement was in New York, McEllrath sent words of encouragement. However, when they shocked the PMA by shutting down the Port of Oakland, November 2, 2011, with a march of some 30,000 to protest police brutality against their City Hall encampment and in solidarity with Longview longshore workers, McEllrath and the International officers refused to participate in this mass outpouring of anger against Wall Street on the waterfront. However, Longview longshore union president, Dan Coffman addressed an Occupy Oakland rally giving his heartfelt thanks to Occupy, commending their action for bolstering his members' morale. When Occupy organized a solidarity rally for Longview longshore workers at the Labor Temple in Seattle with rank-and-file ILWU speakers to build up for a mass mobilization to confront a scab ship docking at the EGT terminal, McEllrath and Sundet supporters made sure the meeting was broken up.

Abridged from Counterpunch, June 6, 2013.

Message from Pres. McEllrath:
We share Occupy's concerns about America, but EGT battle is complicated

Letter sent to longshore local unions on Dec. 6, 2011, from ILWU International President Robert McEllrath:

On October 5, 2011, I published a statement in support of "Occupy Wall Street." In that statement, I thanked the organizers of the "Occupy Wall Street" protest in New York City for shining a light on some of the most pressing issues of our times, corporate influence on democracy, the growing disparity between the rich and the poor, and the failure of accountability for the financial crisis. These issues are linked to issues that concern the membership of the International Longshore and Warehouse Union (ILWU), namely, the attack on Social Security and Medicare, the refusal to level the playing field by supporting workplace democracy and employee free choice, and the failure to implement any kind of meaningful change to an unjust tax system, and we find strength in the courage of the supporters of the Occupy movement.

Since my October 5 statement, the Occupy movement has spread from the East Coast to the West Coast and captured the hearts and minds of the 99% who have had enough. Some in the movement have begun to draw comparisons between the broader struggle against Corporate America and the ILWU's labor dispute with its employer EGT in Longview. The fact is that the story of corporate greed and its impact on the working class is the story of the 99%, and, of course, this reality connects us all.

While there can be no doubt that the ILWU shares the Occupy movement's concerns about the future of the middle class and corporate abuses, we must be clear that our struggle against EGT is just that, our struggle. The ILWU has a long history of democracy. Part of that historic democracy is the hard-won right to chart our own course to victory. As the Occupy movement, which began in September 2011, sweeps this country, there is a real danger that forces outside of the ILWU will attempt to adopt our struggle as their own. Support is one thing, organization from outside groups attempting to co-opt our struggle in order to advance a broader agenda is quite another and one that is destructive to our democratic process and jeopardizes our over two year struggle in Longview.

Most recently, groups directly connected to the Occupy movement and other loosely affiliated social media groups have called for the shutdown of certain terminals and the West Coast ports. At the same time, these groups seek to link these shutdowns to the ILWU's labor dispute with employer EGT. None of this is sanctioned by the membership of the ILWU or informed by the local and International leadership. Simply put, there has been no communication with the leadership and no vote within the ILWU ranks on EGT associated Occupy actions.

Further, since our November 22, 2011, press release clarifying our position regarding third-party protests to occupy West Coast ports on December 12, 2011, we have been the subject of much criticism from individuals affiliated with the Occupy movement. This is shortsighted and only serves the 1%. We ask only that our internal process be respected and that whatever transpires not be in our name as we have not taken part in the call for that action.

With respect to EGT, the International Officers are fully engaged. That struggle, as managed by the Coast Committee and local elected officers, is center stage and will be until victory is achieved.

longshoreshippingnews.com/2011/12/message-from-pres-mcellrath-we-share-occupys-concerns-about-america-but-egt-battle-is-complicated/

Longshore workers say
Occupy Movement crucial to EGT settlement

Press release issued Feb. 11, 2012, from Occupy Oakland, Occupy Portland and Occupy Longview

Members of the ILWU and the labor community named the Occupy movement as key to the settlement reached on Feb. 9, 2012, between ILWU Local 21 and the Export Grain Terminal (EGT). The contract finally provides for the use of ILWU labor in the grain terminal at the Port of Longview.

After staging Dec. 12 port shutdowns in solidarity with Local 21, the West Coast Occupy Movement planned coordinated action together with labor allies for a land and water blockade of an EGT ship in Longview, should it attempt to use scab labor to load. OWS in states where EGT's parent company Bunge has operations were also planning actions against the company on the day of the arrival of the ship.

"This is a victory for Occupy in their involvement in forcing negotiations. Make no mistake, the solidarity and organization between the Occupy movement and the Longshore workers won this contract," said Jack Mulcahy, ILWU officer with Local 8 in Portland, Ore. "The mobilizations of the Occupy Movement across the country, particularly in Oakland, Portland, Seattle and Longview, were a critical element in bringing EGT to the bargaining table and forcing a settlement with ILWU Local 21."

"West Coast OWS had already demonstrated their ability to stage such a blockade by shutting down ports along the West Coast on Dec. 12 as well as the Port of Oakland on Nov. 2," said Anthony Leviege, ILWU Local 10 in Oakland.

The Occupy Movement shut down ports in order to express solidarity with port truckers and Local 21, as well as responding to a nationally coordinated eviction campaign against Occupy.

Negotiations progressed to the point where longshore workers began loading the merchant vessel Full Sources on Feb. 14. "When any company ruptures jurisdiction it is a threat to the entire union. The union jobs wouldn't be back in Longview if it weren't for Occupy. It's a win for the entire class of workers in the Occupy Movement in demonstrating their organizational skills," said Leviege.

Nov. 2 and Dec. 12, and the impending mobilization in Longview, is what made EGT come to the table," said Clarence Thomas, ILWU Local 10 Coastwide Caucus delegate. "When Gov. Chris Gregoire intervened a year ago nothing was settled, non-ILWU workers were still working in the port. It wasn't until rank-and-file and Occupy planned a mass convergence to blockade the ship that EGT suddenly had the impetus to negotiate.

"Labor can no longer win victories against the employers without the community," Thomas continued. "It must include a broad-based movement. The strategy and tactics employed by the Occupy Movement in conjunction with rank-and-file ILWU members confirm that the past militant traditions of the ILWU are still effective against the employers today."

EGT itself made evident the company's concern about Occupy's role in the conflict in the Jan. 27 settlement agreement: "The ILWU Entities shall issue a written notice to The Daily News and the general public, including the Occupy Movement, informing them of this settlement and urging them to cease and desist from any actions.

"The Occupy movement and rank-and-file unionists both within and outside of our ranks have forced the company to settle, but this is not over," said Jess Kincaid of Occupy Portland. "Occupy doesn't sign contracts. We have not entered into any agreements with EGT, nor do we intend to do so. EGT and its parent company Bunge bribe the government for military escorts, use slave labor in Brazil and systematically avoid contributing anything to our social safety net in the U.S. or abroad. There is no ethic here beyond putting money back in the pockets of the 1% at the cost of working people and the sustainability of the earth.

"It was the brave action of members of Local 21, blocking the train tracks this past summer, that inspired the solidarity of the Occupy Movement up and down the West Coast and around the country," said Paul Nipper of Occupy Longview. "It was not until Occupy joined together with Local 21 and its labor allies that the company returned to the table. Gov. Gregoire did nothing but let EGT raid longshore jurisdiction until Occupy responded to the call for support."

CHAPTER 12

THE STRUGGLE CONTINUES!

JUNETEENTH 2020 MARCH IN OAKLAND

'Voices of a People's History'

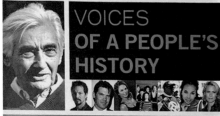

Howard Zinn wrote 'A People's History of the United States' in 1980.

Clarence Thomas, ILWU Local 10 Executive Board member and national co-chair of the MWMM appeared with Howard Zinn in February 2009.

For the occasion he recited Langston Hughes poem, "Ballad of Roosevelt." His second reading was the Rev. Dr. Martin Luther King's speech at the Riverside Church in New York on April 1, 1967, "Beyond Vietnam."

Other presentations were made by Benjamin Bratt, Josh Brolin, Diane Lane, Boots Riley, Stairwell Sisters and Kerry Washington.

.

'When I began work, five years ago, on what would become the present volume, "Voices of a People's History of the United States," I wanted the voices of struggle, mostly absent from our history books, to be given the place they deserve. I wanted labor history, which has been the battleground, decade after decade, century after century, of an ongoing fight for human dignity, to come to the fore. And I wanted my readers to experience how at key moments in our history some of the bravest and most effective political acts were the sounds of the human voice itself.

"To omit or to minimize these voices of resistance is to create the idea that power only rests with those who have the guns, who possess the wealth, who own the newspapers and the television stations. I want to point out that people who seem to have no power, whether working people, people of color, or women – once they organize and protest and create movements – have a voice no government can suppress."

— **Howard Zinn**,
From the introduction

Clarence Thomas and early MWM endorser Howard Zinn at the Mission High School Auditorium, San Francisco in 2009.

Ballad of Roosevelt

The pot was empty,
The cupboard was bare.
I said, Papa,
What's the matter here?
I'm waitin' on Roosevelt, son,
Roosevelt, Roosevelt,
Waitin' on Roosevelt, son.
The rent was due,
And the lights was out.
I said, Tell me, Mama,
What's it all about?
We're waitin' on Roosevelt, son,
Roosevelt, Roosevelt,
Just waitin' on Roosevelt.
Sister got sick
And the doctor wouldn't come
Cause we couldn't pay him
The proper sum—
A-waitin on Roosevelt,
Roosevelt, Roosevelt,
A-waitin' on Roosevelt.
Then one day
They put us out o' the house.
Ma and Pa was Meek as a mouse
Still waitin' on Roosevelt,
Roosevelt, Roosevelt.
But when they felt those
Cold winds blow
And didn't have no
Place to go
Pa said, I'm tired
O'waitin' on Roosevelt,
Roosevelt, Roosevelt.
Damn tired o' waitin' on Roosevelt.
I can't git a job
And I can't git no grub.
Backbone and navel's
Doin' the belly-rub—
A-waitin' on Roosevelt,
Roosevelt, Roosevelt.
And a lot o' other folks
What's hungry and cold
Done stopped believin'
What they been told
By Roosevelt,
Roosevelt, Roosevelt—
Cause the pot's still empty,
And the cupboard's still bare,
And you can't build a
bungalow
Out o' air—
Mr. Roosevelt, listen!
What's the matter here?
— **Langston Hughes**,
New Republic 31, Nov. 14, 1934.

Oakland port truckers gather support

Terri Kay

More than 200 truckers, their families and local supporters of the Port of Oakland Truckers Association (POTA) gathered at Middle Harbor Park in the Port of Oakland for a cookout on Nov. 2, 2013. Local port truckers and Local 10 members addressed the crowd, and nearly $1,000 was raised for a strike fund. Independent operators are legally prohibited from forming a sanctioned union, but Oakland owner-operators have formed POTA to organize and bargain for better conditions and compensation.

A Nov. 4 POTA press release explains the current need for support: "In what organizers are calling a 'major escalation,' the City of Oakland has filed suit against two owner-operator truck drivers for alleged participation in a work stoppage at the Port of Oakland on Aug. 19, 2013.

After truckers shut down the port a second time with pickets on Oct. 21 and followed with a major slow-down, Oakland Mayor Jean Quan requested a meeting with representatives for the Port Truckers to persuade them to return to work.

Mayor Quan asked for 10 days in which to pull together a meeting to discuss Port Truckers' demands with Port commissioners, legislators, and members of the California Air Resources Board (CARB), but has not contacted them since to schedule such a meeting. Now, 11 days later, at least two representatives are being sued for unlimited damages exceeding $25,000. POTA are some of the lowest paid port drayagers in the country.

Abridged from WW, Nov. 13, 2013.

Photos: Alice Loaiza

Port truckers Frank Adams POTA; Clarence Thomas Local 10; Cesar Parra POTA; and Trent Willis Local 10 at Middle Harbor Shoreline Park cookout fund raiser for the POTA, Nov. 2, 2013.

WW photo: Terri Kay

L.V. Ali and Vincent Camp at 'Unity in the Community,' deFremery Park, Oakland 2006.   Photo: Delores Lemon-Thomas

Victor Manuel Lemagne Sánchez, in red cap, Secretary General of Cuba's National Assembly visit with Local 10 members in 2017.

Invitation to the 10th Anniversary Celebration of the Million Worker March

Brothers and Sisters:

It has been ten years since Local 10 Trent Willis conceived the idea of the Million Worker March. Local 10's rank-and-file took the initiative to launch the MWM at the Lincoln Memorial in Washington, D.C. on October 17, 2004.

The Mission Statement described a 'crisis facing working people' in which the vast majority of working Americans are under siege. The call for the March was adopted unanimously at the ILWU Longshore Caucus, representing workers at all 29 ports on the West Coast.

Delores Lemon-Thomas and Charles Jenkins at the MWM Celebration Oct. 17, 2014 at Teamsters Local 808 in Long Island City, Queens, N.Y.
WW photo: Monica Moorehead

The leadership role of Local 10 rank-and-file, national convener Leo Robinson, initiated by MWM co-chairs Trent Willis and Clarence Thomas along with Henry Graham, Jack Heyman, Tommy Silas and retiree Addison Hicks; Local 34 members, MWM secretary-treasurer Keith Shanklin and Russ Miyashiro; Local 19 member Gabriel Prawl; and Local 8 members Jerry Lawrence and Debby Stringfellow. Marcus Holder; MWM administrative assistant Kathy Shanklin; communication chair Ralph Schoenman also contributed. The MWM was manifested by the national and regional centrality of Black and Latino trade union leaders.

The voices of the most oppressed sector of the working class and of the population at large, Chris Silvera chair of the Teamsters National Black Caucus; Brenda Stokely president of AFSCME District Council 1707; Charles Jenkins of TWU Local 100; Saladin Muhammad of Black Workers for Justice; Baldemar Velasquez of Farm Labor Organizing Committee, were conjoined to those of immigrant rights' organizations. Larry Holmes, Monica Moorehead, Sharon Black, Cheryl LaBash, Steve Gillis, Johnnie Stevens, John Parker and Lallan Schoenstein from Workers World, as well as many others organized the march.

The active support and endorsement of Black and Latino worker organizations from the Coalition of Black Trade Unionists; Teamsters National Black Caucus; Black Workers for Justice; Immigrant Rights Association; and Farm Labor Organizing Committee, brought to the fore of the MWMM the most oppressed sectors of the work force.

This was reflected no less in the role played by renowned actor and activist Danny Glover and civil rights leaders Dick Gregory, Martin Luther King III and Rev. E. Randel T. Osburn of the Southern Christian Leadership Foundation.

The aim was to begin mobilizing working people in their own name and around their own agenda. The action was supported by organizations and unions across the country and internationally. In fact, the MWM received statements of support from unions representing close to 50 million organized workers around the globe. It was the first time the anti-war coalition was joined by rank-and-file labor.

Thousands stood at the foot of the Lincoln Memorial and along the sides of the Reflecting Pool on a chilly October afternoon, calling for more jobs, universal health care and an end to the war in Iraq.

On October 17, 2014, the New York MWMM chapter is hosting the 10th Anniversary of the Million Worker March Movement. We will discuss the ten year retrospective of workers' gains and losses.

Hope you are able to join the discussion with your presence in New York.

Note: Retiree Leo Robinson designed the MWM logo and iconic tee shirt worn now by workers throughout the world. Brother Robinson's commitment to the struggle of the working class and the oppressed motivated him to give generously of his time and resources. Without his commitment the MWMM would not have had the profound impact that it did.

In Solidarity,
Delores Lemon-Thomas
MWMM Supporter

MILLION WORKER MARCH
MOVEMENT NY
IS HOSTING A COMMEMORATION OF THE
TENTH ANNIVERSARY MILLION WORKER MARCH
LINCOLN MEMORIAL · OCTOBER 2004

Organizing & Mobilizing In Our Own Name
10 year Retrospective of Workers Gains & Losses
Thurs ▶ **OCTOBER 16, 2014** 6:30 pm -9 pm
Local 808 International Brotherhood of Teamsters Headquarters
22-43 Jackson Avenue · Long Island City, NY 11101

10th Anniversary meeting celebrates Million Worker March Movement

Cheryl LaBash and Monica Moorehead

Founding members of the Million Worker March Movement (MWMM) held a 10th Commemorative Anniversary meeting Oct. 16, 2014, at Teamsters Local 808 in Long Island City, Queens, N.Y. The guest of honor was Clarence Thomas, national co-chair of the MWMM and a long-time rank-and-file leader of Local 10, from California's Bay Area. Charles Jenkins, president of the NYC Chapter of the Coalition of Black Trade Unionists (CBTU), emceed the program.

MWMM leaders expressed their solidarity at the event with Jerome Thompson, who shared his experience of being fired by Cablevision for attempting to organize a union.

The meeting reviewed some of the important contributions that the MWMM has made to the struggles of working and oppressed people here and worldwide. These include helping to revive May Day at Union Square, NYC in 2005, and supporting the one day countrywide General Strike led by millions of immigrant workers on May Day 2006.

The MWMM debuted on Oct. 17, 2004, when some 10,000 workers gathered at the Lincoln Memorial, where the Rev. Dr. Martin Luther King Jr. had declared war on poverty 36 years earlier.

Trent Willis, a young African-American Bay Area longshore worker, had come up with the idea of organizing the MWMM which relit the spark of conscious working class struggle with a program that is even more relevant today.

From left: Chris Silvera, Larry Holmes, Brenda Stokely, Clarence Thomas, Charles Jenkins and Sharon Black were either coordinators or organizers for the MWM rally.

The MWMM call declared: "The time has come to mobilize working people for our own agenda. Let us end subservience to the power of the privileged few and their monopoly of the political process."

Their program demanded universal single-payer health care, enhancement of Social Security with guaranteed pensions, canceling corporate 'free trade' pacts, and an end to privatization, contracting out of labor and deregulation of industry. It demanded workers' right to organize and the repeal of the Taft-Hartley Act, the Patriot Act and the Anti-Terrorism Act.

The MWMM called for slashing the military budget, recovering public funds from war profiteers, and increasing taxes on the corporations and the rich, while prioritizing the building of schools, financing public schools' arts programs, and funding an army of teachers to end illiteracy. Rebuild the cities, it said, with affordable housing to end homelessness.

It also called for an end to the criminalization of poverty and the prison-industrial complex, enforcing civil rights and granting amnesty to all undocumented workers. The call stressed that mobilizations must be held to protest racism and discrimination. Democratize the economy and the media and open the books of the Pentagon and intelligence agencies, it said. The MWMM also demanded an emergency program to restore the environment and end global warming.

Although many in the labor officialdom at that time considered the March to be a good idea, it was an election year. They chose instead to subordinate the needs of working women and men to the capitalist elections, channeling energy away from independent action.

However, thousands of workers traveled from Coast to Coast, to Washington, D.C. to mobilize in their own name, the name of the independent working class. This voice grows stronger today in the fight for a $15 per hour minimum wage and a union, and in the struggles against police killings and mass incarceration.

Abridged from WW, Oct. 30, 2014.

INTERNATIONAL DOCKWORKERS COUNCIL
C/Mar, 97 - 4º · 08003 Barcelona · Spain

RESOLUTION
AN INJURY TO ONE IS AN INJURY TO ALL;
ALL LIVES MATTER WHEN BLACK LIVES MATTER

Whereas, an injury to one is an injury to all is an eight decade credo of the International Longshore and Warehouse Union (ILWU); and

Whereas, IDC on April 11th of this year issued a letter on behalf of itself and over 90,000 affiliates it represents around the world expressing solidarity with the ILWU Local 10 in San Francisco/Oakland and all Bay Area dockworkers who stood united against racism and police violence in the United States on May Day 2016; and

Whereas, on May Day of this year, ILWU Local 10 took brave action in continuity with the long tradition of struggle towards social justice shutting down Bay Area Ports and marching to protest the recent wave of police violence against Black, Latino and immigrant communities in the Bay Area and other US cities; and

Whereas, the August 2016 ILWU Longshore Division Caucus in San Francisco voted unanimously to endorse the Black Lives Matter Movement; and

Resolution written by
GABRIEL PRAWL
president A.P. Randolph Inst. Seattle, vice president Wash. State Labor Council, delegate to MLK Labor Council, Coastwise exec. co-chair African American Longshore Coalition, Puget Sound co-chair MWMM, chair Seattle Committee Against Systemic Racism & Police Terror

Whereas, six US Pacific Coast longshore and maritime workers were slain by law enforcement on behalf of the employers in 1934 during the Great Coast-wide Maritime Strike to win the first Coast-wide Master Contract in the US for longshore workers; and

Whereas, Walter Scott, the brother of an ILA Local 1422 longshoreman, was brutally shot in the back in cold blood by a Charleston, South Carolina cop; and

Whereas, in Charleston, South Carolina relatives of longshoremen were among those slain on June 17, 2015 along with State Senator Reverend Clementa Pinkney at the historic Mother Emanuel AME Church by the openly White supremacist assassin; and

Whereas, unarmed Blacks continue to be killed by law enforcement in the US, including the recent killings this week of disabled father Keith Lamont Scott in Charlotte, North Carolina and Terence Crutcher in Tulsa, Oklahoma; and

Therefore Be It Resolved, the IDC denounces this widespread campaign of contempt for human life being waged by US law enforcement against Black, Latino and other working class people; and

Therefore Be It Resolved, that we call for all killer cops to be arrested, relieved of their badges, and punished for their crimes with no less severity then a person who was not a cop would typically receive in the US if convicted of the same crime; and

Therefore Be It Resolved, that we call upon our employers, who are among the largest corporations on the planet, to call off their police attack dogs in the US and end this disgraceful modern day lynching spree by law enforcement; and

Therefore Be It Resolved, that the next time a union member or community organizer is murdered by law enforcement in the US, the IDC affiliates in whichever ports are closest to the site of that murder shall immediately take economic action and the IDC shall immediately reinforce such action worldwide.

Be It Finally Resolved, that we call upon all labor to take an action worldwide to demonstrate to employers and governments alike that lynching shall no longer be profitable for them, and that ALL LIVES MATTER ONLY WHEN BLACK LIVES MATTER.

INTERNATIONAL DOCKWORKERS
7th IDC GENERAL ASSEMBLY MIAMI
27 -29 September 2016

ILWU endorses Bernie Sanders in 2016 campaign

On Monday, May 30 a reported 60,000 people attended a Bernie Sanders Rally held at Frank Ogawa Plaza (aka Oscar Grant Plaza) in front of Oakland City Hall. Thousands waited in lines circling several blocks to hear the progressive, anti-Wall Street and pro-democracy candidate who is running on a platform in support of the issues affecting working class and people of color.

I had the opportunity to introduce two speakers who spoke at the Rally. Berkeley's former mayor (1978-1986) Gus Newport, served as an avowed Socialist with progressives serving throughout his administration. Mayor Newport's association with Bernie goes back 4 decades. He campaigned for Bernie when he ran for governor of Vermont.

I also introduced Danny Glover acclaimed actor, activist, and humanitarian. My association with Danny dates back to the 60s when we were students at San Francisco State College where we were both members of the Black Student Union and the leadership of the longest student strike in American history which led to the formation of the Black Studies Department and the School of Ethnic Studies. For 4 decades Brother Glover has been in the forefront in the struggle for economic, racial, social, and environmental justice. He has been one of the prominent African-American campaigning for Bernie around the country.

Danny is in the tradition of Paul Robeson, Harry Belafonte, Nina Simone and others who have used their celebrity to advance the struggle for freedom, justice and equality for all.

In Struggle,
Clarence Thomas
Past secretary-treasurer
ILWU Local 10

Clarence Thomas introduces Gus Newport, former mayor of Berkeley and Danny Glover at the rally of 60,000 in Oakland, below.
Photos: Gene Hazzard

MWMM highlights local efforts for equity

Susan Fried

Danny Glover

Spoken word artist Evan Cook with a raised fist isymbolizing "Power to the People."

Sept. 22, 2018 at the Garfield Community Center, in Seattle.

Photos: Susan Fried

Gabriel Prawl

Clarence Thomas

"There is a difference between a moment and a movement," said Gabriel Prawl, the President of the Seattle branch of the A. Philip Randolph Institute. He said, "The meaning of a movement is sacrifice, not a moment that's just here today, we go home and it's over. A movement is when we continue to do something that makes change, we continue to organize, to bring people together, we continue to face the issues and we are not afraid to speak to power."

Prawl shared this sentiment as he introduced the speakers at an event called 'Where Do We Go From Here,' a discussion about what workers can do to meet the goals set at the MWM in October of 2004. The Million Worker March Movement proposed a working people's political agenda independent of any corporate party. The event, held Sept. 22, 2018 at the Garfield Community Center, in Seattle, featured several distinguished speakers who were active in organizing the 2004 MWM.

Speakers included Clarence Thomas,

MWM organizer; esteemed actor and activist Danny Glover and Chris Silvera who all talked about the continued need for a political agenda that addresses the needs of America's working people.

The event also featured a panel of local activists fighting for change locally and for the state of Washington including Andre Taylor, founder of 'Not This Time,' and K. Wyking Garrett, President of the Africatown Community Land Trust, who talked about maintaining the Central District, Seattle's historic Black neighborhood, as a place where the Black community can continue to grow and thrive.

Jesse Wineberry is a key organizer with the 'Initiative 1000' campaign, which aims to restore affirmative action in Washington. Labor activist Trent Wu, talked about the efforts to unionize New Seasons, a high-end grocery store. The meeting ended with the people vowing to continue the movement for a better quality of life for working people.

Abridged from the South Seattle Emerald, Sept. 28, 2018. tinyurl.com/y33eng63

Jesse Wineberry, K. WyKing Garrett, Trent Wu, and Andre Taylor.

Raging Grannies sing "Solidarity Forever."

Teamsters National Black Caucus Educational Conference
Gerald Horne speaks at a TNBC workshop organized by Chris Silvera

Delores Lemon-Thomas, with author Gerald Horne.
Photos: Clarence Thomas and Delores Lemon-Thomas

Chris Silvera greeting Gerald Horne in Houston 2018.

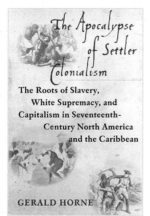

Gerald Horne conducted workshops on his book
The Apocalypse of Settler Colonialism: The Roots of Slavery

Gerald Horne chronicles Europe's colonization of Africa and the Americas, when, from Columbus' arrival until the Civil War, some 13 million Africans and some 5 million Native Americans were forced to build and cultivate a society that extolled 'liberty and justice for all.' The 17th century was an era when the roots of slavery, white supremacy, and capitalism became inextricably tangled into European history. The book evaluates the development of weapons able to ensure Europe's colonial dominance, and the hordes of Europeans whose opportunities in this 'free' land amounted to 'combat pay' for their efforts as 'white' settlers. This essential book will not allow history to be told by the victors. It is needed now.

Gerald Horne is John J. and Rebecca Moores Professor of African American History at the University of Houston. He has published more than three dozen books, including "The Apocalypse of Settler Colonialism." (Monthly Review Press)

Bradford Seymour, Georgina "Gigi" Henson, Clarence Thomas, Kerry Edwards members of Local 10 at the May Day 2018 rally in Oscar Grant Plaza. Photo: David Bacon

Janiero Baltrip Local 10 speaking at press conference for the May Day 2019 rally to be held at Howard Terminal to save the Port of Oakland.

Photo Steve Zeltzer

Presentation by Clarence Thomas on March 16, 2019
The Socialist Unity Conference

Introduction Sharon Black

This is the 100 year anniversary of the General Strike in Seattle, Feb. 6 - 11, 1919. We are celebrating the date because the class struggle is key to us.

Comrade Clarence Thomas, a leader in Local 10 in the Bay Area and of longshore workers throughout the world, will talk about the struggle today. I had the privilege of working closely with him and others in the ILWU on the Million Worker March (MWM) which was an historic event. It was one of the first times that workers spoke in their own voice, developed a program, and went beyond the confines of the Democratic Party.

It took place in Washington, D.C., on Oct. 17, 2004. Many of the people here were extremely active in building that historically significant demonstration. For most of us the first time we met Clarence Thomas was while organizing the courageous, rank-and-file MWM.

The mainstream news media tried to minimize the profound impact of the MWM, an impact empowered by the Black rank-and-file workers expressing independent leadership.

Thomas is retired now, but he hasn't retired from the struggle. He was a member for many decades of one the most powerful unions in the country, not only powerful in terms of the strategic role that this union played in terms of production, but political as well.

In the period preceding the MWM, especially after the collapse of the Soviet Union, the working class struggle had been pushed back. Anti-working class capitalist culture has predominated.

The recent strikes of rank-and-file teachers and the battle of low wage workers like those at Amazon, foretell of bigger and bigger struggles in the future. So it was very important to listen to Clarence Thomas. We want to know about the role of Local 10 and the leadership of Black and Brown workers.

Today he will provide an opportunity, especially for younger folks who didn't have the opportunity to live through great working class struggles to see how change can actually occur, to gain confidence in the multi-national working class to make a revolution.

Thomas' activism started in the 1960s, as a member of the Black Student Union (BSU) at San Francisco State College (SFSC) and as a member of the Black Panther Party (BPP) in Oakland, Calif. At San Francisco State he was part of the leadership of the longest student strike in U.S. history. It resulted in the establishment of the first Black Studies Department and the first School of Ethnic Studies in the country. Both still exist today.

Clarence Thomas: I want to get a few terms out today for those that don't know what the word proletarian means. The proletariat is the class of wage earners in capitalist society whose only possession of significant material value is their labor power.

Young people should also understand the term imperialism, when a nation expands its control outside of its government, through diplomacy or militarily. We saw imperialism in play when Africans were kidnapped and brought here to be placed in hereditary bondage and chattel slavery.

The Million Worker March in 2004, is when I had the opportunity and privilege of meeting comrades Cheryl LaBash, Sharon Black, John Parker, brother Andre Powell, sister Gloria Verdieu and Bill Dores.

I wasn't around for the 1919 Strike, but I was around for another historical strike, the San Francisco State Strike in 1968, the longest strike at an U.S. institution of higher learning, from November 1968 to March 1969.

I know something about strikes. Let me give the young people some background, kind of demistify it.

The nature of a strike is like a small revolution. It's about class struggle. It's about the struggle of the workers taking on the capitalists, the state or the bosses. The struggle is between the bosses who control the means of production, and the workers who generate the profits for the employers. For the workers to gain leverage at the bargaining table they are compelled to develop revolutionary tactics and strategies that have economic and political consequences on the bosses.

BSU activists T.C. Williams, left, Judy Juanita (formerly Judy Hart), Ron Bridgeforth and Jo Ann Mitchell at San Francisco State College in 1967.

Photo: Jerry Varnado

Jerry Varnado strike leader and Thomas Williams, left. George Murray, strike leader, far right, with other BSU members.   Photo: The Militant

Strikes can be violent, bloody and sometimes cause death to the striking workers. Strikes like revolutionary struggles can sometime lead to defeats, setbacks and worker concessions. Strikes can also lead to spectacular victories for the working class leaving historical imprints not just for union members but for the entire working class.

One of the most effective confrontations in the history of the United States student movement, the SFSC Strike will 'no doubt' serve as a precedence for future campus disruption. The SFSC Strike represents the formation of new alliances, the use of new tactics, and the mobilization of unprecedented support. The effectiveness of the Strike can be attributed primarily to the leadership of the San Francisco State College Black Student Union otherwise known as the BSU.

In 1968, Black students at SFSC, of which I was one along with my classmate Danny Glover, formulated 15 working-class centered demands. Here are just two:

1. The establishment of a revolutionary Black Studies Department, that prepared students for self-determination and prepared them to come to grips with the racist capitalist society.

2. Open enrollment that would reflect the makeup of the community of the Bay Area.

One of the most strategic things that we did during that Strike was to help organize the Third World Liberation Front. It was made up of Asian Americans, Fillipino Americans, Mexican Americans, I am sure I am leaving some out. The point is that they were organized because the Black Student Union understood the importance of not only nationalism but internationalism. We understood the importance of solidarity.

You don't take on the State of California, you don't take on the board of trustees of the State College system, you don't take on the City of San Francisco, the tact squad and others without having a commitment to revolutionary struggle. I wasn't even 21 years of age. Everything that I have done since as a community and trade union activist was started at San Francisco State. That was my training ground for revolutionary activism.

When I recently spoke to students at San Francisco State University, I told them we had to think like guerillas in order to win. We made coalitions with various student groups on campus. We gained the support of the American Federation of Teachers. When the AFT received sanctions for a General Strike, it was Local 10 that provided material support.

Solidarity is not an empty slogan. When you provide solidarity you have to give something up. In the case of Local 10 they provided jobs. Casual longshore jobs were filled by professors who were on Strike and by students, because a lot of the students worked as janitors, in the library, and in the cafeteria went on Strike with us.

The role of Black workers

The majority of Black people are workers. Black people and other people of color are more likely to join a union and least likely to lead one. We come from the most oppressed sector. We got the most to gain and the most to lose. That puts us in the position of being in the vanguard. The question today is whether the white proletariat is going to join with the Black proletariat and other workers of color? That's the real question on the table right now.

We have to wake up. We have to be very strategic. I am very encouraged by seeing that young people, unlike my generation, are not afraid of the word 'socialism.' They are not afraid to critique 'capitalism.' We need to be on the front line.

An injury to one is an injury to all. United we stand, divided we fall! Free Mumia Abu-Jamal!

tinyurl.com/yxh4zb9d

Coronavirus protection
Longshore union demands protection for members and community

L eaders and members of the International Longshore and Warehouse Union (ILWU) Locals 10, 34, 75 and 91 protested outside the office of the Stevedoring Services of America (SSA) terminal at the Port of Oakland, Calif., on March 20, 2020, to demand that the company provide personal protective equipment (PPE) for dock workers.

Trent Willis, president of ILWU Local 10, and Keith Shanklin, president of ILWU Local 34, talked about the fight to protect Bay Area longshore workers and their communities from COVID-19.

An issue that poses a grave danger to all port workers and the surrounding community is the disposition of the Grand Princess cruise ship. Over 300 crew members are being held on the ship. Most are Filipino seafarers who have lost their labor and human rights.

Keith Shanklin: Brothers and Sisters, we are requesting members of all our locals to stand with us in solidarity during this crisis and beyond due to the ongoing changes that happen every day with the coronavirus.

We are standing in solidarity with Locals 10, 34, 75 and 91 to demand the Pacific Maritime Association (PMA), SSA and all Bay Area terminals honor the collective bargaining agreement and the safety code book, our contractual rights.

We requested that the PMA clean and sanitize all the equipment that is vital to our ability to provide safe labor to the port without interruptions. It is imperative for us as workers as well as to the public that the

Trent Willis protests the lack of the proper health and safety conditions and equipment for longshore workers loading and unloading the ships on March 20, 2020.

equipment we work with every day be sanitized to prevent the spread of the coronavirus. The employers are obligated under Contract Section 3 of the Pacific Coast Safety Code Book to provide a safe workplace for all operations.

The threat of longshore workers contracting coronavirus and the threat of spreading it to our families and the surrounding community is too great for the employer not to take proactive measures.

The port is a main area for food, medical supplies and basic products for the community to maintain a decent quality of life. Your immediate response is requested. An injury to one is an injury to all.

Now, just to say: All the other terminals have complied with the Pacific Coast Safety Code except for the Stevedoring Services of America Terminal. We want you to understand that we are not trying to target you. It is SSA that is targeting us by not following safety procedures.

Trent Willis: First, I'd like to send solidarity to our sister ILWU locals in this area and to all port workers who are not members of our union, as well as workers in general.

Today, we are here to demand that Stevedoring Services of America as well as Pacific Maritime Association adhere to previously agreed language in our Pacific Coast Safety Code which requires them to make sure that the longshore workers' equipment and facilities are safe for everyday operation.

Now a longshoreman contracting the coronavirus can have a lot of different effects:

• First, we don't want to be responsible for spreading the coronavirus to each other.

• Second, we don't want to be responsible for spreading the coronavirus among port workers.

• Third, we don't want to be responsible for spreading the coronavirus to the community.

If the longshore workers contract the coronavirus because the equipment and the facilities are not being disinfected, we stand the possibility of the Port of Oakland being shut down.

The Port of Oakland is a vital artery to supplying the community in this area. Also, communities that are not in this area. For example the rail system here is directly connected to the main hub of the U.S. rail system in Chicago. There are goods and services that leave this port and get shipped to different communities all across this country.

If this port is shut down because of the coronavirus, it will bring about a health and safety risk to the public and to this entire country. This is a main hub for shipping out agricultural products. This port is responsible for feeding communities all across this nation. We want to be in a proactive position where we are making sure that the equipment and the machines that we operate are sanitized so that longshore workers are protected from contracting this virus.

Disposition of the infected cruise ship Grand Princess

We are also here today to talk about the Grand Princess, which docked at Berth 22. First off, we have not been informed of the condition of the crew members who remain on the Grand Princess. As we speak, there are approximately 300 crew members still aboard. We have no idea if they are receiving the proper medical care. We have absolutely no information whether the terminal in Oakland where the ship was docked for a number of days has been disinfected after they left. That is a risk to the port workers as well as the vitality and the continuation of operations at this port.

We are here standing with our sister locals, the ILWU port workers, together with the community, to demand that these items be addressed:

That our port be sanitized and that we learn the condition of the crew members aboard the Grand Princess.

We hope that the community will stand with us. The ILWU has always been a vanguard for workers all over the world. We stand as the first line of defense here in the Port of Oakland and ports up and down the entire coast.

Bishop Bob Jackson, Acts Full Gospel Church in East Oakland: I'm here to stand with the ILWU to advocate for cleanliness in the terminal so these women and men can work. They're doing essential work. We can't afford to see the ports shut down. We can't afford to see their families and the other people that they have to work with being impacted.

Without them working, without this port being open, without these terminals being able to do what they do, we will be in dire straits in Oakland. I'm here to say: Please do all you can to make sure their environment is cleaned and that they get the things that they request, because we need them to continue to work. We need them to continue to be healthy and for their families to be safe.

We thank you for this opportunity to support the ILWU.

Pres. Trent Willis: We have to recognize one point: We're not just addressing you as longshore workers and ILWU union members, we are also members of the community. The biggest threat to longshore workers and ILWU members is the possibility of infecting the community because we work with ships that are coming from all over the country, from all of these different countries where the coronavirus is spreading. We want to make sure that while we're doing this vital work in the Port of Oakland that all of our members are safe.

Now you hear a lot of talk from the governor and from local elected officials about how essential the Port of Oakland is. Well, the ILWU's position is that the health and safety of the workers and the community are essential. The port being essential is second to that.

We appreciate your supporting us in this time of need. Once again, ILWU Local 10 promises to stand strong with the community and to be the first line of defense at the port.

Steve Zeltzer, "Work Week" on KPFA Pacifica Radio: One of the things that I want to bring up is that of the California Division of Occupational Safety and Health (OSHA). We pay for Cal/OSHA to protect 19 million workers in California. The question we have for Gov. Newsom is: Where is Cal/OSHA when the SSA is not properly protecting the workplace? Cal/OSHA should shut the job down. We have learned that Cal/OSHA has only one doctor and one nurse, with less than 200 inspectors. What kind of protection is that in this dire emergency?

We're calling on Gov. Newsom to staff up Cal/OSHA, to make sure inspectors are down here demanding that the company clean the equipment for the workers or shut this facility down. Cal/OSHA's job is to protect the health and safety of working people who are doing critical work like shipping. They are getting supplies out in this dire emergency and the workers need to be protected.

Pres. Keith Shanklin: If you can put any pressure on, do it for the community, do it for yourself. We have to understand one thing: if this dock continues to go unsanitized and our members get this virus, the dock would shut down immediately. You would not have the goods, the way of life that you enjoy right now. It would not be the same. I guarantee it.

Labor Video: tinyurl.com/y2zlq7bj

YouTube transcript excerpted in Struggle-La Lucha on April 24, 2020.

Washington State Labor Council first to pass resolution
Call for U.S.-Cuba COVID-19 collaboration

Cindy Domingo

While the rate of infections and deaths due to COVID-19 continue to grow in the U.S., the small country of Cuba is making remarkable strides in combating the virus at home as well as throughout the world. For those reasons, the Washington State Labor Council (WSLC) and the Martin Luther King, Jr. Labor Council (MLK Labor) passed resolutions calling for US-Cuba collaboration in the fight against COVID-19.

On September 25, 2020, the WSLC State Convention passed their resolution with overwhelming support from the over 175 delegates in attendance calling on "the U.S. Congress and the President to lift restrictions on access to Cuban medical expertise, including clinical trials of Interferon alpha-2B recombinant (an antiviral medication), in order to more effectively combat the COVID-19 pandemic and to save lives." The WSLC became the first state labor council to pass such a resolution. The resolution was put forth by the three AFL-CIO labor constituencies of color of the WSLC, Asian Pacific American Labor Alliance (APALA), A. Philip Randolph Institute (APRI), and the Coalition of Black Trade Unionists. The Martin Luther King, Jr. Labor Council had passed a similar resolution.

In presenting the resolution to the WSLC delegates, Gabriel Prawl, President of APRI, Seattle called for "All hands to be on deck to save lives … and move to end COVID-19 and allow people to have an opportunity to live longer. In supporting this resolution, this puts us on the right path of history." The WSLC represents more than 600 union locals and councils

with approximately 550,000 rank-and-file union members throughout the state of Washington. The AFL-CIO represents more than 12 million active and retired workers in the U.S.

Cuba's success in fighting COVID-19 is evidenced by their low rate of infections and COVID-19 related deaths. Currently, Cuba has a lower infection rate than most countries in the northern hemisphere and Cubans are 42 times less likely to contract the virus than people in the U.S. Cuba's healthcare system, with an integrated community-based public health and medical care approach, has proven in this time of the pandemic to be effective in identifying, treating, and containing COVID-19. Prevention is a hallmark of Cuba's healthcare system and provides the population with nationwide televised education programs on COVID-19, including safe measures to take and immune bolstering homeopathic medications. Cuba's medical system is also bolstered greatly by a robust biopharmaceutical industry which allows for the development and distribution of medications to its population.

Interferon alpha-2b recombinant, mentioned in the WSLC resolution, is one of the many antiviral medications developed by Cuba, and is utilized to bolster the immune system in some of the most severe COVID-19 cases. It has been used in Italy and China where Cuban medical personnel were dispatched at the height of the pandemic. Both medical treatment and pharmaceuticals are provided free to Cuba's population.

Recently, an international campaign was launched petitioning the

Nobel Peace Prize Committee to award Cuba's Henry Reeve International Medical Brigade for their role internationally in fighting COVID-19. The Brigade of Cuban healthcare professionals who have vowed to serve wherever needed is currently working in over 35 countries. Many members of the Henry Reeve Brigades have previously served in other countries dealing with HIV-AIDS, hepatitis types B and C, SARS, and dengue viruses. The Brigade is renowned for the role it played combating the deadly disease Ebola in West Africa.

Upon the resolution's passage, Karen Strickland, President of American Federation of Teachers, Washington (AFT), who has traveled to Cuba with U.S. Women and Cuba Collaboration, stated, "I have supported an end to the embargo against Cuba for humanitarian reasons for nearly 20 years. In this moment, it is abundantly clear that the Cuban people are not the only people harmed by the embargo. Cuba has much to offer to the U.S. but the stubbornness of politicians has cheated us out of the benefits of collaboration with Cuba." AFT was also a sponsor of the WSLC resolution.

Cindy Domingo, member of Seattle APALA Executive Committee and Chair of U.S. Women and Cuba Collaboration, spearheaded the work on the resolution as part of the Saving Lives Campaign. They call for international cooperation in combating COVID-19. To learn more, visit the Saving Lives website or contact Cindy Domingo at cindydomingo@gmail.com.

Excerpted from the The Emerald southseattleemerald.com

ILWU fights COVID-19

Locals 10 and 34 held a press conference with leaders from the Bay Area's Filipino community in March 2020, to demand that contaminated waste from the Grand Princess cruise ship quarantined in the Port of Oakland, be safely disposed. Also, they demanded adequate medical treatment and a safe repatriation for all workers still aboard the vessel.

Port companies had planned to expose both dock workers and the community to COVID-19 by trucking contaminated waste from the ship through Oakland community. Locals 10 and 34 demanded that the waste be disposed safely through water side offloading and barge removal.

While the dock workers across the West Coast continue to fight for sanitation standards the ILWU is using its power to support the thousands of workers they represent 'on the other side of the gate,' referring to workers outside of the port terminals. From the nearly 400 workers laid off at Powell's Books in Portland to those at Anchorsteam Brewing in San Francisco, to education, veterinarian and warehouse workers, the ILWU is working to ensure safe working conditions and enough cash to survive.

It is courageous for the ILWU to make these demands while it is under intense union-busting pressure from legal proceedings. In Portland, Oregon, a judge rewarded the terminal operator ICTS a $77 million settlement against the ILWU for a 2012 slowdown action. It is more than twice the ILWU's total assets, threatening dock worker's union with bankruptcy.

A union spokesperson said, "The ILWU has been hit with this massive fine that will have a chilling effect not only for the longshoreman's union, but for workers far beyond the waterfront if we don't act. Now is the time to organize in the face of this terrifying disease. As the saying goes, an injury to one is an injury to all. That's never been more true."

COVID-19 took the country by storm. This pandemic exposed the weak underbelly of capitalist America. This virus revealed the importance of certain sectors of the working class and the lack of economic advancement available to them. At the same time, capital continues to concentrate among the ruling elite at the expense of the masses of the people.

Excerpted from Labor Video Project, Steve Zeltzer.

Grand Princess crew member.

Local 10 demanded the medical care and safe repatriation of the Grand Princess workers still aboard the vessel.

Ricki Cox Local 34 listens to Trent Willis speaking about the plight of the crew on Grand Princess cruise ship.

We need to prioritize our medical infrastructure. Medical cargo should come first. Medical cargo must be expedited like an ambulance. The other cargo should stop and wait for it. We need to prioritize our medical system not corporate profits.

– Leith Kahl

Gabriel Prawl's son, Hezekiah Prawl and Leith Kahl Chair of Seattle's Local 19 Education Committee on May 1, 2020.

Teamsters Joint Council #16, provided 300 dinners on May Day 2020, to NY University hospital workers. This was initiated by Teamsters Local 808 in Long Island City, N.Y.

COVID-19 and the impact on the working class

May Day 2020 message from Chris Silvera

In November 2017, workers at Peter Cooper Village and Stuyvesant Town, members of Teamsters Local 808, ratified a Collective Bargaining Agreement that provided one additional holiday, **MAY DAY.**

Starting May 2019, all Teamsters working at PCVST celebrated International Workers' Day. These are the only workers in the USA who enjoy this day as a **contractual holiday.** Local 808 continues to work on behalf of its other members to win May Day in all of its Collective Bargaining Agreements.

Chris Silvera with his son Bashiri on May Day in Union Square, N.Y. 2005.
WW photo: Liz Green

COVID-19 took the country by storm. This pandemic exposed the weak underbelly of capitalist America. This virus revealed the importance of certain sectors of the U.S. working class and the lack of economic advancement available to them. At the same time, capital continues to concentrate among the ruling elite at the expense of the masses of the people.

Who knew that cashiers, warehouse workers and delivery persons would become recognized as essential workers and how long will that recognition last?

This pandemic shows just how important these workers are to our society. They suffer under less than a living wage; the faceless cashiers and warehouse workers at Amazon, Walmart, Krogers and other enterprises around the country.

The U.S., with thousands of missiles, drones and spy satellites, could not provide sufficient personal protective equipment for its nurses and doctors: simple disposable masks, gowns and gloves.

Most of the major hospitals are now a part of what are identified as healthcare systems. With the mergers of hospitals and clinics, healthcare became a super profit center, without creating better outcomes for the patients.

In the decades prior to COVID-19, hospitals were closed resulting in massive decreases in available beds, less nurses and aides, nursing homes with minimalist staffing; all of this to increase profits for the few. COVID-19, has also revealed the reality to working people that the system has failed them. We now see a militancy among the workers at United Parcel Service (UPS), demonstrations by hospital staff and other essential workers all seeking better working conditions in a now more deadly workplace.

COVID-19, has revealed once again the failure of either political party to pass a stimulus bill that benefits the working class instead of a massive bailout of the ruling class and corporations. Just two years ago, trillion dollar tax cuts were given to the ruling class and they are still in need of a bailout, really?

Organized labor must recognize that it is time to separate from the parties of the bosses. Labor must begin to mobilize its members and invest in organizing these essential non-union workers. These workers are exhibiting great degrees of bravery and militancy in the face of their experience with the wanton disregard for their health and safety.

Organized labor in the developed world must recognize that globalization means if it happens here, it will happen there. We must begin to use our resources to not only organize locally, but to organize globally.

What resources one might be tempted to ask? The reallocation of millions of dollars wasted on political parties each year. That money must be used to organize these essential workers who are unorganized. Too many of these essential workers make less than fifteen dollars per hour. For example in New York, Los Angeles, San Francisco, Chicago and other major cities, a living wage is closer to thirty dollars or more. In one of the poorest states, fifteen dollars per hour will still leave you poor in Tupelo, Mississippi. We must organize to fight.

SIERRA CLUB
SAN FRANCISCO BAY

Serving Alameda, Contra Costa, Marin and San Francisco counties   June 18, 2020
2530 San Pablo Ave., Berkeley, CA 94702 (510) 848-0800 Email: info@sfbaysc.org

To Mayor Libby Schaaf and Members of the Oakland City Council   1 Frank H Ogawa Plaza, Oakland, CA 94612

RE: Sale of Coliseum Property to Oakland Athletics

Dear Mayor Schaaf and Members of the Oakland City Council,   *Facsimile of Sierra Club letter*

The Sierra Club is concerned about significant environmental and environmental justice impacts presented by the Oakland A's proposed move from the Coliseum to a new stadium at Howard Terminal at the Port of Oakland. The Coliseum site is already approved for use as a stadium, is transit accessible, and would lift up surrounding East Oakland neighborhoods rather than displacing maritime businesses and workers. Howard Terminal, on the other hand, lacks transit access, is vulnerable to sea-level rise and contamination by toxics, and the A's have challenged environmental oversight in pushing the project forward. Remaining at the Coliseum site and building a new stadium there avoids these risks altogether.

The greenhouse gas emissions from transportation to and from the stadium is a major concern for a site that would attract an average of 20,500 people to each of 80+ home games per season. While both BART and Amtrak have stops right at the Coliseum, the Howard Terminal site is not currently served by public transit. The nearest BART stations are over a mile away and separated from the site by Interstate 880 and busy railroad tracks. The A's have not presented any viable transit solutions, offering up a far-fetched idea for an aerial gondola (which the city "isn't counting on" according to the San Francisco Chronicle) and a "transportation hub" with shuttle to BART — still a quarter mile from the stadium.

Another concern is Howard Terminal's contamination by toxics and the potential, as a result of a large construction project, for human exposure or pollution of the Bay. Prior industrial uses of the site contaminated it with toxics including polycyclic aromatic hydrocarbons, volatile organic compounds, petroleum hydrocarbons, heavy metals and cyanide. The Department of Toxic Substances Control has a Deed Restriction on this site limiting it to industrial and commercial uses (residential uses are explicitly prohibited) and requiring review and approval for any plan that would disturb the existing cap — as the A's plan most certainly would. In internal discussions the A's have indicated they want to avoid remediation to a residential standard.

The project's location right on the waterfront raises another concern on our warming planet. With sea levels expected to rise dramatically in the coming decades, building right on the San Francisco Bay shoreline is foolish in the extreme. A recent report

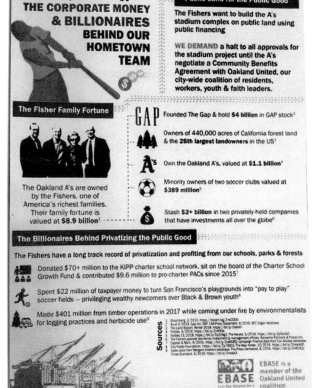

projects that we could see a rise of a half-foot by 2030 and up to seven feet by 2100, which could flood parts of West Oakland, including the Port of Oakland and Howard Terminal. Severe storm events and high tides will produce even higher increases. In addition, rising groundwater could increase the potential for liquefaction-induced damage during earthquakes.

Among the most troubling elements of the Howard Terminal project is its proponents' disregard for environmental review. In pushing their proposal to build at Howard Terminal, the A's have sought shortcuts and exemptions from environmental laws, threatening public health, the San Francisco Bay ecosystem, and the integrity of our system of public oversight.

Black community fights diabolical scheme to push them out of Oakland, Calif.

Dave Welsh

Led by the dock workers union, ILWU Local 10, Oakland's Black community is organizing to stop a baseball stadium project from further gentrifying the city and pushing longtime Black residents out.

"The Black community is under siege, by forces that would like to relocate the Oakland Athletics from the existing Coliseum in East Oakland to Howard Terminal in rapidly gentrifying West Oakland, and drive us out," explained Local 10 organizer Derrick Muhammad at the Forum of the East Oakland Stadium Alliance."'

"This is emanating from City Hall, from real estate developers, from the Fisher family that owns the Gap clothing chain … and from a police department that's working in tandem to drive Black people out."

Speaking at the influential Acts Full Gospel Church, Muhammad asked, "Why are they building a light rail down East 14th Street in East Oakland? Did any of you ask for that? It reminds me of 50 years ago when they destroyed our thriving West Oakland Black community, pushing us out so they could build BART stations, railroad tracks and a huge postal facility smack dab in the middle of our neighborhood, followed by the loss of factory jobs, the introduction of crack cocaine and a wrecking ball for our homes and mom-and-pop stores.

"Now they are promising 6,000 permanent jobs at a new ballpark, hoping to convince a marginalized, oppressed community to support their project," said Muhammad. Ask yourself, "How does 82 home games produce 6,000 jobs? This is a land grab by the rich. This is the de-industrialization of another major urban center, like they did to Detroit. They even want to grab Howard Terminal, which is part of the Port of Oakland."

Danny Glover, actor and activist, whose postal worker family also experienced being pushed out of housing by greedy developers in the San Francisco Bay Area, told the church gathering, "We've seen too much, know too much. There was a time when Oakland was 50 percent

Join actor and activist
DANNY GLOVER
for a community forum
to keep the A's in East Oakland

Saturday Aug. 31, 11 a.m.
Food & drink served

Acts Full Gospel Church
1034–66th Ave, Oakland

WHAT WE NEED:
- AFFORDABLE HOUSING
- GOOD-PAYING JOBS
- COMMUNITY INVESTMENT
- A WORKING PORT

WHAT WE DON'T NEED:
- GENTRIFICATION
- LUXURY HOUSING
- JOB LOSS
- TAXPAYER-FUNDED WASTE

The A's proposal to abandon the Oakland Coliseum for Howard Terminal is a land grab – threatening the thriving maritime industry and worsening gentrification with luxury condos and high-priced office space. Join our coalition to keep the A's in East Oakland and invest in the neighborhood they have called home for decades.

Poster design: Lillian Duong

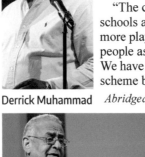

Derrick Muhammad

Black. Now people are living in tent cities. Renters are being forced out.

"The carpetbaggers are coming in, and schools are being privatized. We do not need more playgrounds for the rich, treating Black people as expendable. We have got to fight. We have to take our stand and defeat this new scheme by the rich to steal the people's land."

Abridged from WW, Sept. 20, 2019.

Photos: Phil Meyer

Lawrence Thibeaux

Andy Garcia

Bishop Bob Jackson

Gabriel Prawl and Clarence Thomas with the Local 10 Drill Team at Community Forum of the East Oakland Stadium Alliance on Aug. 31, 2019.

Photos: Phil Meyer

Melody Davis

Keith Shanklin

Aaron Wright

Melvin Mackay

Danny Glover

Lisa Milos

Steve Zeltzer

Proposal to build an A's stadium at the Port of Oakland

Clarence Thomas' remarks on privatization of Howard Terminal

'I am a third-generation longshore worker, who is currently involved in a struggle in the Bay Area to stop, billionaire John Fisher from threatening the Port of Oakland. Fisher owns the Oakland A's, also The Gap and much more. He wants to build 3,000 condominium units for the wealthy. He wants to build a 34,000 seat baseball park, a 400 room hotel, and 1.9 million square foot of retail space at the third busiest port on the West Coast, the Port of Oakland.

The Port of Oakland is the economic engine not only for the Bay Area but for the entire Northern California region. This is a case of privatization of a public resource with some of the best paying blue collar jobs, not only in the Bay Area, but in the entire country.

Longshore workers represent some of the most important workers in the global economy.

Mr. John Fisher is a major funder and supporter of privatization of public schools. He is not a great corporate citizen. We do not understand why the City of Oakland is being held hostage. The commissioner of baseball says that if the Oakland A's do not get their way, they may leave the City of Oakland. Well, that is a threat, OK?

We think that there is plenty of room right now for the Oakland A's to play baseball. The Port of Oakland should not be privatized to accommodate the whims and desires of a multi-billionaire. This deals with the question of gentrification, because after all, who can afford to buy multimillion-dollar condos on the waterfront near a baseball park but multi-millionaires.

If Fisher's proposal is successful, 200 million dollars will come out of taxpayers pockets.

For many, many years, the issue of race has still been highly effective in dividing working class in the United States of America. This not only impacts Blacks, its impacting everyone who lives in the city. If you are not part of the 1%, this is not for you.

We are going to have to continue to be in the streets mobilizing and organizing in our own name to keep the A's out of the Port.

Support Local 10, Local 34 and East Oakland Stadium Alliance in the fight against A's Stadium in the Port of Oakland Howard Terminal."

From: Summer Love Films by Rocky Owens, March 2020. Vimeo.com/402035597

Ryan Coogler on May Day 2018

The following text is a May Day 2018 International Workers' Day message from Ryan Coogler, film director/writer/producer, humanitarian, and activist.

"Hey everybody, what's going on, it's Ryan Coogler, I'm speaking on behalf of my family in support of ILWU, specifically, Local 10. I'm the great grandson, grandson, and nephew of longshoremen who worked for Local 10 in the Bay Area.

"I want to extend my gratitude for everything you guys have done for my family and for the long struggles you have fought for your workers; which my family are in direct benefit of those various struggles.

"I also want to express solidarity for everything you guys are doing around May Day to withhold your work for 8 hours to bring awareness to certain issues you guys deem are important.

"I just want you guys to know we stand with you, my family and I offer our support.

"It is unfortunate we won't be there, for the march. We want to send a special shout out, specifically to my Uncle Buzz (Clarence Thomas) former secretary-treasurer of Local 10 who will be speaking at deFremery Park and Oscar Grant Plaza in Oakland.

"We want to let you know our spirits are with you guys and a special shout out to all the work you guys have done in the past and continue to do.

"Peace Out!"

Ryan Coogler and his grandfather longshoreman C.C. Thomas, Sr. # 6208

Clockwise, Marilyn Thomas, Clarence Thomas, Joselyn Coogler, Cathy Pittman, Charlene Thomas and Carolyn Wingate.

Photo: Eric Marshall

CLARENCE C. THOMAS, SR. #62__
1924 – 1985
Member 17 years 1968–1985

MARELL LOVE #6252
1928 – 1999
Member 35 years 1963–1997

RUDY GARCIA #6260
1933 – 1997
Member 32 years 1963–1995

Jamir Thomas points to the name of his great-grandfather Clarence C. Thomas Sr. in the ILWU hiring hall.

Photo: Clarence Thomas

ILWU family member Charlene Thomas talks about gentrification in her community

Interview by Steve Zeltzer

'I'm Charlene Thomas and I have lived in North Oakland since I was 13 years old and I am 90 now.

"My dad and my son's dad and my son Clarence Thomas were all in the ILWU. So hey, I've been part of this union for a long time. The ILWU is all I know. It means an awful lot to me, through educating my children, having a salary that made it possible for us to own a home while having a living wage and wonderful healthcare. The ILWU continues to be a part of my life.

"So building a stadium on the Port, well that's awful. Why do they want to build a stadium where people are working, where the ships are coming in? I don't understand it. Everything is about money. They want money, money, money. But then after a while that money is not going to mean anything to them. You can have all the money in the world and it still won't mean anything if the work isn't here. It will end up with just a few people having money. That's the only thing that I can see. I'm looking at the situation hoping that they can cool down.

"I noticed that the property is not moving as fast as it was. It used to be that when a house was put up for sale it was gone the same day. Now it's sitting there for a while. There is speculation by house flippers. Everyday the mailbox is full of offers to buy my house. Every day there's a realtor knocking on my door wanting my house. Where am I going to go? I don't want to sell my house. I'm close to the bus stop. I can take it to San Francisco and downtown Oakland, all right on the corner. That's the reason why I'm staying put.

"I'm still staying in the house that I've been in for 64 years. It was old then and it's still old. It's my home and I raised

Juno Thomas and Charlene Thomas at East Oakland Stadium Alliance community forum on August 31, 2019. Charlene Thomas spoke out against the threat of privatization and the building of a new A's stadium at Howard Terminal in the Port of Oakland.

all my five children there and then my grandchildren came along. I'm right across the street from a school. They all went there so why would I move.

"There is a petition that's going around my neighborhood to keep that school open. They want to close it and give it to a 'private charter' school.

"I think if people band together they can keep the public school open. New neighbors are moving in with families and they already started petitions to save that public school. I was tickled to see them do it. Some of them just want to be close to the school so we are hoping that it works out. I have great-grand kids that go over there. One of them is staying with me because her mom has to go to work at 4 o'clock in the morning. We just go across the street to our community school. My kids went across the street, so I was kind of thinking that the grand kids and great-grand kids could go there. I think it's going to work out because the community that's here now is going to fix it."

Excerpts from a August 31, 2019, Community Forum, laborvideo.org. youtu.be/WtflGiITJcE

Charlene Thomas, Clarence Thomas' mother, is originally from Port Arthur, Texas.

She is the daughter, spouse, niece and mother of longshore workers.

She has resided at her home in North Oakland since 1956 when whites were moving out of the City of Oakland. She has been very active in the community for decades including allowing Black Panther Party meetings to be held in her home in the late '60s.

Photo: Delores Lemon-Thomas

Clarence Thomas
and Walter Riley
Civil Rights attorney,
leader of the Black
Folks for Bernie
Bay Area Committee,
and father of
Boots Riley.
Photo:
Delores Lemon-Thomas

Richmond, California 2020
The Bernie Sanders Campaign

Local 10 Membership and the Rank-and-File

Brothers and Sisters:

I would like to salute the action you are taking today of withholding your labor for eight hours to commemorate International Workers Day and the important struggle for fairness in the workplace.

Thank you to Clarence Thomas for his leadership and many thanks to Danny Glover for being such a strong champion.

Mary Jane O'Meara Sanders and Delores Lemon-Thomas. Members of Local 10 and Black Folks for Bernie Bay Area Committee in Richmond, California.

The demands that your Local is putting forward of ending racist policing, guaranteeing a $15 an hour minimum wage, achieving Medicaid health care for all, and ensuring quality education for everyone, are consistent with my campaign platform.

My regards go out to fellow union workers, the interfaith community, and the peace and social justice activists participating with you in the march and rally at Harry Bridges Plaza on the Embarcadero and with workers who stand in solidarity with you all over the country.

These are tough times for working people. But I believe if enough people organize and engage the political struggle, that we can elect leaders who will enact policies for the benefit of ordinary people. When people stand together, and are prepared to fight back, there is nothing that can't be accomplished.

I wish you the very best in your efforts to create a democratic workplace where your voice can really be heard.

Keep up the fight.

Sincerely,

U.S. Senator Bernie Sanders

Excerpts from a 2016 letter.

Dr. Ramona Tascoe Pres. UCSF Medical Alumni Assoc. and Danny Glover, both BSU members. In white coat Dr. Rupa Marya UCSF medical faculty director of the 'Do No Harm Coalition', an organization addressing health issues caused by racism, surrounded by medical students.
Photo: Delores Lemon-Thomas

The most radical union in the U.S. is shutting down the Ports on Juneteenth

Peter Cole

Outrage over the police murder of George Floyd launched Black Lives Matter protests. Most actions are being organized by young Black people. While many are working-class and some are anti-capitalist, few protests are formally part of the labor movement.

That may change this Friday when the most radical union in the U.S. shuts down the country's gateway to the world, West Coast ports, in solidarity with Black Lives Matter on the day commemorating the end of slavery. As Clarence Thomas, a long-time dockworker activist for Black equality and socialism, noted recently, "It will be the first time that an international union has ever taken off from work for the purpose of commemorating Juneteenth."

Thomas, an African American from Oakland, is a proud, third-generation member of the ILWU. Arguably, no union has fought longer and harder for Black equality.

The ILWU's Juneteenth action raises the bar for what worker solidarity with Black Lives Matter looks like.

Harry Bridges, the ILWU's first president, once declared in the 1940s, "If things reached a point where only two men were left on the waterfront, if he had anything to say about it, one would be a black man."

Zack Pattin, a white, rank-and-file activist in ILWU Local 23 (Tacoma), recounted some of his union's history: "We pass down stories about integrating the waterfront, opposition to Japanese internment, fight for immigrant rights, support for the civil rights movement, refusing to handle South African cargo to protest Apartheid, and resistance to the wars in Iraq and Afghanistan."

Trent Willis, Local 10 president, Thomas, Gabriel Prawl of Local 52, Keith Shanklin Local 34 president, and others organized this Juneteenth stop-work prior to Trump's provocation to speak that day, in Tulsa of all places.

Abridged from "In These Times," June 16, 2020.

Dockworker Power:
Race and Activism in South Africa and the Bay Area

Author Peter Cole explores how workers in South Africa and San Francisco ports have harnessed their role in the global economy to promote labor rights and social justice causes.

Clarence Thomas, a third generation Oakland longshoreman and a leader of the Black Student Union during the 1968-1969 San Francisco State strike, will share his first-hand experience on the docks.

FORUM: March 14, 2019
Free and Open to the Public
Wheelchair Accessible

Sponsored by: Labor Archives and Research Center, History Department, Race and Resistance Studies at San Francisco State University

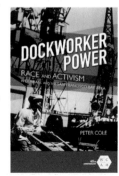

Waterfront battles for rights and justice

A commentary on today's global economy, workers in the world's ports can harness their role, at a strategic choke point, to promote their labor rights and social justice. Peter Cole brings such experiences to light in a comparative study of Durban, South Africa, and San Francisco Bay, California. His research reveals how unions effect lasting change in far-reaching struggles.

Dockworkers draw on radical traditions to promote racial equality. Their commitment to internationalism sparked work stoppages to protest apartheid. They persevered when a new technology, container ships, sent a shockwave of layoffs through the industry. Cole's book brings to light parallels in the experiences of dockers half a world away from each other. And offers a new perspective on how workers can change their conditions and world.

ILWU Local 10 says:
'Unite all working people on May Day'

April 24, 2020 International Longshore and Warehouse Union Local 10

Our union is facing some historic challenges. The collapse of the world economy and the threat of the coronavirus to our members, families and communities have become a life and death question. While we are designated as "essential workers," our lives are not treated as "essential." This, in addition to the dangerous conditions we face daily on the job. We have taken action at the Port of Oakland to ensure the health and safety of our members and the community which is adjacent to the port.

This isn't just about longshore workers here, but throughout the world who face the virus: automation, privatization, deregulation and union busting by governments and employers. Our union has historically been in the forefront of the struggle to unite all working people on May Day. It is precisely because of solidarity with our communities and working people around the world that we have been able to survive.

The Trump government is moving to destroy our union and the lives of all working people. They have weakened and marginalized OSHA protection for maritime workers, as well as other transportation workers, which is leading to the collapse of the global economy and the entire population of the United States. If you cannot protect longshore workers' health and safety, all lives in the country are at risk.

On May 1, we have informed the employer that we will have a stop work meeting as the Longshore Caucus has voted to do every May Day. This will be Local 10's fifth consecutive May Day action.

Donald Trump has designated May 1 as the date to "Reopen the Economy." Let us show the way forward for all working people by our action as we have done in the past.

An injury to one is an injury to all!
ALL OUT FOR MAY DAY!

International Longshore and Warehouse Union
Local 10   400 NORTH POINT, SAN FRANCISCO, CA 94133 • • (415) 776-8100
Fax: (415) 441-0610

Frank Gaskin
SECRETARY TREASURER

PRESIDENT,   **Trent Willis**
VICE PRESIDENT.   **Robert Bradford, Jr.**

June 2, 2020

William Adams, President
International Longshore and Warehouse Union
1188 Franklin Street, 4th Floor
San Francisco, CA 94109

Dear Brother Adams:

We want to express our support for your strong letter to Governor Walz of Minnesota. "We will not sit back and not fight for change." Because now is the time to act it is with the greatest urgency that we, ILWU officials in San Francisco, the birthplace of our union, appeal to you to bring our power to bear now for justice for George Floyd and in defense of the very lives and rights of black and working people. In the best tradition of the ILWU, we can show the way when solidarity and the power of labor are key for workers, youth desperate for a way out, and all opponents of racism and repression. As workers struggle to survive with the pandemic and economic crisis, police terror is taking the lives of our brothers and sisters — and Trump threatens "shootings" of those who protest. In Minneapolis and throughout the country labor has begun speaking out.

This deadly, dangerous surge of racism harks back to the police killing of strikers in our 1934 maritime strike. And as we all know, Bloody Thursday led to the San Francisco General Strike. The mural in front of Local 10 says it clearly: "Police Murder, Two Strikers Shot in the Back". Today working people around the world react in horror at images of George Floyd, a black man, being kneed to death by a Minneapolis police officer. Four other officers protected the killer cop as Floyd pleaded "I can't breathe" — the same haunting last words as Eric Garner. In February Ahmaud Arbery, a black man jogging, was shot down by a former Brunswick, Georgia cop and his son. In Louisville, Breonna Taylor, a frontline EMT worker fighting the Covid-19 pandemic, was killed by the police in her own home. Just yesterday seven people protesting her killing were shot and wounded.

Now President Trump threatens gunfire against protesters, while the Minneapolis mayor and Minnesota governor are bringing in the National Guard. Trump tweeted, *'Just spoke to Governor Tim Walz and told him that the Military is with him all the way. Any difficulty and we will assume control but, when the looting starts, the shooting starts."*

That's what happened when Martin Luther King, Jr. was assassinated during the Memphis strike in 1968, shortly after he was made an honorary member of ILWU Local 10. When African Americans rose up in protest in 100 cities across the country, the National Guard was called out by both Democratic and Republican governors to bloodily repress them. And of course, the National Guard was mobilized in

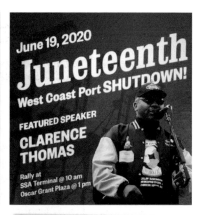

Poster designs: Jeremy Yingling

William Adams
June 2, 2020
Page 2

1934 to break the Maritime Strike. Five years ago, when Minneapolis police shot Jamar Clark in the head and armed KKKers attacked protesters, over 200 union members outside police headquarters, including from the Minnesota Nurses Association, Letter Carriers, SEIU Healthcare MN, St. Paul Federation of Teachers, and CWA Local 7250.

Today, it is urgent that unions respond to the racist upsurge. In fact, it is a matter of life and death. ILWU has a proud record when it comes to taking action for social justice. *The time is now to use our power, for our union to shut down all West Coast ports, in solidarity against racism and repression.* Juneteenth, Friday June 19, is the most appropriate day. It's the day African Americans in the southern states commemorate their emancipation from slavery in Texas in 1865. ILA represents those ports.

As you may already be aware, ILA International President Harold Daggett recently released a statement condemning the brutal murder committed by former Minneapolis police officer Derek Chauvin. He also pointed out that "the grief and outrage expressed on the streets of Minneapolis and other cities across America in the wake of Mr. Floyds murder are the by-product of policies and practices that are discriminatory and seemingly target minorities." We both know that these policies and practices have been crippling African Americans families and progress for generations. We should call on the ILA to join us in shutting down the Gulf and East Coast ports. The fight to extinguish systemic racism in this country is that important! As ILWU's first African American president we are counting on you, in the best tradition of our union. It Is past time for the ILWU to take this crucial stand now showing everyone around the country who risk their lives as "essential workers," and all opponents of racism and oppression the true meaning of solidarity just as we did in 1934 and have continued to do since.

An Injury to One Is An Injury to All! Sincere

Sincerely,

Trent Wills
President
ILWU Local #10

opeiu29/afl-cio: jo

In Solidarity,

Billy Kepo'O
President, ILWU Local 91

Sincerely,

Keith Shanklin
Presdient, ILWU Local 34

Sincerely,

Ryan Murphy
Secretary-Treasurer/Business Agent
ILWU Local 75

'The most effective way to stop police terror is action at the point of production'

Eric Blanc interviews Clarence Thomas

To honor George Floyd, Breonna Taylor, and all victims of police repression, dockworkers on both coasts are taking action at noon to coincide with the funeral of George Floyd in Houston. On the West Coast, members of the ILWU will be stopping work and taking an eight minute, forty-six second moment of silence. We spoke with a protest organizer about the action.

Eric Blanc: Why did ILWU decide to organize this work stoppage today?

Clarence Thomas: Fighting police murders and white supremacy is a class question. Let's not forget that the vast majority of Black people, and the vast majority of victims of police repression, are working class.

For many years now, ILWU, and Local 10 in particular, has been protesting the racist policing of African Americans. And we understand that the way these murders can be stopped is when there are economic consequences. The working class has leverage, and we need to use it.

We think that the most effective way to stop police terror is by the working class taking action at the point of production: **"if the working class is going to be heard, labor must shut it down."**

We believe that labor should strive to be at the vanguard of all social struggles, because labor has a responsibility to fight for those beyond just our own membership. Think about the demand of the eight-hour workday and the elimination of child labor, these were demands that unions a century ago won for the whole working class. It's that kind of spirit we need to revive today.

This is the tradition of the militant labor movement. There is a concerted effort by those in power to give workers amnesia about the history of our class and its militancy. Learning about the past reveals the contradiction between the interests of labor and those who own the means of production.

EB: Do you think the labor movement is doing enough to fight against police repression and racial injustice?

CT: No. Labor cannot continue to remain silent on racist policing. Anytime a Black person or person of color is killed by the police, workers and unions need to be shutting down their workplaces. Protest is one thing, actual resistance and action at the point of production is something else.

Unions should be raising demands for defunding the police and revoking the membership of police associations from our labor councils. The police in many cities are part of the central labor councils, we think this is a major contradiction because cops are not a part of the labor movement.

Whenever there's a strike, the police are called in to defend the bosses, intimidate workers, protect scabs. They always defend the powerful and the privileged.

Unfortunately, labor has forgotten that cops are the enforcers of the bosses. Think about Minneapolis, which has sparked this national revolt. Back in 1934 Minneapolis had a General Strike led by the Teamsters, during which two striking truck drivers were killed by cops on Bloody Friday. And in San Francisco in the 1934 General Strike led by longshore workers, we had Bloody Thursday, when police shot and killed two strikers.

In many instances, trade unionists just don't know about that history of police killings. They don't know how the rank-and-file in places like Minneapolis and San Francisco took on the National Guard, the police, the vigilantes, and the Ku Klux Klan in the 1930s and '40s. The rulers of this country don't want workers to understand our power, to have class consciousness.

EB: Where do you think the movement should go from here?

CT: Young people need to know that no matter how many people are out in the streets, to really win big transformational change you need workers. We need to organize in our own name, independent of the Democratic and Republican Parties.

In cities across the country, we keep on seeing cuts to social services, schools, and hospitals, but never cuts to police departments. They have the advanced military equipment, while people who work in hospitals are forced to use garbage bags and reuse masks.

This year, ILWU will be withholding its labor on Juneteenth, the holiday celebrating the ending of slavery in the U.S. All twenty-nine ports on the West Coast will be shut down Juneteenth for eight hours to demand an end to white supremacy, an end to police terror, and an end to the plans to privatize the Port of Oakland, which would take away essential jobs for working-class African Americans in the Bay Area. And we're calling on unions across the country to join us. Labor must begin to take a lead in the fight against racist police terror.

Abridged from Jacobin, June 9, 2020.

ILWU, ILA and IBT honor George Floyd

Frances Madeson

Today, June 9, 2020, members of the ILWU and the ILA and the Teamsters laid down their tools in a work stoppage on the day George Floyd was buried in Houston.

Trent Willis, Keith Shanklin, and Gabriel Prawl, all members of ILWU's Committee Against Police Terror, conceived of bringing this powerful gesture into union workplaces as a way of honoring Floyd, who earned his livelihood as a truck driver and security guard. In connecting Floyd's struggle for his last breath with workers' struggles for survival in a drastically altered post-pandemic economy, they hope to point the way forward by demonstrating the power of the working class.

"Longshore workers probably understand capitalism better than anyone else," said ILWU spokesman Clarence Thomas. "If the cargo doesn't come off the ship, that's merchandise not sold. Stopping work for eight minutes and forty-six seconds is not a symbol, it's an act that demonstrates the leverage of the working class. The only way that we've been able to get concessions from the bosses is through withholding our labor."

"This is a critical connection between the younger generation who've really been disconnected from labor," explained Kali Akuno, "to expose them to the power of their own creativity and the power of their labor." Akuno says Black youth are struggling as they face a jobless future.

"This step that the ILWU, ILA and Teamsters are taking addresses the issues at the heart of COVID-19," he explained, "the underlying white supremacy, which is the reason why the pandemic has played out so catastrophically for the Black community."

But new threats are on the horizon. Owner of the Oakland A's baseball team, John Fisher, is pushing a real estate deal that would overwhelm the Port of Oakland with a 34,000 seat baseball stadium, 3,000 condominiums, a 400 room hotel and 1.9 million square foot retail space.

"People need to understand it for what it is," Thomas said, suggesting a spectrum of violences against Black people: by police killings, by the denial of jobs, and "against ILWU Local 10 by the owner of the Oakland A's at the only African-American port."

"The longshore jobs represented upward mobility, dignity, Black labor empowerment and influence in the community," Thomas says, "they will not be ceded."

On June 8, it was decided by longshore presidents representing 29 ports up and down the Coast to follow the lead of ILWU Local 10 to withhold its labor for eight hours on Juneteenth.

Abridged from Sprectre, June 9, 2020.

Keith Shanklin, Trent Willis on the mike, starting a car caravan on Bloody Thursday, July 2020. Photo: Jahahara

Cephus X Johnson and Clarence Thomas. Photo: Amir Aziz

Local 13 Port Shut Down 8:46 moments of silence of observance on entire West Coast ILWU June 9, 2020 of George Floyd's funeral. Photo: Dispatcher

Port of Oakland Shut Down Commemorates Juneteenth

"Happy Juneteenth everyone. We are still on the long road to freedom. Whenever the ILWU takes a stand, the world feels the reverberations. A powerful collective thank you to the International Longshore and Warehouse Union.

"We remember your stance against the internment of Japanese Americans in the 1940s. We applaud the fact that you stood with Martin Luther King and the Civil Rights activists in the 1960s. We know that you radicalized the struggle against South Africa apartheid in the 1980s. And, we thank you for supporting Mumia Abu-Jamal; for solidarity with the anti-capitalist Occupy Movement; and for your resounding no to the racist state of Israel; and for your expressions of solidarity with those who called for justice in Palestine.

"I was thinking the other day, that If I had not chosen to become a university professor, my next choice probably would have been to become a dock worker or warehouse worker in order to be a member of the most radical union in the country, the ILWU."

– Angela Davis at the Port of Oakland: Speech to ILWU Juneteenth Work Action, June 19, 2020
youtube.com/watch?v=fWQeDFZBpHE

"You represent the potential and the power of the labor movement."

All 29 ports on the West Coast were shut down on June 19 as dock workers stopped the movement of cargo and rallied to mark Juneteenth by calling for an end to police terror and to honor the lives of George Floyd, Rayshard Brooks, Breonna Taylor and all the others killed by racist cops.

The epicenter was at the Port of Oakland, Calif., where the strike had been initiated by International Longshore and Warehouse Union Local 10.

Ten thousand workers and supporters rallied to hear labor leaders like Willie Adams, the first Black International President of the ILWU, who said: "We're not working today.

We're standing in solidarity." He said dock workers in Genoa, Italy, had also stopped work in solidarity.

"You represent the potential and the power of the labor movement," Angela Davis, a longtime activist and former political prisoner, said at the rally. She said she hopes that other labor unions will join in the effort

Photos: Kelley Kane

of abolishing the police as we know them and re-imagining public safety.

Other speakers included actor Danny Glover and Michael Brown Sr., father of Michael Brown Jr., the 18-year-old Black man who was killed in 2014 by Ferguson, Mo., police officer Darren Wilson.

The protesters drove in a caravan and marched from the port to the Oakland Police Department headquarters and on to Oakland City Hall to rally again. The marchers wore masks and volunteers handed out water and hand sanitizer.

The mood in downtown Oakland was exuberant as cars honked, music by James Brown played and over 100 bikers sped

up and down Broadway with raised fists. A troupe of drummers performed in front of City Hall starting around 1 p.m. as the crowd swelled to thousands more around nearby Oscar Grant Plaza, named for the Black man killed by Bay Area Rapid Transit (BART) police officer Johannes Mehserle on New Year's Eve 2009.

Boots Riley, rapper and the director of the film "Sorry to Bother You" and the musician of the "Coup," said in front of Oakland City Hall that the port work stoppage and other labor efforts would maintain pressure for meaningful change. "We don't want to just ask for things to get better. We're going to say, it's going to get better or else," he said.

Gwendoline Pouchoulin displayed homemade signs that said, "I think if there's a moment to show up, it's now, 'All Black Lives Matter' and a quote from author Alice Walker, "The most common way people give up power is by thinking they don't have any."

Reprinted from SLL, June 21, 2020.

Photos: Brooke Anderson

Photos: Kelley Kane

Pam Price

Photo: D.L.T.

Gene Hazzard

Photo: Clarence Thomas

Melody Davis

D.L.T.

Bill Ross

David Banks, Steve and Phillip Alley, and Frank Jefferson

Gerald Smith, Herb Mills, and Jack Heyman

Mya Shone and Ralph Schoenman.

Photo: Delores Lemon-Thomas

Local 10 leaders and members.

Fred Hampton, Jr and David Newton

Malika Johnson and Kelley Kane

Arthur League

John Hughes and Jack Bryson

Photo: Andrea Mohan

Glen Ford and Chuck Mohan

Judy Juanita,
author Virgin Soul

From Oakland Clarence Thomas
The ILWU Shuts Down the Ports on Juneteenth

John Parker introduction

We had the very inspiring Juneteenth event in the Bay Area with an ILWU shut down which our brother Clarence Thomas is going to talk about.

Whether you're talking about reparations, Juneteenth or the role of police as the right arm of capitalism; these topics are always told through the lens of the ruling class, the financial and industrial monopolies that actually run the politicians and run this country. It's their ideology that pervades the media, TV, movies and so on.

It's so important to give the working-class view, to talk about the necessity of reparations and the importance of Juneteenth. To give the view from the Black liberation struggle, from people who are in the streets fighting racism.

Clarence Thomas: First of all, I'm a third-generation longshore worker retired member of Local 10. Trent Willis president Local 10 and Keith Shanklin president Local 34 initiated the Juneteenth West Coast Port Shut Down. They also organized the Million Worker March at the Lincoln Memorial in Oct. 2004. I, along with Jack Heyman Local 10 pensioner, were part of the 'Committee to Stop Police Terror & End Systemic Racism & Stop Privatization of the Port of Oakland,' the group that was configured to organize the events of Juneteenth.

The International president arranged a teleconferencing call for all longshore presidents on the West Coast to discuss the proposal by brothers Willis and Shanklin to shut down all ports for eight hours to commemorate Juneteenth.

At that time the International president reported that the employer had come up with another date that was suitable to the bosses. The longshore presidents voted to reject the bosses proposal and voted unanimously to shut down for eight hours on Juneteenth.

So now the real work began. Unlike a lot of unions the ILWU has a long history of working

INTERNATIONAL LONGSHORE & WAREHOUSE UNION
COAST LONGSHORE DIVISION

William E. Adams   Robert Olvera, Jr.   Frank Ponce De Leon   Cam Williams

MEMORANDUM

TO:	ILWU Coast Longshore Division Locals
FROM:	The Coast Committee
SUBJECT:	**Juneteenth Stop Work**
DATE:	June 11, 2020

Facsimile of letter

On Friday, June 19, 2020, the ILWU Coast Longshore Division will stop work for eight hours on the first shift in 29 West Coast ports from Bellingham, Washington to San Diego, California in observance of Juneteenth. This action follows on the heels of the June 9, 2020 action in which the ILWU Coast Longshore Division stopped work coastwide at 9:00 a.m. for nine minutes in honor of George Floyd, adding to the chorus of voices protesting police brutality and systematic racism.

Juneteenth commemorates the end of slavery in the United States. On this date in 1865, Black Slaves in Texas were told of their emancipation from slavery two years after the Emancipation Proclamation became effective, changing the legal status under federal law of enslaved African Americans in the Confederate states from slave to free. In the 157 years since the Emancipation Proclamation, our nation has made progress but the changes necessary to end systemic racism have come slowly or not at all, as the murder of Mr. Floyd on May 25, 2020 demonstrated.

On June 19, ILWU workers and their local unions up and down the West Coast will take action to reject racism, hate, and intolerance at this unprecedented moment in time amid a global pandemic, domestic unrest made worse by a President who sows the seeds of division for his own personal gain, and systematic racism laid bare by the recent brutal murder of Mr. Floyd.

As we stop work on Juneteenth, we do so in honor of our African American brothers and sisters and in recognition of the fact that we still have much to achieve as a society in order to carry out the promise of freedom in this country. On Juneteenth, we recommit ourselves to that promise.

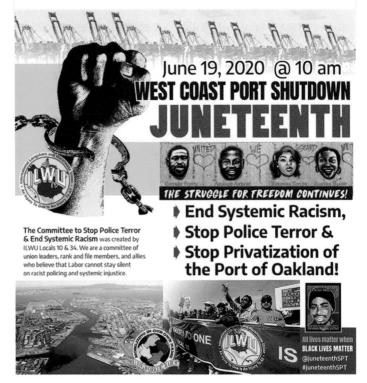

June 19, 2020 @ 10 am
WEST COAST PORT SHUTDOWN
JUNETEENTH

THE STRUGGLE FOR FREEDOM CONTINUES!

▶ **End Systemic Racism,**
▶ **Stop Police Terror &**
▶ **Stop Privatization of the Port of Oakland!**

The Committee to Stop Police Terror & End Systemic Racism was created by ILWU Locals 10 & 34. We are a committee of union leaders, rank and file members, and allies who believe that Labor cannot stay silent on racist policing and systemic injustice.

All lives matter when **BLACK LIVES MATTER**
@juneteenthSPT
#juneteenthSPT

with community organizations as well as with other unions. I think that's one of the things that separates us from others.

Let's go back to Juneteenth. 'The Committee to Stop Police Terror and End Systemic Racism and Stop Privatization of Howard Terminal,' was organized by ILWU Local 10. We had members from progressive organizations throughout the community too numerous for me to outline. We went to work getting the word out. The millennials who are very adept with social media played an important role in the turnout for this particular event. The young people did a fabulous job.

It is critical for us to highlight the issue of the police violence. What is obviously critical is the escalating numbers of murders right before our eyes. Someone described it as murder pornography. The more you look at it in the media the more sickening it is. We have national uprising and uprisings all around the world against racism, in particularly against police killings.

The Juneteenth action was called and organized by ILWU Local 10 and Local 34. The Port of Oakland, where the Local 10 and Local 34 members work is under attack because multi-billionaire John Fisher wants to privatize it.

The Port of Oakland has agreed to give fifty-five acres of the Port to Fisher, a major land owner in the U.S. who owns the Oakland A's, the Gap, the Banana Republic. ...

Fisher wants to build a 34,000 seat baseball park; 3,000 what I call skybox condominiums; a 400 room hotel and nearly 2 million square feet of retail space at the third busiest port on the West Coast where the members of the only predominantly Black longshore local work.

Why do the A's want to move to the Port of Oakland? Well if you've

been to the Port of Oakland where we work you would see the wonderful San Francisco skyline. You're on the beautiful water front. It is a place that has been used for 125 years for maritime and industrial purposes. If Fisher is allowed to privatize the port it is going to eliminate longshore jobs.

An organization has been formed that's called the East Oakland Stadium Alliance. It's made up of maritime unions, shipping interests, environmental groups, trucking, agri-businesses, exporters, interfaith and other community organizations.

The port is the economic engine of Northern California. It is the 'goose that lays the golden egg.' The real estate interests at the port are willing to sacrifice that to accommodate a billionaire's gentrification scheme.

Violence is perpetuated against

Black people by the police; in the denial of health care; in the denial of jobs, housing and education.

That violence is further perpetuated against Black workers when you allow a billionaire to build a baseball park at the port. It is like building an amusement park on an assembly line. It could have devastating impact at the port and also on the remaining Black community.

So, this is an attack on longshore workers, Black longshore workers, the most radical Black workers in the U.S. if not the world. That's the reason why the issue of the privatization is right up there with the issue of stopping the police terror. This action on Juneteenth would not have happened if it were not for the ILWU.

Let's talk about what happened on Juneeteenth. The most remarkable thing was the turnout from the community. I've been told there were 25,000 people and hundreds of cars. There are aerial views of it. See: tinyurl.com/ydalrnmw.

We started with a rally at the Port of Oakland, marched to the Oakland Police Department and ended with a rally at Oscar Grant Plaza in front of City Hall.

At the port, sister Angela Davis appeared following the COVID-19 safety precautions. She stood up in her car and played a message that brought tears to my eyes.

Angela Davis laid out the history of the ILWU and its struggle against white supremacy, going back our stand against Japanese internment in the 1940s, our support for the Civil Rights Movement in the 60s, the boycott of Southern African cargo in the 70s and 80s, solidarity actions in support of Mumia Abu-Jamal, and support for the Palestinian struggle.

She was in a sea of workers it was absolutely astounding. I'll never forget it. All that I could think of was the first African American to be a elected president of Local 10, Cleophas Williams, who knew my grandfather and came into the industry in the same year 1944. In 1971, at the 19th ILWU Bi-Centennial convention in Honolulu Cleophas introduced a resolution calling for justice for Angela Davis, calling for her right to receive bail. Angela never forgot that. So, Angela was not speaking to a history of days gone by she was speaking to the living history of the ILWU.

Danny Glover's activism is in the tradition of other African American artist such as Paul Robeson, Harry Belafonte, and Nina Simone to name a few who have utilized their celebrity to advance the struggle for freedom, justice and equality. Glover spoke from his car following the COVID-19 protocols.

Boots Riley, the director of the film "Sorry to Bother You" and the leader of the rap group the "Coup" spoke about how the bosses couldn't make money for eight hours because of the shutdown.

Michael Brown Sr,, whose son Michael Brown Jr. was killed in Ferguson, Missouri spoke. Cephus X Johnson the uncle of Oscar Grant spoke. We had young people. Labor leaders, Trent Willis, Keith Shanklin, Jack Heyman all spoke.

Juneteenth 2020, was an absolutely extraordinary day, not only for ILWU Local 10, but for the entire working class. It was an expression of the leadership of the Black working class.

Excerpts from a SLL Webinar, June 27, 2020. See Reparations, Capitalism and Fighting Police Terror at Juneteenth, ILWU Workers Shut Down. tinyurl.com/yymxg62p

Cleophas Williams' resolution calls for justice for Angela Davis at the 1971 ILWU Convention

WHEREAS: We know from California history that anti-radical hysteria and frameup are anti-labor weapons; and

WHEREAS: We know that Tom Mooney, a labor organizer, was kept in prison for 32 years before it officially acknowledged that he was framed.
We know that Harry Bridges was persecuted for 20 years because he was an effective and militant union leader; and

WHEREAS: Now there is a relentless crusade to kill Angela Davis, prejudice and frameup is now employed lo crush Black Militancy. The same device has always been used against labor when the powers of big business and government decide that organized workers are 'getting out of line;' and

WHEREAS: When President Nixon, Governor Reagan and the big money press incite the legal lynching of Angela Davis, experience tell us to beware. Those are our enemies too. It could well be us 'next time around,' or it could be you; and

WHEREAS: Angela is also charged with conspiracy. An old gimmick used to repress the labor movement in this country. We defend ourselves by defending Angela Davis;

THEREFORE BE IT RESOLVED: The International Convention of the ILWU goes on record to support Angela Davis and to see that she receives a fair trial and is released on bail pending trial.

Photo: Jack Heyman

Labor's imperative to defend of Black lives

King Downing and Frances Madeson

Black trade unionists are calling on the labor movement to defend Black Lives Matter protesters and to fight racism in their own ranks. The attacks by police and increasingly violent armed racist militias evoke the memory of violent incidents against Black people in earlier periods, from slavery to segregation to the civil rights era.

For Labor Day 2020, *Truthout* reached out to Christophe Silvera, who has found that members of his union who are in what he terms "the militia mindset" have the exact same demands as unions, wages, pensions and healthcare, but their solutions are based on white supremacy.

"Many were in the military, in Afghanistan, and they're frustrated," he says. "They think they can achieve these demands by way of racism and getting rid of immigrants."

Silvera recalls a recent Labor Day parade in New York City with a marcher who had a confederate flag on his Harley-Davison motorcycle.

"Now what is it about being in a union and the Confederacy that you don't understand, when everything that the Klan stood for was anti-union?" he wonders. "But they don't have this knowledge so they have a contradictory relationship with the union."

Some local unions have started to stand up to militias in much the same way as they have against police brutality. Local 10 has passed resolutions and marched against police violence and fascism. They were prepared to counter-protest the Patriot Prayer in San Francisco in August 2017, until the far-right group backed down.

"Once they heard organized labor was marching against them, they were no longer in the mood," Silvera says, adding that this is precisely why national leadership should be in unison with Black Lives Matter. "If the electricians and the building trades were in these marches, it would let people know that this is unacceptable.

Leaderships' inaction is allowing the militias to breathe, the way they allow the Klan to breathe."

Militias and the Klan are on the historical continuum of what Silvera calls "a chronic level of oppression of the Black working class, but ultimately of the whole working class." He thinks the tradition is being ramped up now because "capitalism has become completely desperate."

Labor has to step into this space to push back and become a leader in anti-militarism and anti-vigilantism in its capacity as "military wing of the working class."

"We have to speak up, we have to start leading marches as labor," Silvera argues. "If we don't we're going to continue to have these problems with state fascism. And when fascism rears its head, one of the first things it goes after is the union."

What do we want? We want the national leadership of the AFL-CIO to call the Fraternal Order of Police (FOP) and tell them to 'rein in your boys.' We want them to say, 'These are our workers, our members, and you all can't treat them like this."

He says if the FOP won't take corrective action to stop the police killings of Black workers and future workers, the AFL-CIO should kick them out.

Abridged from Truthout, Sept. 7, 2020.

Chris Silvera, Julette Silvera and Clarence Thomas.
Photo: Delores Lemon-Thomas

ILWU urges labor action to fight police terror

Lallan Schoenstein

On Juneteenth, tens of thousands flocked to the Port of Oakland to participate in the "West Coast Port Shut Down." Then they marched to Oakland City Hall to hear from labor and community leaders.

See: tinyurl.com/yd54xlav The ILWU called the strike for June 19 to shut down all 29 ports on the West Coast for eight hours. They demanded an end to white supremacy, police terror and plans to privatize the Port of Oakland, which would take away essential jobs from African Americans in the Bay Area. They called for unions across the country to join them in the fight against racist police terror.

Juneteenth commemorates the day that news finally reached Texas that the Confederacy had been defeated and that slavery had been abolished more than two years earlier in 1863.

Calling for labor to take action, Willie Adams, the first Black president of the ILWU, said: "Our union has a long history of confronting racism on the job, in our community and around the world."

Trent Willis, president of ILWU Local 10, said: "The wealth gap for Black and Brown sisters and brothers is larger than ever in history. It's time to push back!" The Juneteenth action was initiated by Locals 10 and 34.

Clarence Thomas, a retired ILWU official and an initiator of the MWMM said: "Local 10 is in the vanguard of the labor movement, protesting and resisting acts of racist police terror on African Americans and other people of color for more than a decade. On Juneteenth, the Coastwide action at the point of production will demonstrate the power of the working class for radical change."

The United Auto Workers said that its members and allies across the globe paused work for eight minutes and forty-six seconds to honor George Floyd on Juneteenth. According to United Domestic Workers, AFSCME Local 3930, San Diego labor union members joined in a Juneteenth Black Lives Matter caravan that took them from San Diego to the La Mesa Police Department.

Boots Riley tweeted that some Tesla workers in the Bay Area were doing a direct action at the Tesla factory on Juneteenth. Organizers of an Atlanta protest against the death of George Floyd and Rayshard Brooks called for a general strike.

The Juneteenth strike took place following a rank-and-file wave of walkouts and wildcat strikes to protest unsafe work-

ing conditions. The lack of protection from COVID-19 and the economic disruption the pandemic has impacted Black and brown workers, already suffering from the effects of racism the worst.

When the police murders of George Floyd and Breonna Taylor occurred a national revolt against racist policing was ignited.

Payday Report says the protests against police terror have more than doubled the number of strikes for safer working conditions occurring in every part of the country. "If the size of these strikes last week is any indication, Juneteenth will likely be the largest day of strikes."

When protests erupted in Minneapolis during May against the murder of George Floyd, members of Amalgamated Transit Union Local 1005 refused to help the police transport protesters to jail. Local 1005's statement read: "This system has failed all of us in the working class from the coronavirus to the economic crisis we are facing. ... This system has failed people of color and Black youth more than anyone else."

Bus drivers with support of transit unions in cities like Boston, Cincinnati, Dallas, Philadelphia and New York have refused to transport police to protests or to aid them in transporting arrested demonstrators. They say this is a misuse of public transit.

There is growing call to kick police unions out of the labor movement: "Conflating our mission with that of police unions undermines our solidarity. White supremacy is central to the system of policing — therefore, we urge the labor movement to cut ties with police unions."

Reprinted from SLL, June 21, 2020.

Chris Silvera secretary-treasurer of Teamsters 808 speaks in Union Square to support the Bessemer Alabama Amazon workers on Feb. 20, 2021, as part of a national day of solidarity. Silvera said, "This union drive is a game-changer for the U.S. workers." www.youtube.com/watch?v=6rFcFRShJQk

20 years of fighting for the homeless in New York City

'Picture the Homeless' PTH celebrated the 20th anniversary of their organization in the Harlem, N.Y. State Office Building on Nov. 25, 2019. Leaders of PTH called for a renewed commitment to their work of fighting for the homeless at a time when housing opportunities in the major cities are rapidly deteriorating.

Talks by members of the PTH board recounted personal experiences among a diverse group of all ages, many of whom had gone without housing. They chose the name "Picture the Homeless" because mainstream culture attempts to drive people who are struggling to survive into oblivion. They say: "Housing is a human right!"

MWMM leader Brenda Stokely, in yellow jacket, stands with PTH Board members to help distribute awards after a slide show.

Photo: Lallan Schoenstein

In an exhibit at crowded hall PTH's strategy on a variety of issues was explained such as the fight against police abuse and the reclamation of vacant properties in New York City that people could rehabilitate.

PTH wages a battle for the homeless to speak in their own name and to be able to play a role in determin-

ing a solution to the myriad problems they suffer. Echoing the grim experience of being undermined by the administrators of social services, who are supposed to serve them, they repeated, "If you are not at the table, you'll be on the menu."

Some background on Brenda Stokely

Proud mother, grandmother and human rights activist dedicated to ending all forms of national oppression, racism, sexism and exploitation of the poor, workers and people of color. Served as co-coordinator for the Million Worker March and the MWM Organizing & Justice School providing free classes for labor and community activists. Spent 49 years building organizations, movements and alliances raising the voices of the ignored and forgotten to win needed services, protective laws and policies.

Designed and established the first day care network including family day care providers in Richmond, California. As a student organizer fought to remove discriminatory barriers against people of color at Sacramento State College.

Built a Washington, DC Housing Coalition that won a strong Rent Control laws. Worked with Black People United for Prison Reform to promote alternatives the to incarceration of D.C. youth and adults.

Founding member of the Harlem Reclamation Project to demand community control of vacant owned city property, Member of the Coalition for Justice of Eleanor Bumpers.

Answered the call of Local 10 and served as Regional organizer for the historic 2004 Lincoln Memorial MWM. Co-convened the NY 2001 Labor Against the War, the Troops Out Now Coalition; Blacks In Solidarity Against the War, served as the NY Labor Party Chair, co-convener of the May 1st Coalition for Workers and Immigrant Rights; NY

Solidarity Coalition with Katrina/Rita Survivors, the Coalition to Save Harlem, National Black Independent Political Party and the Black United Front. Co-editor of "Legacy" dedicated to Ida B. Wells and African Descent-women activists.

Current member of Local 371 Social Service Employees Union, DC 37/AFSCME. Former President of Local 215, Social Service Employees and President of the 25,000 human services workers of District Council 1707/AFSCME. Fought and won, just contracts and internal union democracy with unionized co-workers, as well helped non-unionized workers win union recognition.

Honored recipient of PTH Lou Haggins Social Justice Warrior award. She led many other organizations.

Million Worker March 2004
'The Stakes were High'

It was time for workers to take a stand against the bosses and the labor aristocracy, the white men who trade their union members' interests, so that they can live like the parasitic 1%. Partners with imperialist who make profits off the backs of workers.

A new boldness resonated in the workers voices and actions. The Labor Party, built by brothers and sisters from the industrial, public, agricultural, service and transportation unions, asked, "The bosses have two parties why can't workers have their own?"

The creation of Labor Against the War and Troops Out Now represented a powerful denouncement of imperialist wars. There was growing comprehension that aims of the wars was to increase the wealth of the 1% and to establish political control as a means to appropriate global resources.

Across the country, armed service recruiters were allowed into the public schools of the working class, often in the poorest communities. Students and their families began to protest against the armed services presence, exposing lies and unethical tactics used to seduce students to join.

The students knew that it was not realistic to obtain a job paying a livable wage, to get accepted into a college and pay for tuition, housing and healthcare. Instead, their country offered them an opportunity to become 'cannon fodder for the rich, to return home in a coffin or a lifetime coping with a physical or mental disabilities.

"Right to work states" were being challenged by workers fighting for union recognition. They exposed the criminality of bosses who did nothing to correct conditions that were maiming them and causing death.

These workers began to reject sell-out contracts. They took over work places that the bosses were trying close down. They got fired members rehired. And they gained national and international support.

In the course of fighting back workers revisited the heroic history of workers who put their jobs and lives in jeopardy to form a union, and end oppression in work places. They realized there is a broader role for organized labor in the fight for a better life for all workers.

During the rising militancy and consciousness they began to shed the boss' poisonous weapons against the labor movement, divide and conquer; labor aristocracy's maintenance of white supremacy; white men's dominance over women and the discrimination against workers due to language, nationality or being part of the LGBTQ community.

Powerful organizing initiatives in African American communities around the country included the Million Men's, Million Women's, the Millions More Movement and Black youth mobilizations. These monumental gatherings demonstrated the strength of grassroots activism in Black labor movement.

The millions that gathered in these marches inspired a young Local 10 longshoreman, Trent Willis. He envisioned the formation of millions of workers, their allies and international labor at the Lincoln Memorial. He was imbued by Local 10's revolutionary foundation of international solidarity and zero tolerance for white supremacy.

Local 10's leadership put out a call to labor unions across the country and around the world. The rank-and-file began to mobilize, reaching out to other unions in their region, organizations such as Coalition of Black Trade Unionist and labor allies.

The MWM Northeast mobilization led by Chris Silvera Local 808 Teamsters and my District Council 1707, AFSCME, accepted the responsibility of building a regional contingent of employed, unemployed, unionized, unorganized and immigrant workers. Our unions endorsed and provided financial support. Long time allies worked tirelessly holding community meetings in the cities where International unions held their conventions.

We learned from union members, who wanted bus tickets to the MWM their union officials were discouraging participation "because it was an election year," thus revealing that they took their lead from the Democrats or Republicans, not from their members. "The bosses have two parties and workers have none." (Labor Party)

On October 17, 2004, international solidarity with U.S. workers was reflected by the workers who came from the Caribbean, Europe, Africa, Japan.

The MWMM supports workers who are unionizing, standing up to union leaders who collaborate with the bosses in stripping rights to a livable wage, safe work places, benefits and the right to strike.

We must learn from our best efforts to achieve justice and continue to inspire the next generations. A Luta Continua /The Struggle Continues.

I am forever grateful to all who gave their energy and solid political support.

Brenda Stokely
January 25, 2021

About Clarence C. Thomas Jr.

I was born and raised in Oakland, California the eldest of five children. I come from an African American working class family who believed in a tradition of activism. My father introduced me to Malcolm X. He purchased *Muhammad Speaks* newspapers on a regular basis, and it was through reading that newspaper that I learned of the Southern Africa Liberation Struggle. My parents allowed Black Panther Party (BPP) community meetings to be held in their home.

I had a long and profound curiosity about working on the waterfront as a young boy. I was told many times by family members that there were people from all walks of life and various levels of education who worked together there. It was difficult for me to conceptualize such a work environment until years later when I became a longshore worker.

I'm a third-generation longshore worker and a retired member of the International Longshore & Warehouse Union (ILWU) which represents dock workers along the Pacific Coast in 29 ports, including Hawaii and British Columbia, Canada. I was a member of Local 10 for thirty-one years before retiring in 2016.

My maternal grandfather, Lee Edwards came to Oakland with his family during the Great Migration of African Americans from Port Arthur, Texas, to work in the shipyards of Henry J. Kaiser building Liberty ships for World War II. He became a longshoreman in 1944. My father, Clarence Thomas, Sr. came to Oakland with his parents and siblings in 1936 from Merrill, Mississippi , like other families, to escape Jim Crow. He became a longshoreman in 1963, and my great uncle, Robert Harmon became a longshoreman in 1965. They were all members of Local 10.

Clarence Thomas speaks at a December 2011 'Occupy Oakland' press conference.

My earliest memory of being introduced to ILWU was at the home of my maternal grandparents Lee and Jewel Edwards, who resided in West Oakland, minutes from the Port of Oakland. The first time I recall hearing the name Harry Bridges, founding member of the ILWU and its first International President, was at my grandparent's kitchen table. My grandmother Jewel was a gourmet cook that introduced me to Louisiana gumbo, boiled crawfish, fried okra with stewed tomatoes and shrimp. You get the idea?

Grandpa Lee was a Louisiana Creole with dark skin and his hair was straight as any European. He spoke creole, stood 5' 7" and was sturdily built. Grandpa Lee worked in an all-white gang (workers that always work together) and would on occasion bring co-workers to his home for lunch. It was during these meals that there would be discussion about the union, the job, and Harry Bridges. At the time I was 8 years old. I can't recall the particulars of the discussions, but I gathered that Bridges was an important man.

It was my grandfather who introduced me to the importance of Paul Robeson. It was decades later that I learned that the legendary singer, actor, orator and civil rights leader was made a honorary member of ILWU in 1943. I found it rather curious that a Black man that my grandfather held in high esteem, who was world famous in the same way as the Rev. Dr. King and Jackie Robinson, was someone whose name I had never heard at school. Later I came to realize that Paul Robeson had been black-listed. His accomplishments had been hidden from the consciousness of an 8 year old.

My grandfather told me that the government accused him of being a Communist. I didn't quite understand the full ramification of the McCarthy Era and the Cold War.

I attended Oakland Public Schools. I graduated from Oakland Technical High School; as did classmates Congressman Ron Dellums, former mayor of the City of Oakland and Leo Robinson, legendary Local 10 rank-and-file leader. Both men had prominent roles in the anti-apartheid struggles. Aside from being raised in a union household with all the benefits there of, I strongly believe that all three of us having fathers who were members of Local 10, influenced our radicalism and social justice activism.

Accompanying my father, along with grandfathers R.G. Thomas (paternal) and Lee Edwards to see Rev. Dr. Martin Luther King Jr at the Oakland Auditorium to mark the 100th Anniversary of the Emancipation Proclamation on December 28, 1962, was a momentous occasion of my youth.

My post-secondary education included attending City College of San Francisco, San Francisco State College (SFSC) and University of California, Hastings College of the Law. My activism started in the late 60s at SFSC. While there I was part of the leadership that led the longest student strike in U.S. history. The strike was organized by the Black Student Union and ended with the establishment of the first U.S. Black Studies Department and a School of Ethnic Studies. Many other schools followed our example and changed academia forever.

I was introduced to Black radical thinkers such as Franz Fanon, W.E.B. Du Bois and others; learning the power of self-determination. I was radicalized at SFSC. There I experienced the importance of building coalitions such as the 'Third World Liberation Front,' formed by students of color that waged a successful strike for four and a half months. I acquired the knowledge of organizing rallies, writing leaflets, conducting press conferences, public speaking, and most importantly, how to engage in protracted struggle. I was arrested at SFSC challenging white supremacy and systemic racism.

The ILWU expressed strong solidarity during the strike.

The week of December 16, 1969.   PUBLISHED BY THE BLACK STUDENTS UNION, SAN FRANCISCO STATE COLLEGE   Page 1, Volume III, No. 15

BLACK FIRE

FIFTEEN CENTS

15¢

BLACK FIRE The week of December 16, 1969 Page 12

STRIKE AT S.F

One of the most effective confrontations in the history of the U.S. student movement, the San Francisco State College (SFSC) strike will, no doubt, serve as a precedent for future campus disruption. The strike has been unique in many ways. Differing completely from the events at Columbia University 1968 or the recent disruptions at Cornell and Harvard, the SFSC strike witnessed the formation of new alliances, the use of new tactics, and the mobilization of unprecedented support. The effectiveness of the strike can be attributed primarily to the leadership of the SFSC Black Student union.

Excerpted from: Riots, Civil and Criminal Disorders, Hearings before the Permanent Subcommittee on Investigations of the Committee on Government Operations, United States Senate, Ninety-First Congress-first session(Part 22) Pg. 571.

Local 10 provided work on the docks to faculty and students who were going without regular paychecks.

While a student at SFSC, I was also an active member of the Black Panther Party and part of the Black liberation movement and understood the importance of Black revolutionary working class political leadership and the struggle for freedom, justice and social transformation. I learned the importance of grassroots community organizing, building movements, political education, and mobilizing students to utilize their knowledge and skills to serve the needs of the community.

I entered the maritime industry after the passing of my father in 1985.

I have served as an officer and in various other capacities during my membership in Local 10. I have been part of many historical economic and social justice struggles for African Americans, the working class and the oppressed. This anthology documents many of those struggles.

"Although I am retired from the waterfront, I am not retired from the struggle."

Clarence 'Buzz' Thomas   2021

The author of this anthology, Clarence Thomas, is on the right in the photo, head turned left, leading a picket line during the 1968 student strike. Others pictured include: Jo Ann Mitchell, Arnold Townsend, Robert Prudhomme, George Colbert, Jerry Varnado, Sharon Jones.

The Replacement

In a longshoremen's terminology, a "replacement" is a worker that will take over an assigned job, when the original worker is unable to work on that job, to its completion.

Before my retirement in 1996, I begin to seek a good union person to take the baton of unionism from me. Upon getting to know of, and about Clarence Thomas, I saw him as a young man that grew up with a strong union father. Clarence came into ILWU Local 10 very eager and serious to learn and understand all he could about the good and bad of our Maritime Industry.

Then to learn that this man was one of the leaders, who stood up and fought against SFSC (San Francisco State College), S.I. Hayakawa, and the ultra-conservative Ronald Reagan, over students' rights! I recognized that after joining the Local 10 family, Clarence began to demonstrate his high standards and moral convictions, about our rank-and-file's interest and responsibilities.

Many times he would respectfully disagree with leadership. But registrant #8718 would find a way to remain on track, in order to stand up for the Rank and File's position. Sometimes the union's membership and leaders misunderstood why Clarence believed it was important to dedicate his time and energy to fighting for causes he believed in.

Thank you Clarence for not quitting, giving in, or selling out. We know that the families of the late brothers and sisters that have gone to be with the ancestors are pleased. Thank you for your hard work and energy.

Clarence, I respect you, for being my "replacement" even though you didn't know it. You have been the replacement for so many members who didn't even realized that you were there for us all! We hope that there is a replacement that is as serious, dedicated, and determined as you! We pray for your many years of retirement!

Love and Friendship Forever,

AJ and Rochelle Mitchell

A.J. Mitchell, ILWU Local 10 Retiree #7430
April 11, 2015

Index